Mac® OS X All-in-One Desk Reference For Dummies®

Cheat Sheet

P9-DTX-584

Finder Keyboard Shortcuts

Key	Function
⌘+A	Selects all items in the active window
⌘+B	Hides the Finder window toolbar
⌘+C	Copies selected items
⌘+D	Duplicates the selected item(s)
⌘+E	Ejects the selected volume
⌘+F	Displays the Find Items dialog
⌘+H	Hides Finder windows
⌘+I	Shows info for selected item
⌘+J	Shows the view options for the active window
⌘+K	Displays the Connect to Server dialog
⌘+L	Creates an alias for the selected item
⌘+M	Minimizes the active window
⌘+N	Opens a new Finder window
⌘+O	Opens (or launches) the selected item
⌘+R	Shows the original for selected alias
⌘+T	Adds the selected item or location to Favorites
⌘+V	Pastes items from the Clipboard
⌘+W	Closes the active window
⌘+X	Cuts the selected items
⌘+Z	Undoes the last action (if possible)
⌘+1	Shows the active window in icon mode

Key	Function
⌘+2	Shows the active window in list mode
⌘+3	Shows the active window in column mode
⌘+[	Moves back to the previous Finder location
⌘+]	Moves forward to the next Finder location
⌘+Del	Moves selected items to the Trash
⌘+?	Displays the Mac OS X Help Viewer
⌘+Shift+A	Takes you to the application's location
⌘+Shift+C	Takes you to the computer's location
⌘+Shift+F	Takes you to Favorites
⌘+Shift+G	Takes you to a folder that you specify
⌘+Shift+H	Takes you to Home
⌘+Shift+I	Takes you to iDisk
⌘+Shift+Q	Logs you out
⌘+Shift+N	Opens a new untitled folder in the active window
⌘+Shift+Del	Deletes the contents of the Trash
⌘+Option+H	Hides all application windows

Mac® OS X All-in-One Desk Reference For Dummies®

Strange-looking Menu Keys

Symbol	Key
⌘	Command
⌃	Control
⇧	Shift
⌥	Option
⌦	Del

Mark's Mac OS X Maintenance Checklist

Task	Schedule
Check for updates using Software Update	Once a day (automatically, if you like)
Defragment (Norton Speed Disk/MicroMat Drive 10)	Once a week
Scan for viruses (Norton AntiVirus)	Once a week (with automatic scanning)
Check all volumes (Disk Utility/Norton Disk Doctor/Drive 10)	Once a month
Check for the latest drivers for your hardware	Once a month
Delete temporary Internet cache files (Aladdin Spring Cleaning)	Once a month

Copyright © 2003 Wiley Publishing, Inc.
All rights reserved.

Item 1796-1.

For more information about Wiley Publishing,
call 1-800-762-2974.

For Dummies: Bestselling Book Series for Beginners

Mac® OS X

ALL-IN-ONE DESK REFERENCE

FOR

DUMMIES®

Mac® OS X
ALL-IN-ONE DESK REFERENCE
FOR
DUMMIES®

by Mark Chambers
Erick Tejkowski
Michael L. Williams

Wiley Publishing, Inc.

Mac® OS X All-in-One Desk Reference For Dummies®

Published by
Wiley Publishing, Inc.
909 Third Avenue
New York, NY 10022
www.wiley.com

Copyright © 2003 by Wiley Publishing, Inc., Indianapolis, Indiana

Published by Wiley Publishing, Inc., Indianapolis, Indiana

Published simultaneously in Canada

For general information on our other products and services or to obtain technical support, please contact our Customer Care Department within the U.S. at 800-762-2974, outside the U.S. at 317-572-3993, or fax 317-572-4002.

Wiley also publishes its books in a variety of electronic formats. Some content that appears in print may not be available in electronic books.

Library of Congress Control Number: 2002110271

ISBN: 0-7645-1796-1

Manufactured in the United States of America

10 9 8 7 6 5 4 3 2

1B/RY/RS/QS/IN

®Wiley Publishing, Inc. is a trademark of Wiley Publishing, Inc.

About the Authors

Mark L. Chambers has been an author, computer consultant, BBS sysop, programmer, and hardware technician for more than 20 years. (In other words, he's been pushing computers and their uses far beyond "normal" performance limits for decades now.) His first love affair with a computer peripheral blossomed in 1984 when he bought his lightning-fast 300 BPS modem for his Atari 400. Now he spends entirely too much time on the Internet and drinks far too much caffeine-laden soda.

His favorite pastimes include collecting gargoyles, watching St. Louis Cardinals baseball, playing his three pinball machines and the latest computer games, supercharging computers, and rendering 3-D flights of fancy with TrueSpace — and during all that, he listens to just about every type of music imaginable. (For those of his readers who are keeping track, he's up to 1,200+ audio CDs in his collection.)

With a degree in journalism and creative writing from Louisiana State University, Mark took the logical career choice and started programming computers. However, after five years as a COBOL programmer for a hospital system, he decided there must be a better way to earn a living, and he became the Documentation Manager for Datastorm Technologies, a well-known communications software developer. Somewhere in between organizing and writing software manuals, Mark began writing computer books; his first book, *Running a Perfect BBS*, was published in 1994.

Along with writing several books a year and editing whatever his publishers throw at him, Mark has recently branched out into Web-based education, designing and teaching a number of online classes — called *WebClinics* — for Hewlett-Packard.

Mark's rapidly-expanding list of books includes *Building a PC For Dummies, Scanners For Dummies, CD and DVD Recording For Dummies, Microsoft Office v. X Power User's Guide, BURN IT! Creating Your Own Great DVDs and CDs, The Hewlett-Packard Official Printer Handbook, The Hewlett-Packard Official Recordable CD Handbook, The Hewlett-Packard Official Digital Photography Handbook, Computer Gamer's Bible, Recordable CD Bible, Teach Yourself the iMac Visually, Running a Perfect BBS, Official Netscape Guide to Web Animation,* and the *Windows 98 Troubleshooting and Optimizing Little Black Book.*

His books have been translated into 12 different languages so far — his favorites are German, Polish, Dutch, and French. Although he can't read them, he enjoys the pictures a great deal.

Mark welcomes all comments and questions about his books — you can reach him at mark@mlcbooks.com, or visit MLC Books Online, his Web site, at http://home.mlcbooks.com.

Erick Tejkowski is a freelance author and programmer. He is the author of *REALbasic For Dummies* and a regular contributor to popular Macintosh publications such as MacTech, MacWorld, and ResExcellence.com. When not computing, he enjoys spending free time with his wife, Maria, and their children, Mercedes and Leopold.

Michael Williams lives in St. Louis, Missouri with his wife, Sue Goff. He is a Senior Network Analyst for St. John's Mercy and its parent company, Sisters of Mercy Health System, which includes hundreds of hospitals, doctor's offices, and clinics that span five states. His primary responsibilities are monitoring and upkeep of the St. John's LANs, the Mercy WAN, and designing network expansions, particularly those revolving around videoconferencing, Voice-over-IP, and IP telephony implementations. Prior to working with St. John's Mercy, Mike did network consulting for various business, including being part of a core team that migrated the headquarters of MasterCard International to its new facilities in O'Fallon, Missouri.

Michael's background with networking goes back to his days of first using the Internet on the mainframes at the University of Missouri-Columbia in 1988. Later, he worked for the State of Missouri in Jefferson City and became the Internet Coordinator for the Department of Natural Resources before leaving in 1995. In 2000, Mike then decided to focus solely on network engineering and began obtaining Cisco certifications. He is now certified under the CCDA and CCNP programs. He is currently preparing for the CCIE laboratory exam.

Dedication

This book is dedicated to my oldest daughter, Erin Chambers — "Version 1.0" — with all the love and happiness I can give her.

— Mark Chambers

Dedicated to Maria Paredes — my fiercest advocate, my fairest critic, my best friend, and my wife. Without her, this book would not have been possible.

— Erick Tejkowski

Authors' Acknowledgments

It's high time I express my heartfelt thanks to everyone who helped produce the book you're holding!

First, I owe steak dinners to both Erick Tejkowski and Mike Williams, who both contributed important mini-books to this project — and, in doing so, took several hundred pages of pressure off of me, allowing me to write my part of the manuscript at a more comfortable pace.

Copious thanks are also due to our technical editor, Greg Willmore, who checked each and every word of this Desk Reference for technical accuracy . . . and *that*, my friends, is no easy job, especially when you consider that Jaguar was in beta during the development of this book! I was very lucky to have the help of such a knowledgeable technical editor. Kudos also to Teresa Artman for her outstanding work as copy editor.

A book of this size places a huge burden on the publisher's Production team because they have to design over 700 pages and then prepare both the copy and the high-resolution figures. Again, as in the past, the work they've done is wonderful, and I appreciate the hard work of everyone on the Production team.

As with all my books, I'd like to thank my wife, Anne, and my children, Erin, Chelsea, and Rose, for their support and love — and for letting me follow my dream!

Finally, I turn to the two people at Wiley who made this book possible: Bob Woerner, the acquisitions editor who I've been lucky enough to know for several years now; and Linda Morris, the project editor who I had the pleasure to meet and work with on this project. Their talents and ongoing assistance made this project a joy instead of a job as they gave me all the support that every author craves. Many, many thanks to you both from a very grateful Mac owner!

— Mark Chambers

My thanks to Justin Wilson for help with emergency Macintosh surgery, and to Benjamin Schneider for DVD equipment support. Thanks to Jeff and Alicia for comic relief. To Brian, Rik, D, and Chuckie for keepin' it real. To Melanie, Gretchen, Jim, Amanda, Dave, Mom, and Dad for their love and support. To Chris for getting the bad guys. To Mixi and Bubbers for inspiration. And to Lisa, for everything!

— Erick Tejkowski

I would like to take this opportunity to thank everyone who guided and supported me while I was working on this project.

I would like to, first and foremost, give a huge thanks Mark Chambers for asking me to participate in this book with him. I guess hounding you all those years finally paid off, eh?

I would also like to give great kudos and thanks to everyone at Wiley who edited, rewrote, and answered endless silly questions from me. Thanks to Bob Woerner, Linda Morris, Teresa Artman, and Greg Willmore for everything.

Last, but certainly not least, I would like to give my most sincere gratitude to my wife, Susan Goff, whose patience, understanding, and support have allowed me to do and be everything I am.

— Michael L. Williams

Publisher's Acknowledgments

We're proud of this book; please send us your comments through our online registration form located at www.dummies.com/register/.

Some of the people who helped bring this book to market include the following:

Acquisitions, Editorial, and Media Development

Project Editor: Linda Morris

Acquisitions Editor: Bob Woerner

Sr. Copy Editor: Teresa Artman

Technical Editor: Greg Willmore

Editorial Manager: Kevin Kirschner

Permissions Editor: Carmen Krikorian

Media Development Supervisor: Richard Graves

Editorial Assistant: Amanda Foxworth

Cartoons: Rich Tennant (www.the5thwave.com)

Production

Project Coordinator: Dale White

Layout and Graphics: Amanda Carter, Carrie Foster, Gabriele McCann, Tiffany Muth, Jacque Schneider, Mary Virgin, Erin Zeltner

Proofreaders: Laura Albert, John Tyler Connoley, Betty Kish, Susan Moritz, Carl Pierce

Indexer: Sharon Hilgenberg

Publishing and Editorial for Technology Dummies

    Richard Swadley, Vice President and Executive Group Publisher

    Andy Cummings, Vice President and Publisher

    Mary C. Corder, Editorial Director

Publishing for Consumer Dummies

    Diane Graves Steele, Vice President and Publisher

    Joyce Pepple, Acquisitions Director

Composition Services

    Gerry Fahey, Vice President of Production Services

    Debbie Stailey, Director of Composition Services

Contents at a Glance

Introduction *1*

Book 1: Introducing Mac OS X *7*

Chapter 1: Shaking Hands with Mac OS X 9
Chapter 2: Navigating and Running Programs 25
Chapter 3: Basic OS X Housekeeping 47
Chapter 4: Using Sherlock 3: It's Elementary! 75
Chapter 5: Keeping Track with the Address Book 89
Chapter 6: The Joys of Maintenance 101
Chapter 7: Using Classic Mode 121
Chapter 8: Getting Help for the Big X 129
Chapter 9: Troubleshooting the X 137

Book 11: Customizing and Sharing *147*

Chapter 1: Building the Finder of Your Dreams 149
Chapter 2: Giving Your Desktop the Personal Touch 169
Chapter 3: Delving under the Hood with System Preferences 179
Chapter 4: You Mean Others Can Use My Mac, Too? 209
Chapter 5: Setting Up Multi-User Accounts 215
Chapter 6: Sharing Documents for Fun and Profit 227

Book 111: The Digital Hub *239*

Chapter 1: The World According to Apple 241
Chapter 2: Jamming with iTunes and iPod 249
Chapter 3: Focusing on iPhoto 269
Chapter 4: Making Magic with iMovie 285
Chapter 5: Burn Those DVDs! Using iDVD 2 307
Chapter 6: No, It's Not Called "iQuickTime" 323
Chapter 7: Turning Your Mac into a DVD Theater 339

Book 1V: The Typical Internet Stuff *347*

Chapter 1: Getting on the Internet 349
Chapter 2: Using Apple Mail 359
Chapter 3: Staying in Touch with iChat 381

Chapter 4: Expanding Your Horizons with iDisk 393
Chapter 5: Going Places with Internet Explorer 399
Chapter 6: Staying Secure Online 417

Book V: Networking in Mac OS X 427

Chapter 1: Setting Up a Small Network 429
Chapter 2: Using Your Network 447
Chapter 3: You May Even Need AppleTalk 463
Chapter 4: Going Wireless 473
Chapter 5: Sharing that Precious Internet Thing 485

Book VI: Expanding Your System 497

Chapter 1: Hardware that Will Make You Giddy 499
Chapter 2: Add RAM, Hard Drive Space, and Stir 515
Chapter 3: Port-o-rama: Using USB and FireWire 527
Chapter 4: I'm Okay, You're a Printer 533
Chapter 5: Programs that You've (Probably) Gotta Have 543

Book VII: Advanced Mac OS X 565

Chapter 1: . . . And UNIX Lurks Beneath 567
Chapter 2: AppleScript Just Plain Rocks 595
Chapter 3: Forget Hal! Talking and Writing to Your Macintosh 609
Chapter 4: Hosting a Web Site à la OS X 625

Index 647

Table of Contents

Introduction 1

What's Really Required 2
About This Book 3
Conventions Used in This Book 3
    Stuff you type 3
    Menu commands 3
    Display messages 3
    In case you're curious about computers 4
How This Book Is Organized 4
    Book I: Introducing Mac OS X 4
    Book II: Customizing and Sharing 4
    Book III: The Digital Hub 4
    Book IV: The Typical Internet Stuff 5
    Book V: Networking in Mac OS X 5
    Book VI: Expanding Your System 5
    Book VII: Advanced Mac OS X 5
Icons Used in This Book 5

Book 1: Introducing Mac OS X 7

Chapter 1: Shaking Hands with Mac OS X 9

Convince Me: Why Mac OS X? 10
    Pretty to behold 10
    Stable, stable, stable 15
    Multitasking and multithreading for normal human beings 17
    The definition of Internet-savvy 17
    Lots of free goodies 18
    It even runs the old stuff 19
What Do I Really Need to Run the Big X? 20
Upgrading from Earlier Versions of Mac OS 21
    Back up — PLEASE back up 21
    Snuff out disk errors 22
    Plug it, Road Warrior 22
Personalizing the Big X 23

Chapter 2: Navigating and Running Programs 25

Restarting, Sleeping, and Shutting Down 25
A Window Is Much More than a Frame 27
    Opening and closing windows 27
    Scrolling windows 28
    Minimizing and restoring windows 29
    Zooming windows 30
    Toggling toolbars 31

Moving windows 31
Resizing windows 31
Switching windows 31
Menu Mysteries Explained 33
Icons 'R Us 34
Hardware 35
Programs and applications 36
Files 36
Folders 37
Aliases 37
Selecting Icons for Fun and Profit 39
Selecting a single icon 39
Selecting multiple icons 39
Keyboard Shortcuts for the True Power User 40
Houston, We're Go to Launch Programs 42
Running applications from your hard drive 42
Running applications from a CD-ROM or DVD-ROM 42
Switching 'Twixt Programs with Aplomb 43
Opening and Saving Your Stuff in an Application 43
Opening a document 43
Saving a document 45
Quitting Programs 46

Chapter 3: Basic OS X Housekeeping **47**
The Finder: It's the Wind beneath Your Wings 47
Copying and Moving Files and Folders 48
Cloning Your Items — It's Happening Now! 50
Deleting That Which Should Not Be 50
Dragging unruly files against their will 50
Deleting with the menus and the keyboard 50
Emptying that Wastepaper Basket 51
WAIT! I Need That after All! 51
Renaming Your Items 52
Displaying the Facts on Files and Folders 52
Adding comments 53
Displaying extensions 54
Choosing the application to launch with a file 55
Locking files against evildoers 56
Creating an Alias 57
Using the Apple Menu 57
Using Recent Items 57
Playing with the Dock 58
Bad program! Quit! 60
Tracking down your version 61
Specifying a location 61
Availing Yourself of Mac OS X Services 62
Get Thee Hence: Using the Go Menu 63
Monkeying with the Menu Bar 64
Using menu bar icons 64
Doing timely things with the Clock 66
Eject, Tex, Eject! 66

Common Tasks Aplenty 68
    Opening and editing text files 68
    Listening to an audio CD 69
    Recording — nay, burning — a data CD 70
All You Really Need to Know about Printing 72
You Shouldn't Have to Read This, but 73

Chapter 4: Using Sherlock 3: It's Elementary! **75**
Sherlock Is Just Plain Neat 76
Looking for the Scent with the Great Detective 76
You Don't Need a Remote for These Channels 78
Tracking People, Movies, Definitions, and Auctions 79
    Let your mouse do the walking 79
    Scoping local movies 81
    Consulting Sherlock's dictionary 82
    Scouring eBay for Old London 83
Using Internet Search Sites 84
Minding Your Portfolio 85
Translating 'Twixt Languages 86
Finding Flight Information 87

Chapter 5: Keeping Track with the Address Book **89**
Hey, Isn't the Address Book Just a Part of Mail? 89
Entering Contact Information 91
Using Contact Information 93
Arranging Your Contact Cards 95
Using Network Directories 96
Printing Contacts with Flair 97
Swapping Bytes by Using vCards 98

Chapter 6: The Joys of Maintenance **101**
Deleting Applications the Common-sense Way 101
Popping the Hood: Using the Apple System Profiler 103
Tracking Performance with CPU Monitor 105
Fixing Things with the Disk Utility 107
    Displaying the goods on your disks 107
    Playing Doctor with First Aid 109
    Erasing without seriously screwing up 111
    Partitioning the right way 112
    RAID has nothing to do with insects 114
Updating Mac OS X 115
I Demand that You Back Up Your Hard Drive 116
I Further Demand that You Defragment 117
Special Start-up Keys for Those Special Times 118
Crave the Newest Drivers 119

Chapter 7: Using Classic Mode **121**
Classic Mode Explained 121
Cranking Up Classic 122
Reaching that Antique Software 124
Configuring Classic Mode 125
Returning to Your Mac OS 9 Roots 127

Chapter 8: Getting Help for the Big X **129**

Displaying the Help Viewer Window 129
Searching for Specific Stuff 130
Prodding Apple for the Latest Gossip 132
Calling for Help Deep in the Heart of X 132
Other Resources to Chew On 134
        Voice support 134
        Mac publications 135
        Local Mac outlets and user groups 135

Chapter 9: Troubleshooting the X **137**

Don't Panic! 137
The Troubleshooting Process 138
        Step 1: Always try a simple shutdown 138
        Step 2: Check all cable connections 139
        Step 3: Retrace your steps 139
        Step 4: Run Disk Utility 140
        Step 5: Run antivirus software 140
        Step 6: Check the Trash 141
        Step 7: Check online connections 141
        Step 8: Disable troublesome login items 142
        Step 9: Turn off your screen saver 142
        Step 10: Check for write-protection 143
        Step 11: Check your System Profiler 143
        Step 12: Reboot with the Mac OS X Installation CD 143
Troubleshooting Problems with Classic Mode 144
Do I Need To Reinstall Mac OS X? 145
It's Still Not Moving: Troubleshooting Resources 145
        The Mac OS X Help Viewer 146
        The Apple Mac OS X Support site 146
        Your local Apple dealer 146

Book II: Customizing and Sharing **147**

Chapter 1: Building the Finder of Your Dreams **149**

Will That Be Icons or Buttons . . . or Even Columns? 149
Doing the Toolbar Dance 152
        Hiding and showing the toolbar 152
        Hiding and showing the status bar 152
        Giving your toolbar big tires and a loud exhaust 153
Playing Favorites 155
Searching for Files from the Toolbar 155
Searching for Files from the Find Dialog 157
Configuring the View Options 160
        Setting icon view options 160
        Setting list view options 163
        Setting column view options 164
Setting Finder Preferences 165

Chapter 2: Giving Your Desktop the Personal Touch 169

Changing the Background 169
   Picking something Apple 170
   I just gotta have lavender 172
   Selecting your own photo 172
Changing the Screen Saver 172
Changing Colors in Mac OS X 173
Adding Stickies 174
Customizing the Dock 176
   Adding applications and extras to the Dock 176
   Resizing the Dock 177
Arranging Your Precious Desktop 178

Chapter 3: Delving under the Hood with System Preferences 179

The Preferred Way to Display the Preferences 179
Saving Your Preferences 180
Let's Get Personal 180
   Desktop preferences 181
   Dock preferences 181
   General preferences 183
   International preferences 184
   Login Items preferences 185
   My Account preferences 186
   Screen Effects preferences 187
It's All about the Hardware 188
   CDs & DVDs preferences 188
   ColorSync preferences 188
   Displays preferences 189
   Energy Saver preferences 190
   Keyboard preferences 191
   Mouse preferences 192
   Sound preferences 192
Sharing the Joy: Internet & Network 193
   Internet preferences 193
   Network preferences 194
   QuickTime preferences 197
   Sharing preferences 199
Tweaking the System 200
   Accounts preferences 200
   Classic preferences 201
   Date & Time preferences 202
   Software Update preferences 203
   Speech preferences 204
   Startup Disk preferences 205
   Universal Access preferences 206

Chapter 4: You Mean Others Can Use My Mac, Too? 209

How Multi-User Works on Mac OS X 209
Configuring Your Login Screen 211
Locking Things Down 213
Starting Applications Automatically After Login 214

Chapter 5: Setting Up Multi-User Accounts 215

Adding, Editing, and Deleting Users 215
   Adding an account 216
   Editing an existing account 217
   Deleting an existing account 218
Setting Capabilities 218
Using Keychains — NOT 223

Chapter 6: Sharing Documents for Fun and Profit 227

Sharing over a Network versus Sharing on a Single Mac 227
   No network is required 228
   Relying on a guaranteed lock 228
   Most places are off-limits 228
Permissions: Law Enforcement for Your Files 229
Permission and Sharing Do's and Don'ts 232
Sharing Stuff in Office v. X 233
   Document-sharing features 233
   File-level sharing features 235
Password Protection in AppleWorks 237

Book III: The Digital Hub 239

Chapter 1: The World According to Apple 241

First, Sliced Bread . . . and Now the Digital Hub 241
What Does Digital Mean, Anyway? 242
What Can I Digitize? 243
   Photographic images 243
   Music 243
   Video 244
   DVD 244
The Software That Drives the Hub 244
   iPhoto 245
   iTunes 246
   iMovie 246
   iDVD 247
Can I Use All This Stuff at Once? 247

Chapter 2: Jamming with iTunes and iPod 249

What Can I Play on iTunes? 249
Playing an Audio CD 250
Playing an Audio File 251
   Browsing the Library 253
   Finding songs in your Library 254
   Removing old music from the Library 254
Keeping Slim Whitman and Slim Shady Apart:
   Organizing with Playlists 255
Know Your Songs 256
   Setting the song information automatically 256
   Setting or changing the song information manually 257

Ripping Audio Files 257
Tweaking the Audio for Your Ears 258
A New Kind of Radio Station 260
 iTunes Radio 260
 Tuning in your own stations 261
 Radio stations in your Playlists 262
iSending iTunes to iPod 262
Burning Music to Shiny Plastic Circles 263
Changing iTunes Visuals 264
Adding More Visuals to iTunes 266

Chapter 3: Focusing on iPhoto **269**
What iPhoto Can Do 269
Delving into iPhoto 270
Importing Images 101 271
 Importing images from a digital camera 271
 Importing image files 272
Organizing with Photo Albums 273
 Creating a new Photo Album 273
 Adding photos to a Photo Album 273
 Removing photos from a Photo Album 274
 Deleting a Photo Album 275
The Art of Organizing with Keywords 275
 Customizing your own keywords 276
 Searching for keywords 277
Taking Care of Business: Basic Editing 278
 Constrain and crop 279
 Brightness/Contrast 280
 Red-eye removal 280
 Black-and-white 280
 Don't forget to rotate! 281
Producing Your Own Coffee-Table Masterpiece 281
Sharing Photos with Friends and Family 283

Chapter 4: Making Magic with iMovie **285**
The iMovie Interface 285
The Powers of Three 287
 Monitor 287
 Palettes 288
 Viewers 289
The Movie-Making Process 289
Working with Clips (Not the Paper Kind) 290
 Adding clips from media files 291
 Adding clips from your camcorder 291
 Editing clips 293
Basic Composition the iMovie Way 294
 Adding clips to the movie 294
 Removing clips from a movie 295
 Rearranging clips in a movie 295
Transitions for the Masses 295
Even "Gone with the Wind" Had Titles 297

What Good Is a Movie without Special Effects? 299
    iMovie's stock effects 299
    Adding Effects to a movie 300
    Remove an effect 301
Working with Sound 301
    Adding sound to a movie 301
    Removing sound from a movie 304
Completing Your Cinematic Masterpiece 305
    Camera 305
    QuickTime 305
    iDVD 306

Chapter 5: Burn Those DVDs! Using iDVD 2 ....**307**

What Am I Doing, Anyway? 307
Mastering Menus 308
    Themes 309
    Setting the background 311
Adding Media Files to Your DVD 314
    Adding a Movie Button 314
    Setting the Movie Button style 315
    Adding a Slideshow Button 317
Customizing Titles 318
Checking Things Out with a Preview 319
Saving and Burning a DVD 319

Chapter 6: No, It's Not Called "iQuickTime" **323**

QuickTime Can Do That? 323
Playing Media with QuickTime 324
    At the center of the action: The QuickTime Player 324
    Opening QuickTime movies 325
    Operating the QuickTime Player 326
QuickTime: The Super Converter 332
    Importing files 332
    Exporting files 333
Make QuickTime the Center of Your Digital Universe 334
    Favorites 334
    Free content for all 334
    QuickTime and your browser 335
Tweaking QuickTime 336
    Setting the QuickTime Player Preferences 336
    Working with QuickTime Preferences 336

Chapter 7: Turning Your Mac into a DVD Theater **339**

The DVD Hardware 339
The DVD Player: It's Truly Shiny 340
    Using the Controller 340
    Keep your eyes on the Viewer 342
Taking Advantage of Additional DVD Features 342
    Controller extras 342
    DVD Player preferences 343

Book IV: The Typical Internet Stuff 347

Chapter 1: Getting on the Internet 349
Shopping for an ISP 349
Investigating Various Types of Connections 351
Setting Up Your Internet Connection 353
    Using your internal modem 353
    Using Ethernet hardware 354
Connecting with a Dial-up ISP (The Hard Way) 356

Chapter 2: Using Apple Mail 359
Know Thy Mail Window 359
Setting Up Your Account 361
    Adding an account 362
    Editing an existing account 364
    Deleting an account 364
Receiving and Reading E-Mail Wisdom 364
    Reading and deleting your messages 365
    Replying to mail 366
Raise the Little Flag: Sending E-Mail 369
What? You Get Junk Mail, Too? 371
Attachments on Parade 373
Fine-Tuning Your Post Office 375
    Adding sound 375
    Checking Mail automatically 375
    Automating message deletion 375
    Adding signatures 376
    Changing the status of an account 376
Automating Your Mail with Rules 377

Chapter 3: Staying in Touch with iChat 381
Configuring iChat 381
Changing Modes in iChat 384
Will You Be My Buddy? 385
Chat! Chat, I Say! 387
Sending Files Using iChat 390
Eliminating the Riffraff 391

Chapter 4: Expanding Your Horizons with iDisk 393
Grabbing Internet Storage for Your Mac 393
Understanding What's on Your iDisk 395
Opening and Using iDisk 396

Chapter 5: Going Places with Internet Explorer 399
Let's Pretend You've Never Used This Thing 400
Visiting Web Sites 402
Navigating the Web 404
Setting Up Your Home Page 405
Adding and Using Favorites 406
Downloading Files 408

Using Subscriptions and History 410
Saving Web Pages 411
Protecting Your Privacy 413
    Yes, there are such things as bad cookies 413
    Cleaning your cache 415
    Handling ancient history 415

Chapter 6: Staying Secure Online 417

What Can Really Happen? 417
"Shields Up, Chekov!" 419
    Firewall basics 419
    Antivirus basics 423
A Dose of Common Sense: Things Not to Do Online 424

Book V: Networking in Mac OS X 427

Chapter 1: Setting Up a Small Network 429

What Do I Need to Set Up My Network? 430
    Something to network 430
    Network Interface Card (NIC) 430
    Hub or switch 430
    Cables 433
Setting Up Your Network 434
Understanding the Basics of Network Configuration 435
    TCP/IP 435
    Software applications 436
Configuring Network System Preferences 437
    Manually choosing an IP address range 437
    Using DHCP for automatic IP address assignment 440
Verifying Connectivity 442
Troubleshooting Your New Network 444

Chapter 2: Using Your Network 447

It's All about (File) Sharing 447
    Creating an account 447
    Enabling file sharing 449
    Connecting to a shared resource 449
Sharing a Connected Printer 450
Sharing Files to Windows Computers 451
Accessing File Shares on Windows Computers 452
Using FTP to Access Files 453
    Using Mac OS X built-in FTP to share files 454
    Using FTP from your Web browser to transfer files 454
    Using FTP from the command-line interface to transfer files 456
Using the Built-in Firewall 459
Remote Control of Your Mac 460
    Remotely control your Mac (for free, no less!) 461
    How VNC works 461
    Remotely control another computer from your Mac 461

Chapter 3: You May Even Need AppleTalk 463

Setting Up AppleTalk 464
    Automatically configuring AppleTalk 464
    Manually configuring AppleTalk 465
Accessing Files and Printers with AppleTalk 466
    Accessing AppleTalk share points 467
    Accessing AppleTalk printers 471

Chapter 4: Going Wireless 473

Speaking the Wireless Lingo 473
Figuring Out the Different Flavors of Wireless Ethernet 474
    IEEE 802.11b 474
    802.11a 475
    Ahead on the radar: 802.11g 476
Keeping Your Wireless Network Secure 476
    WEP 477
    Other security standards 478
Setting Up Your Wireless Network 479
    Installing an AirPort or other 802.11b network card 479
    Setting up an Ad Hoc wireless network 479
    Setting up wireless networks with an AirPort Base Station 481

Chapter 5: Sharing That Precious Internet Thing 485

Sharing the Internet 485
Using Network Address Translation 486
Ways to Share Your Internet Connection 488
    Using hardware for sharing an Internet connection 488
    Using software for sharing an Internet connection 489
Connecting Everything 491
    Using the software method 491
    Using the hardware method 491
Adding Wireless Support 494
    If you already have a cable/DSL router or
        are using software Internet sharing 494
    If you do not have a cable/DSL router or AirPort Base Station 494

Book VI: Expanding Your System 497

Chapter 1: Hardware that Will Make You Giddy 499

Parading Pixels: Digital Cameras, DV Camcorders, and Scanners 500
    Digital cameras 500
    DV camcorders 501
    Scanners 503
Incredible Input: Keyboards, Trackballs, Joysticks,
    and Drawing Tablets 504
    Keyboards 504
    Trackballs 505
    Joysticks 507
    Drawing tablets 508

Sublime Storage: CD/DVD Recorders and Tape Drives 509
    CD and DVD recorders 509
    Tape drives 510
Awesome Audio: Subwoofer Systems and MP3 Hardware 511
    Subwoofer speaker systems 511
    MP3 players (Well, actually, just the iPod) 512

Chapter 2: Add RAM, Hard Drive Space, and Stir 515

Adding Memory: Reasons for More RAM 515
Shopping for a RAM Upgrade 517
    Finding out the current memory in your Mac 517
    Determining the exact model of your computer 518
The Tao of Hard Drive Territory 519
Internal versus External Storage 520
    External drives 520
    Internal drives 521
Determining How Much Space You Need 522
Shopping for a Hard Drive 523
Installing Your New Stuff 524
    The easy way 524
    The hard way 524

Chapter 3: Port-o-rama: Using USB and FireWire 527

Appreciating the Advantage of a FireWire Connection 527
Understanding USB and the Tale of Two Point Oh 529
Hey, You Need a Hub! 530
Uh, It's Just Sitting There 530
    Common FireWire and USB headaches 531
    Check those drivers 532

Chapter 4: I'm Okay, You're a Printer 533

Meet the Print Center 533
Toolbar Buttons 534
Adding a Funky Printer 536
Managing Your Printing Jobs 538
Sharing a Printer across That There Network 540

Chapter 5: Programs that You've (Probably) Gotta Have 543

The Trundling Microsoft Mammoth 544
Your Mac OS X Toolbox: Drive 10 546
Image Editing for the Masses 548
The Morass of Digital Video 549
Yes, It's Really Called "Toast" 550
If You Positively Have to Run Windows 552
All Hail FileMaker Pro 553
Utilities that Rock 554
    StuffIt 554
    QuicKeys X 555
    BBEdit 556
    REALbasic 558

At Least One Game 559
    Mac OS X Chess 560
    Civilization III 561
    Return to Castle Wolfenstein 562
    WarCraft III 563

Book VII: Advanced Mac OS X 565

Chapter 1: . . . And UNIX Lurks Beneath 567

Why Use the Keyboard? 567
    UNIX keyboarding is fast 567
    UNIX keyboarding is powerful 568
    Go where no mouse has gone before 569
    Automate to elevate 569
    Remote control 570
Uncovering the Terminal 570
    What's a prompt? 571
    A few commands to get started 571
    Using the skills you already have 573
UNIX Commands 101 574
    Anatomy of a UNIX Command 574
    Command line gotchas 575
    Help is on the way! 576
    Autocompletion 576
Working with Files 577
    Paths 577
    Copying, moving, and renaming files 579
    Opening documents and launching applications 581
Useful Commands 581
    Calendar 581
    Processes 583
Fancy-Pants Commands 584
    Finding files 584
    Pipes 585
UNIX Programs that Come in Handy 586
    Text editors 586
    Networking with the Terminal 590
    Cool command-line tools that you can download 591

Chapter 2: AppleScript Just Plain Rocks 595

What's So Great about AppleScript? 595
    Automate common tasks in the Finder 595
    Automate tasks in other applications 596
Running a Script 597
    The kinds of scripts 597
    The Script Editor application 598
    Executing a script 599
Writing Your Own Simple Scripts 600
    Create a script without touching a key 600
    Building your own scripts 602

One Step Beyond: AppleScript Programming 602
    Grab the Dictionary 603
    Anatomy of a simple script 604
    Help is at your fingertips 607

Chapter 3: Forget Hal! Talking and Writing to Your Macintosh 609

Using Ink with a Tablet 609
Computer, Can You Hear Me? 610
    The Speech Recognition tab 611
    Feedback window 615
    Speech Command window 616
The Mac Talks Back! 618
    The Default Voice tab 618
    The Spoken User Interface tab 619
Speaking Your Own Phrases 621
    Speaking text through applications 621
    Speaking text through services 622
    Speaking text through AppleScript 622

Chapter 4: Hosting a Web Site à la OS X 625

Building a Site with .Mac 625
    Registering as a .Mac user 626
    Setting up your site with HomePage 626
    Adding files with iDisk 628
Creating a Home Page with HTML and iDisk 629
Logging into iDisk the Easy Way 630
Using Mac OS X Web Sharing 630
    I love Apache: Confessions of a UNIX Webmaster 631
    Configuring and running Apache 631
Sharing Files with FTP 642
    What does FTP mean and why should you care? 642
    Setting up and using FTP 642

Index...*647*

Introduction

*E*legant.

I remember the first moment that I moved a mouse across a Mac OS X Desktop — at that time, it was the beta of version 10.0 — and I very well remember the word *elegant* as my first impression. (My second impression was *UNIX done better.*)

That's really saying something because I'm an old operating system curmudgeon: I cut my computing teeth on Atari, Commodore 64, and TRS-80 Model III machines, and I still feel much at home in the character-based environment of DOS and UNIX. Of course, I've also used every version of Windows that His Gateness has produced, including the much-improved Windows XP. And yes, I've used Mac OS since before the days of System 7, using a Macintosh SE with a 9-inch monitor (and a built-in handle).

But out of this host of operating systems, could you really call one *elegant* before now? (Even Mac OS 9 didn't deserve such a description, although it did provide the foundation of convenience and simplicity.) Mac OS X — now at version 10.2, affectionately called *Jaguar* — is something different: It's a fine-cut diamond amongst a handful of semi-precious stones. It's the result of an unnatural marriage, I'll admit . . . the intuitive, graphical world of Mac OS 9 and the character-based stability and efficient multitasking of UNIX. Who would have thought that they would work together so well? Mac OS X performs like a Ferrari, and (unbelievably) it looks as good, too.

Therefore, you can imagine just how excited I was to be asked by Wiley Publishing to write this book, and how I immediately jumped at the chance to write a comprehensive guide to Apple's masterpiece. The book that you hold in your hands is a classic *For Dummies* design — it provides you the step-by-step instruction on every major feature of Mac OS X, plenty of which my editors agree is humorous — but it also goes a step further from time to time, delving into why something works the way that it does or what's going on behind the scenes. You can chalk that up to my admiration for everyone in Cupertino and what they've perfected.

What you *won't* find in this Desk Reference is wasted space. All the new features of version 10.2 are here, including iChat, the new Sherlock 3, the latest versions of all the *iApps* (like iTunes 3), and the new incarnations of Address Book and Apple Mail. Everything's explained from the ground up, just in case you've never touched an Apple computer before. By the time you reach the final pages, you'll have covered advanced topics such as networking, AppleScript, Internet security . . . and yes, even an introduction to the powerful world of UNIX that exists underneath.

I sincerely hope that you'll enjoy this book and that it will act as your guide while you discover all the wonderful features of Mac OS X that I use every day. Remember, if a Windows-enslaved acquaintance still titters about your iMac, I'll understand if you're tempted to drop this weighty tome on his foot.

The official name of the latest version is (portentous pause here, please) Mac OS X Version 10.2 Jaguar. But who wants to spit out that mouthful every time? Throughout this book, I refer to the product as OS X, and when I discuss something that's particular to the latest version, I call it Jaguar. Okay with you?

What's Really Required

If you've got a Mac that's either running Mac OS X version 10.2 or is ready to be upgraded to Jaguar, you're set to go. Despite what you might have heard, you *won't* require any of the following:

✦ **A degree in computer science:** Apple designed Mac OS X for regular people, and I designed this book for people of every experience level. Even if you've never used a Mac before, you'll find no hostile waters here.

✦ **A fortune in software:** I do describe additional software that you can buy to expand the functionality of your Mac; however, that section is only a few pages long. *Everything else* covered in this book is included with Mac OS X Jaguar — and by the size of this volume, you get a rough idea of just how complete Mac OS X is! Heck, many folks buy Macs just because of the free software like iTunes and iPhoto. (Tough cookies to the vast unwashed Windows horde.)

✦ **An Internet connection:** Granted, you're not going to do much with Apple Mail without an Internet connection, but computers *did* exist before the Internet. You can still be productive with Mac OS X without receiving buckets of spam.

Oh, you will need a set of Mac OS X version 10.2 installation discs. Go figure.

About This Book

Although this book is a Desk Reference, you can also read it in a linear fashion (straight through) — probably not in one session, mind you. (Then again, Diet Coke is cheap, so it *is* possible.) The material is divided into seven mini-books, each of which covers an entire area of Mac OS X knowledge. For example, you'll find mini-books on networking, the Apple Digital Hub suite of applications, customizing your Desktop, and Internet-related applications.

Each self-contained chapter discusses a specific feature, application, connection, or cool thing about Mac OS X. Feel free to begin reading anywhere or skip chapters at will. For example, if you're already using an Internet connection, you won't need the chapter on adding an Internet connection. However, I recommend that you read this book from the front to the back, like any good mystery novel. (For those that want to know right now, Bill Gates did it.)

Conventions Used in This Book

Even *For Dummies* books have to get technical from time to time, usually involving commands that you have to type and menu items you have to click. If you've read any of my other *For Dummies* books, you'll know that a helpful set of conventions is used to indicate what needs to be done or what you see onscreen.

Stuff you type

When I ask you to type a command or enter something in a text field (like your name or phone number), the text appears like this: **Type me**

Press the Return key to process the command or enter the text.

Menu commands

When I give you a specific set of menu commands to use, they appear in the following format: Edit⇨Copy.

In this example, you should click the Edit menu and then choose the Copy menu item.

Display messages

If I mention a specific message that you see on your screen, it looks like this on the page: `This is a message displayed by an application.`

In case you're curious about computers

No one expects a book in the *For Dummies* series to contain techno-jargon or ridiculous computer science semantics — especially a book about the Macintosh, which has always strived for simplicity and user-friendliness. I hereby promise that I'll do my absolute best to avoid unnecessary techno-talk. For those who are interested in what's happening under the hood, I provide sidebars that explain a little more about what's doing what to whom. If you'd rather just have fun and ignore the digital dirty work, please feel free to disregard these additions (but don't tear sidebars out of the book because there's likely to be important stuff on the opposite side of the page).

How This Book Is Organized

I've done my best to emulate the elegant design of Mac OS X by organizing this book into seven mini-books, with cross-references where appropriate.

Book I: Introducing Mac OS X

This mini-book begins with an invigorating chapter explaining exactly why you should be so happy to be a Mac OS X owner. Then I provide an introduction to the basic tasks that you'll perform — things like copying files, running programs, and the like. Because Sherlock 3 and the Address Book are such important elements of Mac OS X, I also cover them in this mini-book. You'll also find coverage of Classic mode, a guide to normal Mac OS X maintenance and troubleshooting, and instructions on using the Mac OS X Help system.

Book II: Customizing and Sharing

Who wants to stick with the defaults? The material in this mini-book leads you through the steps that you need to customize Mac OS X to your specific needs and desires . . . everything from a tweak to your background or screensaver to a description of how to set up and administer multiple accounts on a single Macintosh. You'll also find coverage of the different settings that you can change in System Preferences, which is an important place in Mac OS X.

Book III: The Digital Hub

Sweet! This chapter jumps right in among the crown jewels of the Digital Hub: iTunes, iPhoto, iDVD, iMovie, QuickTime, and the DVD Player. Taken as a suite, these applications allow you to plug in and use all sorts of electronic gadgets, including digital cameras, digital video (DV) camcorders, and MP3 players — plus, you can edit or create your own DVD discs, audio CDs, and movies.

Book IV: The Typical Internet Stuff

This mini-book contains just what it says. But then again, it's easy to get enthusiastic about Apple Mail, the new instant messaging application *(iChat),* and the online storage provided by iDisk. I also cover an honest-to-goodness (eek!) Microsoft product — Internet Explorer — which somehow ended up included in Mac OS X. Finally, you'll discover more about the built-in Internet firewall and how you can use it to safeguard your Mac from Internet undesirables.

Book V: Networking in Mac OS X

Ethernet, Rendezvous, and AppleTalk are lurking in this mini-book — but I explain them step-by-step, in language that a normal human being can understand. Find out how to use wireless networks like the AirPort from Apple, as well as how to share an Internet connection with other computers in a local network.

Book VI: Expanding Your System

Time to take things up a notch. In this mini-book, I discuss the hardware and software that everyone's adding to Mac OS X and why you might (or might not) need such toys. RAM, hard drives, printers, USB, and FireWire . . . they're all discussed here in detail. Consider this a banquet of expansion information.

Book VII: Advanced Mac OS X

I know that I told you earlier that I was going to avoid techno-talk whenever possible, yet I also mentioned the advanced things that you'll find in this mini-book, like using UNIX within Mac OS X and writing basic AppleScript scripts to automate repetitive tasks. If you don't mind immersing yourself in all that's technical, read here for the skinny on hosting a Web site and communicating with Mac OS X by using your voice and your handwriting.

Icons Used in This Book

The icons in this book are more than just attractive — they're also important visual cues for stuff you don't want to miss.

The Tip icons flag short snippets of information that will save you time or trouble (and, in some cases, even cash).

These icons highlight optional technical information for folks like me — if you also used to disassemble alarm clocks for fun when you were 6 years old, you'll love this stuff.

Always read this information next to this icon first! Something looms ahead that could put your hardware or software at risk.

Look to the Remember icons for those tidbits you need to file away in your mind. Just remember to remember.

Follow these road signs for all the cool updates and innovations in OS X version 10.2 Jaguar.

Book I

Introducing Mac OS X

AFTER INSTALLING OS X JAGUAR, NED AND LORETTA SELECT THE COMPUTER'S BACKGROUND

© RICHTENNANT

"Oh — I like this background _much_ better than the basement."

Contents at a Glance

Chapter 1: Shaking Hands with Mac OS X..9

Chapter 2: Navigating and Running Programs 25

Chapter 3: Basic OS X Housekeeping..47

Chapter 4: Using Sherlock 3: It's Elementary!..75

Chapter 5: Keeping Track with the Address Book 89

Chapter 6: The Joys of Maintenance 101

Chapter 7: Using Classic Mode 121

Chapter 8: Getting Help for the Big X 129

Chapter 9: Troubleshooting the X 137

Chapter 1: Shaking Hands with Mac OS X

In This Chapter

✓ Understanding the advantages of Mac OS X

✓ Checking your system requirements

✓ Upgrading from earlier versions of Mac OS

✓ Installing Mac OS X

✓ Running Mac OS X for the first time

*I*t's human nature to require instant gratification from your software. I've seen it countless times: Someone runs a program and immediately feels comfortable and then spends the rest of his days using that program religiously. Or another person plays with the same program for 120 seconds and dismisses it with the labels *too difficult* or *too confusing*. It's rather like watching a fancy fashion show in Rome or Paris: There had better be eye appeal pretty quickly, or the bucks won't flow.

Ditto for modern computer operating systems. An *operating system* is the basic software that determines the look and feel of your entire computer and usually extends to the programs that you run as well. Microsoft recently felt the pinch of an old-fashioned operating system — Windows 98 and Windows Me were starting to appear rather plain-looking — and promptly released Windows XP, where menus fade in and out like fireflies on a summer night, little puppies help you find files, and animation abounds. To be honest, however, updating a PC by upgrading to Windows XP is a little like putting on a polyester sports coat over the same tired old T-shirt and jeans — most of what changed was on the outside.

Apple doesn't work that way. Sure, Mac OS X looks doggone good . . . forget the minimum requirement of shirt and shoes, this operating system is wearing an Armani suit. What's *really* exciting for Macintosh owners around the world, however, is the heart that beats *beneath* the pretty form. Mac OS X is quite literally an operating system revolution, delivering some of the most advanced features available on any personal computer in use today — while remaining as easy to use as the first Macintosh. (And yes, I do own and use both PCs and Macs — what's important is which computer does the job the fastest in the easiest manner.)

Now, I'm not going to just haul off and proclaim that Mac OS X can run rings around — well . . . you know, the *W* word — without solid proof. In this chapter, I introduce you to the advantages of Mac OS X and why it's such a step ahead for those running Mac OS 9. I also cover the hardware requirements that you'll need to run Mac OS X as well as guidelines on upgrading from Mac OS 9. Finally, I familiarize you with the steps that you'll encounter the first time you fire up the Big X.

Convince Me: Why Mac OS X?

Apple pioneered the graphical approach to computing with the appearance of the first Macintosh, so you'd expect Mac OS X to be simple to use — and indeed it is. For many folks, that's Job One — if you're one of those people, you can happily skip this section without need of further evidence because Mac OS X is undoubtedly the easiest operating system on the planet to use. (And believe me, I'm not knocking simplicity. Computers are *supposed* to be getting easier to use, and techno-nerds like me are *supposed* to be rendered unnecessary as computers advance.) The mantra of the Mac, and the first of Mark's Maxims: **One Mouse, One Button, One King.**™

Still with me? Need more testimony? Or perhaps you're just curious about the engine under the hood. Then read on — and if you're a Macintosh owner, feel free to gloat! (If you're a PC owner, there's always eBay.)

Pretty to behold

Let me illustrate with a screenshot or two: Figure 1-1 illustrates a typical screen from a day spent in Mac OS 9.2, the capable — but rather old-fashioned — version of the Mac OS operating system that shipped in the days before Mac OS X.

Compare that screen with a similar screen from the Big X, as shown in Figure 1-2. As you can see, everything's streamlined in appearance, with maximum efficiency in mind. Tasteful 3-D abounds, from the drop-shadowed windows to the liquid-look scroll bars. Icons look like miniature works of art. Macintosh owners appreciate outstanding design — and can recognize the value of a great computer, even if it is lime-green. After all, many Mac owners are professionals in the graphic arts, and Apple provides the hardware that they need — like the top-of-the-line LCD display used with the new iMac.

Take a look at what's going on behind the curtain — the Great Oz is actually pretty busy back there.

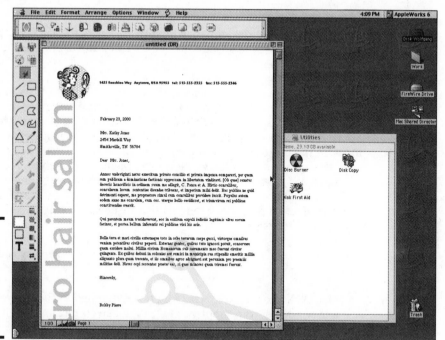

Figure 1-1:
Mac OS 9.2
was a
workhorse,
true, but it
wasn't a
work of art.

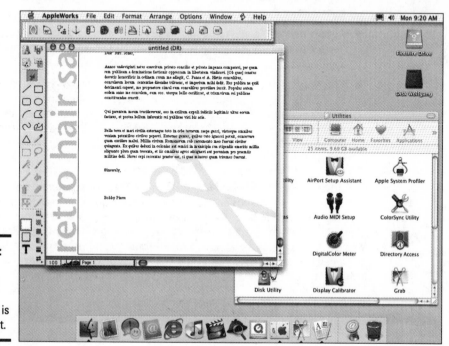

Figure 1-2:
Eye-
catching?
You bet!
Mac OS X is
a knockout.

The allure of Aqua

The Apple software developers who introduced us to Mac OS X designed this new look from the ground up — they call it *Aqua,* and it's the new standard user interface.

Whoops, I just realized that I slipped a ten-cent example of techno-babble into that previous paragraph. Let me explain: A *user interface* design determines how things look throughout both the operating system itself and all applications that are written to run under an operating system (OS). This includes the buttons that you push, the controls that you click or move, and even the appearance of the windows and menus themselves. For example, if you've already begun to use Mac OS X, you've probably stopped right in the middle of a task and exclaimed to yourself, "Why, Self, look at that cool 3-D striping effect on that menu bar!" Those stripes are a tiny part of the Aqua user interface design.

Aqua also extends to the placement of controls and how they're shown to you. For example:

✦ Mac OS X uses Aqua *sheets* (which are attached to their parent dialogs and windows) to prompt you for input, like confirming when you're about to close a document without saving it. Unlike Windows, multiple programs can have multiple sheets open, so you can continue to work in other applications — without being rudely forced to answer the query immediately.

✦ Aqua's new *file selection controls* like the one in Figure 1-3 make it much easier to quickly navigate to a specific file or folder from within an application.

✦ The *Dock* is another Aqua addition, replacing the old Control Strip from Mac OS 9. The Dock launches your favorite applications, indicates what's running on your Mac, and allows you to switch between those programs — and all in a strip that you can relocate and customize at will. I talk about the Dock in greater detail later in the book, in Chapter 2 of Book II.

Consider Aqua the *look-and-feel* of Mac OS X and virtually all applications that it runs; you'll discover how to use these Aqua controls in the pages to come. Of course, Mac owners really don't have to worry about Aqua itself; the Aqua guidelines are a roadmap for those writing applications for Mac OS X. Programs written to the common Aqua interface standard will be easier for you to use, and you'll become a proficient power user of that program much faster.

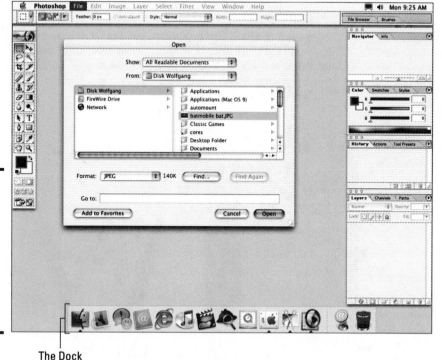

Figure 1-3:
Another
Aqua
original —
the file
selection
controls (in
this case,
in Photo-
shop 7).

The Dock

The quality of Quartz

The second ingredient in the visual feast that is Mac OS X is named *Quartz Extreme* — again, I must ask your forgiveness, good reader, because I have to get a tad technical again. Quartz Extreme is a *graphics engine:* It's the portion of Mac OS X that draws what you see on the screen (in the Aqua interface, natch). Think of the engine in your car, which is responsible for making you move. Whether your Mac is running Microsoft Word or simply idling at the Desktop waiting for you to finish your soda, Quartz Extreme is at work displaying icons, drawing shapes, and animating things in the Dock.

What sets Quartz Extreme apart from the ho-hum graphics engine that Windows uses? It's all about standards . . . you know, those things that Microsoft would *much* rather that you forget. To wit:

✦ **PDF:** The Quartz Extreme engine is built around the Acrobat Portable Document Format (*PDF* for short) developed by Adobe. If you've been spending any time at all on the Internet in the last two or three years, you know that PDF files have emerged as the standard for displaying and printing the highest-quality electronic documents. Plus, Adobe has released a version of the free Acrobat reader for just about every computer on this green Earth. This means that text and graphics displayed in Quartz Extreme are razor sharp, resizable, and easily portable from one computer to another. In fact, Mac OS X displays PDF files without even requiring Acrobat. Figure 1-4 shows a complex PDF document that I opened in Mac OS X.

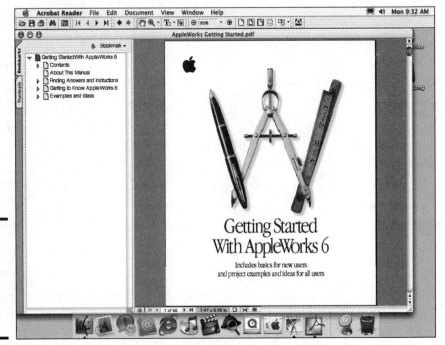

Figure 1-4: Yes, that's a PDF document, not a scanned image!

✦ **OpenGL:** Gamers will get really excited about this one: Quartz Extreme also uses the OpenGL graphics acceleration standard, which delivers the fastest 3-D graphics on the planet. (Think photo-realistic, high-resolution graphics drawn in the blink of an eye.) In fact — and this is a really cool trick — if you have an advanced 3-D card, OpenGL is even used to produce the Desktop in Mac OS X Jaguar.

In English, that means that today's top-of-the-line 3-D gaming and 3-D graphics acceleration can take care of drawing *everything;* forget about waiting for windows to close or menus to appear, even when you're creating the world's biggest honking spreadsheet or building a presentation the size of Baltimore. As the Chairman of the Board would say, "We're talkin' fast, baby, like a rocket ship to the moon!"

Don't forget QuickTime!

If you've recorded or edited digital video (DV), you're probably already familiar with Apple's QuickTime `.mov` format — *QuickTime movies* are high-resolution, relatively small in size, and easily created with iMovie, which I discuss later in Book III, Chapter 4. Although QuickTime isn't "on stage" all the time like Aqua or Quartz Extreme, it's still an important part of Mac OS X: Every time that you display a video clip that you've recorded or watch a streaming TV broadcast from a Web site, you'll be using QuickTime. (Note, however, that you don't use QuickTime to watch DVD movies — that job is reserved for the Apple DVD Player.)

QuickTime is actually not a new Mac OS X feature — it's been around since the days of Mac OS 8 — but the latest version of Mac OS X includes the free QuickTime 6 Player (shown in the figure below), which provides support for the latest broadcast and Web video. In fact, you can set up your own TV station on the Web with the tools included in the Pro QuickTime package.

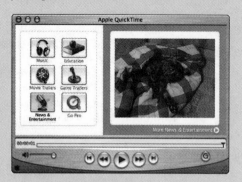

Stable, stable, stable

"So it's elegant in design — that's great, Mark, but what if Mac OS X crashes? Aqua and Quartz Extreme aren't worth a plug nickel if my mouse doesn't move and I lose my document!" Believe me, I couldn't agree more; I make my living from computers, and every time that a misbehaving program locks up one of my machines, I throw a tantrum that would make Godzilla back off. Lockups shouldn't be tolerated in this day and age . . . and, unfortunately, Mac OS 9 crashed almost as often as Windows 98.

Luckily, the folks who designed Mac OS X were just as interested in producing a rock-solid operating system as they were in designing an attractive look. (Think of Tom Cruise's face on The Rock's body.)

Mac OS X is as hard to crash as the legendary UNIX operating system — that's right, the same reliable workhorse that techno-wizards around the world use to power the Internet, where stability is all-important. In fact, Mac OS X is actually built *on top* of a UNIX base. It's just well hidden underneath, allowing you and me to focus on our programs and click with a mouse without learning any of those obscure, arcane keyboard commands. You get the benefits of UNIX without a pair of suspenders, a pocket protector, or the hassle of growing a beard. (Not to mention years of computer programming experience.)

Apple calls this UNIX foundation at the heart of Mac OS X by another nifty title: *Darwin.* I could tell you that Darwin provides the latest in memory and CPU management, but if you're a normal human being, your eyes will glaze over. Suffice it to say that Darwin makes the best use of your computer's memory (RAM) and your computer's brain (CPU). Rest assured that your Web server will stay up, even if your misbehaving Virtual Birdcalling simulation decides to run amok. (Emus running amok . . . how dreadful.)

Yes, yet another standard is at work here — uh-oh, Overlord Gates is truly angry now! For those who do have a beard and are curious about such things, Darwin uses a FreeBSD kernel, so it also inherits all the protocol standards that have made UNIX the foundation of today's Internet. You can find more about FreeBSD at `www.freebsd.org`. Because Mac OS X is developed as an Open Source project, software engineers outside of Apple can actually contribute ideas and code, just like UNIX continues to evolve over time. (And yes, you'll even discover how to access the UNIX command prompt from Mac OS X later in Book VII, Chapter 1!)

To get an idea of just how well armored Mac OS X is, consider Figure 1-5: Note that one program, which I call Titanic 1.0, has locked up like San Quentin. Under Mac OS 9, your only chance at recovering anything would involve divine intervention. However, in Mac OS X, AppleWorks is unaffected because it has a completely protected area of system memory to play in. *Hint:* I show you how to force Titanic 1.0 to go away a little later in Book I, Chapter 3.

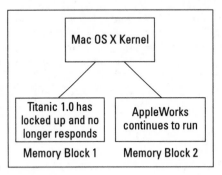

Figure 1-5: Mac OS X keeps programs separate for a reason.

By the way, Darwin makes it easy for UNIX software developers to quickly and easily *port* (or rewrite) all sorts of UNIX applications to work under Mac OS X. I think that you'll agree that a wider selection of applications is a good thing.

Multitasking and multithreading for normal human beings

And now, for your entertainment, a short one-act play. (No, really.)

A Shakespearean Moment of Multitasking and Multithreading

Our play opens with Julius Caesar shaking his head in disgust at his Mac OS 9 Desktop.

> **Caesar:** Anon, I am only one mortal, yet my Desktop doth abound with portals to applications of all different mien. Tell me, foul beast, why thy spirit seems slow and sluggish, and my Excel spreadsheet doth crawl on its belly!

[Enter Romeo, a cocky and rather brash young Apple software developer.]

> **Romeo:** Dude, the problem is, like, your operating system. Y'see, older versions of Mac OS ended up constantly, like, shifting your computer's attention from one app to another — Excel has to cooperate with everything else that's running in the background, like a good little corporate boy. It's less efficient and very, very '90s. Upgrade to Mac OS X, and you get *preemptive* multitasking — the app you're actually using, like, gets the lion's share of the processing time, and everything runs smoother when you need it. That's the way UNIX works.

> **Caesar:** Verily, your strange tongue doth annoy me. Guards, behead him — then obtain for me this Mac OS X.

[Exit Romeo — rather swiftly — stage right.]

> **Romeo:** I'm outta here — I've got a hot date — but don't forget, like, Mac OS X also uses *multithreaded* processing, so if your Mac has more than one CPU, it can handle different operating system tasks at the same time. It's kind of like your computer can both walk and chew gum at the same time: fast, fast, fast!

Fin

As the play closes, we can only hope that Romeo is fast as well. (I told you it was a short play.)

The definition of Internet-savvy

Remember the classic iMac advertisements that touted the one-plug approach to the Internet? That entire campaign was centered on one idea: the Internet was *supposed* to be easy to use. The folks at Microsoft sat up and took notice when the iMac proved so incredibly successful, and Windows XP actually reduced some of the overwhelming folderol that you had to encounter just to connect to the Internet — but Mac OS X still wipes the floor with XP when it comes to easy and complete Internet connectivity. For example:

✦ **Easy configuration:** Mac OS X sets up your entire Internet connection with a simple wizard of four screens. As long as you've got the right information handy (which your Internet Service Provider should supply), it's a snap to set up.

✦ **iDisk:** What if I told you that — for a reasonable yearly subscription fee — Apple can provide you with a chunk of Internet-accessible, private hard drive space — and that you can access this hard drive space from anywhere on Earth? Absolutely, unbelievably, massively cool. This neat trick is called iDisk, and I'll be covering it later in detail in Book IV, Chapter 4.

✦ **All the Internet behind-the-scenes stuff:** The Internet is basically built on a number of *protocols* (read that *rules for exchanging all sorts of data*) — and, as I mention earlier, UNIX machines dominate the Internet. Ergo, adding Mac OS X to your Macintosh also provides you with support for just about every Internet protocol on the planet. Even if you don't know them by name or write your own software, the applications that you buy can use them.

✦ **A gaggle of great Internet applications:** Mac OS X ships with all sorts of Internet magic built-in. For example, there's Sherlock 3 — a supercharged search program that also acts as a doorway to information channels, which I discuss in Chapter 4 of Book I. You also get instant Internet and local network communication with iChat (which I cover in Chapter 3 of Book IV), and Apple Mail, a standard-issue battle-ready e-mail program (which I discuss in Chapter 2 of Book IV). Yup, it's all free.

✦ **And Apache, sweet Apache:** Friends, as a Webmaster myself, I can tell you that I was visibly moved — well, at least exceptionally excited — when I learned that Mac OS X included the industry-standard Apache Web server, which runs over half of the sites on the Web! (Yep, that includes `www.apple.com`.) Get all the details in Chapter 4 of Book VII.

Lots of free goodies

You don't get just Internet applications when you latch your fingers onto a box o' Mac OS X — you can start doing all sorts of neat stuff without investing one extra dollar in more software! Check it out.

✦ **The iStuff:** This suite of easy-to-use integrated programs is practically as well known as the Macintosh itself these days: iDVD, iPhoto, iTunes, and iMovie. Each of these stellar programs is covered in full in Book III. If you've got a digital camera, an MP3 player, or a DV camcorder, you're going to be a very happy individual indeed.

✦ **AppleWorks:** If you've bought a new Macintosh with Mac OS X pre-installed, you'll also receive AppleWorks (Apple's answer to Microsoft Office). Good stuff, indeed. If you don't want to spend the bucks on Office v. X and you don't need the complex geegaws and baroque architecture of Word and Excel, I can guarantee you that AppleWorks is powerful enough to satisfy your office urgings.

✦ **The obligatory games:** Apple couldn't have picked two games that are a better match: the finger-exercising arcade shoot-'em-up challenge of Deimos Rising and the immersive 3-D fun of Otto Matic. Because this book this isn't a game guide, I leave you to explore these two programs at your leisure.

Naturally, there are others that I haven't mentioned here — in fact, bundled programs like Quicken 2002 Deluxe have entire *For Dummies* books devoted to them — but that gives you a taste of what's included.

It even runs the old stuff

Convinced yet? Before I go, I should mention one more outstanding feature of Mac OS X that will undoubtedly please dyed-in-the-wool Mac users: the Big X can run virtually all software written for older versions of Mac OS 8 and 9! (It's rather like Windows XP running Windows 98 programs *without* the hassle and the deluge of error messages.) The good folks at Cupertino are sharp enough to ensure that you can run legacy software if necessary.

In the world of Mac OS X, these applications are called *Classic* programs. To run a Classic application, Mac OS X actually launches a virtual Mac OS 9 session, as you can see in Figure 1-6. You can set Classic to run automatically whenever you turn on your Mac, or Mac OS X can launch it whenever necessary, thus saving the system resources for native Mac OS X applications until you really need Classic. Because I work almost exclusively in Mac OS X now, I've chosen the latter. Face it: This is just downright cool. (For more on Classic, see Book I, Chapter 7.)

If you're a new Mac owner, you can promptly forget about this feature — everything you'll be buying and using from now on will likely be written for the Big X (unless you suddenly stumble upon a gem of a program from a few years back). Oh, and you can also boot cleanly into Mac OS 9 whenever you like . . . usually just for a nostalgic whim, and then you'll reboot right back into Mac OS X.

Figure 1-6:
Waiter,
there's Mac
OS 9 on my
Desktop!

What Do I Really Need to Run the Big X?

I've written three other *For Dummies* books, and I always find the "Hardware Requirements" section a hard one to write. Why? Well, I know what Apple claims as the minimum hardware requirements necessary to run Mac OS X. But, on the other hand, I know what *I* would consider the minimum hardware requirements, and they're substantially different. Oh well, let me list the bare bones, and then I'll give you my take on what you really need. (Of course, if Mac OS X is already preinstalled on your computer, feel free to tear out this page and create a handful of celebratory confetti.)

From *The World According to Jobs*, the minimum requirements are

✦ **Hardware:** You'll need any Mac with a G3 or G4 processor — except for the original PowerBook G3 portable, which is not supported in Mac OS X. This means that any iMac, iBook, Power Mac G3, or Power Mac G4 is eligible to play. I should also mention that Mac OS X doesn't support third-party CPU upgrade cards out of the box.

✦ **RAM:** You'll need at least 128MB of memory (RAM). At today's low prices, that's like buying a pizza.

✦ **Hard drive territory:** Although svelte by Windows standards, Mac OS X still needs about 1.5GB of free space on your hard drive.

From *The World According to Chambers,* the minimum requirements are

✦ **Hardware:** I recommend at least a 600 MHz G3. Remember, this is *my* take on what you'll need to really take advantage of Mac OS X, and I have to say that I don't think it performs well enough on older, slower G3 computers. Any G4 is well suited to run Mac OS X.

✦ **RAM:** Don't settle for anything less than 256MB. Again, with memory as cheap as it is these days, this is like adding extra cheese to that pizza.

Any techno-nerd worth the title will tell you that the single most important key to performance in today's operating systems is RAM — yep, it's actually more effective than a faster processor! Therefore, if you've got any extra spending cash in between your sofa cushions, spend it on RAM.

✦ **Hard drive territory:** I'd recommend 2GB free.

Upgrading from Earlier Versions of Mac OS

Because the installation of Mac OS is as simple as loading a CD-ROM disc and double-clicking on an icon, there's not much to tell. What's important is the steps that you should take care of *before* you start the installation. I cover those in the next section. Pay heed, or pay later. I won't go into detail about the actual installation because there really aren't any details to speak of — you'll answer a question or two, and then hop up to get another cup of coffee or another caffeine-laden soda while the installer does the rest. Would anyone expect any different from Apple?

Pet Peeve Number 1: The round object that you load into your CD-ROM or DVD-ROM disc is a disc, not a disk, like your hard drive or that flimsy floppy. Anyone who pretends to talk oh-so-knowingly about a CD-ROM disk or DVD disk is a dweeb, and you should steer as far away from that dweeb as possible in the future.

Back up — PLEASE back up

I know you're anxious to join the In crowd, and Apple makes the upgrade process as noninvasive and as safe as possible, but SNAFUs like power loss and hard drive failures do happen. With a full backup of your system on CD or DVD (or even to an external hard drive), you can rest assured that you'll get your precious files and folders back in pristine shape if tragedy strikes. To be honest, you need to back up your system on a regular basis anyway. Promise me now that you'll back up your system, won't you?

I recommend a good commercial back up program like Retrospect Backup from Dantz Development Corporation (www.dantz.com), as shown in Figure 1-7 — version 5.0 even supports both Mac OS 9 and Mac OS X, so you can use it both before and after the upgrade!

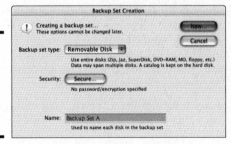

Figure 1-7: Prepare a backup with Retrospect — feel the joy.

Snuff out disk errors

Before you upgrade, I recommend using the Mac OS 9 Disk First Aid utility (Figure 1-8) one last time — upgrading a disk with errors will take longer. You'll find Disk First Aid in the Utility folder.

On the plus side, Mac OS X comes with its own disk check-up program, called *Disk Utility,* which I cover later in the book in Chapter 6 of Book I. Ain't technology grand?

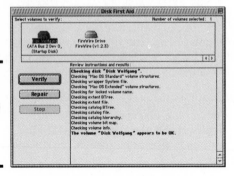

Figure 1-8: Checking the disk one final time before liftoff.

Plug it, Road Warrior

You're on the road with your older G3 iBook, and you've just bought your copy of Mac OS X. You're thinking of installing your brand-spanking new operating system. . . . Stop! *NOW.*

Before you decide to upgrade your Mac notebook, consider what will happen if that magical vessel containing all your files should flicker and. . . . No, on second thought, don't even visualize it. (Even if the battery is fully charged.) If you're installing a Mac OS X upgrade on a PowerBook or iBook, make sure that it's plugged in and receiving its share of good, clean, AC power from a handy, nearby wall socket. The installation process may take an hour, and there'll be constant hard drive and CD-ROM activity — think "Attack of the Energy Draining Installation from Planet Lithium." You don't want to try this while your notebook is operating on battery power.

Heck, a techno-purist would probably recommend that you attach your notebook to an Uninterruptible Power Supply (UPS) for the installation process, but I'm not quite that paranoid about power outages.

If you can't install Mac OS X with your current start-up hard drive, restart your Mac and hold down the C key during the boot sequence. This forces your Macintosh to use the disc as your start-up volume — in this case, the Mac OS X Install disc — which should allow you to launch the install program without any headaches.

Keep one thing in mind while installing Mac OS X: If you format the destination drive — the drive where you'll be installing Mac OS X — you'll lose everything that it stored. No big surprise there, and the installation program will warn you profusely about this beforehand. There's really no reason to do so, unless you just crave a clean installation (which is an installation of a new operating system on a newly-formatted drive, rather than an upgrade of your existing Mac OS System files). Apple gives you the ability to format your drive by using UFS (UNIX File System), which is definitely *not* a good idea unless you're a UNIX techno-wizard already — drives formatted with UFS won't support Mac OS 9 files and folders, and Classic mode won't work. Therefore, if you insist on formatting your destination drive, use Mac OS Extended (or HFS Plus) format.

Personalizing the Big X

After the installation has completed and you've rebooted the beast, stand back and watch those beautiful rounded edges and liquid colors appear. But wait — you're not quite done yet! Mac OS X needs to be personalized for you, just like your toothbrush or your SUV's six-way power seat; therefore, what I call the *First Use Wizard* steps in the first time that you boot Mac OS X.

These wizard screens change periodically — and they're completely self-explanatory — so I won't march you through each one step by step. However, here are a few tips that will provide a bit of additional over-the-shoulder help while you're setting things up.

✦ **How rude!** If you're outside the US or other English-speaking countries, you should know that Mac OS X hides "foreign" country names and keyboard layouts. Rest assured, though, because Mac OS X does indeed provide full support for other languages and keyboard configurations. To display these options in the list boxes, click the Show All button at the bottom of the wizard screen.

✦ **Accounts are important.** When Mac OS X asks you to create your account, don't forget your password — oh, and they're case-sensitive, too, so *THIS* is different from *this* or *ThiS*. It's a good idea to enter a password hint, but don't make that hint too easy to guess — for example, *My first dog's name* is probably preferable to *Plays Frasier on TV.* Mac OS X will use the name and password that you enter to create your account, which you'll use to log in if you set up a multi-user system for several people. (More on this later in Chapter 4 of Book II.) *Never* write down your passwords, either; such crib sheets work just as well for others as for you.

✦ **I need to fix that.** You can click the Back button at any time to return to previous wizard screens. Mac OS X, being the bright child that it is, automatically saves your choices for you, so when you click Continue to return, everything is as you left it.

✦ **Extra stuff.** Whether you decide to accept the news, offers, and related-product information from Apple is your decision — however, it's only right that I point out that you can find this same information on the Apple Web site, so there's no need to engorge your e-mail Inbox unless you so desire. (I turned this off.)

✦ **LAN connections.** If you're connecting your Mac to a Windows Transmission Control Protocol/Internet Procotol (TCP/IP) network (or you're using an Internet router that uses Dynamic Host Configuration Protocol [DHCP]), it's a good idea to click Yes when you're asked whether you should use the configuration supplied by the existing server.

DHCP automatically provides the computers on the network with all the settings that they need to connect — if that sounds like ancient Sumerian, you'll find out more in Chapter 1 of Book VI.

✦ **Do create your .Mac account!** Apple's .Mac service just plain rocks — especially the iDisk storage you'll receive. Again, more on this in Chapter 4 of Book IV, but take my word for it. Join up, trooper. (The trial subscription is free, and it's easy to upgrade to a full membership if you decide you like the .Mac benefits.)

✦ **Have your Mail settings handy.** If you set up your trial .Mac account, you can set up a @mac.com address without any bother — again, this is a good thing. However, if you're setting up an existing account, make sure you have all those silly settings and numbers and names that your Internet Service Provider (ISP) supplied you with when you signed up. This stuff includes your e-mail address, mail server variety, user account ID, password, and outgoing mail server.

Chapter 2: Navigating and Running Programs

In This Chapter

✓ Restarting, sleeping, and shutting down Mac OS X

✓ Using windows

✓ Using menus

✓ Recognizing and selecting icons

✓ Using the keyboard

✓ Running applications

✓ Switching between programs

✓ Opening, saving, and quitting within an application

As the folks in Cupertino will tell you, "It's all about the graphics." They're right, of course — Mac OS X is a highly visual operating system, and using it without a mouse is like building Hoover Dam with a pocketknife. Therefore, most of this chapter will require you to firmly grasp the little rodent. I'll introduce you to little graphical bits like icons and menus, and you'll discover how to open windows that can display anything from the contents of a document to the contents of your hard drive.

On the other hand, any true Macintosh power user will tell you that the keyboard is *still* a useful piece of hardware. Because I want you to be a bona fide, well-rounded Mac OS X power user, I'm also going to demonstrate those key combinations that can save you time, effort, and possible tennis elbow from all that mouse-handling.

Finally, I lead you through the basic training that you'll need to run your programs: how to start them, how to open and save documents, and how to quit an application as gracefully as Fred Astaire moved on his best day.

Restarting, Sleeping, and Shutting Down

First things first. As the guy on the rocket sled probably yelled, "This is neat, but how do you stop it?" Call 'em *The Big Three* — Restart, Sleep, and Shut

Down are the Mac OS X commands that you use when you need to take care of other business. All three appear on the friendly Apple menu at the top left corner of your Desktop (as shown in friendly Figure 2-1).

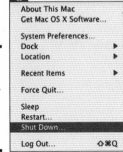

Figure 2-1:
You can choose your path from the Apple menu.

Each of these options produces a different reaction from your Mac:

✦ **Restart:** Use Restart if your Mac has suddenly decided to work "outside of the box" and begins acting strangely — for instance, if your Universal Serial Bus (USB) ports suddenly lock up or your FireWire drive no longer responds. Naturally, you'll need to save any work that's open. You also elect to restart Mac OS X when you switch start-up volumes. (Many applications and Apple software updates require a restart after you've installed them.)

✦ **Sleep:** There's no need for a glass of water or a bedtime story when you put Mac OS X to Sleep, which is a power-saving mode that allows you to quickly return to your work later. ("Waking up" from Sleep mode is much faster than booting or restarting your computer, and it can conserve battery power on laptops.) Depending on the settings that you've chosen in System Preferences — which I'll discuss in Chapter 3 of Book II — your Mac can power-down the monitor and spin-down the hard drives to save wear and tear on your hardware. You can set Mac OS X to automatically enter Sleep mode after a certain amount of inactivity. To awaken your slumbering supercomputer, just click the mouse or press any key on the keyboard. PowerBook and iBook owners may be able to wake their machines by simply opening the computer.

✦ **Shut Down:** When you're ready to return to the humdrum real world and you're done with your Mac for the time being, use the Shut Down option. Well-behaved Mac applications will automatically prompt you to save any changes that you've made to open documents before the computer actually turns itself off. If you've configured your Mac with multiple accounts, you can shut down Mac OS X from the login screen as well.

Besides the Apple Menu command, many Macs have a Power key on the keyboard that you can press to display the dialog that you see in Figure 2-2. If you change your mind and decide to tie up loose ends before you leave, click the Cancel button to return to Mac OS X.

Figure 2-2:
Will that be
Restart,
Sleep, or
Shut Down?

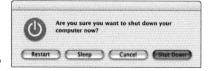

> Are you sure you want to shut down your computer now?
>
> Restart   Sleep   Cancel   Shut Down

If your Mac has a Drive Open key that you use to load and eject discs (like the new G4 iMacs), you can hold down the Control key and press the Drive Open key to display the same options.

A Window Is Much More than a Frame

"And in the beginning, there was the Window." Like older Mac operating systems, most of what you'll do in Mac OS X occurs within these fancy rectangular frames. And, as you might imagine, a number of controls are at your disposal that you can use to control the size, shape, and appearance of these potent portals. In this section, I'll — well, to be blunt, I'll do windows. (No squeegee jokes, if you please.)

Opening and closing windows

Windows are generally opened automatically. Usually, a window gets opened by an application (when you first run it or it needs to display a document) or by Mac OS X itself (when the Finder opens a window to display the contents of your hard drive). The Finder, by the way, is the application that Mac OS X runs to display the operating system's menus and windows.

Some programs even let you open new windows on the fly: For example, Figure 2-3 illustrates a window in its purest form, a new Finder window. To display this window on your own Mac, choose File➪New Finder Window or press ⌘+N. From here, you can reach any file on your Mac or even venture into the Internet.

The Command key has an Apple (🍎) and a rather strange-looking symbol (⌘) on it that I often call *the Spirograph.*

The Close button

Figure 2-3:
A new
Finder
window
allows you
to navigate
your system.

When you're finished with a document or you no longer need a window open, you can close it to free that space on your Desktop. To close a window in Mac OS X, move your mouse pointer over the Close button; it's the red circular button at the top-left corner of the window, as shown in Figure 2-3. An X appears on the button when you're in the zone. When the X appears, just click the mouse. (By the way, if you've been living the life of a hermit in a cave for the last decade or so, pressing the mouse button is called *clicking* the mouse. In the Apple universe, standard mice have only one button.)

Most Mac applications don't want you closing a window willy-nilly if you've changed the contents without saving them. For example, try to close a document window in Word or AppleWorks without saving the file first. The program will ask you for confirmation before it closes the window containing your Great American Novel. Most programs also have a Close command on their File menu.

To close all windows that are displayed by a particular program, hold down the Option key while you click the Close button on one of the windows. Whoosh! They're all gone.

Scrolling windows

Often there's more stuff in a document or more files on your hard drive than you can see in the space available for a window. Guess that means it's time to delete stuff. No, no, **just joking!** You don't have to take such drastic measures to see more in a window.

Just use the scroll bars that you see in Figure 2-4 to move through the contents of the window. You can click on the scroll bar and *drag* it — for the uninitiated, that means clicking on the bar and holding down the button while you move the mouse in the desired direction. Alternately, you can click in the empty area above or below the bar to scroll pages at a time.

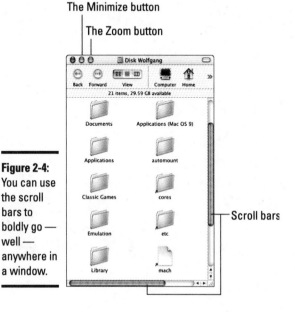

The Minimize button

The Zoom button

Scroll bars

Figure 2-4:
You can use the scroll bars to boldly go — well — anywhere in a window.

Depending on the type of application that you're using, you may be able to scroll a window with your arrow keys as well, or use the Page Up and Page Down keys to move through a window.

Minimizing and restoring windows

The multitalented Figure 2-4 also displays another control that you can use with a window: the Minimize button. When you minimize a window, you elimi-nate it from your Desktop and store it safely in the *Dock* — that strip of icons that appears along the bottom of your Mac OS X Desktop. In fact, a minimized window appears as a miniature icon in the Dock, so you can actually keep an eye on it (so to speak). Figure 2-5 illustrates a minimized window from Internet Explorer, which is actually displaying my Web site at `http://home.mlcbooks.com`. To minimize a window, move your mouse pointer over the yellow Minimize button at the top-left corner of the window — a minus sign appears on the button — and click.

When you're ready to display the window again on your Desktop — a process called *restoring* the window — simply click the thumbnail icon rep-resenting the window in the Dock, and Mac OS X automagically returns it to its former size and location.

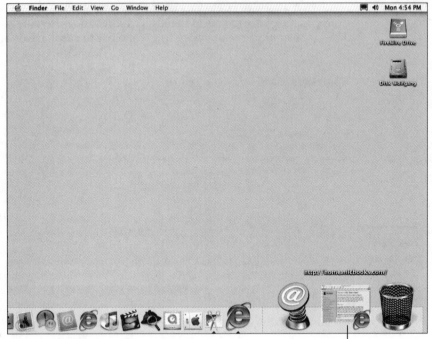

Figure 2-5:
Note the miniature Web page in the Dock — minimizing at work.

A minimized Web page

By the way, some — note that I said *some* — applications will continue to run when minimized, while others will simply stop or pause until you return them to the Desktop. Such is the crazy world we live in.

Zooming windows

Zooming windows has a kind of Flash Gordon sound to it, don't you think? It's nothing quite that exciting — still, when you're trying to view a larger portion of a document, zooming is a good thing because it expands the window to the maximum practical size for the application that you're using. In some cases, zooming a window fills the entire screen; at other times, the extra space would be wasted, so Mac OS X only zooms the window to a larger portion of the Desktop. In fact, the Zoom button can even be disabled by an application that doesn't want you to muck about with the window; for example, I own a game or two that don't allow zooming.

To zoom a window, move your mouse pointer over the green Zoom button at the top-left corner of the window. Again, Figure 2-4 struts its stuff and illustrates the position. (Man, that is one versatile figure.) A plus sign appears on the Zoom button. Click to expand your horizons.

After you've finished with a zoomed window, you can return it to its previous dimensions by clicking the Zoom button again.

Toggling toolbars

If you're wondering what that little lozenge-shaped button is at the right corner of many Mac OS X application windows, I won't leave you in suspense: It toggles the display of the window's toolbar on and off. A *toolbar* is a strip of icons that appear across the top of a window that you can click to perform common commands, like changing the display format or printing the current document. (The toolbar in Figure 2-4, for example, features icons to move Back and Forward, among others.) You'll encounter more toolbar technology throughout the book.

Moving windows

Unlike the rather permanent windows in your home, you can pick up a window and cart it to another portion of the Desktop — typically, this is done when you're using more than one application at a time and you need to see the contents of multiple windows. To grab a window and make off with it, click on the window's *title bar* — the strip at the top of the window that usually bears a document or application name — and drag the window to the new location. Then release the mouse button to plant it firmly in the new location.

By the way, most applications allow you to arrange multiple windows in a graceful swoop with a single click in a menu. Click the Window menu and choose Arrange All to perform this magic.

Resizing windows

Next, consider how to change the width or height of your window. To change the dimensions of a window to your exact specifications, move your mouse pointer over the lower-right corner of the window (which is usually marked with a number of slashed lines to indicate its status as a control), click, and the drag until the window is the size that you prefer.

Switching windows

Before I move to other graphical wonders of Mac OS X, it's important that you master how to switch between windows on your Desktop. First, remember this old Norwegian saying (or is it one of **Mark's Maxims**?):

Only one can be active at once.™

What our Oslo friends are communicating is that only one window can be *active* at any time. The active window appears on top of other windows, and it's the one that you can edit by typing or by moving your mouse. Other windows that you have open may be minimized, as I describe earlier in "Minimizing and restoring windows," or they can be *inactive* (mere ghosts of themselves) and remain on your Desktop. Mac OS X dims inactive windows so that you can tell they're hanging around . . . but you can't use them at the moment. Figure 2-6 illustrates a number of open windows, with the iPhoto window active.

Figure 2-6: How much is that active little window?

I know you're going to get tired of hearing me say this, but here I go again: Certain applications will continue to run while their windows are inactive, like File Transfer Protocol (FTP) clients and such. Most programs, however, will stop or pause until you make their window active.

And how do you switch — *activate* — a different window in Mac OS X? Simply click on any part of that window. I generally click the window's title bar if it's visible, but any part of the inactive window will do. The window that you click leaps like a proud stallion to the fore, and the previously active window now skulks in the background.

You can still use a window's Close, Minimize, and Zoom buttons even when it's inactive.

Menu Mysteries Explained

Next, I move on to menu control in Mac OS X. *Menus* are handy drop-down controls that allow you to select commands that are grouped together logically. For example, an application's File menu will usually allow you to create or open a document, save a document to disk, or quit the program. To *pull down* a menu, click the desired menu group name in the bar at the top of the screen and then click the desired menu option from the extended menu.

Figure 2-7 illustrates the Explorer menu in Internet Explorer: Note the *submenus* designated by right-arrow icons. When you move your mouse pointer over a submenu command, you get another set of even more specific menu commands — in this case, the Services submenu command displays commands like Disk Copy and Grab.

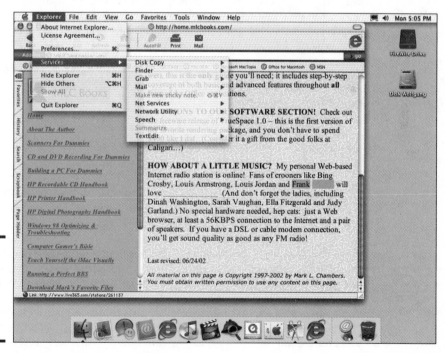

Figure 2-7:
Drilling deeper into Explorer's Services menu.

Some applications allow you to create your own custom menus; naturally, configuring a new menu system takes some time to learn, but imagine the productivity gains that you'll enjoy! For example, my menus in Microsoft Word X feature only the commands that I use often — they're sleeker and easier to navigate. (However, you have to stop short of claiming that you wrote the application — I checked with Microsoft.)

Mac OS X also provides another type of menu: contextual. The *contextual menu* appears when you hold down the Control key and click certain items on the screen, revealing commands that relate specifically to that item. (Unfortunately, the items that sport contextual menus vary from application to application, so it's best to check the documentation for a program before you spend countless hours Control+clicking everything onscreen.)

Many manufacturers sell mice, trackballs, and other pointing things that include a secondary mouse button. This is decidedly a Windows trait — remember, both Apple and I agree that a second mouse button is mere filigree — but if you have one, the device may display contextual menus when you press the secondary button. (This is often called right-clicking because it's typically the left mouse button that's the primary button.) Then again, you may launch Aunt Harriet into a geosynchronous orbit, so double-check the manual for your pointing thing on the default button assignment (and how to change it, if necessary).

You'll note that many commands in menus have keyboard shortcuts — because I'll be holding forth on this subject later in this chapter, I'll hold off on describing them here.

Icons 'R Us

Icons are more than little pictures, they're . . . well . . . actually, I guess they *are* little pictures. However, these graphical WUDs (that's short for *Wonderful User Device*) are really representations of the components of your Mac OS X system, and therefore they deserve a section of their own.

For complete details on what any icon is, what it represents, and what it will do, click the icon once to highlight it and then press ⌘+I. This displays the Information dialog that you see in Figure 2-8, which tells you what kind of icon it is, where the item it represents is actually located, and how big it is. You'll also see a version number for applications — a handy way of quickly checking what version of a program you're running — and when the file was created and last modified. The Info dialog also offers other settings and options that you can display by clicking on the General Information drop-down list box, and I'll cover them in other parts of the book.

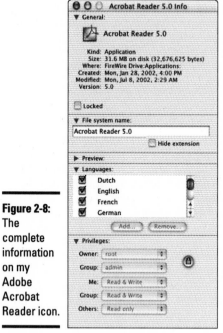

Figure 2-8:
The
complete
information
on my
Adobe
Acrobat
Reader icon.

Hardware

Mac OS X uses icons to represent the various hardware devices in your computer, including your

✦ Hard drive

✦ CD or DVD drive

✦ Printer

✦ Zip drive

You get the idea. Just double-click a hardware icon to display the folders and files that it contains, like with your hard drive and CD/DVD drive.

Generally, you'll only encounter hardware icons on your Desktop or in Finder windows. Figure 2-9 illustrates some of the hardware icons that live in my system.

Figure 2-9:
A wealth of
different
hardware
icons.

Programs and applications

These are the fancy icons, folks — most applications have their own custom icons, and double-clicking one will typically whisk you on your way. Mac OS X also includes a generic icon or two for applications that don't include their own custom icon. Figure 2-10 illustrates a number of my favorite program icons from all sorts of Mac OS X applications.

Figure 2-10:
Most
Mac OS X
applications
are repre-
sented by
custom
icons.

Running a program in Mac OS X can be as simple as double-clicking the application icon — more on this later in the chapter.

Files

Your hard drive will contain many thousands of individual files, and the Big X tries to make it as easy as possible to visually identify which application owns which file — therefore, most applications use a special icon to indicate their data files. For example, Figure 2-11 illustrates several documents and data files created by a range of applications: Microsoft Word, AppleWorks, QuickTime, Quicken, Internet Explorer, and Photoshop. Some cheeky applications even use more than one icon to differentiate between different file types, like documents and templates in Microsoft Word.

Figure 2-11:
File icons
generally
give you a
visual clue
as to their
origin.

There are also a number of generic file icons that indicate text files, including RTF (short for Rich Text Format) documents and PDF (Portable Document File) documents, which use the Adobe Acrobat format.

You can open most documents and data files by double-clicking them, which automatically launches the proper application and loads the document.

Folders

Folders have a 3-D look in Mac OS X — and, as you can see in Figure 2-12, some applications even customize their folder icon!

Figure 2-12:
A selection
of different
generic and
custom
folder icons.

To open a folder within Mac OS X, just double-click it. (Alternately, you can click it once to select it and then press ⌘+O.) Discover more about how to control the look of folder contents later in Chapter 1 of Book II.

Aliases

An alias is a strange beast — although it may look like a standard icon, upon closer examination, you'll notice that an alias icon sports a tiny curved arrow at the base, and the tag alias appears at the end of the icon name. Figure 2-13 has roped in a variety of aliases for your enjoyment, along with one or two actual icons for comparison.

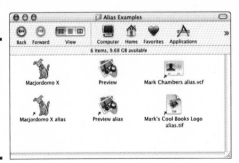

Figure 2-13:
An alias is a
pointer to
another
application,
file, or
folder.

Essentially, an *alias* is a link to something else on your system. For example, a Photoshop alias can run Photoshop just like the actual program icon, but it only takes up a scant few bytes on your hard drive. (If you've crossed over from the Windows Wilderness, think *shortcut* — Windows shortcuts work in a similar manner.) The alias file is just big enough to hold the location of the actual file or folder, allowing it to yell at Mac OS X: "Hey, the Human actually wants you to run *this* or open that *thing* over there!"

Aliases come in handy for a number of reasons:

✦ **They allow you to launch applications and open files and folders from anywhere in your system:** For example, you may want an alias icon in your MP3 folder that runs Roxio Toast so that you can launch Toast and burn an audio CD without laboriously navigating to the Roxio folder, which may be nested in goodness-knows-how-many layers of subfolders.

✦ **They can be easily deleted when no longer needed without wreaking havoc on the original application, file, or folder:** If you decide that you'd rather use iTunes to burn audio CDs, you can simply delete the Toast alias without trashing Toast itself.

✦ **Their tiny size allows you to add multiple aliases (and mucho conven-ience) for a single application without gulping down hard drive space.**

You may be wondering, "Why use aliases when I can just copy the actual application, file, or folder to the desired spot?" Well, indeed you can do that. However, the application may not work in its new location because you didn't copy any of the supporting files that most applications need to run. (An alias actually runs the original application or opens the original file or folder, so things should work just as if you double-clicked the original icon.) Additionally, remember that copying applications willy-nilly throughout your hard drive will eat up territory like a horde of angry Vikings.

If you dislike the *alias* hanging off the end of the icon name, feel free to rename it (as I show you in the next chapter). The alias will continue to function nicely no matter what moniker you give it.

If the original file no longer exists, an alias naturally no longer works, either. However, Mac OS X is sharp enough to automatically "fix" an alias if you rename or move the original file, pointing it to the new location. Slick!

Selecting Icons for Fun and Profit

You'll often find yourself performing different actions on one icon — or a number of icons at one time. For example, you can copy or move files from one location on your hard drive to another or delete a group of files that you no longer need. (The idea of drag-and-drop file management using icons originated on the Macintosh, but I'll wait until the next chapter to describe these operations in detail.) For now, focus on the basics of selecting one or more icons, which specifies which files and folders that you want to use for whatever you're going to do next.

Selecting a single icon

First, here are the various ways that you can select a single icon for an impending action:

✦ Place your mouse pointer over the file and click once; Mac OS X darkens the icon to indicate that it's selected — a mysterious process called *highlighting*.

✦ Type the first few letters of the icon's name — after you type enough characters to identify the icon uniquely (whether it be one or a dozen), Mac OS X highlights the icon that matches the text string.

✦ If an icon in a window is already highlighted, you can move the highlight to the next icon across by pressing the right-arrow key. Likewise, the other three directional arrow keys move the highlight in the other directions. To move through the icons alphabetically, press Tab to go forward and Shift-Tab to go backward.

Selecting multiple icons

To select a gaggle of icons for an action, use one of these methods:

✦ If the icons are next to each other, click and drag to highlight them all. As you drag, Mac OS X displays a selection box, and any icons within that box will be highlighted when you release the mouse button (as shown in Figure 2-14).

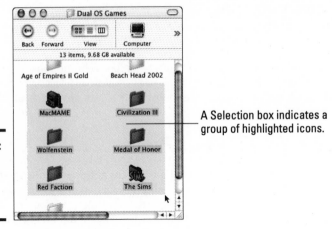

Figure 2-14:
Dragging a
selection
box in
Mac OS X.

A Selection box indicates a
group of highlighted icons.

✦ You can also select multiple adjacent icons by clicking the first item to highlight it and holding down the Shift key while clicking the last icon in the series that you want to select.

✦ If the icons are *not* next to each other, you can hold down the ⌘ key while you click on each item that you want to select.

Selecting an icon doesn't launch or do anything . . . you're just marking your territory.

Keyboard Shortcuts for the True Power User

Virtually all Mac OS X applications have their own *keyboard shortcuts* — a ten-cent term for a key combination that performs the same operation as a menu command or a toolbar button. Although the mouse may seem the easier path when controlling your Mac, it's not always the fastest — those hardy souls who venture to learn common keyboard shortcuts can zip through a spreadsheet or warp through a complex outline at speeds no mere rodent could ever hope to attain.

With that in mind — and with the goal of "pumping you up" into a Mac OS X power user — I hereby present the most common keyboard shortcuts for the Big X in Table 2-1. I've also sprinkled other keyboard shortcuts liberally through the book when I discuss other applications, but these combinations are the classics that appear virtually everywhere.

Table 2-1	Common Mac OS X Keyboard Shortcuts	
Key Combination	**Location**	**Action**
⌘+A	Edit menu	Selects all (works in the Finder too)
⌘+C	Edit menu	Copies the highlighted item to the Clipboard
⌘+H	Application menu	Hides the application
⌘+M	Window menu	Minimizes the active window to the Dock (works in the Finder, too)
⌘+O	File menu	Opens an existing document, file, or folder (works in the Finder, too)
⌘+P	File menu	Prints the current document
⌘+Q	Application menu	Exits the application
⌘+V	Edit menu	Pastes the contents of the Clipboard at the current cursor position
⌘+X	Edit menu	Cuts the highlighted item to the Clipboard
⌘+Z	Edit menu	Undo — reverses the effect of the last action you took
⌘+?	Help menu	Displays the Help system (works in the Finder, too)
⌘+Tab	Finder	Switches between open applications
⌘+Option+M	Finder	Minimizes all Finder windows to the Dock
⌘+Option+W	Finder	Closes all Finder windows

By the way, I should mention that many keyboard combinations use three different keys instead of just two — when these shortcuts appear in a menu, they look something akin to Egyptian hieroglyphics, but you need only hold down the first two keys simultaneously and press the third key. Common "strange" key symbols that you'll see in both the Finder and most applications are shown in Table 2-2.

Table 2-2	Arcane Key Symbols
Symbol	**Action**
Control	⌃
Command	⌘
Delete	⌦
Option	⌥
Shift	⇧

Houston, We're Go to Launch Programs

The next stop on your introductory tour of Mac OS X is the launch pad for your applications — although the Finder is useful, you'll likely want to actually *do* something with your Mac as well.

Running applications from your hard drive

You can launch an application from your hard drive by

✦ Navigating to the corresponding application folder and double-clicking the application icon.

✦ Double-clicking a document or data file that's owned by the application. For example, double-clicking an MP3 audio file will run iTunes.

✦ Double-clicking an alias that you've created for the application. (Get the skinny on aliases in the earlier section, "Aliases." Go figure.)

✦ Clicking the application's icon in the Dock (more on adding items to the Dock later in Chapter 2 of Book II).

✦ Selecting the application icon and pressing the ⌘+O keyboard shortcut.

✦ Adding the application to your Login items list. (I cover this in more detail later in Chapter 3 of Book II.)

Running applications from a CD-ROM or DVD-ROM

After you've loaded a CD-ROM or DVD-ROM, you can display its contents by double-clicking the disc icon that appears on your Desktop (Figure 2-15) — a Finder window opens and shows the files that reside on the disc.

Figure 2-15: The Finder shows the contents of a disc whose icon you've double-clicked.

After you locate the application you want to run on the disc, you can launch it by double-clicking it or selecting it and pressing ⌘+O.

Switching 'Twixt Programs with Aplomb

You may think that juggling multiple applications will lead to confusion, fatigue, and dry mouth, but luckily Mac OS X makes it easy to jump between programs that are running on your Mac. Use any of these methods to jump from open application to application:

✦ Press ⌘+Tab.

✦ Click anywhere in the desired application window to make it the active window.

✦ Click the application icon in the Dock — all applications that are running have an icon in the Dock, and the icon will have an up-arrow underneath it to indicate that the application is open.

Along with the window switch, an astute observer will notice that the application menu bar will also change to match the now-active application.

Opening and Saving Your Stuff in an Application

Almost all Mac OS X applications open and save documents in the same way, whether you're typing a quick letter to your Mom using AppleWorks or expressing your artistic side with Painter 7. Therefore, I'm going to take a moment to outline the common procedures for opening and saving documents. Believe me, you will perform these two rituals dozens of times a week, so no nodding off.

Opening a document

First, the simple way to load a document: Double-click that document in a Finder window, and . . . well, that's it. (This is my preferred method because I'm an admitted Lazy Techno-wizard who would rather use complex hand movements to pour myself another Diet Coke.)

To open a document the hard way — from inside an application — here's the plan:

1. **Choose File⇨Open or press that handy ⌘+O key combination.**

Your Mac OS X program is likely to display the attractive Open dialog that you see in Figure 2-16. In this case, I'm opening a QuickTime movie.

2. **Navigate to the location of the document that you want to open.**

   The From drop-down list allows you to jump directly to common locations — such as the Desktop, your home folder, and your iDisk — as well as places that you've marked as Favorites and places you've recently accessed (Recent Places).

Figure 2-16: The soon-to-be-quite-familiar Open dialog.

Click here and drag to resize the dialog.

Note the Add to Favorites button at the bottom of the dialog — Mac OS X allows you to add Favorites at many points in the program, and this is one of them.

If the target folder isn't in your From list, move the slider at the bottom of the dialog to the far left to display your hard drives, CD-ROM/DVD drives, and network locations.

3. **Click the habitat where the file will be found.**

   You'll note that the right column(s) will change to show you the contents of the item that you just clicked. In this way, you can cruise through successive folders to find that elusive document. (This somewhat time-consuming process is somewhat derisively called *drilling* — hence, the importance of adding Favorites and using Recent Places.)

4. **When you sight the document that you want to load, either double-click it or click once to highlight the filename and then click Open.**

"Hey, the Open dialog can be resized!" That's right, good buddy — you can expand the Open dialog to show more columns and find things more easily. Click and drag the right corner of the Open dialog to resize it.

Note that you can also type the path to the file in the Go To field. I'll cover more about file paths in Chapter 1 of Book VII — however, I find this field to be less than convenient because most folks don't feel like typing a long path by hand unless they've delved into the Linux undercarriage of Mac OS X.

Saving a document

To save a document, follow these steps:

1. **Choose File⇨Save.**

If you've previously saved this document, your application should immediately overwrite the existing document with the new copy, and you get to return to work . . . end of story. If you *haven't* previously saved this document, the program will display a Save dialog that's usually very similar to the Open dialog; it generally has a few more options, however, so stay frosty.

2. **Navigate to the location where you'd like to save the document and type a file name.**

Often, you can use a default name that's already provided by the thoughtful folks who developed the software. Note that you may be given the chance to save the document in several different formats. For example, Figure 2-17 illustrates the AppleWorks Save dialog; you can click the File Format drop-down list to choose other formats, such RTF, HyperText Markup Language (HTML), and even bargain-basement text.

Figure 2-17:
Saving a
work of
art in
AppleWorks.

3. **Click Save (or OK, depending on the application).**

If an application offers a Save As menu option in the File menu, you can, in effect, copy the document by saving a new version of the document under another name. Save As comes in particularly handy when you want to retain the original version of a document.

Quitting Programs

If I had a twisted and warped sense of humor, I'd simply tell you to quit applications by pulling your Mac's power cord from the wall socket. (Luckily, I don't.) There are, however, more sane ways to exit a program — use one of these methods instead:

✦ Press the ⌘+Q keyboard shortcut.

✦ Choose File⇨Quit.

✦ Click the Close button on the application window — note, however, that this doesn't always completely close down the application. For example, Internet Explorer stays running even if you close the browser window.

Chapter 3: Basic OS X Housekeeping

In This Chapter

✔ Copying, moving, and duplicating files

✔ Deleting and recovering files

✔ Renaming files

✔ Finding specific files

✔ Locking files

✔ Using Apple menu commands

✔ Using Services, the Go menu, and menu icons

✔ Printing within Mac OS X applications

✔ Listening to audio discs and recording data discs

After you master basic Mac spell-casting — things like selecting items, using menus, opening and saving documents, working with windows, and launching an application or two — it's time to delve deeper into Mac OS X.

In this chapter, I discuss file management, showing you the hidden power behind the friendly Apple menu. I also discuss some of the more advanced menu commands, how to print within most applications, and how to listen to an audio CD on your Mac. (It makes a doggone good stereo.) Finally, I introduce you to the built-in CD/DVD disc recording features within the Big X.

The Finder: It's the Wind beneath Your Wings

So what exactly is the *Finder* anyway? It's a rather nebulous term, but in essence, the Finder gives Mac OS X the basic functions that you'll use for the procedures I outline in this chapter. This UberOS has been around in one guise or another since the days of System 6 — the creaking old days when a Mac was an all-in-one, tote-able computer with a built-in screen. Come to think of it, some things never change.

The Finder is always running, so it's always available — and you can always switch to it, even when several other applications are open and chugging away. Figure 3-1 illustrates the Dock with the rather perspective-crazy Finder icon at the far left side.

Figure 3-1:
The Finder
is always
there,
supporting
you with a
unique
smile.

The Finder icon

Is that icon supposed to be one face or two faces? I'm still confused, and I've been using the Mac since 1991.

Don't forget that Mac OS X gives you a second method of doing everything I'll cover in this chapter: You can use Terminal to uncover the UNIX core of Mac OS X, employing your blazing typing speed to take care of things from the command line. Of course, that's not the focus of this book, but for those who want to boldly go where no Mac operating system has ever gone before, you'll find more in Chapter 1 of Book VII. Despite what you may have been led to believe, power and amazing speed are to be found in character-based computing.

Copying and Moving Files and Folders

Here's where drag-and-drop makes things about as easy as computing can get:

✦ **To copy a file or folder from one window to another location on the same drive:** Hold down the Option key and click and drag the icon from its current home to the new location. (*Note:* You can drop files and folders on top of other folders, which puts the copy inside that folder.) If you're copying multiple items, select them first (read how in Book I, Chapter 2) and then drag and drop the entire crew.

"Is the Desktop a valid target location for a file or folder?" You're darn tootin'! I recommend, though, that you avoid cluttering up your Desktop with more than a handful of files — instead, create a folder or two on your Desktop and then store those items within those folders.

✦ **To copy items from one window to a location on another drive:** Click and drag the icon from the window to a window displaying the contents of the target drive. Or, in the spirit of drag-and-drop, you can simply drag the items to the drive icon, which places them in the root folder of that drive.

✦ **To move items from one window to another location on the same drive:** Simply drag the icon to the new location, whether it be a window or a folder.

Mac OS X provides you with a number of visual cues to let you know what's being copied or moved. For example, dragging one or more items displays a ghost image of the items (check out Figure 3-2), and when you've positioned the mouse pointer over the target, Mac OS X highlights that location to let you know that you're in the zone. If you're moving or copying items into another Finder window, the window border is highlighted to let you know that Mac OS X understands the game plan.

Figure 3-2:
Icons
appear in
ghostly form
when you're
dragging
them.

In case you move the wrong thing or you port it to the wrong location, press ⌘+Z to undo the previous action.

If the item that you're dragging already exists in the target location, you get a confirmation dialog like the one you see in Figure 3-3 — you can choose to replace the file, leave the existing file alone, or stop the entire shootin' match.

Figure 3-3:
To replace,
or not to
replace —
the choice
is yours.

Cloning Your Items — It's Happening Now!

No need for sci-fi equipment or billions in cash — you can create an exact duplicate of any item within the same folder. (This is often handy when you need a simple backup of the same file in the same folder or when you're going to edit a document but you want to keep the original intact.)

Click the item to select it, and then click File from the Finder menu and choose the Duplicate menu item. To distinguish the duplicate from the original, Mac OS X adds the word *copy* to the end of the duplicate's icon name; additional copies have a number added to the name as well.

Alternately, aficionados of the keyboard can hold down the Option key and drag the original item to another spot in the same window — when you release the button, the duplicate appears.

When you duplicate a folder, Mac OS X automatically duplicates all the contents of the folder as well.

Deleting That Which Should Not Be

Even Leonardo da Vinci made the occasional design mistake — his trash can was likely full of bunched-up pieces of parchment. Luckily, no trees will be wasted when you decide to toss your unneeded files and folders; this section shows you how to delete items from your system.

By the way, as you'll soon witness for yourself, moving items to the Trash doesn't necessarily mean that they're immediately history.

Dragging unruly files against their will

In Mac OS X, the familiar Macintosh Trash can has been moved to the right edge of the Dock — in fact, it's now a spiffy-looking wire can instead of the old clunker that the Mac faithful remember. You can click and drag the items that you've selected to the Trash and drop them on top of the wire can icon to delete them. When the Trash contains at least one item, the wire can icon changes to appear as if it were full of trash.

You can also add a Delete icon to your Finder toolbar — for all the details, see Chapter 1 of Book II.

Deleting with the menus and the keyboard

The mouse isn't absolutely necessary when deleting items. Your other options for scrapping selected files include

✦ Clicking File from the Finder menu and choosing the Move to Trash menu item

✦ Pressing the ⌘+Delete keyboard shortcut

✦ Holding down Control while clicking the item to display the contextual menu and then choosing Move to Trash from that menu

Emptying that Wastepaper Basket

As I mention earlier, moving items to the Trash doesn't actually delete them immediately from your system — believe me, this fail-safe measure comes in handy when you've been banging away at the keyboard for several hours and you stop paying close attention to what you're doing. (I usually also blame lack of Diet Coke.) More on how to rescue files from the Trash in the next section.

Like any folder, you can check the contents of the Trash by clicking the Trash icon in the Dock.

After you double-check the Trash contents and you are indeed absolutely sure you want to delete its contents, use one of the following methods to nuke the digital Bit Bucket:

✦ Click Finder from the Finder menu and choose the Empty Trash menu item.

✦ Press the ⌘+Shift+Delete keyboard shortcut.

✦ Click on the Trash icon in the Dock and hold down the mouse button, and choose Empty Trash from the menu that appears.

✦ Hold down Control while clicking the Trash icon in the Dock and then choose Empty Trash from the contextual menu that appears.

Depending on the method that you select and the settings that you choose in System Preferences (which I cover later in Chapter 3 of Book II), Mac OS X may present you with a confirmation dialog to make sure that you actually want the Trash emptied.

WAIT! 1 Need That after All!

In the adrenaline-inducing event that you need to rescue something that shouldn't have ended up in the scrap pile, first click the Trash icon in the Dock to display the contents of the Trash. Then rescue the items that you want to save by dragging them to the Desktop or a folder on your hard drive. (This is roughly analogous to rescuing your old baseball glove from the family garage sale.)

Feel free to gloat — if someone else is nearby, ask her to pat you on the back and call you a lifesaver.

Renaming Your Items

You wouldn't get far in today's spacious virtual world without being able to change a moniker for a file or folder. To rename an item in Mac OS X, use one of these two methods:

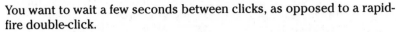

✦ **With the mouse:** Click once on an icon to select it and then click again on the icon's name (or just press Return). Mac OS X highlights the text in an edit box — type the new name and press Return when you're done.

You want to wait a few seconds between clicks, as opposed to a rapid-fire double-click.

✦ **From the Info dialog:** Select the item and press ⌘+I to display the Info dialog; then click the triangle next to Name & Extension to display the field that you see in Figure 3-4. Click in the Name field, drag the mouse to highlight the text that you want to change, and type the replacement text.

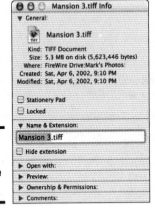

Figure 3-4: Rename a file from the Info dialog.

Naturally, the first method is the easiest, and it's the one I use most often.

Displaying the Facts on Files and Folders

Speaking of the Finder's Info dialog, it's the place to view the specifics on any highlighted item (including drives and aliases). Select an item and press

⌘+I or click the Finder's File menu and choose Get Info (Figure 3-5). If you select more than one item, the Info dialog combines as many properties as possible to give you a summary.

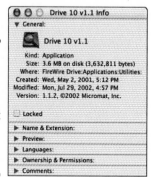

Figure 3-5:
The General Information panel appears first when you display the Info dialog.

Mac OS X displays the General Information panel when you first open the Info dialog, but other panels are usually available (depending on the type of selected items). To display the other panels, click the panel that you want to see.

For most types of files and folders, the Info dialog can tell you

✦ **Size:** The total size of the item (or items) that you select

✦ **Kind:** What type of item it is — for example, whether it's a file, folder, drive, or alias — and what program automatically launches when you open the selected item

✦ **Dates:** The date the item was created and the date it was last modified

✦ **Permission:** The privileges that control who can do what to the file — more on this later in Book II, Chapter 6 — and whether a file is locked in read-only mode

Some of this information you can change, and some can only be displayed. To banish the Info dialog from your Desktop, click the dialog's Close button.

For the rest of this section, I describe a number of tasks that you can accomplish from the Info dialog.

Adding comments

Mac OS X provides you with a comment field where you can add additional text that's stored along with the file. I use this feature to record the version number of manuscript chapters and programs that I create during the course of writing books.

Hey, Martha Stewart — Make stationery with Mac OS X!

If you use a specific document over and over as a basis for different revisions, you can enable the *Stationery Pad* check box on the General Information pane to use the file as stationery. Opening a stationery file automatically creates a new, untitled version of the file in the linked application; this can save you steps compared with duplicating the file or using the Save As procedure I show you in Book I, Chapter 2.

Here's an example: Suppose you save a blank shipping invoice in AppleWorks because you

have to create and print a new invoice for everything that you buy for your company — but you don't need to keep a separate copy on your hard drive of each invoice that you handle. You can simplify everything by creating a blank invoice document file and then turning that document file into stationery. Now all you need to do is double-click the file, make your changes, print, and then close AppleWorks without saving anything. Neat!

To add a comment, follow these steps:

1. **Display the Info dialog for the item by pressing ⌘+I or choosing File⊅Get Info.**

2. **Click in the Comments box and type the comment text.**

If you need to expand the Comments section of the Info dialog, click on the triangle next to the Comments heading — the arrow rotates and the Comments box appears.

3. **Close the Info dialog to save the comment.**

Displaying extensions

Extensions are alien creatures to most Mac owners — however, these three- or four-character add-ons that follow a period at the end of a filename have been a mainstay in the DOS, Windows, and UNIX environments for years. An *extension* identifies what program owns a specific file, and therefore which application launches automatically when you double-click that file's icon. Examples of common extensions (and the applications that own them) include

+ `.pdf` (Adobe Acrobat)

+ `.doc` (Microsoft Word)

+ `.cwk` (AppleWorks)

✦ .psd (Adobe Photoshop)

✦ .jpeg or .jpg (Preview, or your image editor)

✦ .tiff or .tif (Preview, or your image editor)

✦ .htm and .html (Internet Explorer, or your Web browser of choice)

Why would someone want to see a file's extension? It comes in handy when a number of different types of file are linked to the same application — for example, if you install Adobe Photoshop, both JPEG and TIFF images have the same icon, so you can't tell one from the other. With extensions on, it's easy to tell what type of file you're looking at.

Follow this procedure to hide or display extensions with your filenames:

1. **Display the Info dialog for the item by pressing ⌘+I or choosing File⇨Get Info.**

2. **If you need to expand the Comments section of the Info dialog, click on the triangle next to the Comments heading — the arrow rotates and the Comments box appears.**

3. **To display the extension for the selected file, uncheck the Hide extension check box to disable it.**

4. **Close the Info dialog to save your changes.**

Choosing the application to launch with a file

So what's the plan if the wrong application launches when you double-click a file? Not a problem: You can also change the linked application from the Info dialog as well. (I told you this was a handy toy box, didn't I?) Follow these steps to choose another application to pair with a selected file:

1. **Display the Info dialog for the item.**

2. **Click the triangle next to the Open with heading, which expands to show the information that you see in Figure 3-6.**

3. **Click the icon button, and Mac OS X displays the applications that it feels are best suited to open this type of document.**

4. **Click the application that should open the file.**

To go completely hog-wild and choose a different application, select Other from the drop-down list. Mac OS X opens a Choose Other Application dialog where you can navigate to and select the program you want. After you highlight the application, click Add.

5. **To globally update all the documents of the same type to launch the application that you choose, click the Change All button.**

   Mac OS X displays a confirmation dialog asking whether you're sure about making this drastic change. Click Continue to update the other files of the same type or click Cancel to return to the Info dialog.

6. **Close the Info dialog to save your changes.**

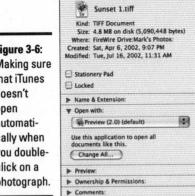

Figure 3-6:
Making sure that iTunes doesn't open automatically when you double-click on a photograph.

Locking files against evildoers

"Holy Item Insurance, Batman!" That's right, Boy Wonder: Before I leave the friendly land of the Info dialog, every Mac owner needs to learn how to protect files and folders from accidental deletion or editing. By locking a file, you allow it to be opened and copied — but not changed, renamed, or sent to the Trash. Locked items appear in the Finder with a small padlock attached to the icon.

To lock or unlock a file, you have to have ownership of the file — I cover privileges in Book II, but on a Mac where you've configured only one administrator account, you should already have ownership. Follow this procedure:

1. **Display the Info dialog for the item.**

2. **Check the Locked check box to enable it.**

   The Locked check box is in the General section of the dialog.

3. **Close the Info dialog to save your changes.**

Creating an Alias

I mention aliases earlier in Chapter 2 of Book 1. As I discuss in that chapter, an alias acts as a link to an application or document that actually exists elsewhere on your system (a handy trick to use when organizing items on your hard drive). You have a number of different ways to conjure an alias after you select an item:

✦ Click File from the Finder menu and choose the Make Alias menu item. (You have to move the alias yourself.)

✦ Press the ⌘+L keyboard shortcut. (Again, you have to move the new alias to its new location.)

✦ Hold down Control while clicking the selected item and then choose Make Alias from the contextual menu that appears.

In addition, you can hold down the ⌘+Option key combination and drag the item to the location where you want the alias.

Although Mac OS X does a great job in tracking the movements of an original and updating an alias, some actions can break the link — for example, if you delete the original, the alias is left wandering in search of a home. However, all is not lost — when you double-click a broken alias, Mac OS X offers to help you fix the alias. This involves browsing through your system to locate a new original.

Using the Apple Menu

The Apple menu is a familiar sight to any Mac owner — although Apple contemplated removing it during the original development and beta cycle for Mac OS X, the ruckus and cry from beta-testers ensured that it remains today. It's amazing how reassuring that little fellow can be when you boot the Big X for the first time.

In this section, I cover the important things that are parked under the Apple menu.

Using Recent Items

If you're like most of us — and I think I'm safe in assuming that you are — you tend to work on the same set of applications and files during the day. Normally, this would be somewhat of a pain because each time you sit down in front of the keyboard, you have to drill down through at least one layer of folders to actually reach the stuff that you need. To make things easier on yourself, you *could* create a set of aliases on your Desktop that link to those files and applications . . . but as you move from project to project, you'd find yourself constantly updating the aliases. As Blackbeard the Pirate was wont to exclaim, "Arrgh!"

Ah, but Mac OS X is a right smart operating system, and several years ago Apple created the Recent Items menu to save you the trouble of drilling for applications and files. Figure 3-7 illustrates the Recent Items menu from my system — note that the menu is thoughtfully divided into both Applications and Documents. As you open documents or launch applications, they're added to the list. (Accountants will revel in this *First In, First Out* technology.) To launch an application or document from the Recent Items menu, just click it.

Figure 3-7: The Recent Items menu makes it easy to open a document or application you've been using.

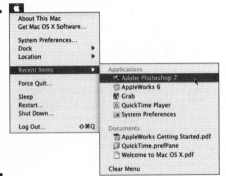

To wipe the contents of the Recent Items menu — for example, if you've just finished a project, and you want to turn over a new digital leaf — click Recent Items and choose the Clear Menu item.

You can specify the number of recent items that will appear in the menu from System Preferences; display the General settings and click the Applications and Documents list boxes in the Number of Recent Items field. (More on this in Chapter 3 of Book II.)

Playing with the Dock

You know how Air Force One acts as the mobile nerve center for the President? And how The Chief can jet all around the world and take all his stuff along with him? Well, the Dock is kind of like that. Sort of.

If you want your Dock to go mobile as well, click the Apple menu and choose the Dock item to display the submenu that you see in Figure 3-8. Here's a rundown of the options that you'll find:

Figure 3-8:
Use the
Dock
submenu
to fine-tune
the oper-
ation of your
friendly
neighbor-
hood icon
strip.

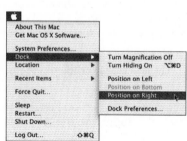

✦ **Magnification:** Click Turn Magnification On/Off to toggle icon magnification when your pointer is selecting an icon from the Dock. With magnification on, the icons in the Dock get really, *really* big . . . a good thing for
Mr. Magoo or those with grandiose schemes to take over the world.
Check out the rather oversized icons in Figure 3-9. (The amount of magnification can be controlled from the System Preferences Dock settings,
which I explain in Chapter 3 of Book II.)

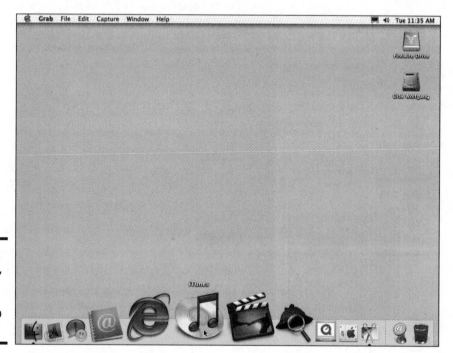

Figure 3-9:
Now those,
my friend,
are some
pumped-up
icons.

✦ **Hiding:** Click Turn Hiding On/Off to toggle the automatic hiding of the Dock. With hiding on, the Dock disappears off the edge of the screen until you move the mouse pointer to that edge. (This is great for those who want to make use of as much Desktop territory as possible for their applications.)

You can press ⌘+Option+D to toggle Dock hiding on and off from the keyboard.

✦ **Position:** Click one of three choices (Position on Left, Bottom, or Right, respectively) to make the Dock can appear on the left, bottom, or right of the screen.

✦ **Dock Preferences:** Click this to display the System Preferences Dock settings, which I explain in Chapter 3 of Book II.

Bad program! Quit!

Once in a while, you're going to encounter a stubborn application that locks up, slows to a crawl, or gets stuck in an endless loop — although Mac OS X is a highly advanced operating system, it can still fall prey to bad programming or corrupted data.

Luckily, you can easily shut these troublemakers down from the Apple menu. Just click Force Quit to display the Force Quit Applications dialog that you see in Figure 3-10. (Keyboard types can press ⌘+Option+Escape.) Click the application that you want to banish and then click the Force Quit button; Mac OS X requests confirmation, after which you click the Force Quit button again.

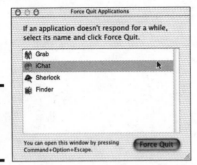

Figure 3-10: Forcing a program to take a hike.

If you select the Finder in the Force Quit dialog, the button changes to Relaunch — this allows you to restart the Finder, which comes in handy if your system appears to be unstable. (This is much faster than actually restarting your Mac.)

Forcing an application to quit will also kill any open documents that you were working with in that application, so save your work (if the program will allow you to save anything). If you relaunch the Finder, some programs may restart as well.

Tracking down your version

This isn't a big deal, but if you choose About This Mac from the Apple menu, Mac OS X displays the About This Mac dialog that you see in Figure 3-11. In case you need to check the amount of memory or the processor in an unfamiliar Mac, the About This Mac dialog can display these facts in a twinkling — however, I primarily use it to check on the Mac OS X version and build number, and to launch the Apple System Profiler (which I discuss in full in Chapter 6 of this mini-book). Click the More Info button to launch the Profiler.

Figure 3-11:
Display your Mac's memory, processor, and Big X version.

Specifying a location

Mac OS X allows you to create multiple network locations — think of a *location* as a separate configuration that you use when you connect to a different network from a different locale. For instance, if you travel to a branch office, you'd assign a location for your desk and a location for the remote branch. A student might assign one location for her home network and another for the college computer lab network.

A location saves all the specific values that you've entered in the System Preferences Network settings, including IP address, AppleTalk zones, proxy servers, and the like. If all this means diddly squat to you, don't worry — it gets explained in Chapter 1 of Book V. For now, just remember that you can switch between locations by clicking Locations under the Apple menu, which displays a submenu of locations that you can choose from.

Availing Yourself of Mac OS X Services

In Mac OS X, *services* allow you to merge information from one application with another. To Mac old-timers, that may sound suspiciously like the Clipboard; however, services can also include functionality from an application, so you can create new documents or complete tasks without running another program! Services can be used in both the Finder and Mac OS X applications.

To illustrate, here's a fun example:

1. **Launch TextEdit (you'll find it in your Applications folder) and type these words:** Hello from your Macintosh!

2. **Highlight those words.**

3. **Click the TextEdit menu — don't switch to the Finder, use the TextEdit Application menu — and choose Services.**

4. **From the Services submenu, choose Speech and then choose Start Speaking Text.**

After you've chuckled a bit at your Mac's accent, consider what you just did — you ran the Speech application from *within* TextEdit, using the selected words! Pretty slick, eh?

A glance at the other services that show up from within most applications gives you an idea of just how convenient and powerful Mac OS X services can be — I often use services to take care of things like

✦ **Sending an e-mail message** from an e-mail address in a text file, AppleScript document, or the Address Book (using the Mail service)

✦ **Capturing a screen snapshot** within an application (using the Grab service)

✦ **Checking the availability of an Internet server** by pinging it (using the Network Utility service)

Remember, you can access the Services menu from a Mac OS X application by picking that program's Application menu (sometimes called the *named* menu). For instance, in the demonstration above, I use the TextEdit menu that appears in the TextEdit menu bar. In Microsoft Word, I would click the Word menu.

Geez, I think the computing world needs another word for *menu* — don't you?

Many third-party applications that you install under Mac OS X can add their own commands under the Service menu, so be sure to read the documentation for a new application to see what service functionality it adds.

Get Thee Hence: Using the Go Menu

Remember the transporter from *Star Trek*? Step on the little platform, assume a brave pose, and whoosh! — you're transported instantaneously to another ship or (more likely) to a badly designed planet exterior built inside a soundstage. Talk about convenience . . . that is, as long as the doggone thing didn't malfunction.

The Finder's Go menu gives you the chance to play Captain Kirk: You can jump immediately to specific spots, both within the confines of your own system as well as external environments like your network or the Internet. (You can leave your phaser and tricorder in your cabin.)

Figure 3-12 illustrates the Go menu and the Favorites submenu.

Figure 3-12:
The Go
menu —
just go
there.

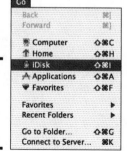

The destinations you can travel to include the following:

✦ **Computer:** This window includes your hard drives, CD and DVD drives, and your network — the same places that appear when you open a new Finder window with the ⌘+N key shortcut.

✦ **Home:** This window displays the home directory for the user currently logged in.

✦ **iDisk:** This window displays the contents of your Internet iDisk storage. (More on the coolness that is iDisk in Chapter 4 of Book IV.)

✦ **Favorites:** Select one of the Favorites that you've set up in Mac OS X — I cover Favorites in Chapter 1 of Book II.

✦ **Applications:** This window includes all the applications that appear in your Mac OS X Applications folder (a neat *Just the programs, ma'am* arrangement that really comes in handy).

✦ **Recent Folders:** This window displays a submenu that allows you to choose from the folders you've recently opened.

You can also type the path for a specific folder (using the Go to Folder command) or connect to a specific network server (using the Connect to Server command).

Note that all the Go menu commands include keyboard shortcuts, proving once again that *the fingers are quicker than the mouse.*

Monkeying with the Menu Bar

Ever stared at a menu bar for inspiration? Fortunately for Mac owners like you and me, people in Cupertino are paid to do just that, and these designers get the big bucks to make the Mac OS X menu bar the best that it can be. Thus were born menu bar icons, which add useful controls in what would otherwise be a wasted expanse of white.

Using menu bar icons

By default, Mac OS X installs two menu bar icons — the Displays icon and the Volume icon — along with the Clock display, which is actually an icon in disguise. Figure 3-13 illustrates these standard icons.

Figure 3-13:
Adjust your
Mac with
these menu
bar icons.

Clicking the Displays menu bar icon (it looks like a monitor) allows you to choose from the recommended resolutions and color depth settings for your graphics card and monitor. For example, Figure 3-14 illustrates the possible settings for my G4 iMac, which has an LCD monitor: I can choose from 800 x 600 or 1024 x 768 resolutions, and my display can be set to thousands or millions of colors. Typically, it's a good idea to choose the highest resolution and the highest color depth. You can also jump directly to the System Preferences Display settings by clicking Open Displays.

Figure 3-14:
The settings offered by my Displays menu bar icon.

To quickly change the audio volume level within Mac OS X, click the Volume icon (it looks like a speaker with emanating sound waves) once to display its slider control, and then click and drag the slider to adjust the level up or down. After you select a level by releasing the mouse button, your Mac thoughtfully plays the default system sound to help you gauge the new volume level.

Depending on the functionality that you're using with Mac OS X, these other menu bar icons may also appear:

✦ **Modem status:** You can turn on the display of the Modem status icon from the Internal Modem panel of the Internet Connect application, which I discuss in Chapter 1 of Book IV. Click this icon to connect to or disconnect from the Internet by using a modem. You can open the Internet Connect application from the menu bar icon, and the icon can be set to show the time that you've been connected to the Internet as well as the status of the connection procedure.

✦ **AirPort:** If you've installed an AirPort card in your Mac, you can check the status of the AirPort connection; click the AirPort icon to toggle AirPort on or off. The icon displays the relative strength of your AirPort signal, whether you're connected to a base station or a peer-to-peer computer network, or whether AirPort is turned off.

✦ **PPoE:** The display of this icon is controlled from the Ethernet panel of the Internet Connect application. Click this icon to connect to or disconnect from the Internet using *Point-to-Point Protocol* (PPP) over Ethernet, which is a type of Internet connection offered by some *Digital Subscriber Line* (DSL) providers.

Doing timely things with the Clock

Even the Clock itself isn't static eye candy on the Mac OS X menu bar —
I told you this was a hardworking operating system, didn't I? Click the Clock
display to toggle the icon between the default text display or a miniature
analog clock.

You can also open the System Preferences Date & Time settings from the
icon. From within the Date & Time settings, you can choose whether the
seconds or day of the week are included, whether the separators should
flash, or whether Mac OS X should display the time in 24-hour (military)
format. More on this in Chapter 3 of Book II.

Eject, Tex, Eject!

Mac OS X makes use of both *static volumes* (your Mac's hard drive, which
remains mummified inside your computer's case) and *removable volumes*
(like Zip disks, DVD-RAM cartridges, and CD/DVD-ROM discs). Mac OS X
calls the process of loading and unloading a removable volume by old-
fashioned terms — *mounting* and *unmounting* — but you and I call the
procedure *loading* and *ejecting*.

Mark's totally unnecessary Computer Trivia 1.0

"Where the heck did *mounting* come from, anyway? Sounds like a line from a John Wayne Western!" Well, pardner, the term dates back to the heyday of Big Iron — the Mainframe Age, when giant IBM dinosaurs populated the computing world. Sherman, set the WayBack Machine. . . .

At the time, disks were big, heavy removable cartridges the diameter of dinner plates (and about as tall as a 100-count spindle of CD-Rs). The acolytes of the mainframe, called *computer operators,* would have to trudge over to a cabinet and swap disk cartridges whenever the program stopped and asked for them — that's right, those mainframes would actually stop calculating and print, "I need you to **mount** cartridge 12-A-34, or I can't go any farther. Have a nice day." (Can you imagine what it would be like loading and unloading a hard drive every time you needed to open a folder?)

Anyway, even though eons passed and mini-computers appeared — which were only the size of a washing machine — the terms *mounting* and *unmounting* still commonly appeared in programs. This time, the removable volumes were 8-inch floppy disks and tape cartridges. Because UNIX (and its offspring Linux) date from the Minicomputer Age, these operating systems still use the terms.

I won't discuss loading/mounting a removable volume — the process differs depending on the computer because some Macs need a button pushed on the keyboard, others have buttons on the drive itself, and some drives have just a slot, with no button at all. However, there are a number of standard ways of unloading/unmounting/ejecting a removable volume:

✦ **Drag the Volume icon** from the Desktop to the Trash, which changes to an Eject icon to help underline the fact that you are *not* deleting the contents of the drive (see Figure 3-15).

✦ **Select the Volume icon** and use the ⌘+E keyboard shortcut.

✦ **Click the Finder File menu** and choose Eject.

✦ **Hold down Control** and click the Volume icon to display the contextual menu; then choose Eject.

✦ **Press your keyboard Eject key** (if it has one).

You can't unmount a static volume from the Desktop, so your internal hard drive icon will stay where it is.

Figure 3-15: Eject a volume by dragging it to the Trash.

The Eject icon

Common Tasks Aplenty

Okay, I admit it — this section is kind of a grab bag of three very common tasks. However, I want to walk you through these three procedures early in the book. Most Mac owners will want to listen to and record CDs as soon as Mac OS X is installed, and you'd be amazed how much information still flows across the Internet in plain, simple text.

Therefore, hang around and take care of business.

Opening and editing text files

Text files would seem to be another anachronism in this age of formatted Web pages, rich text format (RTF) documents, and word processors galore — however, virtually every computer ever built can read and write in standard text, so text files are often used for

✦ **Information files** on the Internet, like FAQs (Frequently Asked Question files)

✦ **Readme and update** information by software developers

✦ **Swapping data** between programs, like comma-delimited database files

Here's the quick skinny on opening, editing, and saving an existing text file:

1. **Navigate to your Applications folder and launch TextEdit.**

2. **Press ⌘+O to display the Open dialog.**

3. **Navigate to the desired text file and double-click the file name to load it (see Figure 3-16).**

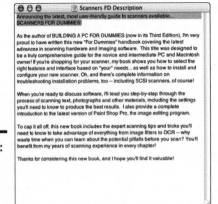

Figure 3-16: A text file open in TextEdit.

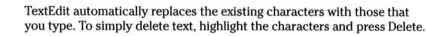

4. **Click the insertion cursor anywhere in the file and begin typing — or, to edit existing text, drag the insertion cursor across the characters to highlight them and type the replacement text.**

   TextEdit automatically replaces the existing characters with those that you type. To simply delete text, highlight the characters and press Delete.

5. **After you finish editing the document, you can overwrite the original by pressing ⌘+S (which is the same as choosing File⇨Save), or you can save a new version by choosing File⇨Save As and typing a new, unique filename.**

6. **To exit TextEdit, press ⌘+Q.**

Listening to an audio CD

By default, Mac OS X uses iTunes to play an audio CD — although I cover iTunes in complete detail in Chapter 2 of Book III, take a moment to see how to master the common task of playing an audio CD (just in case you want to jam while reading these early chapters). Follow these steps:

1. **Load the audio CD into your Mac's CD-ROM/DVD-ROM drive.**

   An Audio CD volume icon appears on your Desktop.

2. **Mac OS X automatically loads iTunes and displays the spiffy window that you see in Figure 3-17.**

   In this case, I've loaded an old favorite of mine: the James Brown album *Live at the Apollo*. (And here's a piece of killer Mac trivia to stump even the hardiest silicon warrior: James Brown performed at the Mac OS 8 rollout party. Get funky with it!)

3. **Click the Play button at the upper left of the iTunes window to begin playing the disc at the beginning.**

   To play an individual track, double-click the track name in the iTunes window.

4. **To adjust the volume from within iTunes, drag the Volume slider to the left or right — it's under the Play button.**

5. **To eject the disc and load another audio CD, click the Eject CD button at the lower-right of the iTunes window.**

6. **To exit iTunes, press ⌘+Q.**

The first time that you run iTunes, you're asked to configure the program and specify whether Mac OS X should automatically connect to the Internet to download the track titles for the disc you've loaded. I recommend that you accept all the default settings and that you allow automatic connection. Is simple, no?

Click to play.   Drag the Volume slider.

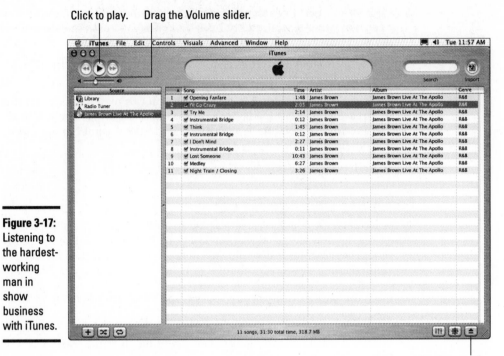

Figure 3-17:
Listening to
the hardest-
working
man in
show
business
with iTunes.

The Eject button

Recording — nay, burning — a data CD

Mac OS X offers a built-in CD recording feature that allows you to burn the simplest forms of CD: a standard Mac format data CD-ROM that can hold up to approximately 660MB of files and folders, or an audio CD that can hold up to about 78 minutes of music. Naturally, you'll need a Mac with a CD or DVD recorder.

If you're interested in recording *all* the exotic CD and DVD formats available today, I can heartily recommend the best book on CD and DVD recording on the shelves: *CD and DVD Recording For Dummies,* written by (surprise!) yours truly and published by Wiley Publishing. *CD and DVD Recording For Dummies* is a comprehensive recording guide that shows you how to burn all types of audio, data, and video by using the latest PC and Mac hardware and the best software on the planet (Roxio Easy CD Creator for the PC and both iDVD and Toast for the Mac). I can honestly say that it's a good read.

Back to the story! To record a disc, follow these steps:

1. **Load a blank CD-R or CD-RW disc into your drive.**

   Mac OS X displays an Untitled CD volume icon on your desktop. (It's marked with the letters *CDR* so you know that the disc is recordable.) You'll be prompted for permission to format it.

2. **Double-click the Untitled CD icon to display the contents — it'll be empty, naturally.**

   As you can see in Figure 3-18, the window tells you that you have 660.7MB of space remaining on the disc.

3. **Click and drag files and folders to the CD window as you normally do.**

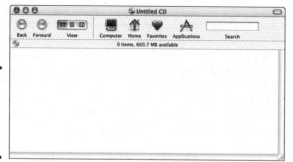

Figure 3-18:
Preparing a data CD for recording in Mac OS X.

4. **Rename any files or folders as necessary — remember, after you've started recording, this stuff is etched in stone, so your disc window should look just like the volume window should look on the finished CD-ROM.**

5. **Click File on the Finder menu and choose Burn CD.**

6. **The Big X displays the confirmation dialog that you see in Figure 3-19 — if you've forgotten something, you can click the Cancel or Eject buttons.**

   Otherwise, click the Burn button and sit back and watch the fun.

Unfortunately, Mac OS X doesn't support recording from the Finder for many of the external and third-party drives available for the Macintosh. If you can't burn from the Finder, I recommend that you buy a copy of Roxio Toast recording software (www.roxio.com).

Figure 3-19:
Are you
positively,
absolutely
sure you
want to
record?

All You Really Need to Know about Printing

To close out this chapter, I turn the attention to another task that most Mac owners need to tackle soon after installing Mac OS X: printing documents. Because basic printing is so important (and in most cases, so simple), allow me to use this final section to demonstrate how to print a document.

Most of us have a Universal Serial Bus (USB) printer — the USB being the favored hardware connection within Mac OS X — so as long as your printer is supported by Mac OS X, setting it up is as easy as plugging it in to one of your Mac's USB ports. The Big X does the rest of the work, selecting the proper printer software driver from the Library/Printers folder and setting your printer as the default power in the universe.

Before you print, preview! Would you jump from an airplane without a parachute? Then why would you print a document without double-checking it first? Click Preview, and Mac OS X opens the Preview application to show you what the printed document will look like. (Once again, some upstart programs have their own built-in Print Preview mode.) When you're done examining your handiwork, close the Preview application to return to your document.

To print from within any application using the default page characteristics — standard 8½-x-11 inch paper, portrait mode, no scaling — follow these steps:

1. **Within your application, click File and choose Print — or press the ⌘+P keyboard shortcut.**

2. **Mac OS X displays the Print dialog that you see in Figure 3-20.**

Some applications use their own custom Print dialogs, but you should see the same general settings.

3. **Click in the Copies field and enter the number of copies that you need — you can also enable or disable collation, just like those oh-so-fancy copiers.**

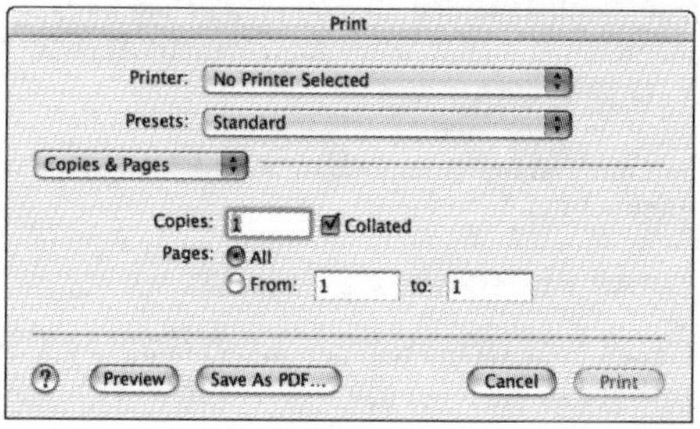

Figure 3-20:
The familiar
Mac OS X
Print dialog,
available
from any
application
with any
real guts.

4. **To print the entire document, use the default Pages radio button setting of All — to print a range of selected pages, select the From radio button and enter the starting and ending pages.**

   Each Mac OS X application provides different panes so that you can configure settings that are specific to that application — it's not necessary to display any of these extra settings to print a default document, but the power is there to change the look dramatically when necessary. To display these settings, click the drop-down list box in the Print dialog and choose one of these panes. For example, if you're printing from the Address Book, you can choose the Address Book entry from the drop-down list and elect to print a phone list or an e-mail list.

5. **When everything is go for launch, click the Print button.**

Of course, there are more settings and more functionality to the printing system within Mac OS X, and I cover more complex printing topics in much more detail in Chapter 4 of Book VI — however, I can tell you from my experiences as a consultant and hardware technician that this short introduction to printing will likely suffice for 90 percent of the Mac owners on Earth. 'Nuff said.

You Shouldn't Have to Read This, but . . .

You will find situations when you have to add a printer manually. (I heartily recommend that you avoid this by buying a printer that's already supported, but this is not a perfect world.) For example, if you own a USB printer that isn't natively supported by Mac OS X but the manufacturer has just released a Mac OS X driver, you can add the printer manually. Follow these steps:

1. **Run the driver installation program or manually copy the driver file into the Library/Printers folder.**

2. **If you're adding a USB printer, make sure that it's connected to your Mac and turned on.**

3. Restart Mac OS X — depending on the driver, this may actually be all you have to do because Mac OS X may automatically detect your printer at this point. If not, continue.

4. Open any application's Print dialog, click the Printer drop-down list, and choose Edit Printer List.

5. Click Add on the Printer List toolbar.

6. Click the Directory Services drop-down list to display USB printers, printers on your AppleTalk network, or available TCP/IP printers, as shown in Figure 3-21.

7. Click the entry for the desired printer and click Add.

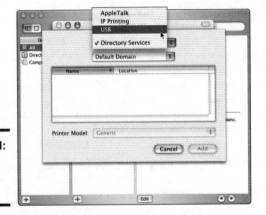

Figure 3-21:
Adding
a printer
manually.

For more troubleshooting information on printers, see Chapter 4 of Book VI.

Chapter 4: Using Sherlock 3: It's Elementary!

In This Chapter

- ✔ Using channels
- ✔ Locating a business
- ✔ Searching for movie listings
- ✔ Checking the definition of a word
- ✔ Following eBay auctions
- ✔ Tracking stock prices
- ✔ Searching with Internet search engines
- ✔ Translating words and phrases
- ✔ Looking up flight schedules

*O*ne of the things that the Internet is *supposed* to provide is (almost) instantaneous access to all sorts of information: news, reference and research material, e-mail addresses, shopping, streaming live video, and even maps that help you chart your way to Grandma's house from wherever you happen to be on the planet. And yes, all that stuff is there — waiting to be used.

However, finding anything in the organized chaos that is the Internet is a completely different matter. A favorite e-mail tagline of mine reads as follows:

What good is a Web search engine that returns 324,909,188 "matches"? That's like saying, "Good news, I've located the information you want. It's on Earth."

In this chapter, I introduce to you to the famous sleuth who makes it easy to search for the proverbial needle in the Internet haystack: Sherlock 3, which is included in Mac OS X. (One note: If you don't have an Internet connection, you can skip this chapter because Sherlock 3 depends entirely upon the Internet while searching for the information you need. There's always a caveat, right?)

Sherlock Is Just Plain Neat

I love Conan Doyle's character Sherlock Holmes — he's one of my favorite fictional figures in literature, as a matter of fact — but even the Bloodhound of Baker Street would be hard pressed to keep up with the great flood of information available online. Apple's Sherlock, on the other hand, was built to do precisely that. To wit:

✦ **Help me, Mr. Wizard!:** Sherlock simplifies the major search engines and allows you to access them all from a single location — no longer do you have to open your Web browser and laboriously visit search engine sites such as Lycos, CNET, and Excite. If you find something on a Web site that you want to explore, a simple double-click of the item automatically launches your Web browser and displays that page.

✦ **Real-time, really:** You can also display real-time information by using Sherlock: Access stock prices, news and headlines, your eBay auctions, and such.

✦ **Plug it in:** Sherlock can provide additional services through the use of *plug-ins* — software add-ons offered by companies, libraries, and Apple itself that expand the functionality of Sherlock.

✦ **Show me:** Depending on the type of information you're seeking, Sherlock can display text, graphics, and even video.

Looking for the Scent with the Great Detective

"By Jove, Watson, the game is afoot!" You can run Sherlock by simply clicking its icon in the Dock, which features Holmes' hat and magnifying glass. To begin, take a look at the Sherlock window itself — Figure 4-1 does the job nicely. The window is divided thusly:

✦ Use the **Channel buttons** displayed along the top of the window to quickly switch between different types of searches. To display all the channels on a single page — complete with descriptions — click the Channels button on the toolbar.

✦ In the **Topic or Description box,** type whatever you're searching for — the fields in this area can change depending on the type of search that you're conducting.

✦ Click the **Search button** — the button bearing the suave-looking magnifying glass — to start searching the selected sites. (Alternatively, you can just poke the Return key.)

Topic or Description   Search button   Channel buttons

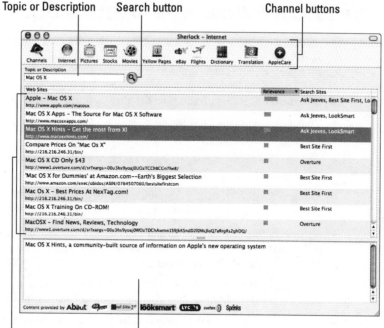

Figure 4-1:
Start the
hunt here
from the
Sherlock
main
window.

Results section   Summary section

✦ The fruits of your search appear in the **results section** — for more information on an item, double-click it.

✦ Clicking an item once often displays a quick summary of the information in the **summary section**.

TIP

Several channels alter the basic look of the Sherlock window, so not every channel will offer all these controls.

Note the *handles* — the double lines — that appear in the separator bars. You can click and drag these handles to resize the dimensions of the channel button display and the results section.

To sort a column in Sherlock, just click the column's heading button. For example, if you're looking at your stock portfolio, click the Name column heading to sort the sites in ascending order — click again to sort in descending order. You can also click and drag the right edge of each column's heading button to resize the width of the column.

You Don't Need a Remote for These Channels

As I mention earlier in this chapter, Sherlock calls each different type (or genre, or class) of search that you can perform a *channel* — for example, the default Sherlock channels include

✦ **Internet:** Click this channel to display popular Web search engines.

✦ **Pictures:** Click this channel to search and select content from the Getty Images online image collection.

✦ **Stocks:** Use this channel to keep track of your stocks and recent headlines concerning each company.

✦ **Movies:** Switch to this channel for movie listings and times in your area or watch the latest movie trailers — now that's techno-*sassy!*

✦ **Yellow Pages:** Use this channel to search for brick-and-mortar businesses — just like that ponderous paper phone book — and even display a map with directions to help you reach a business.

✦ **eBay:** Click this channel and hang onto your wallet as you traverse *the* auction place to hang out — search and track your auctions with aplomb.

✦ **Flights:** Check the major airline schedules by departure and arrival city, as well as flight information like plane type, altitude, and speed — you can even pinpoint the location of a plane in flight!

✦ **Dictionary:** If you use the Internet for research, this channel is, quite simply, your Holy Grail. From this one location, you can peruse the online versions of *The American Heritage Dictionary* and *Roget's II Thesaurus.*

✦ **Translation:** Need to know the word for *taxi* in Portuguese? You can translate phrases and words to and from different languages with this channel.

✦ **AppleCare:** Clicking this channel brings you to the Apple Knowledge Base — a virtual gold mine for Sherlock searches — the Macintosh Product Guide and the Apple Web site.

When researching a troubleshooting issue with Mac OS X, fire up Sherlock and use the AppleCare channel to check out keywords potentially related to your problem.

As I mention earlier, you can display all the default channels and a short description of each channel by clicking the Channels button in the Sherlock toolbar. From this Channel panel — yes, I actually wrote that — click a channel icon to begin your search.

To switch channels, just click the desired channel button at the top of the Sherlock window.

Tracking People, Movies, Definitions, and Auctions

To demonstrate the Fine Art of Search, I show you in this section how to locate a business, how to check movie listings, the definition of the word *sleuth,* and how to locate a print of Old London on eBay. (Something for everyone there, wouldn't you agree?)

Let your mouse do the walking

First, use Sherlock to locate the address and telephone for a popular local pizza restaurant. Follow these steps:

1. **Launch Sherlock 3 and then click the Yellow Pages channel button to display the window that you see in Figure 4-2.**

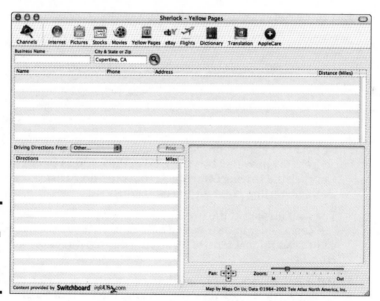

Figure 4-2:
Search for a
business
with
Sherlock.

2. **Type the name** Shakespeare's Pizza **into the Business Name box.**

3. **Type the city and state** Columbia, MO **into the City & State or Zip box and then click the Search button (the magnifying glass button).**

   Figure 4-3 illustrates the results. The business address and phone number is listed, along with the approximate distance in miles from your location.

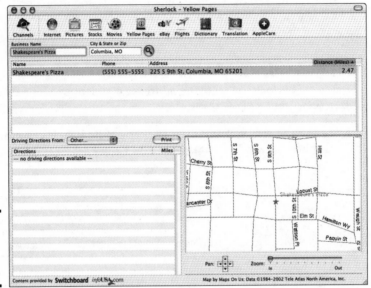

Figure 4-3:
Eureka!
We've
struck pizza.

By default, Sherlock provides directions starting from your home address (as provided by your card in the Address Book). However, you can click the Driving Directions From drop-down list box to select another starting point for the directions.

The map display at the lower-right corner can be zoomed by dragging the Zoom slider in the desired direction. To move the map so that you can see additional territory, click the desired direction on the Pan control.

4. **If the search matches more than one business, click a name in the results section to display the information for that business.**

   To print the results of your search, click the Print button.

Scoping local movies

To search local theaters for information on a movie and watch the trailer to boot, follow these steps:

1. **Click the Movies channel button to display the window that you see in Figure 4-4.**

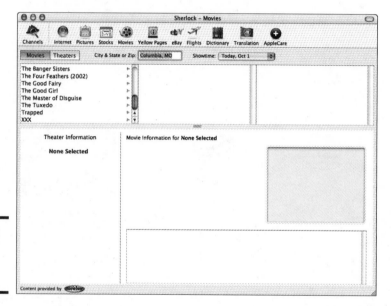

Figure 4-4:
Cinema
searching
simplified.

2. **To search by movie name, click the Movies button at the top-left corner of the window; to search by theater name, click the Theaters button.**

3. **Click the Showtime drop-down list box and then choose the date for your listings.**

By default, today's date is shown.

If necessary, you can also enter a different city/state combination or Zip code in the City & State or Zip box.

4. **Hey, there's one that looks good — click the XXX entry to display the summary text (see Figure 4-5).**

(And no, this isn't a racy film — that's actually the title. It's a great action flick.)

Sherlock automatically begins downloading the QuickTime move trailer for the film. After the movie downloads, click the Play button in the QuickTime viewer window to watch the trailer.

5. **To display the show times for the selected film, click the desired theater in the center column.**

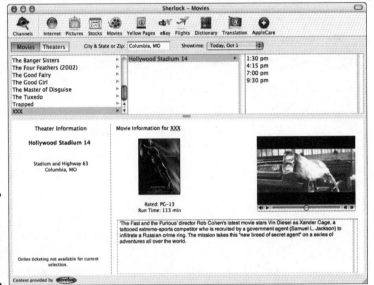

Figure 4-5: More information on a film is a click away.

Consulting Sherlock's dictionary

One of the tasks that I perform most often with Sherlock is searching for word definitions. Follow these steps to find the definition of a word:

1. **Click the Dictionary channel button.**

2. **Type the word** sleuth **into the Word to Define box and then click the Search button.**

3. **To display the definition of any synonyms, click the desired word in the Roget's II Thesaurus column, and Sherlock provides you with the definition in the summary section, as shown in Figure 4-6.**

   Happy hunting!

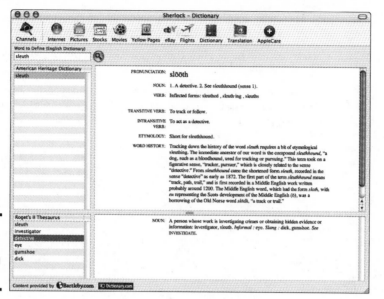

Figure 4-6:
Ferret out
the meaning
of words.

Scouring eBay for Old London

To locate a print of London on eBay, follow these steps:

1. **Click the eBay channel button and then click the rectangular Search button (below the Item Title box and to the left of the Track button) to look for items.**

To track specific auctions, click the Track button instead.

2. **Click the Categories drop-down list to narrow your search to specific categories or leave it set to All Categories to search all eBay.**

3. **Click the Regions drop-down list to show items from a particular area or leave it set to All Regions to search from any locale.**

4. **To limit the price range for matching items, enter values in the Priced Between boxes.**

5. **Type the words** London print **into the Item Title box and then click the Search button — the one with the magnifying glass.**

To display matching items by the newest items first or in a particular price order, click the Items Ending First drop-down list box and choose the desired order.

6. **Click any item, and Sherlock updates the summary section with the specific auction information (see Figure 4-7).**

   • To track this item, click the Track Auction button at the bottom of the Sherlock window.

   • To bid on the item, double-click the item entry, and Sherlock launches Internet Explorer and displays the eBay bidding page for that item.

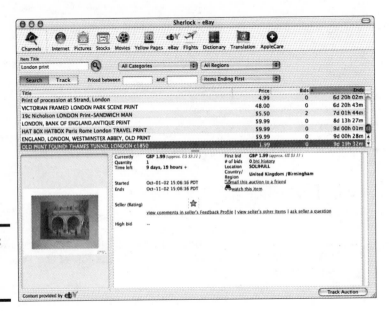

Figure 4-7: Good luck on your bidding.

Using Internet Search Sites

Besides the specialized searches I've already presented in this chapter, Sherlock can make use of existing Internet search engines. Follow these steps to search the Internet for Web sites:

1. **Click the Internet channel button.**

2. **Type the phrase** Scanners for Dummies **into the Topic or Description box and then click the Search button.**

3. **When you find the perfect match for your search, click that entry to display the summary text (see Figure 4-8).**

   Hey, that's quite a coincidence — or is it an obvious plug for another of my books?

4. **To display the entire Web page in all its glory, double-click the entry, and Sherlock launches Internet Explorer.**

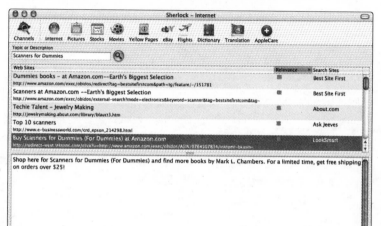

Figure 4-8:
Finding
what you
need is easy
with the
Summary
section.

Minding Your Portfolio

Next, focus your magnifying glass on your stock portfolio. To display information on a stock, follow these steps:

1. **Click the Stocks channel button.**

2. **Type the word** Apple **(or its ticker symbol** AAPL**) into the Company Name or Ticker Symbol box and then click the Search button.**

   Sherlock displays the latest stock quotation and relevant news headlines concerning the company itself.

3. **To display the text of a news item, click the desired headline.**

   Sherlock provides you with the text in the summary section, as shown in Figure 4-9.

4. **To specify a time period for the chart display, click the Chart drop-down list box and pick the desired period.**

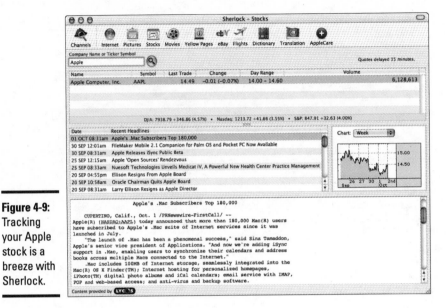

Figure 4-9:
Tracking
your Apple
stock is a
breeze with
Sherlock.

Translating 'Twixt Languages

Although Sherlock can't help you with the word for *bathroom* when you're in the middle of the street in Berlin, you can use the Translation channel to translate words and phrases from the comfort of your computer desk. (And come to think of it, if you have a wireless Internet connection and an iBook, I guess you *could* use it in the middle of a foreign street!)

Follow these steps to translate words and phrases:

1. **Click the Translation channel button.**

2. **Type the word or phrase that you want to translate into the Original Text box.**

(Sorry about the very silly line from *Monty Python and the Holy Grail,* but how could I possibly resist?)

3. **Click the *language-to-language* drop-down list box to specify the starting and ending language for the translation.**

4. **Click the Translate button to translate the text, as shown in Figure 4-10.**

You can highlight and copy the translated text into the Clipboard and then paste it into your word processor or e-mail application.

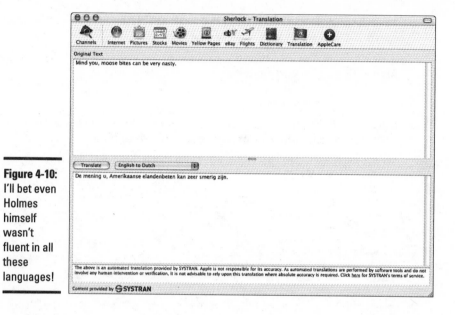

Figure 4-10:
I'll bet even
Holmes
himself
wasn't
fluent in all
these
languages!

Want to experience what I call the Tower of Babel Effect (or TBE)? Start with an English phrase, translate it into a second language, and then continue to translate the results to another language or two. Finally, translate the end result back to English and — voilà! You'll likely be surprised by just how imprecise different languages can be.

Finding Flight Information

Finally, allow me to demonstrate how you can track flight schedules by using Sherlock — truly, gentle reader, this program is as versatile as Apple claims! Follow these steps:

1. **Click the Flights channel button.**

2. **Click the All Airlines drop-down list to narrow your search to specific airlines.**

To display information on a particular flight, type the flight number into the Flight Number box.

3. **To search by departure city, click the Departure City or Airport Code drop-down list and then click the desired location.**

Note that you can also type a city name or airport code directly into the Departure City or Airport Code list.

4. **To search by arrival city, click the Arrival City or Airport Code drop-down list and then click the desired location.**

   Note that you can also type a city name or airport code directly into the Arrival City or Airport Code list.

5. **Click the Search button.**

6. **Click any flight entry, and Sherlock updates the summary section with the specific flight information, as shown in Figure 4-11.**

   To display any leg of the flight, click the Leg drop-down list box.

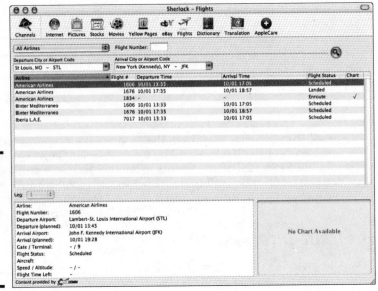

Figure 4-11: Keep track of your arrivals and departures with the Flights channel.

Chapter 5: Keeping Track with the Address Book

In This Chapter

✔ **Adding contact cards**

✔ **Editing contacts**

✔ **Using contact information throughout Mac OS X**

✔ **Creating groups**

✔ **Sending e-mail to a group**

✔ **Printing contacts**

✔ **Importing and exporting vCards**

Do you have a well-thumbed address book stuck in a drawer of your office desk? Or do you have a wallet or purse stuffed with sticky notes and odd scraps of paper, each of which bears an invaluable e-mail address or phone number? If so, you can finally set yourself free and enjoy the "Paperless Lifestyle" of the new millennium with the new Rauncho Digital Address Book! As seen on TV! Only $29.95 — and it doubles as an indestructible garden hose! But wait! If you order now, we'll also send you. . . .

Of course, you and I would tune that stuff out as soon as we heard, "As seen on TV" — but, believe it or not, the Rauncho Digital Address Book does exist (after a fashion), and you already have one if you've installed Mac OS X. It's called the Address Book, and in this chapter I show you how to store and retrieve all your contact data, including iChat information, photographs, and much more.

(And before you ask, operators are not standing by.)

Hey, Isn't the Address Book Just a Part of Mail?

It's true — in older versions of Mac OS X, Address Book was relegated to the minor leagues and usually appeared only when you asked for it within Mail.

Although it could be run as a separate application, there was no convenient route to the Address Book from the Desktop, so most Mac owners never launched it stand-alone.

In Mac OS X Jaguar, however, the Address Book arrives in the limelight, earning a default location in the Dock and available whenever you need it. Although the Address Book can still walk through a meadow hand-in-hand with Mail, it also flirts with other Mac OS X applications and can even handle some basic telephony chores all by itself through the use of services.

Figure 5-1 illustrates the default face of the Address Book, complete with a single address card: your own contact information, which you enter within the First Use Wizard that I mentioned in Chapter 1 of Book I. (This card carries a special me tag indicating that it's your personal card, as well as a suave-looking silhouette next to your name in the Name column.) Other Mac OS X applications use the data in your card to automatically fill out your personal information in all sorts of documents.

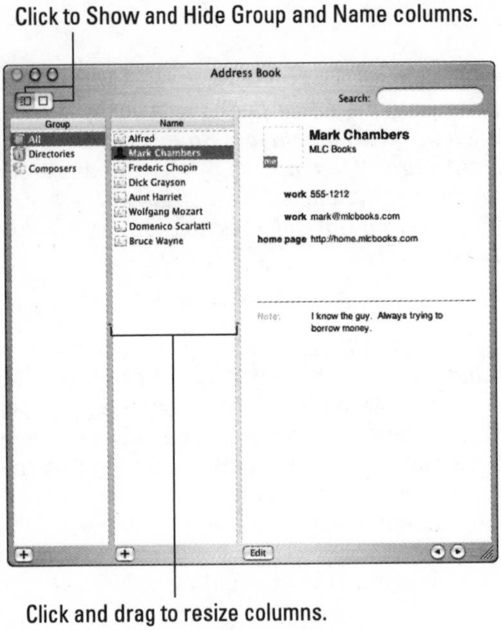

Click to Show and Hide Group and Name columns.

Figure 5-1:
Greetings
from the
Mac OS X
Address
Book!

Click and drag to resize columns.

Note those cool little dimples that mark the Group and Name column dividers — click and drag on the dimples, and you can resize the Group and

Name columns as well as the display window on the right. Plus, you can click the two buttons at the left corner (underneath the window controls) to hide or show the Group and Name columns.

Entering Contact Information

Unless you've actually met and hired a group of DataElves — see the sidebar "I gotta type (or retype) that stuff?" — you'll have to add contacts to your Address Book manually. Allow me to demonstrate here how to create a new contact within your Address Book:

1. **Launch Address Book from the Dock by clicking its icon.**

   The icon looks like an old-fashioned paper Address Book with an "@" symbol on the cover.

2. **Press the ⌘+N shortcut to create a new contact. (Alternatively, choose File⇨New or click the Add a New Person button at the bottom of the Name column.)**

   Address Book displays the template that you see in Figure 5-2, with the First name field highlighted and ready for you to type.

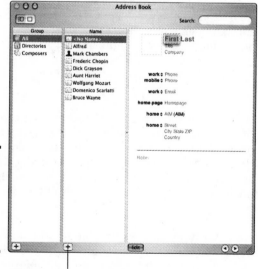

Figure 5-2:
"Hey, I don't know anyone named *No Name!*"

Click to add a new person.

3. **Enter the contact's first name and press Tab to move to the Last name field.**

4. **Continue entering the corresponding information in each field, pressing Tab to move through the fields.**

If a field has no meaning (for example, if a person has no home page), just press Tab again to skip it. You can press Return to add extra lines to the Address field.

When you complete certain fields — like the Address field — a plus symbol pops up to the left of the field. That's the Address Book telling you that there are additional versions of the field that you can enter as well. (Think home and work addresses.) Click this plus sign, and you can enter the other version. For example, if you enter an iChat address for the contact at home, the plus sign appears; click it and then you can enter the contact's work iChat address, too.

5. **To add a photograph to the card, just double-click the thumbnail square next to the person's name.**

Address Book displays a standard Open dialog that you can use to select the image.

6. **When you're done, click Edit to save the card.**

You can edit the contents of a card at any time by displaying it and clicking the Edit button at the bottom (or by pressing ⌘+L, or even by clicking Edit and choosing the Edit Card menu item). You can also add new fields to a card, such as birthdays, anniversaries, and the like.

No need to edit a card to add information to the Note field — just click and type.

You can also add contact cards directly to your Address Book from the Mac OS X Mail application — go figure. Within Mail, click the message (to highlight it) from the person whom you want to add, click the friendly Message menu, and then click Add Sender to Address Book. (Naturally, this doesn't add supporting information — just the person's name and email address. Once again, your nimble fingers will have to manually enter the rest.) For more on Mail, see Book IV, Chapter 2.

If someone sends you a vCard (look for an attachment with a .vcf extension), consider yourself lucky. Just drag the vCard from the attachment window in Mail, drop it into your Address Book, and any information that the person wants you to have will be automatically added!

"I gotta type (or retype) that stuff?"

In my two decades of travel through the computer world, one lovely recurring fantasy shared by computer users keeps cropping up over and over: I call them the DataElves. You see, the DataElves are the hard-working silicon-based gnomes in tiny green suspenders who magically enter all the information that you want to track into your database (or Address Book, or Quicken, or whatever). They burrow into your papers and presto! — out pops all that data, neatly typed and . . . whoa, Nellie! Let's stop there.

For some reason, computer users seem to forget that *there are no DataElves*. I wish I had a dime for every time I've heard a heartbroken computer user say, "You mean I have to *type* all that stuff *in*?" (My usual retort is, "Affirmative . . . unless you want to pay me a hideous amount to do it for you.") Make no mistake — adding a lifetime's worth of contact information into Address Book can be several hours of monotonous and mind-bendingly boring work, which is another reason why many computer owners still depend on paper to store all those addresses. But take my word for it, dear reader, your effort is worth it — the next time that you sit down to prepare a batch of Christmas cards or the next time that you have to find Uncle Milton's telephone number in a hurry, you *will* appreciate the effort you made to enter contact information into your Address Book.

By the way, if you've already entered contact information into another PIM (short for Personal Information Manager), you can re-use that data without retyping everything — that is, as long as your old program can export contacts in vCard format. After you export the records, just drag the vCards into the Address Book window to add them, or import them by pressing ⌘+I — more on this at the end of this chapter.

To delete a card, click the unlucky name to display the card, click Edit, and then choose Delete Person.

Using Contact Information

Okay, now that you've got your contact information in Address Book, what can you actually do with it? Often, all you really need is a quick glance at an address. To display the card for any contact within Address Book, just double-click the desired entry in the Name column. You can move to the next and previous cards by using the directional arrow buttons at the bottom-right corner of the Address Book window.

But wait, there's more! You can also

✦ **Copy and paste:** The old favorites are still around — you can copy any data from a card (press ⌘+C) and paste it into another open application (press ⌘+V).

✦ **Send an e-mail message:** Remember the Mac OS X services feature I told you about in Chapter 3 of this mini-book? Click and drag to select any e-mail address on a card, and then click the Address Book menu and click the Services menu. Choose Mail from the submenu and then choose Mail To. Bingo! Depending on the information that you select, other services may also be available.

✦ **Add an iChat buddy:** From within iChat, click the Buddies menu and click Add a Buddy to display the dialog that you see in Figure 5-3. From here, you can select a contact card that has an Instant Messenger address and add it to your Buddy List.

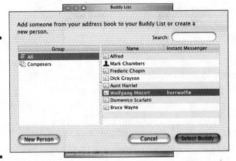

Figure 5-3:
Add a new
buddy
within iChat
using the
Address
Book.

✦ **Export contacts to your iPod (or other applications):** From within the Address Book, select the contacts you want to export, click File, and then choose Export vCards. Address Book displays a standard Mac OS X Save dialog. Navigate to the location where you want to save the cards (for an iPod connected as a FireWire drive, that's the Contacts folder) and click Save.

✦ **Search amongst your contacts:** If you're searching for a specific person and all you have is a phone number or a fragment of an address, click in the Search field at the top right of the Address Book window and type the text. As you continue to enter characters, Address Book shows you how many contacts contain matching characters and displays just those entries in the Name column. Now that's sassy! (And convenient. And fast as all get-out.) Check out Figure 5-4, where many of the characters from my favorite TV shows are gathered — note that a number of very familiar folks share the same address in Gotham City, and I found them using the Search field.

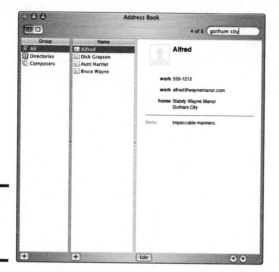

Figure 5-4:
Holy Text
Match,
Batman!

Arranging Your Contact Cards

Address Book also provides you with a method of organizing your cards into groups. A group usually consists of folks with a common link, like your family, friends, co-workers, and others who enjoy yodeling.

To create a group, choose File⇨New Group or press ⌘+Shift+N. (Using the Hollywood method, click the plus sign button at the bottom of the Group column.) Address Book creates a new entry in the Group column, with a highlighted text box so that you can type the group name (see Figure 5-5). After you type the group name, press Return to save it, and then click and drag the entries that you want to add to the New Group icon.

If you've already selected the entries for those contacts that you want to add to the group, choose File⇨New Group From Selection instead — this saves you a step because the group is created and the members added automatically.

After you create a New Group, you can instantly display members of that group by clicking its icon in the Group column. To return to the display of all your contacts, click the All group button.

To further organize your groups, you can drag and drop a group on top of another group — it becomes a sub-group, which is handy for things like branch offices within your company, or relatives who you're not speaking to at the moment.

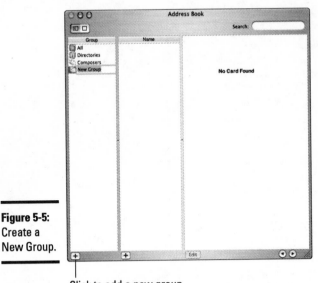

Figure 5-5:
Create a
New Group.

Click to add a new group.

Here's another handy feature of an Address Book group: You can send all
the members of a group the same e-mail message at once. Within Mail,
simply enter the Group name in the To field in the Compose window, and
the same message is sent to everyone.

Using Network Directories

I know, I know, I said earlier that you'd have to enter all your contacts
yourself — but I was talking about your personal contacts! You can also
access two types of external directories from within Address Book:

✦ If you're a member of a company NetInfo network — and if you don't
know, ask your network administrator — you can search network directory servers from within Address Book. These servers are available
automatically, so there's no configuration necessary. Sweet.

✦ You can search Internet-based LDAP directories — sorry, folks, I know
that's pretty cryptic, but others have written entire books on this
technology. Again, suffice it to say that your network guru can tell
you whether LDAP servers are available to you. (In another blazing
display of techno-nerd acronym addiction, LDAP stands for *Lightweight
Directory Access Protocol*.) With LDAP, you can search a central
company directory from anywhere in the world, as long as you have

an Internet connection. To configure this feature, click Address Book from the menu and choose the Preferences menu item; then click on the LDAP tab to enter the specific settings for the server you want to access (see Figure 5-6). Your network administrator or the LDAP server administrator can supply you with these settings.

Figure 5-6:
Enter LDAP
server
information
into Address
Book.

To search either type of network directory, click the Directories entry in the Group column and use the Search field as you normally would. Matching entries will display the person's name, e-mail address, and phone number.

Printing Contacts with Flair

Next, consider how to print your contacts (for those moments when you need an archaic hard copy). Address Book offers two different formats.

By default, Address Book prints on standard US letter-size paper (8 ½-x-11 inches) in portrait orientation. To change these settings, choose File⇨Page Setup or press ⌘+Shift+P. From the Page Setup dialog that you see in Figure 5-7, you can choose exotic settings such as legal-size paper or landscape orientation. Click OK to return to Address Book.

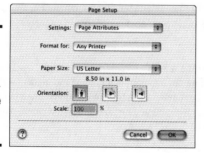

Figure 5-7:
Configure
basic page
characteris-
tics from the
Page Setup
dialog.

Follow these steps to print your contacts:

1. **Choose File⇨Print or press ⌘+P.**

Address Book displays the Print dialog.

If you need more than one copy, enter the desired number in the Copies field. To print a range of cards, click the From option and enter the first and last cards that you want included.

2. **Click the Copies & Pages drop-down list and choose Address Book, which opens the specialized pane that you see in Figure 5-8.**

To print a list based on telephone numbers, choose Phone List in the Print drop-down list box; for a list based on e-mail addresses, choose Email List from the drop-down list.

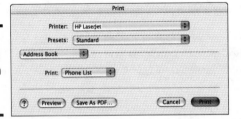

Figure 5-8: Will that list be based on phone or e-mail?

3. **Click the Preview button to check the appearance of the list or click the Print button to send the job to the selected printer.**

Swapping Bytes by Using vCards

A vCard is a standard file format for exchanging contacts between programs like Address Book, Microsoft Entourage, Eudora, and the Palm computer desktop. Think of a vCard as an electronic business card that you can attach to an e-mail message, send via File Transfer Protocol (FTP), or exchange with others using your cellular phone and palmtop computer. vCard files end with the extension .vcf.

In Address Book, you can create a single vCard containing one or more selected entries by clicking File and choosing Export vCards — like any other Mac OS X Save dialog, just navigate to the spot where you want the file saved, give it a name, and click Save. Figure 5-9 illustrates my vCard, saved from my Address Book to my Desktop.

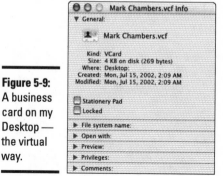

Figure 5-9:
A business
card on my
Desktop —
the virtual
way.

To import vCards into Address Book:

✦ Drag the vCard files that you've received to Address Book and drop
   them in the application window.

✦ Alternatively, choose File➪Import vCards or press ⌘+I. From the Open
   dialog, navigate to the location of the vCard files that you want to add,
   select them, and click Open.

Chapter 6: The Joys of Maintenance

In This Chapter

✔ **Deleting applications**

✔ **Using Apple System Profiler**

✔ **Using CPU Monitor**

✔ **Using the Disk Utility**

✔ **Updating Mac OS X**

✔ **Backing up your system**

✔ **Using a disk defragmenter**

✔ **Using start-up keys in Mac OS X**

✔ **Updating your drivers**

The title of this chapter really sounds like a contradiction in terms, doesn't it? The concepts of *joy* and *maintenance* will likely be mutually exclusive to you — and it's true that most Mac OS X owners would rather work or play than spend time under the hood, getting all grimy. I understand completely.

However, if you do want your work or play uninterrupted by lockups and crashes — yes, believe it or not, the Big X can indeed take a dive if it's not cared for — and you'd like your Mac to perform like Lance Armstrong, you've got to get your hands dirty. That means performing regular maintenance on your hardware, Mac OS X, and your all-important applications, documents, and folders.

Like most techno-types, I actually *enjoy* pushing my system to the limit and keeping it running in top form. And who knows — after you become a Mac OS X power user, you could find yourself bitten by the maintenance bug as well. In this chapter, I cover how to take care of necessary tune-up chores, step-by-step.

Deleting Applications the Common-sense Way

Nothing lasts forever, and that includes your applications — you might no longer need an application or maybe you need to remove it to upgrade to a new version or to reinstall it. Unlike Windows, Mac OS X doesn't have an Add & Remove utility for uninstalling software — nor does it need one because virtually all Macintosh applications are self-contained in a single folder or series of nested folders. Therefore, removing an application is usually as easy as deleting the contents of the application folder from your hard drive.

Always check the application's README file and documentation for any special instructions before you delete any application folder. If you've created any documents in that folder that you want to keep, don't forget to move them before you trash the folder and its contents!

Some programs can leave preference files, start-up applications, or driver files in other spots on your disk besides their home folder. When you're uninstalling a program that has support files in other areas, use the Search box in the Finder toolbar to locate other files that may have been created by the application. (I cover this feature in Chapter 1 of Book II.)

For example, Figure 6-1 illustrates a search that I've run on Microsoft Office X. By searching for the word *office,* I've found a number of files created in other folders, like the settings file that's in my Preferences folder. Typically, you'll want to delete the main application folder first and then remove these orphans.

The Spring Cleaning utility from Aladdin Systems (www.aladdinsys.com) also has the ability to uninstall a program, as well as a feature that can find and remove orphaned files left over from past applications.

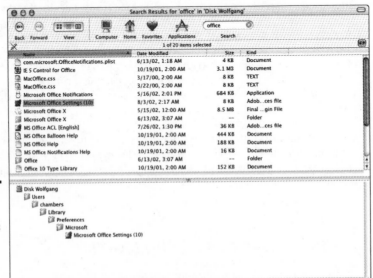

Figure 6-1: Locate support files before deleting an application.

Popping the Hood: Using the Apple System Profiler

Need hard information about your hardware? You might need to determine precisely what hardware is installed in your Mac for the following reasons:

✦ **If you're working with a technical support person to solve a problem:** This person will usually request information about your system, such as what processor you're running and how much memory you have.

✦ **If you're evaluating an application before you buy it:** You'll want to check its minimum system requirements against the hardware on your Mac.

✦ **If you're considering an upgrade to your Mac:** You'll likely need to determine how much memory you have, what type it is, and which memory slots are filled. (The same goes for your hard drive and your video card, for those Macs with video card slots.) For more on upgrading your Mac, thumb through Book VI, Chapter 2.

Apple provides Mac OS X with an all-in-one hardware and software display tool, aptly named *Apple System Profiler,* which you can find in the Utilities folder within your Applications folder. (You can also reach the Profiler through the Apple menu — click About this Mac and then click the More Info button.) As you can see from Figure 6-2, there's a lot to digest from the System Profiler window.

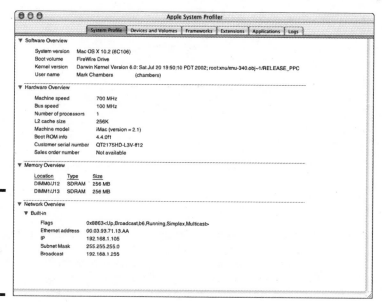

Figure 6-2:
Find your
system
overview in
System
Profiler.

Like the folders in a Finder window in list view mode, you can expand or collapse each major heading that appears in a Profiler screen. Just click the triangle that appears to the left of each Overview heading to expand or collapse that heading.

The System Profiler tabs include

✦ **System Profile:** The heart of the Profiler, this is the screen that you'll use the most (again, feast your eyes on Figure 6-2). It includes information about your Mac OS X version, an overview of your system hardware, a description of the physical memory in your Mac, and an overview of the network connections that you're currently using.

✦ **Devices and Volumes:** This tab tells you volumes — forgive me — about the hard drives, CD and DVDs, and FireWire and USB devices connected to your system. Figure 6-3 illustrates the information from my Devices and Volumes screen, with many of the devices expanded so that you can see them.

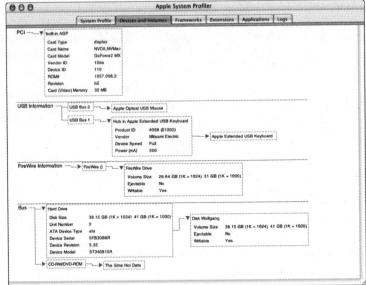

Figure 6-3: See information about the ports and connections on your Mac.

✦ **Frameworks:** This tab is a listing of the *frameworks* — a fancy developer term for shared files (also called *libraries*) — that applications use in Mac OS X. You'll probably only need this screen when asked by a technical support person for the version number of a specific framework.

✦ **Extensions:** This tab shows another rather boring list display with version numbers, along with the *extensions* (or drivers) used by Mac OS X applications.

TIP

You can promptly forget about this screen unless a technical support person asks you to go there.

✦ **Applications:** Okay, this tab shows something useful to the average human being! This screen lists all the applications recognized on your start-up volume, along with their version numbers (see Figure 6-4). If you're wondering whether you need to update an application with a *patch file* (to fix bugs in the software) or update file from the developer, you can look here to check the current version number for the application.

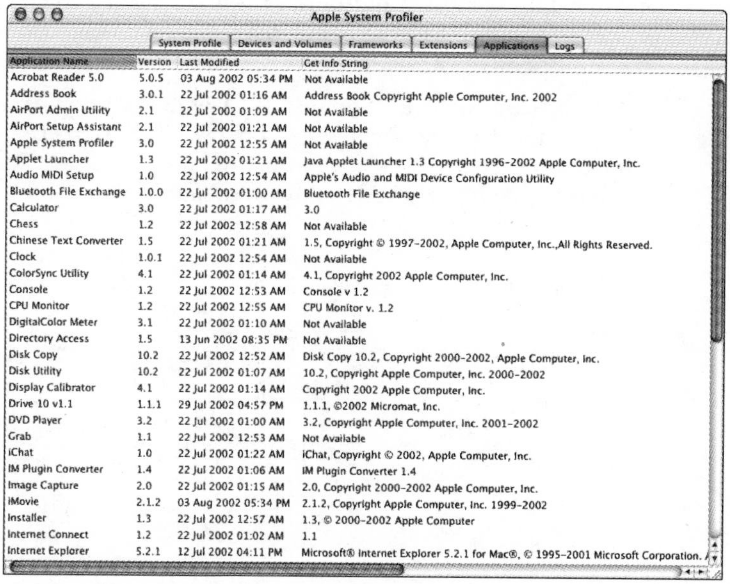

Figure 6-4:
View all
your
applications
and version
numbers.

✦ **Logs:** Although interesting, the highly complex listings on this final tab are usually valuable only to tech support personnel. They document recent lockups, application crashes, and even system crashes.

Tracking Performance with CPU Monitor

Our next stop in Maintenance City is a useful little application called the *CPU Monitor,* which is specially designed to show you just how hard your CPU is working behind the scenes. To run CPU Monitor, open the Utilities folder in your Applications folder; to display the preferences for this application, click on the CPU Monitor menu and then click Preferences. Figure 6-5 illustrates the three different types of displays available within CPU Monitor, from left to right:

✦ **Floating window:** This is the smallest display of CPU usage. You can arrange the floating window in horizontal or vertical mode from the CPU Monitor Preferences dialog.

✦ **Expanded window:** This display is the most informative of the windows, showing the amount of CPU usage over time, and in two ways. The green portion of the bar indicates the amount of processor time used by application software, and the red portion of the bar indicates the CPU time given to the Mac OS X operating system. (These colors are a little tough to see in Figure 6-5 because it's black and white, but just pull up your own CPU Monitor to see what I mean.) You can resize the expanded window, and the colors used can be changed in the CPU Monitor Preferences dialog.

✦ **Standard window:** The standard CPU Monitor window, which uses a blue thermometer-like display, can be displayed in the Dock — you can configure the Dock display from the Preferences dialog. The higher the CPU usage, the higher the reading on the monitor.

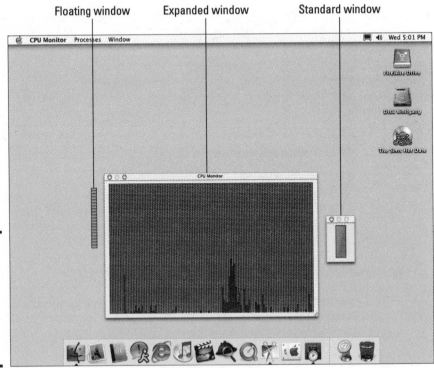

Figure 6-5:
Three different ways to display CPU activity using CPU Monitor.

Whichever type of display that you choose, you can drag the window anywhere that you like on your Mac OS X Desktop. Use the real-time feedback to determine how well your system CPU is performing when you're running applications or performing tasks in Mac OS X. If this meter stays peaked for long periods of time while you're using a range of applications, it's indicating that your processor is running at full capacity.

Note, however, that seeing your CPU capacity at its max *does not* necessarily mean that you need a faster CPU or a new computer. For example, when I'm running applications such as Photoshop or Premiere, the CPU Monitor on my G4 iMac is often pegged (indicating maximum use) for several seconds at a time. The rest of the time, it barely moves. Whether a computer is actually fast enough for you and the applications you run is more of a subjective call on your part.

Fixing Things with the Disk Utility

Another important application in your maintenance toolbox is the Disk Utility, which you'll find — no surprise here — in the Utilities folder within your Applications folder. When you first run this program, it looks something like Figure 6-6, displaying all the physical disks and volumes on your system.

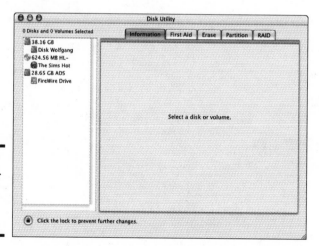

Figure 6-6:
The familiar
face of the
Mac OS X
Disk Utility.

Displaying the goods on your disks

The volume tree structure on the left of the Disk Utility window lists both the physical disks and the partitions that you've set up. A *partition* is nothing more than another word for *volume,* which is the formatted section of a disk that contains data. A single physical hard drive can contain several partitions. The Information tab displays data about both the volumes and the partitions on your hard drive.

To illustrate: On my system, clicking the drive labeled *38.16 GB* (the physical hard drive at the top of the tree) displays a description of the drive itself, including its total capacity, interface (connection type), and whether the drive is internal or external. (See Figure 6-7.) Clicking the tree entry for Disk Wolfgang, however — that's the name of the partition that I created when I formatted the drive — displays information about the type of formatting, the total capacity of the partition and how much of that is used, and the number of files and folders stored on the partition (as shown in Figure 6-8).

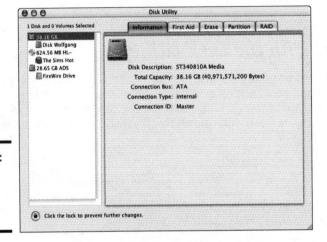

Figure 6-7:
Display data on a physical disk.

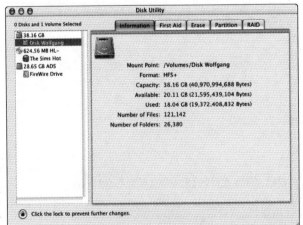

Figure 6-8:
Display data on a volume.

Playing Doctor with First Aid

Click the First Aid tab of Disk Utility to display the controls that you see in Figure 6-9. Disk Utility can be used to *verify* (or check) any disk (well, almost any disk) for errors, as well as repair any errors that it finds. For these two exceptions will the buttons be disabled:

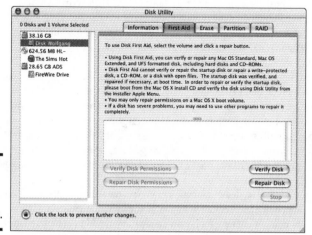

Figure 6-9:
The Disk
Utility First
Aid controls.

✦ **The start-up disk:** Disk Utility can't verify or repair the *start-up disk* — that's Mac talk for the boot drive that contains the Mac OS X system that you're using at the moment — which makes sense if you think about it because that drive is currently being used!

If you have multiple operating systems on multiple disks, you can boot from another Mac OS X installation on another drive to check your current start-up disk. Or, you can boot your system from the original Mac OS X installation CD and run Disk Utility from the Installation menu.

As the Utility so proudly declares, the start-up disk is *automatically* verified and repaired (if necessary) during the boot procedure, so you really don't need to worry about checking the start-up disk.

✦ **Write-protected disks:** Although you can use the Disk Utility to verify CDs, DVDs, and write-protected removable disk drives (like a write-protected Zip disk), it can't repair them.

You also can't repair a disk that has open files — if you're running an application from a drive or you've opened a document that's stored on that drive, you won't be able to repair that drive.

You can also elect to verify and repair *permissions* (also called *privileges*) on a disk; these are the read/write permissions that I discuss in detail in Book II, Chapter 6. If you can't save or move a file that you should be able to access, I recommend checking that drive for permissions problems. Unlike fixing disk errors, you can only verify and repair permissions on the start-up volume.

In order to verify or repair, you must be logged in as an administrator. If you've set up only a single user in Mac OS X, this won't be a problem. If you've set up multiple users, however, you might need to click the lock icon at the bottom of the Disk Utility window and type a valid administrator name and password to continue.

To verify or repair a drive, first select the target volume/partition in the list at the left. To check the contents of the drive and display any errors, click the Verify Disk button. Or, to verify the contents of the drive and fix any problems, click the Repair Disk button. (I usually just click Repair Disk because an error-free disk will need no repairs.) Disk Utility displays any status or error messages in the scrolling list; if you've got eagle eyes, you'll note that the list can be resized so that you can expand it to display more messages.

I generally check my disks once every two or three days — if your Mac is caught by a power failure or Mac OS X locks up, however, it's a good idea to immediately check disks after you restart your Mac. (Remember: The start-up volume is automatically checked and repaired, if necessary.)

A number of very good commercial disk repair utilities are on the market. My favorite is Drive 10 from Micromat (www.micromat.com), shown in Figure 6-10. However, Disk Utility does a good job on its own, and it's free.

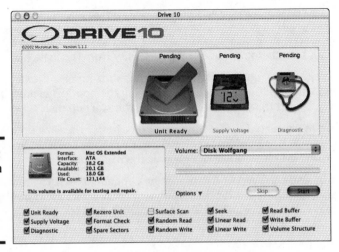

Figure 6-10: Drive 10 is a great Mac OS X native disk repair utility.

Erasing without seriously screwing up

"Danger, Will Robinson! Danger!" That's right, Robot, it is indeed very easy to seriously screw up and get *Lost in Erase.* (Man, I can't believe I actually typed a pun so bad.) Anyway, it's time for another of Mark's Maxims. To paraphrase the rules for handling a firearm responsibly:

Never click this tab unless you mean to use it.™

Figure 6-11 illustrates the Erase tab of Disk Utility. You need only erase a disk or volume when you want to completely wipe the contents of an existing disk or volume. You can also wipe a rewriteable CD or DVD from this tab.

✦ Erasing an *entire disk* deletes **all volumes** on the disk and creates a single new, empty volume.

✦ Erasing a *volume* only wipes the *contents of that specific volume,* leaving all other volumes on the physical disk untouched.

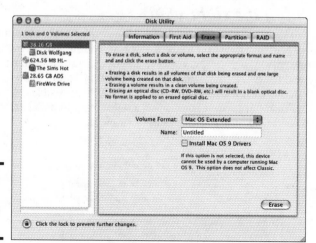

Figure 6-11:
The Disk Utility Erase controls.

To erase, follow these steps:

1. **From the Erase tab of Disk Utility, click the disk or volume icon that you want to erase from the list on the left side of the screen.**

2. **Click the format that you want to use from the Volume Format drop-down list.**

Always choose Mac OS Extended from the Volume Format list unless you have a specific reason to use the MS-DOS File System (for compatibility with PCs running Windows) or the UNIX File System (for compatibility with UNIX/Linux machines). Note that you do *not* need to format a disk or volume with the MS-DOS File System just to read a floppy or a ZIP disk from a PC system — Mac OS X recognizes MS-DOS removable media without a problem.

3. **In the Name field, type the name for the volume.**

If you're erasing an existing volume, the default is the existing name.

4. **If you're erasing a disk, enable the Install Mac OS 9 Drivers check box to specify whether you want to install drivers for native Mac OS 9 machines.**

Without these drivers, the disk can't be used with Mac OS 9 on another Mac or if you reboot your Mac using Mac OS 9. (Note that these drivers are not required to use the disk in Classic mode.)

5. **Click the Erase button.**

In the sheet that appears, click Erase to confirm that you do actually want to do the deleterious deed.

Partitioning the right way

From time to time, just about everyone wishes they had additional volumes handy for organizing files and folders — or at least a little extra space on a particular partition. If you find yourself needing another volume on a disk — or if you need to resize the total space on existing volumes on a disk — click the Partition tab within Disk Utility to display the controls that you see in Figure 6-12. From here, you can choose a volume scheme, creating anywhere from one to eight volume partitions on a single disk.

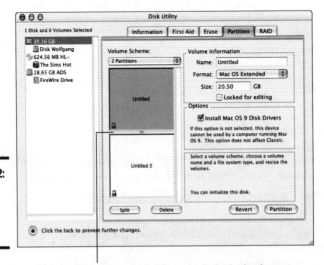

Figure 6-12:
The Disk
Utility
Partition
controls.

Click and drag to dynamically resize unlocked volumes.

You can't monkey around with the partitions on a start-up disk because Mac OS X is currently running on that disk — think about removing your own appendix, and you'll get the idea.

To set up the partitions on a disk, follow these steps:

1. **From the Partition tab of the Disk Utility pane, click the disk icon (left side of the pane) that you want to partition.**

2. **Click the first volume block in the partition list (under the Volume Scheme drop-down list) to select it.**

3. **Click the Volume Scheme drop-down list and choose the total number of volumes that you want on the selected disk.**

4. **Click in the Name field and enter the name for the first volume.**

5. **From the Format drop-down list, choose a format for the volume.**

   Always use Mac OS Extended from the Format list unless you have a specific reason to use the MS-DOS File System (for compatibility with PCs running Windows) or the UNIX File System (for compatibility with UNIX/Linux machines).

6. **Type a total size for this volume in the Size field.**

7. **To install Mac OS 9 drivers on this volume, enable the Install Mac OS 9 Disk Drivers check box.**

   Without these drivers, the disk can't be used with Mac OS 9 on another Mac or if you reboot your Mac using Mac OS 9. (Again, Classic mode doesn't require these drivers.)

8. **After you set up your first volume partition, mark the Locked for Editing check box to prevent any further changes to that volume.**

9. **If you're creating multiple volumes, click the next volume block to select it and repeat Steps 4 through 8.**

10. **To delete a partition from your new scheme, click the unwanted volume and then click the Delete button to remove it.**

11. **To split a partition from your new scheme into two volumes, click the desired volume and then click the Split button.**

12. **When everything is set to your liking, click the Partition button to begin the process.**

   If you suddenly decide against a partition change, click the Revert button to return to the original existing partition scheme — however, the Revert button is only available before you click the Partition button!

Check out the bar(s) with a handle separating the volumes in the partition list. If you leave all your partitions unlocked (by leaving the Locked for Editing check box disabled), you can click and drag these separator bars to dynamically resize the volumes. This makes it easy to adjust the individual volume sizes for the disk until you get precisely the arrangement you want. If a volume is locked, it can't be resized dynamically in this fashion.

RAID has nothing to do with insects

The final stop on the Disk Utility hayride isn't for everyone — as a matter of fact, only a Mac OS X power user with a roomful of hardware is likely to use it. RAID, *Redundant Array of Independent/Inexpensive Disks*, is actually what it says. In normal human English, a *RAID set* is a group of multiple separate disks, working together as a team. Using RAID can

✦ Improve the speed of your system

✦ Help prevent disk errors from compromising or corrupting your data

The RAID tab of Disk Utility is illustrated in Figure 6-13. You'll need at least two additional hard drives on your system besides the start-up disk, which I don't recommend that you use in a RAID set.

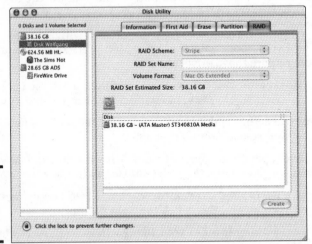

Figure 6-13:
The Disk
Utility RAID
controls.

To set up a RAID array in Mac OS X, follow these steps:

1. **From the RAID tab of Disk Utility, click and drag the disks (or volumes on separate disks) from the list at left to the Disk box.**

2. **Click the RAID Scheme drop-down list to specify the type of RAID that you need.**

   - **Stripe:** Choosing this can speed up your hard drive performance by splitting data between multiple disks.

   - **Mirror:** Choosing this increases the reliability of your storage by creating a mirror backup of that data across multiple disks.

3. **Click in the RAID Set Name field and type the name for your RAID set.**

4. **From the Volume Format drop-down list, choose a format for the volumes.**

   Always use Mac OS Extended from the Volume Format list unless you have a specific reason to use the MS-DOS File System (for compatibility with PCs running Windows) or the UNIX File System (for compatibility with UNIX/Linux machines).

5. **Click the Create button.**

Updating Mac OS X

As any good software developer should, Apple constantly releases improvements to Mac OS X in the form of software updates. These updates can include all sorts of fun stuff, like

- Bug fixes

- Improvements and new features

- Enhanced drivers

- Security upgrades

- BIOS (or firmware) upgrades

Apple makes it easy to keep Mac OS X up-to-date with the Software Update settings in System Preferences (see Figure 6-14). To check for new updates periodically, enable the Automatically Check for Updates When You Have a Network Connection check box. Then from the drop-down list box, choose how often you want these updates. (I suggest at least weekly, if not daily.) For a manual check, make sure that you're connected to the Internet and then click the Check Now button.

If updates are available, Mac OS X displays them with a short description; you can toggle the installation of a specific update by enabling or disabling the check boxes next to it.

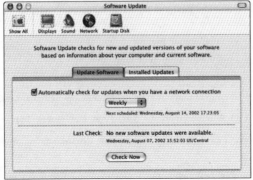

Figure 6-14:
Keep Mac
OS X up-to-
date with
Software
Update.

I recommend installing all updates, even for hardware that you don't have yet. For example, I always install AirPort updates even though I don't use an AirPort connection at home. The reason? Often, the functionality covered by an update may include system software that you do use, so you'll still benefit from installing it.

After you specify the updates that you want to install, click the Install button to begin the update process. You might have to reboot after everything has been installed.

To see which updates you've already installed, click the Installed Updates tab.

I Demand that You Back Up Your Hard Drive

I know we're friends, but there's *no* excuse for not backing up your data. The more valuable and irreplaceable that your documents are, the more heinous it is to risk losing them. (I don't get to use the word *heinous* in many of my books, but it fits really well here.)

Unfortunately, Apple doesn't include a back-up utility in Mac OS X. (Insert sound of stunned silence here.) If you have subscribed to Apple's .Mac service, a backup utility is included, but it's not a part of the default Mac OS X package. Therefore, turn to a commercial back-up application for your salvation — my personal recommendation is Retrospect, shown in Figure 6-15, from Dantz (www.dantz.com). This well-written "software bungee cord" has saved my posterior more than once.

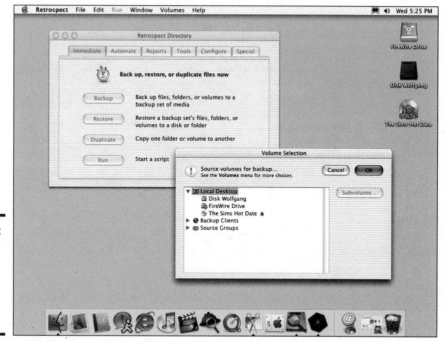

Figure 6-15:
The face of
back-up
security —
Retrospect
Backup
from Dantz.

Using Retrospect is cheap security, but if you can't afford it at the moment, take a second to at least back up your most important documents by copying them to a rewriteable CD or a Zip disk. Don't trust a floppy; they're far too unreliable. With this poor man's backup, even if you lose your entire hard drive, you can still restore what matters the most.

1 Further Demand that You Defragment

Defragmenting your hard drive can significantly improve its performance. Using a *defragmenter* scans for little chunks of a file that are spread out across the surface of your hard drive and then arranges them to form a contiguous file. After a file has been optimized in this way, it's far easier and faster for Mac OS X to read than reassembling a fragmented file.

However, Apple has again dropped the ball on this one and didn't include a defragmenter with Mac OS X. Luckily, version 1.1 of Micromat Drive 10 also includes a defragmenting feature (see Figure 6-16), as does Speed Disk from Norton (www.norton.com). If you have a defragmenter, I recommend that you use it once a month.

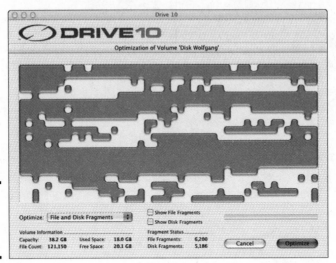

Figure 6-16: Defragment a drive with Drive 10.

Special Start-up Keys for Those Special Times

Mac OS X includes a number of special keys that you can use during the boot process — these keys really come in handy when you need to force your operating system to do something that it normally wouldn't, like boot from a CD instead of the hard drive.

✦ **To boot from a CD or DVD disc:** Restart your Mac while pressing the C key. This is a great way to free up your start-up volume when you want to test it or optimize it using a commercial utility.

✦ **To eject a recalcitrant disc that doesn't show up on the Desktop:** Restart Mac OS X and hold down the mouse button — or if you have a late-model Mac, press the Media Eject key as soon as you hear that magnificent startup chord.

✦ **To force your Mac to boot in Mac OS X:** Hold down the X key while restarting or booting the Mac.

✦ **To display a system boot menu:** Hold down the Option key while restarting or booting the Mac, and you can choose which operating system you want to use.

✦ **To prevent start-up applications from running during login:** Hold down the Shift key while you click the Login button on the Login screen. If you don't see the Login screen during startup, just hold down Shift while Mac OS X boots until the Finder menu appears.

Crave the Newest Drivers

No chapter on maintenance would be complete without a reminder to keep your hardware drivers current. *Drivers* are simply programs that allow your Mac to control hardware devices, like a video card or a Small Computer System Interface (SCSI) card that you've added to your Mac. The Mac OS X Software Update feature that I discuss earlier in the section "Updating Mac OS X" provides most of the drivers that you'll need for things like printers, USB and FireWire peripherals, and digital cameras, but it's still very important to check those manufacturer Web sites.

Like the software updates from Apple, updated drivers can fix bugs and even add new features to your existing hardware, which is my definition of *something for nothing.*

Chapter 7: Using Classic Mode

In This Chapter

✔ **Understanding how Classic mode works**

✔ **Locating Classic applications, files, and folders**

✔ **Configuring Classic mode**

✔ **Restarting in Mac OS 9.2**

To someone as familiar as you are with Mac OS X, using applications in Mac OS 9 is like watching an evening of Lawrence Welk — you know that this music *used* to be cutting-edge, and that tap-dancer *used* to be cool, but now it all seems . . . well . . . horribly *wrong*. (I don't mean to offend the champagne-music crowd — Lawrence and the band were really quite good. Perhaps it's those unspeakable robin's-egg blue tuxedos that give me such a headache.)

We're lucky because most of the popular Mac applications have been updated for the Big X, but the process isn't yet complete. Not every program will run natively in Mac OS X — even a number of programs have only recently hit the shelves, such as QuarkXPress 5.0, still run only in Classic mode — so it's practically a sure thing that sooner or later you'll launch a program, see the bouncing number 9 in the Dock, and realize that means Classic is revving up. For those times, this chapter will prove a soothing balm.

Classic Mode Explained

Let's start with a definition: Classic mode is actually an implementation of Mac OS 9 that runs in Mac OS X. Think of it as a virtual session of Mac OS 9 that runs whenever you need it — although you won't actually see the Mac OS 9 session after it boots up. Instead, Classic runs in the background, providing breathing space for applications that wouldn't otherwise run in Mac OS X.

Of Carbon and Cocoa . . .

First, a word about why Classic mode is required in the first place — you can politely brush past this section if you're not interested in the Grand Design, and I'll catch up with you in a paragraph or two.

Still here? Okay. Here's the chop. Mac OS X applications are written using two software development APIs (nerdspeak for *Application Program Interface*). An *API* specifies the way that a program communicates with the operating system. Read about Quartz in Book I, Chapter 1.

Mac OS X recognizes two programming APIs: Carbon and Cocoa. A *Carbon* application runs in both Mac OS 9.2 and Mac OS X; common

Carbon applications include Adobe Photoshop 7 and Roxio Toast. A *Cocoa* application runs only under Mac OS X, such as Microsoft Office v. X. Cocoa applications perform significantly better than Carbon under Mac OS X, and Cocoa's structure allows software developers to finish an application faster.

If a program supports either Carbon or Cocoa, it'll work like a champ in Mac OS X — however, if the program is older and was exclusively written for earlier versions of Mac OS without Carbon, it won't run in Mac OS X, and Classic mode automatically launches to run the application in a comfortable environment.

The beauty of Classic is that virtually all older applications run fine in Classic mode, and they have absolutely no idea that they're actually working under Mac OS X. Any problems you're likely to experience in Classic mode stem from "confused" hardware that can't communicate through ports that are still controlled through Mac OS X, or the same "shared" memory problems that plagued older versions of Mac OS. (Sigh.) In other words, if a lockup could happen in a "real" Mac OS 9 session, it can also happen in Classic mode . . . but luckily, the only thing that would crash is the Classic environment itself, so the rest of your Mac OS X applications should continue working without a hitch. (In fact, you can launch Classic from System Preferences, as I show you later in this chapter, and try to run the Classic application again without wreaking havoc on the rest of Mac OS X.)

 If you need to use an application from time-to-time that simply won't run correctly under Classic mode at all, you can always take drastic measures and restart under Mac OS 9, which I demonstrate at the end of this chapter.

Cranking Up Classic

The three methods of running Classic mode are

✦ **Double-click on an application without Cocoa or Carbon support:** In other words, launch an older program. As I mention earlier, you'll see the sprightly bouncing Classic mode icon appear in the Dock, and a minimal progress bar appears (Figure 7-1). Click the arrow next to the progress bar to expand the Classic window and watch the boot process, just as if you were actually staring at Mac OS 9. After Classic mode has loaded, the Classic icon disappears from the Dock, the Mac OS 9 boot window/progress bar disappears, and the application menu and window appear.

Figure 7-1:
Starting
Classic
mode with
just the progress bar.

Classic Environment starting from "/Disk Wolfgang/System Folder"

Stop

TIP

Note that applications running in Classic use the Mac OS 9 menu bar, and Classic mode windows have the older Mac OS 9 window controls (Figure 7-2). In fact, there's an easy way to tell whether an application is running in Classic mode: Just to look at the Apple logo in the top left corner of the screen! If it's a solid color Apple, the active application is a native Mac OS X application. On the other hand, if the Apple appears as the traditional six-color logo, the active application is running in Classic mode.

✦ **Launch Classic from System Preferences:** Click the System Preferences icon in the Dock and choose Classic settings to display the dialog that you see in Figure 7-3. Click the Start button.

✦ **Configure Classic to run automatically:** To start Classic automatically when you log in to Mac OS X — on a system where you're the only user, that means when you boot your computer — click on the System Preferences icon in the Dock and choose Classic settings. Mark the Start Classic When You Log In check box to enable it, and then press ⌘+Q to exit System Preferences and save the change.

After Classic mode is running on your Mac, any number of Mac OS Classic applications can use it — you only have to launch Classic once, and it remains running until you log out, Mac OS X is restarted, or Classic mode goes to sleep (more on this nocturnal behavior later in the section "Configuring Classic Mode").

To stop Classic mode — thus freeing up both system RAM and your processor, as well as improving the performance of other Mac OS X applications — open System Preferences, choose Classic settings, and click Stop on the Start/Stop pane.

The six-color Apple means your machine is running in Classic mode.

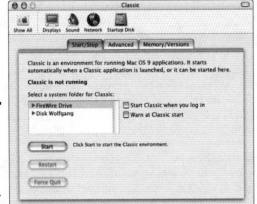

Figure 7-2:
A Classic application is easy to spot in Mac OS X.

Figure 7-3:
The Classic settings within System Preferences.

Reaching that Antique Software

If you upgraded from Mac OS version 8 or 9 to Mac OS X, you'll be happy to know that all those legacy applications that you used before are still available. You can find them in a number of places on your system:

✦ **Applications (Mac OS 9) folder:** Mac OS X places all the applications that existed on your drive in the old Applications folder into this new folder — and, in turn, all the new Mac OS X applications added to your system are stored in the Applications folder. Although slightly schizophrenic, it's a great solution that actually works. After you upgrade to Mac OS X, simply look in the Applications folder for your Mac OS X native applications and open the Applications (Mac OS 9) folder for your older stuff.

Many new Mac OS X native applications that use the Carbon API will also install an alias in your Applications (Mac OS 9) folder so that you can easily run them when you've restarted in Mac OS 9. If a Mac OS X application will run under Mac OS 9 and didn't automatically create an alias (how rude!), it only takes a second to add the alias yourself in the Applications (Mac OS 9) folder. (For more about aliases, see Chapter 2 of Book I.)

✦ **The Mac OS 9 Desktop:** Yep, you heard right, you can still reach the icons and programs on your Mac OS 9 desktop, including folders and aliases. Double-click the Desktop (Mac OS 9) icon on your Mac OS X Desktop to display it, as illustrated in Figure 7-4, and you can run applications or work on documents to your heart's content. (Any changes that you make to this "desktop in a Folder" in Mac OS X will naturally be reflected when you restart in Mac OS 9.)

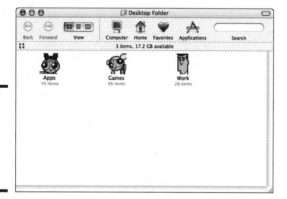

Figure 7-4:
Hey, aren't those my Mac OS 9 Desktop items?

Configuring Classic Mode

The default System Preferences settings for the Classic environment can be tweaked to enhance performance or to change when Classic starts or how it operates. These settings include the following:

✦ **Startup Options:** Click the Advanced tab to display the options that you see in Figure 7-5. By using the drop-down list box, you can elect to start Classic with extensions off, or to start the Classic Extensions Manager to individually toggle Control Panels and Extensions on or off. Choose the Use Key Combination option and type up to five keys — one at a time — that should be simultaneously pressed when you start Classic (which allows you to simulate Mac OS 9 startup keys). Note that these Advanced startup options work only when you launch Classic manually from this panel using the Start Classic button.

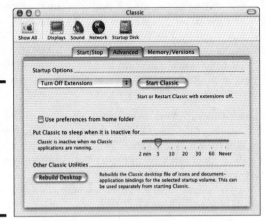

Figure 7-5:
The Advanced configuration options for Classic mode.

✦ **Putting Classic to sleep:** Click and drag the slider to specify the amount of inactivity that will trigger the Classic Sleep option. When Classic is asleep, it uses much less system memory and doesn't bog down your Mac's CPU — when a Classic application is launched, it takes Mac OS X far less time to activate Classic from Sleep mode than it does to start Classic from scratch. To disable the Classic Sleep option, move the slider to Never: After it's running, Classic will continue to remain active in the background until you manually Stop it (as I describe earlier in this chapter).

✦ **Rebuilding your Classic desktop:** Click the Rebuild Desktop button to regenerate the Classic Desktop file, which stores data on what icons go with what Classic applications as well as what types of documents link to which Classic applications. Normally, you need only do this if your Classic applications no longer have the proper icons or if double-clicking on a document created with a Classic application no longer launches the proper application.

To see what's running in the Classic environment — something roughly akin to asking, "I wonder how refrigerant is circulated in my central air-conditioning system?" — click the Memory/Versions tab of the Classic System Preferences dialog. Figure 7-6 illustrates two programs running, showing the amount of memory that they're actually using and the maximum amount of memory that they're allowed to have. To show what's running in the background in Classic mode, mark the Show Background Processes check box to enable it. This dialog also displays the version of Mac OS that Classic is using. (If you're not interested in what's happening behind the curtain in the Classic environment, you can gleefully forget that this tab ever existed in the Classic System Preference settings.)

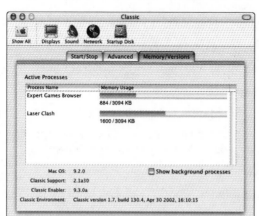

Figure 7-6:
Display memory information for Classic applications.

Returning to Your Mac OS 9 Roots

If you need to take the plunge and travel back in time, you can also restart your Mac in Mac OS 9 for as long as you like — simply change the system Startup Disk! Follow these steps in Mac OS X to return to the days of yore:

1. **Click the System Preferences icon in the Dock.**

2. **Click the Startup Disk icon to display the settings that you see in Figure 7-7.**

Figure 7-7:
Choose a Mac OS 9 System Folder to use.

3. **Click the Mac OS 9 System Folder to select it.**

Note that if you have multiple installations of Mac OS 9 on your system on different hard drives — as I do — you'll have to choose the proper System Folder on the proper drive. For those with only one Mac OS 9 System Folder, all is well.

4. **Click the Restart button and then click the Save and Restart buttons on the confirmation sheet that appears.**

After you finish your fun in Mac OS 9.2 and you want to return to Mac OS X, follow these steps:

1. **Click the Apple menu and choose the Control Panels menu item.**

2. **Click the Startup Disk submenu item.**

3. **Click the Mac OS X System Folder to select it.**

If you have multiple Mac OS X installations or multiple drives, you can click the triangle next to a drive to expand the display.

4. **Click the Restart button.**

Voilá! You've returned to Wonderland. Say hello to the White Rabbit for me.

Mac OS X also provides two neat "Choose your operating system weapon" startup keys you can use when booting or restarting your system. If you hold down the X key while booting or restarting, your Mac boots into Mac OS X — in fact, the Startup Disk choice in System Preferences is actually changed to the Mac OS X System Folder on the current boot drive, so this eliminates the need to follow the steps I just outlined! (Pretty catchy, huh? Holding down X to start the Big X, I mean.) Alternately, if you hold down the Option key while booting or restarting, your Mac displays a menu of all of the available operating systems on your system, and you can pick one. Note, however, that the Option key does not change your Startup Disk setting, so the next time you reboot or restart, you revert to the startup operating system you selected in System Preferences.

Chapter 8: Getting Help for the Big X

In This Chapter

✔ **Using the Mac OS X Help Center**

✔ **Searching for specific help**

✔ **Getting help in applications**

✔ **Finding other help resources**

Whether the voice echoes from a living room, a home office, or a college computer lab, it's all too familiar: a call for help. No matter how well written the application or how well designed the operating system, sooner or later you're going to need support. That goes for everyone from the novice to the experienced Mac owner to the occasional e-mail user to the most talented software developer.

In this short but oh-so-important chapter, I lead you through the various help resources available within Mac OS X as well as native Mac OS X applications. I show you how to tap additional resources from Apple, and I also point you to other suppliers of high-quality (and even questionable) assistance from sources on the Internet and in your local area.

Displaying the Help Viewer Window

Your first line of defense is the Mac OS X Help Viewer, as shown in Figure 8-1. To display the Help Viewer from the Finder menu, click Help and choose Mac Help or press the ⌘+? keyboard shortcut. This Help menu is context-sensitive, so it contains different menu items when you're working inside an application.

As shown in Figure 8-1, the Help Viewer is divided into three sets of controls:

✦ **Toolbar:** You can hide or display the Toolbar from the View menu. The default Toolbar includes navigational controls (Back and Help Center buttons) and the Ask a Question (or Search) text box.

✦ **Quick Clicks:** Clicking these underlined links takes you directly to resources for some of the most frequently asked Help topics for the

Finder (or the application you're using), such as "How do I change my computer settings?" and "Can I send e-mail?" To use a Quick Click, just click once on the question that you want to pursue.

✦ **Go link:** Click this link to display the latest Mac OS X news and the latest Help topics from the Apple Web site.

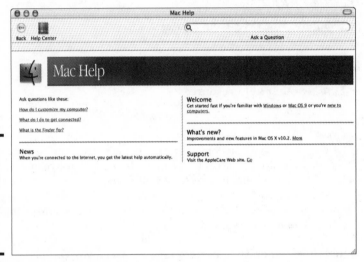

Figure 8-1:
The reservoir of Mac OS X assistance: The Help Viewer.

I know that the Help Viewer looks a little sparse at first glance. However, when you realize how much information has to be covered to help someone with an operating system — check out the size of the book you're holding, for instance — you get an idea of why Mac OS X doesn't try to cover everything on one screen. Instead, you get the one tool that does it all: the Ask a Question text box.

Searching for Specific Stuff

To search for the help topic you need, click in the Ask a Question text box and type one or two words that sum up your question and press Return. (Although you can ask a full sentence question, I've found that the shorter and more concise your search criteria is, the better the relevance of your return.) For example, typing **playing a DVD** displays the topics that you see in Figure 8-2.

Note that the topics are sorted by approximate relevance first — for example, because the topic *Playing DVDs* is smack-on accurate, it appears first because it has the highest relevance. The next topic, *Setting up multiple displays as an extended desktop,* is only distantly related, so the relevance is lower.

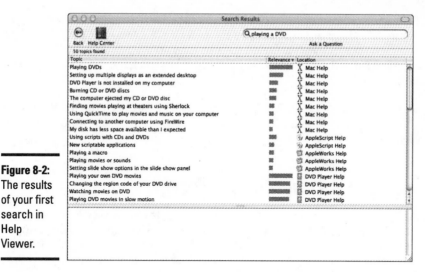
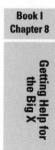

Figure 8-2:
The results
of your first
search in
Help
Viewer.

To sort the topics alphabetically or by their location within the Help system, click the Topic or Location column headings, respectively. You can click a column heading again to toggle the sort order between ascending and descending.

Because the topic *Playing DVDs* sounds quite promising, double-click it to display the topic text — this particular topic displays the text that you see in Figure 8-3. (You can also single-click on a line to display a summary at the bottom of the window.)

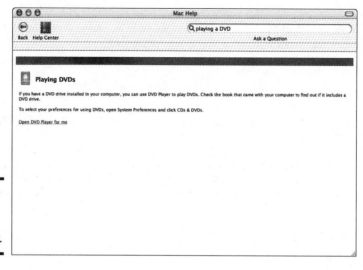

Figure 8-3:
Help result
for *Playing
DVDs* query.

Note the contextual link at the bottom of the Help Viewer window in Figure 8-3: Many topics allow you to open an application or display System Preferences settings that relate to your question. This time, the Help Viewer offers to open the DVD Player application; just click the link to launch the DVD Player.

To move back to the previous topic that you chose, click the Back button on the Help Viewer toolbar. To return to the Help Viewer main window, click the Help Center toolbar button.

Prodding Apple for the Latest Gossip

As I mention in the earlier section "Displaying the Help Viewer Window," you can click the Go link to display the latest Mac OS X help topics from Apple, but I also recommend that you visit the Apple Web site at www.apple.com and surf to your heart's content. You'll often pick up on news and reviews that you won't find anywhere else on the Internet.

From the opening Web screen, you should click these two tabs during every visit to the Apple site: the Hot News tab and the Mac OS X tab. These pages give you

+ Articles about the latest news from Cupertino

+ Downloads of the latest Mac OS X freeware, shareware, and demo-ware

+ The Knowledge Base (an online searchable troubleshooting reference)

+ News about upcoming versions of Mac OS X and Apple applications galore

You'll also find Mac OS X product manuals in Adobe Acrobat PDF format and online discussion forums that cover Mac OS X.

Calling for Help Deep in the Heart of X

A number of different help avenues are available within Mac OS X applications as well. They include

+ **The Help button:** A number of otherwise upstanding Mac OS X windows and dialogs include a Help button, as shown in Figure 8-4. Click the button marked with a ? to display the text for the settings in that dialog or window.

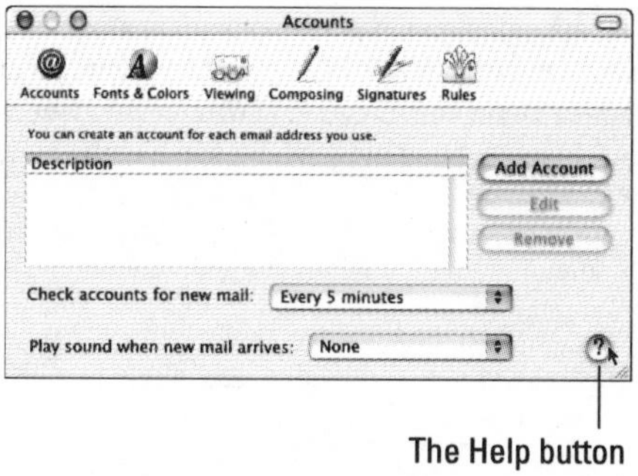

Figure 8-4:
Notice the
not-so-well-
camouflaged
Help button.

The Help button

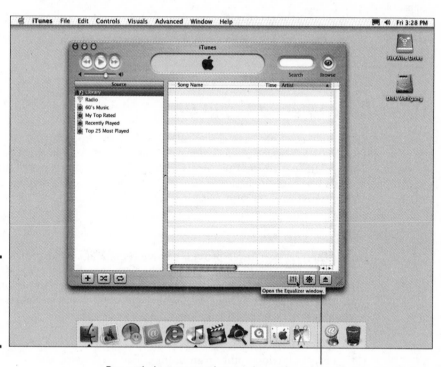

✦ **Pop-up help for fields and controls:** Most Mac OS X applications display a short line of help text when you hover the mouse pointer on top
of a field or control, as shown in Figure 8-5. Sometimes it's just the name
of the item; sometimes it's a full descriptive line. Them's the breaks.

Figure 8-5:
Displaying
pop-up help
within an
application.

Open the Equalizer window.

Pop-up help appears when you hover the mouse pointer over a button.

✦ **Application-specific help:** Applications typically have their own Help system, which may use the Help Viewer, a separate Help display program, or a HyperText Markup Language (HTML; read that *Web-based*) Help system. Figure 8-6 illustrates the stand-alone online Help system for Microsoft Internet Explorer.

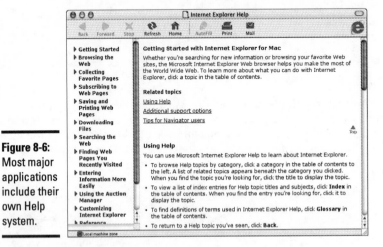

Figure 8-6:
Most major
applications
include their
own Help
system.

Other Resources to Chew On

Although the Help Viewer can take care of just about any question that you might have about the basic controls and features of Mac OS X, you might also want to turn to other forms of help when the going gets a little rougher. In this last section, I cover resources that you can call on when the Help Viewer just isn't enough.

Voice support

As of this writing, Apple provides voice technical support for Mac OS X at 1-800-275-2273 — however, exactly when you qualify for voice support and exactly how long it lasts depends on a number of different factors, like whether you received Mac OS X when you bought a new machine, or whether you purchased a support plan from Apple.

You can also try the general online support site at www.info.apple.com — it's a great starting point for obtaining Mac OS X help.

Mac publications

You can refer to a number of great Mac-savvy publications, both printed and online, for help. My favorites include

✦ *Macworld* (www.macworld.com) and *MacAddict* (www.macaddict.com) magazines, both in archaic hard copy and oh-so-slick online versions

✦ MacGamer (www.macgamer.com), the online gaming resource for the Macintosh

✦ MacFixIt (www.macfixit.com), a well-respected troubleshooting site devoted to the Mac that offers downloads, news and discussion areas

In most of my books, I mention specific Internet newsgroups that cater to the topic I'm discussing — however, virtually all the Mac-specific newsgroups around are devoted to illegally swapping pirated games and applications, so I won't be covering them. Also, the help that you receive from individuals in newsgroups is sometimes misguided — and sometimes downright wrong, so take any claims with a grain of salt.

As a general rule, *never* identify yourself or provide your snail-mail or e-mail addresses in a newsgroup post! These messages are public, and they remain "hanging around" in cyberspace on newsgroup servers for years — you'll be a prime target for spam (or even worse).

Local Mac outlets and user groups

Finally, you can find local resources in any medium- to large-sized town or city: A shop that's authorized by Apple to sell and repair Macintosh computers can usually be counted upon to answer a quick question over the phone or provide more substantial support for a fee. (For example, my local Mac outlet sponsors inexpensive classes for new Mac owners.)

You may also be lucky enough to have a local Macintosh user group that you can join — members can be counted on for free answers to your support questions at meetings and demonstrations. To find a group near you, visit the Apple User Group Support site at www.apple.com/usergroups/ and use the locator.

Chapter 9: Troubleshooting the X

In This Chapter

✔ **Mastering the scientific approach**

✔ **Using troubleshooting techniques**

✔ **Performing the radical solutions**

✔ **Checking troubleshooting resources**

M ac OS X is rugged, stable, and reliable — and as you can read earlier in this mini-book (in Chapter 6), practicing regular maintenance can help eliminate problems caused by everything from power failures to faulty drivers. However, sooner or later you *will* encounter what I like to call *The Dark Moments* . . . a blank screen, a locked Mac, or a device that sits there like an expensive paperweight or a useless keyboard.

How you handle The Dark Moments defines you as a true Mac OS X power-user because most folks seem to fall into one of two categories: Either you panic and beat your head against the wall (which really has little effect on the computer, when you think about it), or you set your brow in grim determination and follow the troubleshooting models that I provide in this chapter to locate (and hopefully fix) the source of the problem.

Don't Panic!

My friend, this is the first — and most important — rule of troubleshooting, and yet another of Mark's Maxims:

Whatever the problem, you *can* fix it.™

Most Mac owners seem to forget the idea that a hardware or software error can be fixed because they panic — they simply see The Problem, and somehow they feel that they'll never be able to use their computer again.

Although the situation may look grim, don't ignore these facts:

✦ **There's no need to scrap your Mac:** As long as you haven't taken a hammer or a chainsaw to your Mac, the problem is only temporary. Sure, components do fail over time — heck, so do people — but the problem is almost certainly something that can be tracked down and fixed without scrapping your computer.

✦ **Don't beat yourself up:** As long as you haven't installed a virus on purpose or deleted half your system files to spite yourself, the problem isn't your fault. Sure, it's possible that you might have done something by accident but don't blame yourself unnecessarily.

✦ **Trust your Apple dealer:** As long as an Apple dealer is in your area, you can get your computer repaired professionally if a component has gone south. (For example, I'd be a fool to try to fix a power supply or a monitor on my own because both can pack a heavy electrical punch.)

✦ **Rely on your backup:** As long as you've made a backup — you *did* back up your hard drive, didn't you? — you won't lose much (if any) work.

Commit these facts to head and heart, and you can rest easy while you track down and attack the *real* enemy — whatever's causing the problem.

The Troubleshooting Process

When I first conceived this chapter, I had originally decided to divide this section into separate hardware and software troubleshooting procedures — however, that turned out to be impractical because often you won't know whether a problem is caused by hardware or software until you're practically on top of it.

Therefore, here's the complete 12-step troubleshooting process that I followed as a consultant and Macintosh hardware technician for more than a decade. Feel free to add your own embellishments in the margin or include reminders with Post-It notes.

If you're not quite sure what's producing the error, this process is designed to be linear — meaning that it's meant to be followed in order — but if you already know that you're having a problem with one specific peripheral or one specific application, feel free to jump to the steps that concern only hardware or software.

Step 1: Always try a simple shutdown

You'd be amazed at how often a reboot (the process of shutting down and restarting) can cure a temporary problem. For example, this can fix the occasional lockup in Mac OS X or a keyboard that's not responding because of a power failure. If possible, make sure that you first close any open documents or you might lose unsaved work. When troubleshooting, always do a shutdown instead of simply restarting the computer because when Mac OS X shuts down, all the hardware components that make up your system are reset.

If your Mac is locked tight and you can't use the Shut Down command from the Apple menu, you have two choices. First, press and hold the Power button on your Mac for a few seconds (which turns your computer off). If this doesn't work — and, from time to time, it actually doesn't — you'll have to physically pull the power cord from the wall (or turn off the surge suppressor, if you're using one).

Step 2: Check all cable connections

Check all connections: the AC power cord and the keyboard cord, as well as any modem or network connections and all cable connections to external peripherals. Look for loose connectors — and if you've got a cat or dog, don't forget to check for chew marks. (Yep, that's the voice of experience talking there.) If you've recently replaced a cable — especially a network cable or a FireWire cable — replace it with a spare to see whether the problem still occurs.

Step 3: Retrace your steps

If the problem continues to occur, the next step is to consider what you've done in the immediate past that could have affected your Mac. Did you install any new software or have you connected a new peripheral? If your Mac was working fine until you made the change to your system, the problem likely lies in the new hardware or software.

✦ **If you added an external device:** Turn off your Mac and disconnect the peripheral. Then turn on the computer to see whether all proceeds normally. If so, then check the peripheral's documentation and make sure that you installed the *driver* — the software provided by the device manufacturer — correctly and that you connected it properly to the right port. Also, to verify that the cable works, substitute another cable of the same type or try the peripheral on another Mac.

✦ **If you installed new software or applied an update/patch:** Follow the guidelines in Chapter 6 of this mini-book to uninstall the application and search for any files that it may have installed elsewhere. (Searching by date created and date modified can help you locate files that you recently installed.) If this fixes the problem, it's time to contact the developer and request technical support for the recalcitrant program; you can always re-install the program after the problem has been solved by the developer.

Not all versions of Mac OS X are created equal. If you've recently upgraded to a major or minor new release of Mac OS X, some of the applications that you've been using without trouble for months can suddenly go on the warpath and refuse to work (or exhibit quirky behavior). If this happens, visit the developer's Web site often to look for a patch file that will update the application to work with the new version of Mac OS X.

Make it a practice to check the manufacturer's Web site for the latest driver when you get new hardware. The software that ships in the box with your new toy could have been on the shelf for months before being sold, and the manufacturer has probably fine-tuned the driver in the interim.

✦ **If you've recently made a change within System Preferences:** It's possible that you've inadvertently "bumped" something. For instance, you might have accidentally changed your modem or network settings or perhaps made a change to your login options. Verify the settings screens that you visited to make sure that everything looks okay. Other locations to check include the Print Center (which I discuss in Book VI, Chapter 4) and your Web browser's Preference dialog (I cover Internet Explorer in Chapter 5 of Book IV).

Step 4: Run Disk Utility

Next, run Disk Utility (as shown in Figure 9-1) to check for disk errors and permissions errors. (Click the Disk Utility icon in the Utilities folder inside your Applications folder. Chapter 6 of this mini-book provides all the details.)

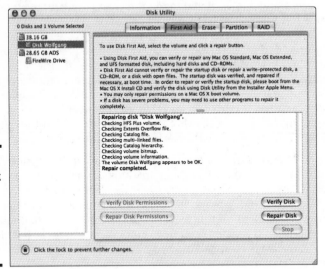

Figure 9-1: Use the Disk Utility to check the integrity of your hard drives.

Step 5: Run antivirus software

Run your antivirus software and scan your entire system for viruses, including all system disks and removable disks. Although Mac OS X doesn't come with antivirus protection built-in, the world-class program Norton AntiVirus (www.symantec.com) that you see in Figure 9-2 constantly scans each file that you open or download for infections.

REMEMBER

Download the latest virus update — usually called a *signature file* or *data file* — to keep your virus protection current.

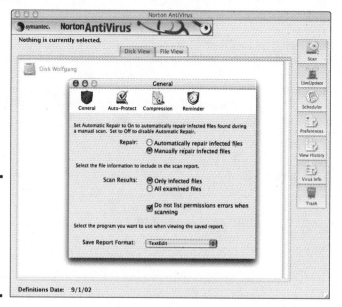

Figure 9-2:
Scan your Mac for viral nastiness with Norton AntiVirus.

Step 6: Check the Trash

Check the contents of your Trash to make sure that you haven't inadvertently tossed something important that could be causing trouble for an application. Click the Trash icon in the Dock to open the Trash window and peruse its contents (switch to List mode to see the file types). To restore items to their rightful place, drag them from the Trash back to the correct folder on your hard drive.

Step 7: Check online connections

If you're connected to an Ethernet network, cable modem, or digital subscriber line (DSL), check your equipment to make sure that you're currently online and receiving packets normally. Your network system administrator will be happy to help you with this, especially if you're blood relatives.

Step 8: Disable troublesome login items

Disable any login items that might be causing trouble. As you can read in Chapter 3 of Book II, login items are automatically launched as soon as you login. For example, an older application that doesn't fully support Mac OS X can cause problems if used as a login item. You can do this from the Login Items settings in System Preferences (as shown in Figure 9-3); click the Apple menu, choose System Preferences, and then click the Login Items icon.

Unfortunately, if a login item doesn't display an error message, your old friend Trial-and-Error is just about the only sure-fire way to detect which item (if any) is causing the problem. Click an item to select it, click the Remove button, and then shut down and reboot your Mac to see whether the problem has been solved. (If not, don't forget to add the item again to the Login Items list.)

Figure 9-3:
A misbehaving login application can cause you a world of grief.

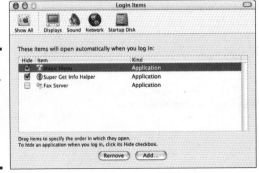

You can also disable login items entirely when you reboot. If the login window appears when you reboot your computer, hold down the Shift key and then click the Login button. If you don't see the login window when you reboot, hold down the Shift key when you see the progress bar in the startup window and continue to hold down the key until the Finder appears.

Step 9: Turn off your screen saver

Another candidate for intermittent lockups is your screen saver, especially if you're running a shareware effort written by a 12-year-old with a limited attention span. Display your System Preferences, choose Screen Effects, and either deactivate the screen saver (on the Activation tab, move the slider to Never) or choose the Computer Name saver (which is provided by Apple) from the Screen Effects list.

Step 10: Check for write-protection

If you're running a multi-user ship, check to make sure that another user with administrator access hasn't accidentally write-protected your documents, your application, or its support files. If possible, log in with an administrator account yourself (as described in Book II, Chapter 5) and then try running the application or opening the document that you were unable to access under your own ID.

Step 11: Check your System Profiler

If you've reached this point in the troubleshooting process and haven't found the culprit, you've probably experienced a hardware failure in your Macintosh. If possible, display the Devices and Volumes tab within the Apple System Profiler (see Figure 9-4) and make sure that it's able to recognize and use all the internal drives, ports, and external devices on your Mac. To start the System Profiler, click the Apple menu, choose About this Mac, and then click the More Info button.

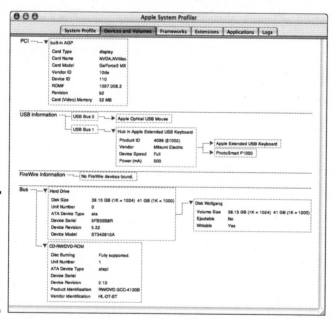

Figure 9-4:
Use System
Profiler to
check the
devices and
ports on
your system.

Step 12: Reboot with the Mac OS X Installation CD

In case your Mac is in sad shape and won't even boot from its hard drive, here's a last step that you can take before you seek professional assistance:

Reboot your Mac from the Mac OS X Installation CD-ROM. Hold down the C key immediately after you hear the startup chord, which boots your system from the CD-ROM or DVD-ROM drive, and then run the Disk Utility from the Installation Apple menu that appears. Because you've booted the system from the CD-ROM, you can verify and repair problems with your startup hard drive. After you're done, restart your system.

Troubleshooting Problems with Classic Mode

If you encounter problems running your older Mac OS 9 applications under Classic mode, here are suggestions that you can follow that might help:

✦ **Check memory allocations:** Classic applications sometimes need additional memory. If a Classic application gets snooty and demands more memory, select the Classic application in the Finder and then press ⌘+I to display the Mac OS 9.2 Info dialog. Click the drop-down list box and choose Memory to display the settings that you see in Figure 9-5; I usually double the suggested size, using that amount for both the Preferred Size and Minimum Size values. Exit the Info dialog to save your changes and then try running the application again.

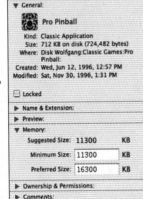

Figure 9-5: Try bumping up the memory allocation for a Classic application.

✦ **Disable extensions:** If a Classic mode extension is wreaking havoc on your system, you can disable extensions entirely from the Classic settings in System Preferences. Usually, this will also end up disabling a significant number of features, perhaps even including FireWire and Universal Serial Bus (USB) support in Classic mode. However, it might help you get Classic running, which will allow you to disable the extension that's causing the problem (or even deleting it entirely from your computer). You can use the Classic Extensions Manager to toggle individual extensions on and off, which makes it easy to test Classic mode to see which specific extension is causing the problem. Reboot in Mac OS 9 and select the Extensions Manager control panel from the Apple menu.

Although many Mac owners have dismissed Conflict Catcher from Casady & Greene (www.casadyg.com), it makes a great debugging tool for Classic mode as well. You can use Conflict Catcher to build custom extension sets for both full Mac OS 9 and Classic mode.

✦ **Move start-up and shut down files:** If a Classic mode start-up or shutdown application is causing problems, you can move the file from the Startup Items and Shutdown Items folders in your Mac OS 9 System folder. (The file itself is usually an alias, so you can simply delete it if you like.)

Do I Need To Reinstall Mac OS X?

To be honest, this is a difficult question to answer. Technically, you should never *need* to reinstall the Big X, but there's also no reason why you *can't*.

I can think of only two scenarios where reinstalling the operating system will likely solve a problem: Namely, if your system files have been so heavily corrupted — by a faulty hard drive or a rampaging virus, for example — that you can't boot Mac OS X at all; or if the operating system displays the death-dealing kernel dump on a regular basis. A *kernel dump* displays several lines of unbelievably technical UNIX terminology on your screen, usually overwriting whatever's on the monitor at the time, ending with the option to Reboot or Continue. (This is analogous to the infamous Windows Blue Screen of Death — I've grown to hate that color of blue with a passion.)

If you receive kernel dumps on an ongoing basis, something is really, *really* wrong. Make sure that your documents are copied to a rewriteable CD or network drive and don't overwrite any existing backup that you have with a new backup because the back-up application is likely to lock up as well.

To reinstall, you must reboot from your Mac OS X Installation CD-ROM. Hold down the C key immediately after you hear your Mac's startup chord. (Read the earlier section "Step 12: Reboot with the Mac OS X Installation CD.")

It's Still Not Moving: Troubleshooting Resources

As I mention earlier in this chapter, you can pursue other avenues to get help when you can't solve a troubleshooting problem on your own. Mind you, I'm talking about professional help from sources that you can trust. Although you can find quite a bit of free advice on the Internet (usually on privately run Web sites and in the Internet newsgroups), most of it isn't worth your effort. In fact, some of it is downright wrong. That said, here are some sources I do recommend.

The Mac OS X Help Viewer

Although most Mac OS X owners tend to blow off the Help Viewer when the troubleshooting gets tough, that's never the best course of action. Always take a few moments to search the contents of the Help Viewer — click Help from the Finder menu — to see whether any mention is made of the problem that you've encountered.

The Apple Mac OS X Support site

Home to all manner of support questions and answers, the Mac OS X Support section of the Apple Web site (`www.info.apple.com/usen/ macosx/`) should be your next stop in case of trouble that you can't fix yourself. Topics include

+ Start-up issues

+ Classic mode problems

+ Internet and networking problems

+ Printing problems

You can search the Apple Knowledge Base, download the latest updates and electronic manuals, and participate in Apple-moderated discussion boards from this one central location.

Your local Apple dealer

Naturally, an Apple dealer can provide just about any support that you're likely to need — for a price — but you can usually get the answers to important questions without any coinage changing hands. Your dealer is also well versed in the latest updates and patches that can fix those software incompatibility problems. Check your telephone book for your local dealer.

Book II

Customizing and Sharing

The 5th Wave   By Rich Tennant

DARRYL PREPARES TO ENGAGE WITH THE AQUA INTERFACE

Contents at a Glance

Chapter 1: Building the Finder of Your Dreams 149

Chapter 2: Giving Your Desktop the Personal Touch 169

Chapter 3: Delving under the Hood with System Preferences 179

Chapter 4: You Mean Others Can Use My Mac, Too? 209

Chapter 5: Setting Up Multi-User Accounts 215

Chapter 6: Sharing Documents for Fun and Profit 227

Chapter 1: Building the Finder of Your Dreams

In This Chapter

✔ Choosing a view mode

✔ Modifying the toolbar

✔ Assigning Favorites

✔ Searching for files from the toolbar

✔ Searching for files using the Find command

✔ Changing view options

✔ Changing Finder preferences

The Finder is the heart of Mac OS X — and we all know how heart surgeons like to tinker, don't we? (*Ouch*. Start again, shall we?)

The Finder is the heart of Mac OS X, and as you might expect, it's highly configurable. You can customize the Finder to present icons, or you can peruse folders with a column view that can pack much more information onscreen at one time. Some folks prefer the default Finder toolbar, and others like to customize it with the applications and features that they use most often.

Decisions like these can help you transform Mac OS X into *Your Personal Operating System* — and every Mac OS X power-user worth the title will take the time to apply these changes because an operating system that presents visual information the way that *you* want to see it is easier and more efficient to use.

No need for a hammer or saw — when you're building the Finder of your dreams, the only tool that you need is your mouse!

Will That Be Icons or Buttons . . . or Even Columns?

The default appearance of a window in Mac OS X uses the familiar large-format icons that have been a hallmark of the Macintosh operating system since Day One — but there's no reason why you *have* to use them. (In fact, most Mac OS X power-users I know consider the icon view mode rather inefficient and slow.) Besides the icon view shown in Figure 1-1, Mac OS X offers two other window view modes: list and column.

Change views here.

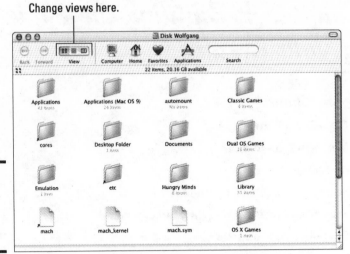

Figure 1-1:
A Finder
window in
icon view
mode.

✦ **List view:** List view displays the folders on the volume in a hierarchical
fashion. To display the contents of a folder, you can either click the right-
facing small triangle next to the folder name — it rotates downward to
indicate that you've expanded the folder — or you can double-click the
folder icon to display the contents in a Finder window. To collapse the
contents of the folder, click the small triangle again; it rotates back to
face the right. Figure 1-2 illustrates the same Finder window in list view.

Figure 1-2:
The
contents of
a volume in
list view
mode.

You can resize a column by dragging the right edge of the column heading button.

✦ **Column view:** Figure 1-3 shows the same window in column view, in which the volumes on your Mac OS X system are displayed on the left. Each column on the right represents a lower level of subfolders. Click the volume, click the desired folder in the second column to display its contents, and so forth. (Personally, this is my favorite view — thanks, Apple! It's efficient and fast as all get-out.) As you drill deeper, the columns automatically shift to the left. When you click an item (rather than a folder), the Finder displays a preview and a quick summary of the selected item in the rightmost column.

Each column has its own individual scroll bar (for those really, really big folders), and you can drag the column handle at the bottom of the separators to resize all the columns. When you hold down Option and drag a column handle, only the column width to the left is adjusted.

**Book II
Chapter 1**

Building the Finder of Your Dreams

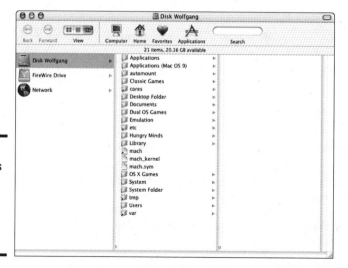

Figure 1-3:
Mac OS X's column view requires very little scrolling.

Another of my pet peeves is cluttered disks. If you're continually having problems locating files and folders, ask yourself, "Self, do I need to organize? Am I — gasp — *cluttered?*" If your answer is yes, take an hour and organize your files logically into new folders. (Remember, I'm talking your documents and such, not your applications, which are usually where they need to be — in your Applications folder.) Often, documents that you create end up as stragglers, usually located in the root folder of your hard drive, which sooner or later ends up looking like a biker bar after Ladies Night. By keeping your root folder clean and saving your files in organized folders, you'll end up wasting less time searching for files and more time actually *using* them.

To switch between the three modes, click one of the three view mode buttons in the Finder window toolbar (the current view is highlighted) or click the View menu and choose As Icons, As List, or As Columns. Mac OS X places a helpful check mark next to the current view mode.

Doing the Toolbar Dance

You can work your customization magic on the Finder toolbar as well! In this section, I show you how to customize that strip of icons across the top of the Finder window that's affectionately called the toolbar. Or, if you like, you'll discover how to dismiss it entirely to gain additional real estate for the contents of your Finder window.

Hiding and showing the toolbar

You can toggle the display of the toolbar in an active Finder window in one of three ways:

+ By clicking the toolbar button at the upper-right corner of the Finder window

+ By pressing ⌘+B

+ By choosing View from the Finder menu and then choosing Hide (or Show) Toolbar

Hiding and showing the status bar

The status bar displays a number of helpful informational-type tidbits about the contents of the Finder window. Depending on what you've opened, the status bar can include

+ **Statistics:** See the number of items in the window and the amount of free space remaining on the volume.

+ **A write-protect icon:** This icon looks like a pencil with a line running through it, as shown in Figure 1-4. This indicates that you don't have write permissions for the contents of the window — or the volume where the contents reside. (Note that this does not necessarily mean that folders at a lower level are write-protected as well.) You'll typically see this icon when you're viewing the contents of a CD or DVD, where everything is write-protected.

+ **The current automatic icon view setting:** For windows in icon view, the status bar can display either a grid icon (indicating that the icons are set to snap to grid) or four tiny icons (indicating that the icons are displayed in a sorted order). You'll discover more about these settings later in the upcoming section "Configuring the View Options."

The toolbar

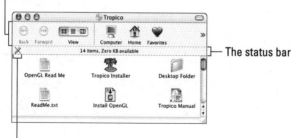

Figure 1-4:
Check the
status bar
for write
permissions.

The status bar

The write-protect icon

To toggle the display of the status bar, choose View from the Finder menu
and then choose Show/Hide Status Bar.

Giving your toolbar big tires and a loud exhaust

The default icons in the toolbar include

+ **Back and Forward:** Like a Web browser, clicking the Back button moves
  you to the previous window's contents. If you use the Back button, the
  Forward button appears — click this to return to the contents that you
  had before clicking the Back button.

+ **View:** Click this control to toggle between the three view modes (icon,
  list, or column).

+ **Computer:** Click this icon to display the top level of your system, just as
  if you had opened a new Finder window.

+ **Home:** Clicking this icon displays the contents of your Mac OS X Home
  folder. (Another user logged in to the same system will see his or her
  Home folder instead.)

+ **Favorites:** Click this icon to display the Favorites that you've added —
  more on this in the next section. (Again, other users will see their own
  Favorites when they're logged in.)

+ **Applications:** Click this to display the contents of your Applications
  folder.

+ **Search:** Okay, I know it's not technically an icon — but the Search box is
  a member of the default Toolbar family nonetheless. You can search for
  a file or folder using this box — more on this later in the section
  "Searching for Files from the Toolbar."

But, as one of my favorite bumper stickers so invitingly asks, "Why be normal?" Adding or deleting items from the toolbar is a great way to customize Mac OS X. Follow these steps:

1. **From the active Finder window menu, choose View⇨Customize Toolbar to display the window that you see in Figure 1-5.**

   Along with controls like Back, Forward, and View, some of the items that you see here are locations on your system — for example, Home or Documents — and others are system functions, like Eject and Burn.

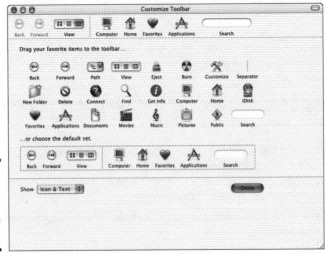

Figure 1-5: Changing the toolbar status quo in Mac OS X.

2. **To add items to the toolbar, drag them from the Customize Toolbar dialog up to the toolbar at the top of the window.**

   To add an item between existing buttons, drop it between the buttons, and they obligingly move aside. If you get exuberant about your toolbar and you add more icons than it can hold, a double-right arrow appears at the right side of the toolbar — a click on the arrow displays a pop-up menu with the icons that won't fit.

   In fact, the Customize Toolbar dialog isn't necessary for some toolbar modifications: You can also drag files, folders, and disk volumes directly from the Desktop or other Finder windows and add them to your toolbar at any time. To remove a file, folder, or disk volume from the toolbar, you can drag it off the top edge of the Finder window, and it vanishes like a CEO's ethics.

3. **To remove an item from the Toolbar, drag it off to the center of the window, amongst the other icons.**

4. **Naturally, you can swap item positions — just click an item, drag it to its new spot, and then release the mouse button.**

5. **To choose the default toolbar configuration or to start over, drag the default bar at the bottom of the window to the toolbar at the top.**

   This is the toolbar equivalent of tapping your ruby slippers together three times and repeating, "There's no place like home."

6. **To toggle between displaying the icons with accompanying text (the default), the icon only, or a text button only, click the Show drop-down list box at the bottom of the Customize Toolbar.**

7. **After you arrange your toolbar as you like, click the Done button.**

Playing Favorites

Next, consider customizing your Favorites in the Big X. *Favorites* are the ultimate shortcut to files and folders in an operating system, and Mac OS X offers them just about everywhere: the toolbar (as I explain in the first sections of this chapter), the Go menu, Open and Save dialogs, and much more.

So how does Mac OS X keep track of Favorites? Well, a Favorite is actually just an alias that's created in your Favorites folder — in turn, the Favorite points to the original file or folder elsewhere on your system. This is my idea of good design — clean, fresh-smelling, and simple to use.

Favorites are easy to use and change. Here's how:

✦ **Creating a favorite:** First click a file or folder to select it. Then from the Finder menu, choose File⇨Add to Favorites. (The handy keyboard shortcut ⌘+T works as well.)

   Alternatively, drag a file or folder to the Favorites toolbar button on any Finder window.

✦ **Deleting a favorite:** Open your Favorites folder and drag the corresponding alias file to the Trash.

✦ **Displaying a favorite:** To display the contents of your Favorites folder, just click the Favorites icon on the default toolbar, or press ⌘+Shift+F.

   Alternatively, click Go on the Finder menu and choose Favorites.

Searching for Files from the Toolbar

Need to find a file fast? The default toolbar has just what you need — the Search field, which offers the ability to search for a string of text within your file names. (In fact, it's a subset of the Find dialog that you see when you press ⌘+F; I'll cover the Find dialog in the next section.) To locate a file using the Search field, follow these steps:

1. Navigate to the starting point for the search in a Finder window.

For example, if you want to search your entire hard drive, select your hard drive in the active Finder window.

To search only a single folder, click that folder name to select it.

2. Click in the Search box in the toolbar and type the text that you want to find.

If you need to clear the field and start over again, click the circular X button, which only appears when there's text in the Search field.

3. When you've entered the desired text, press Return.

The Finder displays the files with names that include the text, as shown in Figure 1-6.

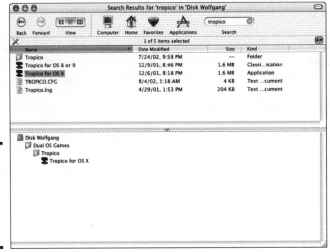

Figure 1-6:
Locate a file with the toolbar Search feature.

4. To display the location of a file, click it once or launch it by double-clicking the entry.

Files can also be moved or copied from the Search results list using the standard drag and Option+drag methods.

5. **To perform a new search, type new text in the Search field and press Return again.**

To return to your original location in the Finder window, click the Back button in the toolbar.

Searching for Files from the Find Dialog

Although the Search box in the toolbar is all that you'll need to find most files and folders, sometimes you need a little more flexibility and power to locate what you need on your system. To do so, enter the Find dialog, where you can create custom file name searches with more complex criteria or even search *within* certain files themselves for the text that you specify. To locate a file using the Find dialog, follow these steps:

1. **With the Finder active, display the Find dialog by pressing ⌘+F (or choose File from the Finder menu and then click Find).**

   Mac OS X displays the Find dialog that you see in Figure 1-7.

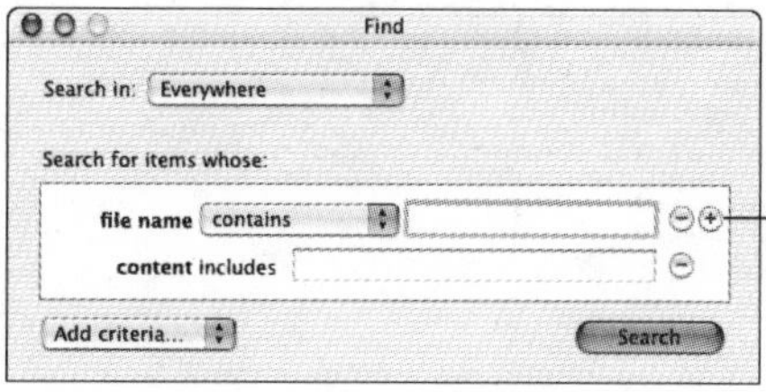

Book II
Chapter 1

Building the Finder
of Your Dreams

Figure 1-7: The Find dialog is ready to pinpoint text within your files.

Click to add a search criteria line.

2. **Click the Search In drop-down list box to specify where you want to search.**

   You can choose Everywhere (your entire system, including network volumes), Local Disks (just the volumes actually inside or connected to your Mac), your Home folder, or Specific Places. When you choose Specific Places, the Find dialog presents you with Add and Remove buttons that you can use to add particular volumes and folders. Typically, you can leave this field set to Everywhere, which is the default.

3. **To search for a specific filename, click in the text box next to the File Name criteria and type all or part of the filename.**

4. **If you want to search for a text string within the document itself, click in the Content Includes text box and type that text.**

The text must appear just as you've typed it, so it's always a good idea to restrict what you're searching for to a minimum of words that you're fairly sure will cause a match. Content searching works only when you've generated an index, which I explain later in this section.

To include additional search criteria lines for either filename or content, click the button with the plus sign next to the Search for Items Whose text fields. You can also remove a search criteria line by clicking the button with the minus sign.

5. **To further narrow your search, click the Add Criteria button at the bottom of the Find dialog.**

You can limit your results based on the date that the file or folder was last modified, when it was created, the file type, the size, the extension, or whether the file or folder is marked visible or hidden (such as a system file). Figure 1-8 illustrates the Find dialog with all search criteria active — if Mac OS X can't find it with all this information, it's just plain not on your system!

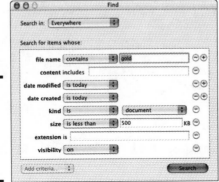

Figure 1-8: The Find dialog revealed in all its full glory.

6. **After you add more specific search parameters, click the Search button to begin the hunt.**

Your search results appear, as shown in Figure 1-9.

Again, you can click an entry name to reveal the location of a matching file or folder, or double-click it to launch it.

7. **Close this dialog to return to the Find dialog, where you can perform another search if you wish.**

8. **Click the Close button on the Find dialog to return to the Finder.**

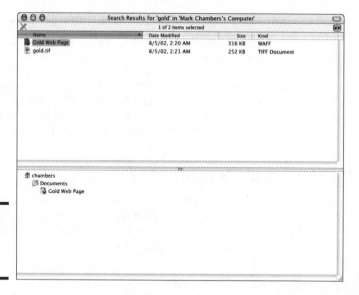

Figure 1-9:
I've struck
gold!
(Literally.)

As I mention earlier, searching by content requires that you index your files. Essentially, this is a humongous database that Mac OS X builds that contains cross-references to words in all the file types with decipherable text. (This includes most word processing documents, text files, and Web pages.) To generate an index for a folder or a disk volume, follow these steps:

1. **Select the item in a Finder window and press ⌘+I to display our old friend the Info dialog.**

2. **Click the triangle next to the Content Index heading to expand that section of the dialog (see Figure 1-10).**

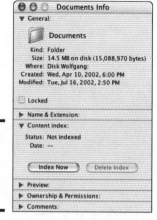

Figure 1-10:
This folder
hasn't been
indexed . . .
yet.

3. **Click the Index Now button to begin the indexing process.**

   After indexing completes, the Info dialog displays the time and date when the item was last indexed.

Indexing can take forever and a day on a full hard drive, so I recommend indexing only the folders that you need to search — like those folders that contain your documents. You can delete an index and re-index at any time, which will freshen the index with the latest changes to your files.

Configuring the View Options

As I discuss at the beginning of the chapter, you've got a lot of control over how Mac OS X presents files and folders in the Finder. In this section, I cover how you can make further adjustments to the view from your windows. (Pardon me for the ghastly cliché posing as a pun.)

Setting icon view options

First, allow me to provide a little detail on housekeeping in the Big X. After a few hours of work, a Finder window in icon mode can look something like a teenager's room: stuff strewn all over the place, as demonstrated with my Applications folder in Figure 1-11. To restore order to your Desktop, click in any open area of the active window and then choose View⇨Clean Up. This command leaves the icons in approximately the same position but snaps them to an invisible grid so they're aligned, as shown in Figure 1-12.

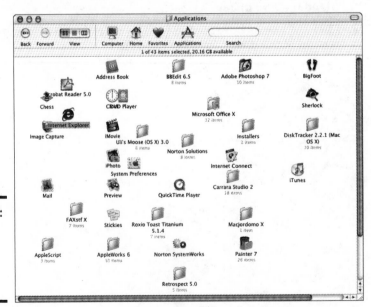

Figure 1-11: Will someone please clean up this mess?

Figure 1-12:
Tidying up is
no problem
with the
Clean Up
menu
command.

Now that things are in alignment, work with the icon view options.
(Naturally, you'll want the active Finder window in icon view first, so click
View and choose As Icons, or press ⌘+1.) From the Finder menu, choose
View➪Show View Options — or press that swingin' ⌘+J shortcut — to display the View Options dialog that you see in Figure 1-13. (Remember, these
are the options available for icon view; I'll discuss the options for list and
column view later in this chapter.)

Figure 1-13:
The settings
available for
icon view.

Note these first two radio buttons, which also appear in the list View Options dialog:

✦ Select the **This Window Only** radio button to apply the changes that you make only to the Finder window that opens when you open the selected item — in other words, the item that appears in the window's title bar.

For example, any changes made to the settings in Figure 1-13 will affect only my Applications folder because it was the active Finder window when I pressed ⌘+ J. (Note that the window name also appears as the title of the View Options dialog.)

✦ Select the **All Windows** radio button to apply the changes that you make to *all* Finder windows that you view in your current mode.

Of course, Mac OS X remembers the changes that you make within the View Options dialog, no matter which view mode you're configuring. Now, on to the other changes that you can make from this dialog, which include

✦ **Resizing your Desktop icons:** Click and drag the Icon Size slider to shrink or expand the icons on your Desktop. The icon size is displayed in pixels above the slider.

✦ **Resizing icon label text:** Click the up- and down-arrows to the right of the Text Size drop-down box to choose the font size (in points) for icon labels.

✦ **Moving icon label text:** Select either the Bottom (default) or Right radio button to choose between displaying the text under your Desktop icons or to the right of the icons.

✦ **Snap to Grid:** Enable this check box to automatically align icons to a grid within the window, just as if you had used the Clean Up menu command.

✦ **Show Item Info:** With this check box enabled, Mac OS X displays the number of items within each folder in the window.

✦ **Show Icon Preview:** If you enable this check box, the Finder displays icons for image files using a miniature of the actual picture. (A cool feature for those with digital cameras — however, this does take extra processing time because Mac OS X has to load each image file and shrink it down to create the icon.)

✦ **Keep Arranged By:** To sort the display of icons in a window, enable this check box and choose one of the following criteria from its drop-down list: by name, by date modified, by date created, by size, or by item type.

✦ **Choosing a background:** To select a background for the window, select one of three radio buttons here:

- **White:** This is the default.

- **Color:** Click a color choice from the color block that appears if you make this selection.

- **Picture:** Select this radio button and then click the Select button to display a standard Open dialog. Navigate to the location where the desired image is stored, click it once to select it, and then click Open.

After all your changes are made and you're ready to return to work, click the dialog's Close button to save your settings.

Setting list view options

If you're viewing the active window in list view, choose View⇨Show View Options to display the View Options dialog that you see in Figure 1-14.

Book II
Chapter 1

Building the Finder
of Your Dreams

Figure 1-14:
List view
settings.

Like in icon view, select from one of the two top radio buttons to apply the changes that you make in this dialog to this window only or to all windows that you view in list mode. The settings include

✦ **Show Columns:** Enable the check boxes under this heading to the display of additional columns in list view, including the date that the item was modified, the creation date, the size, the item type, the version (supplied by most applications) and any comments that you've added in the Info dialog for that item. (In my personal opinion, the more columns that you add, the more unwieldy the Finder gets, so I advise disabling the display of columns that you won't use.)

✦ **Use Relative Dates:** Enable this check box to display modification dates and creation dates with relative terms, such as *Today* or *Yesterday.* If this freaks you out, disable this check box to force all dates to act like adults.

✦ **Calculate All Sizes:** Enable this check box to have Mac OS X display the actual sizes of folders, including all the files and subfolders they contain. *Note:* Using this option takes processing time, so I recommend that you avoid using it unless you really need to see the size.

To save your settings, click the dialog's Close button.

Setting column view options

To make changes to view options in column view mode, choose View➪ Show View Options to display the View Options dialog that you see in Figure 1-15.

Figure 1-15:
Column
view
settings.

You have only three column view options, and any changes that you make to this dialog are always reflected in every column view:

✦ **Resizing icon label text:** Click the Text size drop-down box to choose the font size (in points) for icon labels.

✦ **Show Icons:** Enable this check box to display icons in the columns —
if this option is disabled, the icons don't appear, and you'll gain a little
space.

✦ **Show Preview Column:** If this check box is enabled, clicking a file in
column mode will display a thumbnail and preview information in the
right-most column, as shown in Figure 1-16.

If you store a slew of QuickTime movies and digital images on your
drive, the Preview Column is great. (You can even play a QuickTime
movie from the Preview Column.)

Figure 1-16:
The Preview
column
provides
more
information
on the
selected
file.

The Preview column

Click the dialog's Close button to save your settings and return to the Finder.

Setting Finder Preferences

Finally, you can change a number of settings to customize the Finder itself.
From the Finder menu, click Finder and choose the Preferences menu item
to display the Finder Preferences dialog that you see in Figure 1-17.

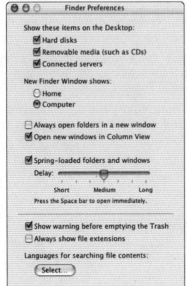

Figure 1-17:
Configure
Finder
preferences.

The preference settings include

+ **Displaying icons on the Desktop:** Enable these check boxes to display your hard disks, removable volumes (including CDs, DVDs, and Zip disks), and connected network servers.

+ **New Finder Window Shows:** Choose from the two radio buttons here to specify whether a new Finder window should show your computer folder — basically, the top level of your system, with disks and volumes — or the contents of your Home folder.

+ **Always Open Folders in a New Window:** When this check box is enabled, double-clicking a folder will open it in a new Finder window, as did earlier versions of Mac OS. (If disabled, the contents of the folder appear in the same Finder window, which makes it easier to focus on just the folder you need at the moment.)

+ **Open New Windows in Column View:** When you enable this check box, each new Finder window that you open automatically uses column view. (If disabled, the new window uses the last view mode you used.)

+ **Spring-loaded Folders and Windows:** It sounds a little wacky, but using this feature can definitely speed up file copying! If this check box is enabled, you can drag an item on top of a folder — *without* releasing the mouse button — and after a preset time (controlled by the Delay slider), a spring-loaded window appears to show you the folder's contents. At that point, you can either release the mouse button to drop the file inside the folder (upon which the window disappears), or you can drag the icon on top of another sub-folder to spring it forth and drill even deeper.

✦ **Show Warning before Emptying the Trash:** By default, this check box is enabled, and Mac OS X will display a confirmation dialog before allowing you to — in the words of Mac OS X patrons around the world — *toss the Bit Bucket.* If you're interested in speed and trust your judgment (and your mouse finger), you can disable this setting.

✦ **Always Show File Extensions:** If this check box is enabled, the Finder displays the file extensions at the end of filenames, à la Windows. This comes in handy for some applications, where everything from a document to a preference file to the application itself all share the same icon — however, I find extensions distasteful and leave things set with the default of extensions off.

✦ **Languages for Searching File Contents:** Click the Select button under this heading to specify which languages the Finder should use when indexing files for the Find dialog — naturally, the fewer the languages you choose, the faster the entire indexing process becomes.

When you've made the desired changes to the Finder Preferences, click the dialog's Close button to save your settings and return to the Finder.

Chapter 2: Giving Your Desktop the Personal Touch

In This Chapter

✔ Picking your own background

✔ Adding and selecting a screen saver

✔ Choosing menu colors and highlights

✔ Keeping track of things with Stickies

✔ Customizing the Dock

✔ Cleaning and sorting the Mac OS X Desktop

"Tweak! Tweak!" It's not the cry of some exotic bird — that's the call of the wild Mac Power User. Power Users like to tweak their Mac OS X Desktops just so, with *that* menu color, *this* background, and *those* applications in the Dock. Non-computer types just can't understand the importance of the proper arrangement of your virtual workplace: When things are familiar and customized to your needs, you're more productive, and things get done faster. In fact, if you've set up multiple users on your computer under Mac OS X, the Big X automatically keeps track of each user's Desktop and restores it when that person logs in. (For example, when you use the Mac, you get that background photo of Farrah Fawcett from the '70s, while your daughter gets Britney Spears.)

In this chapter, I show you what you can do to produce a Desktop that's uniquely your own, including tweaks that you can make to the background and your Desktop icons. I'll also show you how to use Desktop Stickies instead of a forest of paper slips covering your monitor.

With your Mac OS X Desktop clad in the proper harmonious colors — yes, that can be your favorite photo of Elvis himself — and your new Dock icons ready for action, you are indeed prepared for whatever lies ahead in your computing world!

Changing the Background

You may be asking, "Mark, do I really need a custom background?" That depends completely on your personal tastes, but I've yet to meet a computer owner who didn't change his or her background when presented with the opportunity. Favorite backgrounds usually include

✦ Humorous cartoons and photos that can bring a smile to your face (even during the worst workday)

✦ Scenic beauty

✦ Photos of family and friends (or the latest Hollywood heartthrob)

✦ The company logo — I'm not sure it does much for morale, but it does impress the boss

If you do decide to spruce up your background, you have three choices: You can select one of the default Mac OS X background images, choose a solid color, or specify your own image. All three backgrounds are chosen from the Desktop dialog, located under System Preferences (as illustrated by Figure 2-1).

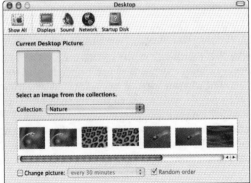

Figure 2-1:
To select a background, get thee hence to the Desktop System Preferences.

You can also hold down Control, click on the Desktop, and choose Change Desktop Background from the pop-up contextual menu (or right-click, if you're using a heathen mouse with multiple buttons).

Picking something Apple

To choose a background from one of the collections provided by Apple, click the Collection drop-down list box and pick one of these groups:

✦ **Apple Background Images:** These default backgrounds range from simple patterns to somewhat strange and ethereal flux shapes. (You'll have to see them to understand what I mean.)

✦ **Nature:** Scenic beauty: blades of grass, sand dunes, snowy hills . . . that sort of thing.

✦ **Solid Colors:** For those who desire a soothing solid shade — more on this in the next section.

✦ **Choose Folder:** You can open a folder containing images and display them instead. (I'll discuss this in more detail in a page or two.)

✦ **Pictures Folder:** This displays the images in the Pictures folder for the active user.

✦ **Abstract:** Even weirder twisting shapes in flux, this time with bright contrasting colors. Good for a psychiatrist's office.

If you see something you like, click the thumbnail and Mac OS X displays it in the well and automatically refreshes your background so that you can see what it looks like. By the way, in the Apple universe, a *well* is a sunken square area that displays an image — in this case, the background image you've selected.

Mac OS X can manipulate the way that the background appears on your Desktop. Click the drop-down list box next to the well and you can choose to

✦ **Tile the background,** which repeats the image to cover the desktop. (This is usually done with pattern images to produce a smooth, creamy, seamless look.)

✦ **Fill the screen,** which can be used with a solid color to get uniform coverage.

✦ **Stretch the background to fit the Desktop.** If your Desktop image is smaller than the Desktop acreage, this works — but be warned, if you try to stretch too small of an image over too large a Desktop, the pixilated result can be pretty frightening. (Think of enlarging an old Kodak Instamatic negative into a 16 x 20 poster. Dots, dots, dots.)

✦ **Center the image on the Desktop.** (This is my favorite solution for Desktop images that are smaller than your resolution.)

Note that this drop-down list appears only if the Desktop picture you select is not one of the standard Apple images — all of the pictures in the Apple Background, Nature, Abstract, and Solid Colors categories are automatically scaled to the size of your screen.

To change your Desktop background automatically on a regular basis, enable the Change Picture check box and choose the delay period from the drop-down list box. To display the images in random order, enable the Random Order check box — otherwise, Mac OS X displays them in the order that they appear in the folder.

How to annoy friends and confuse co-workers

Never let it be said that I can't dish out revenge when necessary. I don't know whether I should call this a *Tip* or a *Devilish Practical Joke that Will Drive People Nuts* — anyway, it's fun as all get-out. Right before you go to lunch, use the Grab utility in your Applications/Utilities folder to take a snapshot of your Desktop with a number of windows open (or an error dialog with an OK or Close button), and then save the image to your Pictures folder. Select the image as your Desktop background, and watch others go crazy trying to click those windows, "buttons," and icons. For an archenemy, try the same trick on *his* Mac! Arrange a slightly embarrassing Desktop on his computer, specify it as the background, and sit back while the fun begins. (Perhaps a Web browser open to a somewhat unusual Web site?)

I just gotta have lavender

As I mention earlier, for those who want their favorite color without the distraction of an image, one can choose from a selection of solid colors — you can choose from these colors in the same way that you'd pick a default Mac OS X background image.

Selecting your own photo

Finally, you can drag your own image into the well from a Finder window to add your own work of art. To view thumbnails of an entire folder, click the Collection drop-down list and choose the Pictures folder (to display the contents of your personal Pictures folder) or click Folder to specify any folder on your system. (Alternatively, you can drag a folder from the Finder to the thumbnail window.) Click the desired thumbnail to embellish your Desktop.

Changing the Screen Saver

Screen savers are another popular item. Because I cover the Screen Saver preferences in Chapter 3 of this mini-book, I'll simply illustrate how to choose one here. Open System Preferences and click the Screen Effects icon to display the settings that you see in Figure 2-2.

To add a third-party screen saver module so that everyone can use it on a multi-user system, copy it into the Screen Savers folder within the top-level Library folder.

Click one of the entries in the Screen Savers column to display a thumbnail of the effect — choosing Random, naturally, runs through 'em all. You can also test the appearance of the saver module by clicking the Test button; the screen saver runs until you move the mouse or press a key.

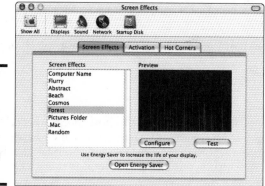

Figure 2-2:
A good screen saver can cancel the effects of a bad boss.

Many screen savers allow you to monkey with their settings — if the Configure button is enabled, click it to see how you can change the effects.

Changing Colors in Mac OS X

I can't understand it, but some people just don't *appreciate* purple menus with gold highlights! (You can tell a Louisiana State University graduate a mile away.) To specify your own colors for buttons, menus, and windows, follow these steps:

1. **Open System Preferences and click the General icon to display the settings in Figure 2-3.**

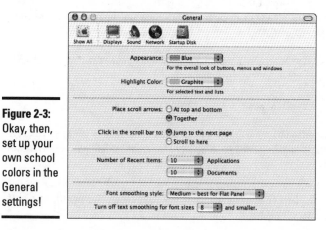

Figure 2-3:
Okay, then, set up your own school colors in the General settings!

2. **Click the Appearance drop-down list and choose the main color choice for your buttons and menus.**

3. **Click the Highlight Color drop-down list and pick the highlight color that will appear when you select text in an application or select an item from a list.**

4. **Press ⌘+Q to exit System Preferences and save your changes.**

Adding Stickies

Stickies are interesting little beasts — I don't know their genus or phyla, but they're certainly handy to have around. To be technical for a moment, a *Stickie* is actually nothing more than a special type of application window, but these windows remain on your Desktop as long as the Stickies application is running.

I use Stickies for anything that a Post-it note can handle, including:

✦ Reminders that you don't want to misplace

✦ Snippets of text that you want to temporarily store while your Mac is turned off (without launching a behemoth like Word or digging for TextEdit)

✦ Boilerplate (repeated and standard) text that you're constantly including in your documents, like your address

✦ A quick note that includes someone's e-mail address or phone number

✦ Today's Dilbert cartoon from `www.dilbert.com`

A Stickie can contain data pasted from the Clipboard, or you can simply type directly into the Stickies application window. Stickie windows can include graphics and different fonts and colors. You can even locate specific text from somewhere in your vast collection of Stickies using the Find command. (And you don't use up our bark-covered friends of the forest, either.)

In Book I, I discuss the Mac OS X Services menu — you can make a Stickie note from the Finder Services menu, as well.

Follow these steps to stick your way to success:

1. **Open your Applications folder, open your Utilities folder, and then run the Stickies application to display the new window that you see in Figure 2-4.**

   The text cursor is already idling in the new window. (The other windows are Stickies, too, but they contain display text from the application. If you like, you can close them.)

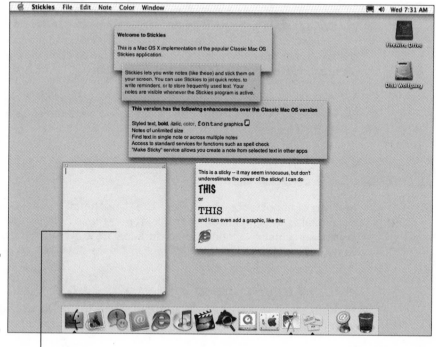

Figure 2-4:
"Look, Ma!
It's a
Stickie!"

Book II
Chapter 2

Giving Your Desktop
the Personal Touch

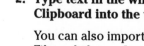

A new Stickie window

2. **Type text in the window or press ⌘+V to paste the contents of the Clipboard into the window.**

   You can also import the contents of an existing file into a Stickie — click File and choose Import text to display a standard Open dialog.

3. **You can add text formatting, change the text font, and change the color of the font from the Note menu.**

   From the same menu, you can also choose to make the Stickie translucent. (No pressing reason, they just look cool.)

4. **To change the Stickie's color, click the Color menu and choose the appropriate hue.**

5. **Resize and drag the Stickie window to the desired location.**

   To shrink and expand the Stickie window, click the icon at the upper-right corner or press ⌘+M to toggle between a miniaturized view (showing only the Title bar) and the expanded view.

To automatically run the Stickies application, open the Login Items settings in System Preferences and add Stickies to the list.

To delete a Stickie, simply click the Close button at the upper-left corner of the Stickie window. Or, click on the Stickie to make it the active note and then click Close. Stickies displays a dialog to confirm that you want to close the note; click Save to save the contents in a file or click the Don't Save button to close the note and discard its contents.

To close the Stickies application completely, click any note and press ⌘+Q — the application will remember the position and contents of each note until you launch it again.

Customizing the Dock

In terms of importance, the Dock — the "launch pad" for applications and documents that appears on your Desktop — ranks right up there with the command center of a modern nuclear submarine. As such, it had better be easy to customize, and naturally Mac OS X doesn't let you down.

Adding applications and extras to the Dock

Why stick with just the icons that Apple places in the Dock? You can add your own applications, files, and folders to the Dock as well.

✦ **Adding applications:** You can add any application to your Dock by simply dragging its icon into the area to the *left* of the separator line (which appears between applications and folders or documents); the existing Dock icons will obligingly move aside to make a space for it wherever you like.

Attempting to place an application on the right of the separator line will send it to the Trash (if the Trash icon is highlighted when you release the button), so beware.

✦ **Adding files and folders:** Folders and volume icons can be added to the Dock by dragging the icon into the area to the *right* of the separator line. (Attempting to place these to the left of the separator line will open an application with the contents, which usually doesn't work.) To open the location in a Finder window, click once on the Dock icon. Then click and hold the mouse button (or press Control when you click) to display a Dock menu like the one you see in Figure 2-5, where you can open documents and run applications. Now that, my friends, is genuine *sassy!*

✦ **Adding Favorites:** You can drag any URL, including one of your Favorites from Internet Explorer, directly into the area to the right of the separator line — clicking that icon automatically opens your browser and displays that page.

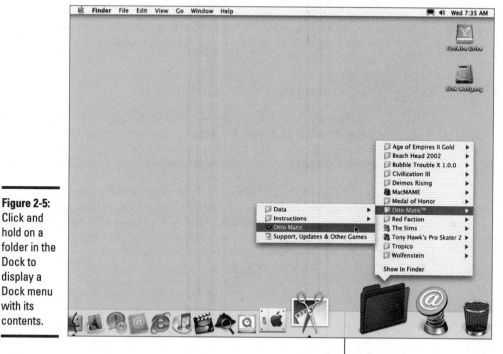

Figure 2-5:
Click and
hold on a
folder in the
Dock to
display a
Dock menu
with its
contents.

The Dock's separator line

To remove an icon from the Dock, just click and drag it off the Dock — you get a rather silly (but somehow, strangely satisfying) animated cloud of debris, and the icon is no more. Note, however, that the original application, folder, or volume is *not* deleted — just the Dock icon is permanently excused. If you like, you can delete *almost* any of the default icons that Mac OS X installs in the Dock; only the Finder and Trash icons must remain in the Dock.

Resizing the Dock

You can change the size of the Dock from the Dock settings in System Preferences — I explain this in more detail in Chapter 3 of Book II — but here's a simpler way to resize the Dock, right from the Desktop.

Move your mouse cursor over the separator line in the Dock, and the cursor turns into a funky line with arrows pointing up and down. This is your cue to click and drag while moving the mouse up and down, which will expand and shrink the Dock, respectively.

You can also hold down the Control key and click when the funky line cursor is visible — this allows you to change your Dock preferences without the hassle of opening System Preferences and displaying the Dock settings.

Arranging Your Precious Desktop

Finally, consider the layout of the Desktop itself. You can set the options for icon placement from the Finder View menu. Just like the options for Finder windows that I cover in Chapter 1 of this mini-book, you can clean up and arrange your Desktop by name, date, size, or kind.

The View Options for the Desktop are slightly different than the View Options for a Finder window in icon view. (Garner the scoop on setting these preferences in Chapter 1 of this mini-book.) First, you choose a background for the Finder from System Preferences. Also, you don't have to worry about whether the options are global or not . . . you only have one Desktop, after all.

Chapter 3: Delving under the Hood with System Preferences

In This Chapter

✔ Displaying and customizing settings in System Preferences

✔ Saving your changes

✔ Changing settings

*L*ike the Mac OS 9 Control Panel before it, the System Preferences window is the place to practice behavior modification in Mac OS X. The settings that you specify in System Preferences will affect the majority of the applications that you use as well as the hardware that you connect to your Mac, your Internet and network traffic, the appearance and activity on your Desktop, and how Mac OS X handles money, dates, and languages. Oh, and don't forget your screen saver.

In this chapter, I discuss the many settings in System Preferences — you'll discover what does what and how you can customize the appearance and operation of Mac OS X.

The Preferred Way to Display the Preferences

Apple has made it easy to open the System Preferences window. Just click the System Preferences icon (looks like a wall light switch, next to the Apple logo) in the Dock, and the window shown in Figure 3-1 appears. You can also open the window by clicking the Apple menu and selecting the System Preferences item.

Note that the System Preferences window has its own toolbar, which you can customize with the icons that you use the most. Simply drag the desired icon from the System Preferences window and drop it on the toolbar to add it. To display all the System Preferences groups at any time, click the Show All button in the toolbar's upper-left corner.

You can also display all the System Preferences panes in alphabetical order — this can make it easier to choose a pane if you're unsure what group it's in. Choose View⇨Show All Alphabetically. (Note that you can also select any pane directly from the View menu.)

Figure 3-1:
Set your
System
Preferences
here.

Click the System Preferences icon.

Saving Your Preferences

You'll note that there's no Save or Apply button on the System Preferences window. Illustrating the elegant design of Mac OS X, simply quitting System Preferences automatically saves all the changes that you make. (However, some panes in System Preferences have an Apply Now button that you can click to apply your changes immediately.) Like any other Mac OS X application, you can quit the System Preferences window by pressing ⌘+Q or by choosing System Preferences⇨Quit System Preferences.

Let's Get Personal

The first stop on your tour of the System Preferences window is the Personal section. No singles ads here — this section is devoted to settings that you make to customize the appearance and operation of your Desktop and login account.

Desktop preferences

Figure 3-2 illustrates the settings in the Desktop group.

**Book II
Chapter 3**

**Delving under the
Hood with System
Preferences**

Figure 3-2:
Change
your
Desktop
picture with
these
settings.

The settings here are

✦ **Current Desktop Picture:** You can drag a picture from the thumbnail strip at the bottom of the screen and drop it into the square well to use it as your Desktop background. To display a different image collection or open a folder of your own images, click the Collection drop-down list box and browse there for your heart's desire. (To add an entire folder of images as a collection, drag a folder to the well.)

✦ **Arrangement:** As I explain in Chapter 2 of this mini-book, you can tile your background image, center it, and stretch it to fill the screen. The Arrangement control appears only when you're using your own pictures, so you won't see it if you're using a desktop image supplied by Apple.

✦ **Change Picture:** Enable this check box to change the Desktop background automatically after the delay period that you set, including each time that you log in and each time that your Mac wakes up from sleep mode.

✦ **Random Order:** To display screens randomly, enable the Random Order check box — otherwise, the backgrounds are displayed in the sequence in which they appear in the thumbnail strip.

Dock preferences

The Dock group is shown in Figure 3-3.

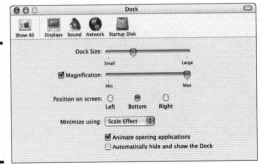

Figure 3-3:
These
settings are
useful for
monkeying
with the
Dock.

Settings here are

✦ **Dock Size:** Move this slider to change the overall size of the Dock.

✦ **Magnification:** With this check box enabled, a Dock icon will magically expand like the national deficit when you move your mouse cursor over it. You can move the Magnification slider to specify just how much magnification is right for you.

This feature is useful for helping you click a particular Dock icon if you've resized the Dock smaller than its default dimensions.

✦ **Position on Screen:** Choose from three radio buttons to make that crazy Dock appear at the left, bottom, or right edge of your Desktop.

✦ **Minimize Using:** By default, Mac OS X animates a window when it's shrunk into the Dock (and when it's expanded back into a full window). From the Minimize Using drop-down list, you can choose from a genie-in-a-bottle effect or a scale-up-or-down-incrementally effect. To demonstrate, choose an effect and then click the Minimize button (the yellow button in the upper-left corner) on the System Preferences window.

If you don't like these minimizing effects or you're running on an older G3 Mac, you can turn minimizing effects off to save processing time and speed up Mac OS X.

✦ **Animate Opening Applications:** By default, Mac OS X has that happy, slam-dancing feeling when you launch an application: The application's icon bounces up and down in the Dock two or three times to draw your attention and indicate that the application is loading. If you find this effervescence overly buoyant or distracting, disable this check box.

✦ **Automatically Hide and Show the Dock:** If you like, the Dock can stay hidden until you need it, thus reclaiming a significant amount of Desktop space for your application windows. Enable this check box to hide the Dock whenever you're not using it.

To display a hidden Dock, move your mouse pointer over the edge of the Desktop where it's hiding.

General preferences

The General group appears in Figure 3-4.

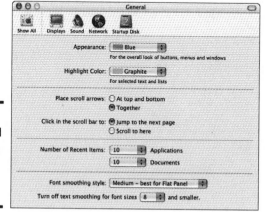

Figure 3-4:
The General settings are generally pretty mundane.

Book II
Chapter 3

Delving under the Hood with System Preferences

These settings are

✦ **Appearance:** From this drop-down list, choose a color to be used for buttons, menus, and windows.

✦ **Highlight Color:** From this drop-down list, choose a color to be used to highlight selected text in fields and drop-down list boxes.

✦ **Place Scroll Arrows:** Select either radio button here to put the scroll bar arrow buttons together (at the bottom of the scroll bar, in the lower-right corner of the window) or at the top and bottom of the scroll bar.

✦ **Click in the Scroll Bar To:** By default, Mac OS X jumps to the next or previous page when you click in an empty portion of the scroll bar. Mark the Scroll to Here radio button to scroll the document to the approximate position in relation to where you clicked.

✦ **Number of Recent Items:** The default number of recent Applications and recent Documents — available from the Recent Items item in the Apple menu, which you can read more about in Book I, Chapter 3 — is 10. To change the default, click either of the drop-down list boxes here and choose up to 50. (Personally, I like 20 or 30 for each.)

✦ **Font Smoothing Style:** Click this drop-down list for choices to make the text on your monitor or flat-panel appear more like the printed page. The best choices are Standard (for a typical CRT monitor) and Medium (for a typical flat-panel LCD display).

✦ **Turn off Text Smoothing for Font Sizes:** Below a certain point size, text smoothing isn't much good for most on-screen fonts. By default, any font displayed at 8 points or smaller isn't smoothed, which is suitable for a high-end video card and monitor. If you have an older monitor or a low-end video card, you can speed up the display of text by turning off text smoothing for fonts up to 12 points.

International preferences

The International group appears in Figure 3-5.

Figure 3-5:
The International settings in Mac OS X.

From left to right, they are

✦ **Language:** Choose the preferred order for language use in menus and dialogs as well as the standards that Mac OS X will use for each script style.

✦ **Date:** You can select a region and use its date conventions (month-day-year versus day-month-year), or you can build a custom format for both the long date (Saturday, September 28, 2002) and short date (9/28/2002) used throughout Mac OS X. The changes that you make are immediately reflected in the sample box at the bottom of the window.

+ **Time:** Like the Date tab, you can select a region to use the preset time conventions. You can choose 12-hour or 24-hour (military) time formats, change the time separator (colons, a period, or a dash), and specify different suffixes for morning and evening.

+ **Numbers:** These convention settings determine the separators used for large numbers or numbers with decimals, as well as the currency symbol that you want to use and where it appears in a number. You can also choose between standard (US) and metric measurement systems.

+ **Input Menu:** Each check box toggles the keyboard layouts available from the Input menu. You can click the Options button to toggle the shortcuts for switching layouts and input methods, as well as toggle automatic synchronization between the active font (where the input cursor is onscreen) and the keyboard layout that Mac OS X uses.

Login Items preferences

The Login Items screen appears in Figure 3-6.

Figure 3-6:
Enable or
disable login
items here.

The applications that you add to this list will launch automatically each time that the current user logs in to Mac OS X. To add an application, click the Add button, navigate to the desired application and select it, and then click the Add button again. To remove an application from the list, click to select it and then click the Remove button.

The order that login items are launched can be changed by dragging entries in the list into the desired sequence.

Each application can be launched in a hidden state — meaning that its window doesn't appear on the Desktop. To toggle an item as hidden or visible, enable the Hide check box next to the desired application.

My Account preferences

The My Account group is shown in Figure 3-7.

Settings here are

✦ **My Password:** Click the Change button here to change your current password. Mac OS X displays a sheet prompting you to type your current password and then a new password, which you have to enter twice in the Verify box as confirmation.

You can also add an optional hint in the Password Hint box, but I strongly recommend that you don't make this hint too suggestive. To keep your current password unchanged, click Cancel.

✦ **My Picture:** This thumbnail image appears on the Login screen — you can choose one of Apple's default pictures, or you can drag a picture from the Finder and drop it into the well. If you know where the image is located on your system, click the Choose Another button to navigate to the location; select the image and then click Open.

✦ **My Address Book Card:** To edit the card that you've marked in the Address Book as My Card, click the Edit button here. Mac OS X launches the Address Book, and you can edit your card to your heart's content. (For the complete scoop on the Mac OS X Address Book, see Chapter 5 of Book I.)

Screen Effects preferences

The Screen Effects group is shown in Figure 3-8.

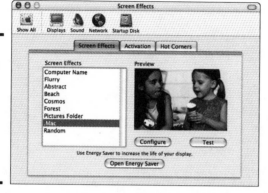

Figure 3-8:
The Screen
Effects
group
controls
the all-
important
screen
saver.

The tabs here are

✦ **Screen Effects:** In the Screen Effects list at the left, click the screen
saver that you want to display an animated Preview of on the right. To
try out the screen saver in full screen mode, click the Test button. (You
can end the test by moving your mouse.) If the screen saver module
that you select has any configurable settings, click the Configure button
to display them. (You can tell whether it has configurable settings by
whether the Configure button is enabled or disabled.) Finally, click the
Open Energy Saver button to jump to the Energy Saver System
Preference settings, where you can control when Mac OS X enters sleep
mode.

✦ **Activation:** Click and drag the slider here to specify the period of inactivity that will trigger the screen saver. To disable the screen saver, choose
the Never setting at the far right of the slider. You can also specify
whether you want Mac OS X to prompt for your account password
before deactivating (awakening from) the screen saver, which is a great
security measure for those who use their Macs in an office environment.

✦ **Hot Corners:** You can click any of the four buttons at the four corners of
the screen to mark one as an activation hot corner (which immediately
activates the screen saver) and another corner as a disabling hot corner
(which prevents the screen saver from activating). As long as the mouse
pointer stays in the disabling hot corner, the screen saver will not kick
in — no matter how long a period of inactivity passes. You can set up to
four corners if you like.

It's All about the Hardware

The next category, Hardware, allows you to specify settings that affect your Macintosh hardware.

CDs & DVDs preferences

The CDs & DVDs group is shown in Figure 3-9.

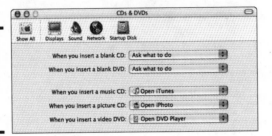

Figure 3-9: Change the automatic launch of CDs and DVDs.

Choices here are

✦ **When You Insert a Blank CD:** Click this drop-down list box to specify the action that Mac OS X should take when you load a blank CD-R or CD-RW disc. You can choose to be prompted or to open the Finder, iTunes, or Disk Copy. Additionally, you can open another application that you select, run an AppleScript that you select, or ignore the disc.

✦ **When You Insert a Blank DVD:** Use this feature to specify the action that your Mac should take when you load a recordable DVD.

✦ **When You Insert a Music CD:** Choices from this drop-down list specify what action Mac OS X should take when you load an audio CD. By default, iTunes is launched.

✦ **When You Insert a Picture CD:** Choices from this drop-down list specify what action Mac OS X should take when you load a picture CD. By default, iPhoto is launched.

✦ **When You Insert a Video DVD:** Choices from this drop-down list specify what action Mac OS X should take when you load a DVD movie disc. By default, DVD Player is launched.

ColorSync preferences

The ColorSync group is shown in Figure 3-10.

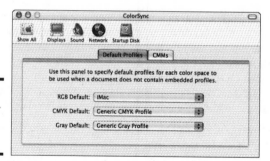

Figure 3-10:
Modify your
ColorSync
profiles.

The two tabs here are

✦ **Default Profiles:** You can select the default color profiles for RGB,
   CMYK, and Gray color models. If that sounded like gibberish, you're
   probably not a graphic artist or a professional digital photographer, in
   which case you can leave these settings as they are.

✦ **CMMs:** (In honest, simple English, *Color Matching Methods*.) Click the
   drop-down list box to select your preferred color matching technology.
   To use ColorSync, leave the option set at Automatic.

Displays preferences

The Displays group is shown in Figure 3-11.

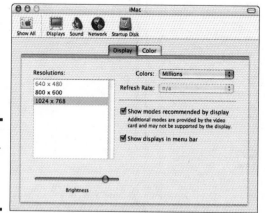

Figure 3-11:
Control your
display with
these
settings.

The two tabs here are

✦ **Display:** Click the resolution that you want to use from the Resolutions
   list on the left and then choose the number of colors (from the Colors

drop-down list) to display. In most cases, you'll want to use the highest resolution and the highest number of colors. (I recommend leaving the Show Modes Recommended by Display check box enabled, which will help ensure that you pick a display configuration that matches your monitor.) You can also choose a refresh rate (from the, ahem, Refresh Rate drop-down list). Again, generally the higher the refresh rate, the better. Move the Brightness slider to adjust the brightness level of your display.

Enable the Show Displays in Menu Bar check box if you'll be switching resolutions and color levels often.

✦ **Color:** Click a display color profile that will control the colors on your monitor. To create a custom ColorSync profile and calibrate the colors that you see on your monitor, click the Calibrate button to launch the Display Calibrator. (You can also launch it from your Utilities folder within your Applications folder.) This easy-to-use assistant will walk you step-by-step through the process of creating a ColorSync profile matched to your monitor's gamma and white-point values.

Energy Saver preferences

The Energy Saver group is shown in Figure 3-12.

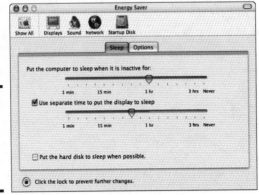

Figure 3-12: Put your Mac to sleep using these settings.

The two tabs here are

✦ **Sleep:** Move the Put the Computer to Sleep When it is Inactive For slider to specify when Mac OS X should switch to sleep mode — the Never setting disables sleep mode entirely. To choose a separate delay period for blanking your monitor, enable the Use Separate Time to Put the Display to Sleep check box and move the delay slider. You can also power down the hard drive to conserve energy and prevent wear and tear (an especially good feature for laptop owners).

✦ **Options:** These settings can toggle events that can wake Mac OS X from sleep mode, including a ring signal from the modem or a network connection by the network administrator. You can also set Mac OS X to restart automatically after a power failure, which is good idea if you'll be running a Web or File Transfer Protocol (FTP) server on your machine. (Read more about this in Book VII, Chapter 4.)

Keyboard preferences

The Keyboard group is shown in Figure 3-13.

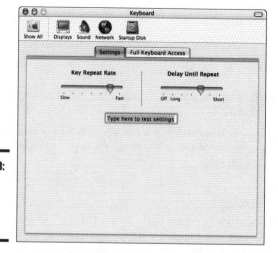

Figure 3-13:
Be the
master
of your
keyboard.

The two tabs here are

✦ **Settings:** Move the Key Repeat Rate slider to alter the rate at which a keystroke will repeat. You can also adjust the Delay Until Repeat slider to alter how long a key must be held down before it repeats. To test your settings, click in the sample box and type some random text.

✦ **Full Keyboard Access:** If you're a power user who appreciates the lure of the keyboard shortcut, you can add additional keyboard controls; enable the Turn on Full Keyboard Access check box to enable the feature. Then click the drop-down list box to choose whether you'll use the Control keys in conjunction with the function keys, letter keys, and custom keys. You can also choose between highlighting only text boxes and drop-down list boxes, or any control on a window or dialog.

Mouse preferences

Figure 3-14 illustrates the Mouse preferences.

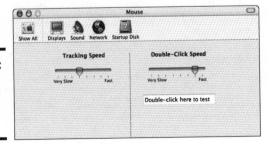

Figure 3-14:
The mouse
is the thing
with these
settings.

The settings here are

✦ **Tracking Speed:** Drag the slider to determine how fast the mouse tracks
across your Desktop.

✦ **Double-Click Speed:** Drag the slider to determine how fast you must
click your mouse to cause a double-click. You can click in the sample
box to test your settings.

Sound preferences

The Sound group is shown in Figure 3-15. To set the overall system audio
volume, drag the Output Volume slider. To mute all sound from your Mac,
enable the Mute check box. I recommend that you enable the Show Volume
in Menu Bar check box, which displays a convenient volume slider menu
bar icon.

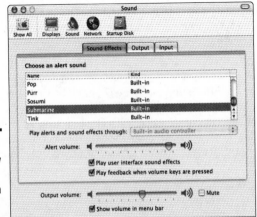

Figure 3-15:
Specify how
your Mac
sounds from
this group.

The three tabs here are

♦ **Sound Effects:** From this panel, you can choose the system alert sound and the volume for alerts. You can also choose to mute application and Finder menu sound effects, as well as toggle the sample sound effect when the volume keys are pressed on your Mac's keyboard (or from the Volume slider).

♦ **Output:** Use these settings to choose which audio controller your Mac should use for playing sound. Unless you've installed additional audio hardware, this should remain set to your Built-in Audio Controller. You can adjust the balance between the left and right channels for the selected output controller.

♦ **Input:** These settings allow you to specify an input source. Unless you've added an input source, leave this set to your Internal Microphone. Drag the Input Volume slider to increase or decrease the input signal volume — the input level display provides you with real-time sound levels.

Book II
Chapter 3

Delving under the
Hood with System
Preferences

Sharing the Joy: Internet & Network

Your Internet & Network connections are controlled from the settings in this category.

Internet preferences

The Internet group is illustrated in Figure 3-16.

Figure 3-16:
Your
Internet
settings are
ready to go
to work.

The four tabs here are

+ **.Mac:** In the .Mac Member Name and the Password text boxes, respectively, type your .Mac member name and password. If you'd like to subscribe, click Sign Up to launch your Web browser — you'll be whisked to the .Mac sign-up page. For more information about joining Apple's .Mac service, see Chapter 1 of Book IV.

+ **iDisk:** This tab displays your current iDisk usage and allows you to subscribe for additional space. You can set your access privileges for your public folder to Read-Only or Read-Write, and you can add a password that others have to enter before they can access your public folder. For a complete description of iDisk, see Book IV, Chapter 4.

+ **Email:** Click the Default Email Reader drop-down list to select the e-mail application that you want to use. To use your .Mac e-mail account information, enable the Use .Mac Email Account check box — otherwise, enter the e-mail account information provided by your Internet Service Provider (ISP).

+ **Web:** Click the Default Web Browser drop-down list box to select the Web browser that you want to use, and then type or paste the home page that you want to use into the Home Page field. You can also click the Select button to specify where you want the files that you download from your browser to be stored.

Network preferences

The Network group is shown in Figure 3-17.

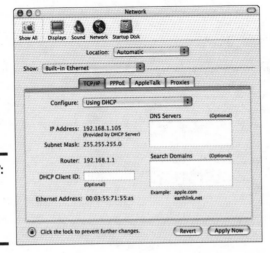

Figure 3-17: Fine-tune Network settings here.

You can create a new Location by clicking the Location drop-down list at the top of the dialog — Mac OS X prompts you for a name — or you can edit your existing Locations by choosing Edit Locations from this list. (Automatic is the default.) As I mention earlier in the book (Book I, Chapter 3), creating Locations makes it easy to completely reconfigure your Network preferences when you connect your computer to other networks: for example, when you take your laptop to a branch office. You can also set up Locations to accommodate different ISP dial-up telephone numbers in different towns.

If you need to create a new Location that's very similar to an existing Location, click the Location drop-down list box and choose Edit Locations. Then select the Location that you want to copy and click the Duplicate button. The new Location that you create will contain all the same settings (without several minutes of retyping), so you can easily edit it and make minor changes quickly.

When you select Built-in Ethernet from the Show drop-down list box, the tabs displayed are

+ **TCP/IP:** These settings are provided either automatically (using Dynamic Host Configuration Protocol [DHCP]) or manually (using settings provided by your network administrator). For more details on TCP/IP settings, see Book IV, Chapter 1 and Book V, Chapter 2.

+ **PPPoE:** The settings that you enter here — if necessary — are used for *Point-to-Point over Ethernet* connections. If you're not using PPPoE to connect to your ISP, you can forget about the settings on this dialog; if you are using PPPoE, see Book IV, Chapter 1 for more details.

+ **AppleTalk:** If you're connecting your Mac to older Macs using an AppleTalk network, enable the Make AppleTalk Active check box and choose an active Zone to join from the AppleTalk Zone drop-down list box. Automatic configuration should work in nearly every AppleTalk environment, but if you want to specify the Node ID and Network ID for your computer manually, choose Manually from the Configure drop-down list box.

   Note that AppleTalk can only be active on one port within a location — for example, if you have AppleTalk active for Ethernet, you can't select AppleTalk for the wireless port in the same location. (You can, however, define different locations for AirPort and Ethernet, both with AppleTalk active.)

+ **Proxies:** Network proxy servers are used as part of a firewall configuration to help keep your network secure, but in most cases, changing them can cause you to lose Internet functionality if you enter the wrong settings.

Most folks using a telephone modem, cable modem, or digital subscriber line (DSL) connection should leave these settings alone. Enable and change these settings only at the request of your network administrator.

If you've enabled your Mac OS X firewall and you use FTP to transfer files, enable the Passive FTP Mode check box on the Proxies tab — I recommend that you enable this setting to allow downloading from some Web pages as well.

When you select Internal Modem from the Show drop-down list box, the tabs displayed are

+ **TCP/IP:** You can configure your Internet connection for Point-to-Point Protocol (PPP), AOL dial-up, or enter the settings manually — the Transmission Control Protocol/Internet Protocol (TCP/IP) dial-up connection that you choose determines what fields are available. Your ISP will supply you with these settings.

+ **PPP:** These settings are used for a *Point-to-Point* connection over a telephone modem. Again, your ISP will provide you with the right values to enter here. If you're supplied with a secondary telephone number to dial when the primary is busy, enter it into the Alternate Number field.

If you're concerned about who's using your Internet connection — or you want to add an extra layer of security when you dial out — disable the Save Password check box, and Mac OS X will prompt you each time for your Internet account password.

+ **Proxies:** Some ISPs use proxy servers for their dial-up accounts to maintain security, but (as I mention earlier in this section) changing these settings willy-nilly is inviting disaster. Leave them disabled unless given specific instructions on what to set by your ISP.

+ **Modem:** Click the drop-down Modem list box and choose the brand and model of your modem. If Mac OS X detects an internal modem, it's used by default.

I strongly recommend that you enable both the Enable Error Correction and Compression in Modem and the Wait for Dial Tone before Dialing check boxes because they will provide you with the best performance and the fastest speeds.

You can also select tone or pulse dialing and whether you want to hear the two modems conversing. (If the caterwauling bothers you, turn the Sound option off.) If you like, Mac OS X can notify you with an alert sound if you receive an incoming call while you're connected to your ISP. If you live outside the United States, click the Change button to select the proper Country Setting; this governs how your modem dials your ISP. Finally, I recommend that you enable the Show Modem status in Menu Bar check box, which gives you a visual reference on your connection status.

To enable and disable your network ports, click the Show drop-down list box and choose Network Port Configurations. You can enable the On check box to toggle individual ports — for instance, if you don't use your internal modem, you can turn it off. And you can drag configurations into any desired order to specify which ports Mac OS X should use first when connecting.

QuickTime preferences

The QuickTime group is shown in Figure 3-18. For complete details on QuickTime, streaming media, and viewing movies downloaded from the Web, see Book III, Chapter 6.

Book II
Chapter 3

Delving under the
Hood with System
Preferences

Figure 3-18:
Tweak
QuickTime
settings
here.

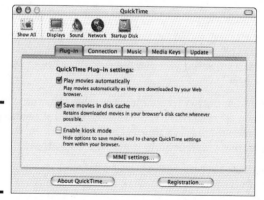

If you've purchased a registration code for QuickTime Pro or Player Pro, click the Registration button to enter it.

The five tabs here are

✦ **Plug-In:** These settings determine how QuickTime acts when it's used as a Web browser plug-in. Enable the Play Movies Automatically check box to toggle automatic playback of movies that you've downloaded from the Web. If you'll be viewing downloaded QuickTime movies often, it's a good idea to enable the Save Movies in Disk Cache check box — this improves the playback performance.

When the Enable Kiosk Mode check box is enabled, the options available from the Player window no longer include the ability to save movies or change QuickTime settings — this is a good idea when your kids will be downloading and watching movies from the Web.

If you need to change the MIME file types that QuickTime will play from a Web page, click the MIME Settings button. (These are the different types of multimedia files you'll encounter on the Web, like video, audio, and photographs.) However, I recommend that you use the default settings because otherwise you might end up downloading a file type that you can't use because you've disabled it.

Often, third-party media players will, in effect, take over the MIME file types from QuickTime — naturally, this is what you want, *if* you like the new player application. However, if you decide that the new player is not your style, you can return QuickTime to its rightful place as Kahuna of the Web Downloads by displaying the MIME settings, clicking the Use Defaults button, and then clicking OK.

✦ **Connection:** Click the Connection Speed drop-down list to choose the data transfer speed closest to your connection rate. This optimizes QuickTime's streaming video performance to match your connection. If you're not using DSL, a network Internet connection, or a cable modem connection, make sure that you disable the Allow Multiple Simultaneous Streams check box.

Click the Instant-On button to enable or disable streaming playback the moment that you start to receive the media (without queuing a significant amount first, which takes time). The faster your Internet connection is, the less time you'll need to queue a media stream.

If you receive protocol error messages from QuickTime, click the Transport Setup button and then click the Auto Configure button. Mac OS X will choose the correct transport protocol and port ID for your connection.

✦ **Music:** You need only visit this tab if you've added a software-based music synthesizer (such as Deck or VST) to Mac OS X — if so, you can click its entry here and click Make Default to use it instead of QuickTime's built-in synthesizer.

✦ **Media Keys:** If you play MP3 or MOV files that require secure media keys, you can click the Add button and enter the category and key from this panel. To edit a key, select it from the list and click the Edit button. To remove a key from the list, select it and click the Delete button.

✦ **Update:** By default, QuickTime checks for new updates automatically, but you can check for new updates immediately by clicking the Update Now button. You can also add QuickTime enhancement software from other companies by clicking the Install New 3rd-Party QuickTime Software button and then clicking the Update Now button.

Sharing preferences

Figure 3-19 illustrates the Sharing preferences.

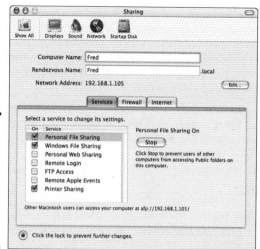

Figure 3-19: These settings control file sharing, FTP access, and printer sharing.

Click in the Computer Name and Rendezvous Name text fields to change the default network names assigned to your Mac during the installation process. (Use Rendezvous to create an instant plug-and-play network of computers and smart devices.) Your current network address is listed, but you can change your network settings by clicking the Edit button.

The three tabs here are

✦ **Services:** Each entry in the services list controls a specific type of sharing, including Personal File Sharing (with other Macs), Windows File Sharing (with PCs running Windows), Personal Web Sharing, Remote Login, FTP Access, Remote Apple Events, and Printer Sharing. To turn on any of these services, enable the On check box for that service. To turn a service off, choose it from the list and click the Stop button that appears.

From a security standpoint, I highly recommend that you enable only those services that you will actually use.

✦ **Firewall:** As I discuss in Chapter 6 of Book IV, Mac OS X includes a built-in firewall. You can enable the firewall from this panel — when the firewall is on, communication to any service not allowed in the list is blocked. (In firewall-speak, these entries are called *rules* because they determine what's allowed to pass through to your Mac.)

To enable communications with a service, select the entry in the list and enable the On check box. Click the New button to specify a new rule by entering a port and assigning it a name. After you create a new rule, it appears in the list, and you can toggle it on and off like any of the default rules. Click the Edit button to edit the selected rule; click the Delete button to remove the selected rule.

If you're using an Internet or network connection, I strongly urge you to enable the firewall (but only after you've reviewed Chapter 2 of Book V). However, if you suddenly can't connect to other computers or share files that you were originally able to share, it's time to review the rules that you've enabled from this panel.

✦ **Internet:** If you want to share the Internet connection from this Macintosh, click Start, and then mark the Share the Connection with Other Computers check box to enable it.

Tweaking the System

The last section of the System Preferences window covers system-wide settings that affect all users and the overall operation of Mac OS X.

Accounts preferences

The Accounts group is illustrated in Figure 3-20.

Figure 3-20:
Manage
user
accounts
with these
settings.

The two tabs here are

✦ **Users:** Each user on your system has an entry in this list. If you choose, you can log in automatically as the selected user by enabling the Log in Automatically as *<Username>*. (If you do use this feature, you'll have to log out after you start or restart your system to allow other users to log in.) For more information about adding and editing users, refer to Book II, Chapter 5.

✦ **Login Options:** You can choose to display either a Name field (followed by a Password field) on the Login screen (which means that the user must actually type in the correct user name) or a list of users, from which a person can select a user ID. If security is a consideration, use the Name and Password option.

You can prevent anyone from restarting or shutting down the Mac from the Login screen by enabling the Hide the Restart and Shut Down Buttons check box. You can also elect to display the password hint after three unsuccessful attempts — again, from a security standpoint, not a good choice.

Classic preferences

Figure 3-21 shows the Classic System Preferences settings. For all the background on Classic, read Chapter 7 of Book I.

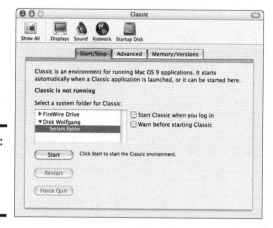

Figure 3-21:
Set up Classic settings here.

The three tabs here are

✦ **Start/Stop:** You can select from multiple Mac OS 9 System folders when launching Classic, and you can elect to start Classic automatically when the current user logs in. (Personally, I don't use Classic often, so I don't run it automatically at login — therefore saving those system resources for my other applications.) If you'd rather be prompted before Classic is launched, enable the Warn before Starting Classic check box. You can launch Classic manually from this panel by clicking Start; if Classic is encountering problems, you can click the Restart or Force Quit buttons as well.

✦ **Advanced:** Three special start-up options are available from the drop-down list — and *only* when you use the Start Classic button on this panel. (As you might expect, these options are typically only for debugging and troubleshooting.) You can elect to start Classic with all extensions turned off, or you can open the Extensions Manager to toggle individual extensions on and off within Classic. Finally, you can choose Use Key Combination from the drop-down list to start or restart Classic when you press a shortcut sequence of up to five keys.

To use preferences from the current user's Home folder, enable the Use Preferences from Home Folder check box. If this is disabled, preferences from the System folder that you choose on the Start/Stop panel are used. You can specify the amount of inactivity before Classic switches to sleep mode, and you can rebuild the Classic Desktop, which is a good idea if custom icons disappear or documents that once had recognized file types are no longer recognized.

✦ **Memory/Versions:** This panel displays information on both Classic and the applications that it's running. To show background processes that would normally be invisible, mark the Show Background Processes check box to enable it.

Date & Time preferences

Click the System Preferences Date & Time icon to display the settings that you see in Figure 3-22.

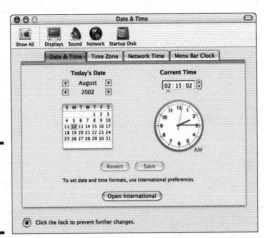

Figure 3-22:
Keep track
of Date &
Time
settings.

The four tabs here are

+ **Date & Time:** To set the current date, click the date within the mini-calendar; to set the system time, click in the Current Time field and type the current time.

  You can't set these values manually if you use a network time server, which I'll discuss in a second.

+ **Time Zone:** Click your approximate location on the world map to choose a time zone or click the Closest City drop-down list and choose the city that's closest to you (and shares your same time zone).

+ **Network Time:** To automatically set your Mac's system time and date from a network time server, enable the Use a Network Time Server check box and then choose a server from the drop-down list that corresponds to your location. (Of course, you need an Internet connection to use a network time server.) You can click the Set Time Now button to immediately update your Mac using network time.

+ **Menu Bar Clock:** If you enable the Show the Date and Time in the Menu Bar check box, you can choose to view the time in text or icon format. You can also optionally display seconds, AM/PM, and the day of the week; have the time separator characters flash; or use a clock based on 24 hours.

Software Update preferences

The Software Update settings are shown in Figure 3-23.

Figure 3-23:
Check for
operating
system
updates on
a regular
basis.

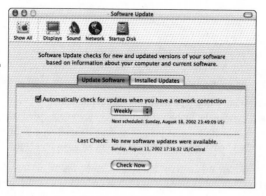

The two tabs here are

+ **Update Software:** I recommend enabling the Automatically Check for Updates when You Have a Network Connection check box. Choose Daily or Weekly from the drop-down list box. To check immediately, click the Check Now button.

✦ **Installed Updates:** Click this tab to display a list of the updates that you've already applied to Mac OS X. You can open the list as a log file as well, which will allow you to cut and paste text.

Speech preferences

Figure 3-24 illustrates the Speech settings — for a discussion of how these settings are used, visit Book VII, Chapter 3.

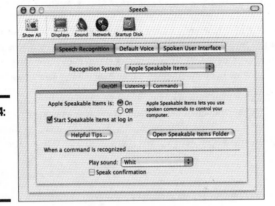

Figure 3-24: Control speech features settings here.

The three tabs here are

✦ **Speech Recognition:** This tab has three tabs of its own: On/Off, Listening, and Commands. Using the Recognition System drop-down list box, you can choose from either the Apple Speakable Items system or a third-party system that you've installed — if you go with a third-party system, the tabs will vary according to the recognition software that you select.

　• **On/Off:** With this feature toggled on (by selecting the On radio button next to Apple Speakable Items), you can control Mac OS X with spoken commands. If you're going to use Apple Speakable Items, enable the Start Speakable Items at Log In check box.

　Click the self-named button to open the Speakable Items Folder from this panel. (I discuss speech in Chapter 3 of Book VII.) From the Play Sound drop-down list, you can indicate what sound effect Mac OS X will play when it recognizes a speech command. (Optionally, Mac OS X can confirm the command by speaking it if you enable the Speak Confirmation check box.)

　• **Listening:** Here you can change the Speakable Items Listening key (Esc by default) and specify whether your Mac should listen only while the key is pressed or whether the Listening key toggles listening on and off. You can also change the name of your computer and whether that name is required before a command. If you have more than one microphone, you can select which one you want to use as well as set the input volume. Otherwise, leave these settings they are.

- **Commands:** Here you can select which types of commands that will be available as well as whether exact wording of command names is required. Read more about these settings in Chapter 3 of Book VII.

✦ **Default Voice:** Here's a fun panel — click a voice in the list at the left, and Mac OS X will use that voice to speak to you from dialogs and applications. You can set the Rate (from Slow to Fast) and play a sample by clicking the Play button. (Try Zarvox, Bubbles, and Pipe Organ.)

✦ **Spoken User Interface:** These settings specify when Mac OS X will talk to you. The Talking Alerts feature actually speaks the text within alert dialogs — to toggle it on, enable the Speak the Alert Text check box.

You can also optionally add a phrase before the text, which you can choose from the drop-down list box. To add a phrase to the list, like *Don't Panic!,* choose Edit Phrase List from the list.

Move the Delay slider to specify how much time your Mac should wait before reading the dialog to you. You can also optionally announce when an application wants your attention, the text that's under the mouse pointer, and the selected text when you press a key that you specify.

Startup Disk preferences

Figure 3-25 illustrates the Startup Disk settings.

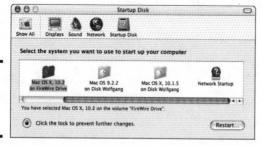

Figure 3-25: Select a start-up disk here.

To select a start-up disk, click the desired start-up folder from the scrolling icon list.

Mac OS 9 System folders have a *9* icon, and Mac OS X folders have the familiar blue X logo. Mac OS X displays the version numbers of each system and the physical drives where each system resides.

If you're planning on rebooting with an external USB or FireWire start-up disk, that disk must already be connected, powered on, and recognized by the system before you display these settings.

Select the Network Startup icon if you'd like to boot from a System folder on your local network — typically, such a folder is created by your network administrator.

After you click a folder to select it, click the Restart button. Mac OS X confirms your choice, and your Mac reboots.

Universal Access preferences

The final group, Universal Access, is shown in Figure 3-26. These settings modify OS X's settings to make them more friendly to disabled users. Note that if you choose the Enable Text-to-Speech for Universal Access Preferences check box, Mac OS X will speak the text for all text and buttons onscreen.

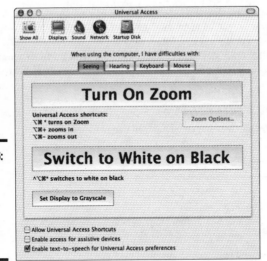

Figure 3-26: You can adjust Universal Access settings here.

If you have an assistive device that's recognized by Mac OS X, click the Enable Access for Assistive Devices check box to allow it to be used throughout the operating system.

The four tabs here are

✦ **Seeing:** These settings make it easier for those with limited vision to use Mac OS X. To turn on the display Zoom feature, click the Turn on Zoom button or press ⌘+Option+* (asterisk). To specify how much magnification should be used, click the Zoom Options button. From the sheet that appears, you can set the minimum and maximum Zoom magnification increments. From the keyboard, use ⌘+Option++ (plus sign) to zoom in and ⌘+Option+– (minus sign) to zoom out. Optionally, you can display a preview rectangle of the area that will be included when you zoom.

Mac OS X can also smooth images to make them look better when zoomed. If you prefer white text on a black background, click the Switch to White on Black button. Note that depending on your display settings, it might be easier on the eyes to use grayscale display mode by clicking the Set Display to Grayscale button.

**Book II
Chapter 3**

**Delving under the
Hood with System
Preferences**

✦ **Hearing:** If you need additional visual cues to supplement the spoken and audio alerts in Mac OS X, click this tab and enable the Flash the Screen whenever an Alert Sound Occurs check box. To raise the overall sound volume in Mac OS X, you can click the Adjust Sound button to display the Sound System Preferences settings, where you can drag the Volume slider to the right.

✦ **Keyboard:** These settings help those who have trouble pressing keyboard shortcuts or those who often trigger keyboard repeats (repetition of the same character) accidentally. If you mark the Sticky Keys radio button, you can use *modifier keys* individually that will be grouped together automatically as a single keyboard shortcut. (You can optionally specify that Mac OS X should sound a beep tone when a modifier key is pressed and whether the modifier keys should be displayed on-screen.)

Sticky Keys can be toggled on from the keyboard by pressing the Shift key five times. Turn Slow Keys on to add a pause (of the length that you specify) between when a key is pressed and when it's actually acted upon within Mac OS X. You can optionally add a key-click sound each time that you press a key. To turn keyboard repeat off entirely, click the Set Key Repeat button, which opens the Keyboard preference settings that I discuss earlier.

✦ **Mouse:** With Mouse Keys active, you can use the numeric keypad to move the mouse pointer across your screen. Mouse Keys can be toggled on and off by pressing the Option key five times. Drag the delay and speed sliders to specify how long you must hold down a keypad key before the pointer starts to move as well as how fast the pointer should move across the screen. You can also click the Open Keyboard Preferences button to turn on Full Keyboard Access, which I mention earlier in the section on keyboard settings.

Chapter 4: You Mean Others Can Use My Mac, Too?

In This Chapter

- Understanding how multi-user systems work
- Configuring login settings
- Changing the appearance of the login screen
- Tightening security during login
- Starting applications automatically when you log in

Whether you're setting up Mac OS X for use in a public library or simply allowing your 12-year-old to use your Mac in your home office, configuring Mac OS X for multiple users is a simple chore. However, you must also consider the possible downsides of a mismanaged multi-user system: files and folders being shared that you didn't want in the public domain, users logging in as each other, and the very real possibility of accidental file deletion (and worse).

Therefore, in this chapter, I show you how to take those first steps — creating users, configuring the personal account that you created when you first installed the operating system, and protecting your stuff. (Network administrators call this security check-up *locking things down.*)

How Multi-User Works on Mac OS X

When you create multiple users in Mac OS X, each person who uses your Macintosh — hence the term *user* — has a separate *account* (much like an account that you might open at a bank). Mac OS X creates a Home folder for each user and saves that user's preferences independently from other users. When you log in to Mac OS X, you select (or provide) a username and a password, which identifies you and tells Mac OS X which user has logged on — and therefore, which preferences and Home folder to use.

Each account also carries a specific *level,* which determines how much control the user has over Mac OS X and the computer itself. Without the proper account, for example, a user might not be able to display many of the panels in System Preferences.

The three account levels are

✦ **Root:** Also called *System Administrator,* this uber-account can change *anything* within Mac OS X — and that's usually not a good thing, so it's actually disabled as a default. (This alone should tell you that the Root account shouldn't be toyed with.) For instance, the Root account can seriously screw up the UNIX sub-system within Mac OS X, or a Root user can delete files within the Mac OS X System Folder.

Enable the System Administrator account and use it only if told to do so by an Apple technical support technician. To enable the Root account, you must launch NetInfo Manager, which is stored in the Utilities folder inside your Applications folder.

✦ **Administrator:** This is the account level that you were assigned when you installed Mac OS X. *Note:* The Administrator account should *not* be confused with the System Administrator account!

It's perfectly okay for you or anyone you assign to use an Administrator account. An Administrator can install applications anywhere on the system, create/edit/delete user accounts, and make changes to all the settings in System Preferences. However, an administrator can't move or delete items from any other user's Home folder.

A typical multi-user Mac OS X computer will have only one Administrator — like a teacher in a classroom — but technically you can create as many Administrator accounts as you like. If you do need to give someone else this access level, assign it only to a competent, experienced user whom you trust.

✦ **Standard:** A Standard account is the default in Mac OS X. Standard users can install software and save documents only in their Home folders and the Shared folder (which resides in the Users folder), and they can change only certain settings in System Preferences. Thus, they can do little damage to the system as a whole. For example, each of the students in a classroom should be given a standard level account for the Mac OS X system that they share.

You can also use the Capabilities feature to fine-tune what a Standard account user can do. For example, you can disable CD/DVD recording and prevent the user from changing the account password, or you can allow the user to open all System Preferences panels and remove items from the Dock.

The next chapter of this mini-book covers the entire process of creating and editing a user account.

Configuring Your Login Screen

Take a look at the changes that you can make to the login process. First, Mac OS X provides three methods of displaying the login screen:

+ **Logging in with a List:** To log in, click your account username in the list, and the login screen displays the password prompt. Type your password — Mac OS X displays bullet characters to ensure security — and press Return (or click the Log In button).

+ **Logging in with Username and Password:** Type your account username in the Name field and press Tab. Then type your password and press Return (or click the Log In button).

+ **Auto Login:** With Auto Login set, Mac OS X automatically logs in the specified account when you reboot. In effect, you never see the login screen unless you click Log Out from the Apple menu. (Naturally, this is an attractive option to use if your computer is in a secure location — like your office — and you'll be the only one using your Mac.)

To specify which type of login screen you see — if you see one at all — head to System Preferences and click Accounts.

+ To set Auto Login, click the account (from the Users tab) that you want to set for Auto Login and click the Set Auto Login button. When Mac OS X displays the user Name and Password sheet that you see in Figure 4-1, type your password and then click OK.

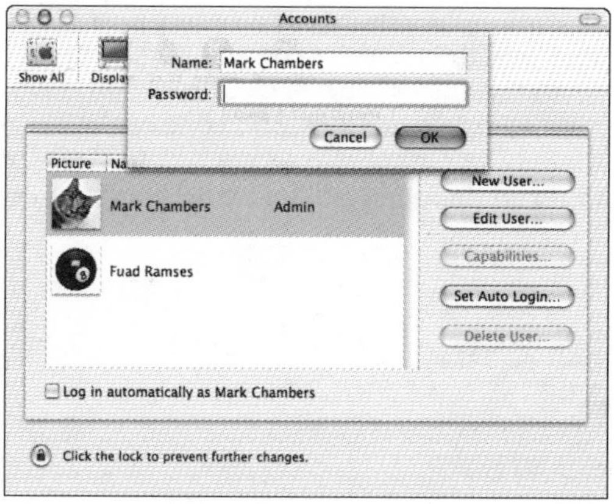

Book II Chapter 4

You Mean Others Can Use My Mac, Too?

Figure 4-1: Configure Auto Login from the Accounts panel.

✦ To determine whether Mac OS X uses a list login screen, click the Login Options tab to display the settings that you see in Figure 4-2. Select the List of Users radio button for a list login screen or select the Name and Password radio button for a simple login screen where you must type your username and password.

Figure 4-2:
Will that be
a list login
screen?

To change settings specific to your account — no matter what your access level — open System Preferences and click My Account. From here, you can change your account password and picture, as well as the card marked as yours within the Address Book.

To log out of Mac OS X without restarting or shutting down the computer, choose the Apple menu and then choose Log Out, or just press ⌘+Shift+Q. You'll see the confirmation dialog shown in Figure 4-3. Although Mac OS X will display the login screen after two minutes, someone can still walk up and click the Cancel button, thereby gaining access to your stuff. Therefore, always click the Log Out button on this screen before your hand leaves the mouse!

Figure 4-3:
Always click
Log Out
before
you leave
your Mac.

Locking Things Down

If security is a potential problem and you still need to share a Mac between multiple users, lock things down. To protect Mac OS X from unauthorized use, take care of these potential security holes immediately:

✦ **Disable the Restart and Shut Down buttons:** Any computer can be hacked when it's restarted or turned on, so disable the Restart and Shut Down buttons on the login screen. (After a user has successfully logged in, Mac OS X can be shut down normally by using the menu item or the keyboard shortcuts I've covered earlier.) Open the Accounts panel in System Preferences, click the Login Options tab, and enable the Hide the Restart and Shut Down Buttons check box. Press ⌘+Q to quit and save your changes.

✦ **Disable list logins:** With a list login, any potential hacker already knows half the information necessary to gain entry to your system — and often the password is easy to guess. Therefore, set Mac OS X to ask for the username and password on the Login screen, as I describe earlier. This way, someone has to guess both the username and the password, which is a much harder proposition.

✦ **Disable Auto Login:** A true no-brainer. Although Auto Login is very convenient, all someone has to do is reboot your Mac and the red carpet is immediately rolled out. This is why I never use Auto Login, even on the Macs in my office. To disable Auto Login, display the Accounts panel in System Preferences; on the Users tab, disable the Log in Automatically as *<username>* check box.

✦ **Disable the password hint:** By default, Mac OS X obligingly displays the password hint for an account after three unsuccessful attempts at entering a password. Where security is an issue, this is like serving a hacker a piece of apple pie. Therefore, head to System Preferences, display the Accounts settings, click the Login Options panel, and disable the Show Password Hint after 3 Attempts to Enter a Password check box.

✦ **Select passwords intelligently:** Although using your mother's maiden name for a password might seem like a great idea, the best method of selecting a password is to use a completely random group of mixed letters and numbers. If you find a random password too hard to remember, at least add a number after your password, like *dietcoke1* — and no, that is not one of my passwords. (Nice try.)

For even greater security, make at least one password character uppercase.

Starting Applications Automatically After Login

Here's one other advantage to logins — each account can have its own selection of applications that run automatically when that user logs in. These applications are called *login items*. (For the Mac OS 9 old-timers, think Startup Items in days gone by.) To set them, open System Preferences and click the Login Items icon (see Figure 4-4).

Figure 4-4:
Hey, why not launch Return to Castle Wolfenstein every time you log in?

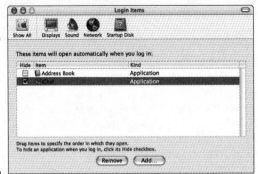

Including an application in your Login Items list is easy: Click Add to navigate to the desired application, select it, and then click Add again. Note that items in the list are launched in order — if something needs to run before something else, you can drag the item entries into any sequence.

To launch the application in hidden mode — which may or may not display it in the Dock, depending on the application itself — click the list entry for the desired item and enable its Hide check box.

Chapter 5: Setting Up Multi-User Accounts

In This Chapter

✔ Adding, modifying, and deleting users

✔ Changing capabilities

✔ Avoiding keychains

In the previous chapter, I introduce you to the different Mac OS X multi-user account levels and the login process. If you're ready to share your Mac with others, you'll discover how to add new accounts and edit existing accounts in this chapter. Oh, and yes, I also show you how to *frag* — that's game-speak for *delete* — accounts that you no longer need. I'll also demonstrate how to add optional powers *(capabilities)* to an individual user account and how to avoid using a keychain to make it easier to store that pocketful of passwords that you've created on the Internet.

Yes, that's right, Mac OS X actually has a feature that I *don't* want you to use. Read on to find out more.

Adding, Editing, and Deleting Users

All multi-user account activity takes place in two panes of System Preferences: the My Account pane, which makes it easy for Standard level users to modify their own personal account preferences; and the Accounts pane. I use the latter pane in this chapter, so open System Preferences and click on the Accounts icon.

If you haven't added any users to your system yet, the Users list should look like Figure 5-1. You should see only your account, which you set up when you installed Mac OS X, set to Administrator (Admin) level.

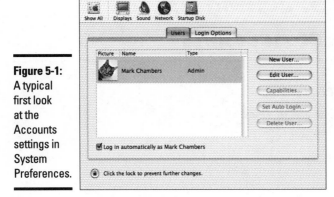

Figure 5-1:
A typical
first look
at the
Accounts
settings in
System
Preferences.

Adding an account

To add a new user account, follow these steps:

1. **In the Accounts pane in System Preferences, click the New User button to display the sheet that you see in Figure 5-2.**

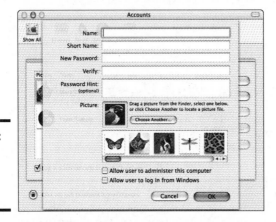

Figure 5-2:
Set up a
new user
account
here.

2. **In the Name text box, type the name that you want to display for this account (both in the Accounts list and on the Login screen) and then press Tab to move to the next field.**

Mac OS X automatically generates a short name for use in iChat and various network applications — it's also the name of the folder that Mac OS X creates on the computer's hard drive for this user. You can keep the default short name or type a new one, but it must not contain any spaces. For more on iChat, jump to Chapter 3 of Book IV. (I'll wait for you here.)

3. **Press Tab again.**

4. **In the New Password text box, type the password for the new account.**

   As always, Mac OS X displays bullet characters for security.

5. **Press Tab, type the password again in the Verify text box, and press Tab again.**

6. **If you decide to use the password hint feature that I describe in the previous chapter, you can enter a short sentence or question in the Password Hint text box (optional).**

   The hint is displayed after three unsuccessful attempts at entering the account password.

   I recommend that you *do not use this option* — if you do, make sure that the hint is sufficiently vague! Press Tab to continue.

7. **Next you can specify the thumbnail image that will appear in the Login list next to the account name by clicking the Choose Another button to navigate to a specific image, selecting it, and then clicking Open.**

   Apple provides a number of good images in the scrolling strip, or you can drag an image from a Finder window and drop it into the well.

8. **To grant this account Administrator-level access, enable the Allow User to Administer This Computer check box.**

9. **To allow this account to log in to Mac OS X through a Windows network connection, enable the Allow User to Log in from Windows check box.**

10. **After all the fields are correct and you've selected just the right image to capture the user's personality — a more difficult task than you might think — click OK to finish and create the account.**

    The new account now shows up in the Accounts list and in the Login screen.

Book II
Chapter 5

Setting Up
Multi-User
Accounts

Editing an existing account

If you need to make changes to an account and it's your account, you can simply click the My Account icon in System Preferences and change your own user settings. However, if it's someone else's account and you have Administrator access, follow these steps:

1. **From the Users tab of the Accounts list, click the account that you want to change.**

2. **Click the Edit User button to display the same settings illustrated in Figure 5-2.**

3. **Edit the settings that you need to change.**

4. **After you make the changes, click Save to save them and return to the Accounts panel.**

Deleting an existing account

To wipe an account from the face of the earth, follow these steps:

1. **From the Users tab of the Accounts list, click the account that you want to delete.**

2. **Click Delete User.**

Mac OS X displays the confirmation sheet that you see in Figure 5-3.

Note that the contents of the user's home folder are saved in a file in the Deleted Users folder (just in case you need to retrieve something).

3. **Click OK to verify and delete the account or click the Cancel button to abort and return to the Accounts list.**

Figure 5-3:
Are you
sure that
you want
to delete
this user
account?

Setting Capabilities

Administrators are special people. Just ask one; you'll see. Anyway, when an administrator creates or edits the account for a Standard-level user, Mac OS X offers another level of specific rights — called *capabilities* — that can be assigned on an individual account basis. *Note:* Capabilities are available only for Standard-level users; administrators don't need them because an Administrator-level account already has access to everything covered by capabilities.

When do you need capabilities? Here are three likely scenarios:

✦ You're creating accounts for corporate or educational users, and you want to disable certain features of Mac OS X to prevent those folks from doing something dumb. Just tell 'em you're *streamlining the operating system.* (Yeah, that's it.) For example, you might not want that one particular kid making CD copies of *The Illustrated Anarchist's Cookbook* in the classroom while you're gone. Therefore, you disable the ability for that account to burn CDs or DVDs.

✦ In the same environment, you might want to give a specific Standard-level account the ability to view all the settings in System Preferences. If Roger in Accounting is both helpful and knowledgeable — oh, and add *trustworthy* in there, too — you might want to give him this capability so that he can make necessary changes to the system while you're on vacation.

✦ You want one or more users to access one — and only one — application on the system, or perhaps just two or three applications. To illustrate: In my years as a hospital hardware technician, we had a number of computers that were used solely to display patient records. No Word, no e-mail, nothing but the one program that accessed the medical records database. We called these machines *dumb terminals,* although they were actually personal computers. (This trick also works well if you're a parent and you'd like to give your kids access without endangering your valuable files. Just don't call your computer a *dumb terminal* lest your kids take offense. That's experience talking there.) If you want to allow access to a specified selection of applications, you can set them in that account's capabilities.

After you get the hang of the capabilities of this feature (sorry about that), review what each of the settings does. To display the capabilities for a Standard account, click the account in the list and then click the Capabilities button (see Figure 5-4).

Book II
Chapter 5

Setting Up
Multi-User
Accounts

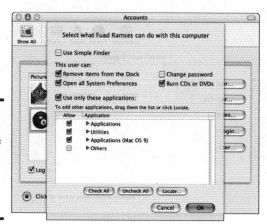

Figure 5-4:
You can set
a number of
capabilities
for a
Standard
account.

The settings are

+ **Use Simple Finder:** The default Simple Finder, shown in Figure 5-5, is a highly simplified version of the regular Mac OS X Finder. The simplified Dock contains only the Finder icon, the Trash, and folders for the user's approved applications, documents, and shared files.

This is the network administrator's idea of a foolproof interface for Mac OS X: A user can access only those system files and resources needed to do a job, with no room for tinkering or goofing off. Enabling the Use Simple Finder check box disables other check boxes on this panel automatically because they can't be used.

Note that a Standard-level user can still make the jump to the full version of the Finder — click Finder and choose Run Full Finder. The user will have to enter a correct Administrator-level username and password.

Figure 5-6 illustrates the simplified screen that appears when you click My Applications; Mac old-timers will recognize this as a variant of the Classic Launcher application. (You'll find out in a second how to specify what applications the user can see.)

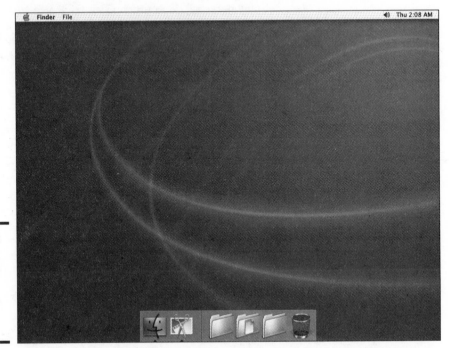

Figure 5-5:
Whoa! It's the Simple Finder — less filling, still runs great!

Figure 5-6:
Select an
approved
application
from the My
Applications
folder.

✦ **Remove Items from the Dock:** Enable this check box, and the user can remove applications, documents, and folders from the Dock in the Full Finder. (If you don't want the contents of the Dock changing according to the whims of other users, then it's a good idea to disable this check box.)

✦ **Open All System Preferences:** When this check box is enabled, this option allows the user to change any setting throughout System Preferences, just as if the account were Administrator level.

✦ **Change Password:** Enable this check box to allow the user to change the account password. If the user isn't allowed to open all System Preferences settings, this check box is disabled.

If you're creating a single Standard-level account for an entire group of people to use — for example, if you want to leave the machine in kiosk mode in one corner of the office or if everyone in a classroom will use the same account on the machine — I recommend disabling the ability to change the account password.

✦ **Burn CDs or DVDs:** Disable this check box to prevent the user from recording CDs or DVDs using the built-in disc recording features in Mac OS X. (Note, however, that if you've loaded a third-party recording program like Toast, the user can still record discs with it.)

✦ **Use Only These Applications:** When this option is enabled, you can select the specific applications that will appear to the user. These restrictions are in effect whether the user has access to the Full Finder or just the Simple Finder.

To allow access to all the programs in the specified folders —
Applications, Utilities, and Applications (Mac OS 9) — click the Check
All button. To restrict access to all applications, click the Uncheck All
button. You can also toggle the restriction on and off for specific applications that Mac OS X finds in these folders; click the right-arrow icon
to expand the list and then either mark or uncheck the Allow check box
for the desired programs.

To add a new application to the Allow list, drag its icon from the Finder and
drop it in the list. Alternatively, click the Locate button and navigate to it,
click the application to select it, and then click Add. After you add an application, it appears in the Others section of the Allow list, and you can toggle
access to it on and off like the applications in the named folders.

After you set the capabilities for a user account, click OK to save them and
return to the Accounts settings.

You can also change the Auto Login account from these settings. Click the
desired account that you want, and then click the Set Auto Login button to
display the password verification sheet that you see in Figure 5-7. Type the
password and then click OK to save the change. This is yet another good
feature for those preparing a Mac for public use — if you set the Auto Login
to your public Standard-access account, Mac OS X automatically uses the
right account if the Mac is rebooted or restarted.

You can always choose Log Out from the Apple menu to log in under your
own account. If you need to temporarily disable the Auto Login feature without changing which account it uses, disable the Log in Automatically as
<username> check box.

Figure 5-7:
Switch Auto
Login to
a new
account.

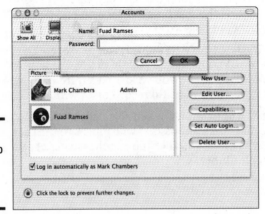

Using Keychains — NOT

Before I leave this chapter, I'd like to discuss a Mac OS X feature that's been around since the days of Mac OS 9: the keychain. Your account keychain stores all the username/password combinations for Web sites, file servers, File Transfer Protocol (FTP) servers, and the like, allowing you to simply waltz in and start using the service (whatever it is). Sounds handy, doesn't it? And it can be, but you'd better watch your step.

I will be perfectly honest here: I **hate** account keychains. With a passion, mind you. As a consultant, Webmaster, and the SYSOP (an ancient Bulletin Board Service acronym meaning *System Operator*) of an Internet-based online system, I know what a hassle it is for users to remember separate passwords, and I feel that pain. However, three *massively* big problems are inherent with using keychains:

**Book II
Chapter 5**

Setting Up
Multi-User
Accounts

+ **Anyone can log on as you:** If your keychain is unlocked, which happens automatically when you log in, all someone has to do is sit at your desk, visit a site or connect with a server, and *bam!* They're on. As *you.* Think about that. And then think how many times you get up from your desk, just for a second, to grab another Diet Coke or a doughnut.

+ **You'll forget your passwords:** If the keychain file is corrupted — and it can happen — your passwords have gone to Detroit without you. Either you've got them on paper hidden somewhere, they're on your recent backup, or it's time to change your online persona.

+ **Keychains need yet another stinkin' password:** Yep, that's right — your keychain can be locked (either manually or, with the right settings, automatically), and you have to remember yet another password/passphrase to unlock your keychain. "When, oh when will the madness end?"

From a security standpoint, keychains should be **completely off-limits** for anyone who's interested in maintaining a well locked-down machine. After all, most folks can completely take care of all their Internet and network connections with a handful of passwords, and that's no big deal for anyone to remember.

However, if you're the only person using your Mac and it resides in your home — personally, I'd prefer a bank vault — and you absolutely must use keychains, you can display them all for the current account from the Keychain Access application (see Figure 5-8), conveniently located in Utilities within your Applications folder. Click the Attributes tab and then click an item in the keychain list to display or edit all its information.

Heck, just think about what I just wrote — anyone can display and *edit* server and site information just by launching this application! That includes your nephew Damien — you know, the one that considers himself the hacker extraordinaire.

Figure 5-8: Take my advice — stay away from the allure of keychains.

Click the Access Control tab to display the settings that you see in Figure 5-9, one of which I strongly recommend. To minimize the damage that someone can do with your keychain, you can enable the Confirm before Allowing Access radio button. Of course, you're probably thinking, "Well, Mark, that pretty much eliminates the purpose of quick, convenient access without passwords, doesn't it?" Yes, indeed it does, but at least your online identity is somewhat safeguarded.

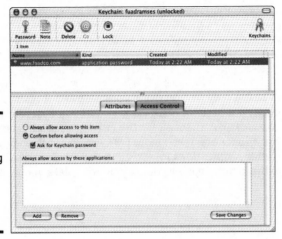

Figure 5-9: I admit that safeguarding a keychain rather dilutes its usefulness.

Click the Password toolbar button to add a new password. Type a name for the item, the username that you typically type to gain access, and the password for that server or site. Then click Add and cross your fingers.

To create a new keychain, choose File➪New➪New Keychain. Mac OS X prompts you for the filename for your new keychain file, as shown in Figure 5-10. In the Keychain dialog that appears, enter a catchy name in the Save As text box. By default, the keychain file is created in the Keychain folder — a good idea — but if you'd like to store it elsewhere, click the down-arrow button next to the Where list box and navigate to the desired folder. When you're ready, click the Create button. Now you need to enter yet another password, type it again to verify it, and click OK.

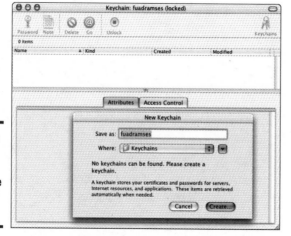

Figure 5-10:
Create a
brand new,
ultra-secure
keychain.
Right.

To lock or unlock a keychain — which, by the way, forces you to enter the password/passphrase that you use when you create the keychain — select the desired keychain in the list (refer to Figure 5-8) and then click the lock icon on the toolbar.

You may be saying to yourself, "Geez, this guy is more than a little paranoid." And yes, dear reader, I suppose that I am. But then again, who's been uploading all those questionable images and MP3 files to the company server . . . using your account?

Chapter 6: Sharing Documents for Fun and Profit

In This Chapter

✔ Comparing network sharing with multi-user sharing

✔ Setting and changing permissions

✔ Sharing documents in Microsoft Office v. X

✔ Sharing documents in AppleWorks

*N*ow here's a topic that any Mac OS X power-user can sink fangs into — the idea that a document on a multi-user system can be *everyone's* property, allowing anyone in your family, workgroup, or highly-competitive mob to make whatever changes are necessary, whenever they like.

Of course, potential pitfalls lurk — even in the Apple world, there's no such thing as an operating system that's both powerful and perfectly simple. However, I think you'll find that the folks from Cupertino have done just about as well as can be expected and that the settings that you use to share documents are fairly easy to understand and use.

Prepare to share!

Sharing over a Network versus Sharing on a Single Mac

First, allow me to clear up what I've found to be a common misconception by using another of Mark's Maxims:

Sharing documents on a single computer is fundamentally different from the file sharing that you've used on a network.™

True, multiple users can share a document over a network, which is a topic that you'll find covered in Book V. But although the results are the same, the way that you share that same document on a single machine betwixt multiple users is a completely different turn of the screw. In this section, I discuss the factoids behind the matter.

No network is required

Although reiterating that no network is required is seemingly the most obvious of statements, many otherwise knowledgeable Mac OS X power-users seem to forget that sharing a document over a network requires an active network connection. Unless you physically copy the document to your hard drive — which defeats the purpose of document sharing — any loss of network connectivity or any problem with your network account will result in a brick wall and a brightly painted sign reading, "No luck, Jack." (Or perhaps it's flashing neon.)

On the other hand, a document shared on a multi-user Mac in the home or classroom is available whenever you need it. As long as the file is located in the Shared folder, the file privileges are set correctly, and you know the password (if one is used), then — as they say on *Star Trek* — "You have the conn" whether your network connection is active or not.

Relying on a guaranteed lock

Sharing documents over a network can get a tad hairy when multiple users open and edit the document simultaneously. Applications such as Office v. X and AppleWorks have methods of locking the document (giving one person exclusive access) when someone opens it or saves it. However, you always face the possibility that what you're seeing in a shared network document is not exactly what's in the document at that moment.

A multi-user system doesn't need such exquisite complexity. You're the one sitting at the keyboard, and you have control: This is what network administrators call a *guaranteed lock* on that document file. Refreshing, isn't it?

Most places are off-limits

Network users are often confident that they can blithely copy and move a document from one place to another with the greatest of ease, and that's true. Most shared network documents created by an application — such as a project outline created in Word, for example — carry their own sharing information and document settings internally. Thus, you can move that same file to another folder on your hard drive, and the rest of the network team can still open it. (Um, if they have the network rights to access the new folder, of course.)

This isn't the case when it comes to multi-user documents. As you can read in Chapters 4 and 5 of this mini-book, Mac OS X places a rather tight fence around a Standard-level user, allowing that person to access only the contents of certain folders. In this case, your document must be placed in the Shared folder for every Standard-level user to be able to open it. If everyone using the document has Administrator access, you can then store the file in other spots on your system; as long as the permissions are set, you're set.

Permissions: Law Enforcement for Your Files

Files are shared in Mac OS X according to a set of rules called *permissions,* the *ownership* of the file (typically the person who saved the document the first time), and an access level specified as a *group.* The combination of privileges, ownership, and group determines who can do what with the file.

You're automatically granted ownership of your Home folder and everything it contains as well as any files or folders that you store in the Shared folder or another user's Public folder.

Three possible actions are allowed through permissions:

+ **Read only:** This action allows the user to open and read the file, which includes copying it to another location.

+ **Read & Write:** This permission grants full access to the file, including opening, reading, editing, saving, and deleting. Read & Write permission also allows the user to copy or move the file to another location.

+ **No access:** This is just what it sounds like — the user can't open the file, copy it, or move it.

No matter what permissions you've set, only the System Administrator (or Root user) can copy items into another user's Home folder. Take my word on this one: Simply consider that this can't be done. (Trust me on this.) Read all about the perils of enabling the System Administrator account in Chapter 4 of this mini-book.

These permissions are set in the Info dialog for a file or folder. If you're setting the permissions for a folder, you can also elect to apply those same settings to all the enclosed items within the folder.

To set permissions, follow these steps:

1. **Click the item to select it, press ⌘+I (or choose Finder⇨File) and then choose the Get Info menu item.**

Mac OS X displays an Info dialog like you see in Figure 6-1.

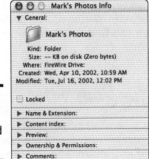

Figure 6-1:
The
compressed
Info dialog.

2. **Click the right arrow next to the Ownership & Permissions heading to expand it, as shown in Figure 6-2.**

   Because I've selected a folder, the Apply to Enclosed Items button appears at the bottom of the section.

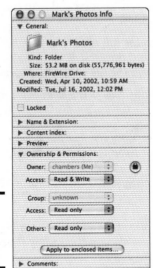

Figure 6-2:
The
expanded
Info dialog.

3. **If you're the file's owner, you can click the lock icon to change the owner.**

   Typically, the Owner drop-down list box is disabled.

   The drop-down list box displays all the users with accounts on this machine, as well as some less savory choices such as *nobody, system,* and *unknown.* Don't choose any of these.

Perhaps I should be a little less tactful here: *Never* choose an owner other than yourself or another recognized Standard-level user — you can potentially prevent yourself from accessing the file in the future!

4. **The first Access drop-down list box determines the access level for the file's Owner.**

   This will likely be set to Read & Write, and it's a good idea to leave it alone. If you're the file's Owner, you're likely not a security risk.

5. **Assign permissions for an entire group — this is a good idea for limiting specific files and folders to only Administrator access.**

   Choose the group from the Group drop-down list and select the desired access permission from the second Access drop-down list box. If you have only Administrator accounts, the drop-down list is disabled.

6. **Set the permission for the Others drop-down list (otherwise known as "I'm going to lump everything else into this category").**

   If a user isn't the Owner of an item and doesn't fit into any group that you've selected, this access permission setting for this file applies to that user.

7. **If you're setting permissions for a folder, Mac OS X can automatically change the permissions for all the items contained in the folder to the same settings. Click the Apply to Enclosed Items button, and Mac OS X displays the confirmation dialog that you see in Figure 6-3.**

   Generally, it's a good idea not to override the permissions for all the items in a folder, so click the Apply to Enclosed Items button only when necessary.

**Book II
Chapter 6**

Sharing Documents for Fun and Profit

Figure 6-3:
Mac OS X
wants to
make sure
you're not
going
permission-
crazy.

Are you sure you want to apply the selected owner, group, and permissions to all the enclosed items?

You cannot undo this.

Cancel   OK

8. **Click OK to proceed or click Cancel to abort the process.**

9. **After all the permissions are correct, click the Close button to save your changes and return to your friendly Finder.**

Permission and Sharing Do's and Don'ts

After you get the basics of sharing files and assigning permissions under your belt, you need to master when to change permissions and why you should (and shouldn't) modify them. Follow these common-sense guidelines when saving documents, assigning permissions, and choosing access levels:

✦ ***Do* use your Shared folder.** The Shared folder is the center of proper document sharing. I know there's a strong urge to create a new document in your Home folder, but you're just making more work for yourself because you'll end up copying that document from your Home folder to the Shared folder. Instead of an extra step, store a document that's intended to be shared in the Shared folder — where it belongs in the first place.

✦ ***Don't* assign permissions just to protect a file from deletion.** Remember, if all you need to do is prevent anyone (including yourself) from deleting an item, you don't need to go to all the trouble of changing permissions. Instead, just display the Info dialog for the item and select the Locked check box to enable it, which prevents the item from being deleted from the Trash until the Lock status is disabled.

✦ ***Do* review the contents of a folder before changing permissions for enclosed items.** That confirmation dialog doesn't appear just for kicks. For example, if you set a highly sensitive private document with permissions of No Access for everyone but yourself and then you apply less-restrictive permissions globally to the folder that contains the document, you've just removed the No Access permissions, and anyone can open your dirty laundry. (Ouch.) Therefore, make sure that you open the folder and double-check its contents first before applying global permissions to the items it contains.

✦ ***Don't* change permissions in the Applications or Utilities folders.** If you have Administrator-level access, you can actually change the permissions for important applications like Mail, Address Book, iTunes, and Internet Explorer, as well as their support files. This spells havoc for all users assigned to the Standard-access level. Be polite and leave the permissions for these files alone.

✦ ***Definitely don't* change System ownership.** Mac OS X is stable and reliable. Part of that stability comes from the protected state of the System folder, as well as a number of other folders on your hard drive. As you can see in Figure 6-4, displaying the Info dialog for the System folder shows that the Owner is set to *system,* and the Group is set to *wheel* (a term from the UNIX world that encompasses all administrator accounts).

Do not change any permissions for any files owned by the System unless specifically told to do so by an Apple support technician. *Do not* monkey with System-owned items.

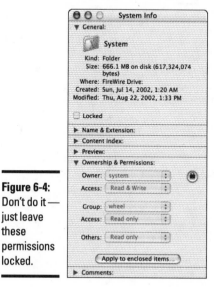

Figure 6-4:
Don't do it —
just leave
these
permissions
locked.

Sharing Stuff in Office v. X

Many Mac OS X applications offer their own built-in document-sharing features. For example, Microsoft Office v. X includes both file-level and document-sharing features. Because Office v. X is the most popular productivity suite available for Mac OS X, I discuss these commands in this final section.

Document-sharing features

You'll find a number of commands that help multiple users keep track of changes that have been made in a shared Office document. Probably the most familiar is the Word revision tracking features (heavily used during the development of this book), but there are others as well:

✦ **Revision marks:** If several users edit a document, how can you tell who did what? By using *revision marks,* which apply different colors to changes made by different editors, those additions and deletions can be accepted or rejected individually at a later date. If Johnson in Marketing adds incorrect material, you can easily remove just his changes. In a worst-case scenario, you can actually reject all changes and return the document to its pristine condition. Figure 6-5 illustrates revision marks in action.

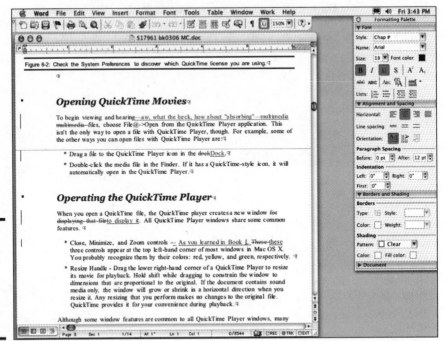

Figure 6-5:
Hey, who's been tracking revisions in my document?

✦ **Compare Documents:** Using this feature allows you to compare a revised document with the original (if, of course, you still have the original file handy). I use Compare Documents only if revision marks weren't turned on before editing began.

✦ **Comments:** Editors can also converse within a document by using embedded Comments. These don't change the contents of the Word file like revision marks do but store commentary and notes in a behind-the-scenes kind of way. (Think of a Mac OS X Stickie that appears within a document.) Again, the author of each comment is listed, allowing for (sometimes heated) communication within the body of a document. Figure 6-6 illustrates the Comments pane in a Word document (see the lower portion of the document).

✦ **Highlighting:** You've heard the old joke about the secretary who. . . . Well, anyway, a traditional highlighter marker is pretty useless on a computer monitor (leaving a nasty mess for the next user to clean), but Word allows multiple highlighting colors for identifying text. (And for the occasional practical joke — nothing like adding eight different highlighting colors to that important proposal. Just make sure your résumé is up-to-date.)

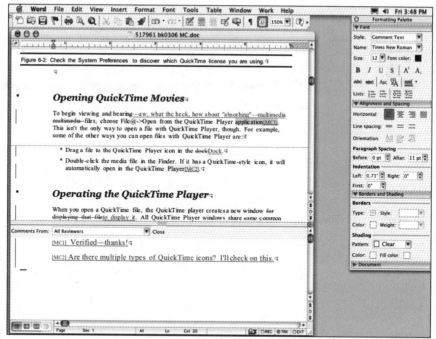

Figure 6-6:
Commentary
is cheap
in Word.

File-level sharing features

Along with the document-level sharing commands, you'll also find that
Office v. X applications also offer sharing features that control access to the
document file itself.

Password protection

You can add password protection to any Office v. X document. Follow these
steps with the document created within Word, Excel, or PowerPoint:

1. **Choose File➪Save As.**

2. **In the Save As dialog that appears, click Options to display the Save
    Preferences panel that you see in Figure 6-7.**

3. **To password-protect the document, enter a password in the Password
    to Open field.**

    This password must be provided when opening the document.

TIP

If you like, you can enter another password in the Password to Modify field. This second password would then also be required to modify the document.

Both passwords are case-sensitive.

4. Click OK to save the preference changes and return to your document.

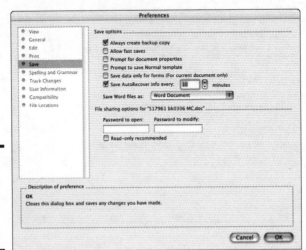

Figure 6-7:
Office v. X
offers two
types of
document
passwords.

Versions

If you like, Word can save multiple versions of a document in a single file. Each version is identified by the date and time it was saved, the user who saved it, and an additional comments line. Choose File⇨Versions to display the Versions dialog that you see in Figure 6-8. Note that you can choose to automatically save a new version of the document whenever it's closed. To save a new version immediately, click the Save Now button.

Figure 6-8:
Different
users can
create
different
versions of
the same
shared
document.

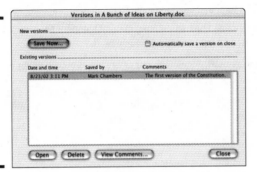

Document protection

Figure 6-9 illustrates the Protect Document dialog in Word, where you can effectively write-protect certain elements. In this Office application, you can protect revision marks, comments, and sections of a document containing forms. A password can be added if desired. To display the Protect Document dialog, click Tools in any of the Office v. X applications and choose Protect Document from the drop-down list that appears.

Figure 6-9:
Set certain elements of a Word document as off-limits.

Password Protection in AppleWorks

As with Office v. X, you can set a password to prevent other users from opening an AppleWorks document. With the document loaded in AppleWorks version 6, follow these steps:

1. **Choose File➪Properties to display the Document Properties dialog shown in Figure 6-10.**

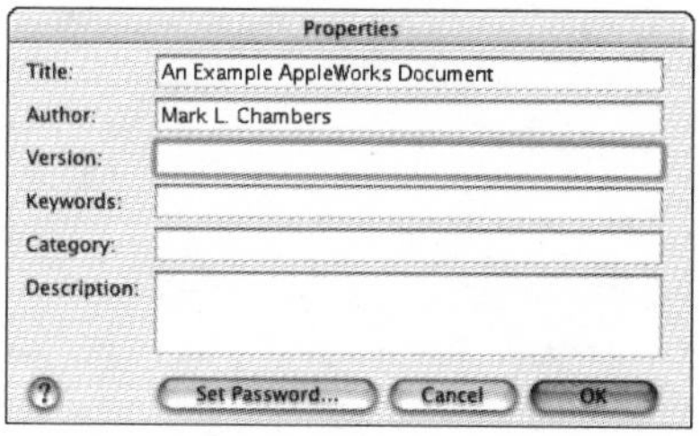

Figure 6-10:
Password-protect an AppleWorks document.

Properties
Title: An Example AppleWorks Document
Author: Mark L. Chambers
Version:
Keywords:
Category:
Description:

Set Password...   Cancel   OK

2. **Click the Set Password button and type the password in the Password box.**

3. **AppleWorks displays a verification box in which you need to type the password again.**

   These document passwords are case-sensitive!

4. **Click OK to save the password and then click OK to return to your document.**

You can edit or remove the password by repeating this process. Use a blank password to remove password protection.

Book III

The Digital Hub

JERRY AND LYLE ATTEMPT TO LOAD THE NEWEST VERSION OF "TOAST", CD BURNING SOFTWARE

©RICHTENNANT

OK, I got the Sunbeam fire-wired to the iMac. Try putting the CD in the slot again.

Contents at a Glance

Chapter 1: The World According to Apple 241

Chapter 2: Jamming with iTunes and iPod 249

Chapter 3: Focusing on iPhoto 269

Chapter 4: Making Magic with iMovie 285

Chapter 5: Burn Those DVDs! Using iDVD 2 307

Chapter 6: No, It's Not Called "iQuickTime" 323

Chapter 7: Turning Your Mac into a DVD Theater 339

Chapter 1: The World According to Apple

In This Chapter

✔ **Doing things the hub way**

✔ **Digitizing your life**

✔ **Making your digital devices work together**

After years of empty promises of professional-quality media features for home and school — most of them coming from that Gates fellow in Redmond — Apple has taken on the challenge and formulated a recipe for digital success.

By using tightly integrated hardware and software, Apple gives you the ability to easily organize your work with digital tools such as iPod and iTunes. That same software also provides fantastic editing capabilities. Finally (and this is very important) — to paraphrase Will Smith in the movie *Men in Black*, "Apple makes these programs look *good*."

First, Sliced Bread . . . and Now the Digital Hub

In today's overloaded world of personal electronic devices, people can juggle as many as five or six electronic wonders. Each device typically comes with its own software, power adapter, and connectors to the outside world. Although managing one or two devices isn't terribly difficult, as the number of devices increases, so do the headaches. When you have a half-dozen cables, power adapters, and software to cart around, the digital life can become pretty bleak. (And quite heavy.)

To combat this confusion, Apple came up with the idea of a *digital hub,* whereby your Macintosh acts as the center of an array of electronic devices. By using standardized cables, power requirements, and built-in software, the Macintosh — along with its operating system, Mac OS X — goes a long way toward simplifying your interaction with all the electronic gadgets that you use.

Given the hub terminology, think of the digital hub as a wagon wheel. (See Figure 1-1.) At the center of the wheel is your Macintosh. At the end of each spoke is a digital device. Throughout the rest of Book III, I give you the skinny on each device, but this chapter gives you the overview and tells you how they all work together.

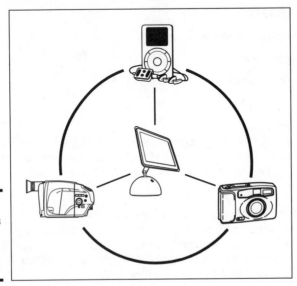

Figure 1-1: Mac OS X is the center of your digital hub.

What Does Digital Mean, Anyway?

Computers are handy machines. They can process information very quickly and never get bored when asked to do the same task millions of times. The problem is that despite their propensity for reliability and speed, they aren't so hot in the intuition department. You have to tell them how to do everything. They know only one thing — numbers — although they do know numbers very well.

In fact, binary (the language of computers) has only two values — one and zero, which represent *on* and *off,* respectively. (Think of a light switch that toggles: The earliest computers were simply banks of switches.) To work with a computer in meaningful ways, you have to describe everything to a computer using numbers — or, if you prefer, *digits*.

By describing audio in numerical digits, you suddenly have something that a computer can work with. Toss a computer as many numbers as you want, and it can handle it. The scientists who figured this out sought to convert anything that they could get their hands on into digits. This resulted in some interesting technologies that you surely recognize:

✦ **Audio CDs:** The music is represented as numbers and stored on a plastic disc.

✦ **Digital video:** Images and sound are stored together on your hard drive or a DVD as one really, *really* long string of numbers.

✦ **Digital fingerprints (no pun intended):** Your fingerprint is converted into numerical data, which a computer can use to compare against fingerprint data from other people.

✦ **Automated telephone operators:** When you call a phone operator these days, you often aren't speaking to a real person. Rather, the computer on the other end of the line converts your voice into digits, which it uses to interpret your words. (At other times, I think I'm talking to a real person, but it's hard to tell.)

What Can I Digitize?

As you've probably guessed by now, practically anything can be digitized. As long as you can represent some data as numbers, you can digitize that data. Whether it's photographs, video, or audio, your Mac is adept at digitizing data and processing it.

Photographic images

Perhaps the most popular of digital devices, the digital camera has transformed photography forever. By using sophisticated electronics, digital cameras convert the image that you see through the camera viewfinder into an image made purely of numbers.

After this numeric information is transferred to your Macintosh, your computer can cut, twist, fade, label, and paint your digital images. Because numbers are the only materials involved, you won't need scissors, paint, or adhesive tape to edit images. Your Macintosh does it all by manipulating those numbers. It cuts down on the messy art supplies and gives you the comfort of being able to go back in time — something anyone who's not so handy with scissors can appreciate.

Music

As I mention earlier in this chapter, audio CDs are one application of music represented as digital data. The physical CD is just a piece of plastic with a metal coating, but you don't even truly need that medium. Your Macintosh can digitize audio for storage on your hard drive, too, which brings up another important point. Not only is digital information palatable to a computer, but it's also very portable. You can store it on any number of storage devices, such as an iPod or an external FireWire drive.

Video

When you photograph a scene multiple times per second and then replay the sequence, you get (tah-dah!) moving pictures. In the analog (as opposed to digital) world, this would be a strip of celluloid film. In the digital world, such a sequence is called *video*. And because video is simply a string of single photographs, video is also something that you can easily digitize. Most often this happens inside your camera. Later you can transfer that data to your Macintosh to further manipulate it: You can edit it, add transitions, text, and other effects.

DVD

Like a CD-ROM or a hard drive, a *DVD* is simply a storage container for digital data. Although you can use it to save many different kinds of data, its most common use is for presenting video content. The Macintosh digital hub can produce DVDs using any digital information that you give it.

The Software That Drives the Hub

At the heart of your digital hub is the Macintosh. To use and manipulate all the data that arrive at your hub (that is, your Macintosh), your computer needs software. *Software* gives your computer the brains to know what to do with the information that you send it. Fortunately, Apple has fashioned some of the most attractive and easy-to-use software to help you manipulate and manage your digital lifestyle. The list of software that belongs to the digital hub includes

+ **iPhoto:** Use iPhoto to download, manipulate, and organize your favorite digital photographs.

+ **iTunes:** As the Apple slogan says, "Rip, Mix, Burn." iTunes offers the ability to create and manage your music collection. It can even burn CDs!

+ **iMovie:** Every film director needs a movie-editing suite. iMovie gives you the chance to set up Hollywood in your living room with outstanding results.

+ **iDVD:** As home video moves toward the digital realm, iDVD becomes an essential tool for authoring your own DVD media. Home movies will never be the same.

+ **iCal:** To help keep your hectic digital lifestyle in order, iCal offers complete calendar features. Besides tracking your dates and appointments on your Mac, you can publish calendars on the Web or share them with different parts of the digital hub.

✦ **iSync:** With so many digital devices at your disposal, it gets hard to keep them all straight. *iSync* is software for automatically synchronizing contact and calendar information between cell phones, your personal digital assistant (PDA), an iPod, the Mac OS X Address Book, and iCal.

iPhoto

What good is a camera without a photo album? *iPhoto,* Apple's photography software, serves as a digital photo album. Check out the cool contact sheet view in Figure 1-2. Use it to help you arrange and manage your digital photos. Beyond its functions as a photo album, iPhoto also gives you the ability to touch-up your images through cropping, scaling, rotating, and red-eye reduction (photographically speaking, not morning-after speaking).

Besides offering editing features, iPhoto also seamlessly integrates with your digital camera. Simply plug in the camera to your Mac's USB port, and iPhoto knows it's there. Need to transfer photos from the camera to your photo album? iPhoto can do that, too.

Figure 1-2: Use iPhoto to edit and manage your digital photo albums.

Book III
Chapter 1

The World According to Apple

When you complete a collection of photographs that you find interesting, use iPhoto to help you publish them on the Internet or even to create your very own coffee-table book. And for those of you who still want that nifty wallet print to show off at work or a poster to hang on your wall, you can print them with your own printer or order them online through iPhoto. Orders made with iPhoto show up in your mailbox a few days later.

iTunes

To help you wrangle your enormous music collection, Apple offers iTunes (see Figure 1-3). For starters, iTunes is a sophisticated audio player for all your digital audio files. But iTunes is also handy for converting audio tracks from audio CDs to a number of popular digital audio file formats, such as MP3 and AIFF. After you import or convert your music into computer files, iTunes helps you manage and maintain your music collection.

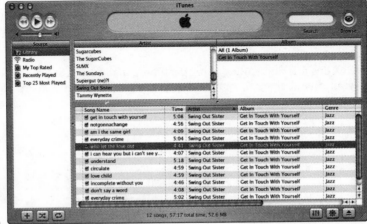

Figure 1-3: Use iTunes to create, organize, and play your favorite music.

Like other parts of the digital hub, iTunes can interface with an iPod. The *iPod* is a versatile, lightweight audio player. It has enough capacity to store your entire collection of music but it's small enough to fit into your back pocket. With iTunes, you can instantly exchange songs between your Macintosh and your iPod. You can also use iTunes to create audio and MP3 CDs for playback elsewhere or for back-up storage. (For the lowdown on iPod, peruse Book III, Chapter 2.)

iMovie

You needn't restrict yourself to still images: Hook up your digital camcorder to your Mac as well. Use *iMovie,* an easy-to-use video editing application, to create and edit digital movies. With features such as transitions, sound effects, and video effects, iMovie turns your home movies into professional productions that you'll be proud to share with friends and family. Finally, you can have a home movie night without putting everyone to sleep — although getting the baby in Figure 1-4 to sleep through the night would be a neat trick.

iDVD

Of course, after you create a video masterpiece (or at least potential blackmail material, in the case of the Figure 1-4), you probably want to save it on a DVD disc for preservation and future viewing. To help you in your endeavors, use iDVD to create — or, as video professionals call it, *author* — DVD movies. With the preset templates, iDVD will have you cranking out stunning DVDs with interactive menus in no time, ready to use with any DVD player.

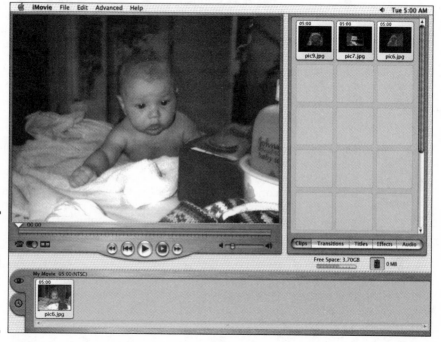

Figure 1-4: iMovie can turn you into Hollywood movie director material.

Can I Use All This Stuff at Once?

What makes the digital hub idea even juicier is that it's an *interoperable* model. "Whoa, Mark, inter-*what?*" In plain English, the digital hub permits you to use digital media from one part of the hub with another part of the hub. Thus, the individual parts of the digital hub can work together to complement each other. To illustrate, consider some digital sharing scenarios:

✦ You shoot a great photograph of your kids. It's so great, in fact, that you'd like to use it as the title page of your family's home movie. With the digital hub, you can use that same photograph in iMovie to create your home flick. When you're done with that, transfer the whole thing to a DVD by using iDVD, and your masterpiece is safe for years of viewing. One image just worked its way through three parts of the digital hub.

✦ Your band just recorded a hit song for its latest album. To get the song into your Mac, you use iTunes to convert the audio CD to MP3 format. From there, you add the song to the soundtrack of the music video that you're creating with iMovie. Then you burn the finished project to DVD to show prospective agents. Again, one piece of media has traveled through three parts of the digital hub!

✦ Your band becomes popular and starts to play some impressive gigs. To document your band's rise to stardom, your friend films a concert with a DV camcorder. You use iMovie to transfer the video to your Macintosh and create clips of your favorite performances of the concert. After that, it's a simple matter to author to DVD with iDVD, extract the audio from the video for use as an MP3, and grab an image from the video for a band scrapbook that you're creating with iPhoto. Now you've attained honest-to-goodness digital hub nirvana. You've traversed the entire hub, easily sharing the media along the way.

Lest I forget, I should mention the other advantage of the digital hub: The media that you swap between all your *iApplications* remains in digital form, so it *never loses quality!* In the previous example of shooting a concert, for instance, that concert footage never lost quality while it was being transferred to DVD, converted to MP3, or pasted into your iPhoto album. Unlike archaic VHS tape, you don't have to worry about whether your source is second-generation — and you can forget degradation and that silly tracking control.

Chapter 2: Jamming with iTunes and iPod

In This Chapter

✔ Playing music with your Mac

✔ Arranging and organizing your music collection

✔ Tuning into the world with Internet radio

✔ Creating eye candy with the Visualizer

Throw out the boombox, ditch the stereo, and toss the CD player. Every installation of Mac OS X comes with the newest gadget in town — a great application called *iTunes*. With it, you can listen to your favorite songs, organize your music collection, listen to radio stations from around the world, burn CDs, and much more! iTunes has so many features that you'll soon find yourself wondering why you even own a stereo at all. In no time, you'll be pondering how much new speakers with a subwoofer will cost for your Mac.

In this chapter, I show you how to play audio CDs and Internet downloads, but that's just the beginning. I show you how to use iTunes' Library to get one-click access to any song in your collection. I even show you how to tune into Internet radio, burn audio CDs (if you have the necessary hardware), and how to make your iTunes interface look just as good as your music sounds.

What Can I Play on iTunes?

Simply put, *iTunes* is an audio player; it plays audio files. These files can be in any of many different formats. Some of the more common audio formats that iTunes supports are

✦ **MP3:** The small size of MP3 files has made it popular for file trading on the Internet. You can reduce MP3 files to a ridiculously small size (at the expense of audio fidelity), but a typical CD-quality three-minute pop song in MP3 format has a size of 3–5MB.

✦ **AIFF:** The standard Macintosh audio format produces sound of the highest quality. The high quality, however, also means that the files are typically large. A typical pop song in AIFF format has a size of 30–50MB.

✦ **WAV:** Not to be outdone, Microsoft created its own audio file format (WAVE) that works much like AIFF. It can reproduce sound at higher quality than MP3, but the file sizes are large, like AIFF.

✦ **CD Audio:** iTunes can play audio CDs. Because you don't usually store CD audio anywhere but on an audio CD, file size isn't a concern.

Playing an Audio CD

Playing an audio CD in iTunes is simple. Just insert the CD in your computer's disk tray, close the tray, start iTunes by clicking its icon in the Dock, and click the Play button. The iTunes interface resembles that of a traditional cassette or CD player. The main playback controls of the iTunes are Play, Previous Song, Next Song, and the Volume Slider, as shown in Figure 2-1.

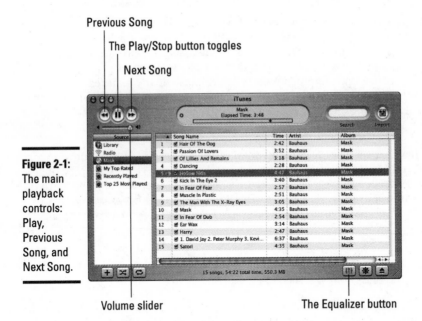

Previous Song

The Play/Stop button toggles

Next Song

Figure 2-1:
The main playback controls:
Play, Previous Song, and Next Song.

Volume slider

The Equalizer button

Click the Play button to begin listening to a song. While a song is playing, the Play button toggles to a Stop button. As you might imagine, clicking that button again stops the music. If you don't feel like messing around with a mouse, you can always use the keyboard. The space bar acts as the Play and Stop buttons. Press the space bar to begin playback; press it again to stop.

Click the Next Song button to advance to the next song on the CD. The Previous Song button works like the Next Song button, but with a slight twist: If a song is currently playing and you click the Previous Song button, iTunes will first return to the beginning of the current song (just like an audio CD player). To advance to the previous song, click the Previous Song button a second time. To change the volume of your music, click and drag the volume slider.

Your mother was right! Listening to loud music can and will damage your hearing, especially considering that most computer speaker systems are much closer to your ears than a typical stereo. Move the volume slider a little to the left to increase your chances of being able to listen to music for years to come.

Like other Macintosh applications, you can control much of iTunes with the keyboard. Table 2-1 lists some of the more common iTunes keyboard shortcuts.

Table 2-1	Common iTunes Keyboard Shortcuts
Press This Key Combination	*To Do This*
Space bar	Play the currently selected song if iTunes is idle.
Space bar	Stop the music if a song is playing.
Right-arrow key (→)	Advance to the next song.
Left-arrow key (←)	Go back to the beginning of a song. Press a second time to return to the previous song.
⌘+up-arrow key (↑)	Increase the volume of the music.
⌘+down-arrow key (↓)	Decrease the volume of the music.
⌘+Option+down-arrow key (↓)	Mute the audio if any is playing. Press again to play the audio.

Playing an Audio File

In addition to playing audio CDs, iTunes can also play the audio files that you download from the Internet or obtain from other sources in the WAV, AIFF, and MP3 file formats. The process of playing an audio file is just slightly more complicated than playing a CD. After downloading or saving your audio files to your Mac, open the Finder and navigate to wherever you stored the files. After you find them, simply drag them from the Finder into the iTunes application. The added files appear in the iTunes Library. If you happened to drop the file somewhere in the Source List, iTunes adds it to that particular Playlist as well as the main Library. Think of the Library as a master list of your music. To view the Library, select it in the left-hand column of the iTunes player, as shown in Figure 2-2.

Select Library in the Source pane.

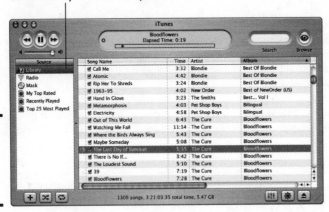

Figure 2-2:
The Library keeps track of all your audio files.

To play a song, just double-click it in the Library. Alternatively, you can use the playback controls (Play, Previous Song, Next Song) that I discuss earlier in this chapter.

Note that the Source list of iTunes lists two possible sources for music: the Library, which I talk about in this section, and iTunes Radio. Radio enables you to listen to Internet radio stations; more on that later in the section "iTunes Radio." When you insert an audio CD into your Mac, that CD also appears in the Source list.

Notice that the Library lists information for each song that you add to it, such as

✦ **Song:** The name of the song

✦ **Time:** The length of the song

✦ **Artist:** The artist who performs the song

✦ **Album:** The album on which the song appears

If some of the songs that you're adding don't display anything for the title, album, or artist information, don't panic; most MP3 files have embedded data that iTunes can read. If a song doesn't include any data, you can always add the information to these fields manually. I show you how later in the section "Setting or changing the song information manually."

Clicking any of the column headings in the Library causes iTunes to reorder the Library according to that category. For example, clicking on the Song column heading will alphabetize your Library by song title.

Browsing the Library

After you add a few dozen songs to iTunes, viewing the Library can become a task. Although a master list is nice for some purposes, it becomes cumbersome if the list is very long. To help out, iTunes can display your Library in another format, too. Besides one huge list, the Library also has a browsing mode. To view the Library in browsing mode, click the Browse button in the upper right-hand corner of iTunes, as shown in Figure 2-3.

Click to browse.

Figure 2-3: Click Browse to view your Library in a more manageable form.

The Browse mode of iTunes displays your library in a compact fashion, organizing your tunes into three sections:

✦ Artist

✦ Album

✦ Songs

Selecting an artist from the Artist list causes iTunes to display that artist's albums in the Album list. Select an album from the Album list, and iTunes displays that album's songs in the bottom section of the Browse window.

Finding songs in your Library

After your collection of audio files grows large, you may have trouble remembering where that favorite song is. To help you out, iTunes has a built-in Search function. To find a song, type some text into the search field of the main iTunes interface. As you type, iTunes tries to find a selection that matches your search text. This will include matching artist, album, song title, and genre in the search results. For example, if you were to type "Electronic" into the field, iTunes might return results for the band named "Electronic" or other tunes that you classified as electronic in the Genre field. (The section "Know Your Songs" later in this chapter tells you how to classify your songs by genre, among other options.) Figure 2-4 shows the iTunes search function in action.

The Search field

Figure 2-4: Use the Search feature to locate your favorite music.

Removing old music from the Library

After you spend some time playing songs with iTunes, you may decide that you didn't really want to add forty different versions of "Louie, Louie" to your Library. To remove a song from the Library, click the song to select it and then press the Delete key on your keyboard.

You can also remove a song from the Library by dragging it to the Trash can in your Dock. Cool!

Removing a song from your Library only removes it from the iTunes Library; it doesn't delete it from the Finder (if it is located anywhere else besides the iTunes music folder). If you mistakenly remove a song that you meant to keep, just drag it back into iTunes from the Finder. If, on the other hand, you delete a song from the Library that is only located in the iTunes music folder, iTunes will prompt you to make sure that you really want to move the file to the Trash.

Keeping Slim Whitman and Slim Shady Apart: Organizing with Playlists

The iTunes Library is a handy feature, but can soon become unruly. Each Library can hold up to 32,000 songs: If your Library grows anywhere near that large, finding all your Paul Simon songs is not a fun task. Furthermore, with the Library, you're stuck playing songs in the order that iTunes lists them.

To help you organize your music into groups, use the iTunes Playlist feature. A *Playlist* is a collection of some of your favorite songs from the Library. You can create as many Playlists as you want, and each Playlist can contain any numbers of songs. Whereas the Library lists all available songs, a Playlist displays only the songs that you add to it. Further, any changes that you make to a Playlist only affect that Playlist. The Library remains intact no matter what operations you perform on a Playlist.

To create a Playlist, you can do any of the following:

✦ Select File⇨New Playlist.

✦ Press ⌘+N.

✦ Click the New Playlist button in the iTunes window (the plus sign button in the lower-left corner). Figure 2-5 shows a newly created Playlist (My Favorite Tunes), before any tunes have been added.

All Playlists appear in the Source List. To help organize your Playlists, name them. For example, suppose that you want to plan a party for your polka-loving friends. Instead of running to your computer after each song to change the music, you could create a polka-only Playlist. Select and play the Playlist at the beginning of the party and you won't have to worry about changing the music the whole night — you can polka 'til you pop. To load a Playlist, select it in the Source List. When you do, iTunes displays the songs for that Playlist.

The same song can appear in any number of Playlists. The songs in a Playlist are simply pointers to songs in the Library, not the songs themselves. Add and remove them at will to any Playlist, secure in the knowledge that the songs will remain safe in the Library. Removing a Playlist is simple: Select the Playlist and press Delete. Removing a Playlist does not actually delete all those songs from your Library.

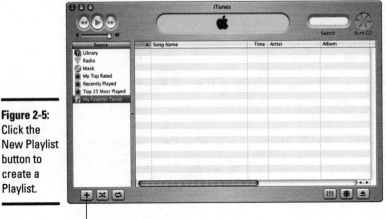

Figure 2-5:
Click the
New Playlist
button to
create a
Playlist.

Click to create a new Playlist.

Know Your Songs

Besides organizing your music into *Elvis* and *non-Elvis* Playlists, iTunes gives you the option to track your music at the song level. Each song that you add to the Library has a complete set of information associated with it. iTunes displays this information in the Song Information dialog with the following fields:

✦ **Song:** The name of the song

✦ **Artist:** The name of artist who performed the song

✦ **Album:** The album where the song appears

✦ **Year:** The year the artist recorded the song

✦ **Track Number:** The position of the song on the original album

✦ **Genre:** The classification of the song (such as rock, jazz, or pop)

Setting the song information automatically

Each song that you add to the iTunes Library may or may not have song information with it. If you add music from an audio CD, iTunes will connect to a server on the Internet and attempt to find the information for each song on the CD. If you download a song from the Internet, it often comes with some information embedded in the file already. The amount of included information depends on what the creator supplied. (And believe me, it's often misspelled as well — think *Leenard Skeenard.*) If you don't have an Internet connection, iTunes can't access the information and will display generic titles instead.

Setting or changing the song information manually

If iTunes can't find your CD in the online database or someone gives you an MP3 with incomplete or inaccurate information, you can change the information yourself. To view and change the information for a song, perform the following steps:

1. **Select the song in either the Library or a Playlist.**

2. **Press ⌘+I or choose File➪Get Info to bring up the Song Information dialog.**

3. **Edit the song's information on the Tags tab, as shown in Figure 2-6.**

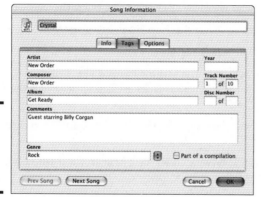

Figure 2-6: Press ⌘+I to alter a song's information.

Keep in mind that the more work you put into setting the information of the songs in your Library, the easier it is to browse and use iTunes. Incomplete song information can make it more difficult to find your songs in a hurry. If you prefer, you don't have to change all information about a song. It just makes life easier later if you do. Normally, you can get away with setting only a song's title, artist, and genre. The more information you put in, however, the more you can get out of it. iTunes tries to help by automatically retrieving known song information, but sometimes you have to roll up your sleeves and do a little work. The good news is that after you set a song's information, you don't have to reset it later.

Ripping Audio Files

You don't have to rely on Internet downloads to get audio files: You can create your own MP3, AIFF, and WAV files with iTunes. The process of converting audio files to different formats is called *ripping*. (Audiophiles with technical teeth also call this process *digital extraction,* but they're usually ignored at parties by the popular crowd.) Depending on what hardware or software you use, each has its own unique format preferences. For example, an iPod likes MP3 files, but your audio CDs are not in that format. Being able to convert files from one format to another is like having a personal translator in the digital world. You don't need to worry if you have the wrong format: You can simply convert it to the format you need. The most common type of ripping is to convert CD audio to MP3 format. To rip MP3s from an audio CD, follow these simple steps:

1. **Launch iTunes by clicking its icon in the Dock.**

   Alternatively, you can locate it in your Applications folder.

2. **Choose iTunes⇨Preferences.**

3. **In the Preferences window that appears, click the Import tab.**

4. **Select MP3 Encoder from the Import Using pop-up menu and click OK.**

5. **Load an audio CD into your Mac.**

   The CD title shows up in the iTunes Source list, which is on the left side of the iTunes interface. The CD track listing appears on the right side of the interface.

6. **Uncheck the check box of any song that you don't want to import from the CD.**

   All songs on the CD have a check box next to their title by default. Unmarked songs will not be imported.

   Notice that the Browse button changes to Import.

7. **After you select the songs that you want added to the Library, click the Import button.**

Tweaking the Audio for Your Ears

Besides the standard volume controls that I mention earlier in this chapter, iTunes offers a full equalizer. An *equalizer* permits you to alter the volume of various frequencies in your music. This can have the effect of boosting low sounds, lowering high sounds, or anything in between. Now you can customize the way your music sounds and adjust it to your liking.

To open the Equalizer (as shown in Figure 2-7), do one of the following:

✦ Select the Window⇨Equalizer menu.

✦ Press ⌘+2.

✦ Click the Equalizer button (refer to Figure 2-1).

Click to select a preset equalizer.

Figure 2-7:
The
Equalizer
window has
11 sliders to
help you
tweak your
audio.

The Equalizer window has an impressive array of 11 sliders. The leftmost slider is for setting the overall level of the Equalizer. The remaining sliders represent various frequencies that the human ear can perceive. Setting a slider to a position in the middle of its travel will cause that frequency to play back with no change. Move the slider above the midpoint to boost that frequency. Conversely, move the slider below the midpoint to reduce the volume of that frequency.

Continue adjusting the equalizer sliders until your music sounds the way that you like it. When you close the Equalizer window, iTunes will remember your settings until you change them again. If you prefer to leave frequencies to the experts, the iTunes Equalizer has several predefined settings to match most musical styles. Click the pop-up menu at the top of the Equalizer window to select a genre, as shown in Figure 2-8.

Figure 2-8:
Use the
iTunes
preset
equalizer
settings or
set them
yourself.

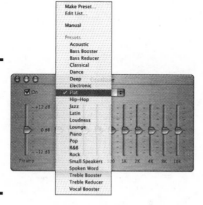

After you adjust the sound to your satisfaction, close the Equalizer window to return to the iTunes interface and jam to the custom sounds that fit your ear just right.

**Book III
Chapter 2**

**Jamming with
iTunes and iPod**

A New Kind of Radio Station

Besides playing back your favorite audio files, iTunes can also tune in Internet radio stations from around the globe. You can listen to any of a large number of preset stations, seek out lesser-known stations not recognized by iTunes, or even add your favorite stations to your Playlists. This section shows you how to do it all.

iTunes Radio

Although it's not a radio tuner in the strictest sense, iTunes Radio can locate virtual radio stations all over the world that send audio over the Internet. iTunes can track down hundreds of Internet radio stations in a variety of styles with only a few mouse clicks.

To begin listening to Internet radio with iTunes, click the Radio Station icon located directly beneath the Library icon in the Source list. The result is a list of more than 20 types of radio stations, organized by genre, as shown in Figure 2-9.

When you expand a Radio category by clicking its triangle, iTunes queries a tuning server and locates the name and address of dozens of radio stations for that category, as shown in Figure 2-10. Whether you like new wave, alternative, or rap, there's something here for everyone. The Radio also offers news, sports, and talk radio.

After iTunes fetches the names and descriptions of radio stations, double-click one that you would like to hear. iTunes immediately jumps into action, loads the station, and begins to play it. Which station you choose might depend on the kind of Internet connection you use.

Figure 2-9:
Radio displays radio stations in specific categories.

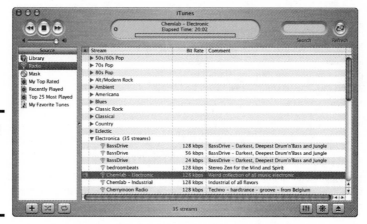

Book III
Chapter 2

Jamming with
iTunes and iPod

Figure 2-10:
Expand the
Radio
category to
view its
stations.

The numbers that appear next to the radio station names in the Radio indicate the amount of information that streams through your Internet connection: The larger the number, the faster your connection needs to be to receive it. For example, cable modem (a fast network connection for the home), DSL (an even faster connection for the home), and T1 (a super fast connection typically used by businesses) users can easily listen to the fastest streams, which typically rate at 128 Kbps. Telephone modem users will want to aim for a station that transmits in slower streams, such as 56 or 24 Kbps. As the stream rate increases, the quality of the sound you hear improves. Therefore, you should choose the fastest rate that your particular connection can handle for the best-sounding audio.

Tuning in your own stations

Although iTunes offers you a large list of popular radio stations on the Web, it's by no means comprehensive. Eventually, you might run across a radio station that you'd like to hear, but it's not listed in iTunes. Luckily, iTunes permits you to listen to other stations, too.

To listen to a radio station that iTunes doesn't list, you'll need the station's Web address. For example, National Public Radio (NPR) has a URL that looks like this:

```
http://stream.qtv.apple.com/channels/npr/refs/nprlive.mov
```

In iTunes, choose Advanced⇨Open Stream (or press ⌘+U). In the Open Stream dialog that appears, enter the URL of your desired radio station and click OK, as shown in Figure 2-11. Within seconds, iTunes will tune in your station.

Figure 2-11:
Press ⌘+U
to hear a
radio station
by using
its URL.

Radio stations in your Playlists

If you find yourself visiting an online radio station more than once, you'll be glad to know that iTunes supports radio stations in its Playlists. To add a radio station to a Playlist from the Radio:

1. **Open the category that contains the station that you want to add to your Playlist.**

2. **Locate the station that you would like to add to your Playlist and drag it from the Radio list to the desired Playlist on the left.**

   If you haven't created any Playlists yet, see the section "Keeping Slim Whitman and Slim Shady Apart: Organizing with Playlists" earlier in this chapter to find out how.

Adding a radio station that doesn't appear in the Radio list is a bit trickier, but possible nonetheless. Even though iTunes allows you to load a radio station URL manually, it doesn't give you an easy way to add it to the Playlist. Follow these steps to add a radio station to a Playlist:

1. **Add any radio station from the Radio to your desired Playlist.**

2. **Press ⌘+I or choose File⇨Get Info to bring up the Song Information dialog for that station.**

3. **In the Song Information dialog that appears, change the URL by clicking the Edit URL button.**

4. **Enter the desired URL.**

5. **Name the station to your liking and click OK.**

   This name is just a reminder for yourself. It doesn't change the actual name of the radio station.

iSending iTunes to iPod

If you're lucky enough to own an iPod, you'll be happy to know that iTunes has features for your personal jukebox as well. The *iPod* is Apple's MP3 player, a portable device that can be purchased for about $299. This great gadget and those like it are likely to soon replace Sony Discman and Walkman as *the* preferred portable music players.

Connect an iPod to your Macintosh with a FireWire cable, available at any computer store. When you connect an iPod to your Mac via a FireWire connection, it automatically synchronizes to the Playlists in iTunes. The iPod device and the iTunes software communicate with each other and figure out what songs are in your iTunes Library versus the iPod Library. If they discover songs in your iTunes Library that are missing from your iPod, the songs automatically transfer to the iPod. Conversely, if the iPod contains songs that are no longer in iTunes, the iPod automatically removes those files from its drive.

Go back and reread that last sentence above about the iPod automatically removing files from its drive. Apple added this feature in an effort to be attentive to copyright concerns. The reasoning is that if you connect your iPod to your friend's computer, you won't be able to transfer songs from the iPod to that computer. Of course, you could always look at it from the marketing perspective as a feature that makes sure your Mac and iPod are always in total sync. Whatever the case, pay close attention and read all dialogs when connecting to another Mac than your own, or you might wipe out your iPod's library.

The great thing I can say about the iPod and iTunes combination is that there isn't anything else to say about them. The auto-sync feature is so easy to use, you forget about it almost immediately.

Burning Music to Shiny Plastic Circles

Besides being a great audio player, iTunes is adept at creating CDs, too. iTunes makes the process of saving songs to a CD as simple as a few mouse clicks. Making the modern version of a mix tape is easy. iTunes lets you burn CDs in one of two formats:

✦ **Audio CD:** This is the typical kind of music CD that you buy at a store. Most typical music audio CDs store 650 megabytes of music (about 15 average three-minute pop songs per disc).

✦ **MP3 CD:** Like a computer disc, an MP3 CD holds MP3 files in data format. Because MP3 files are so much smaller than the digital audio tracks found on traditional audio CDs, you can fit as many as 160 typical pop songs on one disc. Besides being playable in your Macintosh, many commercial CD players now also support MP3 CDs. Keep in mind that you don't buy these types of CD at a store. Rather, this is the kind you burn at home for your own collection.

The first step that you must perform before burning a CD is to set the preferred format. Open the iTunes Preferences by choosing iTunes⇨Preferences. In the Preferences window that opens, click the CD Burning tab. Select the desired disc format by clicking its radio button. Click OK to close the Preferences window when you're finished.

The next step in the CD creation process is to build a Playlist. Create a new Playlist and add whatever songs you would like to have on the CD to it. (See the earlier section "Keeping Slim Whitman and Slim Shady Apart: Organizing with Playlists" if you need a refresher.) With the songs in the correct order, select the Playlist. When you do, the Browse button changes into a Burn CD button, as shown in Figure 2-12. Click that button to commence the CD burning process. iTunes will let you know when the process is over.

Click to burn a CD.

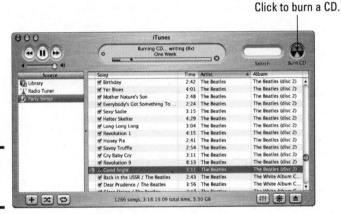

Figure 2-12: Burn, baby, burn.

Changing iTunes Visuals

By now, you know that iTunes is a feast for the ears, but did you know that it could provide you with eye candy, too? With a click or two, you can view mind-bending graphics that stretch, move, and pulse with your music, as shown in Figure 2-13.

To begin viewing iTunes visuals, choose Visuals⇨Turn Visual On. Immediately, most of your iTunes interface disappears and begins displaying groovy lava lamp-style animations, man. To stop the visuals, choose Visuals⇨Turn Visual Off. The usual iTunes interface returns. You can also turn visuals on or off by clicking the button at the bottom right of the interface, as shown in Figure 2-13.

You can also change the viewing size of the iTunes visuals in the Visual menu. From the Visuals menu, select Small, Medium, or Large to alter the size of the visual presentation. Similarly, to view the graphics at full screen size, choose Visuals⇨Full Screen. To escape from the Full Screen mode, click the mouse or press Esc.

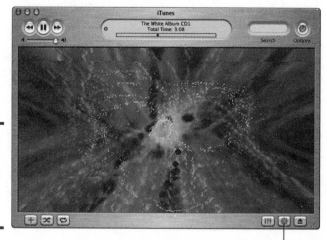

Figure 2-13: iTunes can display some interesting patterns!

Turn visuals on and off.

You can still control iTunes with the keyboard while the Visuals are zooming around your screen. See Table 2-1 earlier in this chapter for a rundown on common keyboard shortcuts.

The iTunes Visualizer has many hidden features. While viewing the Visualizer, press H for Help. When you do, you'll see a list of hidden Visualizer settings. Press H again, and the list changes to reveal more hidden functions. Table 2-2 shows the list of settings that you can change.

Table 2-2	Visualizer's Hidden Keyboard Features	
Press This Key	*To Perform This Action*	*What This Action Does*
H	View a list of hidden features	Displays the list of shortcuts from this table on the screen.
I	Display song information	Displays the song's title, artist, and album.
D	Reset settings to default	Returns all Visualizer settings to a default state.

(continued)

Table 2-2 *(continued)*

Press This Key	To Perform This Action	What This Action Does
F	Toggle frame rate display	Displays how fast your screen is redrawing the animations.
T	Toggle frame rate capping	Lets you set the highest permissible frame rate.
M	Select config mode	Chooses between random, user configuration, and current modes.
0–9	Select user configuration (press Shift to set)	Do you like the way a certain animation looks? Save the settings in a user configuration for later.
R	New random configuration	Creates the animations based on a random configuration.
C	Display current configuration	Shows which configuration is currently in use.

But wait, there are more Easter eggs to be found! Again, while viewing the Visualizer, press one of following keys:

✦ **A:** Changes the Visualizer Pattern

✦ **Z:** Changes the Visualizer Color Scheme

Press either of these keys repeatedly to cycle through the various patterns and color schemes lurking deep within the Visualizer.

Adding More Visuals to iTunes

Although the Visualizer is cool, it's not the only kid on the block. You can expand iTunes' visual functionality with plug-ins. Many iTunes plug-ins are available for download, and most of them are completely free. Some of the more popular iTunes plug-ins include

✦ **ArKaos:** Perhaps the most advanced iTunes plug-in yet, ArKaos offers 60 real-time effects that bump and groove to the bass and percussion of your favorite music. This isn't your average visual effects engine, though. Used by top performers from Bowie to U2 to animate stage imagery, ArKaos provides slick and professional-grade effects that enhance your iTunes experience. Go to `www.ArKaos.net/visualizer/index.html` to download.

✦ **Trinfinity Software**: Don't miss Trinfinity Software's two iTunes plug-ins, Vortex and EasyView. Both are free and offer something a little bit different. Available at `www.trinfinitysoftware.com/itunesplugins.shtml#screen`.

✦ **Zoomify:** Use the Zoomify plug-in for iTunes to view your favorite images while you listen to music. Go to www.zoomify.com/downloads/.

After you download iTunes plug-ins, you need to install them in a specific place to ensures that iTunes can find them. To install a plug-in, follow these steps:

1. **Open a Finder window.**

2. **Click the Home button in the toolbar of the window.**

3. **From the home folder, navigate to the** /Library/iTunes/iTunes Plug-ins **folder.**

4. **Add any new plug-ins that you've downloaded to this folder.**

5. **Restart iTunes to use the new plug-in.**

Of course, some plug-ins have an actual installer application, in which case you don't need to locate the iTunes Plugins folder. The installer should place the necessary files in the appropriate place for you.

Chapter 3: Focusing on iPhoto

In This Chapter

✔ **Organizing images with iPhoto**

✔ **Tweaking the appearance of photographs**

✔ **Importing pictures from your hard drive or digital camera**

✔ **Sharing photos with your friends**

*F*or years, the Macintosh has been the choice of professional photographers for working with digital images. Apple continues this tradition with *iPhoto,* a photography tool for the home user that can help you organize, edit, and even publish your photographs. You can shoot photos with a digital camera, import them into iPhoto, edit them, and publish them. You're not limited to photos that you take yourself, either; you can edit, publish, and organize all kinds of digital image files. You can even create a photo album and use the iPhoto interface to order a handsome hard-bound copy shipped to you.

In this chapter, I walk you through an overview of what iPhoto can do. After that, I give you a brief tour of the iPhoto interface so you can see what features are available to you, including features for managing, printing, and publishing your photos.

What iPhoto Can Do

iPhoto performs many different types of tasks. From your camera to the printed page and everything in between, iPhoto steps you through the process of digital photography:

✦ **Import:** Digital cameras are everywhere these days, so it's important for your Macintosh to quickly and easily connect with them. iPhoto takes the guesswork out of working with a digital camera. Simply plug your digital camera into your Mac's USB port, open iPhoto, and click a button or two. (I give you the details later in the section "Importing Images 101.") iPhoto automatically imports the images that you've taken.

✦ **Organize:** A digital camera has no film; instead, it uses computer memory, which is instantly reusable. For that reason, you may find yourself taking many more pictures than usual. As your collection of photographs grows, you'll need some help keeping them all organized. iPhoto is, at its core, a digital photo album that you can use to organize, sort, and search your photographs in seconds. iPhoto offers many great features to help you manage your digital equivalent of a shoebox full of photos. You'll never lose an important photo again.

✦ **Edit:** After you see the images from your camera on your computer monitor, you realize that your dog has red eyes, your ocean pictures are upside down, and the campfire photos are too dark. With a traditional film camera, you'd probably toss that campfire photograph in the trash. Thankfully, iPhoto has an array of image-editing tools that make the bad photos good and the good ones better.

✦ **Publish:** With all these photographs on your computer, you decide that it would be nice to pass a few on to Grandma, post a couple on your Web site, and print the rest. iPhoto guides you through a number of ways to share your photographs with others. From print to the Internet to e-mail, iPhoto takes away the hassle of working with images on a computer with a simple-to-use interface.

Delving into iPhoto

The iPhoto interface continues in the vein of other *iApps,* using only one window to work all its magic. The main iPhoto window is split into three sections: its toolbar, the Album List, and the Viewer. Figure 3-1 shows the three main sections of the iPhoto window.

✦ **Toolbar:** The iPhoto toolbar is the main control center for iPhoto. At the top of the toolbar is a row of buttons (refer to Figure 3-1). They give you one-click access to the various modes of iPhoto.

When you change modes, the toolbar panel changes to reflect the functions available in that mode. For example, click the Edit button to view the editing functions, such as Crop, Brightness/Contrast, or Black & White. Click the Book button to see the controls necessary to publish a photo album.

✦ **Album List:** To the left side of the iPhoto interface is the Album List (refer to Figure 3-1). This is where you organize your photo albums or select them for viewing.

✦ **Viewer:** The largest portion of the iPhoto interface is the Viewer (refer to Figure 3-1). The Viewer, where you see your photographs when you browse through photo albums, is also the main window for editing individual images and laying out photo books.

The Album List   Viewer

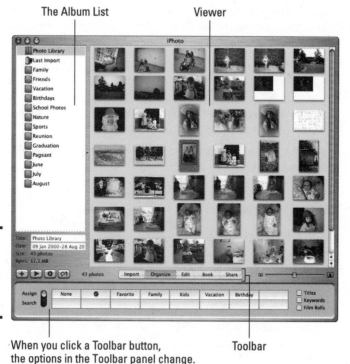

Figure 3-1:
The iPhoto
window has
three main
parts.

When you click a Toolbar button,   Toolbar
the options in the Toolbar panel change.

Importing Images 101

After you have the iPhoto basics under your belt, it's time to get busy.
Before you do anything else with iPhoto, you need to import some photographs into it. iPhoto provides a couple of ways to import photos, depending on the source of the image.

Importing images from a digital camera

To import photographs from your digital camera, follow these simple steps:

1. **Connect your digital camera to your Macintosh.**

   Plug one end of a USB cable into your camera and the other end into
   your Macintosh USB port. Power up the camera.

2. **Launch iPhoto.**

   Launch by clicking its icon in the Applications folder. The first time you
   launch iPhoto, you have the option of setting its auto-launch feature. If
   you turn auto-launch on, iPhoto will launch whenever you connect a

camera to your Mac. If you want to change the auto-launch setting at a later date, you can access it using the Preferences menu of Apple's Image Capture utility, also located in the Applications folder.

3. **Click the Import mode button on the iPhoto toolbar, as shown in Figure 3-2.**

This sets iPhoto in Import mode. While in Import mode, the toolbar panel changes to reflect import operations. At the rightmost side of the toolbar panel is another Import button.

4. **Click the second Import button to import your photographs from the camera.**

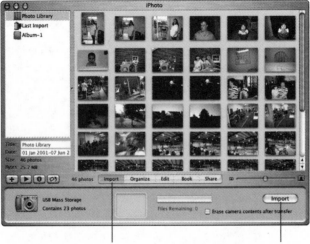

Figure 3-2: Import photos from your camera to iPhoto.

Click to switch to Import mode.   Click to import your photos.

As you import images from your camera, iPhoto displays a small preview in the toolbar panel. iPhoto sticks the newly imported images in the Photo Library, the warehouse for all your images.

Importing image files

Besides images you shot with your digital camera, you can also import any image file on your hard drive into the Photo Library. This could include images that friends have sent you, that you've downloaded off the Internet, or that you've created in a graphics program such as Photoshop. You can import image files in one of two ways:

✦ **Choose File⇨Import:** When you click on the menu, iPhoto displays the standard Open dialog. From there, you can choose your favorite image files for import.

✦ **Drag-and-drop:** Drag files from the Finder and drop them in the iPhoto window. iPhoto instantly adds them to the Photo Library.

If you drag a folder of images into iPhoto, it creates a film roll with the folder name as the roll name. Within that roll are all of your images.

iPhoto recognizes a variety of popular graphics formats, so none of your image files will feel left out. You can add images with the following formats:

✦ JPEG

✦ GIF

✦ PICT

✦ TIFF

✦ PDF

Organizing with Photo Albums

After you build up your Photo Library by importing photographs with your camera and from your hard drive, you might become overwhelmed with the volume of images at your disposal. The easiest way to organize your images for quick access is to use the iPhoto Photo Album feature.

Creating a new Photo Album

To create a new Photo Album, do one of the following:

✦ **Choose File⇨New Photo Album**

or

✦ **Click the + button at the bottom of the Photo Album List, shown in Figure 3-3.**

The name of a Photo Album is editable, meaning you can rename your Photo Album anything you like.

Adding photos to a Photo Album

After you have your newly created, empty Photo Album in place, add some photographs to it. Click the Photo Library icon (refer to Figure 3-3) to view all the images in your collection. Drag any photograph that you want from the Photo Library to your new album in the Photo Album List. iPhoto instantly adds it to the album. Don't worry — you're not making copies of the photograph: iPhoto simply creates a reference to the image in the Photo Library and adds it to your Photo Album.

The Photo Library icon

Figure 3-3:
Click the +
button to
create a
new Photo
Album.

Click to create a new Photo Album.

To view the photographs you've added to a Photo Album, click that album's icon in the Photo Album List. The images instantly appear in the Viewer.

Removing photos from a Photo Album

If you suddenly discover that your boyfriend or girlfriend is now an ex-boyfriend or ex-girlfriend, you'll probably want some way to remove his/her photographs from your Photo Album. Or maybe you just want to change the location of a photo from one Photo Album to another. Whatever the case, iPhoto makes it a cinch to remove photographs from a Photo Album. Follow these steps:

1. **Select the Photo Album from the Photo Album list.**

2. **In the Viewer, select the photo that you want to remove from the Photo Album.**

3. **Press Delete.**

Keep in mind that removing a file from a Photo Album doesn't remove it from the Photo Library. (Remember that the Photo Album is just an assortment of links to your photos.) To really remove that image of your "ex," you need to navigate to the Photo Library and delete the picture there, too.

Deleting a Photo Album

It's just as easy to remove a Photo Album from your collection as it is to remove photos from that Photo Album. To delete an entire Photo Album, here's the process:

1. **Select the Photo Album in the Photo Album list.**

2. **Press Delete.**

Told you it was easy!

If you mistakenly delete a Photo Album, you can always recreate it because the images within that Photo Album still reside in the Photo Library. Simply open the Photo Library folder in the Finder and drag the files into iPhoto again.

The Art of Organizing with Keywords

Using Photo Albums is a great way to organize your photo collection, but it's just the start of what iPhoto can do: You can also assign *keywords* to images to help you organize your collection. Keywords give you the opportunity to quickly search through your photos later. You can use iPhoto's standard keywords or create your own. For example, you could organize your photos according to important family events. Birthdays photos would get one keyword; graduation photos would get another. Later you can search for that birthday shot where the cake caught on fire or the graduation where the valedictorian fainted. Using keywords, they're just a few keystrokes away.

To begin using the keyword features, set iPhoto to Organize mode by clicking the Organize button in the toolbar, as shown in Figure 3-4.

iPhoto comes stocked with a handful of useful preset keywords:

✦ Favorite

✦ Family

✦ Kids

✦ Vacation

✦ Birthday

You'll also note two unusual keywords: None and Checkmark. *None* means that an image has no keyword assigned to it. The *Checkmark* keyword causes a small checkmark icon to appear in the bottom right-hand corner of any image that gets that assignment. For example, you might temporarily mark your favorite photographs with the Checkmark keyword. Then, it's a cinch to retrieve just your favorites by searching for the Checkmark keyword.

You can display keywords set for an image.

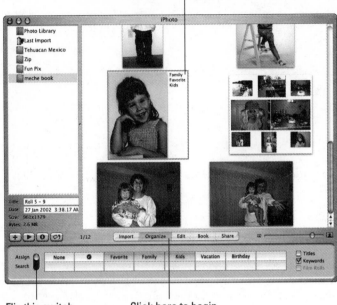

Figure 3-4:
Click
Organize to
use the
iPhoto
keyword
features.

Flip this switch
to assign keywords.

Click here to begin
assigning keywords.

You can also display the keywords assigned to each photo in the Viewer. (Check out Figure 3-4 to see what this looks like.) Enable the Keywords check box at the rightmost side of the Organize panel to display the Keywords for each photo.

Customizing your own keywords

Besides the keywords that are included in iPhoto by default, you can create a number of custom keywords. You're limited to fourteen keywords, plus the checkmark keyword, across the entire Library. Note that in Figure 3-4, the button to the right of the Birthday keyword is blank. You can edit these blank buttons to create any sort of keyword you find useful. To create your own keywords, do the following:

1. **Click the Organize mode button in the iPhoto toolbar to select the Organize mode.**

2. **Click the Assign switch.**

3. **Choose Edit➪Edit Keywords.**

4. **Enter your own custom keyword.**

   Click on any empty button to enter a keyword for that button. You can also change existing keywords, but keep in mind that they will affect all images that already use that keyword.

   Whether you use the supplied keywords or your own, assigning one to a photo is a simple procedure. Simply select a photograph from the iPhoto Library or one of your Photo Albums. Make sure that the Organize button is selected, and click the keywords buttons that pertain to that image. When you select an image later, the Organize panel will reflect the keywords that you've assigned to that image, as shown in Figure 3-5.

Figure 3-5:
Use the
preset
keywords
or create
your own.

Searching for keywords

All that work assigning keywords to your photos isn't in vain. In fact, the more keywords that you assign, the easier it is to use iPhoto. As your photo collection grows, it can become unmanageable. To help you out, iPhoto lets you search for photos by using the keywords that you assigned to the images. To search for images using keywords, do the following:

1. **Click the Organize button in the iPhoto toolbar.**

2. **Click the Search switch.**

   The Search switch is the toggle of the Assign switch, shown in Figure 3-5.

3. **Click as many keywords as you would like to search by.**

   As you click the keywords that interest you, the Viewer refreshes, displaying only the photos that have the keywords that you requested. Figure 3-6 shows the keywords of Favorite, Family, and Kids highlighted, and only photos that have all three keywords assigned to them are displayed in the Viewer.

Figure 3-6:
Click the
Search
switch to
find images
using
keywords.

Use the Search tool as a quick and easy way to build a Photo Album. To create a Photo Album of pictures of your wedding, for example, you could search for the keyword "Wedding," assuming you assigned that keyword to your wedding pictures, and then drag the results of the search to a Photo Album in the Album List.

Taking Care of Business: Basic Editing

Sometimes mere mortals like you and I don't take the greatest photographs. For those times, iPhoto gives you a helping hand with several important editing features that will save your dark photos from the Trash and improve the keepers.

To begin editing your photographs, select the photo that you want to edit and click the Edit button in the iPhoto toolbar. This displays the Edit panel of the toolbar, which has four subsections, as shown in Figure 3-7:

+ **Crop:** This lets you trim off any unwanted edges of the photo and focus on the photo's subject.

+ **Brightness/Contrast:** These features give you the chance to enhance photos that are too dark, too light, or washed-out looking.

+ **Red-Eye and Black & White:** Remove the evil-looking red-eye phenomenon from your photos. For that vintage look, you can also convert color pictures to black and white.

+ **Navigation Arrows:** Click these to advance to the previous or next image.

Figure 3-7:
Click the
Edit button
to start
fixing your
photos.

Constrain and crop

Sometimes your photos have additional clutter around the edges. To get rid
of this problem with traditional photographs, you might use a pair of scissors to cut off the unwanted portion of the image. Professional photographers call this *cropping*. Digital image-editing software packages (including
iPhoto) borrow this term. The Crop feature of iPhoto gives you the ability to
remove unwanted stuff from around the edges of your otherwise perfect
photographs.

To crop a photo, you must first select what portion of the image that you
want to keep. You do this by clicking and dragging on the image in the
Viewer. As you drag, a rectangle appears indicating what part of the image
you want to keep, as shown in Figure 3-8. Everything outside of this rectangle will disappear after a crop operation.

The crop focuses
attention on
the subject's face.

Figure 3-8:
Click and
drag to
select the
part of the
image you
want to
keep.

After you select the portion that you want to remain, click the Crop button
in the Edit panel to remove the rest. If you would like to constrain your

selection to a specific size, select that size from the Constraint pop-up menu to the left of the Crop button. This lets you resize a photograph according to a preset size.

Brightness/Contrast

Shooting photographs that look perfect is a tough task, and sometimes things don't work out the way that you plan. If your images turn out too dark or light, iPhoto can help you clean up after the fact. To adjust the brightness and contrast of an image, simply move the Brightness/Contrast sliders until the image looks the way that you want.

The Brightness and Contrast sliders only work when no part of an image has been selected with the rectangle. That way, the controls will affect the entire image.

Red-eye removal

Have you ever picked up your photographs from the local photo developer only to discover that the subjects in your photographs all look like rather unsettling red-eyed zombies? *Red-eye* is a phenomenon that occurs when the camera captures light reflecting off the retinas of eyeballs. This problem isn't limited only to human eyes, either. Even Spot, your loving canine pal, can have that Demon Doggy possessed look! To help exorcise these red-eye problems from your photographs, iPhoto gives you a Red-Eye filter.

To remove red-eye problem in your photographs, select the eyeball in question by clicking and dragging around the eyeball in the Viewer. Then, click the Red-Eye button in the Edit panel. Your red-eye problem disappears in an instant.

Unlike Brightness and Contrast, the Red-Eye function only works when an image has a selection.

Black-and-white

In the old days, photographers had to cart around two rolls of film if they wanted to shoot in color and black-and-white. These days, you can simply shoot in color because iPhoto can do the black-and-white conversion for you. It's really simple, too! Just click the Black & White button to convert an image from color to shades of gray.

If you change your mind and want to revert to a color image, choose Edit⇨ Undo to see colors again. For an interesting artistic effect, you can select just a portion of a photo with the Crop tool and click the Black & White button to turn just the selected area to black-and-white.

Don't forget to rotate!

Although it's not technically an Edit mode feature, rotation is a sort of edit, so I discuss it here. This feature is useful for viewing those images where you held the camera sideways to fit that tall building into the viewfinder. To rotate an image, simply click the Rotate button at the left-hand side of the toolbar, as shown in Figure 3-9. The default rotation is in a counter-clockwise direction. Hold the Option key while you click the rotate button to rotate in a clockwise direction.

Figure 3-9: Click the Rotate button to spin an image in 90° increments.

Click to rotate an image.

Producing Your Own Coffee-Table Masterpiece

Computerized photo albums are fun and all, but sometimes people long for the real photo albums of the past. They like to turn pages, put it on the shelf, and view it without a computer screen. For those folks, iPhoto offers a way to create and print your own professional quality photo album. Use iPhoto to create a Photo Album (the digital kind), tweak its formatting until you're satisfied, and then transmit your finished product via the Internet to a vendor who will print, bind, and send you a copy of your finished album, for a small fee, of course. Here's how:

1. **Create a new Photo Album in iPhoto by choosing New⇨Photo Album or clicking the + button at the left edge of the toolbar.**

   The name of the album is editable, so you can name it to your liking.

2. **Click the Photo Library icon at the left side of the iPhoto interface and drag your favorite photos into the new Photo Album.**

   These images will appear in your bound photo album.

   When preparing a photo album that will be printed on paper, use the highest quality images available. It takes higher-resolution images to look good on paper (as compared to your Mac's monitor).

3. **After you complete the preparation of your Photo Album in iPhoto, select that Photo Album in the Photo Album List by clicking it.**

   The Photo Album List appears on the left side of the iPhoto interface.

4. **Next, click the Book button in the toolbar, as shown in Figure 3-10.**

   In Book mode, the Viewer changes in subtle ways. It displays the current image at the top of its display and adds a scrolling row of thumbnail images below it, as shown in Figure 3-10. This row of images represents the current order of the various pages in your book. Clicking any of these thumbnails causes the Viewer to load that image into its display area.

5. **Rearrange the page order to suit you by dragging the thumbnail of that page from one location to another in the row.**

6. **In the Book panel below the toolbar, you can adjust a variety of settings for the final book, including the book's theme, page numbers, and comments.**

7. **Make sure that the Show Guides check box is enabled in the Book panel.**

   Besides photos, you can also add text to the pages of your photo album. Selecting Show Guides draws faint blue boxes in the Viewer that show where you can add text.

Figure 3-10: Click the Book button to begin designing a bound photo album.

Click the Book button.

These thumbnails can be clicked and dragged.

8. **Click any one of the Guide boxes and begin typing to add text to that page.**

9. **After you complete the design of your book, preview it by clicking the Preview button at the bottom right of the Book Panel.**

   iPhoto displays the book, allowing you to scan through the pages of your creation to make sure that it looks exactly as you wish. When you're satisfied with the results of the photo book, it's time to publish it.

10. **Click the Share button on the toolbar.**

11. **In the row of buttons that appears in the Share panel, click the Order Book button.**

   In a series of dialogs that appear, iPhoto guides you through the final steps to order a bound hardback book.

A fast connection to the Internet like cable or DSL is very handy for this process. The images you must submit are too large for a slow dial-up connection.

Sharing Photos with Friends and Family

Besides creating a photo book, iPhoto offers many other ways for you to share your photos. Click the Share button in the toolbar to see the possibilities, shown in Figure 3-11.

**Book III
Chapter 3**

Focusing on iPhoto

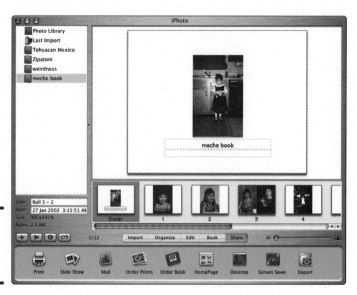

Figure 3-11: Share your photos with iPhoto.

Here are the different ways that you can share your photos using iPhoto:

✦ **Print:** Don't forget about your computer's printer. You can print photographs from iPhoto using your inkjet or laser printer.

✦ **Slide Show:** Display a slide show presentation of your photos in iPhoto, complete with background music.

✦ **Mail:** Send photos to your friends via e-mail. You'll need an active Internet connection for this to work. iPhoto will launch your default e-mail client when you're ready to send your photographs.

✦ **Order Prints:** Order photographic quality prints of your favorite images. Kodak prints the photographs for you and will ship them wherever you want them to go.

✦ **HomePage:** Publish your photos on your Web site.

✦ **Desktop:** Change your Desktop picture to one of your iPhoto images.

✦ **Screensaver:** Use a Photo Album as your screensaver.

✦ **Export:** Export a photo in a different graphics format (such as JPEG, TIF, or PNG).

Chapter 4: Making Magic with iMovie

In This Chapter

✔ Working with iMovie controls

✔ Adding media to your projects

✔ Applying text, transitions, and effects to your movie

✔ Adding audio to your movies

✔ Sharing your movies in many different formats

Alfred Hitchcock, Stanley Kubrick, George Lucas, and Ridley Scott — those guys are amateurs! Welcome to the exciting world of movie-making on your Mac, where *you* call the shots. With iMovie, you can try your hand at all aspects of the movie-creating process, including editing and special effects. Built with ease-of-use in mind, iMovie lets you perform full-blown movie production on your Macintosh with a minimum of effort.

Don't let iMovie's fancy buttons and flashing lights fool you: *iMovie* is a feature-packed tool for serious movie production. The iMovie interface mimics top-notch movie editing tools that professionals use. From basic editing to audio and video effects, iMovie has everything you need to get started creating high quality movies.

The iMovie Interface

To launch iMovie, navigate to the Application folder and double-click the iMovie icon. When you first launch iMovie, perhaps the first thing that you'll notice is that the window isn't like most applications. iMovie takes over the entire screen, concealing the Desktop and even the Dock. (See Figure 4-1.)

This makes the interface clean and orderly, but might throw you for a loop if you're not used to this kind of arrangement. To hide iMovie, press ⌘+H. This instantly hides iMovie and lets you see the desktop again. You can also move your mouse over the location where your Dock normally is. This causes the Dock to reappear so that you can switch to other applications while working with iMovie.

Monitor

Shelf

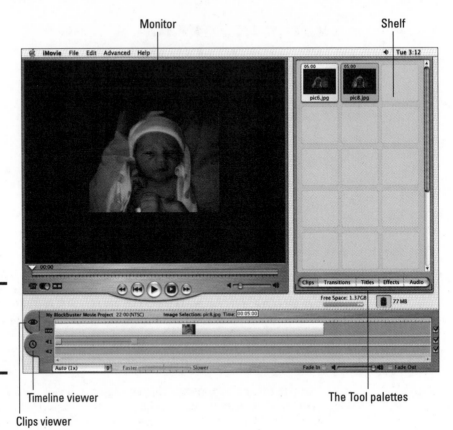

Figure 4-1:
iMovie
takes over
your
Desktop.

Timeline viewer

Clips viewer

The Tool palettes

You'll notice that the interface consists of three main parts:

✦ **Monitor:** The Monitor is the big black square interface where you watch movies.

✦ **Tool Palettes:** The iMovie Tool Palettes appear on the right side of the iMovie interface. They offer one click access to an array of movie-building tools.

Just above the Tool Palettes is the shelf. The contents of the shelf vary, depending on which of the Tool Palette buttons you've selected. Clicking the Clips button displays the Clips shelf, for example, which is where iMovie stores your movie clips for use in full length movies that you create. Clicking the Audio button triggers display of a shelf with audio files in it. iMovie stores your audio clips here, which you can also use in any movie you create. The Transitions, Titles, and Effects tools let you twist, turn, and label your movies like the pros do.

✦ **Viewers:** The Viewers are where you compose your movie masterpiece. There are two main tabs here: the Clips Viewer and the Timeline Viewer. I cover these in more detail later.

The Powers of Three

The minimalist approach of iMovie provides power with simplicity (something that the average Joe can appreciate). Instead of the nested windows and cryptic film jargon of traditional movie editing packages — which also, by the way, tend to cost hundreds or thousands of dollars a pop — iMovie reduces the clutter to three elements. Learn to use this trio of tools and you'll be on your way to movie-making bliss.

Monitor

The Monitor is the largest of all the interface elements in iMovie. The Monitor element is meant to mimic the video monitor and control deck that a traditional film editor uses. You can think of it as iMovie's screen. Here you view clips and preview your movie while you edit it. Check it out in Figure 4-2. When you launch iMovie for the first time, the Monitor appears black, indicating that you haven't created a movie yet. On subsequent launches of iMovie, it displays the most recent movie file.

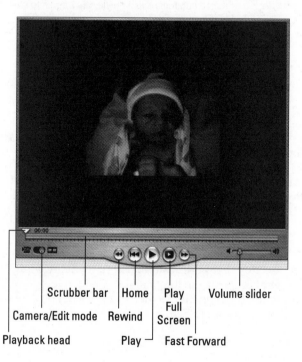

Figure 4-2:
Watch your movies on the Monitor while you edit them.

Scrubber bar   Home   Play
                       Full
                       Screen   Volume slider

Camera/Edit mode   Rewind

Playback head   Play   Fast Forward

Nestled directly beneath the iMovie Monitor are the playback controls (refer to Figure 4-2). Resembling buttons on a conventional CD player, the iMovie playback controls let you play, stop, advance, and rewind movies that display in the Monitor.

In addition to the buttons that control playback, the Monitor sports other important controls. The *scrubber bar* contains the playback head, which tells you visually where you are in the movie. The *playback head* is a white triangle positioned directly below the Monitor. As your movie plays, the playback head moves to indicate the current location of playback. The playback head isn't just a visual indicator, though: It also has an important function. You can also click and drag the playback head to move forward or back in the current movie.

All the remaining Monitor button controls affect the playback head's position with one click. Table 4-1 lists the various playback controls and how they affect the playback head's position.

Table 4-1	iMovie's Playback Controls
Control	*What It Does*
Rewind	Plays the current movie in reverse.
Home	Moves the playback head to the beginning of the movie.
Play	Click to begin playing a movie. Click again to stop playback.
Play Full Screen	Plays the current movie in full-screen mode.
Fast Forward	Advances the playback head at high speed towards the end of the movie.

The Monitor has two remaining controls that demand attention.

✦ **Volume slider:** Adjusts the volume during movie playback

✦ **Camera/Edit Mode switch:** Toggles between video from your camera and the movie that you're editing with iMovie

The DV Camera/Edit Mode switch affects how you import video from a camera. Read more about this in the upcoming section "Working with Clips (Not the Paper Kind)."

Palettes

The Palettes occupy the rightmost portion of the iMovie interface and offer a complete set of tools for creating movies. Divided into five sections, the Palettes house the building blocks that you need to construct your cinematic masterpiece. (Refer to Figure 4-1.)

Throughout the creation process, you'll use the tools located in the Palettes to build the content of your movie. Table 4-2 describes the role that each Palette plays in the movie-making process.

Table 4-2	Palette Roles
Palette	*Role*
Clips	Stores movie clips from your hard drive in a visual library.
Transitions	Adds useful video transitions to your movies for professional-looking edits.
Titles	Offers text editing tools to label and title your movie.
Effects	Adds stunning visual effects that give your movies an edge.
Audio	Gives you audio effects and voiceover tools for making your movie an aural treat as well.

Viewers

The final stops on the iMovie interface tour are the Viewers. Located at the bottom of the screen, the Viewers are the heart of editing operations in iMovie. The *Viewers* are where you add audio and video clips to construct the perfect movie. As shown in Figure 4-3, they offer a visual representation of the order in which the various clips appear in a movie.

Clip viewer

Figure 4-3:
The Viewers
display
audio and
video clip
sequences.

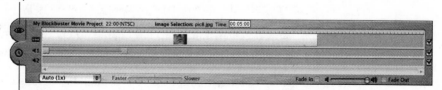

Timeline viewer

As you can see in Figure 4-3, the Viewer interface has two tabs.

✦ **Clip Viewer:** Displays the sequence of video clips in a movie.

✦ **Timeline Viewer:** Displays the location in time of the various audio and video clips in a movie.

The Movie-Making Process

Using the three main sections of the interface, follow this simple six-step process to create professional looking movies in minutes. I go into more detail about each of these steps in the following sections.

1. **Import and edit your movie footage.**

   The first step in creating a movie is to import movie clips into iMovie. You will use these clips to construct a full-length movie.

2. **Add clips from the Clips shelf to the Timeline.**

   After you prepare your movie clips, you can add them to the movie. Using drag-and-drop, it takes only a few seconds to add the movie segments found in the Clips shelf to your full-length movie.

3. **Apply transitions, effects, and text to the movie.**

   With your movie clips in place, it's a snap to enhance them with visual effects and transitions. You might also want to spice up the movie with titles and credits.

4. **Import or record audio clips.**

   Great movies look even better when accompanied by great audio. With iMovie, you can add audio from MP3 files, audio CDs, or even what you've recorded yourself with a microphone.

5. **Add audio from the Audio shelf to the Timeline.**

   Drag audio clips from the Audio shelf to the Timeline to add instant audio to your movie. Now your flick can have a great soundtrack as well as narration.

6. **Preview, build, and burn the final product.**

   After you construct a movie, iMovie makes it a snap to preview your creation. Then it's just a few clicks before your project becomes a movie. iMovie helps you distribute your completed movie as well: You can burn it to a CD-ROM, or import it into QuickTime for online distribution.

The remainder of this chapter guides you through the details of these steps. Before you know it, you'll be producing movies like Hitchcock or Spielberg without setting foot out of your home.

Working with Clips (Not the Paper Kind)

The first step for creating a movie is to add video clips to the Clips shelf. These clips form the bulk of the video that you use in the completed movie. iMovie is flexible in that it permits you to import video clips from more than one source:

✦ **Import from a digital video camcorder:** Connect a DV camcorder to your Macintosh to transfer video.

✦ **Import from files:** Import any DV Stream file directly from your hard drive.

If your favorite movie clip isn't in DV Stream format, you can export it from QuickTime Pro. Then, import into iMovie. See Book III, Chapter 6 for more on QuickTime Pro.

After you import your video, you can perform a variety of editing functions on the clip: You can edit clips together to tell a story, edit out mistakes or bad footage, apply audio, transitions, effects, and even add titles, for that cinematic touch.

Adding clips from media files

iMovie allows you to import many different kinds of media files. From graphics to video to audio files, iMovie has you covered. Table 4-3 lists some of the files that iMovie can import into your project.

Table 4-3	File Types That iMovie Understands
File Type	*What It's Used For*
AIFF	Audio from an audio CD
MP3	Compressed audio
JPEG	Standard for still images from the Web, scanners, or a digital camera
GIF	Standard for still images from the Web, scanners, or a digital camera
PSD	Images from Photoshop
DV	Video

The file type dictates what happens when you import that file. For example, when you import an image or video file, the file goes directly into the Clips shelf. In contrast, importing an audio file automatically places it in the movie at the song pointer's current location. To import an audio or video file, choose File⇨Import. Select a file to import in the Open dialog and click OK. The imported file appears in either the Clips shelf or the Audio shelf, depending on the file type.

Adding clips from your camcorder

Adding clips from your DV camcorder is just as simple as playing a movie. To retrieve video from your camcorder, do the following:

1. **Using a FireWire cable, connect a FireWire-compatible camera to your Macintosh and set it to VTR mode.**

If your camera is not FireWire compatible, you should be able to buy an adapter. Setting your camera to VTR mode allows remote control of the camcorder by iMovie. If you're not sure how to set VTR mode on your camera, consult its manual.

2. **In iMovie, slide the Camera/Edit Mode switch to the Camera position, which is labeled with a DV icon (refer to Figure 4-2).**

   This initiates the camera capture mode. When you set this mode, an Import button appears above the Play button.

3. **Find the video.**

   Click the Monitor's playback buttons to locate the video on your camcorder that you wish to import, fast forwarding or rewinding until you find the correct footage, watching your progress in the Monitor. When you find the video, stop the playback and position the playback head a few seconds prior to the place where the desired video begins. When you're ready, click the Play button again.

4. **When the video that you want to capture appears in the Monitor, click the Import button, shown in Figure 4-4, to begin transferring that video from the camcorder to your Macintosh.**

5. **Stop the video.**

   Click the Import button again to stop the video transfer.

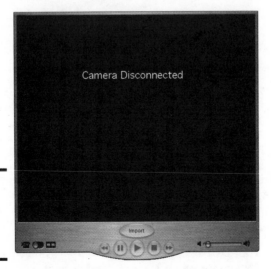

Figure 4-4:
Preview
video and
then im-
port it.

Imported video from a camcorder transfer appears in the Clips shelf.

Editing clips

iMovie gives you several different ways to edit your video clips. You can copy, trim, and crop your video clips to your heart's content, and if you mess up along the way, an instant fix is one click away.

Copying clips

Sometimes you'll want to work on multiple copies of the same clip. This gives you the ability to try out different edits on the same piece of footage without altering the original. To duplicate a clip, do the following:

1. **Select a clip in the Clips shelf.**

   The selected clip turns yellow.

2. **Press ⌘+C or choose the Edit⇨Copy menu.**

3. **Press ⌘+V or choose Edit⇨Paste.**

   A new copy of the clip appears in the Clips shelf.

Of course, you can also follow the Macintosh convention of Option-dragging a clip from its cell on the shelf to an empty cell or to the timeline. Doing so makes a copy wherever you release the mouse.

**Book III
Chapter 4**

**Making Magic
with iMovie**

Cropping, splitting, and trimming clips

Cropping, splitting, and *trimming* are three important editing functions that iMovie affords you. Here's the skinny on the functions:

+ **Crop:** Delete everything from the clip except a selected region

+ **Split:** Breaks a single clip into multiple clips

+ **Trim:** Delete a selected region from the clip

To perform any of these functions, you must first select a region of a clip. Choose a clip in the Clips shelf. This causes the clip to appear in the Monitor. Position the playback head at the beginning of the region that you wish to select. Then Shift+click anywhere on the scrubber bar to the right of the starting point. A region turns yellow when you select it. After you select a region, perform the editing operation.

+ **Crop:** Choose Edit⇨Crop. Everything but the selected region disappears.

+ **Split:** Choose Edit⇨Split Video Clip at Playhead. The clip instantly splits into two clips.

+ **Trim:** Choose Edit⇨Clear. The selected region disappears.

Naming clips

As your movie project grows, you'll want to take care to label your clips. This helps to remind you when you return to the project later. It's also a godsend when you begin working on multiple copies of the same clip. Otherwise, you have no easy way to differentiate two identical clips because they appear the same in the Clips shelf.

To edit the name of a clip, click the text of the clip name near the clip's bottom edge. When the text highlights in gray, type a new name for the clip. Press Return to affix the new name to the clip.

Basic Composition the iMovie Way

After you import and edit some video clips, it's finally time to begin creating a movie. Adding video to your movie is a simple drag-and-drop operation.

Adding clips to the movie

Before you add clips to your movie, select the desired Viewer tab. The Clip Viewer tab displays clips in sequential order, with each clip occupying the same amount of space in the Timeline. The Timeline Viewer tab displays clips with lengths that are relative to their duration. For example, a 30-second clip will appear as half the length of a 60-second clip when you view clips in the Timeline Viewer. See Figure 4-5.

Clips in the Clip viewer   The Playback head

Figure 4-5:
Choose the
Timeline
Viewer or
Clip Viewer
based on
your editing
needs.

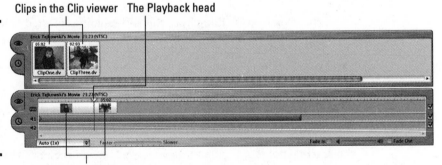

Video clips in the Timeline

To add a clip to your movie, drag it from the Clips shelf to the desired location in the Timeline. Constructing a movie is just a matter of repeating this step with the various clips that you want to add to your movie.

Removing clips from a movie

Eventually you'll add a clip that you don't really want in your movie. To delete a clip from a movie, select the clip in the Timeline and press Delete. The clip disappears, and any clips that follow the deleted selection slide to the left to fill the void.

If you mistakenly remove a clip that you intended to keep, press ⌘+Z or choose Edit➪Undo to cancel the delete operation.

Rearranging clips in a movie

If you decide at some point that certain clips are in the wrong order, it's a cinch to change. Simply drag a clip in the Clip Viewer. Release the mouse when the clip reaches the desired destination.

Transitions for the Masses

Stringing together a bunch of video clips to make a movie is cool stuff, but that's only a small fraction of what iMovie can do. Beyond simple editing, iMovie offers a set of video transitions for you to use in your movies. *Transitions* are video effects that perform their magic at the point where two clips connect. They help smooth out the joint between the two clips. If you're a television viewer, you see transitions all the time. Any time that the screen fades to or from black, you are seeing a transition in action. (Remember the cool swirling bat from the old *Batman* TV series?)

iMovie gives you a small group of transitions from which to choose. These can be accessed by selecting the Transitions button in the Tool palette, shown in Figure 4-6. Clicking on any one of the transitions in the Transitions shelf causes a brief preview of the effect to automatically play in the preview window at the top of the shelf. The list of available transitions provided free with iMovie is short, but it covers most of the basic movie needs. (Hey, no one ever said free didn't have a cost of some kind!)

✦ **Cross Dissolve:** Video dissolves from one clip to the next.

✦ **Fade In:** Video fades in from black.

✦ **Fade Out:** Video fades out to black.

✦ **Overlap:** Video fades from one clip to another.

✦ **Push:** Video slides to an edge of the screen over time. Select which edge by clicking the directional arrows that appear when you select the Push transition.

✦ **Scale Down:** Video shrinks over time to reveal a clip behind it.

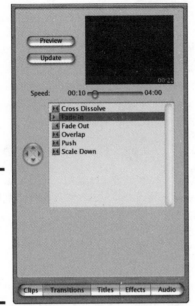

Figure 4-6:
A variety of transitions are available in iMovie's Transitions shelf.

For those who just can't get enough, Apple offers a number of additional transitions, effects, and audio clips for free at www.apple.com/imovie. You can also purchase many transitions and special effects as add-on packages from third-party developers.

To add a transition to your movie, drag the desired transition from the Transitions shelf to the Timeline. A transition merges two clips together, so you'll want to drop the transition in an appropriate location — in between two clips. If you change any settings of a transition, make sure to click the Update button. It refreshes the preview of that transition in your movie.

Transitions are a wonderfully subtle way to improve the look of your movie. Use them judiciously to emulate professional movie and television editing. Just because iMovie offers you many transitions doesn't mean you have to use them all in a two-minute clip. To give you a feel for how the pros do it, pay attention when you watch television or movies. You may even want to occasionally watch television or a movie on DVD or video with the sound turned down to focus on the transitions. Sometimes the simplest transition can have dramatic effects on a movie.

Even "Gone with the Wind" Had Titles

Besides transitions, professional movies and videos have text, and lots of it. From the title at the beginning of a movie to the litany of names that scroll by in the credits after the movie, movie editing clearly demands sophisticated text-editing abilities. With over a dozen title styles to choose from, iMovie can handle most text tasks that you throw at it.

The Title shelf is where you can find the text features of iMovie. Figure 4-7 shows you the basic layout of the Title shelf.

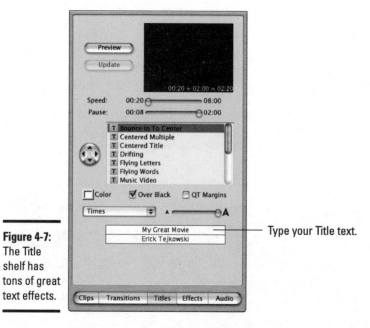

Figure 4-7: The Title shelf has tons of great text effects.

Type your Title text.

The Title shelf changes to accommodate different amounts of text depending on which title style you choose. Otherwise, the controls for the title styles are identical for each effect. Table 4-4 lists the settings and functions that are common to all title styles.

Table 4-4	Title Shelf Features
Setting	*What It Does*
Speed	Slider that adjusts how quickly the text effect executes.
Pause	Slider that adjusts the length of time that the text remains on the screen after the effect has completed its animation.

(continued)

Table 4-4 *(continued)*

Setting	What It Does
Color	Palette pop-up that changes the color of the text in the title style. When you click the Color box, a palette of colors that you can choose from pops up.
Over Black	Check box that displays the text on a black background if checked. If not enabled, a movie appears behind the text.
Font menu	Drop-down list that changes the font that the Title style uses to display the text.
Font Size	Slider that increases or decreases the size of the font.
QT Margins	Check box that alters the position of the text based on standardized QuickTime margins.

To begin working with Titles, select a text style from the shelf. At the bottom of the Title shelf you can change the text for any title style, as shown in Figure 4-7. As you alter the text of the style and any of its parameters, the miniature preview at the top of the Title shelf updates to reflect the changes. When you've successfully adapted the text style to match your needs, you can add it to a movie by dragging the title style from the list to the Timeline (see Figure 4-8). When you do, the title appears in the Timeline as a movie segment.

Figure 4-8: Drag a text effect from the Title shelf to the Timeline to make it part of your movie.

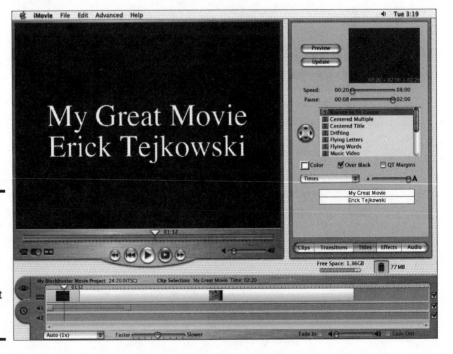

Like deleting a movie clip, removing a title from your movie requires just a click of the mouse and one key press. Click the title in the Timeline to select it and press then Delete to remove it from the movie. If you delete a title accidentally, press ⌘+Z to undo the operation.

What Good Is a Movie without Special Effects?

Although iMovie can produce some nice transitions and titles, it doesn't stop there. It also comes stocked with a handful of cool video effects for you to use in your movies.

iMovie's stock effects

Click the Effects button to reveal the Effects shelf (Figure 4-9), which houses the various video effects. Selecting an effect from the list causes that effect's controls to appear in the Effects shelf. The available controls vary based upon the effect.

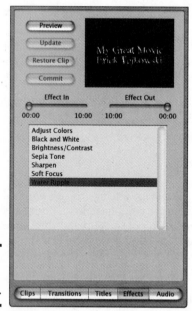

Figure 4-9:
Add movie effects here.

Table 4-5 lists the names and features of the built-in iMovie effects. If these effects don't fit the bill for your movie, you'll be happy to know that you can find third-party effects on the Internet, too.

Table 4-5	iMovie Effects
Effect	*Does This*
Adjust Colors	Tweaks colors to reduce yellow or blue casts; also works great for spooky results.
Black and White	Takes your movie back in time with the nostalgic look of black and white video; good for simulated security camera shots, too.
Brightness/Contrast	Adjusts the brightness and contrast to lighten up a dark movie or to take the edge off harsh footage; used creatively, also works well for special effects purposes.
Sepia Tone	Adds a sepia-colored tint on your movie; can give movies rustic, old-fashioned, or romantic moods.
Sharpen	Defines edges in a blurry movie; makes everything look more crisp.
Soft Focus	Makes a movie blurry; fun for I-lost-my-eyeglasses shots.
Water Ripple	Simulates water ripples; great for your next *Jaws* movie!

Adding Effects to a movie

To work with Effects in your movies, follow these five easy steps:

1. **In the Timeline, click a movie clip.**

   The clip changes to a yellow color to indicate that you selected it successfully.

2. **Open the Effects shelf by clicking the Effects button in the Tool palette and then select an Effect.**

   In the Effects shelf, choose from the list of available effects by clicking the effect's name.

3. **Adjust the Effect.**

   Using the effect's controls, tweak its settings to suit your needs. The Effect In and Effect Out sliders let you phase in an effect a certain amount of time from the beginning of the clip and then phase it out before it ends. As you adjust the effect's parameters, the results appear in the miniature preview window at the top of the Effects shelf.

4. **Preview the Effect at full size.**

   After you choose and adjust the effect to your liking, you might want to see what it will look like in action. Click the Preview button to see a preview of the effect in the Monitor.

5. **Apply the Effect.**

   If you're happy with the results of the effects preview, it's easy to permanently add it to the movie clip by clicking the Apply button.

When you apply an effect to a movie clip, iMovie begins building the movie effect — the faster your Mac is and the more memory you have, the faster the effect is finished. To track the progress of an effect being built, iMovie displays a small red line in the movie clip found in the Timeline. As the build progresses, this red line grows until it spans the entire length of the clip. If you try to preview the clip before it's built, you'll still be able to view it, but at a lower quality. This temporary preview permits you to view the effect while iMovie builds the real effect.

Remove an effect

If you decide later on that you don't really like an effect that you've applied to a movie, it's easy to remove it from the clip. Select the clip by single-clicking it in the Timeline. Then, navigate to the Effects shelf and click the Restore Clip button. Your movie instantly returns to its pre-effect appearance.

Working with Sound

In addition to video and graphics, iMovie is adept at working with sound. With iMovie, you can use your favorite audio files, music CDs, and microphone to create professional-sounding soundtracks. (Sorry, John Williams is not included.)

Adding sound to a movie

All audio that you add to a movie resides in one of the two audio tracks in the Timeline. The audio tracks (see Figure 4-10) are visible only in the Timeline Viewer tab.

Figure 4-10:
Audio tracks contain music and sound.

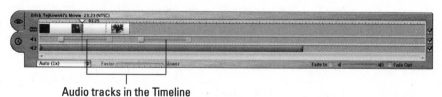

Audio tracks in the Timeline

To begin working with audio in iMovie, open the Audio shelf by clicking the Audio button in the Tool palette. Note that the Audio shelf is split into three sections:

✦ Sound Effects

✦ Voice Recorder

✦ Music Recorder

Using the built-in sound effects

To get you started with audio in your movies, iMovie gives you a set of pre-recorded sound effects, as shown in Figure 4-11. These make great background noises to enhance your movies. To preview any one of the sounds, click that sound.

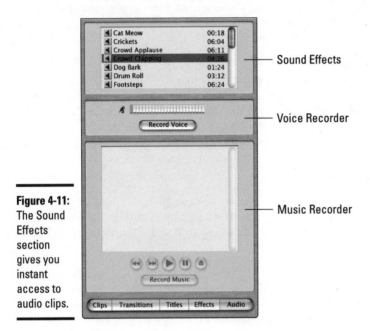

Figure 4-11:
The Sound
Effects
section
gives you
instant
access to
audio clips.

To add the sound to your movie, drag the sound effect from the Audio shelf and drop it on the Timeline at the bottom of the screen. When you do, the audio clip appears in one of the audio tracks for the movie. Feel free to move the sound effect clip anywhere in the track by dragging it. This gives you precise control over when the sound plays so you can synchronize it with video events.

Adding your own sound effects

If you'd like to add your own sound effects to the Audio shelf, you need to do a little work in the Finder. Drag your favorite AIFF files in the Finder to your Sound Effects folder (which is located in the home folder under Library⇨iMovie⇨Sound Effects).

Restart iMovie to see your new sound effects in the Audio shelf. With a quick drag, you can add the new audio files to your movie.

Recording voice-overs for your movie

Sometimes you might want to narrate a segment of your movie rather than rely on sound effect files. Fortunately, iMovie gives you the ability to do just that. By using the Voice Recorder section of the Audio shelf (refer to Figure 4-11), you can record your voice and add it to the audio track of your movie. What's more, you can record your voice as you watch the movie playing in real-time. This allows you to perfectly synchronize any narration you speak with the video onscreen. Truly sassy!

To record your voice, perform the following steps:

1. **Position the playback head at the place in your movie where you'd like to begin recording narration.**

   The playback head tells you where you are in the movie. You can position the playback head in either the Monitor or the Timeline Viewer.

2. **Open the Audio shelf by clicking the Audio button.**

3. **(Optional) On the Monitor playback controls, click Play.**

   By clicking Play, you are able to view the video in your movie. By watching the video as you narrate, you can synchronize your speech to the video track. This step is optional, since you don't have to play a movie while recording a narration. Slower Macs may have trouble playing and recording audio at the same time.

4. **Back in the Audio shelf, click the Record Voice button to begin recording.**

   As you speak, the meter in the Audio shelf will help you monitor the incoming volume level.

5. **Click Stop in the Audio shelf.**

   When you complete the recording process, iMovie displays the newly recorded segment in the Timeline in an orange color. Now you can manipulate the audio in the Timeline just as you would any other movie or audio clip. If you aren't happy with the result, you can always press Delete to remove the audio clip and return to Step 4.

Importing audio from a CD

The bottom section of the Audio shelf is for working with audio CDs in iMovie. See Figure 4-12.

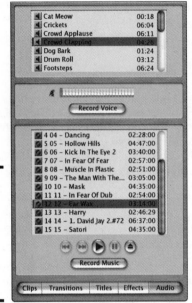

Figure 4-12:
The Audio shelf gives you easy access to CD recording features.

To import clips from an audio CD, follow these steps:

1. **Insert an audio CD into your Mac's CD drive.**

2. **Open the iMovie Audio shelf.**

   If your Mac is connected to the Internet, the song titles appear in the Audio shelf. Without the connection, you see generic track titles, such as 1 Audio Track, 2 Audio Track.

3. **Click whichever song you'd like to import into iMovie.**

4. **Click the Record Music button to begin recording the song.**

5. **Click Stop to finish the CD import.**

   The Play button toggles to a Stop button while import is in progress.

When you're finished importing a song from an audio CD, it appears in the Timeline in one of the audio tracks.

Removing sound from a movie

To remove an audio clip from your movie, select it in the Timeline and press Delete. Removing an audio clip does not have any effect on the position of other audio clips. This ensures that your audio clips stay in sync with existing video clips.

Completing Your Cinematic Masterpiece

You've made it through the movie-making process. You've shot, composed, and edited your own movie, but now what? Like any good filmmaker, the goal of creating a movie is to have people watch it. Luckily, iMovie gives you more than one way to export your movies for viewing.

✦ **Digital Video Camcorder:** Transfer your completed movie back to the camcorder to take it with you.

✦ **QuickTime movies:** Millions of computers around the world have QuickTime software. These computers can view iMovie movies, too! The great part about QuickTime movies is that you can use them in a variety of applications, from Web pages to PowerPoint presentations.

✦ **iDVD:** iMovie can prepare your movies for use with iDVD. The iDVD application lets you create a DVD. Read more about iDVD in Book III, Chapter 5.

Each type of export has its specific purposes and uses. What you'll use depends on your audience, video quality needs, and desired format. Whatever path you choose, iMovie can help you get there.

Camera

To export your completed movie to a DV camcorder, choose File➪Export Movie. In the dialog that appears, choose To Camera in the Export pop-up menu. iMovie presents you with settings (as shown in Figure 4-13) for exporting to the camcorder. As the dialog warns you, be sure your camera is in VTR mode and has a tape in it.

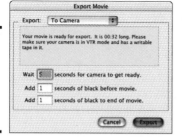

Figure 4-13:
Export
to your
camcorder
for port-
ability.

QuickTime

QuickTime is a multimedia engine in use on millions of computers every-where. Its popularity makes it a natural for many different uses:

✦ CD-ROM video

✦ Internet delivery

✦ High-quality playback from hard drive or removable disk

To export your completed movie to a QuickTime file, choose File➪Export Movie. In the dialog that appears, choose To QuickTime in the Export pop-up menu. iMovie presents you with settings for exporting to QuickTime. From the Formats pop-up, shown in Figure 4-14, choose the option that best fits the intended use of your movie. You can also maintain backwards compatibility with users of older versions of QuickTime by clicking the QuickTime 3.0 Compatible checkbox.

Figure 4-14: Export to QuickTime so millions of users worldwide can view your movie.

iDVD

To export your completed movie in preparation for iDVD, choose File➪Export Movie. In the dialog that appears, choose To iDVD in the Export pop-up menu. iMovie presents you with settings for exporting to an iDVD-compatible file (see Figure 4-15). For a full discussion of iDVD, run — don't walk — to Chapter 5 of Book III.

Figure 4-15: Export to iDVD for playback on your television.

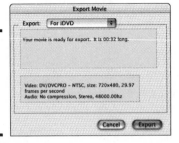

Chapter 5: Burn Those DVDs!
Using iDVD 2

In This Chapter

✔ **Putting together your DVD Menu**

✔ **Adding media to a DVD**

✔ **Burning a DVD for your friends and family**

A pple made history when it became one of the first companies around to include the SuperDrive in a computer. The *SuperDrive* is a drive capable of creating and viewing CDs and DVDs. To make it easy to create your own DVDs, Apple includes iDVD with today's Macs. *iDVD* is a sophisticated authoring utility that enables you to create beautiful DVD presentations with professional results.

What Am 1 Doing, Anyway?

Creating a DVD is a unique process. Combining talents in art, video, and presentation, DVD authoring demands multiple skills of its users. At its core, a *DVD* is simply a collection of digital video files. Unlike a CD-ROM or videotape, however, a DVD also has a fancy presentation and navigation system built into it. By using the DVD authoring tools of iDVD, you can

✦ Create a menu with buttons, text, and background music and images to enable viewers to navigate your DVD.

✦ Add still and moving images to your DVD.

✦ Burn the DVD to a disc for permanent storage and distribution to friends, family, and co-workers.

Apple overcomes the complexity of DVD authoring with its powerful iDVD software. With iDVD, you can create professional-looking menu systems to present your videos and digital slideshows. Then, when you're ready, a few clicks will burn the presentation, videos, and slideshows onto a DVD using your Super Drive. In fact, iDVD will run only on a system that has a Super Drive.

Use iDVD to reduce the process of creating a DVD to three simple steps:

1. **Customize the Menu.**

   The *Menu* of a DVD is the main screen that viewers use to navigate the completed DVD. You can use one of the menus supplied by Apple or you can create your own.

2. **Add media.**

   What's a DVD without movies? Use drag-and-drop to fill your DVD with movie files from iMovie or photographs from iPhoto. (Read more on these in Chapter 4 and Chapter 3 of this mini-book, respectively.)

3. **Preview and burn a DVD.**

   You can preview your DVD at any point during the design process. When you're satisfied with the results, slip a blank DVD-R in the drive and click the mouse to burn a finished product.

I go into more detail on each of these steps throughout this chapter.

Mastering Menus

As a Macintosh user, you're no doubt familiar with the term *menu*. When it comes to DVD authoring, though, *menu* takes on a new meaning. Instead of the traditional menus that display when you click towards the top of your screen in Mac OS X, a *DVD Menu* is the name of the entire interface.

When you launch the iDVD application, you immediately see a default DVD Menu, as shown in Figure 5-1. Like that of any commercial DVD movie, you'll see this DVD Menu when you load the completed DVD in your favorite DVD player.

Three components make up a typical DVD Menu:

+ **Background image or movie:** The backdrop picture that appears behind all the controls.

+ **Buttons:** Icons that represent the video clips and slideshows on the DVD.

+ **Titles:** Text that appears in your DVD Menu.

You can change the look and style of the background, buttons, and titles by using one of the Apple-provided themes, or you can customize all parts of the DVD Menu by using your own images, fonts, and buttons.

Background image   Title

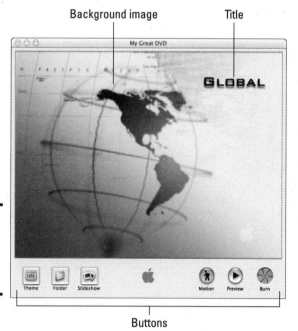

Figure 5-1:
A DVD
Menu is the
heart of
your DVD.

Buttons

Themes

If you can't draw a stick figure and you didn't have a single class in graphic arts — like yours truly — you'll be happy to know that iDVD offers several professional-looking, prepackaged themes for you to use. A *theme* is just a group of settings that determine the look and feel of your DVD Menu. (*Many thanks, Apple.*)

To view the included themes, click the Theme button in the iDVD window (lower-left). When you do, a drawer pops out from the side of the window, as shown in Figure 5-2.

The Themes drawer contains a tabbed panel, which subdivides the drawer into three tabbed sections:

✦ **Themes:** The Themes panel is where you select one of the included themes for your DVD Menu.

✦ **Customize:** Select the Customize tab to tweak the settings of your theme.

✦ **Status:** The Status tab gives you some extra information about the files in your DVD presentation.

Figure 5-2:
Whoa!
We've got
Themes,
dude!

Click to extend the Themes drawer.

Use choices from the Themes and Customize tabs in the iDVD drawer to personalize your DVD Menu to match your tastes. Start with the Themes tab panel to choose from a list of professional themes.

Clicking any one of these themes updates the DVD Menu to reflect your selection. A *theme* contains a background image, a button style, and settings that affect the onscreen text. Table 5-1 lists some of the 14 included themes and the uses to which they might apply.

Table 5-1	Popular Themes and Their Uses	
Theme Name	*Common Use*	*What It Looks Like*
Global	General purpose	A map of the world
Family	Vacations and family events	An earth-tone background
Wedding	A wedding, bridal shower, or anniversary	White roses
Sports	Sporting events	A runner
Sky	General purpose	A cloud-filled sky
Kids Blue	Boys' videos	A subdued blue background
Kids Pink	Girls' videos	A subdued pink background

Of course, those are only suggestions for using the themes. You can use them in whatever fashion you find useful.

After playing around with the iDVD themes, you might begin to wish for more of them. Fortunately, iDVD doesn't lock you into using one of its themes. You can customize one of the included themes to match your own style.

Setting the background

The first thing that you see when you pop your DVD disc into your DVD player is the background image. On top of this image hang out the rest of the DVD Menu controls. Besides the beautiful images that iDVD provides in its themes, you're free to use any other image that you prefer: You can use still or motion images as a background and even add background music.

Adding a still background

To change the background of your DVD Menu, perform the following steps:

1. **Click the Theme button in the main iDVD window.**

   This causes the iDVD drawer to open, revealing the Themes, Customize, and Status tabs.

2. **Click the Customize tab in the Theme drawer, as shown in Figure 5-3.**

   The Customize tab enables you to set the various aspects of your DVD Menu.

Drag your background image or movie here.

Drag an audio file here.

Figure 5-3:
Change the background image to anything you want.

Click to view motion effects.

Click to preview audio effects.

3. **Drag an image from the Finder and drop it into the Image/Movie box of the Background section.**

iDVD updates the DVD Menu to reflect your new background choice.

Adding a moving background

The fun doesn't stop there, though. Not only can you use any image from your collection as the backdrop to your DVD Menu, but you can also use any QuickTime movie to animate the background. Outstandingly *sassy*!

When you choose a movie to use as a background, make sure that it's a short clip, preferably no longer than 30 seconds. To make it look really professional, try making the end of the movie clip sync with the beginning of the movie. Because the short clip loops continuously, you don't want too much of a visual difference between the first and last frames of the clip.

To liven up your background with a movie, follow these steps.

1. **Click the Theme button in the main iDVD window.**

The iDVD drawer opens.

2. **Click the Customize tab in the Theme drawer.**

The Customize tab enables you to set the various aspects of your DVD Menu.

3. **Drag a movie from the Finder and drop it into the Image/Movie box.**

4. **In the main DVD window, click the Motion button (bottom-right) to see how your background video looks in action.**

5. **Click the Motion button again to stop the background motion.**

Adding audio to your menu

You can make your customized background even cooler — oops, I meant *more professional* — by adding some audio to the mix. To add some background music or audio to your DVD Menu, follow these steps:

1. **Click the Theme button in the main iDVD window.**

The iDVD drawer opens.

2. **Click the Customize tab in the Theme drawer.**

Use choices here to change the background audio that plays while viewing your DVD Menu.

3. **Drag an audio file from the Finder and drop it into the Audio box.**

iDVD will accept AIFF, MP3, and WAV files. If you're using a moving Menu, its audio track will appear in the Audio well. You can choose to either keep that audio or to delete it and use another audio file in its place. If you're a .Mac subscriber, you can download dozens of free, professional-quality audio clips that make good background audio for a DVD.

4. **Click the Motion button in the main iDVD window (bottom-right) to hear the background audio of your DVD Menu.**

5. **Click the Motion button again to stop the audio.**

When your DVD is complete, your viewers will hear the custom audio play whenever the main DVD Menu is displayed. Here are some suggestions for adding some extra style or mood to your DVD Menu system:

✦ Play a rendition of "Happy Birthday" for a birthday DVD.

✦ Play the "Wedding March" or the song you first danced to as the background for a wedding DVD.

✦ Bring back memories of the family vacation in the backseat of the car with a DVD that plays "99 Bottles of Beer on the Wall" as the background music.

A word on image dimensions

For best results, make sure that your background image has the same dimensions as digital video — 720 x 480 pixels. If the dimensions of your image don't match the dimensions of digital video, iDVD will stretch or shrink the image to fit, which might have undesirable effects. When your image is stretched and skewed to fit the DVD Menu, Aunt Harriet might end up looking like the Ogre from *Shrek*. Don't forget that you can resize images in iPhoto to help you with this step.

Because no two televisions are exactly alike, it's also a good idea to activate the Show TV Safe Area option, which you can find under the Advanced menu. This draws a smaller rectangle within the larger full-screen. If you place your buttons within this smaller rectangle and make sure that the important parts of the background image also appear within it, you can be certain that any television will be able to display the DVD properly. Go outside of this "safe area" and you might end up cutting Aunt Harriet's head off in the background image or losing some of your most cherished clips.

You can use QuickTime player or iPhoto to change the dimensions of your background image for import into iDVD. For example, you can use the iPhoto crop feature to alter the overall shape of the image and then resize it within iPhoto. Use the Size setting when you export the image from iPhoto and then save the file in the Pictures folder located in your Home folder so that you can find it easily later. For more on working in iPhoto, see Book III, Chapter 3.

With a little imagination, you can probably come up with numerous ideas to personalize the audio that accompanies your DVD projects.

Adding Media Files to Your DVD

With the background of your DVD Menu in place, now start adding some content to the project, either video or images. With iDVD, you can add your movies or photographs to a DVD presentation. What a great way to present and preserve your photographs and videos for years to come . . . and never again will your guests groan when you announce that you want to show them home movies.

Adding a Movie Button

iDVD displays video clips in the Menu with small buttons. These Movie Buttons display small previews of the video. To play the video, the user just selects the Button. To create a Movie Button, you need to add some video content to your DVD. To do so, drag a QuickTime movie file from the Finder and drop it into your DVD Menu. When you do, a Movie Button appears in the DVD Menu, as shown in Figure 5-4.

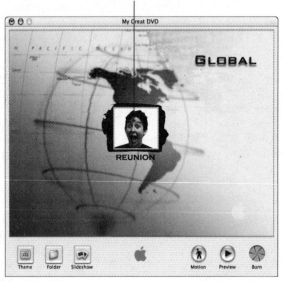

A Movie Button appears.

Figure 5-4: Drag a movie file into your project to create a Movie Button.

A Movie Button serves two important purposes:

+ **Preview:** Displays a small thumbnail image of the movie to the user.

+ **Navigation:** Permits a user to navigate the DVD.

After you drag a movie file into your DVD Menu and create a Movie Button, you can place the button anywhere in the DVD Menu that you wish. To reposition a Movie Button, simply click it and drag it to the desired destination. By default, Movie Buttons snap to an imaginary grid when relocated. To position Movie Buttons outside the confines of this grid, select the Free Position option in the Customize drawer.

An iDVD Menu limits you to six Movie Buttons. If you'd like to have more than that, create a folder in the Finder, drag six movie files into that folder, and add that folder as a Movie Button by dragging it into the DVD Menu like you would a single movie file.

Setting the Movie Button style

Like the Menu backgrounds, you can also customize Movie Buttons. To adjust your Movie Buttons, do the following:

1. **Click the Theme button in the main iDVD window.**

The iDVD drawer opens.

2. **Click the Customize tab in the Theme drawer.**

3. **Click any Movie Button from the DVD Menu to select it.**

When you select a Movie Button, a small slider appears above it. Move this slider to set the default thumbnail picture for that Button in the Menu. If you select the Movie check box, the Movie Button animates in the Menu.

4. **Adjust the button's properties in the Button section of the Customize tab, shown in Figure 5-5.**

You can customize Movie Buttons in several different ways. Table 5-2 describes the settings and what they do.

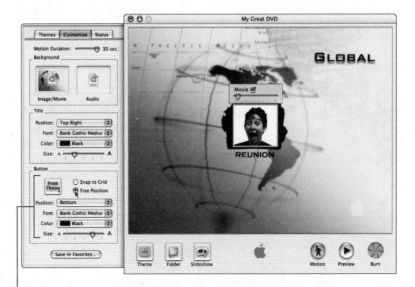

Figure 5-5:
Customize
a Movie
Button here.

Adjust a Movie Button's properties.

Table 5-2	Movie Button Customization Features
Movie Button Property	*What It Does*
From Theme	Changes the frame shape of the Movie Button.
Snap to Grid	Forces placement of a Movie Button on an imaginary grid.
Free Position	Unlike Snap to Grid, allows Movie Buttons to be placed in a more freeform arrangement.
Position	Places the text for a Movie Button in a specific location.
Font	Changes the font that a Movie Button uses for its caption.
Color	Adjusts the color of a Movie Button's frame and text caption.
Size	Adjusts the size of the text of a Movie Button's caption: Move the slider to the right to increase caption size.

One of the more unusual customization features of Movie Buttons is the Button Shape setting, which you can use to change the look of all Movie Buttons in your DVD Menu. Choose from several different styles (by clicking the From Theme button) to match your artistic needs.

Adding a Slideshow Button

In addition to movies, iDVD gives you the chance to place your favorite digital images on the DVD. In the same way that iDVD handles movies as Movie Buttons in the DVD Menu, you can add a group of images to the Menu as Slideshow Buttons. Slideshow Buttons are nearly identical to Movie Buttons, with one exception: They playback a sequence of digital photographs instead of a movie.

When you add a Slideshow Button, iDVD rearranges the buttons in the DVD Menu to account for the new button.

Add images to the slideshow

With a new Slideshow Button in place, you can add images to it by following these steps:

1. **Double-click the Slideshow Button that you just added to the Menu to open the Slideshow window.**

2. **To add images to the slideshow, drag your favorite images from the Finder to the Slideshow window.**

   Feel free to drag several photos at once. After the photos are in the Slideshow window, you can drag them around to change their order of appearance as shown in Figure 5-6.

Figure 5-6: Arrange your Slideshow photos in any order you desire.

Book III
Chapter 5

Burn Those DVDs! Using iDVD 2

3. **To add some audio, simply drag your favorite audio file from the Finder and drop it on the Audio Button of the Slideshow window.**

4. **When you've completed setting up your Slideshow, click the Return button to return to the main Menu.**

Setting the Slideshow Button preview

Because multiple images comprise a slideshow, iDVD gives you the opportunity to select which image you want for the DVD preview. To choose an image as the preview, click the Slideshow Button that you added to the Menu to select it. A slider appears above the Slideshow Button. Move this slider to scroll through the various images in the slideshow. When you find the image that you want to use for the Slideshow Button in the DVD Menu, click the Slideshow Button again to finish the task.

Customizing Titles

Your DVD Menu isn't just a container of images, movies, and sound. It can do text, too! Labeling items in your DVD Menu makes it easier to use, and iDVD makes it a cinch. You can find titles in your DVD Menu in two different locations:

✦ **Main Title:** The main Title usually appears at the top of the DVD Menu. It's the text that uses the largest font.

✦ **Button captions:** Each Movie Button and Slideshow Button has its own caption (a *Title*).

Use a Title to label a video clip with a description or add a date for future reference. As your collection of DVDs grows, you'll be glad that you took the time to properly label your Menu and Movie Buttons.

To change the text of the Title or the captions below Movie Buttons, select the text by clicking it. When you do, a rectangle with a cursor appears to indicate that you can now edit the text. Type the text that you want to appear and press Return when you're finished, as shown in Figure 5-7.

As I mention earlier in the chapter, you can also customize the font, color, and position of the various Titles by clicking the Theme button at the bottom of the iDVD window.

Edit a title by selecting it and typing new text.

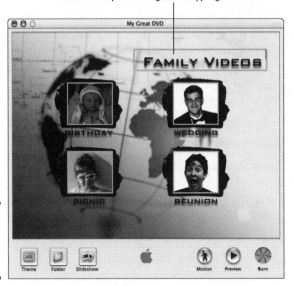

Figure 5-7:
Edit a Title
by clicking
its text.

Checking Things Out with a Preview

After you toil to design your DVD — hey, you're now a DVD-authoring professional! — you'll no doubt want to see the results. (Yet another great hat
you can wear as a Mac owner.) Don't forget that you're creating a DVD that
others will view. *Hint:* Review your work to make sure that the results are
up to your stellar ambitions. To help you out, iDVD gives you a full-featured
Preview mode, where you can view your DVD creation much as you would
with a traditional DVD player. To preview your DVD, just click the Preview
button (bottom-right) at the bottom of the main iDVD window.

Previewing your DVD project also gives you the opportunity to check your
content. After all, you don't want the "Wedding March" to play in the background of your birthday party footage or "The Old Gray Mare" at your in-
law's anniversary bash. Because you eventually want to commit this DVD
presentation to real DVD media, it makes sense to scrupulously preview
your presentation; you'll avoid wasting DVD-R discs.

Saving and Burning a DVD

After your DVD Menu is complete and the project looks great in Preview, it's
time for the final step in the process. iDVD makes it just as easy to burn
your DVD as it was to lay out the interface and add media to it.

**Book III
Chapter 5**

**Burn Those DVDs!
Using iDVD 2**

1. **Click the Burn button at the bottom of the iDVD window to begin recording a DVD.**

   When you click it, the Burn button changes into something that looks like a serious nuclear warning. No need to run for cover, though. iDVD is powerful . . . but not *that* powerful.

   iDVD asks you to insert a blank DVD-R disc into the SuperDrive. When this happens, you might see a message that reads like this:

   ```
   Disc Insertion... Waiting for Device to Become Ready...
   ```

2. **Insert a blank DVD-R into the SuperDrive.**

3. **After you load the disc, wait a moment for iDVD to recognize that the ball is in its court.**

   iDVD begins the process of burning the DVD. The length of this process varies depending on a few factors:

   - **DVD burner speed:** The faster the drive, the shorter the wait.

   - **Amount of material:** The more content on your DVD, the longer the wait.

   As the burning proceeds, iDVD updates you with progress messages. Don't worry if you don't understand all the messages that it displays. The language of the DVD creation process is a technical one, and sometimes iDVD speaks this language. Just ignore the messages as the burning proceeds.

   Because iDVD has to encode all the content before the burn can take place, it might take a couple hours to create a DVD. After the first DVD is done, though, iDVD lets you create additional DVDs at a fraction of the time. It will keep asking you for additional discs until you cancel the operation.

   If you want to find out what all these messages mean — as well as how to burn all sorts of data, audio, and exotic CD and DVD formats — then I heartily recommend *CD and DVD Recording For Dummies,* by Mark Chambers. It's a comprehensive guide to everything optical for both Mac and Windows computers, published by Hungry Minds, Inc.

4. **When iDVD completes the burning process, remove the disc from the drive and pop it into any consumer-grade DVD player.**

   Alternatively, you can leave the DVD in the drive, fire up DVD Player by clicking its icon in the Applications folder, and view your new work of art right on your Mac.

If you have any experience with DVDs at all, you'll soon notice one big difference between a copy of *Spiderman* that you rent from your local video store and the DVDs that you create with iDVD. Although the iDVD software is great for presenting video clips and image slideshows in a menu format, iDVD cannot create a DVD that plays all video clips on the disc as one continuous movie. Whereas Spidey will play from the beginning to end of the movie, iDVD limits users to video clips accessible from the main menu. Apple produces software called DVD Studio Pro, which is a piece of software that permits you to author DVDs like those that you find in the store, but the Pro in its title should be taken to heart. Although it has professional features, it also has a professional learning curve and, perhaps more importantly, a professional price tag. Hovering around the $1,000 mark, it's clearly not a solution for most casual home DVD producers.

Chapter 6: No, It's Not Called "iQuickTime"

In This Chapter

✔ Viewing movies

✔ Listening to audio

✔ Converting media to different formats

✔ Keeping track of your favorite media

✔ Tweaking QuickTime preferences

*Q*uickTime is a set of exciting technologies that gives you access to the greatest multimedia experience around. Despite its power, don't be surprised if you don't even realize that you're using it sometimes. Built with the average Joe in mind, QuickTime takes multimedia to new heights without forcing its users to become rocket scientists in the process. And dig that *sassy* chrome sheen — not bad for a software application!

QuickTime Can Do That?

QuickTime was created by Apple Computer to perform all sorts of multimedia functions. Although it's normally associated with movie playback, QuickTime can do much more. Whether it's movies, audio, animation, or music, QuickTime acts as the main engine that drives all your multimedia needs.

✦ **Media player:** QuickTime's main claim to fame is playing all sorts of media — and I do mean *all* sorts. Table 6-1 lists some of the media types that QuickTime can play.

The real beauty of QuickTime is that it transparently handles playback of all of these media formats and more. You don't even really have to know what each of these formats is to play them. QuickTime takes care of that for you.

✦ **File converter:** The world of multimedia includes all kinds of file formats: So many, in fact, that it can take a rocket scientist to figure them all out. Fortunately, beyond its abilities as a world-class media player, QuickTime also has a full suite of conversion tools at its heart. QuickTime can import many kinds of media and spit them back out into practically any other format it supports. Again, QuickTime handles the messy details behind the scenes for you. You don't need to know a .mov from a .mp4 to import and export to and from either format. QuickTime's got you covered.

✦ **Internet media tool:** When it comes to using media from the Internet, QuickTime is in a league all its own. With its plug-in feature, QuickTime takes its functionality to the Web browser. In addition to playing the usual movies and audio files found on the World Wide Web, QuickTime can play (or display) 3-D scenes and animations. If that weren't enough, QuickTime even lets you interact with some media. For example, with QuickTime, you can navigate within 3D worlds or play Flash games.

Table 6-1	QuickTime Playback Formats
Media Type	*File Types*
Movie	.mov, .avi, .mpg, .dv, .mp4
Audio	.aiff, .wav, .mp3, .au, .sfil
Graphics	.jpg, .tif, .pct, .bmp
Music	.mid, .kar
3D	QTVR (QuickTime Virtual Reality)
Animation	.swf

Playing Media with QuickTime

QuickTime makes a world of movies, audio, graphics, and music instantly available to you. Whether you want to view professional movie trailers or listen to a garage band's new single, QuickTime faithfully reproduces nearly any media format that you feed it.

At the center of the action: The QuickTime Player

At the heart of QuickTime's playback functionality is the QuickTime Player application. To launch QuickTime Player, double-click its icon in the Finder, which appears in the following figure. You can also launch the QuickTime Player from the Finder by double-clicking a media file that QuickTime can play. (See Table 6-1 earlier in this chapter for a listing of these file types.)

QuickTime Player

Don't make the mistake of thinking that QuickTime and QuickTime Player are the same thing: QuickTime is a technology that hides in the background waiting for instructions to do something with media; the QuickTime Player is an application that uses the QuickTime technologies. You'll do media conversions, playback, and editing with QuickTime Player. What you won't see is the QuickTime technology in action behind the scenes.

You can also launch QuickTime Player from its oh-so-convenient Dock icon. For more on the Dock, read in Chapter 3 of Book II.

QuickTime has two versions: free or Pro. The main differences between the free and Pro versions of QuickTime lie in the QuickTime Player application itself. The free version just plays media, and the Pro version adds extra features to QuickTime Player, such as exporting and full screen playback. If you're using QuickTime Pro, all items listed in this chapter will work as described. If, however, you notice that a feature is dimmed out or missing altogether, you might be using the free QuickTime license. To find out whether you're using a free or Pro license, open the System Preferences and navigate to the QuickTime panel. If you've registered as a QuickTime Pro user, you can find its registration information here, as shown in Figure 6-1. If you're not a registered user, you can purchase the upgrade at www.apple.com/quicktime. The upgrade will cost you $29.99, at the time of this writing.

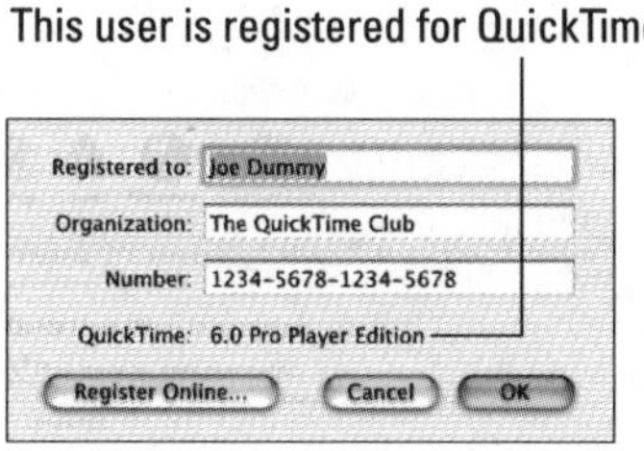

Figure 6-1:
Check the System Preferences to discover which QuickTime license you have.

This user is registered for QuickTime Pro.

Registered to:	Joe Dummy
Organization:	The QuickTime Club
Number:	1234-5678-1234-5678
QuickTime:	6.0 Pro Player Edition

(Register Online...) (Cancel) (OK)

Opening QuickTime movies

To begin viewing and hearing — aw, what the heck, how about *absorbing* — multimedia files, choose File⇨Open from the QuickTime Player application. This isn't the only way to open a file with QuickTime Player, though. Some of the other ways to open files with QuickTime Player are

✦ Drag a file to the QuickTime Player icon in the Dock.

✦ Double-click the media file in the Finder. If it has a QuickTime-style icon (a blue letter Q), it will automatically open in the QuickTime Player.

Operating the QuickTime Player

When you open a QuickTime file, QuickTime Player creates a new window to display it. All QuickTime Player windows share some common features.

✦ **Close, Minimize, and Zoom controls:** These three controls appear at the top left-hand corner of most windows in Mac OS X. You probably recognize them by their colors: red, yellow, and green, respectively.

✦ **Resize handle:** Drag the lower right-hand corner of a QuickTime Player to resize its movie for playback. Hold Shift while dragging to break free from constrained resizing. If the document contains sound media only, the window will grow or shrink in a horizontal direction when you resize it.

Any resizing that you perform makes no changes to the original file. QuickTime provides it for your convenience during playback.

Although some window features are common to all QuickTime Player windows, many features depend on the type of media that you wish to play. Table 6-2 lists some of the window features you may find and the media types associated with those features.

Table 6-2	QuickTime Player Window Features Based on Media
Window Feature	*Media Type that Uses this Feature*
Play button	All time-based media: movies, audio, animations, and MIDI
Rewind button	All time-based media: movies, audio, animations, and MIDI
Fast-forward	All time-based media: movies, audio, animations, and MIDI
Timeline	All time-based media: movies, audio, animations, and MIDI
Volume slider	All media with one or more audio tracks
Audio controls	All media with one or more audio tracks
Video controls	All media with one or more video tracks
Zoom buttons	QTVR 3-D media
Equalizer display	All media with one or more audio tracks

To make your life easier, QuickTime does a lot of work for you behind the scenes each time that it opens a media file. Although you might think that there are different combinations of controls in QuickTime Player, the reality is that the various media windows are more similar than they are different. Figure 6-2 shows the location of various QuickTime Player controls.

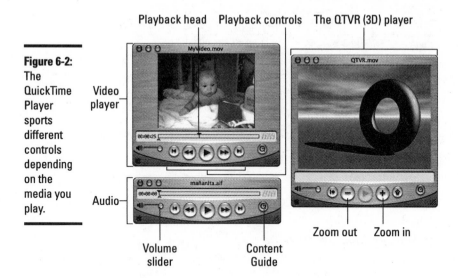

Figure 6-2: The QuickTime Player sports different controls depending on the media you play.

Playing media

Playback begins like you might suspect — by clicking the Play button. While a file is playing, the Play button toggles to a Stop button. Click that button to stop playback, which toggles the button back to Play.

Clicking the buttons with double-arrows on them advances the playback head at high speed in the direction of the arrows. If the file has audio in it, you will hear the playback at high speed, which sounds like an episode of Dave Seville and his helium-inhaling Chipmunks. Despite its comical sound, it's helpful for quickly scanning through a file. Click the buttons with a single arrow to advance to the beginning or end of a file.

You can also advance through the file by dragging the playback head in either direction. This action is permissible while the file is playing or when it's stopped. Unlike when you use the buttons, however, you miss out on the high-speed sound and video.

To adjust the volume of a movie, simply move the volume slider left or right.

You can control playback using the keyboard as well. Table 6-3 summarizes the keyboard shortcuts for playback.

Table 6-3	Keyboard Shortcuts for Common Playback Functions
Keyboard Shortcut	*What It Does*
Space bar	Starts or stops the player
Left/right arrow (←/→)	Advances the playback head (in slow motion)
Option+←/→	Moves the playback head to the beginning or end of the file
Option+↑/↓	Sets the volume to maximum and minimum respectively
Control+click Play	Plays a movie with the audio muted
Up/down arrow (↑/↓)	Increases/decreases the volume of the current movie

Advanced playback features

QuickTime Player offers advanced playback features that go beyond simple play and stop functions. Keep in mind, however, that some of the advanced features of QuickTime Player are meant only for registered QuickTime Pro users. The general rule of thumb is that registered Pro users of QuickTime Player can modify QuickTime content. If you aren't registered as a QuickTime Pro user, you can take advantage of only playback features in QuickTime Player.

Video playback

To adjust video playback quality, choose Movie⇨Show Video Controls or press ⌘+K. When you do, a small adjustment bar arises like magic from the bottom edge of your movie. The first setting that you'll probably see is Brightness. Click the text in this adjustment to select the next setting, Contrast. The video settings that you can change are

- ✦ Brightness
- ✦ Contrast
- ✦ Tint
- ✦ Color

To change a setting, click the colored lines that span the adjustment bar. You can immediately view the results of any video changes that you make. Figure 6-3 demonstrates one of the video controls in action.

Figure 6-3:
Set the
Brightness,
Contrast,
Tint, and
Color of
your movie
to improve
its look on
playback.

Audio playback

You can also tweak the audio playback of any file that has one or more soundtracks. To open the audio playback controls, either click the miniature equalizer to the right of the timeline or choose Movie⇨Show Sound Controls. With the audio controls, you can alter the following:

✦ Balance

✦ Bass

✦ Treble

After you change the audio to your satisfaction, click the miniature equalizer again or choose Movie⇨Hide Sound Controls. Figure 6-4 shows the advanced audio controls.

Looping features

Sometimes you may want to play a piece of media more than once. In these situations, you need to loop the playback. To force a movie to loop, choose Movie⇨Loop or press ⌘+L. Press ⌘+L again to turn the looping off.

Figure 6-4:
Set
Balance,
Bass, and
Treble to
enhance
audio during
playback.

If you want to get fancy, you can also play a movie in a forward direction followed by playback in reverse. Apple calls this *looping back and forth*. To do this, choose Movie⇨Loop Back and Forth.

Movie info

To see more information about the files that you're playing, ask the expert: QuickTime Player. To view basic information about a movie, choose Window⇨Show Movie Info or press ⌘+I. The resulting window displays the following data:

✦ **Source:** Location of the file

✦ **Format:** Compressor and dimensions of the file

✦ **Movie FPS:** Preferred rate of playback in frames per second (fps)

✦ **Playing FPS:** Actual rate of playback in fps (available during playback only)

✦ **Data Size:** Size of the file

✦ **Data Rate:** Preferred rate of playback (in bytes per second)

✦ **Current Time:** Position of the playback head (in units of time)

✦ **Duration:** Length of the movie file (in units of time)

✦ **Normal Size:** Default movie dimensions

✦ **Current Size:** Actual movie dimensions (if you've resized the movie since opening the file)

Back on track

Every file that you open with QuickTime Player consists of one or more tracks. A *track* contains one (and only one) type of media. For example, a typical QuickTime movie might comprise two tracks:

✔ **Video track:** Stores the video data of the movie

✔ **Sound track:** Stores the audio data of the movie

In contrast, opening an audio file with QuickTime Player might have only a single sound track. Other files don't have a video or sound track at all: Shockwave and Flash (.swf) files, for example, usually contain only one Flash track. MIDI files have yet another type of track. Luckily, QuickTime makes it simple for you to ignore these technical trivia facts altogether (which most of us prefer).

These bits and pieces of information are *read-only,* which means that you can't change them from the Movie Info window.

Movie properties

In addition to general movie information, you can also peek inside a QuickTime movie to see what makes it tick. To display the Movie Properties window, choose Movie⇨Get Movie Properties or press ⌘+J. Figure 6-5 shows the Movie Properties window when you first open it.

Figure 6-5:
Use the Movie Properties window to view its track information.

The Movie Properties window displays the tracks using the pop-up menu on the top left of the Movie Properties window. Selecting a track causes the pop-up menu on the top right to display a set of properties that pertain to the selected track. Figure 6-6 demonstrates the Track and Properties pop-up menus in action.

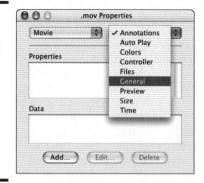

Figure 6-6:
Select Tracks and their Properties from the pop-up menus of the Properties window.

Unlike the Movie Info window, the Movie Properties window does let you change many aspects of a movie. For example, to resize, skew, or even rotate a movie's video track, follow these steps:

1. **Using the QuickTime Player, open a QuickTime movie.**

2. **Press ⌘+J to open its Movie Properties window.**

3. **From the Tracks pop-up menu of the Properties window, choose the first available Video Track.**

4. **From the Properties pop-up menu, select Size.**

5. **Click the Adjust button.**

   Red adjustment handles appear in the movie player. Resize and rotate to your heart's content!

6. **When you've adjusted the track's size to your liking, click the Done button.**

Using a similar approach, you can change many other properties of a track, such as Annotations settings.

QuickTime: The Super Converter

QuickTime also makes a great tool for converting media files. As your collection of multimedia grows, you'll eventually find yourself wishing that certain files were in a different format. For example, you might want to convert a QuickTime movie to a DV file for use with iMovie. With a few clicks, QuickTime can open a media file in one of dozens of formats and convert it to most any other format that QuickTime understands. To do so, you must import the file into QuickTime, and then export it into the format you prefer.

Importing files

For most operations, you can open a file with the QuickTime Player by using the usual File⇨Open menu item. For some formats, however, this won't work. In these instances, QuickTime gives you the chance to import a file. The difference between *open* and *import* is subtle but important. If QuickTime can handle a file's media natively, you can use the Open menu. If it can't handle a media's data natively, it must import the file. The import process converts the file to a format that QuickTime can use. To start the import process, just select File⇨Import.

For example, QuickTime doesn't normally display text files. Using the Import command, however, converts a text file into a movie file. Then you can view the text in a traditional movie player window. Figure 6-7 shows an imported text file movie.

Figure 6-7:
Choose
File➪Import
to import a
file.

Table 6-4 lists the file types that QuickTime can import.

Table 6-4	QuickTime Import File Types
Category	*File Types*
Audio	AIFF/AIFC, Audio CD, MP3, Sound Designer II, System 7 Sound, uLaw (AU), WAV
Video	AVI, DV, Motion JPEG, MPEG-1, MPEG-4
Images	BMP, GIF, JPEG/JFIF, MacPaint, PICT, PNG, Photoshop (with layers), SGI, Targa, FlashPix, TIFF
Animation	3DMF, Animated GIF, FLC/FLI, Flash, PICS
Other	KAR (Karaoke), MIDI, QuickDraw GX, QuickTime Image File, Text

Exporting files

After you open or import a media file, QuickTime Player will let you export it to one of many formats. To export a movie, choose File➪Export. In the dialog that appears (shown in Figure 6-8), select the desired output format from the Export pop-up menu. Each export type also has a set of options. To view them, click the Options button on the right side of the Export dialog.

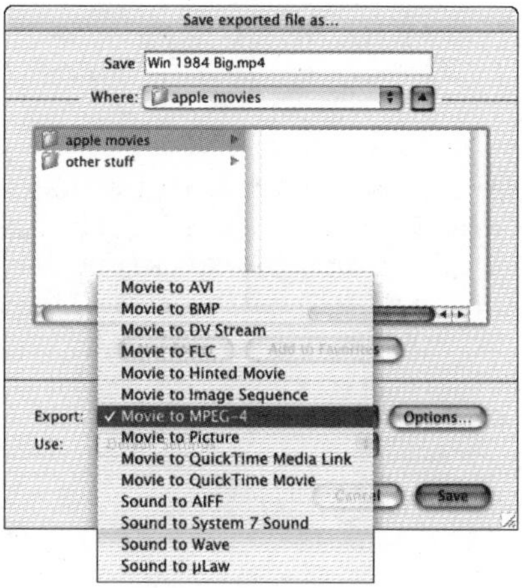

Figure 6-8:
Use
QuickTime
to export
your media
files to a
variety of
formats.

Make QuickTime the Center of Your Digital Universe

Although QuickTime is great at actively importing, exporting, and altering all kinds of media, most Mac OS X owners don't care about these features. For those who could care less what the media type is for an e-mail attachment, QuickTime transparently handles the chore of displaying the file without having to know all the technical details behind it. With QuickTime as your ally, you can watch the latest *Star Wars* movie trailer, view an image in a Web page . . . or, if you're like me, you can listen to Bob Hope jaw with Bing Crosby (if you have a collection of classic radio shows in MP3 format). QuickTime makes a great tool for viewing and exploring all sorts of exciting multimedia content.

Favorites

The quickest way to keep track of your media files is with the Favorites menu. It offers one-click access to the media files that you use most. To add a file to the Favorites menu, do the following:

1. **Open your favorite media file.**

2. **Press ⌘+D or choose Favorites➪Add Movie as Favorite.**

Now, anytime you want to watch and/or hear this file, you simply choose it from the Favorites menu.

You can remove files later from the Favorites menu by performing these steps:

1. **Choose Favorites➪Show Favorites.**

2. **In the Favorites window that appears, select the file that you wish to remove.**

3. **Press the Delete key to remove the file from the Favorites.**

Free content for all

The QuickTime Player offers you one-click access to a variety of multimedia content, including news, entertainment, and educational features. Naturally, an Internet connection is required. To view the QuickTime Player Content Guide, click the Q button in the lower right-hand corner of the Player (see Figure 6-9).

Figure 6-9:
Click the Q
button to
view free
content.

Click to bring up the Content Guide.

When you do, a new window opens in the Player, shown in Figure 6-10. This is the content guide's main menu. From here, you can click any of the provided links just as you might click on a link in a Web page.

Figure 6-10:
The
QuickTime
Player
content
guide gives
you instant
access to a
variety of
topics.

Clicking any item in the content guide opens a Web page in your preferred browser.

QuickTime and your browser

QuickTime is equally at home in a Web browser. Like the QuickTime Player application, the QuickTime Web plug-in offers convenient playback utilities directly in your Web browser. To view a movie in a browser window, simply navigate to a Web page that contains a QuickTime movie; QuickTime automatically loads the movie and plays it in the Web page. In many cases, you can even save a movie from a Web page — just click the triangle icon at the far right of the movie controller. A menu appears, giving you two options to save the movie, shown in Figure 6-11. Save as Source saves the file in the format in which you originally downloaded it. Save as QuickTime converts the file to a QuickTime movie.

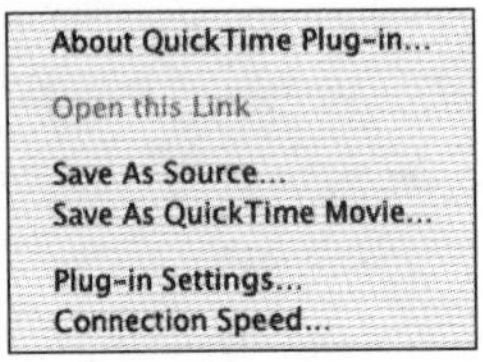

Figure 6-11:
Save
movies from
a Web page.

About QuickTime Plug-in...

Open this Link

Save As Source...
Save As QuickTime Movie...

Plug-in Settings...
Connection Speed...

To aid your quest for QuickTime content on the Web, Apple hosts a vast array of materials on its site. You can find movie trailers, free tunes from your favorite artists, game trailers, and Internet radio news at this site:

`www.apple.com/quicktime/`

Tweaking QuickTime

After you become comfortable with using QuickTime for media playback, you may want to expand your horizons. QuickTime has many features — so many, in fact, that it requires two different Preference windows to handle them all.

Setting the QuickTime Player Preferences

To open the QuickTime Player Preferences, choose QuickTime Player⇨ General Preferences. A General Preferences window appears with a number of settings that affect how the QuickTime Player application works.

Working with QuickTime Preferences

To open the Preferences for QuickTime, do one of the following:

✦ Open the System Preferences and navigate to the QuickTime panel.

✦ Using the QuickTime Player application, choose QuickTime Player⇨ QuickTime Preferences.

Click the various tabs of the QuickTime Preferences, shown in Figure 6-12, to change its settings.

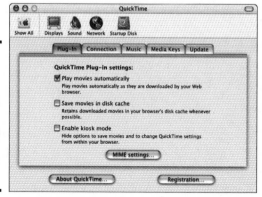

Figure 6-12:
Open the
QuickTime
dialog of the
System
Preferences
to change
QuickTime's
settings.

The QuickTime Preferences consist of five tabs of settings.

✦ **Plug-In:** To play QuickTime content, your browser uses a QuickTime
Plug-In. Configure the Plug-In's settings here.

✦ **Connection:** QuickTime can tailor your online multimedia experience to
the speed of your Internet connection. Tell QuickTime what speed your
connection uses and it takes care of the rest.

✦ **Music:** QuickTime can do music! Select QuickTime's synthesizer in this
panel. You can also take advantage of SoundFont and DLS files, which
are popular in the Windows world.

✦ **Media Keys:** The Media Keys panel lets you set authentication for
secure media. So far this hasn't taken off, but it may in the future.

✦ **Update:** Wondering if you have the most current version of QuickTime?
Let QuickTime look for you! In this panel, you can force QuickTime to
update itself.

**Book III
Chapter 6**

**No, It's Not Called
"iQuickTime"**

Chapter 7: Turning Your Mac into a DVD Theater

In This Chapter

✓ **What you need to watch DVDs on your Macintosh**

✓ **Using the DVD Player software**

✓ **Mysteries of the hidden controls unearthed!**

All the authoring capabilities of the Mac OS X digital hub are a lot of fun, but at some point, you're going to want to take a break from work. In recent years, DVDs have exploded onto the home entertainment scene. Because of its high fidelity, convenience, and seemingly limitless storage capacity, the DVD has taken consumers by storm. The idea of an honest-to-goodness theater in your home is now within the grasp of mere mortals. Mac OS X has everything that you'll need to enjoy a night at the movies without ever leaving home. In fact, I can highly recommend the new 17-inch iMac G4 for those wide-screen classics.

The DVD Hardware

Before you watch one second of film, it's a good idea to get your setup in order. Playing DVDs requires a bit of hardware; fortunately, most recent Macintosh computers come equipped with the stuff that's necessary to watch DVDs.

To play DVD movies, you'll need either an internal DVD-compatible drive in your Macintosh or an external DVD drive with a FireWire connection. ***Note:*** DVD-ROM drives can only play discs, while others, like the SuperDrive, can both play *and* record discs. Either type of drive will work fine for watching movies on your Mac.

You can watch any standard DVD that you purchase at your local video store, as well as any DVD that you create with iDVD.

The DVD Player: It's Truly Shiny

To watch Frodo Baggins, Don Corleone, or Citizen Kane, you'll need DVD Player software. Mac OS X comes stocked with the perfect tool for the task: DVD Player.

Apple's DVD Player application is included with Mac OS X. You can find DVD Player here:

```
/Applications/DVD Player
```

But instead of rooting through the Finder, you can launch DVD Player an even easier way. Simply insert a DVD into the drive. As soon as you do, your Mac recognizes the disc and launches DVD Player by default for you. (Time for another round of well-deserved gloating about your choice of personal computer.)

However you choose to start DVD Player, you'll notice that it offers two windows:

✦ **Controller:** The small silver-colored remote control-looking interface that holds all of the controls for the player.

✦ **Viewer:** The large window where you will view your DVD movies.

If you're already using a traditional DVD player, you'll be right at home with Apple's DVD Player. Even if you've never used a traditional DVD player, it's not much different than using a software-based audio player like iTunes.

Using the Controller

The Controller is the command center of the DVD Player software. Arranged much like a VCR or tape deck, all of the familiar controls are present. Check it out in Figure 7-1.

Play Rewind

Stop | Fast Forward

Figure 7-1:
Use the
Controller
for common
playback
functions.

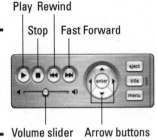

Volume slider   Arrow buttons

Table 7-1 details the fundamental commands present in the DVD Player controller. Apple software usually has some goodies hidden beneath the surface, and DVD Player is no exception. The controls in DVD Player have a few functions that might not be obvious to the casual user. These are listed in the third column of Table 7-1.

Table 7-1	Basic DVD Controls	
Control Name	*What It Does*	*Other Functions*
Play	Plays the DVD	It also toggles into a Pause button anytime a movie is playing.
Stop	Stops playback of the DVD	
Rewind	Skips to the previous chapter	Click and hold the Rewind button to quickly scan through the movie in reverse.
Fast Forward	Skips to the next chapter	Click and hold the Fast Forward button to quickly scan forward through the movie.
Volume Slider	Adjusts the volume of the DVD audio	
Arrow Button	Navigates through the menu items of the DVD	
Enter	Selects the currently highlighted menu item	
Eject	Ejects the DVD from the drive	
Title	Toggles display of the subtitles	
Menu	Displays the menu of the current DVD	

Movies on DVD are divided into *chapters* that enable you to jump directly to that point. That way you can skip right to the scene, say, where the flying monkey guards march, chanting, into the Wicked Witch's castle in *The Wizard of Oz*. You can navigate to chapters, play the movie from the beginning, or check out special bonus features (such as trailers and documentaries) from the DVD's main menu.

You can switch the Controller between horizontal and vertical orientation, which can make it easier to fit onscreen. Choose Controls➪Controller Type and then choose either Horizontal or Vertical orientation. (Those with keyboard shortcut fever can use ⌘+Shift+H or ⌘+Shift+V, respectively.)

Keep your eyes on the Viewer

As soon as you begin playing around with the DVD Player controls, you'll notice activity in the Viewer window, as shown in Figure 7-2.

Figure 7-2:
The Viewer is the main screen of the DVD Player.

You can think of the Viewer window as a television inside your Macintosh if it helps, but DVD Player goes one step further. Unlike a television screen, the Viewer has some nice tricks up its sleeve: For example, you can resize the Viewer window by using one of the four sizes listed in the Video menu (half, normal, maximum, and full-screen sizes). This is useful for watching a movie in a small window on your Desktop while you work with other applications.

If you're in it for the entertainment factor only, you'll probably want to resize the Viewer to fill the screen. You can resize the Viewer by clicking and dragging, or you can adjust its settings by choosing Window⇨Viewer. I like to watch movies in full-screen mode, which you can toggle with the ⌘+0 keyboard shortcut.

Taking Advantage of Additional DVD Features

As anyone with a little DVD experience knows, DVD discs can do a lot more than those archaic tapes you used to feed your VCR. Apple has included several functions that allow you to explore the extra features and content provided with a DVD movie.

Controller extras

To use the additional Controller features, click the small vertical lines at the rightmost edge of the DVD Player Controller. When you do, a small drawer slides out displaying the extra controls. (See Figure 7-3.)

Figure 7-3:
Expand the
Controller
window to
view the
additional
controls.

Table 7-2 summarizes the functions that you can perform with these additional controls.

Table 7-2	Additional Controller Features
Control	*What It Does*
Step Button (Half Speed)	Steps through a DVD in slow motion at half of the original speed
Step Button (Frame Speed)	Steps through a DVD in slow motion, one frame at a time
Previous Menu	Navigates to the previous menu
Alternate Tracks - Subtitles	Displays alternate subtitle tracks on the DVD
Alternate Tracks - Audio	Plays alternate audio tracks on the DVD
Alternate Tracks - Video Angle	Displays the current video footage from different camera angles

DVD Player preferences

The DVD Player application has a variety of settings that you can access and adjust via its Preferences window. To open the Preferences window, choose DVD Player➪Preferences. This brings up the DVD Preferences dialog, as shown in Figure 7-4.

Figure 7-4:
Use the
Preferences
to customize
your DVD
Player.

Preferences

Player | Disc | Windows

On Start Up
☑ Go To Full Screen Mode If Disc Is Mounted
☑ Start Playing Disc

On Disc Insertion
☐ Start Playing Disc

Full Screen Mode
Default Viewer Size [Maximum Size]
☐ Enable Viewer Resizing In Full Screen
☑ Hide Controller If Inactive For [10] Seconds

Cancel | OK

The Preferences window consists of three main tabs:

+ **Player:** Settings that affect how DVD Player operates.

+ **Disc:** Settings for Audio, Subtitles, Language, and the Web.

+ **Windows:** Settings for displaying onscreen information during playback.

The advantage of these Preference settings is that you can customize your copy of DVD Player to match your needs or desires. Everyone has different needs, so Apple tries to help out by providing you with some options. Nice of Apple, eh?

Player

Despite its moniker, the Player settings tab of DVD Player seems to have more to do with discs than the player. As you can see in Figure 7-4, three subsections make up the Player tab settings, yet only two of them have something to do with discs. Strange, but true!

+ **On Start Up:** These two settings affect what happens when you launch the DVD Player application. You can force DVD Player to play in full screen mode and automatically begin playback every time you start the application.

+ **On Disc Insertion:** One lonely option appears in this subsection. Besides automatic playback on startup, you can also make DVD Player start playing whenever you insert a disc into your Mac.

+ **Full Screen Mode:** These three options let you set the default viewer size, enable resizing in full screen, and make the controller disappear after a defined time of inactivity.

Disc

The second tab of the Preferences window consists of two sections, shown in Figure 7-5.

+ **Default Language Settings:** Sprechen Sie Deutsch? DVDs are designed to be multilanguage aware. Feel like brushing up on your German, Spanish, or Chinese? You can control the language the audio and menus appear in this section; of course, your choices are limited to those options included on the DVD. For the nonmultilingual, turn on the subtitles here, too.

+ **Features:** One lonely setting resides in the Features section. Some DVDs can access information on the Internet. Mark this check box to permit that function.

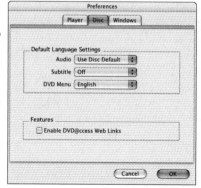

Figure 7-5:
The Disc tab lets you change the language that you hear and see during playback.

Multiple languages and Web access are not mandatory features of a DVD, so don't be surprised if you see variations of support when it comes to these settings.

Windows

The third, and last, tab of the Preferences window gives you the chance to toggle the help text for the Controller and status information for the Viewer window. Figure 7-6 shows the Windows tab of the Preferences window.

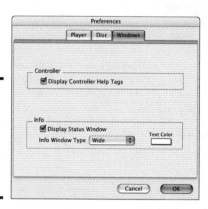

Figure 7-6:
The Windows tab holds Controller and Info settings.

✦ **Display Controller Help Tags:** Need some help using the Controller? Mark this check box to have DVD Player give you hints when you place your mouse over the Controller. Hold your cursor over a button for a brief moment, and a Help Tag will appear near the cursor.

✦ **Display Status Window:** Mark this check box, and DVD Player displays a small text box at the top-left corner of the Viewer window. In this text box, you see the name of the last task that you performed with DVD Player. For example, click the Stop button to see the word *Stop* displayed in the Viewer on top of the video beneath it.

✦ **Info Window Type:** Choose from two sizes with which to display your Status Window: Standard and Wide. If you select Wide, you can also change the color of the text that appears over your DVD. The Info Window shows the chapter, timing information, and subtitle settings about the video that's playing.

Figure 7-7 gives you a glimpse at what the Display Status Window looks like in the Viewer window.

Figure 7-7:
See the last executed command in the Viewer window.

Now that you have your DVD Player customized to your liking, get out the popcorn, pull up your favorite recliner, and let the movies roll!

Book IV

The Typical Internet Stuff

The 5th Wave — By Rich Tennant

"Wow, I didn't know OS X could redirect an email message like that."

Contents at a Glance

Chapter 1: Getting on the Internet 349

Chapter 2: Using Apple Mail 359

Chapter 3: Staying in Touch with iChat 381

Chapter 4: Expanding Your Horizons with iDisk 393

Chapter 5: Going Places with Internet Explorer 399

Chapter 6: Staying Secure Online 417

Chapter 1: Getting on the Internet

In This Chapter

✔ Selecting an Internet Service Provider (ISP)

✔ Understanding how your Mac gets on the Internet

✔ Setting up your Internet connection

I'll be honest — the Internet is a terribly complex monster of a network. If you tried to fathom all the data that's exchanged on the Internet and everything that takes place when you check your e-mail for Aunt Harriet's cookie recipe, your brain would probably melt like a chocolate bar in the Sahara Desert. There's a shoebox full of archaic things tucked under the Internet: communications protocols, routing addresses, packets, servers, and other hoo-hah that's beyond the grasp of just about everyone on the planet.

Luckily for regular folks like you and me, Mac OS X closes the trapdoor on all these details, keeping them hidden (as they *should* be). You don't have to worry about them, and the obscure information that you need in order to establish an Internet connection is kept to a minimum. In fact, the happiest computer owners that I've met think that the Internet is a little blinking light on their modem: If the light blinks in the proper manner, all is well. (I don't argue with them.)

In this chapter, I provide help and advice to those who are searching for an on-ramp to the Information Superhighway — and I lead you through the procedure of adding an Internet connection under Mac OS X.

Note: If you entered your Internet configuration information while you were in the First Use Wizard during the installation of Mac OS X — or if you upgraded to Mac OS X from Mac OS 9, and you already had a working Internet connection — *you can skip this chapter!* The information contained herein is only for those who add or change their Internet connectivity after installing Mac OS X.

Shopping for an ISP

Before you can connect to the Internet, you must sign up for Internet access. If you already have an ISP (acronym-speak for an *Internet Service Provider*) or your company provides Internet access, then smile quietly to yourself and skip to the next section. Otherwise, hang around while I discuss what to look for in an ISP and how to locate one in your local area.

ISPs are as thick as Louisiana mosquitoes these days, and often they're judged solely by the amount that they charge for basic access. Cost definitely is a factor — but it's not the *only* thing that should determine your choice in a service provider. Consider these guidelines when choosing or switching ISPs:

✦ **Local calling rates:** If you live in a rural area, check to make sure that all prospective ISPs offer local calling rates — believe me, no matter how much fun and how useful the Internet is, it's not worth hours of long-distance charges.

✦ **Broadband service:** Many ISPs now offer DSL *(Digital Subscriber Line)* and cable modem access. Collectively, these connections are called *broadband* because they offer the fastest method of transferring information to and from the Internet. If you have a home business, a large family, students, or you telecommute to your office, using broadband can make your life much simpler.

✦ **Quality technical support:** A 24-hour/7-day telephone support line is a godsend for the Internet novice — don't settle for voice support during business hours. Forget e-mail support, too; your e-mail application will be dead and gone if your Internet connection gives you problems. (Sound of palm whacking forehead.)

✦ **Static IP addresses:** A *static IP address* — the unique number that identifies your computer on the Internet — allows you to set up a professional Web server or File Transfer Protocol (FTP) server. (More on these adventures later in the book.) Suffice it to say that a business or organization running one of these services will benefit from a static IP address.

✦ **E-mail accounts:** Investigate how many individual accounts you receive with various ISPs. Also, find out whether you can maintain them yourself through a Web site. If so, that's a good sign. Additionally, if the prospective ISP provides a Web site where you can read and send e-mail messages, you can stay on top of your e-mail even while you're on the road or vacationing halfway across the globe.

✦ **Web space:** If you want your ISP to host your Web site, this is a no-brainer: the more space you get, the better. A minimum of 5MB is acceptable, but most ISPs provide 10MB or 20MB these days. Also, beware of ISPs that will charge you for your Web site if it receives a large amount of traffic, so it can be expensive to host a popular Web site if you join one of these ISPs.

✦ **Domain name service:** Finally, the better class of ISP also offers a domain name service, which allows you to register something like `yournamehere.com`. For the most professional appearance, you can usually pay a yearly fee, and the ISP takes care of all the details in setting up your own `.com` or `.org` domain name.

Locating an ISP is much easier in the modern Internet-savvy world than it was just two or three years ago. In the order you should try them, here are the tricks that I recommend for finding your local ISPs:

✦ **Check with your cable or telephone companies.** If you're already subscribing to cable service in your area, you're likely to be a candidate for cable Internet access. Also, many local phone companies offer DSL access. Call the customer service numbers for these companies and check out what they offer.

✦ **Get recommendations from friends and neighbors.** Folks love to give free advice — ask them how much they're paying, how reliable the connection has been, and how well they rate the ISP's technical support.

✦ **Check your phone directory.** Check the phone book for Internet service.

✦ **Investigate Internet ISP Web sites.** If you have Internet access at work, a friend's house, or your local public library, you can surf to The List (`thelist.internet.com`) where you can search for ISPs within your area code and location.

Investigating Various Types of Connections

Next, consider the types of connections that are available under Mac OS X to link your Mac to said ISP. You can choose from four pathways to digital freedom:

✦ **A dial-up connection:** Old-fashioned, yes. Slow as an arthritic burro, indeed. However, an *analog* (or telephone modem) connection is still the primary method for reaching the Internet for most computer owners. It's the cheapest method available, and all you need for this type of connection is a standard telephone jack and a modem. If you remember your classic iMac commercials, any Mac that can run Mac OS X should have a built-in modem.

✦ **A broadband connection:** Be it through DSL (which uses a standard telephone line) or cable (which uses your cable TV wiring), broadband Internet access is many times faster than a dial-up connection. Plus, both these technologies are *always-on,* meaning that your computer is automatically connected to the Internet when you turn it on and that connection stays active. With DSL or cable, there's no squeaky whine that accompanies your modem making a connection each time that you want to check your movie listings Web site. Both DSL and cable require a special piece of hardware (commonly called a *modem* as well, but it really isn't); this box is usually thrown in as part of your ISP charge.

Book IV
Chapter 1

Getting on
the Internet

✦ **A satellite connection:** If you're really out there — miles and miles away from any cable or DSL phone service — you can still get high-speed Internet access. The price for a satellite connection is usually much steeper than a standard DSL or cable connection, but it's available anywhere you can plant your antenna dish. Plus, a satellite connection is actually faster than other types of broadband access. Older satellite technologies actually require you to use a dial-up connection — the antenna could only receive, not send — but recently, a number of ISPs have started to offer satellite systems that both send and receive through the dish.

✦ **A network connection:** The last type of connection concerns those Macs that are part of a local area network (LAN) either at the office or in your home. If your Mac is connected to a LAN that already has Internet access, then you don't need an ISP at all, and no other hardware is required: Simply contact your network administrator, buy that important person a steak dinner, and ask to be connected to the Internet. On the other hand, if your network currently has no Internet access, you're back to Square One: You'll need one of the previous three types of connections.

After you've connected one of your computers on your network to the Internet, you can use an Internet sharing device to allow all the computers to share that Internet connection. Chapter 5 of Book V goes into all the details on sharing an Internet connection on a network.

Oh, Please! Not ISDN!

If you're thinking, "Hey, Mark, you forgot ISDN!" — allow me to reply, "So did everyone else." I don't mean to anger all those prophets who predicted that we'd all be using Integrated Services Digital Network (ISDN) by now, but the truth is that ISDN has turned into a joke. Essentially, ISDN was the ancestor of DSL, which actually realized the potential of the idea. ISDN, the first broadband connection method using regular phone lines, was supposed to revolutionize the Internet five or six years back, along with curing male pattern baldness and explaining UFO abductions.

Unfortunately, ISDN technology requires all sorts of very complex and expensive hardware, and it really isn't as fast as all that — most cable modem Internet access is much faster. ISDN was quickly eclipsed by the other broadband technologies . . . therefore, its acronym has come to mean *It Still Does Nothing*, and anyone with an option to use DSL or cable should give ISDN a wide berth.

Setting Up Your Internet Connection

Okay, so you've signed up for Internet access, and your ISP has sent you a sheet of paper covered with indecipherable stuff that looks like Egyptian hieroglyphics. Don't worry, those are the settings that you need to connect to your ISP — after you get them in Mac OS X, you should be surfing the Web like an old pro.

Before you jump into this configuration, make sure that you've configured the Internet settings within System Preferences, as I discuss in Chapter 3 of Book II. That way, you'll already have entered your default e-mail and Web settings.

Using your internal modem

Follow these steps to set up your Internet connection if you're using your Mac's internal modem:

1. **Click the System Preferences icon in the Dock and choose Network.**

2. **Select Internal Modem from the Show drop-down list and then choose to display the settings for a dial-up connection, as shown in Figure 1-1.**

Figure 1-1: The Network settings for an internal modem Internet connection.

3. **Enter the settings for the type of connection that your ISP provides:**

- **If your ISP tells you to use PPP** *(Point-to-Point Protocol):* Click the Configure drop-down list and choose Using PPP. If your ISP provided you with DNS Server or Search Domain addresses, click in the corresponding box and type them now.

- **If you're using AOL:** Click the Configure drop-down list and choose AOL Dialup. If AOL provided you with DNS Server or Search Domain addresses, click in the corresponding box and type them now.

- **If you'll use a manual connection:** Click the Configure drop-down list box and choose Manually. Then click in the IP Address, DNS Servers, and Search Domains fields and enter the respective settings provided by your ISP.

4. **Click the PPP tab to display the settings shown in Figure 1-2.**

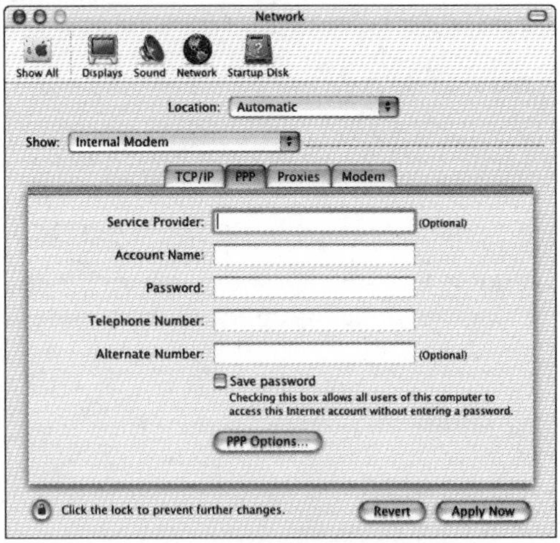

Figure 1-2:
Adding PPP
settings.

5. **In their respective fields, enter the account name, password, telephone number, and (optionally) the service provider name and an alternate telephone number provided by your ISP.**

6. **Press ⌘+Q to exit System Preferences and save your changes.**

Chapter 1 of Book V discusses these Internet settings in depth.

Using Ethernet hardware

Follow these steps to set up your Internet connection if you're using a network, cable modem, or DSL connection:

1. **Click the System Preferences icon in the Dock and choose Network to display the settings that you see in Figure 1-3.**

Figure 1-3:
The
Network
settings for
an Ethernet
Internet
connection.

2. **Select Built-in Ethernet from the Show drop-down list.**

3. **Enter the settings for the type of connection that your ISP provides:**

   - **If your ISP tells you to use Dynamic Host Configuration Protocol (DHCP):** Select Using DHCP from the Configure drop-down list, and your ISP can automatically set up virtually all the TCP/IP settings for you! (No wonder DHCP is so popular these days.)

   - **If you won't be using DHCP:** Select Manually from the Configure drop-down list box. Then enter the settings provided by your ISP in the IP Address, Subnet Mask, Router, and DNS Servers fields.

4. **If your ISP uses PPPoE *(Point-to-Point over Ethernet)*, click the PPPoE tab to display the settings shown in Figure 1-4.**

5. **Mark the Connect Using PPPoE check box to enable it and then enter the account name and password.**

   If your ISP includes the Service Provider name and a PPPoE Service Name, you can enter those as well.

6. **To allow everyone who uses your Mac to access the Internet with this account, mark the Save Password check box to enable it.**

   I recommend that you enable the Show PPPoE Status in Menu Bar check box. When you do, Mac OS X displays a menu bar icon that lets you know the status of your PPPoE connection.

7. **Press ⌘+Q to exit System Preferences and save your changes.**

**Book IV
Chapter 1**

**Getting on
the Internet**

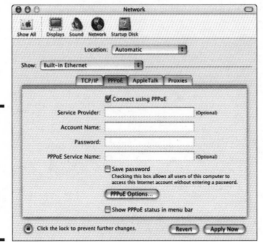

Figure 1-4:
Entering
PPPoE
data —
geez, that
just sounds
ridiculous,
doesn't it?

If you need help entering Internet settings or you want to know more about what you're actually doing, Chapter 1 of Book V discusses these settings in depth.

Connecting with a Dial-up ISP (The Hard Way)

Before you leave the serene confines of this chapter, I'd like to demonstrate how to use the Internet Connect application to connect to your ISP using your internal modem. (As I mention earlier in this chapter, most connections made over a network, DSL line, or cable modem won't need to use Internet Connect.) You can also use this application to connect if you're using a DSL line with PPPoE or an AirPort connection. Many ISPs provide high-speed access for Macs using PPPoE, which provides more efficient communications than the older PPP protocol that you might have used in the past. Further, if you're using an AirPort wireless connection, you can launch Internet Connect to take advantage of an existing Internet connection available through your wireless network.

To be honest, I always like Mac OS X to connect automatically when I'm using a modem — I hate excess mouse movements, which usually lead to a bad case of Rodent Elbow. To automate your connection, follow these steps:

1. **Re-open the Network settings in System Preferences and choose Internal Modem from the Show drop-down list.**

2. **Select the PPP tab and then click the PPP Options button and enable the Connect Automatically When Needed check box.**

3. **Click OK.**

4. **Press ⌘+Q to exit System Preferences.**

   You can forget about using Internet Connect! (The same trick works with PPPoE, which you can reach from the PPPoE tab on the Built-in Ethernet settings.)

Follow these steps to connect to the Internet manually:

1. **Open your Applications folder and launch the Internet Connect application, which displays the Internal Modem dialog that you see in Figure 1-5.**

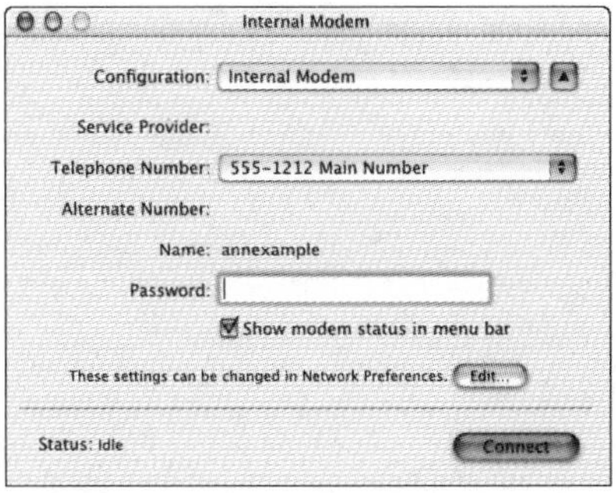

Figure 1-5:
Doing things manually with Internet Connect.

2. **From the Configuration drop-down list box, choose Internal Modem, Built-in Ethernet (for a DSL PPPoE connection), or AirPort.**

3. **Select the connection options for the hardware that you're using:**

   • **Modem connection:** Choose a telephone number for your ISP from the Telephone Number drop-down list box and then type your password in the Password box (if prompted). I recommend that you enable the Show Modem Status in Menu Bar check box, too.

   • **PPPoE connection:** Type your password in the Password text box (if prompted).

   • **AirPort connection:** Click the Turn AirPort On button (if AirPort is currently powered off) and select the network that provides your Internet access from the Network drop-down list box.

4. **Click the Connect button, sit back, and watch the fun!**

   Note that you don't have to click the Connect button if your AirPort base station is already connected to your ISP.

**Book IV
Chapter 1**

**Getting on
the Internet**

Chapter 2: Using Apple Mail

In This Chapter

✔ **Adding and configuring mail accounts**

✔ **Receiving and reading e-mail**

✔ **Sending e-mail**

✔ **Filtering junk mail**

✔ **Opening attachments**

✔ **Configuring Apple Mail**

✔ **Automating Apple Mail**

O kay, how many of you can function without e-mail? Raise your hands. Anyone? Anyone at all?

I suppose that I *can* function without my Internet e-mail, but why should I? Mac OS X includes a very capable and reliable e-mail client, which has been substantially improved for version 10.2 (affectionately called *Jaguar* by everyone but Bill Gates).

In this chapter, I discuss the features of Apple Mail and show you how everything hums at a perfect C pitch. However, you'll have to sing out, "You've got mail!" yourself. Personally, I think that's a plus, but I show you how you can add any sound you like.

Know Thy Mail Window

Figure 2-1 illustrates the Mail window. Besides the familiar toolbar, which naturally carries buttons specific to Mail, you'll find the following.

✦ **Status bar:** This heading bar displays information about the current folder — typically, how many messages it contains, but other data can be included as well. You can hide and show the Status bar from the View menu, or you can press the ⌘+Option+S keyboard shortcut to hide and show it.

✦ **Message list:** This resizable scrolling list box contains all the messages for the folder that you've chosen. To resize the list larger or smaller, drag the handle on the bar that runs across the window; you can also resize the columns in the list by dragging the edges of the column heading buttons.

To specify which columns appear in the message list, choose View⇨ Columns. From the submenu that appears, you can toggle the display of specific columns. You can also sort the messages in the message list from the View menu; by default, messages are sorted by the Date Received.

✦ **Drawer:** The extension to the right of the main Mail window is the Drawer. You can click any of the folders to switch the display in the message list. The Drawer can be hidden or shown from the View menu by clicking the Mailbox button in the toolbar, or you can press the ⌘+Shift+M keyboard shortcut to hide and show it. The Drawer is also automatically hidden when you maximize the Mail window.

✦ **Preview box:** This resizable scrolling list box displays the contents of the selected message, including both text and any graphics or attachments that Mail recognizes.

Toolbar

Status bar

Drawer

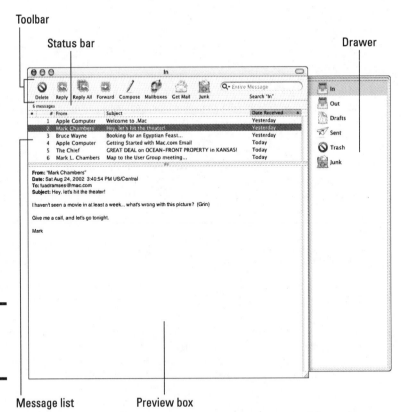

Figure 2-1:
The Apple
Mail
window.

Message list   Preview box

Mail uses the following folders:

✦ **In:** Mail you've already received.

✦ **Out:** Messages that Mail is waiting to send.

✦ **Drafts:** Draft messages waiting to be completed.

✦ **Sent:** Mail you've already sent.

✦ **Trash:** Deleted mail. Like the Trash in the Dock, you can open this folder and retrieve items that you realize that you still need. Alternatively, you can empty the contents of the Trash at any time by pressing the ⌘+K shortcut or by choosing Mailbox⇨Erase Deleted Messages.

✦ **Junk:** Junk mail. You can review these messages or retrieve anything you want to keep by choosing Message⇨Transfer. After you're sure there's nothing left of value, you can delete the remaining messages straight to the Trash.

You can add new personal folders to the Drawer to further organize your messages. Choose Mailbox⇨New Mailbox menu item and then type the name for your new folder in the Name box. Click OK to create the new personal folder.

Messages can be dragged from the message list and dropped into the desired folder in the Drawer to transfer them. From the Message list, select the messages that you want to move, click Message, choose the Transfer submenu, and then click the desired destination folder.

Also note that the Search box (upper-right) in the Mail toolbar looks a little different. Click the down arrow in this field, and from the drop-down list that appears, you can specify whether Mail should search for the text that you've entered there within the entire text of a message or just in the From, To, or Subject fields.

Setting Up Your Account

By default, Mail includes one (or more) of these accounts when you first run it:

✦ **The account that you entered when you first installed Mac OS X:** Go back to the beginning — literally, Book I, Chapter 1 — to read about the first use wizard that I discuss at the beginning of this book. If you entered the information for an e-mail account, it's available.

✦ **Your .Mac account:** If you registered for a .Mac service account, it will be included.

✦ **Upgraded accounts:** If you upgraded an existing Mac OS system, your existing Mail accounts will be added to the Accounts list in Mail.

Speaking of the Accounts list, choose Mail⇨Preferences to display the Accounts dialog that you see in Figure 2-2. From here, you can add an account, edit an existing account, or remove an account from Mail. Although most folks still have only one e-mail account, you can use a passel of them. For example, you might use one account for your personal e-mail and one account for your business communications. To switch accounts, just click the account that you want to use from this list to make it the active account.

Figure 2-2:
The
Account list,
where all is
made clear
(about your
e-mail
accounts).

Adding an account

To add a new account within Mail, click the Add Account button (refer to Figure 2-2) to display the dialog that you see in Figure 2-3 and then follow these steps:

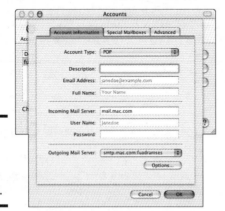

Figure 2-3:
Add an
account
within
Apple Mail.

1. **On the Account Information tab, click the Account Type drop-down list box and choose the protocol type to use for the account.**

You can select an Apple .Mac account, a POP (Post Office Protocol) account, or an IMAP (Internet Message Access Protocol) account. If you're adding an account from an Internet Service Provider (ISP), refer to the set-up information that you received to determine which is right. Most ISP accounts are POP accounts.

2. **In the Description field, name the account to identify it within Mail and then press Tab to move to the next field.**

   For example, *Work* or *Mom's ISP* are good choices.

3. **In the Email Address field, type the e-mail address supplied by your ISP and then press Tab to move to the next field.**

4. **In the Full Name field, type your full name — or, if this is to be an anonymous account, enter whatever you like as your identity — and then press Tab.**

   Messages that you send will appear with this name in the From field in the recipient's e-mail application.

5. **If you're entering a POP or IMAP account: In the Incoming Mail Server field, type the name of the incoming mail server (supplied by your ISP) and then press Tab.**

6. **In the User Name field, type the user name supplied by your ISP for login to your e-mail account and then press Tab.**

   This is sometimes different from the username and password you use to connect to the Internet.

7. **In the Password field, type the password supplied by your ISP for login to your e-mail account.**

   Again, this might be different from your connection password.

8. **Click the Outgoing Mail Server drop-down list box; if the outgoing server appears in this list, select it.**

   This is often the case if you're adding another new account provided by your ISP.

   If the outgoing mail server doesn't appear in the list, click Add Server in the list, enter the server address provided by your ISP in the Server Options dialog, and then click OK to return.

   Luckily, the defaults for the Outgoing Mail Server settings will work like a charm for 99 percent of us. However, if your ISP or network administrator tells you that you must make changes to your outgoing mail server settings, click the Options button (either while adding or editing an account). You can specify a port number, toggle SSL (Secure Sockets Layer) support, and select your authentication type. Because all that stuff sounds like a medieval Gregorian chant to most computer owners, just enter these server settings if you're told to do so.

9. Click OK.

You're done! The new account appears in the Accounts list.

You can specify advanced settings for an account. I cover those in the section "Fine-Tuning Your Post Office" later in this chapter.

Editing an existing account

Need to make changes to an existing account? Choose Mail⇨Preferences, click the account that you want to change, and then click the Edit button. Mail displays the same settings that I explain in the previous section. After you make your changes, click OK to return to the Preferences window.

Deleting an account

If you change ISPs or you decide to drop an e-mail account, you can remove it from your Accounts list. Otherwise, Mail can annoy you with error messages when it can no longer connect to the server for that account. Display the Mail Preferences window, select the account that you want to delete, and then click the Remove button.

Naturally, Mail will request confirmation before deleting the folders associated with that account. Click OK to verify the deletion or click the Cancel button to prevent accidental catastrophe.

Receiving and Reading E-Mail Wisdom

The heart and soul of Mail — well, at least the heart, anyway — is receiving and reading stuff from your friends and family. (Later in this chapter, I show you how to avoid the stuff you get promising free prizes, low mortgage rates, and improved . . . um . . . performance. This is a family-oriented book, so that's enough of that.)

After you set up an account (or selected an account from the Accounts list), it's time to check for mail. Use any of these methods to check for new mail:

✦ Click the Get Mail button on the toolbar.

✦ Choose Mailbox⇨Get New Mail or press ⌘+Shift+N.

✦ Choose Mailbox⇨Get New Mail in Account and then choose the specific account to check from the submenu.

This is a great way to check for new mail in another account without going through the trouble of making it active in the Preferences window.

Mail can also check for new messages automatically — more on this in the upcoming section "Checking Mail automatically."

If you do have new mail in the active account, it appears in the Message list. As you can see in Figure 2-4, new unread messages appear marked with a dot (it's blue) in the first column, and the number of unread messages is displayed next to the In folder icon in the Drawer.

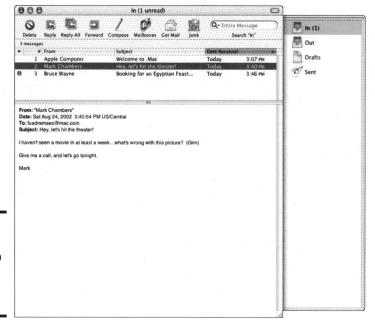

Figure 2-4: A new message to read... oh, joy, and no spam!

Mail also displays the number of new messages that you've received on its Dock icon. If you've hidden the Mail window or sent it to the Dock, you can perform a quick visual check for new mail just by glancing at the Dock.

Reading and deleting your messages

To read any message in the message list, you can either click the desired entry (which displays the contents of the message in the preview box) or you can double-click the entry to open the message in a separate message window, complete with its own toolbar controls.

To quickly scan your mail, click the first message that you want to view in the list, and then press the down-arrow key when you're ready to move to the next message. Mail displays the content of each message in the preview box. To display the previous message in the list, press the up-arrow key.

Book IV Chapter 2

Using Apple Mail

Displaying all Mail headers

Mail actually hides the majority of the heading lines that help identify and route an e-mail message to its rightful destination. By default, all you'll see is the *filtered heading*, which includes only the From, Date, To, and Subject fields. This is great unless for some reason you need to display the entire message header in all its arcane madness. If you do, choose View⇨Show All Headers or press ⌘+Shift+H. You can toggle back to the filtered heading by pressing the same shortcut or visiting the same spot on the View menu.

To delete a message from the message list, click the desired entry to select it, and then click the Delete button in the toolbar (or press the Del key). To delete a message from within a message window, click the Delete button in the toolbar.

Replying to mail

What? Aunt Harriet sent you a message because she's forgotten where she parked her car last night? If you happen to know where her auto is, you can reply to her and save her the trouble of retracing her steps.

If Aunt Harriet isn't in your Address Book yet, this is a good time to add her. With the message entry selected in the list, choose Message⇨Add Sender to Address Book or just press the convenient ⌘+Y keyboard shortcut. The person's name and e-mail address are automatically added to your Address Book. To add more information in the Address Book, however, you have to open that application separately.

To reply to a message in Mail, follow these steps:

1. **To respond to a message from the message list, click the desired message entry and then click the Reply button in the toolbar.**

To respond to a message that you've opened in a message window, click the Reply button in the toolbar for the message window.

If a message was addressed not just to you but also to a number of different people, you can send your reply to all of them. Instead of clicking the Reply button, click the Reply All button in the Mail window toolbar. (This is a great way to quickly facilitate a festive gathering, if you get my drift.)

You can also add carbon copies of your message to other new recipients, expanding the party exponentially; more on carbon copies later in the section "Raise the Little Flag: Sending E-Mail."

Mail opens the Reply window that you see in Figure 2-5. Note that the address has been automatically added and that the default Subject is Re:*<the original subject>*. Mail automatically adds a separator line in the message body field that reads `On <day><date>at<time>, <addressee> wrote:`, followed by the text of the original message; this is done so that the addressee can remember what the heck he or she wrote in the first place to get you so happy/sad/angry/indifferent. The original text is indented and colored blue to set it apart. If you like, you can click in the Subject line and change the default subject line; otherwise, the cursor is already sitting on the first line of the text box, so you can simply start typing your reply.

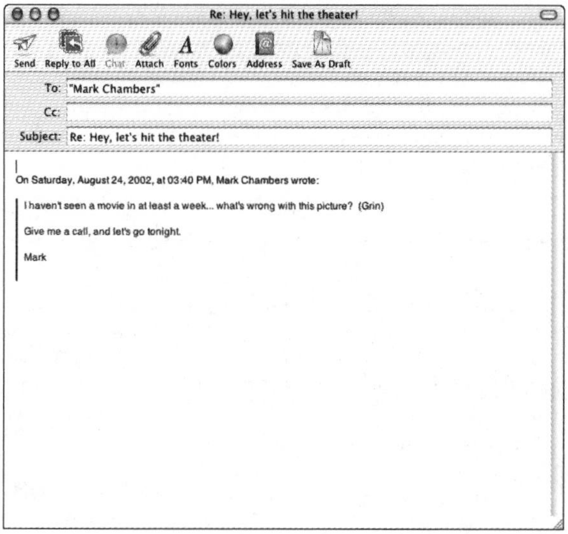

Figure 2-5:
Reply to an e-mail message.

2. **After you complete typing your reply, you can select text in the message body and apply different fonts or formatting.**

   To change your reply's formatting, click the Fonts button in the message window toolbar. From the window that appears, you can choose the font family, the type size, and formatting such as italic or bold for the selected text. Click the Close button on the Fonts window to continue. (If you like menus, you can also choose Format from the menu and make changes from there.)

   To apply color to the selected text, click the Colors button in the message window toolbar and then click anywhere in the color wheel that appears to select that color. You can also vary the hue by moving the

**Book IV
Chapter 2**

Using Apple Mail

slider bar at the right of the Colors window. After you find the color that expresses your inner passion, click the Close button on the Colors window to continue.

3. **To add an attachment, click the Attach button on the toolbar.**

    Mail displays a familiar file Open dialog. Navigate to the to-be-attached file, select it, and click the Open button to add it to the message. (More on attachments in the upcoming section "Attachments on Parade.")

4. **When you're ready to send your reply, you have two options. You can click the Send button to immediately add the message to your Out folder, or you can click the Save as Draft button to store it in your Drafts folder for later editing.**

    After a message is moved to the Out folder, it is sent either immediately or at the next connection time that you specify in Mail Preferences (more on this in the section "Checking Mail automatically" later in the chapter.) However, saving the message to your Drafts folder will not send it. Read the next section for the skinny on how to send a message stored in your Drafts folder.

Hey, what does MIME mean?

First, a note of explanation about Internet e-mail. Decades back, Internet e-mail messages were pure text, composed only of ASCII characters — that means no fancy fonts, colors, or text formatting. However, as more and more folks started using e-mail, the clarion call rang forth across the land for more attractive messages (as well as attachments, which I cover in the section "Attachments on Parade.") Therefore, the MIME encoding standard was developed. In case you're interested, MIME stands for *Multipurpose Internet Mail Extensions* — a rather cool (and surprisingly understandable) acronym.

Originally, virtually all e-mail programs recognized MIME, but then the Tower of Babel principle kicked in, and now there are actually multiple versions of MIME. Apple Mail uses the most common variant of MIME, so most folks who receive your e-mail should be able to see them in all their glory (even under Windows).

However, if one of your addressees complains that he got a message containing unrecognizable gobbledygook and a heading that mentions MIME, he's using an e-mail client application that either doesn't support MIME or supports a different version. (Of course, that person could have unknowingly turned MIME support off as well.) You have two possible solutions: You can ask the addressee to double-check whether MIME is enabled on his end in their e-mail application, or you can disable MIME when sending a message to that particular person. When you're composing an original message or a reply, you can use pure text by choosing Format➪Make Plain Text. (Naturally, this prevents you from doing anything fancy, and you shouldn't attach any files to a plain text message.)

When you reply to a message, you can also forward your reply to another person (instead of the original sender). The new addressee receives a copy of both the original message that you received and your reply. To forward a message, click the Forward button on the Mail toolbar instead of Reply or Reply to All.

If you don't want to include the text of the original message in a reply, choose Mail⇨Preferences⇨Composing and disable the Quote the Text of the Original Message check box.

By default, Mail checks your spelling as you type and also underlines any words that it doesn't recognize. (Very Microsoftian.) I like this feature, but if you find it irritating, you can turn it off. Just choose Mail⇨Preferences⇨ Composing and disable the Check Spelling as I Type check box.

Raise the Little Flag: Sending E-Mail

To compose and send a new message to someone else, follow these steps:

1. **Click the Compose button on the Mail toolbar or choose File⇨New Message (or avail yourself of the handy ⌘+N keyboard shortcut).**

Mail opens the New Message window that you see in Figure 2-6.

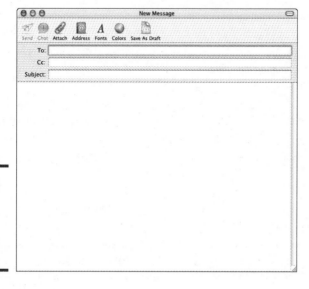

Figure 2-6:
An empty
Mail
message,
waiting to
be filled.

2. **Enter the recipient's (To) address by**

- **Typing it in directly**

- **Pasting it in after copying it to the Clipboard**

- **Or (my favorite) clicking the Address button, which shows you the scaled-down version of the Address Book (the Addresses window) that you see in Figure 2-7.**

Figure 2-7:
Select an
e-mail
address
from the
Address
Book.

From the Addresses window, click the address that you want to use and then click the To button. To pick multiple recipients, hold down the Shift key while you click the multiple addresses. Click the Close button on the Addresses window to close it and then press Tab.

If you've got a huge number of entries in your Address Book, use the Search field in the Addresses window toolbar, which operates just like the Finder window Search box.

3. **When Mail highlights the Cc field (the spot where you can send optional carbon copies of the message to additional recipients), you can type the addresses directly, use the contents of the Clipboard, or display the Addresses window.**

If you use the Addresses window, select the addresses that you want to use and click the CC button. Then click the Close button on the Addresses window and press Tab.

4. **In the Subject field, enter the subject of the message and then press Tab.**

Your text cursor now rests in the first line of the message text box — type, my friend, type like the wind! It's considered good form to keep this line short and relatively to the point.

5. **When you're done typing your message, select any of the text that you've entered and use the toolbar features I describe in the earlier section "Replying to mail" to apply different fonts or formatting.**

Click the Fonts button in the message window toolbar to open a window of formatting choices. (Click its Close button to continue.) If you like menus, you can also click Format and make changes from there.

6. **Add color to any selected text, if you like.**

   Just click the Colors button in the message window toolbar and make choices there; when the hue is perfect, click the Close button on the Colors window to continue.

7. **To add an attachment, click the Attach button on the toolbar, navigate to the to-be-attached file in the dialog that appears, select the file, and then click Open to add it to the message.**

8. **When your new message is ready to post, either click the Send button to immediately add the message to your Out folder or click the Save as Draft button to store it in your Drafts folder (without actually sending it).**

To send a message held in your Drafts folder, click the Drafts folder in the Drawer to display all draft messages. Double-click the message that you want to send, which will display the message window — you can make edits at this point, if you like — and then click the Send button in the message window toolbar.

If you don't have access to an Internet connection at the moment, Mail allows you to work off-line. This way, you can read your unread messages and compose new ones on the road to send later. After you regain your Internet connection, you might need to choose Mailbox⇨Go Online (depending on the connection type).

What? You Get Junk Mail, Too?

Spam — it's the Crawling Crud of the Internet, and I hereby send out a lifetime of bad karma to those who spew it. However, chucking the First Amendment is *not* an option, so I guess we'll always have junk mail. (Come to think of it, my paper mailbox is just as full of the stuff.)

Thankfully, the latest version of Apple Mail has a net that you can cast to collect junk mail before you have to read it. The two methods of handling junk mail are

✦ **Manually:** You can mark any message in the message list as Junk Mail. Select the unwanted flotsam in the message list and then click the Junk Mail button on the Mail window toolbar, which marks the message as you see in Figure 2-8. (Ocean-front property in Kansas . . . yeah, right.) If a message is mistakenly marked as junk and you actually want it, display the message in the preview box and then click the Not Junk button at the top of the preview box.

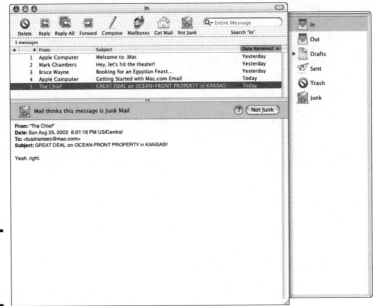

Figure 2-8:
"Be gone,
demons of
Junk Mail!"

✦ **Automatically:** Apple Mail has a sophisticated Junk Mail filter that you actually train to better recognize what's junk. (Keep reading to discover how.) After you train Mail to recognize spam with a high degree of accuracy, turn it to full Automatic mode, and it will move all those worthless messages to your Junk folder.

You customize and train the Junk Mail filter from the Mail menu; click Junk Mail to show the submenu choices. By default, Mail starts in Training mode, which means that it takes its best shot at determining what's junk. As you receive more mail and mark more messages as junk (or mark them as *not* junk), you're actually teaching the Junk Mail feature how to winnow the wheat from the chaff. In Training mode, junk messages are not actually moved anywhere — they're just marked with a particularly fitting grungy brown color.

After you're satisfied that the Junk Filter is catching just about everything that it can, display this submenu and choose Automatic. Mail creates a Junk folder and prompts you for permission to move all junk messages to this folder. After you review everything in the Junk folder, you can delete what it contains and send it to the Trash folder. To save a message from junkdom, click the Not Junk button in the preview window and then drag the message from the Junk folder message list to the desired folder in the Drawer.

If you don't receive a lot of spam — or you want to be absolutely sure that nothing gets labeled as junk until you review it — then display the Junk Mail submenu and then choose the Off menu item.

To reset the Junk Mail filter and erase any training that you've done, choose Junk Mail⇨Reset. Then click the Yes button to confirm your choice. To display the Junk rule and edit it if necessary, choose Junk Mail⇨Custom. (I discuss filtering rules at length at the end of this chapter.)

Attachments on Parade

Attachments are a fun way to transfer files through e-mail. However, remembering these three very important caveats is imperative:

✦ **Attachments can contain viruses.** Even a message attachment that was actually sent by your best friend can contain a virus — either because your friend unwittingly passed one along or because the virus actually took control of your friend's e-mail application and replicated itself automatically. (Ugh.)

Never send or receive attachments unless you have an up-to-date antivirus scanning application running.

✦ **Corpulent attachments don't make it.** Most corporate and ISP mail servers have a 1–3MB limit for the total size of a message — and the attachment counts toward that final message size. Therefore, I recommend sending a file as an attachment only if it's less than 1MB (or perhaps 2MB) in size. If the recipient's e-mail server sends you an automated message saying that the message was refused because it was too big, this is the problem.

✦ **Not all e-mail applications and firewalls accept attachments.** Not all e-mail programs support attachments in the same way, and others are simply set for pure text messages. Some firewalls even reject messages with attachments. If the message recipient gets the message text but not the attachment, these are the likely reasons.

With that said, it's back to attachments as a beneficial feature. Follow these steps to save an attachment that you receive:

1. **Click the message with an attachment in your message list.**

Having trouble determining which messages have attachments? Choose View⇨Columns and then click the Attachments item from the sub-menu that appears to toggle it on. Now messages with attachments appear with a tiny paper clip icon in the entry.

**Book IV
Chapter 2**

Using Apple Mail

Figure 2-9 illustrates the preview window for a message with an attachment that Mail recognizes. In this case, it's a JPEG image. If Mail recognizes the attachment format, it displays or plays the attachment in the body of the message; if not, the attachment is displayed as a file icon.

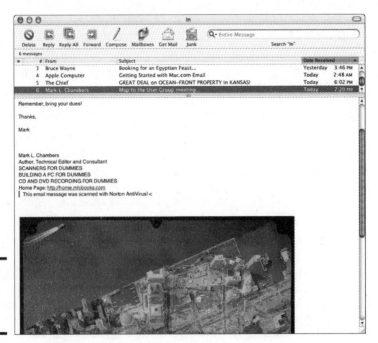

Figure 2-9:
Time to
check this
baggage.

2. **To open an attachment that's displayed as a file icon, hold down Control, click the file icon, and then choose Open Attachment from the pop-up menu that appears.**

If you know what application should be used to open the attachment, click the Open With button and choose the correct application from the submenu that appears.

3. **To save an attachment: Hold down Control, click the attachment (however it appears in the message), and then choose Save Attachment from the pop-up menu.**

In the Save dialog that appears, navigate to the location where you want to save the file and then click Save.

Fine-Tuning Your Post Office

Like all other Apple software, Mail is easily customized to your liking. In this section, I discuss some of the preferences that you might want to change.

Adding sound

To choose a sound that plays whenever you receive new mail, choose Mail⇨Preferences⇨Accounts. Either click the New Mail Sound drop-down list box and choose one of the sounds that Apple provides or choose Add/Remove from the drop-down list to choose a sound file from the Sounds folder (which, in turn, is located within your Library folder). Choose None from the drop-down list to disable the new mail sound altogether.

Checking Mail automatically

By default, Mail automatically checks for new mail (and sends any mail in your Out folder) every five minutes. To change this delay period, display the Accounts list in the Preferences window, choose the Check for New Mail drop-down list box, and then choose one of the time periods. To disable automatic mail checking, choose Manually; you can click the Get Mail toolbar button to manually check your mail any time you like.

Automating message deletion

If you like, Mail can be set to automatically delete sent mail and Junk messages (as well as permanently erase messages that you relegate to the Trash). To configure these settings, display the Accounts list in the Preferences window, click the desired account, and then click Edit. From the Accounts sheet, click the Special Mailboxes tab.

To delete Sent messages automatically, enable the Delete Sent Messages When drop-down list box and choose the delay period or action. You can choose to delete mail after a day, a week, a month, or immediately upon quitting Mail. Alternatively, you can leave this field set to Never, and Mail will never automatically delete any messages from the Sent folder.

To delete Junk messages automatically, click the Delete Junk Messages When drop-down list box and choose the delay period or action. (They're the same as the options available for Sent mail.)

To delete messages from the Trash, click the Permanently Erase Deleted Messages When drop-down list box and choose the delay period or action — again, the choices are the same as those for Sent messages.

**Book IV
Chapter 2**

Using Apple Mail

Adding signatures

To add a block of text or a graphic to the bottom of your messages as your personal signature, follow these steps:

1. **Choose Mail⇨Preferences⇨Signatures.**

2. **From the Signatures pane that appears, click the Add Signature button.**

3. **Type a descriptive name for the signature in the Description box and then press Tab.**

4. **Type the signature itself in the text entry box or copy the signature to the Clipboard and paste it into the text entry box.**

   Because downloading a graphic in a signature takes long — and because some folks still use plain text e-mail — avoid large graphics.

   If you enter a block of formatted text, click the Make Plain Text button to reduce those fancy fonts to plain text.

5. **Click OK to save the signature.**

   If you have multiple signatures, click the Select Signatures drop-down list to choose which one you want to use or to use them all randomly or in sequence.

If you use specific signatures for different subjects, you can also enable the Show Signature Menu on Compose Window check box, which allows you to switch signatures from the Compose window.

Changing the status of an account

Sometimes you won't be able to reach one of your accounts. For example, maybe you're on the road with your laptop and you're unable to access your office network. Apple Mail allows you to enable and disable specific accounts without the hassle of deleting an account and then having to add it again.

To disable or enable an account, choose Preferences⇨Accounts, click the desired account, and then click the Edit button. From the Accounts sheet that opens, click the Advanced tab and then enable (or clear) the Enable This Account check box as necessary.

If you disable an account, you should also disable the Include When Automatically Checking for New Mail check box to make sure that Mail doesn't display an error message. You can always check any account for new mail by choosing Mailbox⇨Get New Mail in Account and then choosing the desired account name from the submenu.

Automating Your Mail with Rules

Before I leave the beautiful shores of Mail Island, I'd be remiss if I didn't discuss one of its most powerful features: the ability to create *rules,* which are automated actions that Mail can take. With rules, you can specify criteria that can perform actions such as

✦ Transferring messages from one folder to another

✦ Forwarding messages to another address

✦ Highlighting or deleting messages

To set up a rule, follow these steps:

1. **Choose Mail⇨Preferences and then click the Rules button on the toolbar.**

Mail displays the Rules dialog, as shown in Figure 2-10.

Figure 2-10:
The Rules
list.

2. **To duplicate an existing rule, highlight it in the list and then click the Duplicate button. (For this demonstration, however, create a rule from scratch by clicking the Add Rule button.)**

Mail displays the settings on the sheet shown in Figure 2-11.

Figure 2-11:
Create a
new rule
within Apple
Mail.

3. **In the Description field, type a descriptive name for the new rule and then press Tab to move to the next field.**

**Book IV
Chapter 2**

Using Apple Mail

4. **Click the If drop-down list to specify whether the rule will be triggered whether *any* of the conditions are met or whether *all* conditions must be met.**

5. **Because each rule requires at least one condition, click the target drop-down list boxes to see the target for the condition.**

These include whom the message is from or to, which account received the message, whether the message is marked as junk, and whether the message contains certain content. Select the target for the condition.

6. **Click the criteria drop-down list box to choose the rule's criteria.**

The contents of this drop-down list box change depending on the condition's target. For example, if you choose From as the target, the criteria include Contains, Does Not Contain, Begins With, and so forth.

7. **Click in the expression box and type the text to use for the condition.**

For example, a completed condition might read:

```
Subject Contains Ocean-Front
```

This particular condition will be true if I get an e-mail message with a subject that contains the string `Ocean-Front`.

8. **Add more conditions by clicking the plus sign button at the right of the first condition.**

To remove any condition from this rule, click the minus sign button next to it. Remember, however, that every rule needs at least one condition.

9. **To specify what actions will be taken after the condition (or conditions) has been met, click the first Perform the Following Actions drop-down list box to see the action that this rule should perform. Then click the second drop-down list box and then select the action for the rule.**

Choices include transferring a message from one folder to another, playing a sound, automatically forwarding the message, deleting it, and marking it as read.

Each rule requires at least one action.

10. **Depending on the action that you select, specify one or more criteria for the action.**

For instance, if I select Set Color as my action, I must then choose whether to color the text or the background as well as what color to use.

Like the plus button next to the conditions, you can also click the plus button next to the first action to perform more than one action. To remove an action, click the minus button next to it.

11. **When the rule is complete, click OK to save it.**

Figure 2-12 illustrates a complex rule that I've set up that performs the following:

If the message were sent by someone in my Address Book AND the Subject field contains the text FORWARD ME, forward the message to the e-mail address fuadramses@mac.com.

Figure 2-12:
A forwarding rule created within Mail.

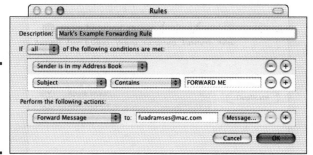

This is a good example of an automated forwarding rule. With this rule in place and Mail running on Mac OS X, any of my friends, family, or co-workers can forward me urgent e-mail to my .Mac account while I'm on vacation. To trigger the rule, all the sender has to do is include the words FORWARD ME in the message subject. And if the sender isn't in my Address Book, the rule doesn't trigger, and I can read the message when I get home. Mondo *sassy*.

Each rule in the Rules dialog can be enabled or disabled by toggling the Active check box next to the rule. You can also edit a rule by selecting it in the Rules dialog and then clicking the Edit button. To delete a rule completely from the list, select it and then click the Remove button; Mail will prompt you for confirmation before the deed is done.

Chapter 3: Staying in Touch with iChat

In This Chapter

✔ Setting up iChat

✔ Changing modes in iChat

✔ Adding Buddies

✔ Inviting a Buddy to chat

✔ Sending an Instant Message

✔ Sending and receiving files via iChat

✔ Ignoring those who deserve to be shunned

Throughout man's history, our drive has been towards communication — from the earliest cave paintings, through written language, to the telegraph, the telephone, and the cellular all-in-one PDA that the guy in the SUV in front of you is using . . . and he's arguing with someone and he's not paying attention and . . . (whump).

So much for the learned and scholarly introduction — forget that silly cellular phone and your complicated calling plan! As long as you have Mac OS X and an Internet connection, you can *instantly* chat with your friends and family, whether they're across the aisle in another cube or halfway across the world. This modern marvel is *iChat,* and in this chapter, I show you how to gab with the following folks:

✦ Others using iChat (either on your local network or on the Internet)

✦ Anyone using AIM — that's short for *America Online (AOL) Instant Messaging*

✦ Folks participating in AOL Chat rooms

Configuring iChat

When you first run iChat, you'll see the dialog shown in Figure 3-1. Type the first name (your name) that you want to use in the First Name field, press Tab, and then type the surname that you want to use. (Yes, you can even use *Bullwinkle Moose* — just leave out the middle initial *J.*)

Figure 3-1:
iChat needs
a little
information
before
things
begin.

Welcome To iChat

To set up iChat enter the information below.
Enter your Mac.com email address and password. Or, you can enter
an AOL Instant Messenger (AIM) screen name and password.

First Name:

Last Name:

Account Type: Mac.com

Account Name: fuadramses

Password: ••••••••

Sign up for Mac.com   Cancel   OK

By default, iChat uses the .Mac account that you set up when you first installed Mac OS X. In this case, your .Mac Account Name and Password are automatically entered for you, and you're good to go. However, if you're already using AIM and you'd like to use your existing AIM account, click the Account Type drop-down list and choose AIM; then enter your AIM name and password instead.

iChat will also ask whether you'd like to enable Rendezvous messaging. As you can read in Chapter 1, Book V, think of Rendezvous as plug-and-play for your local network. In iChat, *Rendezvous messaging* displays a separate window where you can see (and yak with) anyone on your local network without having to know his iChat name because Rendezvous automatically announces all the iChat users who are available on your network. If you have others using iChat or AIM on your local network, go for this option; if you're not connected to a local network, however, Rendezvous messaging isn't necessary. Also, if you're on a public AirPort network or you're connecting to the Internet with a modem through dialup, I recommend disabling Rendezvous messaging. (For all that's cool about AirPort, see Chapter 4 of Book V.)

After you finish these configuration necessities, iChat displays the Buddy List window (or, if you enabled Rendezvous messaging, two windows) that you see in Figure 3-2. Remember that your Rendezvous window displays only those iChat folks on your local network.

A few things to note here about the Buddy List window:

✦ **If you don't have a picture, don't panic.** You can add a picture to your iChat iDentity — sorry, I couldn't resist that — by dragging an image to the well next to your name at the top of the Buddy List window. If necessary, iChat will ask you to position and size the image so that it will fit in the (admittedly limited) space. This picture is then sent along with your words when you chat. In later figures for this chapter, I borrow the smiling face of Wolfgang Amadeus Mozart.

✦ **Check out the buttons along the bottom of the window(s).** In order, these buttons are

- **View** options (with things like sorting and turning pictures on and off)

- **Add a New Buddy** (which I cover in the next section)

- **Show Info** (for the selected Buddy)

- **Compose Email** (where you can launch Mail and send e-mail to the selected Buddy)

- **Send Instant Message**

Using these buttons can handle about 90 percent of the commands you need to give while using iChat, so use 'em! (Note that the Rendezvous window has fewer buttons: only View Options, Compose Email, and Send Instant Message. This is because the Buddy List in the Rendezvous window is automatically populated by other iChat folks on your local network.)

✦ **Hey, look, there's a new menu bar icon!** When you're running iChat, the application adds a balloon menu bar icon next to the clock display in the upper-right corner of your screen. Click it to display the options that you see in Figure 3-3. You can change your online/offline status, immediately invite a Buddy for a chat, or display the Buddy List (which I discuss later in the section "Will You Be My Buddy?").

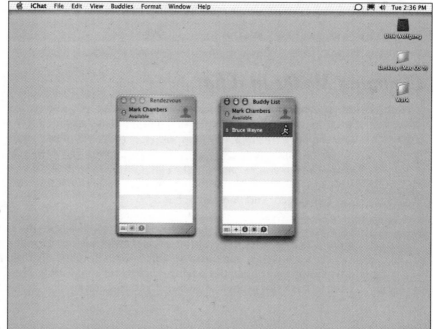

Figure 3-2:
iChat and Rendezvous: Instant communication at its finest.

**Book IV
Chapter 3**

Staying in Touch with iChat

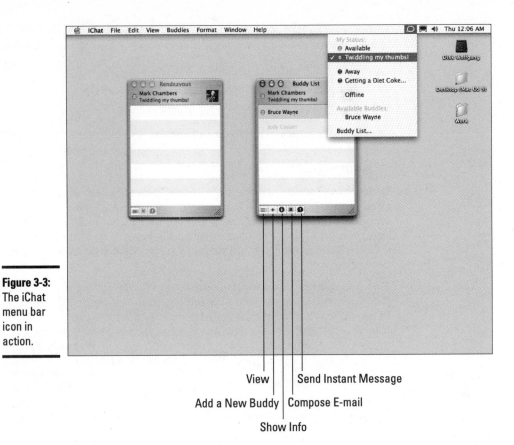

Figure 3-3:
The iChat
menu bar
icon in
action.

View | Send Instant Message

Add a New Buddy | Compose E-mail

Show Info

Changing Modes in iChat

To launch iChat, you can click its icon from the Dock or launch it from its iChat application icon (which you'll find in your Applications folder). Or, you can click its menu bar icon, which is grayed out when you're offline. If you're not already familiar with the terms *online* and *offline*, here's the scoop: When you're *online*, folks can invite you to chat and communicate with you. When you're *offline*, you're disconnected: iChat isn't active, you can't be paged, and you can't chat.

Even when you're offline, you can choose Available from the friendly balloon menu bar icon, which will automatically switch iChat to online mode. Or you can click a Buddy name directly, which will automatically switch iChat to online mode and open the paging window for that Buddy. (Naturally, you have to have the proper network or Internet connection first.)

You can use another mode, *Away*, whenever iChat is running and you're still online but not available. For example, if I'm away from my Mac for a few minutes, I leave iChat running but I switch myself to Away mode. My Buddies get a message saying that I'm Away, so they won't bother trying to contact me. When I return to my computer, I use the menu bar icon to switch from Away to Available (or my other favorite mode, *Twiddling My Thumbs!*). Refer to Figure 3-3 to see these choices.

Speaking of modes, you, too, can create a custom mode — like *Bored stiff!* or *Listening to the Pointy-Haired Boss* — and use it instead of the somewhat mundane choices of *Available* and *Away*. To do this, display the Buddy List window, click the word *Available* beneath your name (refer to Figure 3-2), and a drop-down list appears. To choose an existing mode, click it; modes with a green bullet are online modes, and red bullet modes are offline modes. Click the Custom menu item for either color to open an edit box; type the new mode there and then press Return. The new mode is automatically added to your mode list. You can also switch modes using this drop-down list.

Will You Be My Buddy?

I know that question sounds a little personal, but in iChat, a *Buddy* is anyone whom you want to chat with, whether the topic is work related or your personal life. iChat keeps track of your Buddies in the Buddy List. You can also add them to your Address Book or use the AIM entry in an Address Book contact to generate a new Buddy identity.

To add a new Buddy, follow these steps:

1. **Choose iChat⇨Buddies⇨Add a Buddy, or click the Add a New Buddy button at the bottom of the iChat window, or press ⌘+Shift+A.**

iChat displays the sheet that you see in Figure 3-4.

Figure 3-4: Add a Buddy from your Mac OS X Address Book.

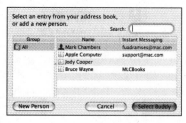

2. **To create a Buddy entry from an Address Book contact who has an Instant Messaging user name, click the entry to select it and then click the Select Buddy button.**

3. **To add a brand-new person who's not already in your Address Book, click the New Person button to display the sheet that you see in Figure 3-5.**

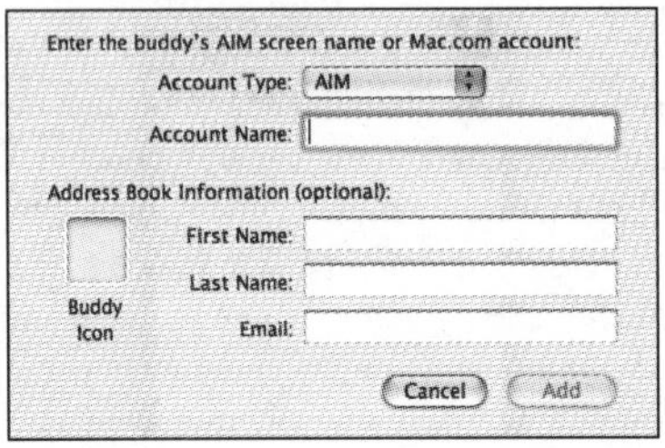

Figure 3-5: Enter information for a new Buddy.

Enter the buddy's AIM screen name or Mac.com account:

Account Type: AIM

Account Name:

Address Book Information (optional):

Buddy Icon

First Name:

Last Name:

Email:

Cancel   Add

4. **In this new sheet, select the proper account type (either .Mac or AIM), press Tab, and then type the person's Instant Messaging account name.**

   If you like, you can also add your own picture to represent that person (instead of using the icon that he provides). Just locate the image file that you want to use within a Finder window and drag the image to the Buddy Icon well.

   You can also optionally enter the person's real name and e-mail address.

5. **Click Add to save the Buddy information.**

Even when you add a new Buddy and that name appears in the Buddy List, don't be surprised if the name actually fades out after a few seconds — that indicates that the person is offline and unavailable. You can also tell when a person is available if her name appears with a green bullet in the Buddy List.

You can also specify a number of actions that iChat should take if a Buddy logs in or out of Instant Messaging, or if a Buddy changes his or her status to Available. To display these actions, click the desired Buddy's entry in your Buddy List and then click the Show Buddy Info button at the bottom of the list. Choose the event that should trigger the action from the Event drop-down list, select the Enable These Actions check box, and then choose whether iChat should play the sound that you select, speak a line of text, and/or bounce the iChat icon in the Dock.

Chat! Chat, 1 Say!

Turn your attention to getting the attention of others — through inviting others to chat. You don't have to actually invite someone to chat. For example, you can send an Instant Message just by double-clicking the desired entry in the Buddy List. However, good chatting etiquette implies inviting someone to a conversation rather than barging in unannounced. Also, using the invitation method opens a true Chat window, which makes it easier to engage in longer conversations.

If you want to join an AIM or Rendezvous chat already in progress, choose File⇨Go to Chat (or press ⌘+G). You'll have to specify both the type of chat and the specific chat room name.

To invite someone, click the desired Buddy from the Buddy List, click Buddies, and then choose Invite to Chat (or press ⌘+Option+C). iChat displays the Group Chat window that you see in Figure 3-6, which also doubles as an Invitation window.

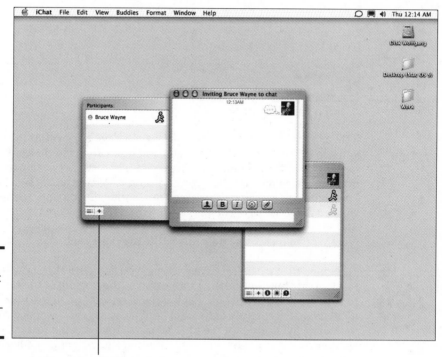

Figure 3-6:
Inviting that special someone — well, me.

Invite another Buddy to chat.

TIP

You can invite additional Buddies to enter the chat by clicking the plus button at the bottom left of the Participants list and choosing another Buddy.

Type your invitation text into the entry box at the bottom of the window. If you'd like to use bold or italic text, highlight the text and click the Bold **(B)** or Italic *(I)* button. You can also add a Smiley face to your invitation text: Click in the desired spot in the text, click the Smiley button, and then choose the proper Smiley from the list. To send the invitation text, press Return.

The recipient of your chat invitation can decline or accept your chat invitation. As you can see in Figure 3-7, you'll be notified if the chat has been declined.

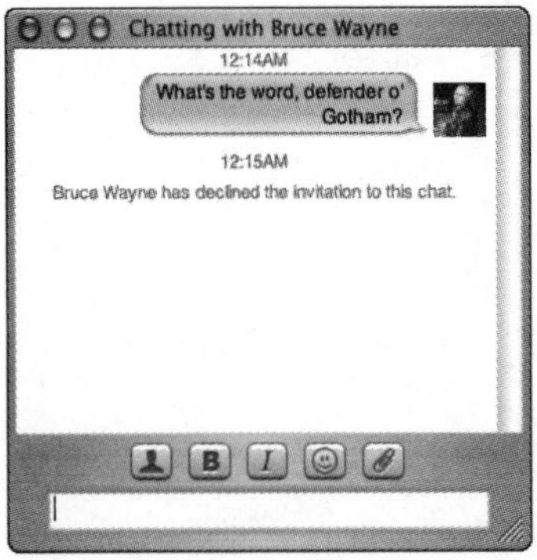

Figure 3-7:
Okay, I
didn't want
to chat with
myself
anyway!

If the chat is accepted, iChat displays a message saying that the Buddy whom you invited has joined the chat, and you now can begin the chat. You don't have to alternate sending messages back and forth between participants — everyone in a chat can compose and send messages at the same time — but I personally like to alternate when I'm chatting one-on-one. See the volley in Figure 3-8. By the way, you may notice that AIM users are represented by the AIM "Running Dude" icon (unless they change it, or you assign an icon picture of your own as I describe in the previous section).

TIP

To reduce the size of the Chat window, you can click the Show or Hide Participants button (it's the first button at the bottom of the Chat window) to stow the Participants list behind the Chat window. Click View from the iChat menu and choose Hide Chat Toolbar to regain the space used by the toolbar at the bottom of the Chat window. You can also resize the Chat window by using the handle at the bottom-right corner, just like most other application windows in Mac OS X.

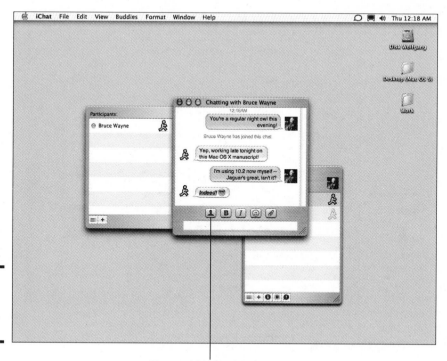

Figure 3-8:
A typical chat in progress.

Show or Hide Participants

As you can see in Figure 3-9, you can change fonts and colors while composing a line of text. Simply select the text and then choose Format⇨Show Fonts and Format⇨Show Colors (or press ⌘+T and ⌘+Shift+C) to display the Fonts and Colors windows, respectively. These windows can be resized and moved wherever you like.

To save the discussion in a chat, choose File⇨Save a Copy As. In the dialog that appears, type a name for the chat file, select a location where you want to store the file, and then click Save.

When the iChat window is active, a number of display choices can be made from the View menu, including

✦ **Text display:** Each line that you write and receive in a chat can be displayed in *balloons*, just like your favorite comic — the default — or as simple text.

✦ **Buddy ID:** Each line can be displayed with the individual's picture, just the name, or both the name and picture.

✦ **Background display:** Choose the Set Chat Background menu item to choose a graphic to use for the Chat window. To return to the original appearance, choose the Clear Background menu item.

**Book IV
Chapter 3**

**Staying in Touch
with iChat**

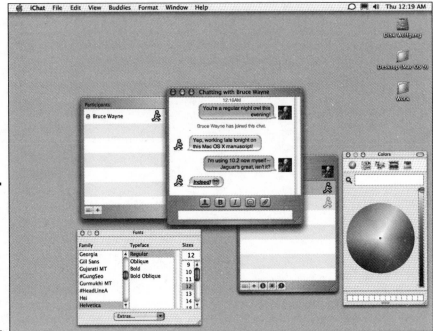

Figure 3-9:
For the truly creative, leave the Fonts and Colors windows open during your chat.

Click the Buddy List, and the View menu offers a different set of controls: You can sort your Buddy List by first name, last name, and availability, and you can also toggle the display of offline Buddies. These options are also available from the Buddy List toolbar.

To close a chat, click the Close button on the Chat window.

Sending Files Using iChat

To send a file to a Buddy, click the desired entry in the Buddy List and then choose Buddies⇨Send a File, or use the ⌘+Option+F keyboard shortcut, or click the paper clip icon at the bottom of the Chat window. You'll see the dialog shown in Figure 3-10, which indicates that the recipient is being offered a file transfer request. If the file request is accepted by your Buddy, the transfer begins and is saved where the recipient specifies on their system.

Figure 3-10:
A moment of
suspense —
will my
Buddy
accept a file
from me?

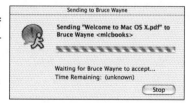

Figure 3-11 illustrates the reverse: I'm receiving a file from a Buddy. From the Incoming File Request pane that appears when someone sends me a file, I can either click the Decline button (to decline the file transfer) or the Save File button (to save the incoming file to any spot on my system).

Always check any files that you receive from iChat with your antivirus scanning software before you run them!

Figure 3-11:
My Buddy
returns the
favor with
a file of
his own.

Eliminating the Riffraff

Here I need to explain something that I hope you won't have to use — what I like to call the *Turkey Filter.* (iChat is a little more subtle — you just *ignore* people.)

To ignore someone in a chat group, choose Buddies⇨Ignore<*username*>. When someone is ignored in a chat group, you won't see anything that he types or have to respond to any file transfer requests from that person.

If only it were that easy to ignore someone when he's standing close to you.

Chapter 4: Expanding Your Horizons with iDisk

In This Chapter

✔ Setting up iDisk

✔ Using files and folders on your iDisk

✔ Using public files

*I*f you ask the average Mac owner what's available on the Internet, you'll likely hear benefits such as e-mail, Web surfing, and instant communication using iChat. What you probably *won't* hear is "Convenient, trouble-free storage for my files and folders."

You might have tried to use one of the dozens of storage sites on the Internet that allow you to upload and download files from a personal file area via your Web browser. Unfortunately, these Web-based storage sites are slow in transferring files and typically offer only a small amount of space. As a result, most computer owners decide that the idea of online storage is neat . . . but impractical.

In this chapter, I show you what real online storage is all about. I'm talking about *iDisk,* the online storage feature that's integrated into the Mac OS X Finder. No jury-rigged Web site is necessary (although you can use one if you're not on a Mac). I'll admit that online storage won't replace the hard drives on your Mac, but with a .Mac subscription, you can easily make use of online storage for backups and sharing files with your friends . . . from anywhere on the planet!

So how do you actually *use* iDisk? That's the simple part! To use iDisk within Mac OS X, just do what comes naturally — it works like any other removable volume's Finder window. You can copy and move files and folders to and from your iDisk, create new sub-folders (except in the Backup and Software root folders, which are read-only) and delete whatever you don't need.

Grabbing Internet Storage for Your Mac

To set up iDisk on your Mac OS X system, you'll need a .Mac account. You did create one during the installation of the Big X, but these accounts are limited to 20MB of storage, and the trial account is active for only 60 days.

Therefore, if you decide that you like iDisk, you should subscribe to .Mac; a subscription increases your online treasure chest to 100MB of iDisk storage. To subscribe, visit `http://mac.com` and follow the prompts to join from there. (At the time of this writing, the subscription fee is $100 per year.)

With a .Mac account active, iDisk is automatically available. To see how much storage you're using and to configure access to your Public folder, open System Preferences, click the Internet icon, and then click the iDisk tab to display the settings that you see in Figure 4-1. (You can also click the Buy More button on this panel to subscribe to Apple's .Mac service.)

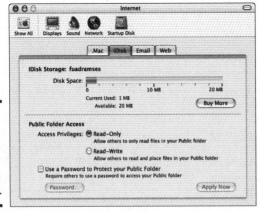

Figure 4-1:
Your iDisk information is available from System Preferences.

The iDisk Storage bar graph illustrates how much of your current iDisk territory you're using.

So where exactly are your files kept when you use your iDisk? Behind-the-scenes, your acre of storage farmland sits on one of Apple's iDisk *file servers* — perhaps in Cupertino, perhaps elsewhere. These server computers are especially designed to store terabytes (TB) of information (1 TB equals 1,000 GB), and they're connected to the Internet via high-speed trunk lines. (And yes, they do have a firewall.)

You can specify the access privilege level for other .Mac users from this panel as well. Select the Read-Only radio button to prevent any other .Mac user from copying files to your Public folder, or select the Read-Write radio button to allow others to save files there. No matter which privilege level you choose, you can also set a password that other .Mac users must type before they're allowed access to your Public Folder. (More on the Public folder in the next section.) If you've already set a password, you can change it by clicking the Password button and typing the new word in the Password box. Retype the word in the Confirm box to verify it, then click the OK button to save the change.

Understanding What's on Your iDisk

Unlike the physical hard drive in your Mac, your iDisk never needs formatting or defragmenting, and you'll never have to check it for errors — however, the structure of an iDisk is fixed, so you can't just go crazy creating your own folders. In fact, you can't create new folders at the root — the top level — of your iDisk at all, but you can create new folders inside most of the root folders.

Now that you're thoroughly *rooterized,* here are the folders that you'll find hanging out in your iDisk:

✦ **Documents:** This folder holds any application documents that you want to store . . . things like spreadsheets and letters. No one but you can access these items.

✦ **Pictures:** This folder is the vault for your JPEG and GIF images, including those that you want to use with iCards or your Web pages.

✦ **Movies:** QuickTime movies go here — again, you can add the movies stored here to your Web pages. (I cover QuickTime like a blanket in Chapter 6 of Book III.)

✦ **Public:** This is the spot to place files that you specifically want to share with others, either directly through iDisk or with your Web pages. If you've allowed write access, others can copy files to your Public folder as well.

✦ **Sites:** The Web pages you store here can be created with Apple's HomePage utility — which is available to all .Mac members — or you can use your own Web page design application and copy the completed site files here.

✦ **Music:** This is the repository for all of your iTunes music and playlists — the contents can be added to your Web pages. (iTunes is the star of Chapter 2 in Book III.)

✦ **Backup:** This is a read-only folder that contains the backup files created with the .Mac Backup application. You can, however, copy the files in this folder to a removable drive on your system for an additional level of safekeeping.

✦ **Software:** Apple provides this read-only folder as a service to .Mac members; it contains a selection of the latest freeware, shareware, and commercial demos for you to enjoy. To try something out, open the Software folder and copy whatever you like to your Mac OS X Desktop. Then you can install and run the application from the local copy of the files.

**Book IV
Chapter 4**

**Expanding
Your Horizons
with iDisk**

Opening and Using iDisk

When you're connected to the Internet, you can open your iDisk in one of the following ways:

✦ **From the Finder menu, choose Go⇨iDisk or use the ⌘+Shift+I keyboard shortcut.**

✦ **Add an iDisk button to your Finder window toolbar by clicking View and choosing Customize Toolbar.**

   After you add the button, you can click it to connect to your iDisk from anywhere in the Finder.

Your iDisk opens in a new Finder window, as shown in Figure 4-2. After you use one of these methods in a Mac OS X session, your iDisk icon appears on the Mac OS X Desktop; Figure 4-3 shows both the iDisk icon and its properties in the Show Info dialog. The iDisk volume icon remains until you shut down or restart your Mac.

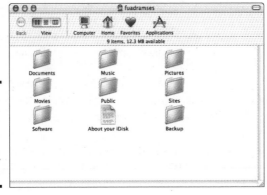

Figure 4-2:
The contents of my iDisk — pretty iNeat, I'm thinking.

If you're using a remote computer with an Internet connection, you can log in to the .Mac page at www.apple.com and use your Web browser to access the contents of your iDisk. (Hey, sometimes this is the only choice you have.)

However, you don't actually need to open your iDisk in a Finder window to use it because you can also load and save files directly to your iDisk from within any application. Simply choose your iDisk as you would any of the hard drives on your system when using the application's Load, Save, or Save As commands.

The iDisk icon

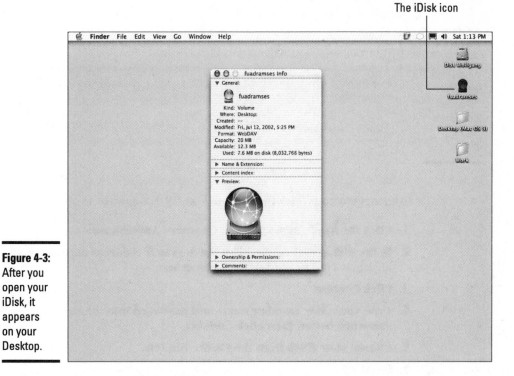

Figure 4-3:
After you
open your
iDisk, it
appears
on your
Desktop.

You can also open an iDisk's Public folder — either yours or the Public folder inside another person's iDisk — as if it were an Internet file server. As I explain earlier, if that person has set a password, you'll need to enter that password to gain access to their Public folder. From the Finder menu, choose Go➪Connect to Server. In the Connect to Server dialog that appears, click in the Address text field (see Figure 4-4) and enter the following:

```
http://idisk.mac.com/username/Public
```

where *username* is the person's .Mac account name. This opens the .Mac member's Public folder.

You can also use the server address `http://idisk.mac.com/username` to connect to an iDisk from computers running Windows and Linux. Check the Help for your operating system to determine how to connect to a WebDAV server. When prompted for your access username and password, use your .Mac account name and password.

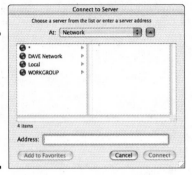

Figure 4-4:
You can
connect to
any iDisk
using the
Connect to
Server
dialog.

To connect to your iDisk from within Mac OS 9, follow these steps:

1. **Click the Apple menu, choose Chooser⇨AppleShare.**

2. **In the dialog that opens, click the Server IP Address button and type** idisk.mac.com **in the Server Address box.**

3. **Click Connect.**

4. **Type your .Mac member name and password into the User name and Password boxes; then click Connect.**

5. **Choose your iDisk from the Finder window.**

6. **Click OK.**

Chapter 5: Going Places with Internet Explorer

In This Chapter

- Introducing the Explorer window and controls
- Visiting Web sites with Explorer
- Moving between sites
- Creating and using Favorites
- Receiving files with Explorer
- Using subscriptions and the History file
- Saving Web pages to disk
- Protecting your privacy on the Web

When I was designing the Table of Contents for this book, I seriously considered leaving this chapter out — after all, more people use a Web browser now than any other software application. Who really needs a guide to mowing a lawn?

But then again, I suddenly thought of all the hidden features that folks don't know about Internet Explorer — for example, the tips and tricks that can help you organize your online visits. It's a little like learning more about the lawn mower itself: Even though you might not need tips on mowing, many people don't know how to remove the sparkplug in the winter or how to sharpen the blade so you can handle taller grass. Remember, *magic is nothing more than technology that someone understands.*

In this chapter, I show you how to use those other toolbar buttons in Internet Explorer — you know, the ones *besides* the Forward and Back buttons — and you'll discover how to keep track of where you've been and where you'd like to go.

One note: Many authors have written entire books on Internet Explorer. As you might guess, this chapter is far narrower in scope than those books, and it doesn't include every feature. However, I think the coverage that you find here will explain all that you're likely to need for most surfing sessions.

Let's Pretend You've Never Used This Thing

Figure 5-1 illustrates version 5.2 of Internet Explorer, which runs under both Mac OS 9 and Mac OS X and matches the Windows version in most respects. (Then again, it wasn't even written by Apple... that *other group* is responsible for Internet Explorer.) You can launch Explorer directly from the Dock, or you can click the Internet Explorer icon within your Applications folder.

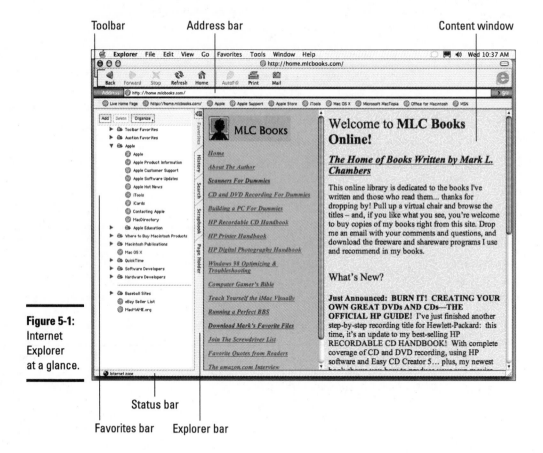

Figure 5-1: Internet Explorer at a glance.

Major sections of the Explorer window include

✦ **The toolbar:** (Or, as Microsoft so quaintly calls it, the *button bar*.) You'll find the most often-used commands on the toolbar for things like navigation, printing, and sending e-mail. At the right side of the toolbar is the animated Internet Explorer icon, which moves when the program is loading information from a Web site. The toolbar can be collapsed to the left side of the Explorer window, as shown in Figure 5-2, to provide you with more real estate in your browser window for Web content. To toggle collapsed mode, press ⌘+B or choose View⇨Collapse/Expand Toolbars.

Explorer allows you to customize its toolbar in a fashion quite similar to customizing the Finder window toolbar; just choose View⇨Customize Toolbars. From here, you can drag individual buttons to the toolbar or drag either the Default set or the Basic set to the toolbar to adopt a complete, prefabricated set of buttons. After you finish creating the browser toolbar of your dreams, click the Go Back button to return to the Web.

✦ **The address bar:** Next on the Hit Parade is the address bar, where you can type or paste the address for Web sites you'd like to visit. To toggle the display of the address bar, choose View⇨Address Bar.

✦ **The Favorites bar:** Consider this a toolbar that allows you to jump directly to your favorite Web sites with a single click. I show you later in the section "Adding and Using Favorites" how to add and remove sites from your Favorites bar. For now, remember that you can toggle the display of the Favorites bar by choosing View⇨Favorites Bar.

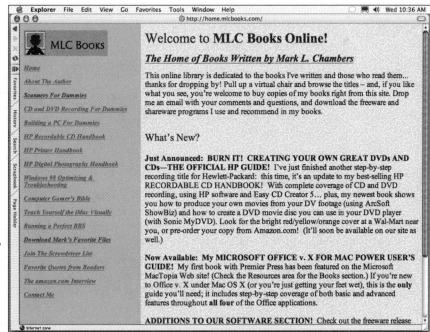

Figure 5-2:
Create more space by collapsing toolbars.

Book IV
Chapter 5

Going Places with Internet Explorer

✦ **The Explorer bar:** This series of tabs appears down the left side of the Content window. You can reach your Favorites from here, as well as the History of sites that you've recently visited. You can also search for a specific site, map, or address; add items to your Internet Scrapbook; or even place a page in the Page Holder so that you can navigate easily to the links on that page. (More on these features in the upcoming section "Using Subscriptions and History.")

To expand the Explorer bar, simply click the desired tab. To collapse it, click the tab again. Refer to Figure 5-2 to see what the Explorer bar looks like in collapsed mode. You can also completely hide the Explorer by using the ⌘+T keyboard shortcut or by choosing View⇨Explorer Bar. To resize the width of the Explorer bar, move your mouse pointer over the right edge of the separator until it turns into a pipe with arrows pointing to the left and right, click, and then drag the separator.

✦ **Content window:** Congratulations! At last, you've waded through all the controls that Microsoft offers — many Mac power users complain that there are *too* many controls, in fact — and you've reached the area where Web pages are actually displayed. Like any other window, the Content window can be scrolled; and when you minimize Explorer to the Dock, you get a thumbnail image of the Content window.

The Content window often contains underlined text and graphical icons that transport you to other pages when you click them. These underlined words and icons are *links*, and they make it easy to move from one area of a site to another or to a completely different site.

✦ **Status bar:** Although tiny, the Status bar includes important stuff; for example, it displays a tiny lock icon when you're connected to a secure Web site. A *secure* site encrypts the information that you send and receive, making it much harder for those of unscrupulous ideals to obtain things like credit card numbers and personal information. The Status bar also displays information about what the mouse pointer is currently resting upon, like the address for a link or the name of an image.

Visiting Web Sites

Here's the stuff that virtually everyone over the age of 5 knows how to do . . . but I get paid by the word, and some folks might just not be aware of all the myriad ways of visiting a site. You can load a Web page using any of the following methods:

✦ **Type (or paste) a Web site address into the address bar and then press Return.**

If you're typing in an address and Explorer recognizes the site as one that you've visited in the past, it helps by completing the address for you. (Explorer jargon: AutoComplete.) If this is a new site, just keep typing.

If this (cough) *helpful* feature drives you up the wall, you can turn it off by either choosing Explorer➪Preferences or by pressing ⌘+; (semicolon). In the Preferences window that opens, click the triangle next to the Web Browser category to expand it and then click Browser Display. Click (uncheck) the Use Address AutoComplete check box to disable it.

✦ **Click a Favorite entry within Explorer.**

✦ **Click the Home button, which takes you to the Home page that you specify.**

More on this in the section "Setting Up Your Home Page" elsewhere in this chapter.

✦ **Click a page link in Apple Mail or another Internet-savvy application.**

✦ **Click a page link within another Web page.**

✦ **Use the Search panel in the Explorer bar.**

Select the Find a Web Page radio button and then type the contents that you want to find in the Find a Web Page Containing box.

Explorer displays any matches that it finds as underlined links in the Explorer bar. Figure 5-3 illustrates a search that I've performed and one of the sites that Explorer found.

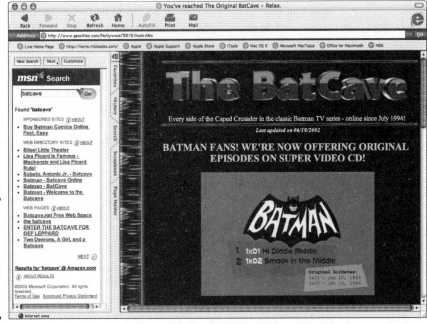

Figure 5-3: Locate a page on a specific subject from the Search panel.

✦ **Click an Explorer page icon in the Dock or in a Finder window.**

For example, Mac OS X already has an icon in the default Dock that takes you to the Mac OS X page on the Apple Web site. Drag a site from your Favorites list or the Favorites bar and drop it on the right side of the Dock. Clicking the icon that you add launches Internet Explorer and automatically loads that site.

This trick works only on the side of the Dock to the right of the vertical line.

If you minimize Explorer to the Dock, you'll see a miniature thumbnail of the page with the Explorer logo superimposed on it. Click this thumbnail in the Dock to restore the page to its full glory.

Navigating the Web

A typical Web surfing session is a linear experience — you bop from one page to the next, absorbing the information that you want and discarding the rest. However, after you visit a few sites, you might find that you need to return to where you've been or head to the familiar ground of your Home page. Internet Explorer offers these navigational controls on the toolbar:

✦ **Back:** Click the Back button on the toolbar to return to the last page that you visited. Additional clicks take you to previous pages, in reverse order. The Back button is disabled if you haven't visited at least two sites. From the keyboard, press ⌘+[(left square bracket) to go Back.

✦ **Forward:** If you've clicked the Back button at least once, clicking the Forward button takes you to the next page (or through the pages) where you originally were, in forward order. The Forward button is disabled if you haven't used the Back button. Press ⌘+] (right square bracket) to move Forward using the keyboard.

✦ **Stop:** Click this button to stop the loading of the content from the current page. This is a real boon when a download takes *foorrevverr,* which can happen when you're trying to visit a very popular or very slow Web site, especially if you're using a dial-up modem connection to the Internet. Using Stop is also handy if a page has a number of very large graphics that are going to take a long time to load. Keyboard buffs can use the ⌘+. (period) shortcut.

✦ **Refresh:** Click Refresh to reload the contents of the current page. Although most pages remain static, some pages change their content at regular intervals or after you fill out a form or click a button. By clicking Refresh, you can see what's changed on these pages. (I use Refresh every hour or so with CNN.com, for example.) To refresh from the keyboard, press the ⌘+R keyboard shortcut.

✦ **Home:** Click this button to return to your Home page. If you're like me and you've chosen a search engine as your Home page, you can zip back for a quick search at any time!

✦ **AutoFill:** If you fill out a lot of forms online — when you're shopping at Web sites, for example — you can click the AutoFill button to complete these forms for you. If you haven't filled out your AutoFill Profile, Explorer displays the AutoFill Profile section of the Explorer Preferences dialog, where you can type in data such as your name, phone numbers, and e-mail and street addresses.

To be honest, I'm not a big fan of releasing *any* of my personal information to *any* Web site, so I don't use AutoFill often. If you do decide to use this feature, make sure that the connection is secure (look for the padlock icon in the Status bar) and read the site's Privacy Agreement page first to see how your identity data will be treated.

✦ **Print:** Click the Print button to print the contents of the current Web page to your default printer. To display the Page Setup and Print Preview commands, you can click and hold on the Print toolbar button.

Some combinations of background and text colors might conspire together to render your printed copy practically worthless. In a case like that, use your printer's grayscale setting (if it has one). Alternatively, you can simply click and drag to select the text on the page, press ⌘+C to copy it, and then paste the text into Word or AppleWorks, where you can print the page on a less offensive background (while still keeping the text formatting largely untouched). You can also save the contents of a page as plain text — more on this later in the section "Saving Web Pages."

✦ **Mail:** Click this toolbar button to automatically launch Apple Mail and open a New Message window. By clicking and holding on the Mail toolbar icon, you can also choose to read your mail or send a link to the current page to someone in e-mail.

Setting Up Your Home Page

Choosing a Home page is one of the easiest methods of speeding up your Web surfing, especially if you're using a dial-up modem connection. However, a large percentage of the Mac owners who I've talked to have never set their own Home page, simply using the default Home page provided by their browser! With Internet Explorer running, take a moment to follow these steps to declare your own freedom to choose your own Home page:

1. **If you want to use a specific Web page as your new Home page, display it in Explorer and select the page address in the address bar. Press ⌘+C to copy the address to the Clipboard.**

It's a good idea to select a page with few graphics or a fast-loading popular site — my Home page, Google.com, is both.

2. **Choose Explorer⇨Preferences or press ⌘+; (semicolon).**

3. **Click the triangle next to the Web Browser category in the scrolling list at the left; from the expanded category list, click Browser Display.**

   You'll see the settings shown in Figure 5-4.

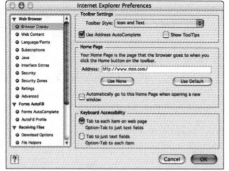

Figure 5-4: Adding your own Home page is an easy (and often time-saving) change you can make.

4. **Click in the Home Page Address field and erase its current contents — probably that doggone MSN.com that I dislike so much — and then press ⌘+V to paste the address from the Clipboard.**

   You can even do things the old-fashioned way and actually type the Web address manually.

5. **Alternatively, click the Use None button if you want Explorer to load with a blank page.**

   This is the fastest choice of all for a Home page.

6. **Click OK.**

Adding and Using Favorites

No doubt about it: Favorites make the Web a friendly place. As you collect Favorites in Internet Explorer, you're able to immediately jump from one site to another with a single click on the Favorites menu or the Favorites panel on the Explorer bar.

To add a Favorite, first navigate to the desired page and then do any of the following:

✦ **Choose Favorites⇨Add Page to Favorites.**

✦ **Press the ⌘+D keyboard shortcut.**

✦ **Press the ⌘+K keyboard shortcut to create a new untitled Favorite.**

> If you use this method, you must enter everything manually. Figure 5-5 illustrates the Info dialog that appears for a new, untitled Favorite.

Figure 5-5:
You can add a Favorite manually, but I prefer to create a Favorite from the page itself.

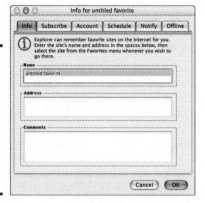

✦ **Click the Add button in the Favorites panel.**

✦ **Choose Favorites⇨Subscribe.**

> More on subscriptions later in the section "Using Subscriptions and History."

To add a Favorite to the Favorites bar, navigate to the page, click the icon next to the page address in the Address bar, and then drag the icon to the desired spot on the Favorites bar. You can also drag a link on the current page to the Favorites bar — but note that doing this only adds a Favorite for the page corresponding to the link, not the current page.

To jump to a Favorite:

✦ **Choose Favorites⇨Favorite.**

> If the Favorite is contained in a folder, which I discuss later in this section, move your mouse pointer over the folder name to show its contents and then click the Favorite.

✦ **Click the Favorite on the Favorites bar.**

If you've added a large number of items to the Favorites bar, click the More icon on the edge of the Favorites Bar to display the rest of the Favorites buttons.

✦ **Display the Favorites panel in the Explorer Bar and then click the desired Favorite.**

The more Favorites you add, the more unwieldy the Favorites menu and the Favorites panel become. To keep things organized, use either of these two methods:

- Choose Favorites⇨Organize Favorites. From the submenu that appears, you can add a new folder or a *divider*, which is a dividing line that separates different groups of Favorites on the Favorites panel. A divider appears as an empty line on the Favorites menu.

- Choose Favorites⇨Organize Favorites. From the submenu that appears, click New Folder to create an untitled Favorite folder. *Note:* You have to use the Favorites panel to actually move or manage a divider or a new folder . . . go figure.

Using the Favorites panel of the Explorer bar to organize things is much easier. Simply click the Organize button to add a new divider or folder. To then move the divider where you like, click and drag it to the proper spot in your Favorites list. You can also click and drag Favorites icons into folders or rearrange them by dropping them into a different order.

If you've created a new folder, you'll naturally want to change its name. Just hold down Control while you click the folder and then pick Edit Name from the pop-up menu that appears. The folder name appears in an edit box, and you can type the new name; press Return when you're done.

To delete a Favorite, a folder, or a divider, hold down Control and click it, and then pick Delete from the pop-up menu that appears.

Downloading Files

A huge chunk of the fun that you'll find on the Web is the ability to download images and files. If you've visited a site that offers files for downloading, typically you just click the Download button or the download file link, and Explorer takes care of the rest. See the Download Manager window shown in Figure 5-6, which keeps you updated with the status of the download. While the file is downloading, feel free to continue browsing or even download additional files; the Download Manager window helps you keep track of what's going on and when everything will be finished transferring.

Figure 5-6:
Monitoring
downloaded
files is easy
with the
Download
Manager.

By default, Explorer saves any downloaded files on your Mac OS X Desktop, which I like and use. To specify the location where downloaded files are stored — for example, if you'd like to scan them automatically with an antivirus program — follow these steps:

1. **Choose Explorer➪Preferences or press ⌘+; (semicolon).**

2. **Click the triangle next to the Receiving Files category in the scrolling list at the left; then from the expanded category list, click Download Options.**

3. **Click the Change Location button.**

4. **Navigate to the location where you want the files stored.**

5. **Click the Choose button.**

6. **Make sure that the Always Download Files to the Download Folder radio button is selected.**

7. **Click OK.**

To download a specific image that appears on a Web page, move your mouse pointer over the image and hold down Control while you click. Then choose Download Image to Disk from the pop-up menu that appears, as shown in Figure 5-7. Explorer prompts you for the location where you want to store the file.

Luckily, Internet Explorer has matured to the point that it can seamlessly handle virtually any multimedia file type that it encounters. However, if you've downloaded a multimedia file and Explorer doesn't seem to be able to play or display it, try loading the file within QuickTime. As you can read in Book III, Chapter 6, QuickTime is the Swiss Army Knife of multimedia players, and it can recognize a huge number of audio, video, and image formats.

**Book IV
Chapter 5**

**Going Places with
Internet Explorer**

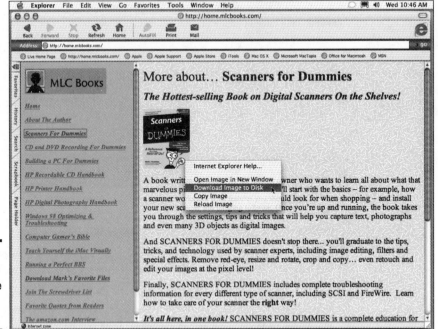

Figure 5-7:
Download
single image
files from a
Web page.

Using Subscriptions and History

Although using the Refresh button is one way of checking for changes in a Web page, it's not the best way. (I discuss the Refresh toolbar button in the earlier section "Navigating the Web.") Explorer offers a feature called *subscriptions,* in which a Favorite site is checked for updates on a regular schedule; updated pages with new content are displayed on the Favorites menu and in the Favorites panel with a blue star. You can also choose to update subscribed sites manually by pressing ⌘+U within Explorer or by clicking Favorites and choosing the Update Subscriptions menu item.

To set up a page with a subscription, display the desired page and then choose Favorites➪Subscribe. Explorer displays the dialog that you see in Figure 5-8. Click the Subscribe button there.

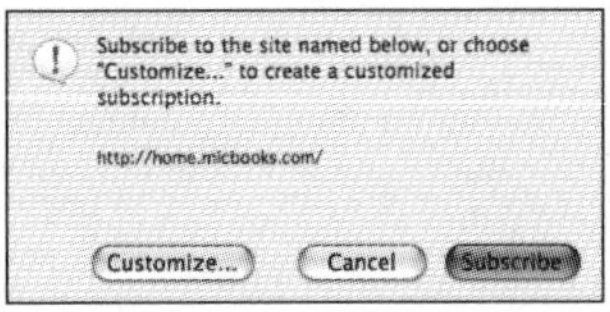

Figure 5-8:
Subscribe to
a Web page.

> Subscribe to the site named below, or choose "Customize..." to create a customized subscription.
>
> http://home.mlcbooks.com/
>
> (Customize...)   (Cancel)   (Subscribe)

To set the update period, follow these steps:

1. **Choose Explorer⇨Preferences.**

2. **Click the triangle next to the Web Browser category in the scrolling list at the left; from the expanded category list, click Subscriptions.**

3. **To check for updates each time that you launch Explorer, mark the Each Time Explorer Is Launched radio button.**

4. **To set a schedule period, mark the Every radio button, click the Time Period drop-down list box (you can choose Minutes, Hours, or Days), click in the value field, and then enter the desired number.**

5. **Enable one or more check boxes to choose how Explorer will alert you to updated subscriptions, including playing a sound of your choice or sending an automated e-mail message to the address that you specify.**

6. **Click OK to save your changes.**

To keep tabs on where you've been, you can display the History list either by clicking the History panel in the Explorer bar or by choosing Window⇨ History. (The keyboard shortcut ⌘+3 works well, too.) To return to a page in the list, just click it from the History panel (or double-click, if you're viewing the stand-alone History window). Explorer also searches the History list when it fills in an address you're typing — that's the AutoComplete feature I mention in the earlier section "Visiting Web Sites."

You can specify how many site entries Explorer should save in the History file by following these steps:

1. **Choose Explorer⇨Preferences.**

2. **Click the triangle next to the Web Browser category in the scrolling list at the left; from the expanded category list, click Advanced.**

3. **Click in the Remember the Last Places Visited field and enter the number of places that you want to retain in the History list.**

   By default, Explorer remembers the last 300 places.

4. **Click OK to save your changes.**

I show you how to clear the contents of the History file in the upcoming section "Handling ancient history."

Saving Web Pages

If you've encountered a page that you'd like to load later, you can save to disk in its entirety. Follow these steps:

1. **Display the desired page.**

2. **Choose File⇨Save As.**

Explorer displays the slightly newfangled Save dialog that you see in Figure 5-9.

Figure 5-9:
Save a Web
page as
a file.

3. **In the Save As text field, type a name for the saved page.**

4. **From the Where field, navigate to the location where you want to store the file on your system.**

5. **From the Format drop-down list, choose one of the three options.**

I recommend choosing Web Archive, which stores images and frame designs, allowing you to display the page from the file just as it appeared online.

You can also either choose to save just the HyperText Markup Language (HTML) source code or to just save the text on the page as plain text. Either of these two formatting choices, however, can result in an incomplete file because Web designers employ a host of different methods to put text and multimedia on a Web page.

6. **If you choose Web Archive as the format, click the Options button to display the sheet that you see in Figure 5-10.**

Here you can specify what types of multimedia you want to include on the page, as well as any pages that are provided as links. (The farther down you drill — by choosing multiple levels deep — the more space this monster of a Web Archive file will take.) To prevent the inclusion of other sites at different addresses from links, enable the Skip Links to Other Sites check box. When you're finished making your selections, click OK to save your changes.

Figure 5-10: Determine what to save in a Web Archive file.

Site Download Options

NOTE: Downloading a site may take a long time and consume a lot of hard disk space. The fewer options you use from below, the faster and smaller the download will be.

☑ Download images
☑ Download sounds
☑ Download movies
☑ Download links
　　1 ⬍ Levels deep
　☑ Skip links to other sites

Cancel　　OK

7. Click Save to begin the download process.

After the Save file has been created, double-click it to load it in Explorer.

Protecting Your Privacy

No chapter on Internet Explorer would be complete without a discussion of security, both against outside intrusion from the Internet and prying eyes around your Mac. Hence this last section, which covers protecting your privacy.

Yes, there are such things as bad cookies

First, a definition of this ridiculous term: A *cookie,* a small file that a Web site automatically saves on your hard drive within Explorer's folder, contains information that the site will use on your future visits. For example, a site might save a cookie to preserve your site preferences for the next time or — in the case of a site such as Amazon.com — to identify you automatically and help customize the offerings that you see.

In and of themselves, cookies aren't bad things. Unlike a virus, a cookie file isn't going to replicate itself or wreak havoc on your system, and only the original site can read the cookie that it creates. However, many folks don't appreciate acting as a gracious host for a slew of little snippets of personal information. Also, if you do a large amount of surfing, cookies can occupy a significant amount of your hard drive space over time. (Not to mention that some cookies have highly suggestive names, which could lead to all sorts of conclusions. 'Nuff said.)

You can choose to accept all cookies — the default — or you can opt to disable cookies altogether. You can also set Explorer to ask you for confirmation before saving a cookie on a case-by-case (or is that cookie-by-cookie?) basis. To change your Cookie Acceptance Plan (or CAP, for those who absolutely crave acronyms), follow these steps:

Book IV
Chapter 5

Going Places with Internet Explorer

1. **Choose Explorer⇨Preferences.**

2. **Click the triangle next to the Receiving Files category in the scrolling list at the left; from the expanded category list, click Cookies.**

   Explorer displays the scrolling list of all cookies on your drive, as shown in Figure 5-11.

Figure 5-11:
Exploring
the contents
of my
cookie
jar.

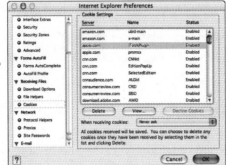

3. **To view the properties of an individual cookie file, click the cookie entry in the list and then click the View button.**

   You'll see things like the date that the cookie expires and whether it's encrypted (which is displayed in the Secure field).

4. **To delete a cookie file, select the entry and then click the Delete button.**

   The site that used that cookie will forget any information that it stored in the file, meaning that you might have to take care of things manually, like providing a password on the site that used to be read automatically from the cookie.

5. **To set how you want to keep cookies, click the When Receiving Cookies drop-down list box and then choose from the following:**

   • **Never Ask** (to allow all cookies)

   • **Ask for Each Site**

   • **Ask for Each Cookie**

   • **Never Accept Cookies**

6. **Click OK to save your changes.**

Cleaning your cache

Explorer speeds up the loading of Web sites by storing often-used images and multimedia files in a temporary storage, or *cache,* folder. Naturally, the files in your cache folder can be displayed (hint), which could lead to assumptions (hint, hint) about the sites you've been visiting (hint, hint, hint). (Tactful, ain't I?)

Explorer makes it easy to dump the contents of your cache file. Follow these steps:

1. **Choose Explorer⇨Preferences.**
2. **Click the triangle next to the Web Browser category in the scrolling list at the left; from the expanded category list, click Advanced.**
3. **Click the Empty Now button in the Cache section of the dialog.**
4. **Click OK to return to Explorer.**

Handling ancient history

As you might imagine, your History file leaves a very clear set of footprints indicating where you've been on the Web. Follow these steps to delete the contents of the History file:

1. **Choose Explorer⇨Preferences.**
2. **Click the triangle next to the Web Browser category in the scrolling list at the left; from the expanded category list, click Advanced.**
3. **Click the Clear History button.**
4. **Click OK to return to Explorer.**

You can also effectively disable your History file by entering a zero in the Remember the Last Places Visited field.

You can also selectively delete individual items from the History file — open the History list (as I demonstrated earlier), select the items you want to eliminate, and then press the Delete key.

Chapter 6: Staying Secure Online

In This Chapter

✓ **Understanding the dangers of going online**

✓ **Using a firewall**

✓ **Avoiding trouble online**

know that you've heard horror hacking stories: Big corporations and big government installations seem to be as open to hackers as a public library. Often, you read that even entire identities are being stolen online. When you consider that your Mac can contain very sensitive and private information in your life — such as your Social Security numbers and financial information — it's enough to make you nervous about turning on your computer long enough to check your eBay auctions.

But how much of that is Hollywood? How truly real is the danger? And how can you protect yourself? The good news is that you can easily secure your data from all but the most determined hacker — in fact, depending on the hardware that you're using to connect yourself to the Internet, you might be well guarded right now without even knowing it.

In this chapter, I continue a quest that I've pursued for over a decade now — to make my readers feel comfortable and secure in the online world by explaining the truth about what can happen and telling you how you can protect your system from intrusions.

One quick note: This chapter is written with the home and small business Mac owner in mind. Macs that access the Internet through a larger corporate network are very likely already protected by that knight in shining armor, the network system administrator. Of course, if you're using Mac OS X in your office, you're still welcome to read this material — however, check with your system administrator before you attempt to implement any of the recommendations that I make.

What Can Really Happen?

Before I begin, I want to offer you a moment of reassurance and a little of my personal background to explain that I'm well qualified to be your guide through this online minefield. (After all, you don't want Jerry Lewis lecturing you on how to maintain your Internet security.)

✦ I've been running and managing all sorts of online systems since the days of the BBS (Bulletin Board System), the text-based dinosaurs that used to rule the online world in the late '80s and early '90s. (In fact, my first book was on this very subject — and it contained a chapter on viruses long before they were the darlings of the techno-media.)

✦ As a consultant, I run Web sites and handle virus attacks for a number of organizations.

✦ I keep my own office network of six computers safe from attack while still providing readers all over the world with a Web site and a BBS.

With that understood, here's what can happen to you online *without* the right safeguards:

✦ **Hackers can access shared information on your network.** If you're running an unguarded network, it's possible for others to gain access to your documents and applications or wreak havoc on your system.

✦ **Your system could be infected with a virus or dangerous macro.** Left to their own devices, these misbehaving programs and macro commands can delete files or turn your entire hard drive into an empty paperweight.

✦ **Unsavory individuals could attempt to contact members of your family.** This kind of attack may take place through iChat, e-mail, or Web discussion boards, putting your family's safety at risk.

✦ **Hackers can use your system to attack others.** Your computer can be tricked into helping hackers as they attempt to knock out Web servers and public access File Transfer Protocol (FTP) sites on the Internet.

✦ **Criminals can attempt to con you out of your credit card or personal information.** The Internet is a prime candidate for identity theft.

Yes, that's a frightening list, and to be absolutely honest, some danger is indeed present every time that you or any user of your Macintosh connects to the Internet. However, here's the good news. With the right safeguards, it's literally impossible for most of those worst-case scenarios to happen on your Macintosh, and what remains would be so difficult that even the most die-hard hacker would throw in the towel long before reaching your computer or network.

I also want to point out that virtually everyone reading this book — as well as the guy writing it — really doesn't have anything that's worth a malicious hacking campaign. Things like Quicken data files and genealogical data might be priceless to us, of course, but most dedicated hackers are after bigger game. Unfortunately, the coverage that the media and Hollywood give to corporate and government attacks can turn even Aunt Harriet more than a little paranoid. Therefore, time for another of Mark's Maxims:

More of Mark's totally unnecessary computer trivia

The term *hacker* dates far back in the annals of the personal computer — in fact, it originally had nothing to do with networks, the Internet, or illegal activities at all . . . because In The Beginning, there was no Internet!

"Explain yourself, Chambers!" All right. The original hackers were electronics buffs, ham radio operators, computer hobbyists, and engineers who built (hacked) a working computer out of individual components with a soldering gun and a whole lotta guts. At the time, you didn't simply order a computer from Gateway or visit your local Maze o' Wires store in the mall to select your favorite system.

No, I'm talking about the mid-'70s, in the halcyon time before IBM even introduced the IBM PC (and when the only folks using the Internet, which wasn't called that back then,

were military folks and researchers). Even the simplest computer — really nothing more than a glorified calculator by today's standards — had to be lovingly assembled by hand. These early personal computers didn't run software as we know it. Instead, you programmed them manually through a bank of switches on the front, and they responded with codes displayed on a bank of lights. (Think about that next time you launch Microsoft Word.)

Today, of course, the need to assemble a computer from individual transistors is nonexistent, and the word *hacker* has an entirely different connotation — but don't be surprised if you meet an older member of your Macintosh user's group who's proud to be an old-fashioned hacker! (Look for the soldering gun, usually worn in a holster like a sidearm.)

It's not really necessary to consider the NSA or Interpol each time you poke your Mac's power button.™

A few simple precautions are all that's required.

"Shields Up, Chekov!"

"Okay, Mark, now I know the real story on what can happen to my computer online. So what do I do to safeguard my Macintosh?" You need two essential tools to protect your hardware (besides a healthy amount of common sense, which I cover in the upcoming section, "A Dose of Common Sense: Things Not to Do Online"): a *firewall* and an *antivirus* program.

Firewall basics

A *firewall* is a piece of hardware or software that essentially builds an impermeable barrier between the computers on your side of the wall (meaning your Mac and any other computers on your network) and all external computers on the other side of the wall (meaning the rest of the Internet).

"But wait a second, Mark — if other computers can't reach me and my Mac can't reach them, how can I use the Internet at all?" Ah, that's the beauty of today's firewalls. By using a series of techniques designed to thwart attacks from the outside, a firewall allows you to communicate safely, even monitoring what you send and what you receive for later examination. Figure 6-1 illustrates the basics of a firewall.

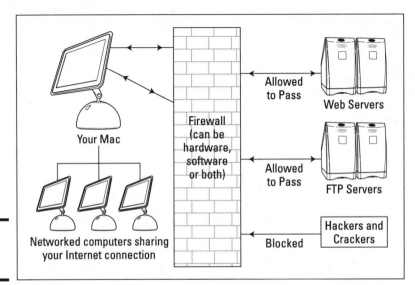

Figure 6-1:
A firewall
at work.

A firewall sounds grand and incredibly complex and highly technical — and sometimes it is — but it can also be incredibly simple. For example:

✦ You can spend thousands of dollars installing sophisticated firewall hardware and software.

or

✦ You can activate your firewall by disconnecting your dial-up, Digital Subscriber Line (DSL), or cable modem from the wall socket.

Believe it or not, both of those examples technically involve a firewall. In the first case, the firewall is a physical, tangible presence on the network; in the second case, the lack of a connection to the Internet actually acts as a firewall. (Think of it as the Air Firewall.) I've spoken to a number of readers who actually do this — however, if you're running a Web site or downloading a file from your company's FTP site, yanking the connection when you head to bed isn't an option. Therefore, most of us will install a physical firewall through hardware or software.

Do I already have a firewall?

In some cases, you might already be using a hardware firewall and not even know it. For example, many Internet-sharing devices include a built-in NAT firewall. NAT stands for *Network Address Translation,* and it's the most effective and popular hardware firewall standard in use by consumer devices. If you're using an Internet sharing hub or router, check its manual to determine whether it offers NAT as a firewall feature — and if so, turn it on if NAT isn't enabled by default. (See Book V, Chapter 2 for more on Internet sharing, routers, and firewalls.)

For instance, Figure 6-2 illustrates the configuration screen for my Internet router. Note the options to disable port scanning and ping responses, which are two tricks that hackers often use to detect what's often called a *hot computer* — meaning that the computer can be identified and is accessible to attack.

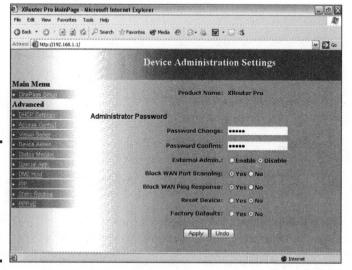

Figure 6-2: My Internet router can be set to be downright un-neighborly.

Using the internal Mac OS X firewall

Mac OS X includes a powerful internal firewall called *IPFW*. I'm happy to say that the latest version of Mac OS X makes IPFW very simple to use, and I can now recommend it! (In earlier versions of Mac OS X, IPFW — actually a UNIX application — was completely command driven from the Terminal.) The Mac OS X firewall is now configured through System Preferences — find more information on setting up IPFW in Chapter 2 of Book V.

Several developers have written user-friendly front-ends that provide alternate methods of configuring IPFW; you can try the shareware applications BrickHouse (shown in Figure 6-3), available from `http://personalpages.tds.net/~brian_hill/brickhouse.html`, or Firewalk X 2, available from `www.pliris-soft.com`.

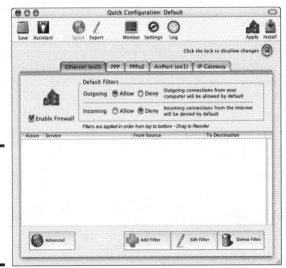

Figure 6-3:
BrickHouse
provides
another
route for
configuring
IPFW.

Using a commercial software firewall

You'll also find a number of popular alternatives to IPFW on the market. Here are two commercial software firewall applications that are proven to be both effective and easy-to-use:

✦ **Symantec, Norton Personal Firewall, $70** (`www.symantec.com`): Symantec provides both antivirus and firewall protection for the PC and Macintosh. Frequent updates and top-of-the-line technical support ensure that your firewall stays current and that you can get help when you need it.

✦ **Intego, NetBarrier X, $60 (**www.netbarrier.com**):** NetBarrier X comes with a number of preset configurations that allow you to choose a basic firewall for your network environment with a single click.

After you set up IPFW or a commercial firewall, visit a favorite site of mine on the Web: http://grc.com, the home of Gibson Research Corporation. There you'll find the free online utility ShieldsUP!, which will automatically test just how tight your firewall is and how susceptible your Mac could be to hacker attacks. Visit this site often because this service is updated periodically to reflect new hacking techniques.

Antivirus basics

Next, consider your antivirus protection. *Viruses* are typically transmitted through applications — you run a program, and the virus is activated. (Although not the traditional definition of a virus, both scripts and macros can be used to take control of your system and cause trouble, as well.) Therefore, you need to closely monitor what I call *The Big Three:*

✦ **Web downloads:** Consider every file that you receive from the Internet as a possible viral threat.

✦ **Removable media:** Viruses can be stored on everything from CD-ROMs and DVD-ROMs to Zip disks and even archaic floppy disks.

✦ **E-mail file attachments:** An application sent to you as an e-mail attachment is an easy doorway to your system.

Mac OS X has no built-in antivirus support, but a good antivirus program will take care of any application that's carrying a virus. Some even handle destructive macros within documents. However, make sure that the antivirus program that you choose offers *real-time scanning,* which operates when you download or open a file. Periodic scanning of your entire system is important, too, but only a real-time scanning application like Norton AntiVirus can immediately ensure that the StuffIt archive or the application you just received in your e-mail Inbox is actually free from viruses.

Virus technology continues to evolve over time, just like more beneficial application development. For example, recently a virus has been discovered that's actually contained in a JPEG image file! With a good antivirus application that offers regular updates, you'll continue to keep your system safe from viral attack.

I heartily recommend Norton AntiVirus from Symantec, as shown in Figure 6-4. This program includes automatic updates delivered while you're online to make sure that you're covered against the latest viruses.

**Book IV
Chapter 6**

**Staying Secure
Online**

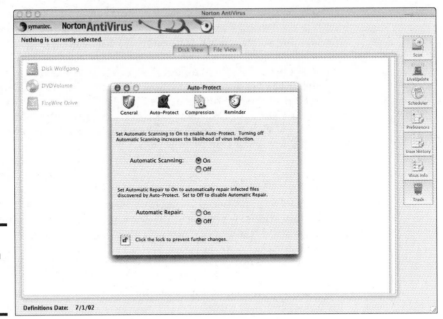

Figure 6-4:
The Norton
AntiVirus
control
center.

A Dose of Common Sense: Things Not to Do Online

One more powerful weapon that you can use to make sure that your Mac stays safe from unlawful intrusion is this: Practicing common sense on the Internet is just as important as adding a firewall and an antivirus application to Mac OS X.

With this in mind, here's a checklist of things that you should never do while you're online:

+ **Never download a file from a site you don't trust.** And make sure that your antivirus software is configured to check downloaded files before you open them.

+ **Never open an e-mail attachment until it's been checked.** Even if the person who sent the message is someone you trust. (Many of today's macro viruses actually replicate themselves by sending copies to the addresses found through the victim's e-mail program. Of course, this problem crops up regularly in the Windows world, but it's been known to happen in the Macintosh community, as well.)

✦ **Never enter any personal information in an e-mail message unless you know the recipient.** Sure, I send my mailing address to friends and family but no one else. In fact, even e-mail can be intercepted by a determined hacker, so if you're sending something truly important, use an encryption application like PGP Freeware (www.pgp.com) shown in Figure 6-5. It's a Mac OS 9 application, but it works fine in Classic mode. (For more on Classic mode, read Book I, Chapter 7.)

Figure 6-5:
PGP allows
you to
encrypt
information
for safe
delivery
through
e-mail.

✦ **Never include any personal information in an Internet newsgroup post.** After all, these posts can be viewed by anyone with a newsgroup account, so there's no such thing as privacy in a newsgroup.

✦ **Never buy from an online store that doesn't offer a secure, encrypted connection when you're prompted for your personal information and credit card number.** If you're using Internet Explorer or Netscape, you can tell when you're using a secure connection by checking the status bar at the bottom of the Web browser window: If a small padlock icon appears (as shown in Figure 6-6), the connection is encrypted and secure.

✦ **Never divulge personal information to others over an iChat connection.**

✦ **Never use the same password for all your electronic business.** Use different passwords that include both letters and numbers, change them often, and never divulge them to anyone else.

✦ **Never give anyone else administrative access to your Web or FTP server.**

✦ **Never allow any type of remote access to your Macintosh or your network without testing that access first; restrict that access to visitors whom you trust.**

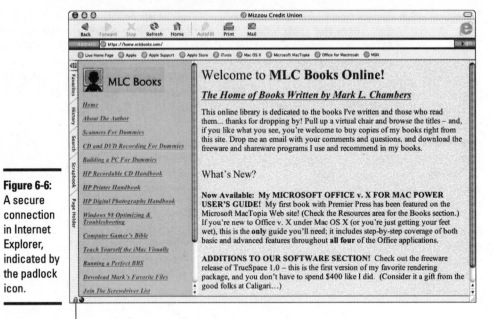

Figure 6-6:
A secure
connection
in Internet
Explorer,
indicated by
the padlock
icon.

The padlock icon indicates a secure connection.

Find more details on securing your network from intrusion — including
Internet hacker attacks — in Book V. And in Book II, I cover System
Preferences that can affect the security of your system.

Book V

Networking in Mac OS X

The 5th Wave   By Rich Tennant

"If it works, it works. I've just never seen network cabling connected with Chinese handcuffs before."

Contents at a Glance

Chapter 1: Setting Up a Small Network 429

Chapter 2: Using Your Network 447

Chapter 3: You May Even Need AppleTalk 463

Chapter 4: Going Wireless...473

Chapter 5: Sharing that Precious Internet Thing 485

Chapter 1: Setting Up a Small Network

In This Chapter

✔ **Finding out what a network is and why you might want one**

✔ **Setting up the network hardware**

✔ **Configuring network system preferences**

✔ **Troubleshooting your network**

In the not-so-distant past, networks were found only in huge companies that had the money and workforce to pay for and maintain it. But now, as technology rolls on, having a network of your own has become very affordable and relatively easy to create. In this chapter, I talk about what networks are, what you can do with them, and how to set up a small network of your own for your home or small business.

In a nutshell, a *network* is a combination of hardware, cables, and software that allows computers and printers to talk to each other. To have a network, you need the right hardware and software. Some of the hardware and most of the software that you'll need probably came with your Mac, depending on which Mac you have. As you progress through this chapter, you will discover everything that's required to set up your network so you can pick up any additional parts you need. Don't worry too much about getting additional parts: Virtually any local or online computer store has everything you need to get up and running.

Networks can be used for many things. A network allows computers to talk or exchange data. The data that's exchanged could be anything: files that you want to send between computers or to networked printers; streaming audio or video; data that allows you to remotely control another computer on the network; or data sent between a game server and people on other computers who are playing a game together. Basically, anything you can imagine that would involve moving data between multiple computers can be done using a network.

What Do I Need to Set Up My Network?

You'll need the right hardware and software to make your network sing. This section covers each component with a description about the role that each part plays on the network and other good stuff that you'll want to know to get your network right the first time.

Something to network

Okay, I know this is pretty basic, but the first thing that you need to build a network is . . . stuff to network together. That's right, you need to have devices that you want to network as your starting place. Most times this will be computers, whether Macs or Windows/UNIX PCs, printers, PDAs, and other stand-alone network-capable devices.

Network Interface Card (NIC)

A *Network Interface Card,* or NIC, is a hardware device that your computer uses to talk to the rest of the network. The NIC is what you connect the network cable into that speaks the language of electronics, sending data around the network. Nowadays, most networks use the Ethernet networking protocol, and most NICs are Ethernet-compatible. Most modern Macs have an Ethernet NIC built right in and in fact aren't really cards at all, but something built right onto the Mac's main system board. If you have an older Mac, say one bought before 1998, you can purchase an add-on NIC at any computer store.

Hub or switch

So you have an assortment of devices in your home or small office that you've decided to network. How do you make them all interconnect? Although you could connect just two computers together using nothing more than a single *crossover* cable, you need fancier hardware to connect more than two computers: namely, a hub or a switch. The hub or the switch, used to connect everything together, is the focal point of the network. Without a hub or switch, you wouldn't have a network.

Hubs

A *hub* is a small box that has a bunch of Ethernet ports on it. A *port* is really just like an Ethernet NIC on your computer, but a hub or switch has lots of them. Inside, a hub connects all those Ethernet ports together so that the talking (sending) wires from each port connect to the listening (receiving) wires on all other ports. Thus, in true E.F. Hutton style, when one computer talks, all others listen. As a side effect of how hubs work, if more than one computer tries to talk at once, a *collision* happens. Collisions are a Bad Thing: The data that was being sent by the two computers is destroyed and has to be re-sent.

39 flavors of Ethernet

Ethernet standards allow for operation at different speeds. Because the Ethernet standard improved over time, some older Ethernet devices only support the older (slower) speeds. Ethernet's speed is rated by how much data it can transfer in a second — usually in millions of bits per second, or megabits per second (Mbps). Originally, Ethernet was designed to run at 10 Mbps. Now there are three different speeds of Ethernet: 10 Mbps, 100 Mbps, and 1000 Mbps.

1000 Mbps Ethernet — also called *Gigabit Ethernet* or just *Gigabit* for short — is still a bit on the expensive side for small home or office networks. All consumer-level Gigabit Ethernet NICs also support running at 10 Mbps or 100 Mbps, so you will hear them called 10/100/1000 Ethernet NICs. PowerBook G4s and G4 Towers come with a 10/100/1000 Ethernet built in, but the iMac, iBook, and eMac still come with just 10/100 Ethernet NICs built-in. Although Gigabit NICs are now priced under $100, the devices

that can connect Gigabit NICs together are still in the thousands of dollars. That fact, coupled with the reality that most computer systems can't really even handle or dish out that much data, make Gigabit Ethernet a choice for only those wanting an extremely high-end and costly network.

NICs and other Ethernet equipment that only handle 10 Mbps are rapidly becoming obsolete because virtually all the modern NICs and other Ethernet hardware support both 10 Mbps and 100 Mbps. Most times, you will see this labeled as *10/100 Ethernet*. For your home networking, you probably want to invest in 100 Mbps or 10/100 Mbps. You can pick up a 10/100 Ethernet NIC for as low as $19.

Keep your eye out for Ethernet NICs and equipment that only handles 100 Mbps. You won't see it much, but be wary because it can't interconnect with 10 Mbps Ethernet NICs and equipment. I advise against buying it.

Although they may seem relatively harmless, collisions can really take a toll on your Ethernet network. When data starts flying around your network, collisions *will* take over and limit the amount of data that you can get through the network. Typically you'll only be able to use about 40 percent of the total speed, or *bandwidth*, of the hub. With the cost of switches barely above that of hubs, you really have little reason to get a hub instead of a switch.

Usually setting up a hub, and therefore giving birth to your network, means simply connecting a power cable to the hub and then plugging your computers in. Voilà! You have a network! Congratulations! You'll see various lights on the hub, usually a power light indicating that the hub is powered on and operational. But you'll also see lights that correspond to each port on the hub. These lights are meant to show you certain information about things that are happening in the hub. For instance, you will normally see the following types of lights:

+ **Link light:** Each port on a hub should have a link light. A *link light* simply tells you, by looking at a hub, which ports have something alive connected to a given port: that is, a device is connected and powered on. On hubs that support 10 and 100 Mbps, the speed light is also used to indicate a link, so there isn't a separate link light.

+ **Speed light:** Each port on the hub should have a speed light. On hubs that support both 10 Mbps and 100 Mbps, this tells you the speed of the device at the other end. Some hubs have different lights for different speeds, and some use a single light and make it different colors for different speeds.

+ **Activity light:** When one computer speaks, they all hear it. Typically, an entire hub has only one activity light for the entire hub, indicating that someone is speaking. With heavy traffic, the light could appear solid.

+ **Collision light:** Just like the activity light, collisions affect everything connected to the hub, so logic dictates having only one collision light for the entire hub. This light will flash whenever a collision occurs, which can happen even with only two devices attached. When you add more devices, you get more collisions. When this light stays on most of the time, look into getting a switch (which I describe in the next section).

Switches

A hub is a relatively simple way to connect a bunch of cables together to allow computers to talk. Hubs don't think about the actual data that travels through it; they just receive information on one port and send a copy out to all the other ports. Simple. A *switch,* although it also doesn't do anything to the data going through it, uses the information in the data to help it be more efficient.

When an Ethernet switch receives a *frame* — a small package that Ethernet equipment uses to send the data in — it reads the label on the frame to see the return address of the computer that sent the frame. In a short amount of time (after being turned on and watching the data move around), a switch learns which computer is located on which port. Then, whenever data comes into the switch, it looks at the *header* (some information on the front of all frames, much like a label on a package you might send) and sees which computer the data is going to. The switch then sends the frame out the port for that computer only.

This is a Good Thing because instead of having to let one computer speak and forcing all others to listen (as a hub does) — known as *half-duplex* — a switch can actually send the data directly to the only computer that needs to hear it. This gets rid of the evil collisions, allowing all the computers to speak and talk at the same time *(full-duplex).* Now, twice as much information can be shoved around because a computer can now send and receive data at the same time. This is a major breakthrough and can happen *only* on a switch.

Just how much of a performance improvement do you get with a switch compared with a hub? On average, you'll move from a 100 Mbps hub that can handle an average of 5 Mbps of traffic per device (assuming eight computers are communicating at once) to a 100 Mbps switch that can handle 200 Mbps per device (no matter how many devices are connected). That's a speed increase of 4,000 percent!

Cables

Cables are the ties that bind, literally. *Cables* are used to connect the NIC card on each computer to the central hardware of the network: namely, hubs and switches. Before you know it, you'll be a cable-wielding maniac with thousands of feet of cable draped across every piece of furniture in your place for your first LAN party. (A *LAN party*, by the way, is when way too many techies bring their computers into a very small space, connect them up together, and play games for 48 hours straight. Good stuff!)

Here's the scoop on what kind of cables to use. Technically, you can run 10 Mbps Ethernet over *Cat5* cable (like a super version of the wire that you use for your telephones) or *coaxial* cable (the kind of cable that you use to connect your TV to your cable service). You can run 100 Mbps Ethernet over Cat5 cable or fiber-optic cable.

I'm sure that you noticed that the common denominator here is the Cat5 cable. Although you could get by using coaxial cable, it's pretty much gone out of style as a network cable because it's limited to 10 Mbps Ethernet and virtually all NICs have stopped coming with a coaxial connection on them. Fiber-optic cable, although supporting speeds of 100 Mbps, 1 Gbps, and even 10 Gbps, is more expensive and more difficult to install.

Although you can do 10/100 and most times 100Mbps Ethernet over Cat5 cable, any new cables that you buy should be Cat5E — which I talk about a little later — because it is specifically meant to be used with 1000Mbps Ethernet.

Be sure to buy *straight-through* Cat5E cables (also called *patch* cables) and not *crossover* cables, which are only used in certain circumstances. *Crossover cables* are mainly used to connect two computer directly together to form a network, connect a cable/DSL modem directly to a computer, or connect multiple hubs or switches together.

Cat5 cable supports speeds of 100 Mbps. Of course, 1000 Mbps Ethernet is designed to run ten times faster than that; luckily enough, it was engineered to be compatible with 90 percent of Cat5 installations. Having said that, some Cat5 cable doesn't stick to the stringent specifications that 1000 Mbps Ethernet requires. There is a newer version of Cat5 cable called *Category 5 Enhanced,* or Cat5E for short. Cat5E is recommended for any new installation because it can easily handle 10/100 Mbps Ethernet and yet can handle 1000 Mbps Ethernet as well. Even if you're using 10/100 Mbps Ethernet, you can upgrade someday to 1000 Mbps without having to worry about upgrading your cabling.

Setting Up Your Network

After you collect the hardware components listed earlier in this chapter, you're ready to connect things. Here's a quick list of things to do to get your network fired up:

1. **Find the best location for placing your hub or switch.**

To keep costs down, try to place the hub or switch in a location close to a power socket that's centrally located, so you can use the least amount of cable. If cost isn't an issue, hide the unit in a closet and just run all the cables along the walls to the hub or switch. And if cost *really* isn't an issue, get your house fully wired with Cat5E cable.

2. **Plug the hub or switch into the power socket.**

Some hubs and switches come on automatically when you plug them in and can never be turned off. Others have a power switch that you need to turn on the first time that you plug them in.

3. **Verify that the hub or switch is working by looking at the lights on the front. Check the manual that came with the hub or switch to see what light configuration is normal for that particular unit.**

Until you have computers or printers attached to it, you might just have a status light that shows the hub is powered on. But if your lights on your unit don't match up with what the manual says, you could have a bum unit that you need to return.

4. **Verify that all your devices are near enough to the hub or switch to be connected by your cables and then turn them all on.**

5. **Get one of your Cat5E cables and connect one cable from the Ethernet jack on your computer, usually on the side or back, to an open port on the hub or switch.**

You should see a link light or speed light come on that verifies that the two devices sense each other. (You might also have a link light on your NIC where you plug in the cable, but that depends on the Mac that you're using.)

6. **Repeat Step 5 until each device is attached to the hub or switch.**

Congratulations! The first phase of the network, the physical connection, is complete. After the hardware part is connected, you need to configure the software side of the network.

Understanding the Basics of Network Configuration

After you've physically hooked together your network, you need to configure it, which basically just involves entering a lot of numbers and other stuff in dialogs. But just so you'll understand what you're getting into, this section explains what those numbers are, what they do, and why you ought to know it. Because this is an OS X book, I stick with configuring Macs running the Big X.

TCP/IP

Protocol is just the techno-weenie word for a set of rules or a language. A *protocol* is a language that computers use to communicate. Without protocols, the computers would never be able to speak to each other even though you have NICs, cables, and a hub or a switch. The Internet Protocol (IP) part of the TCP/IP suite is really what I want to talk about because that's the main thing that you need to configure to make these darn computers all talk with each other.

IP addresses

IP addresses are like street addresses for computers on a network. Each computer on the network has an IP address, and it needs to be unique because no other computer can share it. When a computer wants to communicate with another computer, it can simply send the data on the network in a nice package that has its address as well as the address of the computer that it's trying to talk to.

An IP address is just a number, but it's written in a strange way (what a surprise). An IP address is written as four numbers between 0 and 255 with a dot (period) between them: For instance, a common IP address that you might run into is 192.168.0.1. As everyone knows, techno-nerds can't sleep unless they have three or four ways to write the same thing, including IP addresses. The form shown above, which is by far the most common and what you will be dealing with, is called *dotted notation*. Each number, like 192, is called an *octet*.

Don't worry too much about this stuff: You don't have to remember all these terms (like octet) to create your own network. They could be helpful, however, if something goes wrong and you need to place a call into tech support. You can impress the computer wonk at the other end of the line with your mastery of techno-babble.

IP addresses at home versus on the Internet

One very important thing to keep in mind is that the almighty IP address police — *Internet Assigned Numbers Authority* (www.iana.org) — have broken IP addresses into groups. The two main types of IP addresses are public and private. *Public* IP addresses are ones that can be used on the Internet and are unique throughout the whole world. *Private* IP addresses are used in homes or businesses and cannot be used to talk to the public Internet. Private IP addresses are used over and over by many people and most commonly take the form 192.168.*x.x*.

You will almost always get a public IP address from your Internet Service Provider (ISP), whether you're using a cable modem, Digital Subscriber Line (DSL), or a regular dial-up modem. If you use a cable/DSL router or something like IPNetShareX to share your Internet connection among multiple computers, you'll be using private IP addresses on your network while using a single public IP address to talk to the Internet (more on that later in Book V, Chapter 5).

"Great! I get an IP address, put it into my Network settings in System Preferences, and off I go. Right?" Well, you're close, but here are a few other pieces of information that you'll need before you can go surfing around the world:

+ **Default gateway:** When you send information to other networks, whether in another building or on the Internet, your computer needs to know the IP address of the gateway that will forward your data down the line. The *default gateway* is really just the IP address of a *router,* which is a device that connects multiple networks together. A *gateway* gets its name because it really is your gateway to all other networks.

+ **Subnet mask:** A *subnet mask* is a number that helps your computer know when it needs to send stuff through the router. It's a group of four octets with dots, just like an IP address, but almost always it uses 0 or 255 as the four octets. Most often, the subnet mask will be 255.255.255.0. If the wrong number is entered for the subnet mask, it could keep you from talking to the Internet or even computers on your own network!

Software applications

After you have the hardware in place and you've chosen and configured a protocol to allow the computers to all talk to each other, you need software on each computer that enables them to perform a specific task working together. A lot of the software that you'll need to move data on your network is already included in Mac OS X. Here is a quick list of some of the network software and protocols already built into OS X and what they're used for:

+ **FTP:** *File Transfer Protocol* (FTP), part of the TCP/IP protocol suite, is used to enable computers of any type — Mac, PC, UNIX, mainframe, or whatever — to transfer files back and forth between them.

+ **Telnet:** *Telnet* is also part of the TCP/IP suite that enables you to remotely connect to a computer and execute commands on the remote machine.

✦ **Samba:** *Samba,* an open source software suite, enables Mac OS X users to share files to people using Windows computers and also allows the Mac user to connect to files that the Windows computers share.

✦ **HTTP:** *HyperText Transfer Protocol* (HTTP), also part of the TCP/IP suite, is used by Web browsers to provide access to all the various pages on the World Wide Web.

Configuring Network System Preferences

In this section, I show you how to configure your Mac to communicate with other computers on a local network. This configuration means two things: You need to manually configure the Transmission Control Protocol/Internet Protocol (TCP/IP) Properties, and you don't need an address for a router (the gateway to the outside world). Keep in mind that for now, you're not concerned with the Internet — just computers on the local network.

A result of being on a *local* network — because it's not connected to the Internet, it's also called a *private* network — is that you must use IP addresses that are reserved for private network use. You can use a few different ranges of IP addresses, but I recommend that you choose an address range from the 192.168.*x.x* networks. In the next section, I show you how.

Manually choosing an IP address range

I recommend that you use IP addresses in the 192.168.*x.x* range. What does this mean exactly? Well, here's the scoop:

✦ **Use IP addresses where the first two octets are 192 and 168 (192.168).**

Octet numbers are conjoined by periods.

✦ **For the third octet, choose any number between 1 and 254.**

It doesn't matter which one you choose as long as you use this same third number on all computers on your network.

✦ **For the fourth octet, choose any number between 1 and 254.**

Make sure that every computer on your local network has a different fourth octet number. This is very important — your network will not work otherwise.

✦ **Use 255.255.255.0 as your subnet mask.**

For instance, suppose that you're using three computers on your network. All the IP addresses that you use will start with *192.168.* Next, suppose you choose *123* for the third octet. (Remember, you can choose any number between 1 and 254.) Finally, for the fourth octet, choose the numbers 100, 105, and 110 for the three computers, respectively. (Again, you can choose any numbers between 1 and 254.) The resulting IP addresses used on the three computers are

192.168.123.100

192.168.123.105

192.168.123.110

After you know the IP addresses and the subnet mask that you're going to use, start setting up each computer. I'll walk you through the process of configuring Mac OS X with the 192.168.123.105 address as an example. Be sure that you have all the physical portion of your network powered up and connected as outlined in the earlier section "Setting Up Your Network."

1. **Select any of your Macs to start with and open the System Preferences (either choose System Preferences from the Apple menu or from the Dock, as shown in Figure 1-1).**

2. **From the System Preferences dialog that appears (Figure 1-2), choose Network.**

   The Network dialog appears.

Figure 1-1: Open the System Preferences from the Dock.

Click to begin configuring your network.

Choose Network.

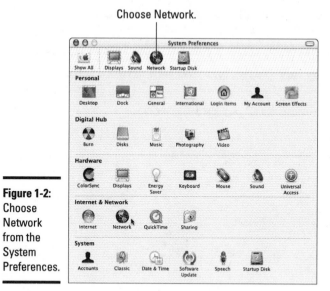

Figure 1-2:
Choose
Network
from the
System
Preferences.

3. **Make sure that the Built-in Ethernet option is selected in the Show drop-down list.**

   The Location drop-down list needs to be set to Automatic. The TCP/IP tab should already be active by default; if not, click it to bring it forward.

4. **Choose Manually from the Configure drop-down list of the TCP/IP tab.**

   Figure 1-3 shows how things should look at this point.

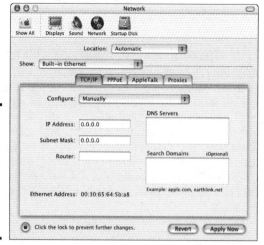

Figure 1-3:
Manually
configure
TCP/IP
properties
for a built-in
Ethernet
adapter.

5. **Enter the IP address for this machine (192.168.123.105 in this example) in the IP Address text box.**

6. **Enter the subnet mask of 255.255.255.0 in the Subnet Mask text box.**

7. **Click the Apply Now button, and your new network settings will take effect.**

   Figure 1-4 shows the result of your hard work.

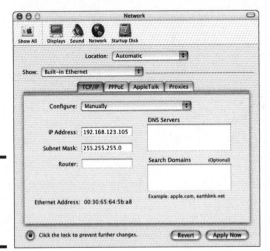

Figure 1-4: TCP/IP configuration is complete.

8. **Press ⌘+Q to quit System Preferences.**

Repeat this same procedure using the other IP addresses for each of the other Macs that are connected to your network.

Using DHCP for automatic IP address assignment

Dynamic Host Configuration Protocol, or DHCP for short, is a protocol that enables a computer to automatically get all the information that I've talked about to this point. This sounds like a godsend, and it does work great. If you're wondering, "Why didn't you just tell me about this in the first place instead of making me mess around with IP addresses and subnet masks?" here's the reason. Using DHCP requires something that most people don't have lying around on their local network: namely, a DHCP server. Luckily, most Internet connection-sharing hardware and software provide a DHCP server as part of the price of admission. (*Internet connection sharing* is letting all your network computers access the Internet through a single Internet connection. I cover it more in Book V, Chapter 5.)

If you plan to use Internet connection sharing or you know you have a DHCP server on your network, you can set up your Mac to automatically obtain the required IP address and information. Open the System Preferences from the Dock or the Apple menu and choose Network. From the Network dialog that appears, choose Using DHCP from the Configure drop-down list on the TCP/IP tab. Click the Apply Now button, and Mac OS X will contact the DHCP server to obtain an IP address, a subnet mask, a gateway router IP address, and Domain Name Server (DNS) IP addresses (which are used to convert a user-friendly address like www.yahoo.com to a computer-friendly IP address like 66.218.71.86).

A few seconds after clicking the Apply Now button, you should see the information come up, as shown in Figure 1-5. Notice the addition underneath IP Address: *(Provided by DHCP Server)* — this lets you know that the process worked and configuration is complete. You might also notice that the DNS information is empty, but OS X is really using DNS information provided by the DHCP server.

Figure 1-5:
Use
DHCP for
automatic
TCP/IP
configura-
tion.

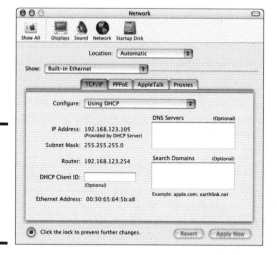

If you ever make a network change that screws things up, like entering the wrong subnet mask or an IP address that isn't in the same range as others on your LAN, you can always click the Revert button to get back your old settings.

Connecting directly to the Internet with a DSL or cable modem

If you have a DSL or cable modem, you can connect it to your computer directly so that your single computer can access the Internet without using any of the Internet Sharing methods that I talk about in Chapter 5 of this mini-book. All you need to do is to connect the LAN port on your DSL/cable modem to the Ethernet port on your Mac using a *crossover* cable. (Your DSL/ cable modem probably came with one just for this purpose.) Then configure your Mac to obtain an IP address automatically using DHCP. Depending on your ISP, you might have to give your Mac a specific network name or use other specific settings to get it to work right — you'll just need to call or check the instructions from your ISP.

Verifying Connectivity

After you have your Macs connected and your TCP/IP configuration is done, you need to check to make sure that everything is working. After you have at least two computers on your network, each with a TCP/IP address, you can use a simple little utility called `ping` to test the connection.

`ping` is a very simple yet extremely helpful utility that's the first connectivity-testing tool out of the box, even for network professionals. When you use the `ping` utility — referred to as *pinging* something — the application sends out a small packet of data to whatever destination you're trying to reach. When the receiving computer hears the ping, it answers with a ping reply. If original computer receives the ping reply; you know that the connection between the computers is good.

To ping a computer, you use a little program built in to OS X called *Network Utility.* This utility allows you to work various network wonders, including checking connectivity, watching the route that your computer takes to get to another computer, looking up information about Internet domain names, and even scanning other computers for network holes. To use the Network Utility to check network connectivity, follow these steps:

1. **Double-click your hard drive to open it and then choose Applications⇨ Utilities⇨Network Utility, as shown in Figure 1-6.**

2. **In the Network Utilities dialog that opens, click the Ping tab (see Figure 1-7).**

3. **In the Please Enter the Network Address to Ping text field, enter the IP address of the computer that you want to ping.**

4. **To simply verify connectivity, select the Send Only *x* Pings radio button
   and enter a low number, such as 5, in the text field to the right.**

   Five or ten pings are plenty to see whether the connection is good.

5. **Click the Ping button.**

   Your Mac sends five ping packets to the IP address that you entered.

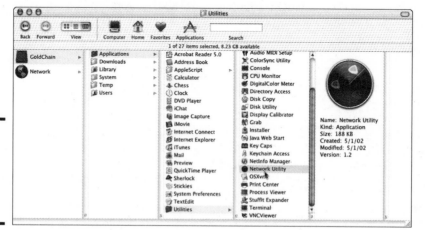

Figure 1-6:
Find the
Network
Utility in
the Utilities
folder.

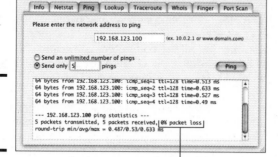

Figure 1-7:
The
Network
Utility tool.

A successful ping

If the pings are successful, text appears in the text box at the bottom of the
Ping tab, one line for each ping reply received from the other computer.
The end of each line reads `time=` with a number at the end. That number
is the amount of time, in $\frac{1}{1000}$ of a second (milliseconds [ms]), that it took for
the ping packet to go from your computer to the other computer and back.
Refer to Figure 1-7 to see a successful ping.

If your ping is unsuccessful, you will see nothing, at least for a little bit. Each ping that you send takes two seconds before it's considered missing in action. So, if you chose five pings, you'll need to wait ten seconds before you see the results. After all the pings time out — a ping *times out* when it doesn't get returned in the proper amount of time if at all — you'll see a line of text appear that reads `100% packet loss`, as seen in Figure 1-8, meaning that all the ping packets that you sent out are now in the packet graveyard, never to be seen again. This is not a good sign for your network connectivity: Flip ahead to "Troubleshooting Your New Network" to find out where to start addressing this problem.

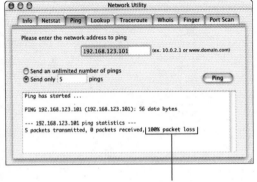

Figure 1-8:
An unsuccessful ping in the Network Utility tool. Rats.

An unsuccessful ping

If you can ping all the other computers on your network from one of the computers, you don't need to go to each computer and ping all the others. You can logically assume that all the computers can communicate. For instance, if you can ping computers B, C, and D from computer A, you don't need to bother with ping tests from computer B, C, or D.

After you have your computers configured and you've verified connectivity between them, start doing the fun stuff that a network allows you to do, like sharing data, printing, and most importantly, playing games with users on other computers.

Troubleshooting Your New Network

After a network is set up, it rarely has problems. Still, sometimes the darn thing just won't work right. When you do have problems, I recommend using a standard, consistent approach to finding and fixing the problem. This section breaks down troubleshooting into two areas. The first area, and always the best place to start troubleshooting a network problem, is checking the actual equipment, such as the Network Interface Cards (NICs), cables, and hubs/switches. The second place to check for problems is in the configuration of the computers on the network, specifically the configuration on the computer(s) having the problem that you're troubleshooting.

Physical problems

Although many things on a network can go bad or cause problems, most of the time, network problems are caused by faulty equipment or wiring. Sometimes it's something as simple as a cable not being plugged in snugly. Looking at the physical cables, connections, and equipment is always the best place to start looking for problems. Here is a quick list of physical things to check while trying to fix network problems:

✦ **Make sure that both ends of the network cable are firmly connected.**

First check the end that plugs into the computer and then check the end that connects to the hub/switch.

✦ **Turn on the problematic computer to be sure that it's connected to a hub or switch.**

Check the port on the hub/switch to see whether the link/speed light is lit. (Depending on the hub or switch that you have, you might not have a link light. Many hubs and switches use a speed light to indicate a link. Check the manufacturer's manual for your model.) If your computer is on and connected but no link/speed light is lit, try replacing the network cable.

✦ **If you replace the network cable and there is still no light, try unplugging the cable from the hub/switch and plug it into another port.**

Choose one of the other computers connected to the hub/switch that works, unplug it, and plug the broken computer into that port for testing. Occasionally, a single port on a hub or switch will go bad; just mark it as bad and don't use it anymore. But if all computers connected to the hub/switch stop working, it's probably the hub or switch that has gone south. If the hub/switch is still under warranty, I recommend getting it fixed or replaced.

✦ **If you replace the cable, try a different port on the hub, and other computers work fine on that hub/switch, the NIC inside your computer has possibly gone bad.**

If you reach this determination, call your local service center to have it looked at and repaired. If you have an older model where the NIC was added instead of built-in, you can simply replace the NIC yourself.

 The key when troubleshooting physical problems is the link/speed light on the hub or switch. If the link/speed light still won't work, the problem isn't likely a physical problem. You need to start troubleshooting the network configuration on the computer itself.

Network configuration problems

After checking the physical layer, look for problems in the network settings. When using TCP/IP on your network, look for these specific things: the TCP/IP configuration mode, IP address, subnet mask, and router IP address (if you're using a router to connect to the Internet or other networks). To check these settings, choose Apple➪System Preferences➪Network to bring up the Network dialog.

✦ Make sure the Configuration drop-down list on the TCP/IP properties tab is set to the appropriate option. Choose the Using DHCP option only if you're using a cable/DSL modem/router or other DHCP server. Otherwise, set this to Manually.

✦ If you're set up for DHCP and your TCP/IP properties sheet looks like Figure 1-9 (with the DHCP fields blank), make sure that your DHCP server — which could be your cable/DSL modem/router — is turned on and working properly.

✦ If the configuration is set to Manually, check the IP Address and Subnet Mask fields to make sure that they're correct. If you're not sure whether your Subnet Mask field entry is correct, you can usually make it the same as other computers on the same network with you. Most times, the subnet mask is 255.255.255.0.

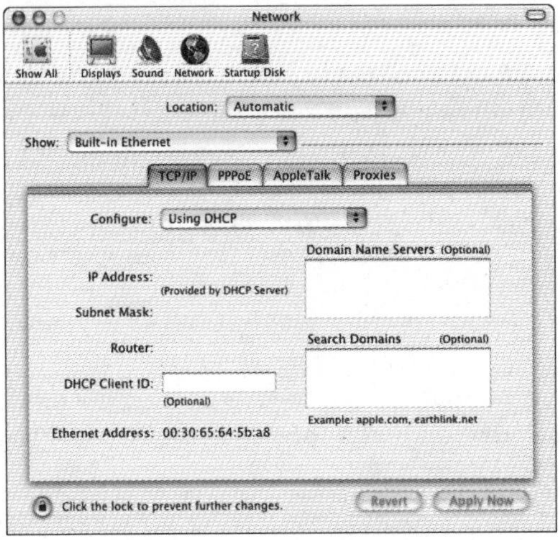

Figure 1-9:
If DHCP settings are blank, check the physical connections on the failing computer and DHCP server.

Chapter 2: Using Your Network

In This Chapter

✔ **Finding out what you can do with your network**

✔ **Sharing your files and printers with other Macs**

✔ **Sharing your files with Windows computers**

✔ **Accessing files on Windows computers**

✔ **Configuring the built-in firewall**

✔ **Remotely controlling your Mac from afar**

After you have your network all set up and ready to go, you can do all kinds of things with your network. You can use your network to share files, share printers, remotely control your Mac, or even play multi-user games like Quake III or Unreal Tournament against other friends. To keep your files safe from unwanted snoops, you can configure OS X's built-in firewall. In this chapter, I cover the basics of file sharing, sharing printers, and using the firewall to protect yourself from intruders.

It's All about (File) Sharing

One of the main reasons for having a network is so that you can share files between computers. You may even want to set up a *server,* which is a computer with shared files that are always available to anyone on the network. Think of a server as a common file storage area for the rest of the network. Really, any computer that shares files is technically a server, because it's *serving,* so to speak. But usually most people only use the word *server* to mean a computer that's dedicated solely to serving files, printers, and so on for the rest of the network.

Creating an account

Sharing files on your Mac with other Mac users is a piece of cake. Keep some basic things in mind, though, to make everything go smoothly. First off, you need to create an account, with a user name and password, on your computer to allow others access to the files on your Mac. Second, you need to create an account for anyone whom you want to have access to your files. The accounts that you create can only access two folders, shown in Figure 2-1:

✦ **The account's Home folder:** That specific account's Home folder is a folder named with the short version of the username that's in the Users folder on your hard drive. Figure 2-1 shows the Home folder, which is noted with an icon that looks like a house, for the gc account (where *gc* is the short account name for GoldChain).

✦ **The Shared folder:** This folder is also in the Users folder on your hard drive. Anyone with an account on your Mac can access the Shared folder, so it's a great place to keep common files that everyone wants to copy or use.

The home folder for the gc account

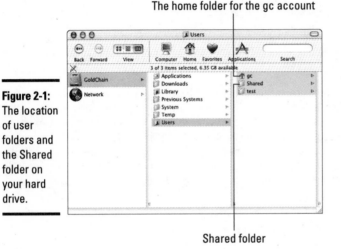

Figure 2-1:
The location of user folders and the Shared folder on your hard drive.

Shared folder

To create an account, follow these steps:

1. **Open System Preferences from the Apple menu or the Dock.**

2. **Click Accounts under the System section.**

3. **On the Users tab, click the New User button, which opens a dialog that you can fill in to create a new user account.**

4. **Fill in the appropriate information including the name for the account and a password, and then choose an image for the account, as shown in Figure 2-2.**

Note that the name that appears as the short name will determine name of that user's Home folder.

5. **Click Save to finish creating the account.**

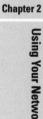
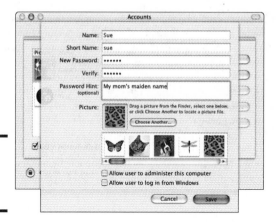

Figure 2-2:
Adding a
new user
account.

Enabling file sharing

When you enable file sharing, your files will be shared using Transmission
Control Protocol/Internet Protocol (TCP/IP) and/or AppleTalk, depending on
which protocols you've enabled. (To enable AppleTalk for compatibility with
older Macs on your network, see Book V, Chapter 3.)

Regardless of which protocol you use to share your files, enabling file sharing on your Mac can be accomplished through a few simple steps:

1. **Open System Preferences either from the Apple menu or from the
    Dock.**

2. **Click the Sharing icon under the Network & Internet section to open
    the Sharing Preferences.**

3. **On the Services tab, mark the Personal File Sharing check box.**

    After the computer thinks for a second, you see the message `Personal
    File Sharing On` appear just above the Stop button. This lets you
    know that file sharing is enabled.

Connecting to a shared resource

Toward the bottom of the Sharing dialog, you can see that other Macintosh
users can access your computer at `afp://<ip address>`, where `ip
address` is the IP address for your specific computer. The initial `apf` repre-
sents AppleTalk file protocol, but it can also use TCP/IP. When another Mac
user wants to connect to your shared files, that person can do the following:

1. **Open the Finder and select Go⇨Connect to Server.**

2. **After the Connect to Server dialog opens, other Mac users can type**
    afp://*<ip address>* **(where** *ip address* **is the IP address of your
    Macintosh) and then click the Connect button.**

After clicking the Connect button of the Connect to Server dialog, you'll be prompted to choose whether you want to connect as a Guest or a Registered User. To connect to the server as a Registered User, you must supply the right username and password. If you connect as Guest, you don't have to supply a password, but you will have restricted access only to the folder called Shared that appears in the Users folder on each system you connect to. If you connect as a Registered User, you need to get the correct username and password from the person who is in control of user accounts on a given Mac.

Give the username and password that you created to the person using the other Mac, and he can now access files in his Home folder on your Mac as well as any files in other user's folders that have been defined as Public.

Sharing a Connected Printer

Sharing your printer for others to use is one of the best reasons to have a network. Setting up your Mac to share your printer is very easy under Mac OS X. Here's a quick rundown of what you need to do:

1. **Open System Preferences either from the Apple menu or from the Dock.**

2. **Click the Sharing icon under the Network & Internet section to open the Sharing Preferences.**

3. **On the Services tab, mark the Printer Sharing check box.**

There will be a slight pause while OS X gets everything ready, but when it's done, you see the message Printer Sharing On appear just above the Stop button. This lets you know that printer sharing is enabled.

After Printer Sharing is enabled, follow these steps to connect to that printer from other computers on your network:

1. **From your hard drive, choose Applications⇨Utilities and then double-click the Print Center icon to open Print Center.**

2. **If you have a local printer attached, click the Add icon.**

Otherwise you'll be prompted to add a printer automatically when Print Center opens. Click the Add button to begin the addition. (For more on adding a printer with Print Center, see Book VI, Chapter 4.)

3. **From the dialog that opens, click the Add button.**

4. **From the top drop-down box, choose IP Printing (see Figure 2-3).**

5. **Enter the IP address of the Macintosh that's already connected to the printer that you want to connect to and then click the Add button.**

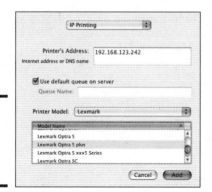

Figure 2-3:
Enable
shared
printing
here.

With Rendezvous, it's even easier — printers just appear in your Printer List automatically. It doesn't get any easier than that!

Sharing Files to Windows Computers

If you happen to have computers running Windows on your network, you'll probably want to share files with those computers, too. Sharing files with a Windows computer — actually a Windows user — is very similar to sharing files for other Mac users. However, be aware of one very important difference. (Refer to the earlier section "Enabling file sharing" about Sharing Preferences and turning on Personal File Sharing.) Chances are that you saw no option called *Windows File Sharing*. This is because before you can use Windows File Sharing, you must have at least one user account on your computer that allows logins from Windows computers.

To enable Windows sharing, create an account on the local Mac similar to what I did above. (Refer to Figure 2-2.)

1. **Open System Preferences from the Apple menu or the Dock.**
2. **Click Accounts under the System section.**
3. **On the Users tab, click the New User button.**
4. **In the dialog that appears, fill in the appropriate information including the name for the account and a password, and then choose an image for the account.**
5. **Mark the Allow User to Log in from Windows check box.**
6. **Click Save to finish creating the account.**

After you create at least one Windows account, you see a new option appear in the Sharing Preferences. To get to the Sharing Preferences, open System

Preferences and click Sharing to bring up the Sharing dialog. In this dialog, you see the new option that allows you to share to Windows computers — Windows File Sharing — shown in Figure 2-4.

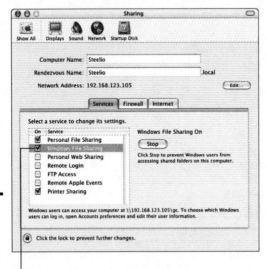

Figure 2-4:
Enable
Windows
File Sharing
here.

Check to enable Windows file sharing.

After you mark the Windows File Sharing check box on the Services tab to enable it, the label Windows File Sharing On appears just above the Stop button. Just like when sharing files with other Mac users, you will see a helpful reminder toward the bottom that tells you what the Windows users will need to type to gain access to your Mac. At the bottom of Figure 2-4, you can see that the Windows user needs to enter **\\192.168.123.105\gc** to access the file share on this Mac. *Note:* The IP address that you enter here changes for each computer you want to access.

Accessing File Shares on Windows Computers

Just like when you want a Windows computer to have access to your files, you'll also probably want to access files on a Windows computer. Easy.

Accessing files on Windows computers relies on the Samba component (a part of the UNIX foundation of Mac OS X). Follow these steps:

1. **Choose Go⇨Connect to Server from the Finder.**

The Connect to Server dialog opens.

2. **In the Address box, enter** smb://<*ip address*>, **where** *ip address* **is the IP address of the Windows computer that you want to connect to.**

3. **Click the Connect button.**

4. **From the prompt to select which Windows shared drive you wish to mount, choose the desired shared drive from the drop-down box.**

5. **If you're accessing a file shared on a Windows 95 or Windows 98 computer, simply click OK to mount the share.**

   If you're accessing a file shared on a Windows NT, 2000, or XP computer, click the Authenticate button. Then enter your username and password, click OK, and then click OK again to mount the share.

After you mount the shared drive, you'll see it appear on your Desktop, just like a Mac volume. You can use this drive just like any other drive on your system. To disconnect from the Windows share, you can drag the icon to the Trash on the Dock (which changes to an Eject icon when you start dragging); press ⌘+E; or hold Control, click the icon, and then choose Eject from the menu that appears.

Using FTP to Access Files

FTP is part of the TCP/IP protocol suite. The hoary acronym FTP stands for *File Transfer Protocol* — big surprise there. FTP is one of the oldest methods for sharing files between computers. However, because it's part of the TCP/IP protocol suite, it can be used on many different kinds of computers, including those running just about any type of strange and arcane operating system. You can still manage to exchange files regardless of whether you're using Mac OS X, Windows, or UNIX.

Using FTP on the Internet

Because FTP is a part of the TCP/IP suite, it works on virtually every type of computer and on the Internet as well as a local area network (LAN). So, assuming that you have your computer connected to the Internet through a modem or a LAN connection, everything that I discuss about FTP and how to use it will apply to connecting to FTP servers on the Internet as well. When you connect to FTP servers on the Internet, you can use the Fully Qualified Domain Name (or FQDN for short) like ftp.apple.com instead of an actual IP address. You can also use the FTP server in Mac OS X to make files available to friends on the Internet just as you would to make them available on a LAN.

FTP is a *client/server* application. In plain English, this means that two pieces make things tick: the *server* (which hosts the connection, rather like a file server) and the *client* (which connects to the server). Mac OS X, thanks to its UNIX foundation, has both FTP server and client built-in. To use FTP, you need a computer running the FTP server software to give others access to files; then the other computer, or client, can connect to the FTP server. After the connection is made, the client can either send files to the server *(uploading)* or get files from the server *(downloading)*. In this section, I cover how to use FTP to give others access to your files as well as talk about the FTP applications that come with Mac OS X.

Using Mac OS X built-in FTP to share files

One way to give other access to your files is to run an FTP server on your Mac. Mac OS X comes with an FTP server built in, so you just have to activate it. You might wonder why you'd use FTP to share files when you can use Personal File Sharing or Windows File Sharing. The main advantage to using FTP to share files is that not only can people on your LAN access files, but anyone on the Internet can also access your files regardless of the type of machine that they're using.

Just like with the other file sharing methods, you need to create a user account on your computer before someone can connect to and get files from your Mac. After you have an account created for the people/person that you want to give access to, you can enable FTP sharing like this:

1. **Open System Preferences either from the Apple menu or from the Dock.**

2. **Click the Sharing icon under the Internet & Network section to open the Sharing Preferences.**

3. **Mark the FTP Access check box.**

You see the message FTP Access On appear above the Stop button. This lets you know that FTP access is enabled. Also you can see toward the bottom of the dialog that people can use ftp://<ip address>, where ip address is the IP address of your Mac.

If you're using an AirPort or other cable/digital subscriber line (DSL) router to share your Internet connection, you need to place the Mac that you want people on the Internet to access in the *DMZ,* or demilitarized zone. Check your cable/DSL router documentation for more information.

Using FTP from your Web browser to transfer files

Another way to transfer files between you and the FTP server is to use the FTP functionality in Internet Explorer (IE) that's installed with OS X.

Unfortunately, you can use IE only to *get* files from an FTP server, not *send* files to it. To connect and get files with IE, follow these steps.

1. **Open Internet Explorer from the Dock or from the Applications folder on your hard drive.**

2. **Type** ftp://username@ip address **in the Address field to open your connection to the FTP server.**

   You can leave out username if you're connecting as an anonymous user.

3. **If you're logging in anonymously, IE will connect to the FTP server, and you will see the contents of the root folder on the FTP server in your IE window.**

4. **If you're using a username (which you would obtain from the person who set up the FTP server) to log in to the FTP server, you'll be asked for a password, as seen in Figure 2-5.**

   For regular FTP, you don't need to type anything in the Account field of Figure 2-5.

   After you provide the correct password and click OK, you'll be shown the contents of the root folder on the FTP server.

Figure 2-5:
Log into an
FTP server
with your
username
and pass-
word.

5. **Navigate through the folders to find the file that you want.**

   The files and folders that you see are on the FTP server, not your computer.

6. **To download a file, just click the file.**

   Download Manager will open, and the file will download to the Desktop.

7. **Close Internet Explorer to end your FTP session.**

After you get the hang of using FTP to download files from an FTP server, you might find that sometimes you want to send files as well. To gain that functionality, you have to move on to the command-line version of FTP that's part of Mac OS X.

Using FTP from the command-line interface can be a bit daunting at first, but after you get used to it, it's great. Plus, if you can use the command line version of FTP, you can use it on Macs, Windows computers, UNIX boxes, or virtually anything that supports FTP.

Using FTP from the command-line interface to transfer files

The other way to use FTP to transfer files around is to go character-based by using the command-line interface (CLI). To use the CLI, you need to open a Terminal, or shell, session. To use a Terminal session, click the Terminal icon in the Utilities folder inside of the Applications folder, as shown in Figure 2-6. When you open a Terminal session, you'll be presented with a window that uses a text interface. You'll see a prompt that consists of your computer's name and the folder that you're currently in, followed by the user ID that you are currently logged in as. It's at this prompt where you type various commands to make the computer do things for you.

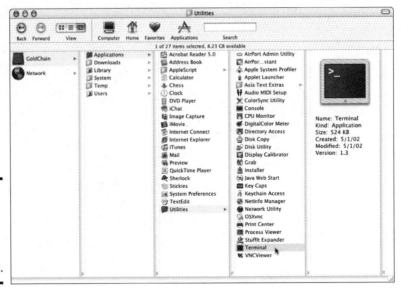

Figure 2-6:
Open a
Terminal
session to
use FTP
from the CLI.

Figure 2-7 shows a quick FTP file transfer. If you look at the Terminal session, you'll see the complete process of connecting to an FTP server, logging in, changing both the local and remote folders, and downloading a file.

```
000                          tcsh (ttyp1)
[localhost:~] gc% ftp 192.168.123.174
Connected to 192.168.123.174.
220-Microsoft FTP Service
    +------------------------------------------+
    I IIII    Welcome to GoldChain's FTP   IIII I
    I If you do not have a username/password,  I
    I please disconnect now.                   I
220 +------------------------------------------+
Name (192.168.123.174:gc): goldchain
331 Password required for goldchain.
Password:
230 User goldchain logged in.
Remote system type is Windows_NT.
ftp> lcd /temp
Local directory now /Temp
ftp> cd Files
250 CWD command successful.
ftp> bin
200 Type set to I.
ftp> get c64.zip
local: c64.zip remote: c64.zip
500 'EPSV': command not understood
227 Entering Passive Mode (192,168,123,174,4,28).
125 Data connection already open; Transfer starting.
100% |*********************************************|  5020 KB   4.57 MB/s   00:00 ETA
226 Transfer complete.
5140700 bytes received in 00:01 (4.47 MB/s)
ftp> quit
221 Catch ya later!
[localhost:~] gc% ▊
```

Figure 2-7:
An FTP file
transfer
session
from the CLI.

The ftp prompt

After you're in the Terminal session, you'll use a series of commands to connect to, move in and out of folders, and transfer files. Below is a list of the basic commands that you need to use FTP as well as a brief description of what each command does.

✦ ftp: This command starts the FTP command-line interface session. You can tell that you're in the FTP client application when you see ftp> as your command prompt (see Figure 2-7). This is where you will type all other FTP commands to do things.

✦ open: This command is used to start your connection to another computer. Type this command followed by the IP address of the FTP server that you want to connect to.

✦ ls: Use this command to see a listing of all files and folders in the current folder on the FTP server.

✦ cd: This command allows you to change the folder that you're in. Type **cd <*folder*>** (where *folder* is a specific folder name) to move into a subfolder on the FTP server. Type **cd ..** to go back out a folder level.

✦ lcd: This command acts exactly like cd except that it changes the folder that you're currently in on your local system, not the FTP server. Use this command to put yourself in the folder on the local drive that you want to transfer files to and from.

- ✦ `bin`: Type this command to get in binary mode to transfer files that aren't plain text files. (*Always* use binary mode unless you're specifically transferring plain text files.)

- ✦ `ascii`: This command puts you in ASCII mode for transferring text files.

- ✦ `get` or `mget`: To retrieve a single file, use the `get` command followed by the filename of the file that you want to retrieve. If you want to get multiple files at once, use the `mget` command followed by a filename containing * and/or ? as wildcards.

- ✦ `put` or `mput`: To send a single file, use the `put` command followed by the filename to send a file to the FTP server. To send multiple files, use the `mput` command followed by a filename containing * and/or ? as wildcards.

- ✦ `quit`: Use the `quit` command to end your FTP session.

To end a Terminal Session at any time, type **exit** and press Return.

Many FTP servers will let you send files only to certain folders. Most times this folder is named *Upload* or *Uploads* or something to that effect.

Using these commands will enable you to send and receive files from an FTP server. You need to do some things in the right order for it to all work out. Here is a rundown of how to use these commands:

1. **Type** ftp **to get into FTP mode.**

2. **Type** open *<ip address>* **to open your connection to the FTP server.**

3. **At this point, you'll be asked for a username and password.**

For many FTP servers, using the username `anonymous` and your e-mail address as the password is enough to get you logged in. On others, you must use an assigned username and password provided by the administrator of that particular server.

4. **Use the** lcd *<folder>* (where *folder* is a specific folder name) **command to change into the folder on your local drive that you want files to come to/from.**

5. **Use the** ls **and** cd **commands to place yourself into the desired folder on the FTP server.**

6. **Use the** ascii **or** bin **commands to set your file transfer mode to ASCII or binary, respectively.**

This is important because choosing the wrong type will likely cause the transfer to fail. Unless it's a plain text file, use binary mode.

7. **Use the** `get/mget/put/mput` **commands to send or receive the desired files.**

8. **Use the** `quit` **command to close the connection and exit the FTP session.**

Using the Built-in Firewall

One of the new features in OS version 10.2 is the built-in firewall. A *firewall* watches all the network communications coming into your computer and can block or deny certain traffic from coming into your computer that you may want to avoid. It acts as another layer of security to help keep you safe from unwanted attacks. You need to be very careful when using this: A configuration mistake could make your Mac inaccessible from the network.

Having said that, the main purpose of the firewall is to allow or block certain kinds of traffic. For instance, if you want to enable FTP access on your Mac but you also want to keep all other traffic from coming into your Mac, you can tell the built-in firewall to allow only FTP traffic. The firewall on the Mac will block or allow only TCP/IP traffic, not AppleTalk, so AppleTalk traffic is always able to get in. Here is how this is done.

When enabled, the firewall by default will block all traffic that comes into your Mac. But, by default, the firewall is turned off. So, your first mission is to enable the firewall, following these steps:

1. **Open the System Preferences from the Apple menu or the Dock.**

2. **Click the Sharing icon.**

3. **Click the Firewall tab, shown in Figure 2-8.**

4. **Click the Start button.**

This will enable the firewall and, by default, all incoming TCP/IP traffic will be blocked. You must enable each sharing method that you want to be able to use. As you enable different sharing methods, such as Personal File Sharing or FTP Access, you might notice that under the Firewall tab, those types of traffic now have a check mark in the box for each type of traffic. In other words, when you turn on a sharing method, the firewall automatically allows traffic for that sharing method.

Sometimes you might want to allow other traffic that isn't in the list through your firewall. At that point, you can click the New button to create a new definition for your firewall to use. The resulting dialog has a drop-down menu with some common things that you might want to allow, such as America Online (AOL) Instant Messenger, ICQ, and MSN Instant Messenger.

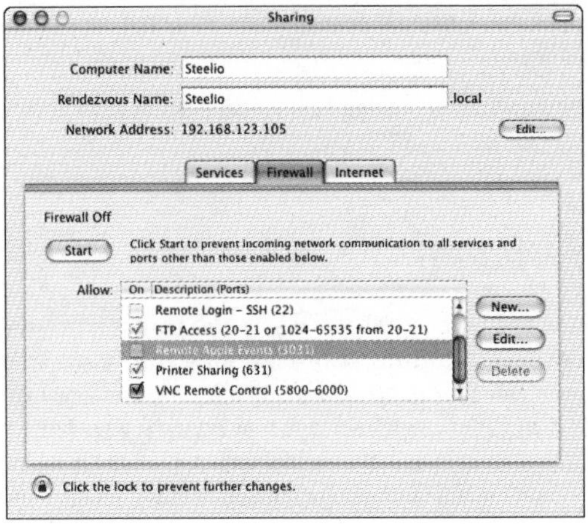

Figure 2-8:
Enabling the firewall in OS X.

If you need to add ports for another application that's not in that drop-down list — for instance, VNC for remote control (which I cover in the next section) — you need to choose Other from the Port Name drop-down list (as shown in Figure 2-9). Then you can enter a port number, a port range, or series of ports. You might need to check the documentation for a specific application to see which ports it uses.

Ports are like an extension to an IP address. For instance, when you communicate with a Web server, you send a request not only to that Web server's IP address, but you send it on port 80 — the standard port for HyperText Transfer Protocol (HTTP) traffic. Different applications use different port numbers, so you need to check which ports are used when you want to adjust your firewall to allow that traffic. In this example, I set up a hole in the firewall for VNC, which uses ports 5800–6000. You can enter this information in the dialog, as seen in Figure 2-9, and then click OK.

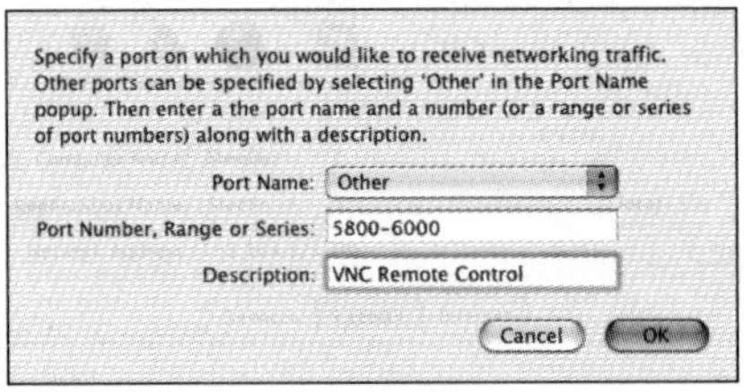

Figure 2-9:
Configure a hole in the firewall for a specific application.

Remote Control of Your Mac

One of the absolute coolest things about having a network is being able to take control of one computer from another computer. Sometimes you might need to access files on your Mac, but you don't have Personal File Sharing enabled. What can you do? You can remotely connect into your Mac and then — just as if you were sitting in front of it — do what you need to do to enable Personal File Sharing or whatever service you need. Perhaps you have a file on your computer with someone's phone number that you need access to. With remote control, it's at your fingertips. Ah, technology.

Remotely control your Mac (for free, no less!)

Designed by Olivetti Research Labs and then purchased by AT&T, Virtual Network Computer (VNC — www.uk.research.att.com/vnc/) is a very nice application that enables you to remotely control a computer from pretty much anywhere that has an Internet connection. VNC is easy to install and configure, but the best feature is that it's free. VNC can run on many different platforms from Mac OS X and UNIX on desktop computers and servers to Palm OS and Windows CE on personal digital assistants (PDAs). So you could be at a friend's house on her wireless network with your PDA and remotely control your Mac at home over the Internet. Too cool.

Some networks have proxies and firewalls that might interfere with VNC's operation. You can remotely control a computer that's behind a firewall or cable/DSL router, but the firewall/router needs to be configured properly. Because the process varies from one manufacturer to the next, check your cable/DSL router manual for instructions on how to do this.

How VNC works

In a nutshell, VNC takes the graphical interface on your monitor, turns it into data, and sends it to the computer that you're using to remotely control it. The computer that you're using sends keyboard presses, mouse movement, and clicks to it, acting just the same way it would if you were sitting right in front of it.

A specific version of VNC is available for Mac OS X which, ironically enough, is called OSXvnc. You can download OSXvnc at netmath.math.uiuc.edu/VNC-osx.htm. There you'll find instructions on how to install and set up OSXvnc. Figure 2-10 shows a screenshot of a Mac running OSXvnc being remotely controlled from a computer running Windows 98.

Remotely control another computer from your Mac

A few different VNC viewers exist for Mac OS X. A VNC viewer is just an application you use to remotely control your computer running VNC. You can download them at www.uk.research.att.com/vnc/platforms.html. If you find yourself on a computer without the viewer, VNC server actually runs a little Web server that serves up a Java client. As long as the computer that you're using has a Web browser that supports Java — which all newer versions of Internet Explorer and Netscape do — you can still remotely control your computer.

Figure 2-10:
Use OSXvnc
to remotely
control
your Mac.

When you connect to the computer running VNC using a Web browser, the Web server sends a default page that contains a Java applet. That Java applet asks you for the password to connect, and upon entering the correct password, it brings up the remote control session right in the Web browser. It doesn't get any easier than that!

Chapter 3: You May Even Need AppleTalk

In This Chapter

✔ Describing AppleTalk

✔ Configuring the AppleTalk network preferences

✔ Using Mac OS X to access AppleTalk resources

*W*hen talking about networking and Macs, I'd be remiss not to discuss *AppleTalk,* a communications protocol created by Apple that allows a network of Macs to share files and printers. AppleTalk performs functions similar to that of TCP/IP, such as giving each Mac a unique logical address and allowing a Mac to see what's available on the network. AppleTalk is used in a variety of environments such as homes, offices, and college campuses. However, AppleTalk is disappearing because it simply cannot scale, or grow, to handle large networks like Transmission Control Protocol/Internet Protocol (TCP/IP) can.

When Apple first introduced AppleTalk, it also introduced a network cabling system and a protocol to move the AppleTalk data through the network: LocalTalk. LocalTalk was basically Apple's version of Ethernet that ran over special cables that connected to each Mac's printer port. Because it used the Mac printer port to communicate, it ran at a not-so-speedy 230 Kbps, or 230,000 bits per second, compared with Ethernet running at 10 Mbps, or 10 million bits per second. Eventually LocalTalk went away, but AppleTalk still remains and is now run over Ethernet networks, just like TCP/IP.

Although Apple finally made the move to TCP/IP as its primary network protocol — I mean, who hasn't — Apple still includes AppleTalk in the Mac OS, even up to its newest version, Mac OS X. About the only time you might need to use AppleTalk is if you find yourself trying to access a network that is running only AppleTalk. But, like I said, most networks are using TCP/IP anymore, so this should be a rare occurrence. This chapter shows you how to enable the AppleTalk protocol on your Mac as well as how to access files and printers on a network running AppleTalk.

Setting Up AppleTalk

Just like most network configuration tasks under the Big X, configuring your Mac to use AppleTalk and participate in an AppleTalk network isn't very difficult. In this section, I talk about how to configure the settings in your Network Preferences so that you can join in the file sharing and network printing.

Before you can configure and use AppleTalk on your network, you need a network — go figure. For more information on setting up your network, see Chapter 1 of this mini-book.

You can configure AppleTalk on OS X in two ways: manually or automatically. Unless you're designing your AppleTalk network to work through routers with other AppleTalk networks or you're given specific AppleTalk settings by a network administrator, I highly recommend using the automatic AppleTalk configuration. However, I cover both methods in this chapter just to be on the safe side.

Automatically configuring AppleTalk

To automatically configure AppleTalk, follow these steps.

1. **Choose System Preferences from the Apple menu or the Dock.**

2. **From the System Preferences dialog that appears, click either of the Network icons to open the Network Preference dialog.**

3. **Click the AppleTalk tab to display the AppleTalk settings page, as shown in Figure 3-1.**

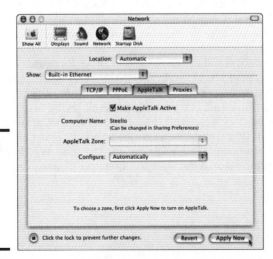

Figure 3-1:
Using AppleTalk automatic configuration is a breeze.

4. **Select (mark) the Make AppleTalk Active check box and then click the Apply Now button.**

   OS X defaults to using the automatic AppleTalk configuration mode, as shown in the Configure drop-down menu in Figure 3-1. Now, I know this is going to be hard to believe, but you're done!

Now your Mac is configured to use the AppleTalk protocol to share and access files and printers. AppleTalk is ready to go as soon as you click the Apply Now button. But you won't see anything special when you turn AppleTalk on. AppleTalk is invisible until you try to use it. Check the "Accessing Files and Printers with AppleTalk" section later in this chapter to actually start using AppleTalk to do stuff.

Manually configuring AppleTalk

Although not as simple as using the automatic configuration, manually configuring AppleTalk is quite easy as well. To manually configure AppleTalk, follow these steps:

1. **Choose System Preferences from the Apple menu or the Dock.**

2. **From the System Preferences dialog that appears, click the Network icon to open the Network Preference dialog.**

3. **Click the AppleTalk tab to display the AppleTalk settings page; refer to Figure 3-1.**

4. **Mark the Make AppleTalk Active check box.**

5. **From the Configure drop-down list, choose Manually.**

   When you do, two more text boxes appear where you can enter information, as Figure 3-2 illustrates: the Node ID and the Network ID. Unless you are the network administrator, you must obtain these two ID numbers from whoever is administering your network.

   Only use manual configuration if you're designing an AppleTalk network or you have information from a network administrator on the correct settings to use. But even if you enter the wrong settings, the worst thing that can happen is that you won't be able to communicate with other Macs on your network, so don't worry about blowing something up or killing your Mac.

6. **After you enter the appropriate Node ID and Network ID, click the Apply Now button to save those settings.**

A word about Zones

The final option on the AppleTalk settings page is the AppleTalk Zone property. *AppleTalk Zones* are logical groupings of computers that a network administrator creates for ease of use. Take the example of a large company that employs many graphic artists. This company has many buildings, but because of how the business has grown, the graphic artists are spread between several different locations in different buildings. The network administrator can create a Graphics Zone that would contain all the Macs and servers and printers that make up the graphics department. This way, the artists can get to files on servers or print to printers that are meant for them simply by putting themselves in the Graphics Zone. This is a handy way to keep people who are physically separate logically grouped into a common area, or *Zone*.

When you configure AppleTalk, you might or might not need to set the AppleTalk Zone property. If you're on a network where the administrator has configured AppleTalk Zones, you'll see a list of all the Zones by clicking the AppleTalk Zones drop-down list. From there, simply choose the name of the Zone that you want to participate in. If you're on a network where no Zones are configured, the AppleTalk Zones drop-down box will be grayed out and unavailable — and if you can't choose a Zone anyway, don't worry about it!

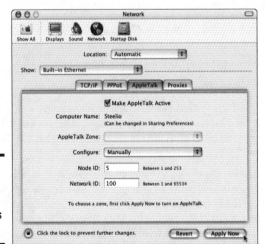

Figure 3-2:
Manually configuring AppleTalk is easy, too.

Accessing Files and Printers with AppleTalk

After you have AppleTalk configured and ready to go, you can share files and printers from your Mac. If you're wondering what to do after AppleTalk is enabled, the following sections show you how to share your files and printers as well as how to access files and printers that others have shared on the network.

Accessing AppleTalk share points

Accessing *share points* — collection of files that are shared to the network —
by using AppleTalk is much like accessing other shared files with Internet
Protocol (IP). In this section, I talk about finding AppleTalk servers, connecting to AppleTalk share points, and how to disconnect when you are done.
Follow these steps each time when you start your computer or if you get
disconnected for any reason.

Although a server version of OS X that is meant to run on corporate servers
that do nothing but serve up files does exist, in this section, I use the word
server to simply mean any Mac or other computer that has AppleTalk running and is sharing files or printers.

Choosing an AppleTalk server

To choose an AppleTalk server, perform the following steps:

1. **From the Finder, choose Go⇨Connect to Server or press Option+K
   on the keyboard.**

   This brings up the Connect to Server dialog.

2. **From this dialog, click the * item in the left pane, as shown in
   Figure 3-3.**

Figure 3-3:
Finding
available
AppleTalk
servers.

When you click the *, your Mac will search the local network for any
AppleTalk servers and display a list of all the servers found in the right
pane of the Connect to Server dialog. In Figure 3-3, you can see that I have
two AppleTalk servers on my network — one called *AppleTalk-FileServer*
and one that is my own Mac, *Steelio* — because I have AppleTalk running
and have file sharing enabled.

3. **Choose the appropriate AppleTalk server that contains the share point you want to access by clicking its name in the right pane of the Connect to Server dialog.**

4. **After you've chosen the AppleTalk server, click the Connect button.**

Connecting to the AppleTalk server

Each time that you want to access files or printers via AppleTalk, you must connect to the server. To connect to an AppleTalk server, you need to connect as a Guest or, if you have a username and password for that server, as a Registered User. After clicking the Connect button of the Connect to Server dialog, you'll be prompted to choose whether you want to connect as a Guest or a Registered User, as shown in Figure 3-4.

Figure 3-4:
Choose how
to log in
to an
AppleTalk
server.

In Figure 3-4, I'm connecting to the server as a Registered User, so I must supply the right username and password. If you connect as Guest, you don't have to supply a password, but you will have restricted access only to the folder called Shared that appears in the Users folder on each system that you connect to. If you connect as a Registered User, you need to get the correct username and password from the person who is in control of user accounts on a given Mac.

Using PC MACLAN to access Windows networks

Of course, those Windows people won't let us forget that there are a lot more Windows users out there than Mac users. Sigh . . . you'll probably find yourself sometime on a network with people running Windows. True, it's easy for OS X users to get to files on Windows systems (see Book V, Chapter 2). However, you might want access available for those Windows folks to get to your Mac files or to perhaps share printers between the Mac and Windows. One of the best ways to do that is to install PC MACLAN (http://www.miramarsys.com) on the Windows computer(s). PC MACLAN allows bidirectional file sharing using both IP and AppleTalk, as well as allowing Macs and PCs to share printers both ways.

You might want to check out some other connection options before clicking the Connect button to complete the connection. Click the Options button to display the preferences page shown in Figure 3-5. Here is a list of each preference and what it does:

✦ **Add Password to Keychain:** Enabling this check box saves the username and password for this connection so that you don't have to type it in each time that you reconnect to this particular share point.

✦ **Allow Clear Text Password:** Enabling this means that your Mac doesn't attempt to encrypt your password when it sends it across the network. Although encryption is a good thing, you need to choose this option when you're not 100 percent sure that the AppleTalk file server is using encryption.

✦ **Warn when Sending Password in Clear Text:** Select this check box, and a dialog warning comes up every time that your computer sends a password in clear text. These warnings are supposed to be helpful, but I find them annoying, especially if most of the AppleTalk share points that you access don't use encryption. I recommend that you turn this option off if you're not absolutely sure that your AppleTalk servers are using encryption.

✦ **Allow Secure Connections Using SSH:** Again, this is a security thing. *SSH* is a secure protocol that allows computers to talk over the network without worrying about anyone else listening in on it. However, unless your network administrator has instructed you to, leave this option unchecked.

Figure 3-5:
Different options you have before connecting to an AppleTalk share point.

After you choose the options that you want, click the Save Preferences button to save them for the future. (I recommend this Good Idea.) Then click OK.

From the preferences dialog, you can also click the Change Password button if you'd like to change your password — assuming that you're connecting as a Registered User and not as a Guest. Click the Change Password button, and you're presented with a dialog in which you type your old password, your new password, your new password again (as confirmation), and then click OK. Simple enough, eh?

Choosing a share point from the AppleTalk server

Whether or not you chose to play with the connection options, finalize the connection by clicking the Connect button after choosing to log in as a Guest or a Registered User. After you click Connect, you see a list of share points on AppleTalk server, as shown in Figure 3-6.

Figure 3-6:
Choose a share point from the AppleTalk server.

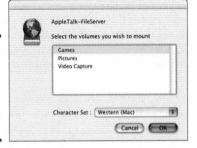

Click the name of the share point that you want and then click OK. You see a network drive appear on your Desktop, which you can treat as you would any other attached drive.

Disconnecting from the share point

When you're done using the share point, you can disconnect from the share point in a few different ways:

✦ Control+click the network drive Desktop icon and choose Eject from the contextual menu that appears.

✦ Click the network drive Desktop icon to highlight it and then choose Eject from the File menu.

✦ Click the network drive Desktop icon to highlight it and press Option+E on the keyboard.

✦ Click and drag the network drive Desktop icon to the Trash can on the Dock — the Trash can will change into a Disconnect icon when dragging a network drive.

Accessing AppleTalk printers

The other major thing (besides file sharing) that you can do with AppleTalk is to connect to and use AppleTalk network printers. Again, like most things under Mac OS X, it's pretty straightforward and easy.

Adding an AppleTalk printer

Before you can print to an AppleTalk printer, you first need to add that printer to your setup. Follow these steps to add a printer:

1. **Open your hard drive from the Desktop, double-click the Applications folder, double-click the Utilities folder, and then double-click the Print Center Icon.**

This opens the Print Center.

You can drag a copy of the Print Center to the Dock or Toolbar Favorites for easy access for checking print jobs and so on.

2. **When you're prompted to add a printer the first time that you open the Print Center, as seen in Figure 3-7, click Add to start the process.**

Figure 3-7:
Add printers
the first time
you open
the Print
Center.

If you've already opened Print Center and have already added printers in the past, you add another network printer by clicking the Add icon in Print Center.

3. **From the resulting Printer List dialog, choose AppleTalk from the top drop-down box.**

You see a list of all the AppleTalk shared printers that your Mac sees on the network, as shown in Figure 3-8.

4. **(Optional) If you're on a network with more than just the local Zone, you might need to choose the appropriate Zone from the second drop-down box before you will see the desired printer.**

5. **After you choose the desired printer, choose the proper printer from the Printer Model drop-down list at the bottom of the Printer List dialog.**

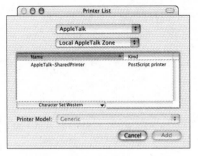

Figure 3-8:
Choose a
printer from
the list of
printers
your Mac
sees on the
network.

If the needed printer model isn't in this list, you might have to select
Other from this list and provide your Mac with the right printer files to
use this new printer. Choosing Generic from the list will work with most
printers, but you're restricted to text-only output and don't have access
to special features like tray selection.

6. **Click the Add button to complete the process.**

    You can now treat this as any other printer that could be connected
    directly to your machine. You can view the print queue and hold,
    resume, and delete print jobs from the Queue menu.

Removing an AppleTalk printer

Removing an AppleTalk printer that you've connected to is very simple.
From the Print Center, click once on the printer that you wish to remove and
then either click the Delete icon or choose Delete Printer from the Printers
menu. The Delete icon is one of the four icons at the top of the Printer List
windows in Print Center.

Chapter 4: Going Wireless

In This Chapter

✔ **Finding out how wireless networking works**

✔ **Discovering wireless security**

✔ **Connecting to other Macs without a Wireless Access Point**

✔ **Connecting to and disconnecting from AirPort networks**

Nowadays, connectivity is king. Cell phones have gone from being something only the technological elite could afford to being a permanent fixture on the hip of the common man. The shorts I'm wearing right now have a special pocket just for a cell phone to ride in. (Perhaps that was too personal . . . sorry.)

Because people have become accustomed to being able to keep in touch wherever they are, they also want to be able to have access to their network, at least within their house or workplace, without the hassle of cables. This desire for convenience and the advances in wireless technology have combined to bring you the concept of the wireless network.

Now you can be connected to your home local area network (LAN) and your shared Internet connection (covered in Book V, Chapter 5) from your balcony, deck, lounge chair in the yard, or even your bedroom. In this chapter, I talk about how wireless networks work and give you a lot of information to help you get the right pieces to free yourself from the world of the wired, at least to some degree.

Speaking the Wireless Lingo

Wireless networks aren't all that different from their wired siblings. In this chapter, I discuss some of the features and limitations of wireless networking, but you must first be familiar with a foundation of information.

Because of the technology involved in wireless networks and how things are changing rapidly in this area, you'll find yourself swimming in a sea of acronyms and other technobabble. Although you don't need to know every little detail to be able to set up your own wireless network, you should know some of these terms so that you can avoid getting stung by hackers or stuck with equipment that is on the verge of obsolescence. Here is a quick list of terms that you'll see on your road to becoming a wireless network guru:

✦ **WLAN:** WLAN stands for *Wireless LAN.* A *LAN* (local area network) is just a bunch of computers and other devices connected together.

✦ **IEEE:** The Institute of Electrical and Electronics Engineers. This is an organization that approves standards which allow computers, network equipment, and just about anything else electronic to play nicely together. Sometimes IEEE helps create these standards before approving them, and sometimes it just approves standards that others have come up with.

✦ **802.11:** This is the part of the IEEE standards that deals specifically with wireless networking. Although wireless is generically usually referred to as *wireless networks,* it's all really a wireless form of Ethernet.

✦ **Wireless Access Point:** A *Wireless Access Point,* or WAP, is a device that allows wireless network devices to connect to a wired Ethernet network.

✦ **Service Set Identifier:** The *Service Set Identifier,* or SSID, is used to tell your computer the name of the wireless network to participate in.

✦ **Wired Equivalency Protocol:** *Wired Equivalency Privacy,* or WEP, is an encryption that wireless networks can use to keep your wireless network more secure from snoopers and hackers.

✦ **Ad Hoc mode:** An *Ad Hoc* wireless network is one where each wireless device talks directly with all other wireless devices. Apple calls this mode a *computer-to-computer network.*

✦ **Infrastructure mode:** This is where all wireless devices talk to a WAP, and the WAP then talks to other wireless devices and the wired network.

As I cover the different parts of wireless networking and how to set it up, you'll find yourself using these terms over and over. Before you know it, you'll be spouting these wireless-related acronyms like a pro. (No, really.)

Figuring Out the Different Flavors of Wireless Ethernet

One of the first things that you might notice when you start looking into wireless networking is the different wireless standards. You should at least be aware that these different standards exist. Be sure to get wireless network components that will work together because some of the different wireless standards are not compatible. (Feel free to photocopy this list and stick it on your fridge door.)

IEEE 802.11b

IEEE 802.11b has another name that you'll likely see on product advertisements, literature, or boxes in stores: *Wi-Fi,* which stands for Wireless Fidelity.

(Kinda like that good ol' Hi-Fi stereo where *Hi-Fi* stood for *High Fidelity.*) When you see Wi-Fi, you know it's 802.11b. Wi-Fi was the first version of wireless Ethernet. This version of wireless runs at speeds up to 11 million bits per second, or 11 Mbps. The reason I say that it runs at speeds *up to* 11 Mbps is because the actual speed at which the data is transferred depends on things like signal strength and quality. When the conditions are such that your signal strength or quality is decreased, you might find your wireless connection change down to 5.5 Mbps, 2 Mbps, or even as low as 1 Mbp.

Most available wireless Ethernet equipment, including Apple's AirPort network cards and AirPort Base Station, uses 802.11b.

In general, Wi-Fi network cards have the ability to communicate with other Wi-Fi devices and WAPs that are up to 1,000 feet away. Having said that, realize that 1,000 feet is a generous estimate when outdoors on a clear day with no wind blowing — you see what I'm getting at. In reality, when you set up your wireless network, things such as walls — especially concrete walls, like in basements — decrease the distance that you can cover. If you use a WAP, plan on no more than 150 feet between wireless computers in an Ad Hoc network between your wireless computer and the WAP. However, your mileage may vary.

Wireless Ethernet networks operate just like a wired Ethernet network using a hub (see Book V, Chapter 1 for more info on hubs). This means that the 11 Mbps bandwidth is shared between all computers using it. Collisions can also occur if more than one computer tries to speak at the same time. If you have a lot of people on your wireless network, the network can and will get noticeably slower because of increased collisions and because the bandwidth is shared. This applies not only to Wi-Fi but also to 802.11a (which I cover in the next section) and the forthcoming 802.11g standards.

One last thing about 802.11b networking: Wi-Fi uses the 2.4 GHz frequency range. It actually uses 11 different channels, but they're all around the 2.4 GHz range. I bring this up because if you're using a 2.4 GHz cordless phone or even a microwave, using either device can definitely interfere with or even shut down your wireless network. Keep this in mind when you buy your next phone or wonder why your file transfers stop when you make popcorn in the microwave.

802.11a

802.11a is a newer version of wireless Ethernet. No, I didn't get my letters mixed up. For some reason that I don't know or understand, 802.11b came out first, and 802.11a came out next. (I guess someone ran into a doorframe.) Anyway, 802.11a doesn't yet have a handy nickname like Wi-Fi, so just call it 802.11a.

802.11a isn't all that much different than Wi-Fi, but the few differences make a big impact. First off, 802.11a can run at speeds up to 54 Mbps — almost *five times* faster than Wi-Fi. This is because 802.11a uses the 5 GHz frequency range instead of the cluttered 2.4 GHz range that Wi-Fi uses. The powers that be set aside the 5 GHz range just for wireless networking, so cordless phones and microwaves (or any other wireless devices for that matter) can't interfere with the network. The downside to using the higher 5 GHz range, though, is that the distances that can be covered are even less than that of Wi-Fi — no more than about 60 feet to maintain the highest speeds.

802.11a equipment is starting to become easier to find. However, 802.11a equipment isn't compatible with Wi-Fi, so don't make the mistake of buying network equipment that's Wi-Fi and then trying to move to 802.11a later. Having said that, some manufacturers are making equipment that does both, but I wouldn't bother investing in that stuff because 802.11g is around the corner.

Ahead on the radar: 802.11g

Some manufacturers are starting to make equipment that will handle both Wi-Fi and 802.11a. Although this sounds like a great way to get both the speed of 802.11a and the compatibility with Wi-Fi, another standard is just around the corner that will provide both of those things without having to try to use two incompatible standards together. That new standard, *802.11g,* will operate at speeds up to 54 Mbps, like 802.11a, but will operate at the same frequency ranges and be interoperable with 802.11b that exists now.

Feelings in the wireless networking community are mixed on this standard. 802.11g will go back to using the 2.4 GHz range and will be backward compatible with Wi-Fi, so you don't have to throw everything out to move to faster speeds. However, going back to the 2.4 GHz range also means that your cordless phone and microwave can also do the same damage to your network that they do to Wi-Fi.

Keeping Your Wireless Network Secure

One aspect of wireless networking that has people standing at attention is security. As you might (or might not) know, the government has said that intercepting calls made from wireless phones isn't a violation of privacy. Because of the similarities between wireless phones and wireless networks, it stands to reason that if/when a court has to make a determination, it will most likely determine that it's not illegal for someone in the next apartment or house — or standing right in your street — to listen to and intercept your data from your wireless network.

But before you decide to toss the idea of a wireless network, keep this in mind: Even though it *is* technically possible that someone might camp out on your doorstep in order to gain access to your wireless network, for most home networks, this possibility isn't very likely. Even if someone tries to gain access to your wireless network and perhaps even *sniff* your network — a techno-nerd term meaning to record all the data flying around a network — there isn't a whole lot someone can do with that information.

You might say, "But I use my credit card on the Internet to buy stuff." Well, this is a valid concern. However, if you purchase things on the Internet with your credit card, you should already be using a secure connection provided by the Web site for your personal information so that the data you're sending across your wireless network is already encrypted and relatively safe from thieves. "But I have shared out my files on my computer. Can they access those file shares?" Another good question, but if you read Book V, Chapter 2, you know that you have to create an account for those whom you want to access your files. Unless the would-be hacker is very good at guessing usernames and passwords, your files are pretty safe, too.

This is not to say that you bear absolutely no risk of being hacked. If a legitimate user on your wireless network connects to your computer and starts transferring a file, a would-be hacker could potentially record all the traffic and then reconstruct the file that was sent from the data that was recorded. In other words, a hacker could grab that user's username and password. That's where WEP comes in.

WEP

Wired Equivalency Protocol, or WEP, is a good acronym — it's an encryption scheme that can be used on your wireless network. WEP is a part of 802.11b, so all your Wi-Fi equipment supports using WEP. WEP comes in two varieties: 40-bit and 128-bit. The more bits used in the encryption, the better it is.

To use WEP, you just have to use a WEP *key*, which is really just a code word. The longer the key, the better. Also, when making a key, be sure to use something like *ab8sher7234ksief87* (something that's random with letters and numbers) as opposed to something like *mykey* that's easily guessed. If you're using an Ad Hoc wireless network, all the computers need to have their wireless network card configured with the same WEP key in order to communicate. If you're using a WAP to connect to the rest of the network, you need to use the same key on your computers that you have set on your WAP.

One thing to note about WEP is that it has been *broken,* meaning that someone has figured out how to undo the encryption that WEP provides. For businesses, especially those with sensitive data, WEP is not a good security solution.

However, for home users, WEP can be just enough of a deterrent to keep people out. In order for someone to crack your WEP key, that person needs to record somewhere around 1 million encrypted packets or more. For a business, that might only be a hour or so of monitoring for a hacker, but for most home networks, this could take much longer because most home networks have much less traffic than business networks. So, not only would someone need to pitch a tent outside on your porch, he would need to be able to record at least a million of the packets going over your network and then have the knowledge to crack your encryption key. Although WEP isn't going to ward off the spies at the National Security Agency, it's good enough to protect home networks like yours and mine.

Other security standards

Although all Wi-Fi network equipment supports WEP, a few standards are worth mentioning: LEAP and 802.11x.

LEAP, *Lightweight Extensible Authentication Protocol*, is a protocol developed by Cisco Systems. To use LEAP, you need to have a server that's set up to enable users to log in to gain permission to the wireless network. What makes LEAP so good is that after you initially log in (authenticate) to your network, LEAP changes encryption keys on the fly at a time interval that you determine. You could set it so that every 15 minutes your encryption key is changed: Even if someone is in that hypothetical tent on your front lawn, he would never be able to record enough packets to figure out your key because it changes so often.

Setting up a server so that you can use LEAP isn't something for the novice to attempt. I would encourage you to read up on LEAP only if you are very serious about airtight security on your WLAN. The Cisco Web site (www. cisco.com) is a good place to read about LEAP.

All the Apple AirPort 2.0 wireless network cards and base stations are compatible with Cisco's LEAP for higher security.

The other thing worth mentioning is the new upcoming wireless security standard from IEEE: 802.11x. This new standard will take care of the weaknesses in WEP. Right now, IEEE is still trying to hammer out many of the fine details; however, the final 802.11x standard will probably be based on a system very similar to Cisco's LEAP. After 802.11x is ratified (agreed on and finalized) by IEEE, expect to see it integrated with the other 802.11 standards. For most 802.11b/a hardware, a simple software update will be all that's required to support the new standard.

Setting Up Your Wireless Network

On to the good stuff. This section describes installing an AirPort card as well as how to setup an Ad Hoc or infrastructure-based WLAN (wireless LAN).

Installing an AirPort or other 802.11b network card

Some Macs come with an AirPort card built-in, especially if you ordered one pre-installed. However, if your Mac doesn't have an AirPort card installed, you can usually add one yourself. A couple of Macs don't have a slot or antenna for an AirPort card, specifically the Indigo iMac with a 350 MHz CPU. However, all other iMacs do have a slot for an AirPort card. You just need to check www.info.apple.com/applespec to see whether your particular Mac can use an AirPort card.

In case you have any issues using AirPort, or need more information about anything related to AirPort, check this page at Apple's Web site: (www.info. apple.com/usen/airportAirPort/).

You should be able to use any standard 802.11b Wi-Fi card, but you might run into some issues with drivers and such. Be sure that any non-AirPort card that you might buy comes with Mac drivers.

A variety of 802.11b wireless network devices are available, many of which come with drivers for the Mac. Some of these devices connect using Universal Serial Bus (USB), which could be handy if you want to be able to move it between a desktop PowerMac or iMac to an iBook and back (without the hassle of opening the case each time). Before you can set up your wireless network, you have to install the card, which you can pick up at virtually any Apple store or Apple-authorized reseller, such as CompUSA. Because of the differences between manufacturers, check the installation instructions that come with whichever device that you choose.

After you have your AirPort or other 802.11b wireless network card installed, you're ready to connect up.

Setting up an Ad Hoc wireless network

Using an Ad Hoc network — also called a *computer-to-computer* network — is a fairly easy thing to accomplish in Mac OS X. Not only can you use this kind of network with your Macs but also with PCs and personal digital assistant's (PDAs) that have 802.11b Network Interface Cards (NICs) installed. This Ad Hoc network is great for setting up an impromptu network in a classroom, exchanging recipes and pictures at a family reunion in a park, or blowing your friend up while gaming across the aisle of a 757 at 30,000 feet.

Using non-Apple 802.11b equipment with AirPort equipment

Because of Apple's implementation of AirPort, keep in mind some things when trying to mix Apple wireless equipment with other vendors' 802.11b equipment. As you discover elsewhere in this chapter, using AirPort wireless networks can require a password. This corresponds to the 802.11b WEP key for encryption. However, the password that you enter for AirPort networks isn't exactly the same as the WEP key for that same network. If you're using an AirPort network card and are trying to connect to a non-Apple 802.11b WAP, you need to follow a specific procedure. You can find this procedure by going to www.info.apple.com/usen/AirPort/ and searching on the number 106250 (the Apple Knowledge Base article number). If you're using a non-Apple 802.11b network card and are trying to connect to an Apple AirPort Base Station, go to the same URL and search on *106864*. These articles will show you how to convert the Apple AirPort password to a WEP key and vice versa.

But because of the issues of using non-AirPort 802.11b stuff with AirPort stuff, I recommend that you stick with using Airport if possible.

To set up an Ad Hoc network, you first have to create the computer-to-computer network on one of your Macs. This takes advantage of the AirPort Software Base Station that's built into Mac OS X. To create a computer-to-computer network, follow these steps:

1. **From the Applications folder on your hard drive, open the Internet Connect application.**

2. **From the Internet Connect window, choose AirPort Network from the Configuration drop-down menu.**

3. **Choose Create Network from the Network drop-down menu.**

   Alternatively, if you're using AirPort, you can reach the same dialog from the AirPort status icon on the menu bar, as seen in Figure 4-1.

4. **In the resulting dialog, enter a name for your network, enter a password twice, and then choose a channel.**

   Although you can leave the password blank, I highly recommend that you choose a password for that extra bit of security.

   Out of the 11 channels available for 802.11b networks, channels 1, 6, and 11 are the only ones that don't overlap other channels — and are therefore the best choices to use. If you're close to other WAPs, AirPort Base Stations, or other Ad Hoc networks, you need to try to find a channel that's not being used or performance can be degraded.

The AirPort status icon

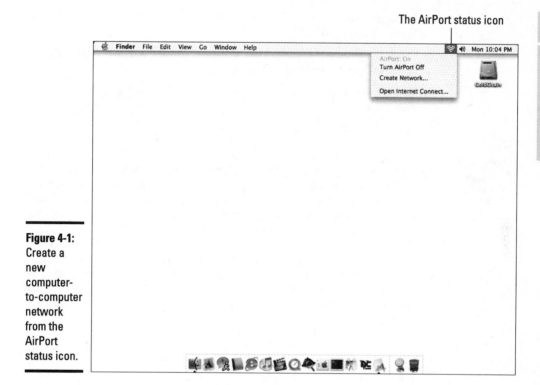

Figure 4-1:
Create a
new
computer-
to-computer
network
from the
AirPort
status icon.

5. **When you finish filling out the dialog, click OK.**

Creating a computer-to-computer network gives the illusion of having an
AirPort Base Station. So for people to join your network, they would follow
the same steps that they would to join any other AirPort network, as covered in the next section.

Setting up wireless networks with an AirPort Base Station

After one computer is running a computer-to-computer network or you've
set up and configured an AirPort Base Station, you're ready to invite other
computers with wireless hardware to the party.

Joining in an existing AirPort network

After you have a network set up on one of your wireless-enabled computers,
you just need to have the other wireless-enabled computers join that network.
You can use the same process, described below, to join any Ad Hoc wireless
network.

1. **From the Applications folder on your hard drive, open the Internet Connect application.**

2. **From the Internet Connection window, choose AirPort Network from the Configuration drop-down menu.**

3. **Choose an existing AirPort network from the Configuration drop-down menu.**

4. **Click Connect.**

If you want to join a network whose name doesn't appear in the drop-down — also called a *closed network* — choose Other from the Network drop-down menu and then enter the name of the network that you want to join and the password (if any is required). A closed network is another added measure of security — one that's good enough for most people because it's very unlikely a hacker is going to try to hack a network that he can't see.

If you're using AirPort for your wireless networking, you can also join a network from the AirPort status icon on the menu bar as seen in Figure 4-2. Just select the name of the network that you'd like to join — or select Other if you're joining a closed network. In this figure, the network is called GoldChain.

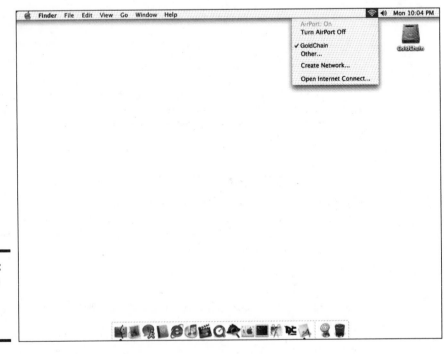

Figure 4-2:
Joining an existing AirPort network.

Disconnecting from an AirPort network

To disconnect from an AirPort network, you can do one of a few things. One way is to turn off your AirPort card altogether, which I cover in the next section. Another way is to simply connect to another AirPort network. This option is really only useful if you really want to connect to another network.

Turning your AirPort card on or off

You might want to use your Mac, usually your laptop, in a place where your wireless card shouldn't be used, like on an airplane (when they tell you to turn all cell phones off) or in a hospital in an area that doesn't allow cell phones or other wireless devices. Being able to turn your AirPort card on and off actually has its uses.

Just like with creating and joining a network, you have two ways that you can turn your AirPort card on and off. One way is in the Internet Connect application found in your Applications folder on your hard drive. In the Internet Connect application, choose New from the File menu, choose AirPort from the Configuration drop-down menu, and then click the Turn AirPort On/Off button. The other way to turn your AirPort card on or off is from the AirPort status icon on the menu bar. If you click the AirPort status icon, you can choose Turn AirPort On/Off from the resulting menu.

If you would like to control exactly which wireless network cards can access your wireless network, go to www.info.apple.com/usen/AirPort/ and search on *58571,* which is the Apple Knowledge Base article number of a document that explains exactly how to limit access to your network to specific wireless network cards.

Chapter 5: Sharing That Precious Internet Thing

In This Chapter

✔ Finding out how Internet sharing works

✔ Discovering the difference between hardware and software Internet sharing

✔ Connecting your Macs to a cable/DSL router

✔ Adding wireless support to your shared Internet connection

Although I've discussed lots of fun stuff that you can do with your network in previous chapters, this has to be my favorite: sharing a single Internet connection between all the computers on your network. If you have more than one computer, I'm sure you've had to deal with the dilemma that pops up whenever more than one person wants or needs to access the Internet at the same time.

Luckily, because most small home and office local area networks (LANs) use Transmission Control Protocol/Internet Protocol (TCP/IP) for network communications, connecting an entire network to the Internet isn't as large of a task as you might think. In this chapter, I talk about different hardware and software options for sharing your Internet connection as well as how to include your wireless devices.

Sharing the Internet

Sharing a single Internet connection between all your computers can be a boon simply because of the reduced chances of random acts of violence due to Internet deprivation. Although I won't claim that Internet sharing will save lives, it can indeed save you from headaches and arguments when more than one person wants to use the Internet at once.

Throughout this chapter, I talk a lot about cable modems and Asynchronous Digital Subscriber Line (ADSL) modems. Both of these are high-speed Internet connections, offered by your local cable company and your local phone company, respectively. The phone company offers different kinds of Digital Subscriber Line (DSL) connections, the most common of which is ADSL. However, because different kinds of DSL connections exist, in this chapter, I refer to them all generically as DSL.

To share your Internet connection, you need a few things, so here's a quick checklist:

✦ **An Internet connection:** This could be a dial-up Internet connection that's accessed via a standard analog modem, or it could be a cable or DSL modem connection.

✦ **A local area network (LAN):** A LAN is the main mechanism that allows Internet connections to be shared. This LAN could be a standard LAN with wires or a wireless LAN. See Book V, Chapter 1 for more information on setting up a LAN and Book V, Chapter 4 for more on setting up a Wireless LAN (WLAN).

✦ **An Internet-sharing device:** I use the word *device* because the method that you use to share your Internet connection could be software that you run on one of your computers or hardware that is standalone, depending on how you connect to the Internet and what fits your needs best.

When you have these three things ready to go, you can share your Internet connection. However, you need to know some background information to help you choose the right components and get everything up and running.

Using Network Address Translation

One thing that you must be aware of when configuring your LAN and preparing for an Internet connection is the set of IP addresses that you'll use. If you used Book V, Chapter 1 to set up and configure your LAN, you might recall that I suggest a specific range of Internet Protocol (IP) addresses to use on your LAN. In case you missed out on Chapter 1, I briefly cover this important topic again so that you can share your Internet connection smoothly.

When talking about IP addresses, the ruling body that tracks IP addresses and where they are used has broken all IP addresses up into two parts: public and private IP addresses. *Public* IP addresses are used to communicate on the Internet, and only one device in the entire world can use a given public IP address at any given time. *Private* addresses, on the other hand, are only supposed to be used on networks (like your home LAN) and do *not* connect to the Internet. Lots of people can use the same private address because their networks never go public: That is, they never access the Internet, so their IP addresses never conflict. Most times, you'll use addresses in the form of 192.168.*x.x* on your LAN. See Book V, Chapter 1 for an overview of IP addresses and how they work.

You might be wondering that if you use private IP addresses on your LAN at home or office and you have to use a public IP address to communicate on the Internet, how can your private IP addresses on your LAN communicate with public IP addresses on the Internet? That is an excellent question, and the answer is Network Address Translation (NAT).

NAT acts as a gatekeeper between your private IP addresses on your LAN and the public IP addresses on the Internet. When you connect to the Internet, your Internet Service Provider (ISP) gives you one — and usually only one — public IP address that can be used on the Internet. Instead of one of your computers using that public IP address and depriving all the other computers on the LAN, the hardware or software that you use to share the Internet will take control of that public IP address. Then, when any computer on your LAN tries to communicate on the Internet, your NAT software/hardware intercepts your communications and re-addresses the traffic so that it appears to be coming from your allotted public IP address.

When the Web site, File Transfer Protocol (FTP) server, or whatever strange Internet intelligence you're using on the Internet replies, it replies to your NAT device. The NAT device remembers which private IP address it should go to on the LAN and sends the information to that computer. See NAT at work in Figure 5-1.

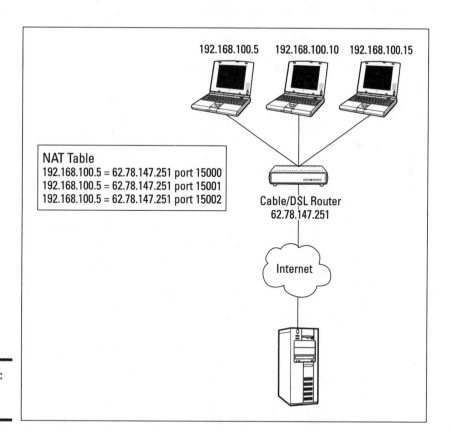

Figure 5-1:
NAT at
work.

Ways to Share Your Internet Connection

After you have an Internet connection and your LAN is set up, you need something to make this NAT thing work. You have a couple of different options to take care of NAT for your shared Internet connection. You can buy hardware or software. Each has pros and cons, so take a look at each option individually.

If you've already read Chapter 4 of this mini-book, you know that Mac OS X version 10.2 Jaguar has AirPort software built in. So, if you have an AirPort wireless network card in your Mac and you're using Jaguar, you can have your Mac act like an AirPort Base Station for all the wireless computers on your network, which in turn can use a software NAT.

Using hardware for sharing an Internet connection

Probably the most popular way to share an Internet connection is to buy a hardware device that connects to your Internet connection, which then connects to your LAN. These devices are referred to as *cable/DSL routers*. The main downside to a hardware Internet connection-sharing device is that it costs more than a software solution.

Don't let the name throw you: Although these devices are usually used to share cable/DSL connections, many have the ability to use an external analog modem to connect to a standard dial-up Internet account.

These devices are nice because they're easy to set up and configure — and you can leave them on, which means constant Internet access for those on your LAN. You don't have to worry about turning on another computer to connect to the Internet like you do with a software solution.

Apple's AirPort Base Station is not only a Wireless Access Point (WAP) for your network, as I discuss in Chapter 4 of this mini-book, but it's also an Internet connection-sharing device. The AirPort Base Station has not only a built-in V.90 modem for sharing up to 56 Kbps connections using dial-up accounts, but it also has two Ethernet connections for sharing a high-speed Internet connection: one to connect to a cable/DSL router and one to connect to the LAN.

If you think that a cable/DSL router or an AirPort Base Station could be the route for you to achieve your goal of sharing your Internet connection, here are some things to consider when deciding which device to buy for your LAN.

Most cable/DSL routers have a small 3-, 4-, or 5-port switch built-in — refer to Chapter 1 of this mini-book to discover more about hubs and switches.

This is nice because the same cable/DSL router that shares your Internet connection is also the centerpiece of your LAN where all your connections meet, thus saving you from having to buy a hub or switch on top of the cost of the cable/DSL router.

Some cable/DSL routers, however, like the AirPort, have only a single Ethernet connection to connect to your LAN. So keep in mind that if you choose a device with a single LAN connection, you must supply your own hub or switch that would then connect the cable/DSL router to the rest of your LAN.

On your cable/DSL router, look for either a built-in analog modem, like the AirPort has, or at least a serial port that an external analog modem can connect to. If your only Internet connection is through a dial-up modem account, you must have this feature if you want to use a hardware device to share your Internet connection. The AirPort is great for this because the modem is built-in. Even if you have cable/DSL service, most ISPs include a dial-up account with it. So you can connect both your cable or DSL service to the cable/DSL router as well as use the dial-up account as a backup in case your main service has problems.

Some cable/DSL routers also have a port for connecting a printer. This is also a great feature to have because it allows you to leave the printer connected and turned on so that anyone on the network can print to it anytime they need to. This is advantageous over connecting the printer to a computer and sharing it because then the computer doing the sharing must always be on in order to make the printer available. Mac OS X can send a print job to a printer using TCP/IP, so just make sure that your printer is compatible with TCP/IP printing, also called *LPR* (Line Printer Remote).

Using software for sharing an Internet connection

As I mention earlier, if you're using Mac OS X version 10.2 Jaguar and have an AirPort wireless network card installed, your Mac can act like an AirPort Base Station, providing both wireless Ethernet connectivity for other computers on the LAN *and* a shared Internet connection.

Mac OS X version 10.2 Jaguar also has built-in software that allows a single computer on your network to share its Internet connection with others on the LAN. To share your Internet connection, follow these quick steps:

1. **Open System Preferences either from the Apple menu or from the Dock.**

2. **Click the Sharing icon.**

This brings up the Sharing dialog, shown in Figure 5-2.

3. **Click the Internet tab of the Sharing dialog.**

4. **Mark the Share the Connection with Other Computers on Built-in Ethernet check box.**

When you do, you will be issued a warning that enabling this could affect your ISP or violate your agreement with your ISP. In my experiences, this neither violates your agreement with your ISP nor causes problems with them. However, if you have any doubts, contact your ISP and verify this.

5. **Click OK in the warning dialog to continue.**

You go back to the Sharing dialog, which now has a Start button.

6. **Click Start to enable Internet sharing.**

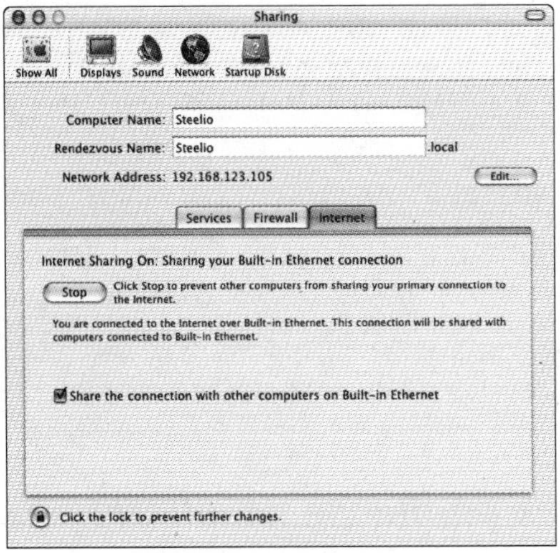

Figure 5-2:
Use Internet
Sharing
under
Mac OS X.

If you're using a dial-up modem to access the Internet, you need to also make sure that the computer that has the modem also has an Ethernet LAN connection. The iMac is a great example of a computer that can do this because it has both a built-in modem and an Ethernet connection.

If you're using a cable or DSL modem for your Internet connection, the Mac that you want to run the sharing software on should have two Ethernet connections: one to connect to the cable/DSL modem and one to connect to the rest of the LAN.

The main disadvantage to using a software solution for Internet connection sharing is that the computer that connects to the Internet must be turned on and ready to go all the time so that others on the network can get to the Internet. And although the sharing software operates in the background on the machine it's running on, it still takes up some of the processing power and memory, so it could make things a little slower on the machine that it's running on.

Connecting Everything

After you decide whether to use a software or hardware solution, you need to get all the pieces set up and connected. In this section, I tell you how to connect things for either the software or hardware method of sharing the Internet connection.

Using the software method

When you use the software method to share your Internet connection, this means that one of the computers on your network will have both the connection to the Internet and a connection to the LAN. Figure 5-3 shows a typical setup for software Internet sharing, whether you're using a dial-up modem account or cable/DSL modem for your Internet connection.

Keep in mind, though, that when using a cable/DSL modem for your Internet connection, the computer running the sharing software *must* have two Ethernet connections. If you're using a standard dial-up modem for Internet access, chances are that it's built into the computer used for sharing the Internet connection.

Using the hardware method

Using a hardware device for sharing an Internet connection, to me, is the best option. It is a bit more costly, but it's well worth the extra cost for the convenience that it adds. Not only does using a dedicated piece of hardware relieve a computer from having to run sharing software, but it also keeps you from having to have more than one Ethernet connection on a single computer if you're using a cable/DSL modem for your Internet access. Figure 5-4 shows how you would connect your devices for hardware Internet sharing using either a cable/DSL router with a built-in Ethernet switch or a cable/DSL router with a stand-alone Ethernet hub or switch, like you would need to use the AirPort.

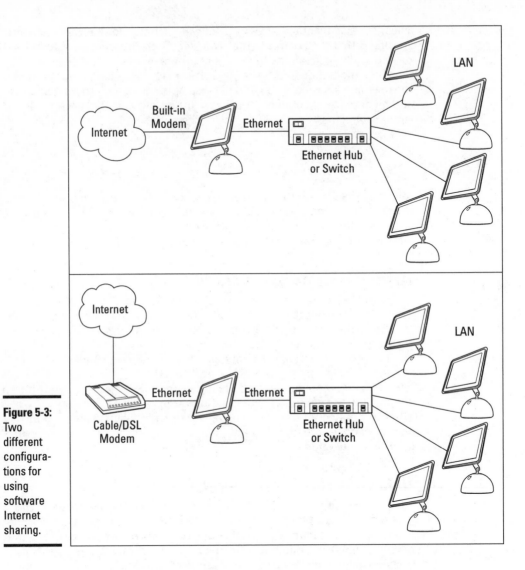

Figure 5-3:
Two
different
configura-
tions for
using
software
Internet
sharing.

If you choose to buy a cable/DSL router that has a built-in Ethernet switch, you can simply connect all your computers on the LAN to the built-in switch. However, if you buy a cable/DSL router that has only a single LAN connection, like the AirPort, you must connect that single LAN connection to an external hub or switch in order to get all the computers on the same network.

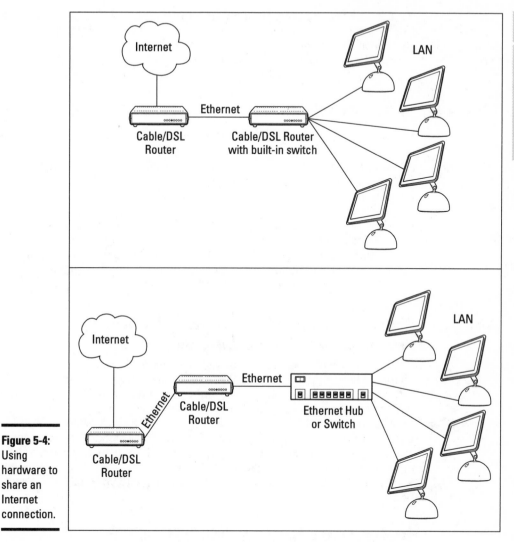

Figure 5-4:
Using
hardware to
share an
Internet
connection.

Regardless of whether you use the hardware or software method to share
your Internet connection, all the computers on your LAN — except the
one that's doing the sharing if you're using software sharing — should be
configured to obtain its IP address automatically through Dynamic Host
Configuration Protocol (DHCP). (See Chapter 1 for detailed instructions on
how to do this in Mac OS X.) Although it's not a requirement that you set up
your other devices with DHCP, it is recommended unless you understand

the IP addressing scheme required by your cable/DSL router and are willing to set up the addresses manually. You need to follow the instructions that come with the cable/DSL router or software that you purchase for detailed information on how to configure that.

Adding Wireless Support

You might have noticed that I mention wireless here and there in this chapter. This section is going to cover in a bit more detail what you can do to add wireless capabilities to your shared Internet party. To discover more about how wireless networks work and how to set one up, see Book V, Chapter 4.

Basically, you'll encounter a couple of situations when trying to add wireless capabilities into the mix. Either you already have an Internet connection-sharing mechanism in place (either hardware or software) or you don't yet have your Internet connection shared. Your situation will play a role in which way you choose to integrate wireless into your network.

If you already have a cable/DSL router or are using software Internet sharing

If you already have a cable/DSL router or if you're using software Internet sharing, like that built into Mac OS X version 10.2 Jaguar, you can simply buy a Wireless Access Point (WAP) and connect it to your LAN. Adding a WAP will enable anyone using wireless Ethernet access to your network and thus to your shared Internet connection. There are many WAPs that you can buy to add wireless to your network. The AirPort is a good example; however, because the AirPort also can do Internet sharing, make sure that you *don't* enable the Internet sharing on the AirPort card! (In this case, you don't want or need this feature because it can conflict with your cable/DSL router operation.)

If you do not have a cable/DSL router or AirPort Base Station

If you don't have a cable/DSL router or an AirPort Base Station for Internet sharing, you have a few options. Each option has an upside and downside.

One option is to get an AirPort Base Station, which will provide both wireless access for AirPort-enabled wireless computers and Internet sharing for the entire network. The downside to the AirPort Base Station is that it has only a single LAN Ethernet connection, so if you have more than one computer using wired Ethernet, you must buy an additional hub or switch to connect them all together.

The other option is to buy a combination cable/DSL router, which has a built-in WAP. Most cable/DSL routers — including the ones that have wireless built-in — also have multiple Ethernet ports on them, so connecting computers using wired Ethernet can be done without buying an external hub or switch.

The final option is that you can use the AirPort software built-in to Mac OS X to turn your Mac into an Airport Base Station — if you have an AirPort wireless card on that particular Mac. This is a great, low-cost way to add wireless and Internet sharing to your network. However, many Macs don't come with an AirPort wireless card built in, and you still can eat up processor time and memory by running the AirPort software. For more on wireless networking, read Chapter 4 of this mini-book.

Book VI

Expanding Your System

The 5th Wave   By Rich Tennant

©RICHTENNANT

"Come here, quick! I've got a new iMac trick!"

Contents at a Glance

Chapter 1: Hardware that Will Make You Giddy 499

Chapter 2: Add RAM, Hard Drive Space, and Stir 515

Chapter 3: Port-o-rama: Using USB and FireWire 527

Chapter 4: I'm Okay, You're a Printer 533

Chapter 5: Programs that You've (Probably) Gotta Have 543

Chapter 1: Hardware that Will Make You Giddy

In This Chapter

✔ Using digital cameras, digital video camcorders, and scanners

✔ Adding keyboards, trackballs, joysticks, and drawing pads

✔ Using optical recorders and tape drives

✔ Adding speakers, subwoofers, and MP3 hardware

*H*ardware. We love it. To a Mac power-user, new hardware holds all the promise of Christmas morning, whether your new toys are used for business or for pleasure. We pore over magazines and visit our favorite Mac Web sites like clockwork to check on new technology.

These hardware devices don't come cheap, however, forcing you to make the painful decision of deciding which new hardware you really *need* in order to accomplish what you want and which hardware is a luxury. Also, if you're a new Mac owner, you might not know what's available. For example, I constantly get e-mail from readers, asking, "What can I connect to my new computer?" I guess I could reply, "Why, the kitchen sink!" To that end, I decided to add this chapter to the book to let you know how you can expand the hardware for your Mac OS X powerhouse.

Each section in this chapter provides a description of what a particular device does, approximately how much it costs, and a set of general guidelines that you can use when shopping. Although this isn't in-depth coverage — after all, the book is supposed to be about Mac OS X — it will serve to get you started if you've just become a Mac owner. If you're especially interested in a specific piece of hardware, I recommend other books that you can read for the exhaustive details.

Ready? To quote a great line from the first Batman film: "Alfred, let's go shopping!"

Parading Pixels: Digital Cameras, DV Camcorders, and Scanners

The first category of hardware toys revolves around images — hardware for creating original images, capturing images in real-time, and reading images from hard copy.

Digital cameras

A digital camera like the Hewlett-Packard PhotoSmart 912 (shown in Figure 1-1) shares most of the characteristics of a traditional film camera. It looks the same, and you use the same techniques while shooting photographs. The difference is in the end result. With a digital camera, instead of a roll of film that has to be developed you have an image in JPEG or TIFF format that's stored on a memory card. The contents of the memory card can be downloaded to your Mac, and then the real fun begins. With a digital photograph, you can

+ Edit with an image editor such as Adobe Photoshop

+ Print with an inkjet or color laser printer

+ Record to a CD or DVD

+ Add to a Web page

+ Print in a coffee-table book (using iPhoto)

+ Mail to friends and family

What they cost

Consumer-level digital cameras typically sell for anywhere from $200 (for a 2-megapixel model) to $400 (for a 3-megapixel camera). *Megapixel* is a general reference to the resolution (the size of the image, measured in individual dots called pixels) and detail delivered by the camera. Such digital cameras can produce photographs that are well suited for just about any casual shutterbug. Professional digital cameras in the 4- or 5-megapixel range can set you back one or two thousand dollars, but I wouldn't recommend them for someone who's just discovered digital photography because of their cost and complexity.

What to look for

Here are some general guidelines that I recommend when selecting a digital camera:

+ **At least a 2-megapixel camera.** As a general rule, the higher the megapixel value, the better the camera.

✦ **At least an 8MB memory card.** The *memory card* stores the images that you capture.

✦ **A Universal Serial Bus (USB) connection to your Macintosh.** (USB is covered in all its glory in Chapter 3 of this mini-book.)

✦ **An optical zoom feature.** Optical zoom allows you to draw closer to subjects that are farther away.

✦ **A self-timer.** With a self-timer, your camera can snap a photo automatically, allowing you to finally be seen in your own pictures!

✦ **A manual flash setting.** Although automatic flash is a good thing most of the time, a manual setting allows you to disable your camera's flash for artistic shots (or just to prevent the glare on subjects with polished surfaces).

**Book VI
Chapter 1**

Hardware that Will
Make You Giddy

TIP

For a complete guide to digital cameras, I heartily recommend the *Digital Photography Handbook,* published by John Wiley & Sons, Inc. — and written by some guy named Mark L. Chambers. (It really is a good book.) For a full exposé of everything in digital photography, check out *Digital Photography Bible,* also published by John Wiley & Sons, Inc.

Figure 1-1:
Although it looks like a film camera, a digital camera is a different breed altogether.

DV camcorders

Like digital cameras, digital video (DV) camcorders are the counterpart to the familiar video camcorder. A *DV camcorder* looks and operates like a VHS camcorder, but you can connect it to your Macintosh via a FireWire cable and download your video clips directly into iMovie. (Chapter 4 of Book III explains all about iMovie, and FireWire is tackled in Chapter 3 of this mini-book.) Figure 1-2 illustrates the Panasonic PV-DV401 DV camcorder.

Figure 1-2:
A digital camcorder produces digital video clips for iMovie.

Besides the higher quality of digital video, it has a number of other real advantages over analog video:

✦ Digital video can be edited with applications such as iMovie or Adobe Premiere.

✦ Digital video can be recorded to a CD or DVD.

✦ Digital video can be posted for downloading on a Web page.

What they cost

A typical DV camcorder starts at about $500, with the more desirable MiniDV camcorders selling for around $1,000.

If a DV camcorder is too costly of an investment, you can convert *analog video* — video from your current VHS camcorder or VCR — into digital video using an inexpensive device called an *AV converter*. I've used the Hollywood DV-Bridge from Dazzle (www.dazzle.com), — it's available on the Web for about $250.

What to look for

I recommend the following when shopping for a DV camcorder:

✦ **The highest optical zoom in your price range.** Again, like a digital camera, it's important to be able to capture subjects and action when you can't get any closer — think the lion exhibit at the zoo.

✦ **Image stabilization.** This helps steady the picture when you're holding the camcorder.

✦ **On-board effects.** These effects generally include some snazzy things like black and white footage, fades, and wipes.

✦ **AV connectors.** Use these to display your video by connecting the camcorder directly to your TV.

✦ **Support for FireWire (or IEEE-1394) connectivity.** For more details on FireWire, see Chapter 3 of this mini-book.

✦ **Digital still mode.** This enables you to take still photographs if your digital camera isn't handy; however, the image quality isn't as good as a bona-fide digital camera.

For an in-depth look at digital video, check out *Digital Video For Dummies,* by Martin Doucette, published by Hungry Minds, Inc.

Scanners

Figure 1-3 illustrates a typical flatbed scanner, the tool of choice for those Macintosh owners who want to digitize images and text from printed materials. Although you can also connect a sheet-fed scanner, flat-bed models are much more versatile and produce better quality scans.

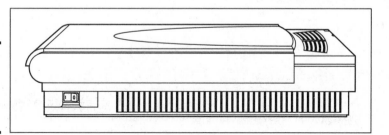

Figure 1-3:
The flatbed
scanner,
King of
Digitizing.

Images produced by a scanner can be edited, mailed, displayed on the Web, or added to your own documents, just like the images from a digital camera.

What they cost

A good-quality scanner should cost anywhere from $100 to $200, with the best models — featuring the fastest scanning speeds, best color depth, and highest resolutions — going for around $1,000.

What to look for

Try to get the following features in a scanner:

+ **The highest color depth that you can afford.** Get a minimum of 36-bit.

+ **The highest resolution that you can afford.** Get a minimum of 600 dots per inch (dpi) (optical).

+ **Single-pass scanning.** This feature results in a faster scan with less chance of error.

+ **Transparency adapter for scanning film negatives.** If you're a traditional film photographer, you'll find that a transparency adapter turns a standard flatbed scanner into an acceptable negative scanner.

+ **One-touch buttons for e-mailing your scanned images or uploading them to the Web.** These are controls of convenience — pressing one of these buttons automatically scans the item and prepares the image to be e-mailed or uploaded to a Web site.

+ **USB or FireWire connection.** I cover the advantages of both in Chapter 3 of this mini-book.

Another shameless plug. My best-selling book *Scanners For Dummies* offers comprehensive coverage of all types of scanners, as well as chapters devoted to advanced features, image editing, and step-by-step projects. It's published by Hungry Minds, Inc.

Incredible Input: Keyboards, Trackballs, Joysticks, and Drawing Tablets

Although your Mac is already equipped with a keyboard and a mouse, you can replace them with enhanced hardware that will add functionality and precision to your work. (Or, you can buy a joystick and spend your days wreaking havoc on your enemies.)

Keyboards

If you're using the latest iMac or G4 tower model, you don't really need to upgrade your keyboard. These new machines come with excellent keyboards already, replete with volume controls and a Media Eject key. However, if you're using an older Macintosh — or you have an iBook or PowerBook and you want to add an external keyboard — then you can take advantage of the convenience of a USB keyboard like the one in Figure 1-4.

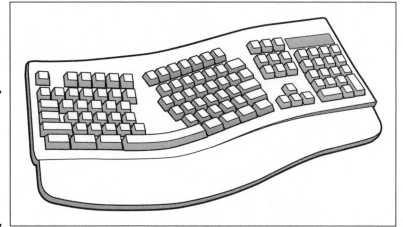

Figure 1-4:
An
ergonomic
upgrade —
the
aftermarket
USB
keyboard.

What they cost

Aftermarket (nonstandard-issue) keyboards generally cost anywhere from
$40 to $100.

What to look for

Look for the following keyboard features when shopping for a keyboard:

✦ **Programmable buttons.** Configure these to launch applications or run
   macros.

✦ **Additional USB ports.** Use these to turn your keyboard into a USB hub.

✦ **One-touch buttons to launch your browser or e-mail application.**
   Press one of these buttons to launch your Web browser or Mail.

✦ **Ergonomic wrist pad.** Helps prevent wrist strain and repetitive joint
   injuries.

Trackballs

Some folks prefer using a trackball, like the one shown in Figure 1-5, over a
mouse any day. Graphic artists find that trackballs are more precise and
offer better control, usually including a secondary button to display
contextual menus. (One model on the market has eight buttons. Who
needs a keyboard?)

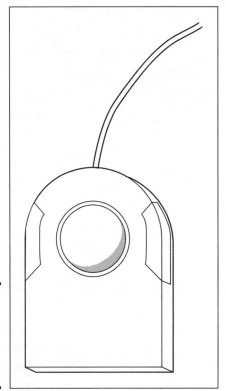

Figure 1-5:
Many
power users
prefer a
trackball to
a mouse.

What they cost

Trackballs range in price from $50 to $90 — most are optical, so they need little cleaning, and they'll last for many years of precise pointing at things.

What to look for

Look for the following feature when shopping for a trackball:

✦ **More programmable buttons.** Opt for at least two buttons!

✦ **Optical tracking.** An optical trackball — one that doesn't use rollers, instead using a photosensitive sensor to record the movement of the ball — is more precise and easier to keep clean.

✦ **A scroll wheel.** Use this gizmo to scroll documents up and down.

✦ **Ergonomic design.** Look for a wrist pad or slanted buttons.

Joysticks

Game players, unite! For arcade and sports games, using a joystick results in increased maneuverability, more realistic action, higher scores, less wear and tear on your keyboard . . . and just plain more fun. Joysticks range from the traditional USB aircraft controller shown in Figure 1-6 to USB controllers and gamepads that rival anything offered on the PlayStation 2 or the Xbox.

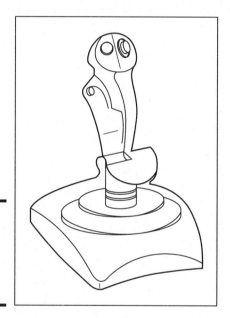

Figure 1-6: The secret weapon of Mac gamers — a joystick.

What they cost

Joysticks vary in price from $30 to $120 — at the low end, you'll usually find the gamepad-type controllers, and aircraft controllers carry the highest price tag.

What to look for

Get the following features in a joystick:

- ✦ **Yet even more programmable buttons.**
- ✦ **Pitch and yaw controls.** These are for the flight simulator crowd.
- ✦ **Force feedback.** A *force feedback joystick* rumbles and moves in tandem with the action in the game, providing an extra feeling of realism.

Drawing tablets

A drawing tablet like the one you see in Figure 1-7 might be pricey, but if you're a graphic artist or a designer, using a tablet will revolutionize the way that you work with your Mac — especially with the new Inkwell technology built-in to the latest version of Mac OS X. Rather than use a mouse or trackball to sketch, you can draw on the tablet freehand, just like you would draw on paper or canvas. Tablets can recognize different levels of pressure, allowing applications such as Photoshop and Painter to re-create all sorts of photo-realistic brush effects.

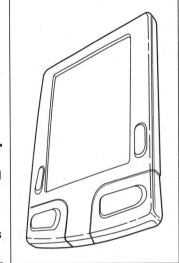

Figure 1-7: Professional artists and designers swear by the graphics tablet.

What they cost

Depending on the size of the tablet, you'll pay anywhere from around $100 to a whopping $500, depending on the size and the pressure levels you need.

What to look for

I recommend the following tablet features:

- ✦ **Programmable buttons.** See a trend here?

- ✦ **Accessory mouse.** Some high-end tablets include a mouse that you can use along with the tablet.

- ✦ **A cordless stylus.** Make sure that it doesn't require batteries.

✦ **The highest number of pressure levels possible.** The more levels that the tablet offers, the more subtle and precise your control is over painting effects.

Sublime Storage: CD/DVD Recorders and Tape Drives

I don't include Zip and Orb drives in this category because the arrival of cheap, reliable optical storage has rendered a 250MB cartridge obsolete. Even the once awesome 2.2GB capacity of an Orb drive seems a little insignificant next to a rewriteable DVD-RW drive, which can store 4.7GB on a single disc.

If you'd like to trade data with another Mac or a PC using floppy disks, you can get an external USB floppy drive for under $100 — however, I personally eschew floppy disks, which are very unreliable and carry a mere 1.44MB of data.

CD and DVD recorders

Virtually all recent Mac models include a rewritable optical drive — either a CD-RW or the DVD-R SuperDrive — but if your computer is older and didn't come equipped with a recorder, you can always add an external model, like the external CD-RW drive shown in Figure 1-8.

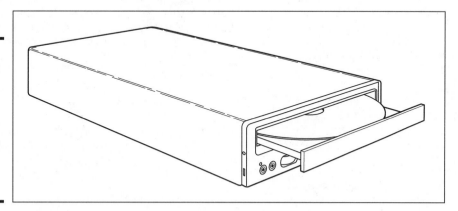

Figure 1-8:
An external CD-RW drive is perfect for backups and recording both audio and data CDs.

What they cost

A typical USB or FireWire CD-RW drive costs about $150. A FireWire DVD-RW drive averages about $500.

What to look for

Get the following features in an external CD-RW drive:

✦ **An internal buffer of at least 2MB.** The larger the buffer, the less chance you'll encounter recording errors and the faster your drive will burn.

✦ **At least 8X recording speed.** A no-brainer here. The faster the recording speed, the less time you'll wait for the finished disc.

✦ **AC power through the USB or FireWire cable.** This eliminates the need for a separate AC power supply.

✦ **Burn-proof technology.** This virtually eliminates recording errors due to multitasking so you can continue to work on other applications while you record.

Okay, just one more. I'm very proud of another of my books in the *For Dummies* series, *CD and DVD Recording For Dummies*. Published by Hungry Minds, Inc., it covers everything that you need to know about producing all sorts of discs — everything from basic data and audio CDs to DVDs and more exotic formats such as CD Extra. Mac owners will be happy to know that this book covers the Mac like a blanket, too.

Tape drives

If you're looking for a real high-capacity backup solution, use a tape drive. A *tape drive* is a storage device that uses a tape cartridge (much like a music cassette). A Travan tape drive (which averages about 40–60GB of storage) is much less expensive than a Digital Audio Tape (DAT) drive, which has a higher capacity of 120GB or more.

What they cost

Travan drives typically range around $500 (storing around 60MB per tape), and most DAT drives start at $1,000 (and can store gigabytes of data on a single tape).

What to look for

Get the following features in a tape drive:

✦ **Hardware data compression.** This provides a faster backup on fewer tapes.

✦ **Automatic head cleaning.** Head cleaning helps reduce errors while writing data (and reading it back later).

✦ **FireWire connection.** A FireWire drive provides much faster data transfer, so your backups take a fraction of the time needed by a USB tape drive.

✦ **A transfer rate of at least 6 Mbps.** The faster the transfer rate, the shorter the time necessary to backup your drive!

Awesome Audio: Subwoofer Systems and MP3 Hardware

Some Macintosh models don't come with speakers — like the current low-end iMac G4 — and even those Macs that do ship with speakers don't measure up to the standards of a true audiophile. For those who really enjoy their music and their game audio, this last section covers the world of Macintosh after-market sonic enjoyment.

Subwoofer speaker systems

The ever-popular USB port again comes to your rescue. This time, it enables you to connect a more powerful speaker system with a subwoofer (like the one shown in Figure 1-9). If you've never heard a subwoofer — think chest-rattling *thump, thump, thump* — they provide the basement-level bass that can add power and punch to both your music and your games. Being hit by an asteroid is a rather flat, tinny experience with a pair of battery-powered speakers that you salvaged from your Walkman years ago. With a new set of speakers and a subwoofer, you'll swear that Han Solo is sitting in the cockpit chair next to you!

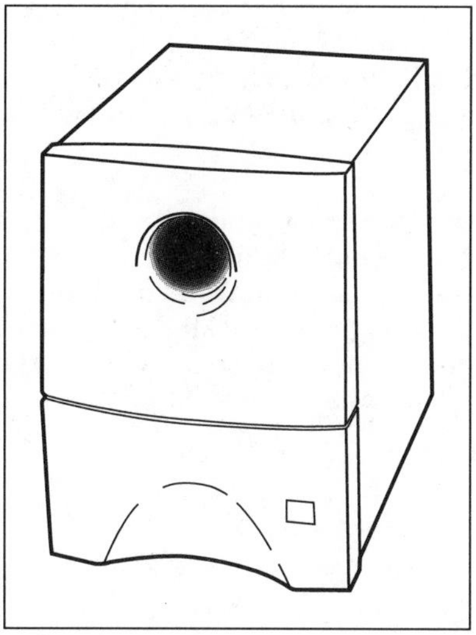

Book VI Chapter 1

Hardware that Will Make You Giddy

Figure 1-9: Whether your passion is games or music, a subwoofer will deliver the goods.

With the growing importance of the computer as a replacement for your home entertainment center, investing in a more powerful set of speakers will help you enjoy all those audio CDs and MP3s that you've added to your iTunes playlists. (Read all about iTunes in Book III, Chapter 2.)

What they cost

Most USB-powered speakers with a subwoofer are priced below $200, but true audiophiles looking for surround sound can spring for a $500 system that includes several satellite speakers and a subwoofer.

What to look for

Get these features in a subwoofer:

+ **At least 30 watts of power.** The higher the wattage rating, the more powerful the speakers (and the louder your music can be).

+ **Additional headphone jacks and stereo mini-plug input jacks.** Use these for connecting your iPod or MP3 player directly to your speaker system. (Read all about iPods in the next section.)

+ **Magnetic shielding.** This helps prevent your speakers from distorting your monitor display.

MP3 players (Well, actually, just the iPod)

I've lusted after Apple's iPod MP3 player ever since it arrived on campus. Depending on which model you get, this incredible device can hold anywhere from 5MB to 20GB of MP3 digital audio — that's over 4,000 songs of average length in the 20GB version! Plus, the iPod also acts as your personal data butler by carrying your files; it's an honest-to-goodness, external FireWire drive. And the latest firmware updates allow you to download your contacts and appointments from Mac OS X. Just think: Carry your files to and from your office *and* carry Devo and the Dead Kennedys as well!

All this fits into a beautiful, stylish package about the size of a pack of cigarettes, with a 10-hour lithium rechargeable battery, high-quality earbud headphones, and automatic synchronization with your iTunes MP3 library. Life just doesn't get any better for a technoid like me. If you think your Mac is a well-designed piece of equipment, then you'll understand why this little box is so alluring. (And why I have one now.)

Sure, there are other MP3 players out there, but most of them share the same following problems:

- ✦ They use digital memory cards, which offer far less capacity.
- ✦ They use standard batteries, or you have to furnish rechargeable batteries (which don't last 10 hours).
- ✦ They use USB connections, which take forever to download your files and audio.
- ✦ They don't operate as an external hard drive or a contacts/appointment database.

I say forget 'em. The iPod is worth every cent you'll pay.

The 5GB iPod runs $299 at the time of this writing, the 10GB costs $399, and the 20GB model costs $499.

If you're shopping for a great MP3 player *and* you happen to need an external drive for backing up your Mac's internal hard drive, the iPod is perfect — I mean, it's literally a double-play!

**Book VI
Chapter 1**

**Hardware that Will
Make You Giddy**

Chapter 2: Add RAM, Hard Drive Space, and Stir

In This Chapter

✓ Understanding the advantages of extra RAM

✓ Shopping for a RAM upgrade

✓ Choosing between internal and external hard drives

✓ Determining your hard drive needs

✓ Shopping for a new hard drive

✓ Installing your upgrades

Most Macintosh owners will make two upgrades — adding more memory (RAM) and additional hard drive space — during the lifetime of their computers. These two improvements have the greatest effect on the overall performance of Mac OS X. By adding RAM and additional hard drive space, you not only make more elbow room for your applications and documents, but everything runs faster: Think of the Six Million Dollar Man, only a heck of a lot cheaper to operate.

In this chapter, I steer you around the hidden potholes along the way for those who aren't well versed in selecting memory modules or weighing the advantages of different types of hard drives. However, if you buy the wrong piece of hardware, remember that using a hammer to make it fit is not a workable option.

Adding Memory: Reasons for More RAM

Of all the possible upgrades that you can make to your Macintosh, adding more random access memory (RAM) is the single most cost-effective method of increasing the performance of Mac OS X. Here is exactly what Mac OS X uses available RAM for:

✦ **Applications:** Naturally, Mac OS X needs system RAM to run the applications that you launch. The more memory in your machine, the larger the applications that you can open and the faster they'll run.

✦ **Overhead:** This includes the operating system itself, Classic mode (if it's running), as well as various and sundry buffers and memory areas devoted for temporary work. As you would guess, the more memory here the merrier. (For the complete scoop on Classic mode, see Chapter 7 of Book I.)

✦ **Virtual memory:** Aha! Now here's something that I mention lightly and politely in Book I but didn't really amount to a hill of beans until this moment. (Can you tell I'm a big fan of Bing Crosby?) Virtual memory allows Mac OS X to use empty hard drive space as temporary system memory, as shown in Figure 2-1. Data is written to your hard drive instead of being stored in RAM, and then it's erased when it's no longer needed. It's a neat trick that's also used by Windows, Linux, and dear old Mac OS 9 (just nowhere near as well as Mac OS X). Virtual memory works automatically within Mac OS X, so you don't have to enable it manually as you did in Mac OS 9.

Figure 2-1:
The mysterious beauty of virtual memory — but it still can't beat the real silicon thing.

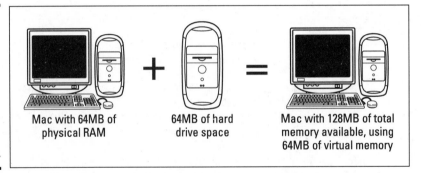

Mac with 64MB of physical RAM   64MB of hard drive space   Mac with 128MB of total memory available, using 64MB of virtual memory

At first, virtual memory sounds like absolute bliss, and it does indeed allow your Macintosh to do things that would otherwise be impossible, like running an application that requires 300MB of RAM in just 128MB of actual physical RAM. However, here come the caveats:

✦ **Virtual memory is slow as molasses in December.** Even today's fastest hard drive is many, many times slower than real silicon, so any use of virtual memory instead of RAM slows down Mac OS X significantly.

✦ **Virtual memory abuses your hard drive.** If you've ever run Photoshop on a Windows PC with 64MB of RAM, you're having flashbacks right now — whenever your Macintosh is using virtual memory, your hard drive remains almost constantly active. (Hardware types like myself call this phenomenon *thrashing* because we know what's happening inside that poor hard drive.) Over time, running any computer with insufficient RAM and behemoth applications will result in a significant increase in hard drive wear and tear.

✦ **Virtual memory costs you processing power.** With sufficient RAM, Mac OS X gleefully runs as efficiently as it can — when virtual memory kicks in, however, your Mac has to spend part of its quality time shuttling data to and from the hard drive, which robs your computer of processing power.

The moral of the story is very simple, so it's time for another of Mark's Maxims:

The less that Mac OS X needs to use virtual memory, the better.™

To put it another way, physical memory (meaning memory modules) is always a better choice than virtual memory. This is why power users and techno-types crave as much system memory as possible.

A mere two years ago, 128MB of RAM was a quite comfortable figure for most folks, but most of today's Macs can accept a whopping 512MB, 1GB (that's short for *gigabyte,* or 1,024 megabytes), or even more system RAM.

If you'll be keeping your current Macintosh for a few years more, then install as much memory as you can afford — you'll thank me every time Mac OS X boots.

Shopping for a RAM Upgrade

Before you click your mouse on some online computer store's Buy button, you need to determine two things that will help you determine which memory module to buy — how much RAM you've already got and how much more your system can handle.

Finding out the current memory in your Mac

Memory modules are made in standard sizes, so you need to determine how much memory you already have and which of your memory slots are filled. To do this, open an old friend you might have used in Mac OS 9, the Apple System Profiler. Here, open your Applications folder and then open the Utilities folder to locate this gem, which is shown in Figure 2-2. Alternatively, click the Apple menu, choose About this Mac, and then click the More Info button.

After you launch this application, it takes a few seconds to scan your Macintosh and display all sorts of identifying information about the hardware and software that you're using. Check out the Memory Overview section. Here you can see exactly how many memory modules you have, what type they are, and how much memory each provides. For example, in Figure 2-2, my iMac G4 has two memory slots — labeled DIMM0 and DIMM1 — and each of those slots is filled with a 256MB module, giving me a total physical memory of 512MB. Jot down the name and contents of each slot on a piece of paper — or, if you're a real Mac OS X power user, add a Stickie to your Desktop with this information. (Stickies are covered in Chapter 2 of Book II.)

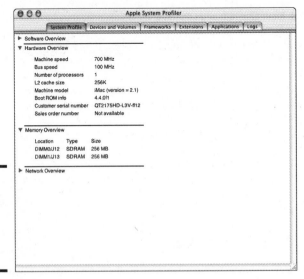

Figure 2-2:
Look under
the hood
with Apple
System
Profiler.

However, on my particular machine, only one of those memory modules can be upgraded by a mere mortal: DIMM1. DIMM0 is an internal module and can only be upgraded by an Apple technician. (Insert sound of harps playing here.) The only module that I can subdue and upgrade is DIMM1.

Unfortunately, this arrangement differs on just about every model of Macintosh ever made — some have more memory slots, and others allow you to upgrade all the system memory, instead of just one module. The only way to determine which modules are accessible on your Mac is to identify the exact model of your computer.

Determining the exact model of your computer

Most folks know the type and model of their computers, but there's a catch here, too — sometimes the memory that you need varies by the processor in your Macintosh. For instance, many different versions of iMacs have been made since the Bondi Blue Beast debuted, and over the course of those years, Apple has made a slew of changes inside. Your eye should be on the actual processor speed and *bus speed* — the transfer speed that data reaches whilst speeding across your motherboard — because they're the identifying factors here. An iMac with a 333 MHz G3 processor, for example, will use a different type of memory from an iMac with a 700 MHz G4 processor.

Again, your salvation turns out to be Apple System Profiler — look again at that talented image Figure 2-2 to see that both the Machine Speed (or *processor speed*) and the Bus Speed are both listed: In this case, this machine has a 700 MHz G4 running at 100 MHz bus speed. Grab that same piece of paper (or open that same Stickie) and add these two figures to your list.

Now you're armed with the information that you need to go online and buy the right memory — or, if you'd rather work directly with a human being, you can visit your local Apple dealer, present him with the list, and have him order the memory upgrade for you.

Buying memory online is much cheaper. I recommend the following online stores:

✦ **MacMall:** `www.macmall.com`

✦ **MacWarehouse:** `www.macwarehouse.com`

✦ **MacConnection:** `www.macconnection.com`

The Tao of Hard Drive Territory

Next, turn your attention to the other popular Mac upgrade — adding extra hard drive space. With today's cutting-edge 3-D games using 600MB of space each and Photoshop expanding to 250MB, IDC (short for *Insidious Data Creep*) is a growing problem. (Bad pun most certainly intended.)

You can save space by deleting those files and folders that you don't need — but what fun is that? To reduce your Mac's waistline before you consider adding more room, I recommend using Spring Cleaning from Aladdin Systems, which you can find at `www.aladdinsys.com` — it's a great tool for locating duplicates, removing empty folders, and uninstalling old programs that you no longer use.

To determine how much free space remains on a hard drive, click the drive's icon on your Desktop and press ⌘+I to display its information, as shown in Figure 2-3. (I'm a major-league Mozart fan-boy, hence the name of my hard drive.)

Figure 2-3:
Check a
drive's free
space.

As a general rule, the following factors indicate that you're ready to upgrade your hard drive territory:

✦ You have less than 2GB of space on your current hard drive.

✦ You've cleaned off all unnecessary files, and your Mac is still lagging.

✦ You need to share a large amount of data between computers that aren't on the same network. (Read on to discover why.)

Internal versus External Storage

Just about everyone who upgrades their existing hard drive does so because they need extra space; however, you might also need to add a hard drive to your system that can go mobile whenever necessary. Unlike an *internal* drive — which resides hidden inside your Mac's case — an *external* drive is a lean, mean, self-contained traveling storage machine that's perfect for road warriors.

External drives

External removable cartridge drives, such as a Zip or an Orb drive, are fine for folks who have to send cartridges to other locations. Unfortunately, however, the capacities of these drives are rapidly falling behind conventional, nonremovable external hard drives. Also, most Macs now have either a CD-RW or DVD-R drive, which basically render Zip and Orb technology obsolete. Therefore, if you're considering an external unit, go with the most popular pick — a high-capacity nonremovable hard drive, which offers the most storage for your dollar.

Most external drives are *shock-mounted* (meaning they can take more abuse than an internal hard drive), and they carry their own power supply. In fact, some external drives actually don't need a separate power supply — they draw their power through your Mac's Universal Serial Bus (USB) or FireWire port. (The next chapter in this mini-book tells all about USB and FireWire.)

External drives also have a number of other advantages:

✦ **No installation hassle:** You can easily install a USB or FireWire drive in seconds. Simply plug in the drive to the proper connector on the side or back of your Mac, connect the power supply (if necessary), and turn it on. (As the folks in Cupertino are fond of saying, "Look, Ma — no drivers!")

✦ **No extra space needed:** Many Macs simply don't have the internal space for another drive — laptops and iMacs are good examples. Therefore, if you want to keep your existing internal drive as-is while you're adding more storage, an external drive is your only choice.

✦ **Share files with ease:** With an external drive, you can share your data between multiple computers or bring your files with you on your next trip.

✦ **Safe from prying eyes:** Unlike an internal drive, external drives are easy to secure. Take your sensitive information home with you or lock it in a safe.

After you plug in an external drive, Mac OS X displays it just like any other hard drive volume — Figure 2-4 illustrates my 30GB FireWire drive in action.

Figure 2-4:
See your external hard drives.

Internal drives

Your other alternative is to upgrade your internal drive, which can be a hassle. Like a memory upgrade, adding or swapping an internal drive involves opening your Mac's case. In fact, it's a somewhat more complex procedure than adding memory.

I usually recommend that folks add a second drive rather than swap out their existing drive — you'll avoid the hassle of backing up and restoring your system on a new drive or (even worse) reinstalling Mac OS X and *then* reinstalling all the applications that you use. (Swapping a hard drive should be the definition of the word *hassle*.) Instead, add a second drive and leave your current hard drive as-is.

However, here are a number of very important reasons why many Mac owners choose updating internal drives, even with the hassle of swapping:

+ **They're cheaper.** You'll spend significantly less on an internal drive because it doesn't need the case and additional electronics required by an external drive.

+ **They're faster.** Even a FireWire or USB 2.0 drive isn't as fast as an internal drive.

+ **They take up less space in your work area.** An internal drive eliminates the space taken by an external drive, which can range anywhere from the size of a paperback to the size of a hardback book.

After you establish that you are in fact ready for more space — and you've decided whether you want to add an internal drive, an external drive, or (if you enjoy punishment) upgrade your existing internal drive — you're ready to consider how big a drive you need.

Determining How Much Space You Need

Your next step is to decide just how much hard drive space is enough — I suppose that if your last name is Gates and you live in Redmond, you can probably pick just about any drive on the market. However, I have a family, a mortgage, and a car payment; therefore, I must be a little more selective.

I have two hard-and-fast rules that I follow when I'm determining the capacity of a new drive:

+ If you're buying a replacement for your existing drive, shop for a drive with at least twice the capacity of the existing drive (if possible).

+ If you're buying an external USB or FireWire drive, shop for a drive with at least half the capacity of your existing internal drive (if possible).

Those rules seem to work pretty doggone well in most circumstances with these two exceptions: gamers and desktop video gurus. These folks need to shoehorn as much space as they possibly can into their systems. If you're a hardcore gamer or if you work primarily with digital video, you need a wheelbarrow's worth of hard drive capacity. Trust me, buy as big a hard drive as you can afford.

Shopping for a Hard Drive

Ready to brave the local Wireless Shed superstore (or perhaps its Web site)? Here's a list of guidelines to keep handy while you're shopping for a new internal or external hard drive:

✦ **Faster is indeed better.** You'll pay more for a 7,200 revolutions per minute (rpm) drive than a slower 5,400 rpm drive, but the extra cash is worth it. Faster drives can transfer more data to your Mac in less time.

✦ **Avoid used or refurbished drives.** Hard drives are one of the few components in your computer that still have a large number of moving parts — therefore, buying a used drive isn't a good idea unless it's priced very low.

Because the prices on new hard drives are constantly dropping, make sure that you check on the price for a new, faster drive of the same capacity before you buy that bargain used drive.

✦ **Pick FireWire over USB 1.x every time.** A USB 1.x external hard drive is simply a joke when it comes to performance. Because most Macs with USB ports also have FireWire ports, make very sure that you buy a FireWire drive! (If your Mac has USB 2.0 ports, then you can buy a USB 2.0 drive without being embarrassed.)

✦ **Watch the size of the drive when buying internal drives.** Most Enhanced Integrated Drive Electronics (EIDE) drives are standard half-height 3.5-inch units, but check to make sure that you're not investing in a laptop drive — unless, of course, you're upgrading a laptop.

✦ **Do I need SCSI?** In most cases, the answer is *no* — Macs built within the last two or three years all use EIDE drives. However, older Macs do use Small Computer System Interface (SCSI) hardware, so make sure you check before you buy. (SCSI and EIDE are the two different types of internal hard drive interfaces — a fancy word for *connection* — used on Macs that can run Mac OS X.) Again, you can use the Apple System Profiler to determine what type of drives you have — click the Devices and Volumes tab and then display the information for your hard drive, as shown in Figure 2-5.

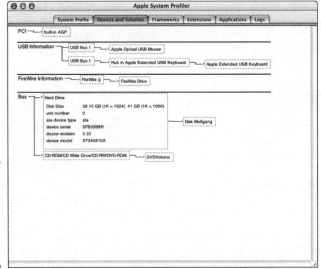

Figure 2-5:
Check
which type
of hard drive
you have
installed.

Installing Your New Stuff

After you get your memory modules or hard drive, pick from one of two methods of installing them: easy and hard. Guess which method will cost you money?

The easy way

Your Apple dealer can perform either type of hardware installation for you — you can rest easy knowing that the job will be done right, but money will definitely change hands.

Personally, I always recommend that owners of iBooks and Titanium PowerBook laptops allow their dealers to install memory upgrades and hard drives — these laptops are much more complex than a desktop, and they're much easier to damage.

The hard way

If you're familiar with the inside of your Macintosh, you can install your own upgrade and save that cash. A memory upgrade is one of the simpler chores to perform, but that doesn't mean that everyone feels comfortable taking the cover off and jumping inside a computer; hard drives are a tad more complex.

If you have a knowledgeable friend or family member who can help you install your hardware, buy 'em the proverbial Nice Steak Dinner and enlist him in your cause. Even if you still do the work yourself, it's always better to have a second pair of experienced eyes watching, especially if you're a little nervous.

Because the installation procedures for both memory modules and hard drives are different for every model of Mac — heck, even removing the cover on each model of Macintosh involves a different challenge — I can't provide you with any step-by-step procedures in this chapter. Many online stores include installation instructions with their hardware. Other sources for installation instructions include the Apple Web site (www.apple.com) or your Apple dealer. You can use Sherlock 3 (more about this in Book I, Chapter 4) to scan the Internet for installation information for your particular model. However, here are guidelines to follow during the installation:

✦ **Watch out for static electricity.** When opening your Macintosh and handling hardware, make certain that you've touched a metal surface beforehand to discharge any static electricity on your body. (You can also buy a static wrist strap that you can wear while working within the bowels of your Mac.)

✦ **Check the notches on memory modules.** Most types of memory modules have notches cut into the connector — these notches make sure that you can install the module only one way, so make certain that they align properly with the slot.

✦ **Make sure that you're using the right memory slot.** As I mention earlier in this chapter, most Macs have multiple memory slots, so check the label on the circuit board to make sure that you're adding the memory to the correct slot. (Naturally, this won't be a problem if you're installing a module into an unoccupied slot.)

✦ **Take good care of older hardware.** If you replace an existing memory module or hard drive with a new one, put the old hardware in the left-over anti-static bag from your new hardware and immediately start thinking of how you'll word your eBay auction . . . *Used 128MB Memory Module for 333MHz iMac*, for example.

✦ **Check your hard drive jumper settings.** If your Mac uses EIDE hard drives, you must set the Master and Slave jumpers correctly on the back (or underside) of the new drive. (This indicates to your Mac which drive is the primary drive and which is the secondary drive. I don't know how engineers got into the whole Master/Slave thing . . . they're normally not quite so exotic when naming things.)

If you're adding a second drive to a G3 or G4 tower, you'll probably have to change the jumper settings on the original drive as well. (If you're replacing the existing drive, you're in luck; simply duplicate the jumper settings from the old drive and use them on the new drive.) A *jumper* is simply a tiny metal-and-plastic connector that is used to change the configuration on a hard drive. Because the configuration settings are different for each hard drive model, check the drive's documentation for the correct jumper position.

✦ **Leave the cover off while testing.** After you install the upgrade, leave the cover off your Mac while you boot the computer and test to see how well you did. That way, if you have to replace the original hardware for some reason, you won't have to remove the cover a second time.

To determine whether a memory upgrade was successful, you can again turn to the Apple System Profiler. Open the Profiler again and compare the memory overview specifications with the original list that you made earlier. If the total amount of memory has increased and the memory module is recognized, then you've done your job well — if not, switch off the Mac and check the module to make sure it's completely seated in the slot.

Chapter 3: Port-o-rama: Using USB and FireWire

In This Chapter

✔ Using FireWire under Mac OS X

✔ Using USB under Mac OS X

✔ Adding and updating drivers

✔ Troubleshooting FireWire and USB connections

✔ Adding a USB or FireWire hub

Apple's list of successes continues to grow over the years — hardware, applications, and (of course) Mac OS X — but the FireWire standard for connecting computers to all sorts of different devices is in a class by itself. That's because FireWire has been universally accepted all over the world as the port of choice for all sorts of digital devices that need a high-speed connection. Even Windows owners have grudgingly admitted that FireWire just plain rocks. Ya gotta love it.

In this chapter, I discuss the importance of FireWire to the digital hub discussed in Book III, and I compare it with both version 1.1 and version 2.0 of Intel's USB connection technology. I also talk troubleshooting and expansion using a hub.

Appreciating the Advantage of a FireWire Connection

So what's so special about FireWire, anyway? Why does Apple stuff at least two FireWire ports in virtually all its current Macintosh models? Heck, even the iPod (Apple's MP3 player, which you can read more about in Book III, Chapter 2) uses FireWire! (Its *official* name is IEEE-1394, but even the Cupertino crew don't call it that — at least very often.)

First things first. As countless racing fans will tell you, it's all about the *speed,* my friend. FireWire delivers a blazing fast 400 Mbps (megabits per second), which is fast enough for all sorts of peripherals to communicate with your Macintosh. The following list includes a number of hardware toys that are well known for transferring prodigious file sizes:

✦ Digital video (DV) camcorders

✦ High-resolution digital cameras

✦ Scanners

✦ External hard drives and CD/DVD recorders

✦ Networking between computers

For example, consider the sheer size of a typical digital video clip captured by one of today's DV camcorders. DV buffs commonly transfer several hundred megabytes of footage to their computers at one time. Check out the relative speeds of the different types of ports in Table 3-1, and you'll see a big attraction of FireWire.

Table 3-1	Transfer Speeds for Ports through the Ages	
Port	*Appeared on Personal Computer*	*Transfer Speed (in Megabits)*
PC Serial	1981	Less than 1 Mbps
PC Parallel	1981	1 Mbps
USB (version 1.1)	1996	12 Mbps
FireWire (version A)	1996	400 Mbps
USB (version 2.0)	2001	480 Mbps
FireWire (version B)	2002	800 Mbps

Ouch! Not too hard to figure that one out. Here are three other important benefits to FireWire:

✦ **Control over Connection:** This is a 10-cent term that engineers use, meaning that you can control whatever gadget that you've connected using FireWire from your computer. This is pretty neat when you think about it — for example, you can control your DV camcorder from the comfort of your computer keyboard, just as if you were pressing the buttons on the camcorder.

✦ **Plug-and-play:** You don't have to reboot your Mac or restart Mac OS X every time you plug (or unplug) a FireWire device. Instead, the FireWire peripheral is automatically recognized (as long as the operating system has the correct driver) and ready to transfer.

✦ **Power through the port:** FireWire can provide power to a device through the same wire — typically, there's enough power available for an external drive or recorder — so you don't need an external AC power cord. (Apologies to owners of DV camcorders, but those things eat power like a pig eats slop.)

However, FireWire isn't finished evolving yet — the new, cleverly named IEEE-1394 B (called *FireWire 2* by anyone with any sense) is designed to deliver a whopping 800 Mbps. That, dear reader, oughta be fast enough for both you *and* your loved ones. These ports aren't in general circulation yet, but when they are, you'll have to wear racing goggles to use 'em. (Oh, and as you would expect from Apple, the new ports will be backwards-compatible with older FireWire hardware.)

Understanding USB and the Tale of Two Point Oh

The other resident port on today's Apple computers is the ubiquitous USB, which is short for *Universal Serial Bus*. (By the way, ubiquitous means *ever-present* or *universal,* which I quickly looked up using Sherlock 3 — read all about this super sleuth in Book I, Chapter 4.) Although version 1.1 of the USB standard is nowhere near as fast as FireWire, USB has taken the world by storm. It's used for everything from mice to keyboards, speakers, digital cameras, and even external drives and CD recorders. (A friend of mine never misses the chance to point out that USB — which was originally developed by Intel — was given its first widespread implementation on the original iMac. You're welcome, Intel.)

Book VI Chapter 3

Port-o-rama: Using USB and FireWire

Unfortunately, those last two are somewhat problematical: Technically, you *can* add an external hard drive, but don't expect response times anywhere near what you'd enjoy with an internal hard drive. Ditto for a CD recorder — 4x is about the limit for the recording speed with a USB 1.1 connection. (Don't even think about recording DVDs over a USB connection.) Now, compare this performance with that of similar equipment using a FireWire connection, which provides nearly the speed of an internal hard drive and CD and DVD recording at the fastest pace possible.

Like FireWire, USB connections are plug-and-play and provide power over the connection — a USB port also offers a more limited version of Control over Connection as well, making it a good choice for virtually all digital cameras.

The average two- or three-megapixel digital camera creates a JPEG image that's about 200–300K, so USB is the connection of choice for all but the five- and six-megapixel camera models. Why is it the connection of choice, even thought it's slower than FireWire? Most PCs still don't come standard with FireWire ports, and transferring a 300K file doesn't take long over USB. (On the other hand, try transferring a 20MB file, and FireWire suddenly makes a lot of sense.)

Not to be outdone, a new USB 2.0 specification has arrived that delivers even better performance than the original FireWire standard — USB 2.0 can transfer 480 Mbps. These ports are backwards-compatible — meaning they work with the original USB 1.x ports as well — but don't look for Apple to jump through any hoops to support the new, faster, even-fresher-smelling USB standard. In fact, none of the Mac models in Apple's current stable have USB 2.0 ports. Mac OS X, however, does support USB 2.0 with the proper drivers, which should be supplied by the manufacturer.

If you have an expandable tower G3 or G4 machine, you can use an empty PCI slot to add USB 2.0 ports to your Mac. For example, Orange Micro sells the OrangeUSB 2.0 Hi-Speed PCI card for a mere $50 (www.orangemicro.com); if you have a PowerBook, you can add a USB 2.0 port using a PC Card.

Hey, You Need a Hub!

Suppose that you've embraced FireWire and USB and you now have two FireWire drives hanging off the rear end of your Mac — and suddenly you buy an iPod. (Or you get another FireWire device that's as much fun as an iPod, if that's actually possible.) Now you're faced with too many devices for too few ports. You *could* eject a drive and unhook it each time that you wanted to connect your iPod, but there *must* be a more elegant way to connect. Help!

Enter the hub. Both the FireWire and USB specifications allow you to connect a device called a *hub,* which is really nothing more than a glorified splitter adapter that provides you with additional ports. Note that this device has nothing — repeat, *absolutely nothing* — to do with the network hubs that I discuss in Book V. With a FireWire or USB hub at work, you do lose a port; however, most hubs multiply that port into four or eight ports. Again, all this is transparent, and you don't need to hide anything up your sleeve — adding a hub is just as plug-and-play easy as adding a regular FireWire/USB device.

I should also mention that both USB and FireWire support *daisy-chaining* — a word that stretches all the way back to the days of the Atari and Commodore computers, when devices had extra ports in the back so that additional stuff could be plugged in. (Today's parallel-port Zip drives have similar ports.) However, not every USB or FireWire drive has a daisy-chain port (also called a *passthru* port). With daisy-chaining, you can theoretically add 63 FireWire devices to your Mac, and a whopping 127 USB devices — talk about impress 'em at your next Mac user group meeting!

Uh, It's Just Sitting There

Man, I *hate* it when FireWire and USB devices act like boat anchors. FireWire and USB peripherals are so doggone simple that when something goes wrong, it really aggravates you. Fortunately, I've been down those roads many a time before, so in this section, I'll unleash my experience. (That sounds a little frightening, but it's a *good* thing.)

Common FireWire and USB headaches

Because FireWire and USB are so alike in so many ways, I can handle possible troubleshooting solutions for both types of hardware at once:

✦ **Problem:** Every time I turn off or unplug my external peripheral, Mac OS X gets irritated and displays a nasty message saying that I haven't properly disconnected the device.

Solution: This happens because you haven't *ejected* the peripheral — I know that sounds a little strange for a device like an external hard drive or a digital camera, but it's essentially the same reasoning as ejecting a CD or DVD disc from your Desktop. When you click your USB or FireWire device and hold the mouse button down, you'll see that the Trash icon turns into an Eject icon; drag the device icon to the Eject icon and drop it, and the external device disappears from your Desktop. (You can also click on the device icon to select it and press ⌘+E.) At that point, you're safe to turn it off or unplug the FireWire/USB cable.

✦ **Problem:** The device doesn't show a power light.

Solution: Check to make sure that the power cable is connected — unless, of course, you've got a device that's powered through the connection itself. This can sometimes pose its own share of problems, however, when using USB devices. Not all USB ports provide power because some are designed only for connecting mice, keyboards, and joysticks.

To check whether an unpowered USB port is your problem, connect the device to a USB port on the back of your Mac, or connect it to a hub or another computer. If the device works when it's connected to another port, you've found the culprit.

✦ **Problem:** The device shows a power light but just doesn't work.

Solution: This can be because of problems with your cable or your hub. To check, borrow a friend's cables and test to see whether the device works. If you're testing the hub, try connecting the device directly to your Mac using the same cable to see whether it works without the hub.

If you're attempting to connect a device through another USB or FireWire device, try connecting it directly to see whether it works. If so, the middleman device either needs to be switched on to pass the data through or it doesn't support daisy-chaining at all — in which case, you'll have to connect both devices directly to your Macintosh.

Book VI
Chapter 3

Port-o-rama: Using
USB and FireWire

✦ **Problem:** Mac OS X reports that I have a missing driver.

Solution: Check the manufacturer's Web site and download a new copy of the USB or FireWire drivers for your device because they've been corrupted, overwritten, or erased entirely. Since Mac OS X loads the driver for a USB or FireWire device when it's connected, sometimes just unplugging and reconnecting a peripheral will do the trick.

Check those drivers

Speaking of drivers . . . old and worn-out drivers are a sore spot with me. *Drivers* are simply programs that tell Mac OS X how to communicate with your external device. Each new version of Mac OS X contains updated drivers, but make certain that you check for new updates on a regular basis. That means using both the Software Update feature in Mac OS X (which I cover in Chapter 3 of Book II) *and* going to the Web sites provided by your USB and FireWire hardware manufacturers.

Chapter 4: I'm Okay, You're a Printer

In This Chapter

✔ Using the Print Center

✔ Adding a non-USB printer

✔ Managing print jobs

✔ Setting up a shared printer

*O*f all the improvements made in Mac OS X over Mac OS 9, one of the most important is the simplified printing process — no Chooser, no strange printer ports . . . just a heap of Universal Serial Bus (USB) and network printing goodness. As I discuss in Book I, if your USB printer is recognized by Mac OS X, you can print within seconds of plugging it in, with no muss or fuss. A USB printer is connected physically to your Mac, but you send print jobs over the network to a network printer. (And yes, if that network printer is in another room, you *do* have to get up out of your comfortable chair to retrieve your printed document . . . not even Mac OS X is *that* powerful.)

But what if you want to print to an AppleTalk printer or perhaps send documents to a printer over Transmission Control Protocol/ Internet Protocol (TCP/IP)? (For more on AppleTalk, read Chapter 3 of Book V.) To take care of tasks like that, you need to dig a little further — and I do so in this chapter. You'll also discover how to use the features of the Print Center and how to juggle print jobs like a circus performer.

Meet the Print Center

The Print Center runs automatically whenever it's needed by Mac OS X — for example, when you print a document — but you can also run it at any time from the Utilities folder inside your Applications folder. Although it doesn't look like much (as shown in Figure 4-1), power lurks underneath.

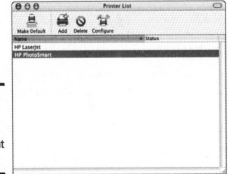

Figure 4-1:
The rather
plain-
looking Print
Center.

If you find the Print Center hard to reach and you need to manually launch it often, add it to the Dock — that way, you can launch it with a single click.

Toolbar Buttons

Along the top of the Print Center, you'll find four default toolbar icons. They are

✦ **Make Default:** If you have more than one printer listed in the Print Center, you can select which printer Mac OS X will use by default. Click the desired entry — in my case, it's the HP PhotoSmart — and click the Make Default icon. (You can also use the ⌘+D keyboard shortcut.) The entry for the default printer appears in bold type.

When you add a new printer to the list, it automatically becomes the default printer. (Some folks like this feature; others would banish the person responsible to Siberia for a decade.)

✦ **Add:** In Chapter 3 of Book I, you can read how to add a typical USB printer (both with and without an installed driver). In the next section, I show you how to add a non-USB printer.

If your USB printer is already natively supported within Mac OS X, you might not need to go through the trouble of clicking the Add icon on the toolbar. Mac OS X can add a new USB printer automatically, so don't be surprised if your Mac swoops in and does it for you as soon as you plug in a new printer. Also, the manufacturer's installation program for your printer might add the printer for you in a behind-the-scenes way, even if Mac OS X lies dormant.

✦ **Delete:** First click a printer in the list to select it and then click this icon to remove a printer from your list of installed printers. This isn't something you're likely to do often, but if a printer is no longer available, it helps keep your list nice and tidy.

✦ **Configure:** A click on this icon displays the model-specific configuration settings and features available for the specific printer that's selected in the list. Of course, these settings vary for every printer produced by the hand of Man — they're actually determined by the manufacturer's printer driver — but they usually include actions such as cleaning and alignment, and settings such as print quality. Figure 4-2 illustrates some of the configuration settings for my HP printer, which appear in their own dialog after you click the Configure icon.

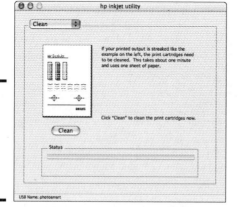

Figure 4-2:
Most printers have their own configuration dialog.

Other features of the Print Center include

✦ **Preferences:** Click the Print Center menu and choose Preferences to display the Print Center Preferences dialog that you see in Figure 4-3. Make choices from the Default Paper Size drop-down list for use with all your printers. Enable the Show Printers Connected to Other Computers check box to display *remote* printers (those that aren't physically connected to your Mac but shared by other computers on the network) here.

Figure 4-3:
Choose global preferences for the Print Center.

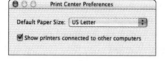

✦ **Show Info:** From the Print Center menu, click Printers and then choose the Show Info menu item (or press the ⌘+I keyboard shortcut) to display information on the selected printer. Figure 4-4 illustrates choosing Name & Location from the lone drop-down list in this dialog; you can change the printer name in this list, but you have other options, too. Many Mac printers use the PostScript standard printing language; if your printer uses PostScript, click the drop-down list box to display the PPD (Postscript Printer Description) data files for the printer (the PPD list will be empty if the printer doesn't use PostScript) as well as any installable options, such as a paper feed or scanning upgrade.

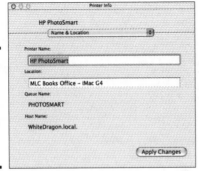

Figure 4-4:
Display printer information by using the Show Info command.

✦ **Show Jobs:** Choosing this from the Print Center Printers menu displays the job list for the selected printer — more on this later in the upcoming section "Managing Your Printing Jobs."

Adding a Funky Printer

"And what," you might ask, "is a *funky* printer?" Well, you have a number of possibilities, but they all add up to a non-USB connection:

✦ **An AppleTalk printer:** If you're sharing a printer on another Mac using AppleTalk, you can print to that device. For more on AppleTalk, read Chapter 3 of Book V.

✦ **IP printing:** Sending a job to an Internet Protocol (IP) printer actually shoots the document across a network or Internet connection using a target IP address or domain name. Generally, it's best to have a static (unchanging) IP address for a network printer; if the IP address changes often, for example, you'd have to reconfigure your connection to your IP printer each time it changed.

✦ **Directory Services:** This connection uses Rendezvous or Mac OS X Directory Services to share a printer. Rendezvous is largely an automatic deal. Any shared printers simply show up in the Rendezvous connection list, but if your network uses Directory Services, your network system administrator will have to set up *mappings* (essentially configurations that point the way to a shared printer). Many network system administrators favor Directory Services, which provide a much higher level of security and make it easy to limit access to a printer by user ID or location.

✦ **Application printer drivers:** Some printers aren't actually physical devices at all. For example, you can print directly to a fax program such as FaxSTF, which then dials, connects, and sends the document to a fax machine.

Although you can install Adobe Acrobat under Mac OS X, the operating system provides built-in support for printing documents in Adobe's PDF format (which can then be viewed and printed on any other computer with the Acrobat Reader, or added to your Web site for downloading). In fact, you don't even have to install a PDF print driver or display Print Center! To print a document in PDF format, click the Save as PDF button in the application's Print dialog, navigate to the desired folder and enter a file name, and then click Save.

No matter which type of funky printer you add, it will need a driver installed in the Printers folder, which resides inside your Library folder. (A *driver* is a software program provided by the printer manufacturer that tells Mac OS X how to communicate with your printer.) Also, if the printer is PostScript compatible, it will need a PPD file installed in your PPD folder, which also appears in the Printers folder. Luckily, Mac OS X comes complete with a long list of drivers and PPD files already installed and available — bravo, Apple dudes and dudettes!

To add a funky printer, follow these steps:

1. **Launch the manufacturer's installation application, which should copy the driver and PPD files for you.**

If you have to do things the hard way, manually copy the driver file into the Library/Printers folder and then copy the PPD file (if required) into the Library/Printers/PPD folder.

2. **If you're adding a physical printer — rather than an application printer driver — verify that the printer is turned on and accessible.**

If you're printing to a shared printer connected to another Mac, that computer has to be on. Luckily, most network printers remain on all the time.

3. **Launch Print Center and then click the Add icon on the toolbar to display the Printer List sheet that you see in Figure 4-5.**

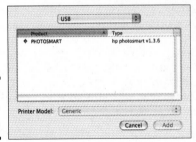

Figure 4-5:
Add a new
printer here.

4. **Click the drop-down list at the top of the sheet and choose AppleTalk, Directory Services, IP Printing, or the application name.**

   • **AppleTalk:** If you choose AppleTalk, click the second drop-down list and choose the correct AppleTalk Zone. After a scan of the specified Zone, Print Center displays the list of printers that it can access from that Zone. Click the desired printer and then click Add.

   • **Directory Services:** If you choose Directory Services, click the second drop-down list and choose the correct service — for example, Rendezvous or NetInfo Network. After a scan of the specified service, Print Center displays the list of printers that it can access. (Again, your access to specific printers might be limited by your network system administrator.) Click the desired printer and then click Add.

   • **IP Printing:** If you choose IP Printing, type the printer's IP address or Domain Name System (DNS) name, which should be provided by your network administrator or the person running the print server. You can use the default queue on the server — which I recommend — or disable the Use Default Queue on Server check box and type a valid queue name on the server.

   If you don't know a valid queue name, you're up a creek — hence, my recommendation to use the default queue.

   Finally, click the Printer Model drop-down list, choose the brand and model of the remote printer, and then click Add.

   • **Application name:** If you choose an application name, like FaxSTF, the application's driver will display its own settings. Set the configuration as necessary and then click Add.

Managing Your Printing Jobs

As I mention earlier in this chapter, you can also exercise some control over the documents — or, in technoid, *print jobs* — that you send to your printer. To display the jobs that are queued (in line) for your printer, click Printers on the Print Center menu and choose Show Jobs, or press ⌘+O. Figure 4-6 illustrates the Jobs dialog in idle mode.

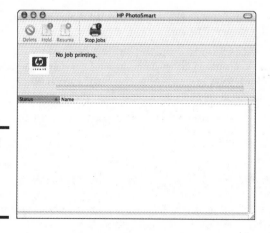

Figure 4-6:
Monitor
pending
print jobs
here.

The actions that you can perform from the Jobs dialog are

+ **Delete:** When you click a print job in the list and then click the Delete icon, the print job is removed from the queue. You might need to delete a print job if you discover a mistake in the document.

If the job is currently printing, several additional pages might be printed before the job is finally cancelled. In other words, information already sent to the printer might have to be printed before the cancel request can be processed.

+ **Hold:** Click the Hold toolbar icon to pause printing of the current print job. The status of the print job changes to Hold, as shown by the document named Sample Chapter in Figure 4-7.

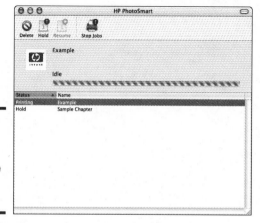

Figure 4-7:
One
document
prints while
another is
held tight.

✦ **Resume:** Click a print job in Hold status in the list and then click the Resume icon to resume printing.

✦ **Stop Jobs:** Click this icon to stop all printing. Note, however, that unlike using the Delete command, Stop Jobs doesn't *remove* any print jobs from the list. When jobs are stopped, the Stop Jobs icon morphs into Start Jobs — click it to restart all jobs in the queue list.

This is a good feature to use when your printer is about to run out of paper.

Sharing a Printer across That There Network

Before we leave the Island of Big X Printing, I'd like to show you how to share a printer with others on your local network.

If you decide to share your printers, don't be surprised if Mac OS X seems to slow down slightly from time to time. This is because of the processing time necessary for your Mac to store queued documents from other computers. The hard drive activity on your Mac is likely to significantly increase as well.

To share a printer, follow these steps:

1. **Click the System Preferences icon in the Dock.**

2. **Click the Sharing group to display the dialog that you see in Figure 4-8.**

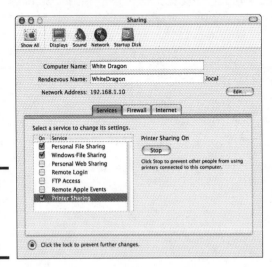

Figure 4-8: Sharing a printer is easy in Mac OS X.

3. **Enable the On checkbox next to Printer Sharing in the Services tab list.**

4. **Click the Firewall tab and make sure that the Printer Sharing check box is enabled.**

This will allow print jobs to pass through the firewall (see Figure 4-9).

Figure 4-9:
Allow
documents
to pass
through
your
firewall.

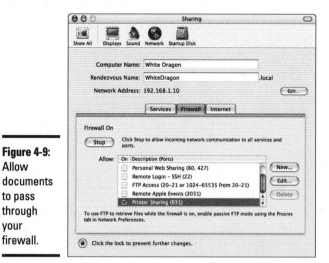

5. **Close System Preferences to save your changes.**

The printers in your Print Center list will be available to other computers within the same IP subnet — in other words, someone in your local network will be able to use your printers, but no one outside your network will have access.

If you haven't already assigned a printer a descriptive name, launch the Print Center, select the printer, and press ⌘+I. This launches the Show Info dialog for that particular printer. With Name & Location chosen from the drop-down list, simply enter the name of your printer in the Printer Name text field. You can also identify that printer's location in the Location text field. For example, in an office environment, I like to add the room number to a shared printer name (as well as the Location field).

Chapter 5: Programs that You've (Probably) Gotta Have

In This Chapter

✔ Using Microsoft Office v. X and AppleWorks

✔ Using disc repair applications

✔ Editing images

✔ Editing digital video

✔ Using Internet applications

✔ Burning discs with Toast

✔ Running Windows with Virtual PC

✔ Adding third-party utilities

✔ Playing games with Mac OS X

*I*n Chapter 1 of this mini-book, I present you with an overview of the most popular hardware that you can add to your Mac — and where there's hardware, software can't be far behind. (Somebody famous said that — I think it was either Bill Gates or Dennis Miller. I consider both of them famous comedians.)

Anyway, Mac OS X comes with a full suite of software tools right out of the box. You get Internet connectivity, disk repair, basic image editing, digital video editing, and — depending on the price that you paid — even games and a complete set of productivity applications. However, if you're willing to pay for additional features and a manual (at least what passes for a manual in the manufacturer's opinion), you can make all these tasks easier and accomplish them in shorter time.

Read on for an overview to the most popular third-party software applications for Mac OS X: what everyone's using, how much they cost, and why they're (usually) better. But before you drop a wad of cash on a fancy new application, though, remember yet another of Mark's Maxims:

If a program you already have does everything you really need, you *don't* have to upgrade. Honest and truly.™

The Trundling Microsoft Mammoth

Yes, I know I've been poking fun at His Gateness for much of this book — you have to admit, he makes a pretty good target — but he did pull PC owners out of the character-based world of DOS, and I'll be the first to say that he does get things right from time to time.

For example, I've always been more impressed with Microsoft Office than I have been with Microsoft Windows. (At least Windows XP Professional is a step in the right direction, but it still has a long way to go to match Mac OS X.) Office has long been the productivity suite of choice in the Windows world, and it's also been a popular favorite in years past on the Macintosh side.

A lot of hard work was put into the latest version of Microsoft Office, and it shows. Office v. X was completely rewritten for Mac OS X, using the rules that Apple recommends for the Aqua user interface — as you can see in Figure 5-1, it looks as much like a native Mac OS X application as AppleWorks 6, Apple's competing office productivity suite.

However, like Mac OS X itself, Office v.X isn't just an attractive exterior. Consider some of the advantages of Office v.X:

✦ **Perfect document compatibility with the Windows version of Office:** You can both read and write documents with transparent ease, no matter which platform gets the file. Documents can be shared between platforms on the same network.

✦ **Mirrored commands:** Both the Windows XP and Mac OS X versions of Office share virtually identical menu items, dialogs, and settings, thus making Mac OS X instantly familiar to anyone who's used Office on a Windows PC.

✦ **Support for native Aqua features:** This includes transparent graphics within your documents, input and confirmation sheets, and palettes for formatting.

✦ **Tons of templates, samples, and support files:** Microsoft doesn't scrimp on ready-to-use documents and templates, as well as additional fonts, clip art, and Web samples.

✦ **Entourage:** Entourage (shown in Figure 5-2) is the Macintosh counterpart to Windows Outlook — it combines most of the same features that you'll find in the Apple Mail, iCal, and Address Book applications. (Read about Apple Mail in Book IV, Chapter 2; read about the Address Book in Book I, Chapter 5.) Use Entourage to participate in Internet newsgroups; it also includes a Mailing List Manager to help you keep track of the deluge of list messages that you receive every day.

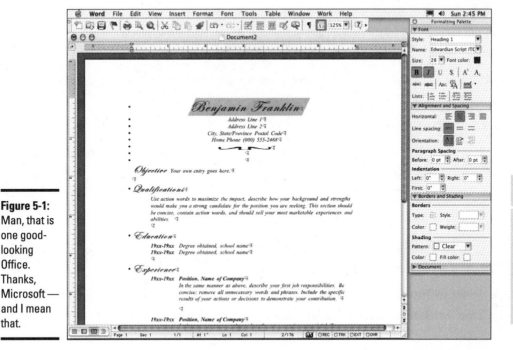

Figure 5-1:
Man, that is one good-looking Office. Thanks, Microsoft — and I mean that.

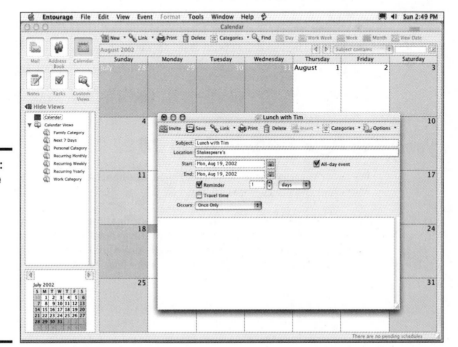

Figure 5-2:
Entourage makes it easy to track contacts, manage your calendar, and take care of e-mail.

What about AppleWorks?

If you're already using AppleWorks, you might have noticed that the Office applications provide roughly the same features. (The drawing and painting elements of AppleWorks are integrated into the Office v. X suite.) Therefore, you might wonder whether you should scrap AppleWorks.

Remember my maxim — if the AppleWorks suite that you're familiar with is doing the job, I recommend that you keep it. After all, AppleWorks is a powerful productivity suite on its own, capable of producing results that are easily as good as Office v. X. Also, Apple does provide conversion filters that can allow you to open and save Office documents, so you're not isolated from the Office crowd. If you're still using Mac OS 9 on one or more of your Macs, I should

also point out that Office v. X doesn't run under Mac OS 9 — but AppleWorks runs like clockwork on both Mac OS 9 and X.

On the other side of the coin, I *would* recommend that you buy Office if

✔ You prefer the Office menu design and features.

✔ You'd like to keep the same commands replicated in the same places as the Windows version of Office.

✔ You want to seamlessly share documents with co-workers using Windows Office on your network or through e-mail.

Besides Entourage, Office v. X includes three other applications:

✦ **Word:** The word processing application that rules the planet

✦ **Excel:** The leading spreadsheet application

✦ **PowerPoint:** A favorite presentation development application

The Office v. X suite costs a little over $400 at the time of this writing.

Your Mac OS X Toolbox: Drive 10

My favorite native Mac OS X disk repair application is Drive 10 from Micromat (www.micromat.com).

More than just about any other type of application, it's important for a disk maintenance program to be built "from the ground up" for Mac OS X. **Never** attempt to repair a disk in Classic mode, nor should you try to use an older repair utility that was written for use under Mac OS 9.

With Drive 10 (shown in Figure 5-3), you can thoroughly check a hard drive for both *physical* errors (such as faulty electronics or a bad sector on the disk surface) and *logical* errors (incorrect folder data and glitches in the file structure). The Disk Utility that's included with Mac OS X does a fine job of checking the latter, but it doesn't perform the physical testing — and Drive 10 does both.

I should note, however, that Drive 10 doesn't take care of viruses. Pick up a copy of Norton AntiVirus (www.norton.com) to protect yourself against viral attack.

Drive 10 also takes care of disk optimization, which is a feature that's been conspicuously absent from Mac OS X ever since the beginning. As I explain earlier in Book I, Chapter 6, defragmenting your disk will result in better performance and a faster system overall.

Version 1.1 of Drive 10, which will set you back about $70, comes on a self-booting CD-ROM so you can easily fix your startup volume by booting your system from the Drive 10 disc.

**Book VI
Chapter 5**

**Programs that
You've (Probably)
Gotta Have**

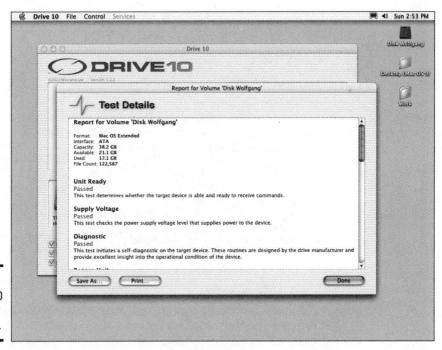

Figure 5-3:
Use Drive 10
to check for
drive errors.

Image Editing for the Masses

The only one true King of the Retouching Hill in Mac OS X, Adobe Photoshop, has been the digital-image editing favorite of Mac owners for many years now. Like Office v. X, Photoshop 7 has been reassembled for Mac OS X, and it also takes full advantage of the Aqua standard (see Figure 5-4).

You can find more three-pound Photoshop books on the shelf than politicians in trouble, so it's no surprise that I can't provide you with a sweeping list of its features in this section. However, here's a summary of what you can expect from Adobe's crown jewel:

✦ The most **sophisticated image editing** possible for a digital photograph — if you can accomplish an image-editing task in software, it's very likely that Photoshop can do it.

✦ **Image retouching tools** that help you rescue images with problems such as overexposure and color imbalance. (You can also use tools like the new Healing brush to erase imperfections in the photograph's subject.)

✦ Photoshop has been a standard for **plug-in functionality** since it first appeared — if you need features that aren't in the application out of the box, you can add them through third-party plug-ins.

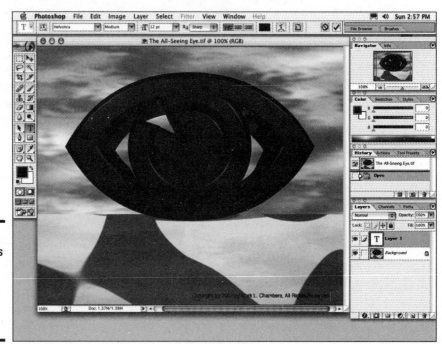

Figure 5-4: Photoshop's performance will put an Indy race car to shame.

✦ Prepare images for use **on the Web**.

✦ **Combine and splice parts** of different images to produce a new work of art.

✦ **Distort and liquefy** an image to produce a new look.

✦ **Painting tools** that you can use to simulate different types of inks, paints, and brushes on different types of media.

Although Photoshop is a hefty $600 for the full package, Adobe has also created a kid brother, Photoshop Elements 2.0, that sells for a mere $85. Designed for the novice or intermediate level photographer, Elements has most of the functionality of the full package that you're likely to need. Elements also provides a number of very helpful wizards to help automate the most common image editing tasks, as well as one of the most comprehensive Help systems that I've ever used.

The Morass of Digital Video

Two types of applications make up the DV market: *digital video editing* (where you create a movie) and *DVD mastering* (where you take that movie and create a DVD movie disc). You can find a number of great applications on the market in both of these categories, all at different price points and different levels of complexity. They include

✦ **iMovie:** I cover this easy-to-use video editing iApp in Chapter 4 of Book III. A good choice for any novice, it's usually bundled for free with today's new Mac models. You might also receive it with Mac OS X.

✦ **iDVD:** This is the DVD mastering counterpart to iMovie. Although it's a snap to use, it doesn't offer a lot of advanced features. (Chapter 5 of Book III explains iDVD in detail.) Again, you'll receive it free with your Mac if you bought a model with a SuperDrive.

✦ **Premiere 6.5:** This is the latest update to the DV editing application from Adobe that's been a standard on both the Mac and PC. Premiere is much more complex than iMovie and offers far more features and control over the finished footage, but learning it is a bear compared with iMovie. Premiere sells for around $600.

✦ **DVD Studio Pro:** Apple's entry into the ranks of DVD mastering (see Figure 5-5) can produce a commercial-quality DVD movie disc, but don't expect any hand-holding or assistants with this application. This is a serious tool for professionals, and it'll set you back $1,000. With DVD Studio Pro, you can add interactive, animated menus, subtitles, multiple audio tracks, and Web interactivity to your DVD projects.

Figure 5-5:
DVD Studio
Pro is a
heavy-duty
tool for
professional
DVD
mastering.

✦ **Final Cut Pro:** At $1,000, you'd assume Final Cut Pro to be the best DV editing package on the market for Mac OS X . . . and you won't get any argument from me. It offers real-time playback — no waiting for rendering, like you have to within iMovie and Premiere — and *OfflineRT,* an offline hard drive storage format that lets you park over 40 minutes of digital video in a single gigabyte of hard drive space. Sweet.

Yes, It's Really Called "Toast"

Time to turn your attention to a subject near and dear to my heart: recording data CDs, audio CDs, and DVDs on the Macintosh (which I cover in detail in another of my *For Dummies* books, *CD and DVD Recording For Dummies*). Of course, Mac OS X can burn basic data CDs without any add-on software, but what if you need an exotic format, like CD Extra? Or perhaps you need a self-booting disc, or an ISO 9660 disc that you can share with your Windows and UNIX friends?

There's one clear choice: When you're ready to seriously burn, you're ready for Roxio Toast, the CD and DVD recording choice for millions of Mac owners. (No snickering about the name, please.) Figure 5-6 illustrates this powerhouse of an application, which is an elegant design that's both simple to use and perfectly Aqua. Files, folders, and digital audio tracks that you want to record are simply dropped into the application window.

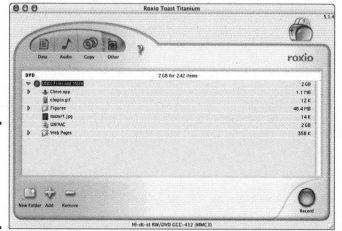

Figure 5-6:
Toast: the classic Mac CD and DVD recording application.

As for exotic formats, here's a list of what types of discs that you can record with Toast:

✦ Standard data CDs and DVDs

✦ Standard audio CDs

✦ Video CDs

✦ MP3 discs (which store MP3 audio tracks)

✦ Discs recorded from an image file

✦ Mac volumes

✦ Hybrid PC/Mac discs

✦ ISO 9660 discs

✦ Multisession discs

✦ CD Extra discs

Toast works with both internal and external CD and DVD recorders, taking advantage of the latest features on today's drives — in particular, *burn-proof* recording, which can practically eliminate recording errors. You can also copy existing discs, using one or multiple drives.

Toast is quite affordable at $90 — you can buy it directly from the Roxio online store at www.roxio.com.

If You Positively Have to Run Windows . . .

Here's where Mac power-users usually start grinning from ear to ear like Santa's elves on the day after Christmas, because — get this — the great Unwashed Windows Horde actually thinks that you *can't* run Windows XP on a Macintosh! Can you believe that? Obviously, they haven't heard of Virtual PC from Connectix (`www.connectix.com`), which without a doubt is one of the coolest applications ever written for the Mac.

No, my friend, your eyes are not deceiving you — you are indeed looking at Windows running on my iMac G4 in Figure 5-7. Virtual PC 5 provides a near-perfect PC environment for any version of Windows from 95 all the way up to XP; literally, Windows has *no* idea that it's not running on a typical piece of PC iron.

Figure 5-7: Take *that*, Bill! I get to play in your pool.

Virtual PC simulates everything necessary for you to get the full functionality out of Windows. For example, this jewel automatically (and transparently) handles your Windows Internet connection, network tasks, and CD and DVD access. Heck, it even allows you to use your single-button mouse as a two-button PC mouse (by holding down the Control key as you click). You can run full-screen or run Windows in a window. (Pun joyfully intended.)

If that weren't enough, you can also run multiple operating systems. So, if you need Linux or Windows 2000 along with your XP system, no problem — all it takes is the install disc for those operating systems and the hard drive space to hold 'em. And yes, it does run under both Mac OS 9 and Mac OS X. Just plain *sassy*.

Naturally, performance is an issue — and, to be honest, Virtual PC isn't for the PC gamer, even with the newest Macs and their super-duper GeForce and Radeon video cards. Because today's PC games push an actual PC to the limit, they just run too sluggishly on a Mac emulating a PC — they do run, just too slowly. (Also, virtually all of today's blockbuster PC games are also being ported to Mac OS X, so why not just run the Mac version?)

However, when it comes to just about any other type of application, Virtual PC running on a late-model G4 Mac can deliver performance equal to a Pentium III. The more memory that your Mac has, the more you can give your virtual PC, so it also pays to have 512MB or more of RAM. (And naturally, a dual-processor Mac runs Virtual PC much faster.) I use Virtual PC with niche Windows programs that have never appeared on the Mac as well as native Mac versions of all other applications. Again, you don't need to use Mac to run the Windows version of Photoshop because Photoshop 7 is also available for the Mac.

**Book VI
Chapter 5**

**Programs that
You've (Probably)
Gotta Have**

If you're tired of the undeserved taunts from your clueless Windows friends, run — don't walk — to your browser and order a copy of Virtual PC 5 (www.connectix.com). The program comes prepackaged with fully licensed copies of several different flavors of Windows and Linux. For example, the version with XP Home costs around $200 — or you can buy the DOS version and supply your own copy of Windows for about $90.

All Hail FileMaker Pro

If databases are the name of your game, you've already been using FileMaker Pro for years (on both Mac and Windows, more than likely). For the uninitiated, FileMaker Pro is the premier database creation, editing, and maintenance application for Mac OS X. It comes with dozens of ready-made database templates for business, home, and education use, or you can construct your own database in surprisingly short order.

Right out of the box, FileMaker Pro 6 (as shown in Figure 5-8) can create

✦ **Business** databases and forms for inventory, personnel, purchase orders, and product catalogs

✦ **Home** databases for budgeting, recipes, music CDs, DVD movies, family medical records, and event planning

✦ **Education** databases for student records, expense reports, field trip planning, book and multimedia libraries, and class scheduling

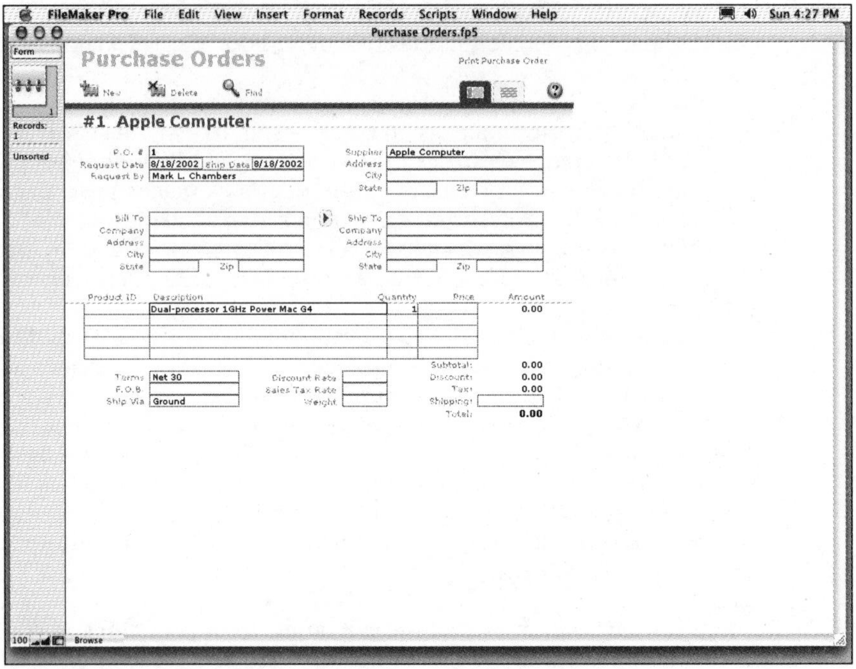

Figure 5-8:
All Hail
FileMaker
Pro 6!

FileMaker Pro 6 can add images and multimedia to your database, and you can quickly and easily publish your databases on your Web site by using one of the built-in theme designs. (In fact, visitors to your Web site can update your database online, if you like.) FileMaker Pro 6 can also allow multiple users to share data across your network, no matter whether they're running the Mac or Windows version.

At $299, FileMaker Pro 6 is one of the least expensive — and most powerful — applications that you can buy.

Utilities that Rock

The next stop on this Cavalcade of Software is an assortment of the absolute best you've-got-to-get-this utility applications. Sooner or later, you're likely going to buy (or register) these utilities because you'll use them every day.

StuffIt

In the Windows world, the Zip archive is the king of archiving formats — an *archive* contains one or more compressed files that you can uncompress whenever you need them. Folks store files in archives to save space on their hard drives; archiving is also a neat way to package an entire folder's worth of files in a single convenient file, which you can attach to an e-mail message or send via File Transfer Protocol (FTP).

On Planet Macintosh, the archiving format of choice is StuffIt. Manage your archives with StuffIt Deluxe, from Aladdin Systems, (www.aladdinsys.com), as shown in Figure 5-9. StuffIt Deluxe can both archive and unarchive .sit files (the common name for StuffIt archives), as well as Zip archives from your Windows friends. The application runs $80 at the Aladdin Systems online Web store.

QuicKeys X

QuicKeys X, from CE Software (www.cesoft.com), is another example of someone thinking properly. This time, the idea is to automate repetitive tasks by allowing Mac OS X to memorize what you do. Think of QuicKeys X as a system-wide macro playback application. Unlike AppleScript, however, QuicKeys X works within any application and can play back mouse movement and clicks/double-clicks. Figure 5-10 illustrates the QuicKeys application menu.

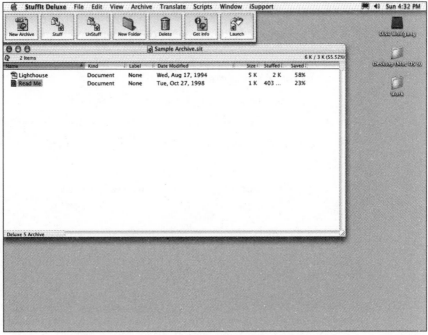

Figure 5-9:
Checking
the contents
of a StuffIt
archive.

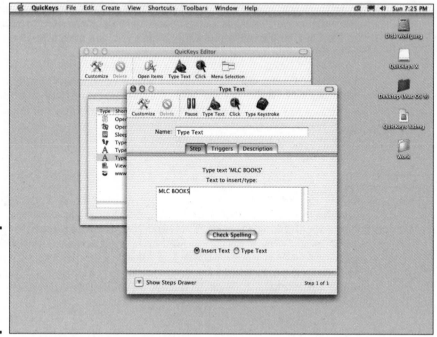

Figure 5-10:
Automate a
set of
keystrokes
with
QuicKeys X.

I've used QuicKeys X for a number of different tasks, including

✦ Typing a commonly used block of text (like my address) into applications that don't support macros

✦ Launching applications at specific times and dates

✦ Operating menus within programs to automate complex tasks

✦ Launching Classic or choosing a specific startup disk with a single key sequence

QuicKeys X sells for $79 on the CE Software Web site.

BBEdit

Although we all know and love Mac OS X as a graphical operating system, folks still need a powerful text editor for creating and modifying text files. For example, software developers and Webmasters still use text editors daily to write applications or apply a quick fix to the HyperText Markup Language (HTML) that makes up a Web page. (I use a text editor to make minor changes to my Web site, MLC Books Online, without firing up a horrendous Web design application. Talk about overkill!)

At first, you might think of TextEdit, the free application that ships with Mac OS X. It's not a bad editor, either, with features that are very similar to Notepad in the Windows environment. However, serious text and code editing requires a more powerful tool, and the text editor of choice for Mac owners is universally considered to be BBEdit, from Bare Bones Software (www.barebones.com). Figure 5-11 shows a document open within BBEdit.

**Book VI
Chapter 5**

**Programs that
You've (Probably)
Gotta Have**

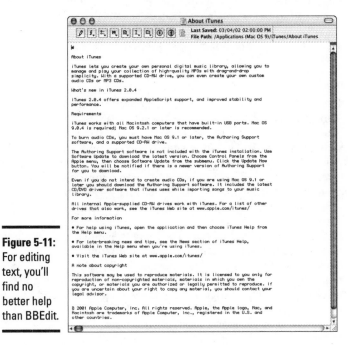

Figure 5-11: For editing text, you'll find no better help than BBEdit.

Bare Bones Software pulls no punches in describing BBEdit — its advertising proclaims, "It doesn't suck." Gotta give Bare Bones credit; this incredibly popular editor includes features like

✦ **Compatibility with both Mac OS X and Mac OS 9.**

✦ **Support for DOS/Windows, Mac, and UNIX text files.** (Yes, differences do exist between the platforms, even with a so-called *pure* text file.)

✦ **Works with text files up to 2GB in size.** (Try that with TextEdit. Hmm . . . on second thought, please don't.)

✦ **HTML tools for Web design.** These tools include syntax checking and browser preview.

✦ grep **pattern-based, multi-file search and replace.** In nonprogrammer/ non-UNIX English, that means a very sophisticated search-and-replace function that can span more than one text file.

✦ **Syntax coloring.** Use this to help you quickly locate commands and qualifiers in programming languages.

✦ **Built-in FTP transfer commands, integrated spell-checking, and highly configurable custom keymaps.**

You can even expand the functionality of BBEdit with plug-ins, many of which are free extensions written by programmers and developers specifically for languages like C/C++, Java/JavaScript, Perl, and Pascal.

BBEdit is available from the Bare Bones Software site for $119.

REALbasic

The final application I want to mention really isn't a utility as such — however, you can use it to write your *own* software, so I guess that it should qualify. As an ex-COBOL programmer, reluctant Visual Basic shareware developer, and recalcitrant dBASE coder, I can tell you that REALbasic, from REAL Software, is definitely the easiest visual drag-and-drop programming environment that I've ever used. If you want to develop your own productivity applications, Mac OS X utilities, or — dare I say it? — your own game, award-winning REALbasic is the way to go. (See Figure 5-12.)

Development in REALbasic is as simple as designing the application window by first simply adding controls, text, and multimedia wherever you like. Then just fill in the blanks, like setting variables and specifying what happens when the controls are triggered, by using a new implementation of the tried-and-true BASIC language. Of course, some programming knowledge is required but far less than you'd need with Visual Basic. And the results look as good as anything you can accomplish in those so-called *real* programming languages.

Check out these features:

✦ Cross-platform support so that you can write your program once and compile it for Mac OS 9, Mac OS X, *and* Windows. Insert Mark's Maxim here:

Code it once, release three versions with no extra work — this is a *very* good thing.™

✦ Support for all sorts of multimedia, including QuickTime.

✦ Ability to animate and rotate text and objects, or tap the 3-D power of QuickDraw3D and OpenGL graphics.

✦ Capability to allow printing, network, and Internet communications within your application.

✦ Automation of Microsoft Office applications and connection of your REALbasic application to business databases (like FileMaker Pro 6).

✦ Completely royalty-free applications, so you can give them away or release them as shareware.

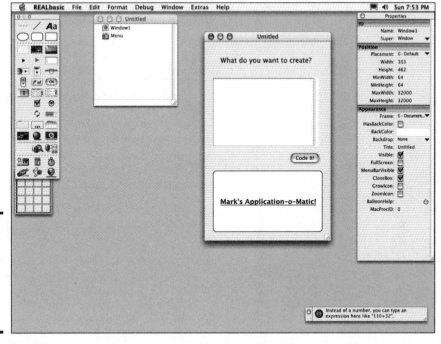

**Book VI
Chapter 5**

**Programs that
You've (Probably)
Gotta Have**

Figure 5-12:
Program-
ming for the
common
man with
REALbasic
4.5.

REALbasic has been such a popular development tool on the Macintosh that dozens of user-supported Web sites and mailing lists have sprung up, offering all sorts of REALbasic plug-ins, tutorials, and sample code for you to use in your own projects.

I would be seriously remiss if I didn't mention the bestselling *REALbasic For Dummies,* written by Erick Tejkowski (who also wrote several excellent chapters of this book) and published by Hungry Minds, Inc. I've practically worn out my copy, and it never leaves my desk. If you're looking for a complete tutorial on writing your own applications in REALbasic, I give *REALbasic For Dummies* my highest recommendation!

REALbasic 4.5 comes in two versions — the Standard Edition ($149.95) and the Professional Edition ($349.95). You can order either version from the REAL Software site at www.realsoftware.com.

At Least One Game

To be completely accurate, Mac OS X already comes with one game — a very good version of chess, which I cover in the next section — but the Macintosh has never been considered a true gaming platform by most computer owners. Until recently, many popular Windows games were never ported (or converted) for the Mac, and only the most expensive Mac models had the one important component that determines the quality of today's games: a first-rate 3-D video card.

However, within the last two years or so, all that has changed dramatically. *All* of today's Mac models feature muscle-car quality video cards using the nVIDIA GeForce or ATI Radeon chipsets so they can handle the most complex 3-D graphics with ease. Match that with the renewed popularity of the Macintosh as a home computer and the performance of the current crop of G4 processors, and — wham! Suddenly you've got the best game developers in the business — id Software (www.idsoftware.com), Firaxis (www.firaxis.com), and Blizzard (www.blizzard.com), to name a few — releasing Macintosh versions of their newest games concurrently with the Windows version.

For the gamer in you, allow me to take you on a tour of the best of the new generation of entertainment.

Mac OS X Chess

No mercenaries, no rail guns, and no cities to raze — but chess is still the world's most popular game, and Mac OS X even includes a little 3-D as well. Figure 5-13 illustrates the Chess application at play; you'll find it in your Applications folder.

Figure 5-13: Mac OS X asks, "How about a nice game of chess?"

The game features speech recognition, move hints, take back (or undo) for your last move, and a 2-D or 3-D board. You can also list your games in text form and print them or save games in progress. Maybe it's not a complete set of bells and whistles like commercial chess games, but the price is right, and the play can be quite challenging when you set it at the higher skill levels.

Civilization III

Sid Meier's original Civilization is considered by many hard-core gamers to be one of the top three or four best games ever written, so Civilization III (*Civ 3* for short) has some pretty big shoes to fill. Like previous versions, your job is to lead a civilization through its development and ultimately win the game by colonizing another star system, assimilating all the other civilizations, or being voted supreme leader of the planet. Sounds like a nice, quiet afternoon's diversion, right?

Well, be ready for a typical turn-based game to last well into the night. Civ 3 is a complex game, but after you learn the basics, you'll be instantly addicted. (Those who have played the first two versions of Civilization will feel comfortable right off the bat.) You establish towns that slowly grow into cities, research new technology, build alliances with other players (and tear them down), and wage war if necessary. Your people must be kept happy and entertained — as well as taxed. One way to keep the peace is to build Wonders like the Pyramids or to assign some of the populace as entertainers. Figure 5-14 shows a typical screen from Civ 3.

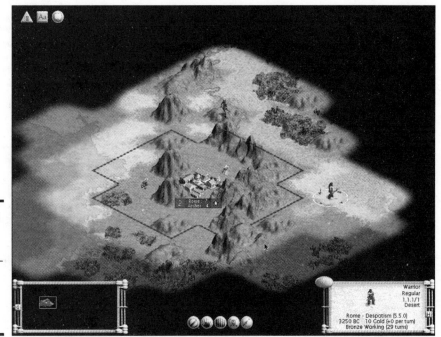

Figure 5-14:
Lead a civilization to victory — or watch your cities get trounced.

The game sells for around $40 on the Web — for screenshots and additional description, visit the game's official site at www.civ3.com.

If you're looking for a game that involves strategy and management — as well as practically unlimited replay value because you can configure entirely new worlds to inhabit — then I can heartily recommend Civilization III. You won't be disappointed!

Return to Castle Wolfenstein

You can just hear Indiana Jones: "Nazis. Why did they have to be Nazis? I hate 'em!" Those of us with a long computing past remember the original Castle Wolfenstein, which ran on the Atari, Commodore, and Apple II computers. (I still have a copy that runs on my antique Atari 800 and Commodore 64 computers.) Playing an American GI imprisoned in a Nazi castle, you had to find your way out, reducing the Nazis to zero and relieving them of their secret Axis plans in the process. Along with the cutting-edge gameplay — pixellated rooms and stick-figure guards — the game actually *spoke* (albeit very fuzzy, hard-to-understand German).

Next came Castle Wolfenstein 3-D, which was an immediate predecessor to DOOM and one of the first classic 3-D games. Suddenly the old building and its occupants were far more realistic. . . . I remember creeping around corners and flinching when I was attacked by a German Shepherd for the first time.

Now id Software brings the legendary Castle Wolfenstein cutting-edge graphics, gameplay, and the best weapon and level designs in the business, as shown in Figure 5-15. You'll encounter evil in many forms: human, zombie, and far worse. Besides the interior of the castle, you'll travel through environments like underground labyrinths, ancient churches, Nazi research laboratories, and even a cable car.

Most of the weapons in this 3-D shooter are realistic recreations of Allied and Axis machine guns, rifles, pistols, and grenades. You also get imaginary weapons like a top-secret Axis chain gun and something that looks and operates like the WWF version of a taser. Enemies are smart and hard to beat, using most of the same tactics that you'll use: using cover, ducking to reload, and working together in teams. The single-player story is well written, with just the right amount of tension. Multiplayer mode allows you to play on either the Axis or the Allied side over both an Internet connection and a local network.

Graphics are literally the best you can get on the Mac, using all the tricks offered by those GeForce and Radeon cards. Optional graphics features that will make any Windows gamer nervous include

✦ Highest-quality, 32-bit textures

✦ Dynamic light maps

✦ Complex reflections

✦ OpenGL support

✦ Support for hardware-specific extras (like fog on GeForce cards and Truform on ATI cards)

The game averages about $50 at most Web stores — for more information, check the official site at www.activision.com/games/wolfenstein.

If you crave the best in first-person 3-D combat, you won't find better. Long live Wolfenstein!

**Book VI
Chapter 5**

**Programs that
You've (Probably)
Gotta Have**

Figure 5-15: The one, the only, the legendary Castle Wolfenstein.

WarCraft III

To finish my survey of must-have games, I'll end with Blizzard's best: WarCraft III. This heady mixture of RTS (short for real-time strategy) and RPG (short for role-playing game) is yet another sequel in another popular game series. WarCraft III puts you in the boots of human princes, Orc battle generals, undead champions, and elven lords — in fact, in single player mode, you'll play each of these warrior races in turn. My recommendation: Stick with the Night Elves, friend.

Combat, however, is only half of the job. Each mission is different; typically, you also have to gather resources by mining gold and cutting trees while you build new structures and train new troops. You can take to the air, buy goods from mercenaries, or even hire goblins to do your dirty work (if you have the gold handy). Spells abound, as do siege weapons and mounted warriors. (Personally, my favorite units have to be the living guardian trees of the Night Elves, which toss boulders. I want one of those — a friendly one, mind you — in my backyard.)

Although visually stunning, WarCraft III is no first-person game. Instead, you view the action from an overhead perspective, as you can see in Figure 5-16. Control is by both keyboard and mouse; the game is easy to learn, but you'll always find someone to kick your posterior in multiplayer games, both over the Internet and across your own local area network (LAN).

You'll find the storyline in this game riveting — it keeps you playing with its twists and turns. Your units include heroes, which are no static figureheads. As they gain experience, you can teach them new skills and outfit them with all sorts of magical items.

You'll pay about $50 online for WarCraft III, and it'll be worth every single penny you spend — for all the details and some great desktop backgrounds, check the official site at `www.blizzard.com/war3`.

Figure 5-16: A grand tale of warfare, magic and alliances — it must be WarCraft III.

Book VII

Advanced Mac OS X

The 5th Wave   By Rich Tennant

"Oh, Anthony loves working with AppleScript. He customized all our Word documents with a sound file so they all close out with a 'Badda Bing!'"

Contents at a Glance

Chapter 1: . . . And UNIX Lurks Beneath 567

Chapter 2: AppleScript Just Plain Rocks 595

Chapter 3: Forget Hal! Talking and Writing to Your Macintosh 609

Chapter 4: Hosting a Web Site à la OS X 625

Chapter 1: . . . And UNIX Lurks Beneath

In This Chapter

✔ Why use UNIX?

✔ Doing things with the keyboard

✔ Introducing UNIX commands

✔ Creating text files

✔ Recording your favorite radio stations

✔ Exploring deep inside Mac OS X

*U*NIX lurks deep beneath the shiny Aqua exterior of Mac OS X. UNIX is a tried-and-true operating system that has been around for decades. If you don't believe that it's a powerful (not to mention popular) operating system, consider that over half of all Web servers on the Internet use some variety of UNIX as their operating system of choice.

Besides being well tested and having a long history, UNIX also offers some fantastic features. Unlike the Mac OS, the keyboard plays an integral role in using a UNIX-based operating system. Because of this tradition for using the keyboard, UNIX has evolved a large set of useful keyboard-driven commands that can perform powerful feats that a mouse user could never do. This chapter examines the role of the keyboard in UNIX operating systems and describes how to execute standard file system commands, use Apple's additional set of commands, and install your own commands from the Internet.

Why Use the Keyboard?

To begin benefiting from the UNIX underpinnings of Mac OS X, get used to doing things with the keyboard. Although mouse skills can be applied to UNIX, it has an historical link to the keyboard, and you'll generally find performing UNIX functions faster and easier with the keyboard.

UNIX keyboarding is fast

Why on Earth would any red-blooded Macintosh user want to leave the comfort of the mouse to use a keyboard? After all, the graphical user interface is what made the Macintosh great in the first place. With the Finder, you can navigate and manage the various files your hard drive with a few clicks. This sounds simple enough, but for some tasks, using the keyboard can be just as fast, if not faster.

Suppose, for example, that you need to copy a file from somewhere on your hard drive to somewhere else on that same drive. To do so with the Finder, you must first open a Finder window (presumably by clicking the Finder icon in the Dock). Then, by using a succession of mouse clicks, you navigate to where the file that you wish to copy resides. Next, you might open another Finder window (***Note:*** Opening the second finder window requires pressing ⌘+N; clicking the Finder icon in the dock does not open a second finder window) and navigate to the folder where you wish to copy the file. Finally, you duplicate the original file and drag that copy to its intended destination.

By using the keyboard and the power of UNIX, you can accomplish the same task with a one-line command. For some tasks, the mouse is definitely the way to go, but you can perform some tasks just as quickly, if not quicker, with the keyboard. For the skinny on one-line commands, skip down to the upcoming section, "Uncovering the Terminal."

UNIX keyboarding is powerful

So maybe you're not an expert typist and using the mouse still sounds inviting. For many scenarios, you'd be correct in assuming that a mouse can handle the job just as quickly and easily as a bunch of commands that you have to memorize. Using the keyboard, however, offers some other distinct advantages over the mouse. To facilitate using a keyboard to control your computer, all UNIX operating systems offer the *command-line* tool. With this tool, you can enter commands one line at a time; hence, its name. Mac OS X ships with the command-line application, Terminal. You can find it here:

```
/Applications/Utilities/Terminal
```

One feature of the command line that really shines is its power. When you use a mouse, one mouse click is equal to one command. When you use the command line, on the other hand, you aren't limited to entering one command at a time. Rather, you can combine commands into a kind of *super command* (minus the silly cape, but with bulging muscles intact), with each command performing some action of the combined whole. By using the command line, you can string together a whole bunch of commands to do a very complex task.

For example, consider how many times you'd have to click a mouse in the Finder to do the following:

✦ Find all files that begin with the letters *MyDocument*

✦ From this list of files, add a number to the beginning of the file name indicating its size in kilobytes

✦ Save the names of all altered files to a text file

By using the command line, you could accomplish all these tasks by typing only one super command: that is, a collection of three simple commands combined to form one instruction.Going into much detail on super commands is not for the faint hearted. Pretty ugly stuff, really. If your thirst for UNIX dominance so compels you, do a little independent study to bone up on all-things-UNIX.

The best thing about the command line is that if you have Mac OS X, you also have a program called Terminal, which gives you everything you need to start using the command line. I show you how in the section "Uncovering the Terminal," later in this chapter.

Go where no mouse has gone before

The Finder is generally a helpful thing, but it makes many assumptions about how you work. One of these assumptions is that you can't handle (or don't have any need to handle) some of the files on your hard drive. (Sometimes being helpful translates to being too simple.) To keep clumsy hands from screwing up the delicate innards of Mac OS X, Apple purposely hides some files from view. What? Apple has hidden files from you! What's a techno-nerd to do?

The command line comes to the rescue! Yep, you guessed it. You can use the command line to peer inside every nook and cranny of your Mac's vast directory structure on your hard drive. It also has the power to edit files that aren't normally accessible to you as a plain ol' user (that's *user*, not *loser*). With the command line, you can pretend to be other users — even users with more permissions. Ooh. By temporarily acting as another more powerful user, you can perform actions with the command line that would be impossible in the Finder.

Automate to elevate

If all these benefits are beginning to excite you, you ain't seen nothing yet! Not only can you perform complex commands with command line, you can go even one step further: automation. If you find yourself using the same set of commands more than once, you're a likely candidate for using automation to save time. Instead of typing the list of commands each time, you can save them to a text file and execute the entire file with only one command. Now that's power!

Of course, you probably don't like doing housekeeping tasks while you're busy on other things, so schedule that list of commands to run in the middle of the night while you're fast asleep. The command line lets you do that, too. (Note that automation of UNIX commands is totally separate from automation of Mac OS X applications with AppleScript, which I cover in Book VII, Chapter 2.)

Remote control

Of course the command line is also handy for accessing and working with the various files on your computer, but there's no reason to stop there. By using the command line, you can also access and control computers anywhere in the world. After you log into another computer, you can use the same commands for the remote computer.

UNIX was created with multiple users in mind. Because computers used to be expensive and physically huge machines, UNIX was designed so that multiple users could remotely use the same machine simultaneously. In fact, if Mac OS X is your first encounter with UNIX, you might be surprised to know that many UNIX beginners of the past weren't even in the same room, building, state, or even country as the computer they were using.

Not only can you work with a computer that's in a different physical location, but it's also very fast to do so. Instead of the bandwidth hog that is the Internet, the command line is lean and mean. This permits you to use a remote computer nearly as fast as if it were sitting on the desk in front of you.

Uncovering the Terminal

The best way to learn how to use command line is to jump right in. Mac OS X comes stocked with an application named *Terminal*. The Terminal application is where you enter commands in the command line. It is located in the Utilities folder within the Applications folder on your hard drive — choose Applications⇨Utilities⇨Terminal.app.

Double-click the icon shown in Figure 1-1 to launch Terminal.

Figure 1-1: Find the Terminal application in the /Applications /Utilities directory.

By the way, feel free to make Terminal more accessible by dragging its icon to the Dock or the toolbar. That way, you won't have to dive this deep into the Applications folder in the future.

What's a prompt?

Upon launch of the Terminal application, you'll immediately notice some text in the window that appears onscreen.

```
Last login: Sun Jun 23 17:51:14 on ttyp1
Welcome to Darwin!
[BV1-24:~] erick%
```

As you might guess, this text details the last time that you logged into the Terminal, followed by a greeting from the Darwin underbelly of Mac OS X. *Darwin* is Apple's name for the UNIX underpinnings of Mac OS X. The last line, however, is the most important one. It's called the *prompt*.

The prompt serves some important functions. First, it lists the current directory, which is listed as ~. A tilde character (~) denotes a user's home directory. By default, you will always be in your home folder each time that you begin a new session on the Terminal. After the current directory, the Terminal displays the name of the current user, which is erick in this example.

The final character of the prompt is a %. Immediately after this character is where you enter any command that you wish to execute. Go ahead, don't be shy. Try out your first command by typing **uptime** in the Terminal application. Your text appears at the location of the cursor, denoted by a small square. If you make a mistake while entering the command, press the left- or right-arrow key to move the cursor to the location of the error. After you type the command, press Return to execute it.

```
[BV1-24:~] erick% uptime
 6:24PM  up  2:42, 4 users, load averages: 2.44, 2.38, 1.90
[BV1-24:~] erick%
```

If all goes well, you should see a listing of how long your Mac has been running since the last reboot or login. In the example listing, the computer has been running for 2 hours and 42 minutes (2:42 in line 2). Simple, eh? Immediately following the listing of the uptime command, you are greeted with another prompt for you to enter more commands. I examine many more commands later in this chapter.

A few commands to get started

Using the command line is simply a matter of entering simple instructions — commands — into the Terminal application and pressing Return to execute them. One of the main reasons that you'll use the command line is to navigate through the various folders on your hard drive. You'll become accustomed to using two vital commands: ls and cd. The ls command is shorthand for *list* and it does just that: It lists the contents of the current directory. Enter **ls** at your prompt, and you should see a listing of your home folder as shown in Figure 1-2.

Figure 1-2:
See the contents of your Home directory after entering the ls command.

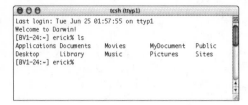

```
 ● ● ●                    tcsh (ttyp1)
Last login: Tue Jun 25 01:57:55 on ttyp1
Welcome to Darwin!
[BV1-24:~] erick% ls
Applications Documents   Movies      MyDocument  Public
Desktop      Library     Music       Pictures    Sites
[BV1-24:~] erick%
```

The complementary cd command (lowercase), which incidentally stands for *change directory*, opens any folder that you specify. It works much the same as double-clicking a folder in the Finder. The difference is that following the cd command, you don't immediately see all the folder content. However, the cd command requires a parameter so your Mac knows which folder to open.

For example, to open the Documents folder that resides in your home directory, type **cd Documents** (Documents should be uppercase) and press Return. When you do, you might be surprised to see another prompt immediately displayed. So where are all the files in the Documents folder? You must enter another command to see what items are in the folder that you just opened. Type **ls** again to see the contents of the Documents folder, as shown in Figure 1-3.

If you try to open a folder that has a space in its name, make sure to enclose the folder's name in quotes.

```
cd "My Picture Folder"
```

To return to your Home folder, enter a modified version of the cd command:

```
cd ..
```

This causes your Mac to move back up the folder hierarchy one folder to your Home directory. By using these three simple commands — ls, cd *foldername*, and cd .. — you can traverse your entire hard drive.

Change to Documents folder

```
000                    tcsh (ttyp1)
Last login: Tue Jun 25 03:10:49 on ttyp1
Welcome to Darwin!
[BV1-24:~] erick% cd ~/Documents
[BV1-24:~/Documents] erick% ls
02-28-02_stego.jpg              dkit
02-28-2002                      dummy.html
9Desktop Folder                 environment.mine
AboutBox                        epson drover!
Acrobat User Data               iTunes
BEST Dev Reg Tool               jnjn.tiff
CLI                             maya
CarApp                          my iPhoto collection
Comm Dev Home Page.url          myImage.tif
DLL Plugin PostLinker v1.3.1    myprefspane
Microsoft User Data             olddownload2.html
MyPicoDocument                  osxguide2_11hq.pdf
MyService                       perltest.pl
OMS Spec.pdf                    screens
```

List Documents folder contents

After you successfully enter a command, you can recall it by pressing the up-arrow key. Press the up-arrow again to see the command prior to that, and so forth. This is an extremely useful trick for retyping extra long file paths.

Using the skills you already have

Just because the Terminal is text-based, doesn't mean that it doesn't act like a good Macintosh citizen. All the usual Mac features that you know and love are there for you to use. Copy and paste functions work as you might expect, but only at the prompt position.

Drag-and-drop is also at your disposal. After you play around with the Terminal for a while, you'll find yourself bored to tears typing the long paths that represent the files on your hard drive. To automatically enter the path of a file or folder to a command, simply drag it to the active Terminal window, as shown in Figure 1-4. The file's full path instantly appears at the location of your cursor. (Thanks, Apple!)

You can even use the mouse while entering commands in the Terminal. Click and drag your mouse over text to select it. From there, you can copy to the Clipboard as you might expect with any other application.

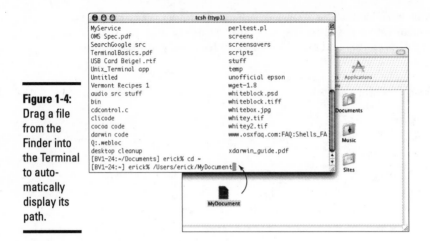

Figure 1-4:
Drag a file
from the
Finder into
the Terminal
to auto-
matically
display its
path.

UNIX Commands 101

To use the command line effectively you'll need to familiarize yourself with the commands that are available to you. After all, how can you use a tool without knowing what it can do? Despite having to memorize a few commands, UNIX usually makes it easy on you by abbreviating commands, by following a standard grammar (so to speak) and by providing you with extensive documentation for each command.

Anatomy of a UNIX Command

UNIX commands can perform many amazing feats. Despite their vast abilities, all commands follow a similar structure:

```
command <optional flag(s)> <optional operand(s)>
```

The simplest form of a UNIX command is the command itself. For a basic discussion on UNIX commands such as ls, see the earlier section, "A few commands to get started." You can expand your use of the ls command by appending various *flags*. Flags are preceded by a dash (-) and always follow the command. For instance, you can display the contents of a directory as a column of names by tacking on an -1 flag to the ls command.

```
ls -1
```

Besides flags, UNIX commands sometimes also have operands. An *operand* is something that is acted upon. For example, instead of just entering the ls command, which lists the current directory, you can add an operand to list a specific directory:

```
ls ~/Documents/myProject/
```

The tilde (~) denotes the user's Home directory.

Sometimes a command can take multiple operands, as is the case when you copy a file. The two operands represent the source file and the destination of the file that you want to copy, separated by a space. The following example copies a text file from the Documents folder to the Desktop folder using the cp command (short for copy).

```
cp ~/Documents/MyDocument ~/Desktop/MyDocument
```

You can also combine flags and operands in the same command. This example displays the contents of a specific folder in list format:

```
ls -l ~/Documents/myProject/
```

Command line gotchas

In earlier sections, I describe a few simple command line functions. All these commands have something in common: You may not have noticed, but every example thus far involved folder and file names that contained only alphanumeric characters. What happens if you have a folder name that has a space in it? Try the following example, but don't worry when it won't work.

The cd command stands for *change directory*.

```
cd /Desktop Folder
```

The result is an error message:

```
cd: Too many arguments.
```

The problem is that a space character is not allowed in a path. To get around this problem, simply enclose the path in double quotation marks, like this:

```
cd "/Desktop Folder"
```

Mac OS X lets you use either double OR single quotation marks to enclose a path with spaces in it. Standard UNIX operating systems, however, uses double quotation marks for this purpose.

In a similar vein, you can get the space character to be accepted by a command by adding an escape character. To *escape* a character, add a backslash (\) immediately prior to the character in question. To illustrate, try the last command with an escape character instead. Note that this time, no quotation marks are necessary.

```
cd /Desktop\ Folder
```

You can use either quotes or escape characters because they're interchangeable.

Help is on the way!

By now, you might be wondering how a computer techno-wizard is supposed to keep all these commands straight. Fortunately, you can find generous documentation for nearly every command available to you. To access this built-in help, use the man command. Using the man command (shorthand for *manual*) will display a help file for any command that it knows about. For example, to read the available help information for the ls command, simply type man ls at the prompt. Figure 1-5 illustrates the result.

Figure 1-5:
Using
the man
command
provides
documen-
tation for
many
different
commands.

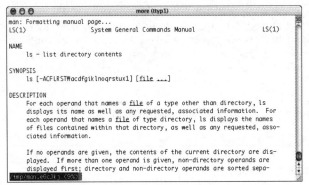

Autocompletion

To expedite your command line use, the *tcsh* shell can complete your input for you as you type. Although the Terminal permits you to enter commands via the keyboard, it is the shell that interprets those commands. There are many kinds of shells available to UNIX users. The shell that Mac OS X uses by default is named *tcsh*. Use the autocompletion features of *tcsh* to autocomplete both commands and file names. To demonstrate, begin by typing the following:

```
cd ~/De
```

Then press the Tab key. This result is that the shell predicts that you will want to type

```
cd ~/Desktop/
```

Of course, if you have another folder that begins with the letters *De* in the same folder, you may need to type a few additional characters. This gives the autocompletion more information to help it decide which characters you want to type. In other words, if you don't type enough characters, autompletion can't do its job of intelligently guessing what you want to type. Kind of ironic, eh?

Working with Files

If you've used a computer for any time at all, you're no doubt familiar with the idea of files. Ever since the first floppy drive appeared in personal computers, operating systems have stored data in files. Mac OS X is no exception. And although you might be familiar with the idea of files, you might be less knowledgeable about how Mac OS X arranges them into folders and how you go about accessing them via the command line. This section describes the basic file and folder information that you need to know to tame the beast that is UNIX.

Paths

Before you dive into UNIX commands, you should first know a few facts . . . nasty things, facts, but you can't earn your pair of power-nerd suspenders without 'em. For starters, as a Mac user, you may not be familiar with how paths work in UNIX. A *path* is simply a textual representation of a folder or file. The simplest path is your home directory. It is denoted by a tilde character. Any folder within the home directory is represented by the folder's name preceded by a forward slash (/). For example, a document entitled `myDoc` that resides in the current user's Documents folder would have a path like this:

```
~/Documents/myDocument
```

Similarly, a folder named *myFolder* that resides in the current user's Documents folder would have a path like this:

```
~/Documents/myFolder/
```

If you haven't figured it out yet, a *folder* and a *directory* are two different names for the same thing. *Folder* is the name with which most Mac users are familiar, and *directory* is a term that UNIX power-nerds prefer. I use the terms interchangeably throughout the remainder of the chapter.

Because Mac OS X is a multi-user environment, you might sometimes want to work with folder or files somewhere other than in your Home folder. Starting from your Home folder, enter the following command:

```
cd ..
```

This will move you to the folder right above your Home folder, which happens to be the Users folder. Using another quick `ls` command will show you all users who are permitted to use to the machine, as shown in Figure 1-6. In this figure you can see the three users that are allowed to use this machine: erick, lisa, and Shared.

Figure 1-6:
The Users folder displays all user names permitted to use this machine.

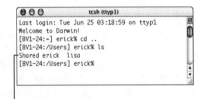

The response to the ls command shows you all users permitted to use a machine.

Enter **cd ..** once again, and you find yourself at the root of your main hard drive. The *root directory* is what you see in the Finder when you double-click your hard drive icon on the desktop. A user's Home directory is represented by a tilde character (~), and the root of the hard drive is denoted by a forward slash (/), as displayed by the prompt:

```
[BV1-24:/] erick%
```

It's easy to return to your Home directory by following this sequence:

```
[BV1-24:/] erick% cd Users
[BV1-24:/Users] erick% cd erick
[BV1-24:~] erick%
```

Instead of moving through each successive folder until you reach your intended destination, you can specify the path by using one `cd` command:

```
[BV1-24:/] erick% cd /Users/erick
[BV1-24:~] erick%
```

Of course, the Home directory is a special folder in that you can also navigate there by simply entering **cd ~**, but the main point here is that you can navigate directly to specific folders by using that folder's path in conjunction with the cd command.

Furthermore, when you navigate your hard drive by using paths, you can jump directly to your desired destination from any place. When you enter **cd ..**, it is in relation to your current position, whereas entering

```
cd /Users/erick
```

will always take you to the same directory, regardless of your starting point.

Copying, moving, and renaming files

After you're comfortable with moving around the hierarchy of your hard drive, it's a cinch to copy, move, and rename files and folders.

To copy files from the command line, use the cp command. Because using the cp command will copy a file from one place to another, it requires two operands: first the source, and then the destination. For instance, to copy a file from your home folder to your Documents folder, use the cp command like this:

```
cp ~/MyDocument ~/Desktop/MyDocument
```

Keep in mind that when you copy files, you must have proper permissions to do so. Here's what happens when I try to copy a file from my Desktop to another user's Desktop:

```
[BV1-24:~] erick% cp ~/Desktop/MyDocument
    /Users/lisa/Desktop/MyDocument

cp: /Users/lisa/Desktop/MyDocument: Permission denied
```

If you can't copy to the destination that you desire, you will need to precede the cp command with sudo. Using the sudo command allows you to perform functions as another user. The idea here is that the other user who you're "emulating" has the necessary privileges to execute the desired copy operation. When you execute the command, the command line will ask you for a password. If you don't know what the password is, you probably shouldn't be using sudo. Your computer's administrator should have given you an appropriate password to use. After you enter the correct password, the command executes as desired.

In case you're curious, sudo stands for *set user and do*. It sets the user to the one that you specify and performs the command that follows the username.

```
sudo cp ~/Desktop/MyDocument /Users/lisa/Desktop/MyDocument
Password:
```

A close cousin to the cp (copy) command is the mv (move) command. As you can probably guess, the mv command moves a folder or file from one location to another. I told you all this character-based stuff would start to make sense, didn't I? To demonstrate, this command moves MyDocument from the Desktop folder to the current user's home folder:

```
mv ~/Desktop/MyDocument ~/MyDocument
```

Ah, but here's the hidden surprise: The mv command also functions as a rename command. For instance, to rename a file MyDocument on the Desktop to MyNewDocument, do this:

```
mv ~/Desktop/MyDocument ~/Desktop/MyNewDocument
```

In this case, you can see that the mv command is really copying the original file to the destination and then deleting the original. Because both folders in this example reside in the same folder (~/Desktop/), it appears as though the mv command has renamed the file.

Again, like the cp command, the mv command requires that you have proper permissions for the action that you wish to perform. Use the sudo command to perform any commands that your current user (as displayed in the prompt) is not allowed to execute. On UNIX systems, not all users are necessarily equal. Some users can perform functions that others can't. This is handy for keeping your child's mitts out of important files on your computer. It also creates a hurdle should you choose to work on files while using your child's restricted user account. The sudo command lets you temporarily become another user — presumably one that has permission to perform some function that the current user can't.

What would file manipulation be without the ability to delete files? Never fear, UNIX can delete anything that you throw at it. Use the rm (short for *remove*) or rmdir (short for *remove directory*) to delete a folder or file. For example, to delete MyDocument from the Desktop folder, execute the rm command like this:

```
rm ~/Desktop/MyDocument
```

Once again, deleting files and folders requires that you have permission to do so. In other words, anytime you manipulate files with the command line, you are required to have the proper permission. If your current user is lacking these permissions, `sudo` will help in these cases.

Opening documents and launching applications

Launching applications and opening documents is child's play for a UNIX pro like you. The `open` command does it all. For example, to bring the Finder to the foreground without touching the mouse, use

```
open /System/Library/CoreServices/Finder.app
```

To open a document from the command line, follow a similar scheme. For example, to view an image named `myImage.tif` that's stored in the your Documents folder, use

```
% open ~/Documents/myImage.tif
```

Useful Commands

Manipulating files and viewing folder content is fun, but the command line is capable of so much more! Now I focus the attention on some of the other useful tasks that you can perform with the command line.

Mac OS X comes stocked with a full set of commands for you to use. You can discover what commands are installed by viewing the files in `/usr/bin`. Type **cd /usr/bin** to navigate there.

Calendar

One of my favorite command line functions is the `cal` command, which displays a calendar in text form. Simply entering **cal** at the prompt displays a calendar for the current month, as shown in Figure 1-7.

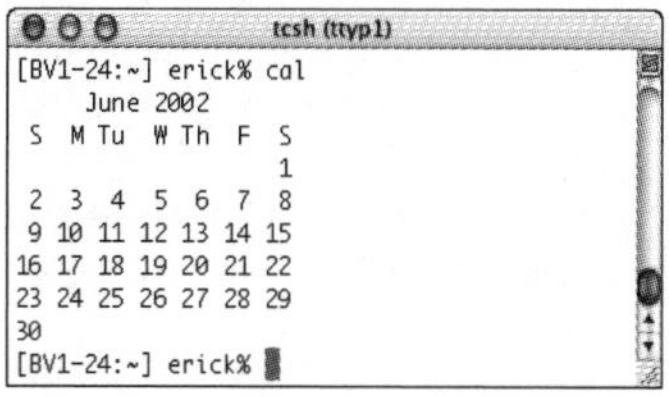

Figure 1-7:
Type **cal**
to view a
calendar for
the current
month.

```
● ● ●          tcsh (ttyp1)
[BV1-24:~] erick% cal
      June 2002
 S  M Tu  W Th  F  S
                   1
 2  3  4  5  6  7  8
 9 10 11 12 13 14 15
16 17 18 19 20 21 22
23 24 25 26 27 28 29
30
[BV1-24:~] erick% █
```

Append a number to the `cal` command to display a 12-month calendar for that year. The number that follows the `cal` command is the year for which you'd like to see a calendar. For example, to view a calendar for 1970, type `cal 1970`. The result appears in Figure 1-8.

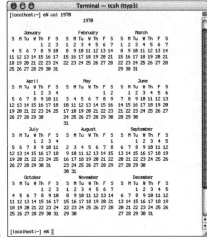

Figure 1-8:
Type **cal** followed by a year to view a 12-month calendar for that year.

Append a month number and a year number to display the calendar for that month. For example, to view a calendar for November 1997, type **cal 11 1997**. The result appears in Figure 1-9.

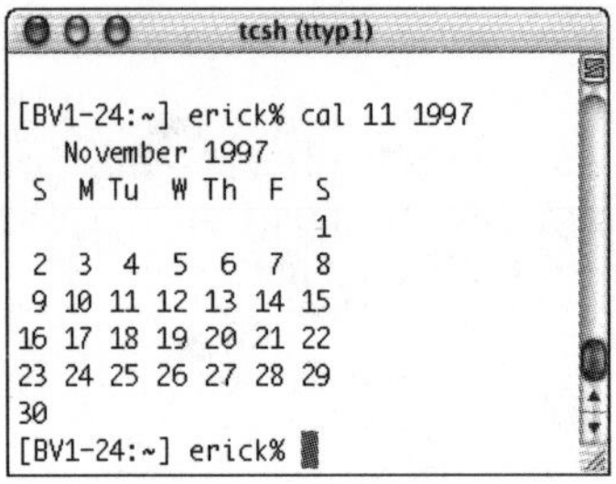

Figure 1-9:
Type **cal** followed by the month and year to view a calendar for that month.

```
[BV1-24:~] erick% cal 11 1997
   November 1997
 S  M Tu  W Th  F  S
                   1
 2  3  4  5  6  7  8
 9 10 11 12 13 14 15
16 17 18 19 20 21 22
23 24 25 26 27 28 29
30
[BV1-24:~] erick%
```

Another useful command that is related to the `cal` command is `date`. Type **date** at the command line to display the day, date, time, and year based on your computer's settings.

```
[BV1-24:~] erick% date
Mon Jun 24 11:32:20 CDT 2002
```

Processes

Have you ever been curious as to why your hard drive seems to spin and grind on occasion while your system is seemingly inactive? Mac OS X sometimes has a lot of stuff going on behind the scenes. To discover just what your computer is busy doing at any time, use the `top` command to display all the actions that your computer is currently performing, as shown in Figure 1-10. These activities are called *processes*; some are created when you launch applications, and others are simply tasks that Mac OS X has to take care of to keep things running smoothly.

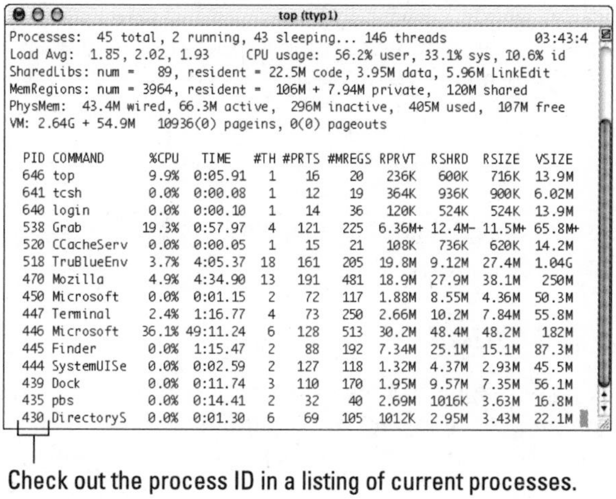

Figure 1-10: Using the `top` command displays all running processes.

```
● ● ●                          top (ttyp1)
Processes:  45 total, 2 running, 43 sleeping... 146 threads        03:43:4
Load Avg:  1.85, 2.02, 1.93      CPU usage:  56.2% user, 33.1% sys, 10.6% id
SharedLibs: num =    89, resident = 22.5M code, 3.95M data, 5.96M LinkEdit
MemRegions: num = 3964, resident = 106M + 7.94M private,  120M shared
PhysMem:  43.4M wired, 66.3M active,  296M inactive,  405M used,  107M free
VM: 2.64G + 54.9M  10936(0) pageins, 0(0) pageouts

PID COMMAND     %CPU   TIME    #TH #PRTS #MREGS RPRVT  RSHRD  RSIZE  VSIZE
646 top          9.9%  0:05.91  1   16    20    236K   600K   716K   13.9M
641 tcsh         0.0%  0:00.08  1   12    19    364K   936K   900K   6.02M
640 login        0.0%  0:00.10  1   14    36    120K   524K   524K   13.9M
538 Grab        19.3%  0:57.97  4   121   225   6.36M+ 12.4M- 11.5M+ 65.8M+
520 CCacheServ   0.0%  0:00.05  1   15    21    108K   736K   620K   14.2M
518 TrueBlueEnv  3.7%  4:05.37  18  161   205   19.8M  9.12M  27.4M  1.04G
470 Mozilla      4.9%  4:34.90  13  191   481   18.9M  27.9M  38.1M  250M
450 Microsoft    0.0%  0:01.15  2   72    117   1.88M  8.55M  4.36M  50.3M
447 Terminal     2.4%  1:16.77  4   73    250   2.66M  10.2M  7.84M  55.8M
446 Microsoft   36.1% 49:11.24  6   128   513   30.2M  48.4M  48.2M  182M
445 Finder       0.0%  1:15.47  2   88    192   7.34M  25.1M  15.1M  87.3M
444 SystemUISe   0.0%  0:02.59  2   127   118   1.32M  4.37M  2.93M  45.5M
439 Dock         0.0%  0:11.74  3   110   170   1.95M  9.57M  7.35M  56.1M
435 pbs          0.0%  0:14.41  2   32    40    2.69M  1016K  3.63M  16.8M
430 DirectoryS   0.0%  0:01.30  6   69    105   1012K  2.95M  3.43M  22.1M
```

Check out the process ID in a listing of current processes.

Besides listing the names of the various processes currently in use, `top` also tells you how much of your CPU is being devoted to each process. This lets you know what process is currently hogging all your computing power.

Sometimes, a process stalls, effectively freezing that action. By using the `top` command to find the Process ID (PID) of the offending process, you can halt the process. Simply use the `kill` command followed by the PID of the process that you want to stop, as shown in Figure 1-11.

Do *not* go killing processes willy-nilly! Although Mac OS X is extremely stable, removing the wrong process @such as `init` or `mach_init` — is rather like removing a leg from one of those deep-sea drilling platforms: Not good. You could lock up your system and lose whatever you're doing in other applications. If you simply want to shut down a misbehaving program, then use the Force Quit menu command from the Finder menu.

Book VII Chapter 1

...And UNIX Lurks Beneath

Figure 1-11:
Using the
`kill`
command
stops a
process
using its PID
number.

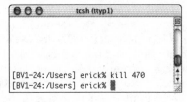

Like `top`, another handy command for examining process info is `ps` (short for *process*). Most often, you will want to append a few flags to the `ps` command to get the information that you desire. For example, try the following command:

```
ps -aux
```

The `man` page for `ps` explains what each flag means.

Fancy-Pants Commands

Besides working with files and processes, the command line has all kinds of sophisticated commands as well. For example, with the command line, you have instant access to a variety of tools for finding files or even stringing together commands.

Finding files

The command line also gives you a number of ways to search for files on your hard drive. The two most commonly used commands are `find` and `locate`.

To use `find`, specify a starting point for the search followed by the name of the file or folder that you wish to find. For example, to find the Fonts folder that belongs to your user, enter the command like this:

```
% find ~/ -name "Fonts"
```

You should see at least one result of the `find`.

```
/Users/erick//Library/Fonts
```

One great feature of the `find` command is that you can look for a file or folder in more than one location. Suppose you want to find a file named

`MyDocument` that you know resides either in your Documents folder or on your Desktop. For this kind of search, use the `find` command like this:

```
% find ~/Documents ~/Desktop\ Folder -name "MyDocument"
```

In this example, you are telling the find command which folders it should search when looking for the file named `MyDocument`.

Besides `find`, another useful command for searching your hard drive is `locate`. Using the `locate` command is many times faster than the `find` command because it relies on a built-in database to do its search. Mac OS X updates this database for you automatically. To find any folder with the name `Fonts` by using the `locate` command, format your syntax like so:

```
%locate /Fonts
```

Pipes

Nearly all UNIX commands can take on greater abilities by using a construct called the *pipe*. A pipe (|) is represented by that funny little vertical line that shows up when you press Shift+\. The purpose of the pipe is to route data from one command to another one that follows. For example, many UNIX commands produce large amounts of information that can't all fit on one page. (You might have noticed this behavior when you used the `locate` command.) Joining two commands or functions together with the pipe command is *piping*. To tame the screens full of text, pipe the `locate` function to the `less` command. The `less` command provides data one page at a time.

```
% locate /Fonts | less
```

When the results fill up one page, the data stops and waits for you to press any key (except the Q key) to continue. When you reach the end of the results, press Q to quit and return to a command-line prompt.

Pipes can be used with nearly every UNIX command around to produce some truly wild results. For example, suppose you want to search for a file in your Home folder named `MyDocument` *and* then count how many words are in that file. Whenever you see the word *and,* you should automatically be thinking of pipes because that indicates that you want to execute more than one command. To perform these search and count tasks, use a command like this:

```
find ~/ -name "MyDocument" | wc
```

The `find` command searches for the file named `MyDocument` in the Home folder (~/). The result of this search is then fed to the `wc` (word count) command, which returns the word count of that file.

UNIX Programs that Come in Handy

As a Macintosh user, you might be surprised to know that many applications on your hard drive don't reside in one of the typical Applications folders of Mac OS X. These applications, in fact, don't have any graphical user interface like you're accustomed to. They're only accessible from the command line. The remainder of this chapter will cover some of these applications. I will also show you how to use the Internet to download a powerful new command-line application, Steamripper, and use it.

Text editors

UNIX has many text-editing applications for use at the command line. Some of the more popular ones include pico, vi, and emacs. Each of these text editors has its pros and cons. For my examples here, however, I use pico because it's simple to use and sufficient for our needs.

Creating a new document

To create a text file using pico, simply type **pico** at the command line. The result should look like Figure 1-12.

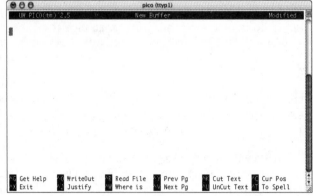

Figure 1-12:
The pico program is a full-featured text editor built into the command line.

At the bottom of the screen is a menu of common commands. Above the menu is a large empty space where you can enter text, much like the word processors that you already know and love (or, for those of us that remember the halcyon character-based days of DOS, older versions of Word and WordPerfect). Type some text in that area. Anything will do . . . a letter to a friend, a grocery list, or a paper for your school homework.

When you're finished entering your desired text, save the document. To do so, you must use the WriteOut command in the pico menu. Directly next to each command in the pico menu is a keyboard sequence used to perform that command. (Refer to the bottom of Figure 1-12.) The ^ character is shorthand for the Control key on your keyboard. Thus, to save a file, press Control+O. This flies in the face of standard Mac keyboard conventions, where the letter *O* is traditionally used to mean *Open*.

This is the rough and tumble world of UNIX, which preceded the Macintosh by many years. Perhaps this will also help you to appreciate why the Macintosh was so revolutionary when it was introduced. You can just hear the designers crowing, "We'll call this a 'menu'! Yeah, that's the ticket!"

After pressing the Control+O sequence, pico prompts you for a filename. Like most UNIX files, you're permitted to enter a simple file name here or a full path to a file, as shown in Figure 1-13. For this example, save the file to your Documents folder, naming it MyPicoDocument.

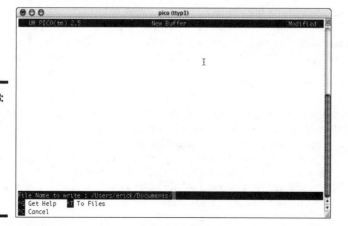

Figure 1-13: After you save your document, pico prompts you for a filename.

Book VII Chapter 1

...And UNIX Lurks Beneath

After you've completed and saved the document, pressing Control+X will transport you away from Planet Pico and back to the command line.

Customizing the prompt

In the previous example, I show you how to launch pico, create a new document, and save it to your Documents folder. For this example, you will again launch pico, but this time the document will be very different. The document won't just hold some plain old letter to your mother. Rather, stick with me to create a file to control some settings of the Terminal.

To get started, navigate to your Home directory.

```
cd ~
```

Then use the `ls` command to list the items in that directory. This time, however, add an `-a` flag. This will cause the listing to display all invisible files. Mac OS X tries to make things safe for average users by hiding files that you don't normally need, but you aren't just an average user anymore! In particular, you are looking for a hidden file named `.tcshrc`. The `.tcshrc` file stores settings for the `tcsh` shell that you use in the Terminal. By altering its contents, you can adjust settings for your shell sessions each time that you use the Terminal application.

All invisible files in UNIX begin with a period.

```
ls -a
```

If you do find a `.tcshrc` file, open it with `pico` by entering the following:

```
pico .tcshrc
```

If you don't find a file named `.tcshrc`, simply launch `pico`. (Later, when you're finished creating the `.tcshrc` file, you can save it as `.tcshrc`.) The prompt already displays some useful information, but you can take that one step further. To the new or existing `.tcshrc` text file, add the following line:

```
set prompt = "Command  %h %"
```

This syntax creates a command counter that keeps track of how many commands you've executed. When you're finished, press Control+O and save the file as described earlier. Make sure that it's named `.tcshrc` and that it's located in your Home directory. To see your handiwork, open a new Terminal session window by pressing ⌘+N. If everything went off without a hitch, you should now see something like Figure 1-14 — a prompt that displays the number of commands that you've executed.

Figure 1-14: Customized prompts can display useful information.

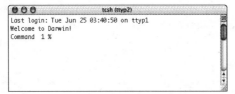

```
Last login: Tue Jun 25 03:40:50 on ttyp1
Welcome to Darwin!
Command  1 %
```

Enter a command, like `ls`, to view the contents of your Home directory. When you do, the next prompt automatically increases the command counter for you!

So, what's actually happening here and why all the % characters? A % character, in UNIX lingo, is an escape character. It denotes a sequence that has special meaning to the Terminal. Table 1-1 shows some other common escape sequences for sprucing up your command line prompt.

Table 1-1	Terminal Prompt Escape Sequences for .tcsh
Escape Sequence	*What It Represents*
%n	The current user's name
%h	The current command count; h stands for *history*
%t	The time
%d	The date
%~	The current directory

In the previous example, I added the text Command to the prompt followed by %h, which represents the current command count. Last, I finish off the prompt with a % character. Recall that that a % character is customary at the prompt to show you where to enter a command. In this case, the % has no special meaning; it's simply meant to display the % character.

With a little experimentation, you can create some really cool, not to mention useful, prompts, as shown in Figure 1-15. For example, you can add the date or command count.

Figure 1-15: Your prompt can be as complex as you like. This one displays the current day of week.

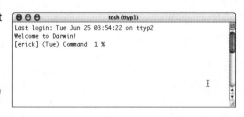

```
tcsh (ttyp1)
Last login: Tue Jun 25 03:54:22 on ttyp2
Welcome to Darwin!
[erick] (Tue) Command  1 %
```

Of course, you aren't limited to geeky UNIX-style prompts. Be as creative as you want. It's your computer, after all! Figure 1-16 is an example of a fun prompt.

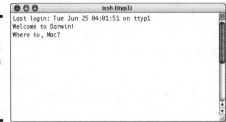

Figure 1-16:
Your prompt
can even be
informative.
It's your
decision!

```
● ○ ○           tcsh (ttyp1)
Last login: Tue Jun 25 04:01:51 on ttyp1
Welcome to Darwin!
Where to, Mac?
```

Networking with the Terminal

Because UNIX isn't a new phenomenon, it has many useful networking abilities built into it. In fact, UNIX was instrumental in creating much of what we
now take for granted: e-mail, the Internet, and the World Wide Web. Thus,
you will be happy to know that you can communicate over networks with
the Terminal in practically any manner you can dream of . . . and then some!

WWW and FTP

If you've used the Internet for any time, you're probably familiar with the
various means to transport data over a network. From FTP (short for *File
Transfer Protocol*) and Telnet to e-mail and the Web, UNIX can handle it all.
In fact, UNIX has a command for each of these functions and many more.
Rather than use each individual command to send and retrieve data with
the Terminal, Apple has conveniently provided a command that can handle
them all: curl. The curl command is competent at all the standard network
protocols. To see it in action, pass a Web address (or URL, to The
Enlightened) to the curl command:

```
curl http://www.dummies.com
```

The result is that you will see the HyperText Markup Language (HTML) page
that's located at www.dummies.com. Because this isn't particularly useful for
most people (it's not very easy to read), you need to add the letter o as a
flag. This specifies where you would like to save this file upon download. To
save the HTML page to your Home directory, add the -o flag and a path to
the destination file.

Don't forget to precede all flags with a hyphen. For this example, it would
be -o.

```
curl -o ~/dummies.html http://www.dummies.com
```

If you now perform an ls command, you will see that curl has, in fact,
downloaded the HTML found at www.dummies.com and saved it to a file
named dummies.html in your Home directory.

The beauty of `curl` is that it does much more than just retrieve Web pages. It is equally comfortable with FTP transfers. FTP is used to grab files from a server as well as upload them. Like the previous HTTP examples, you only have to provide an FTP address in URL format and `curl` will take care of the rest. Of course, most people want to save any files that they download via FTP, not view it in the Terminal as I did the HTML file. Therefore, like the previous example, you should add the `-o` flag and a path to the destination of your download. This time I'll download a README file about `curl` directly from the makers of `curl`.

```
curl
-o ~/Desktop/ README.curl ftp://ftp.sunet.se/pub/www/utilities/curl/README.curl
```

If you're familiar with FTP, you might be wondering whether `curl` can upload, too. Yes, indeed! Instead of using the `-o` flag, you will need to use two flags: `-T` and `-u`. The `-T` flag denotes which file you wish to upload. The `-u` flag denotes the username and password. Then, specify the FTP destination address of where you want to upload it. Because this example deals with an upload, the remainder of this example is for an imaginary FTP server. In real life, you'd use the appropriate FTP address, username, and password for an FTP server where you are allowed to upload.

```
curl -T /Desktop/README.curl -u username:passwd ftp://ftp.yoursitehere.com
/myfiles/README.curl
```

This example uploads the `README.curl` file from the Desktop folder that I downloaded earlier to an imaginary FTP server.

How do you spell success? C-u-r-l!

Sure, HyperText Transfer Protocol (HTTP) and FTP are handy, but did you know that there are many other protocols for network communications? One of the niftier ones is called the *Dictionary protocol*. With it, you can look up words from any server that understands the protocol. Suppose, for example, that you would like to know the meaning of the term *CD-ROM*. Enter the following command to find out:

```
% curl dict://dict.org/d:CD-ROM
```

The results are shown in Figure 1-17. You may never use a real dictionary again!

Cool command-line tools that you can download

Thus far in this chapter, I've used commands and programs that ship with nearly every UNIX (and thus Mac OS X) distribution. The truth is that this is only a small fraction of what is possible by using the command line. Now, focus your attention on some interesting programs that you can download or that Apple provides for us Mac users that make the command line

**Book VII
Chapter 1**

**...And UNIX
Lurks Beneath**

super-powered. My hope is that these examples will entice you to explore the many other commands and programs that are available — usually for free.

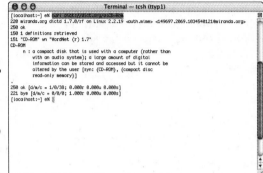

Figure 1-17:
The `curl`
tool can
even look up
words in the
dictionary.

Streamripper

One of my favorite command-line tools is Streamripper. With it, you can record all those great online radio stations that iTunes affords you. Streamripper records a radio station and saves it to your hard drive as an MP3 file. (See Book III, Chapter 2 for more on MP3s and iTunes.) The great part about saving a broadcast is that you can listen to it later as many times as you want.

To download and install Streamripper by using only the command line, use the following:

```
cd ~
curl -o streamripper-1.32.tar.gz
http://streamripper.sourceforge.net/dl
/streamripper-1.32.tar.gz
gnutar xzf streamripper-1.32.tar.gz
cd streamripper-1.32
./configure
make
make install
```

First, navigate to the Home folder by typing **cd ~**. The second line of code downloads the source code for Streamripper to the current folder, which in this case is Home(~). Then, `gnutar`, a compression utility, unzips the download. Next, navigate to the folder that results from unzipping the download. The remaining commands compile the source code into an application that you can use. Now Streamripper is installed on your system, and you can begin using it.

To record a Web radio station, you need an address for that station. Launch iTunes by clicking its icon in the Dock and navigate to the Radio section. A list of radio station categories appears. Expand a category to view the stations available for that category. After you see the names of radio stations, select one and press ⌘+I to bring up the Song Information dialog. In the Info tab of that dialog, you can find the URL for that station, as shown in Figure 1-18.

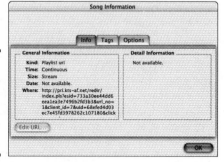

Figure 1-18:
Press ⌘+I
to view the
URL of an
iTunes radio
station.

Back at the command line, enter one simple command to begin recording the radio station. I use an address for Monkey Radio to illustrate.

```
streamripper http://205.188.245.132:8038
```

The resulting MP3 files appear in a folder named `Monkey Radio` within the `streamripper` folder.

If for some reason the Streamripper installation was unsuccessful, you might see an error like this when attempting to capture a stream:

```
streamripper: Command not found.
```

Just because the install failed doesn't mean you can't still use Streamripper. It just requires a few extra steps. First, navigate to the streamripper directory. Then, issue the same `streamripper` command as before, but this time precede it with a `./` sequence. This forces the command to execute despite not being installed.

```
cd streamripper-1.32
./ streamripper http://205.188.245.132:8038
```

Apple's command-line tools

Apple provides a host of command-line tools that are specific to Macintosh use. They come with the Developer Tools that accompany Mac OS X.

Apple's command-line tools are part of the Mac OS X Developer Tools installation.

To see a list of the command-line tools that Apple installs with the Developer Tools, enter this:

```
cd /Developer/Tools
ls
```

These tools are generally intended for developers, but a few gems in there can help nondevelopers, too: in particular, the `GetFileInfo` and `SetFile` commands. Because these commands are so handy and they're not in the standard command folder, the first step is to link them to `/usr/bin`. Normally, command-line tools must reside in the `/usr/bin` directory for them to be operational. If you would like to use a particular command that does not reside in the proper directory, one solution is to link the command to the appropriate folder. Then, when the system loads the usual commands for you to use, it includes the commands that you have linked.

The `sudo` command requires an administrator password. For more on `sudo`, read the earlier section, "Copying, moving, and renaming files."

```
sudo ln -s /Developer/Tools/GetFileInfo /usr/bin/GetFileInfo
sudo ln -s /Developer/Tools/SetFile /usr/bin/SetFile
rehash
```

Now you can safely use these commands. These two commands simulate the Get Info window that is part of the Finder. For example, to view a file's information, use the `GetFileInfo` command:

```
GetFileInfo ~/myDocument
```

The result is a display like this:

```
% GetFileInfo ~/MyDocument
file: "/Users/erick/MyDocument"
type: "TEXT"
creator: "R*ch"
attributes: avbstclInmed
created: 06/23/2002 22:25:04
modified: 06/23/2002 22:25:04
```

Conversely, `SetFile` sets one or more bits of the file's information. For example, to change the creator for this file, the `-c` flag is necessary.

```
SetFile -c "ttxt" ~/MyDocument
```

Although neither of these new commands have a `man` page, Apple does provide some documentation. Enter either command without any parameters to view the documentation for that command.

Chapter 2: AppleScript Just Plain Rocks

In This Chapter

✔ Simplifying your life with AppleScript

✔ Letting AppleScript create scripts for you

✔ Creating scripts on your own

✔ Searching for AppleScript help elsewhere

*U*sing a Macintosh is supposed to make your life easier, and in many ways, it does. When it comes down to it, though, you still have to move the mouse, press keys on the keyboard, and read information on the screen to get things done . . . or do you? Why not let your computer do the dull chores — such as renaming a thousand digital photographs from your family vacation and organizing them into folders based on the subject of each photo — for you? Although most people are familiar with controlling their Macs with the mouse and keyboard, few realize that they can operate their machines without touching a key, a mouse button, or even glancing at the screen.

What's So Great about AppleScript?

If one word could describe what AppleScript is all about, it would be *automation*. *AppleScript* is a technology for automating practically any action that you perform with your Macintosh, such as common tasks in the Finder and in other applications.

Automate common tasks in the Finder

If you've ever found yourself repeating some task more than once, you're an ideal candidate for becoming an AppleScript techno-wizard. AppleScript is particularly good at taking the boredom and tedium out of using your Macintosh. It permits you to perform all sorts of tasks automatically. To illustrate, consider a few jobs that would take a fair amount of time to do by hand but are a snap with AppleScript:

✦ While writing your best-selling novel, you make a mistake and misnumber the chapters. All the chapters have a file name bearing the chapter number, but they're all off by one. Sure, you could rename each file by hand, but your book is a large tome and renumbering forty-two chapters manually doesn't sound like much fun. Using a simple AppleScript of only a few lines of code, you can rename the chapters in seconds. On the other hand, performing the same task by hand would require several minutes and lots of tedious attention on your part, not to mention introduce the likelihood of human error.

✦ You're a neat freak and think that your Mac should reflect your penchant for order. In fact, you like your Desktop icons to be placed just so. Being left-handed, you prefer the icons over on the left side of the Desktop, like some of those (ahem) other operating systems. In this situation, an AppleScript can help you do things that aren't humanly possible. Not only can you rapidly rearrange the icons on your desktop, but you can do so with pixel-point accuracy. Without AppleScript, it would be nearly impossible to precisely align dozens of icons. And if you could, it would take a long time and probably cause you to go blind.

✦ After a font-download binge, you find yourself with hundreds of fonts. You really want to organize them into separate folders based on the date that you downloaded them. AppleScript comes to the rescue again! With a brief script, you could knock out this challenge without ever looking at a single date. Add a couple more lines of code to the script and AppleScript will take care of creating the folders, too.

Automate tasks in other applications

Using AppleScript, you can also automate your work in many other applications. You can often automate your work from beginning to end, despite the fact that you need multiple applications to do so. Look at a few scenarios, and you'll begin to appreciate why AppleScript is such a powerful technology:

✦ You've just completed creating the ultimate library of bagpipe songs in iTunes and you want to share the list with your friends at the next Bagpipers Anonymous meeting. You could easily send everyone in the group an iTunes playlist, but not everyone in the club has a Macintosh, let alone a computer. This is going to require creating a hard copy for those members without a computer. Because your bagpipe song list contains thousands of songs, you don't want to retype the name of each song. AppleScript can save the day by extracting the song titles for you and compiling them into a list just in time for your meeting.

✦ AppleScript can take care of your computer-owning bagpipe friends, too. With a few extra steps, you can e-mail all of them the list as well.

✦ Being so fond of bagpipes, you want to send your bagpipe friends a special note during the holidays. To help manage your holiday greeting cards, you can create a record in FileMaker Pro or some other database listing the name and address of each person who should receive a card. If you've entered their street addresses in the Contacts section of your e-mail application, AppleScript can aid in transferring the addresses from your e-mail application to the database. Never again will your bagpiping friends miss a holiday greeting . . . and the world is a much better place.

As you can imagine, there are literally thousands of ways that you can use AppleScript to automate your workflow. Whatever your needs are, AppleScript can often deliver.

Running a Script

The easiest way to get started with AppleScript is to use some scripts that others have already written. *Scripts* are small files that contain a list of commands. This list of commands tells your Mac what function to perform and when to perform it. Fortunately, Apple is kind enough to provide you with several completed scripts with your installation of Mac OS X. You can find a large cache of scripts in the scripts folder, found here in the Library folder, under Scripts.

Many scripts (but not all) end with the extension .scpt. Before you get started running scripts, however, you should know a few things first.

The kinds of scripts

Each script that you encounter will be in one of these three formats:

✦ **Script application:** Some AppleScripts act much like an application. To use one, simply double-click it in the Finder, and off it goes to perform whatever tasks it was meant to do. Depending on an internal setting of the script, it may or may not quit when it's finished doing its thing. Most often, the script completes its mission and quits. You can identify these kinds of scripts in the Finder by their unique icon, shown in Figure 2-1.

**Book VII
Chapter 2**

**AppleScript Just
Plain Rocks**

Figure 2-1: To run some AppleScripts, just double-click their icon.

✦ **Compiled script:** You might also encounter AppleScripts that won't run without the aid of another application. Apple calls these *compiled*

scripts. Although they're not able to execute on their own, they do have the abilities of a script built-in. They just require a host application to use them. Compiled scripts also have their own unique icon, as shown in Figure 2-2.

Figure 2-2:
To execute a compiled AppleScript, you need to use a host application.

✦ **Text file:** In addition to compiled scripts and those that act like applications, a third category of AppleScript that you might encounter is a script stored in a text file. Scripts that are stored in a text file also need a host application before they'll do anything. The main difference between a text file script and a compiled script is that you can read a text file script with any application that can open a text file. Just like all other types of scripts, those stored in text files have a special icon, shown in Figure 2-3.

Figure 2-3:
You can read text file scripts with any word processor.

The Script Editor application

Two of the three possible script types (compiled scripts and text files) require some sort of host application before they'll perform any action. Luckily, Mac OS X provides you with just such a host. The AppleScript Script Editor application comes with Mac OS X and can execute any AppleScript that you throw at it. With the Script Editor you can also do much more, including

✦ View or modify an AppleScript

✦ Create a new AppleScript

✦ Check an AppleScript for errors

✦ Save scripts in one of any of the three possible formats

To launch the Script Editor application, navigate to the AppleScript folder (choose Applications➪AppleScript➪Script Editor) and double-click the Script Editor icon, as shown in Figure 2-4. The Script Editor application displays an empty script editing window.

Figure 2-4:
Script Editor
slices,
dices . . .
even
checks
syntax,
fulfilling
all your
AppleScript
needs.

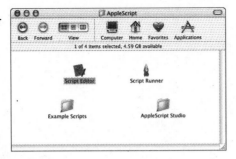

**Book VII
Chapter 2**

**AppleScript Just
Plain Rocks**

Executing a script

After you have the Script Editor application running, you can run any AppleScript that can you find. To get you started, Apple has conveniently provided a handful of useful scripts. Navigate to the Scripts folder, which is located in the Library folder.

The scripts are divided into folders based on functionality, such as fonts, mail, color, and navigation. Figure 2-5 shows the script categories that Apple provides with Mac OS X.

Figure 2-5:
Your Scripts
folder
contains
many
sample
scripts with
which
you can
experiment.

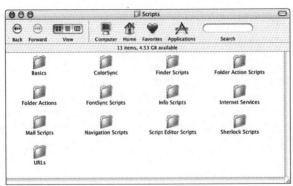

For example, open the Internet Services folder, where you'll find a script named `Current Temperature by Zipcode.scpt`.

You'll need an active Internet connection to test this script.

Double-click the script to open it. Because it's a compiled script and not an application script, the Script Editor automatically loads the script and comes to the foreground. This particular script prompts a user for their zip code and then displays the current temperature, which it retrieves from a Web site. To see the script in action, click the Run button or press ⌘+R. Figure 2-6 shows the location of the Run button.

Figure 2-6:
Click the
Run button
to execute a
script that's
loaded in
the Script
Editor.

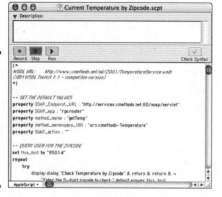

Writing Your Own Simple Scripts

Using someone else's scripts is fun and all, but the real joy of AppleScript comes when you create your own. Not only can you customize a script to your own needs and desires, but saving all those keystrokes can really produce a feeling of euphoria.

Create a script without touching a key

You needn't wear a pocket protector or tape the bridge of your glasses to become proficient with AppleScript. In fact, the Script Editor can get you up and running with AppleScript in no time at all. The secret weapon of the AppleScript author is the Record function of the Script Editor. You click the Record button, perform one or more actions in a recordable application, and then return to the Script Editor where you click the Stop button. The Script Editor stores each of your actions and compiles the whole list into an AppleScript.

In theory this is how it should all work, but in reality, finding recordable Macintosh applications is not always so easy. The Finder is, perhaps, the most recordable application on the Mac. Although there are some other applications that support recording, so few do that Finder may be the only recordable application most Mac users ever see.

To try it yourself, do the following steps to automate actions in the Finder:

1. Bring Script Editor to the foreground.

If Script Editor isn't currently running, double-click its icon in the Finder. If it is running, click its icon in the Dock.

2. Create a new script by pressing ⌘+N.

3. Click the Record button.

The Record button is one of three buttons positioned near the top of a new script window.

4. Switch to the Finder and perform the actions you want to automate.

When the Finder is active, you can select some icons on the Desktop and move them around, resize any open Finder windows, or navigate to your home directory. Any action that you perform in the Finder should be acceptable fodder for the Script Editor. Figure 2-7 shows what the Script Editor looks like while recording icon movements in the Finder. As you perform tasks in the Finder, Script Editor automatically generates a script that replicates your actions.

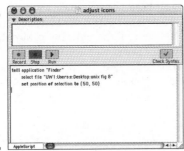

Figure 2-7:
Click Record
to make
Script Editor
automatic-
ally
generate
a script.

5. Return to Script Editor and click the Stop button.

To reactivate Script Editor, click its icon in the Dock. Click the Stop button to cease the recording of your script.

When you're finished, you should be looking at a complete AppleScript. To test your work, return to the Finder and revert any icons or windows that you may have moved or repositioned (you don't want to run a script that doesn't appear to have any effect). Then, return to the Script Editor and click the Run button to watch your automated Finder tasks being performed.

Building your own scripts

An AppleScript novice can perform all kinds of amazing feats with recording features of the Script Editor. Because AppleScript uses a kind of pseudo-English language, it's usually pretty easy to figure out what's going on behind the scenes. Consider the following script for an example:

```
tell app "Finder"
    activate
    set windowList to every window --save list of open windows
    repeat with theWindow in windowList
        tell theWindow
            if collapsed is true then
            --do nothing, because the window is collapsed
            else
                set collapsed to true
            end if
        end tell
    end repeat
end tell
```

The first thing that you may notice about this script is the first line: The `tell` command. This indicates that this script relates to the Finder. This script activates the Finder, creates a list of open windows, and then examines the state of each window: Is it collapsed or not collapsed? (In Mac OS X, a *collapsed* window appears in the Dock.) If the window is already collapsed and in the Dock, nothing happens and the script continues through the list of windows. If the window isn't collapsed, the script collapses it. This continues until the script has examined all open windows. The end result? All open windows end up collapsed in the Dock.

Another thing to note about this script is that it has two comments in it (`save list` and `do nothing`). Comments are your friend! They can help you remember what you were thinking months later when you open the script again. *Comments* help us humans know what's happening, but don't really have any other function. An AppleScript comment begins with two dashes (- -).

One Step Beyond: AppleScript Programming

Creating AppleScripts can soon become very involved, bordering on programming. Don't let that term *programming* scare you away, though. You needn't be a computer scientist to take advantage of AppleScripts. Apple provides a lot of help to get you started along the AppleScript trail.

Grab the Dictionary

Perhaps the greatest resource for AppleScript novices and experts alike is the AppleScript Dictionary. Although many applications are scriptable, not all are. To be scriptable, an application must contain an AppleScript Dictionary. An AppleScript Dictionary details the various commands and objects of an application that you can access via AppleScript.

The Script Editor application allows you to peer inside an application and view its AppleScript Dictionary. To open an application's dictionary, choose File⇨Open Dictionary. Mac OS X searches through your installed applications and presents you with the Open Dictionary dialog, shown in Figure 2-8, which lists all applications that have a dictionary and are therefore scriptable.

Figure 2-8:
Select the
File⇨Open
Dictionary
menu to
view a list of
scriptable
applications.

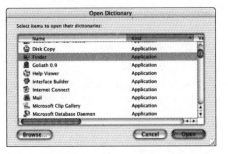

Book VII
Chapter 2

If you don't see your favorite application in the list, alas, it's probably not scriptable. To make certain, click the Browse button and select the application in question.

After you select an application, Script Editor displays that application's AppleScript Dictionary. An application's dictionary lists all the features of that application that are scriptable. Perhaps the most voluminous Dictionary is that of the Finder.

Scriptable features are divided into categories, called *Suites,* which you can see on the left side of the AppleScript Dictionary. Every Mac application is supposed to support the Standard Suite, which lists common terms that most applications should support.

Click an item in the Suite on the left side of the Dictionary to view detailed information about its capabilities, as shown in Figure 2-9.

Figure 2-9:
Select an
item in a
Suite to
view details
about its
capabilities.

The left pane lists an application's Suites.

By surveying the various Suites of an application, you begin to see what tasks you can automate. The Finder, with its huge AppleScript Dictionary, is perhaps the most scriptable of all applications.

Anatomy of a simple script

Although a full discussion of AppleScript programming is beyond the scope of this book, that doesn't mean that you can't produce some quick and useful scripts. Most AppleScripts begin with a command that addresses the application you want to automate. Enter this command into a new AppleScript document, which you create by pressing ⌘+N.

```
tell application "Finder"
```

This is like saying, "Hey, Finder, listen up! I'm going to send commands your way!" Similarly, after you finish instructing the Finder what tasks you want performed, you must also tell it to stop listening. As such, typical scripts end with

```
end tell
```

With the shell of a script in place, all you have to do is add commands in between the `tell` and `end tell` commands of the script. If you want your script to force an application to the foreground, an `activate` command is usually the first line within the shell of your script.

```
tell app "Finder"
  activate
end tell
```

Believe it or not, this is technically a complete and valid script! It doesn't do much, though, so add some more functionality to make it accomplish something worthwhile. For example, suppose that you would like to perform some housekeeping chores each time that you login to your Macintosh. Some desirable tasks might include

+ Emptying the Trash
+ Cleaning up the Desktop icons
+ Having your Mac say "Hello!" to you

Okay, maybe saying "Hello!" isn't a housekeeping chore, but it makes the whole script that much more fun. No one ever said programming had to be boring.

To add these functions, you can do so by using a language you already know: English. Apple tries (and sometimes succeeds) to make AppleScript as English-like as possible. That way, you don't have to learn some silly computer language; just use your native tongue. For example, to empty the Trash, tell the Finder to do so.

```
empty trash
```

Similarly, cleaning up the Desktop is a no-brainer.

```
clean up desktop
```

The trickiest line of code may be the speech, and that's only because you need to remember to add quotes. AppleScript thinks that anything without quotes is an AppleScript command.

```
say "Hello!"
```

The result is a super-simple script that anyone can read but that performs several powerful functions. The completed script looks like this:

```
tell app "Finder"
  activate
  empty trash
  clean up desktop
  say "Hello!"
end tell
```

When you've completed the script, choose File⇨Save to save your script. The Save dialog appears, which is shown in Figure 2-10. Because you want the script to execute and then quit, use the Form field to save it as an application. Also, make sure that the Stay Open check box is not checked and that the Never Show Startup Screen check box is checked. And don't forget to name your script in the Save text field.

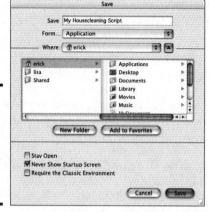

Figure 2-10: Save your script as an application so that you can run it again later.

You can save the script wherever you choose. To have the script automatically run each time that you log in to your Mac, save the script anywhere you wish. (Assign its home folder in the Where field of the Save window.) Then open System Preferences by clicking its icon in the Dock. To add the new script to the Login Items, click the Login Items button in the System Preferences. Then click the Add button and navigate to your script in the Open dialog that appears. After you dismiss the Open dialog, you'll see the script in the Login Items window. In Figure 2-11, see the Login Items dialog after a new script called My Housecleaning Script has been added.

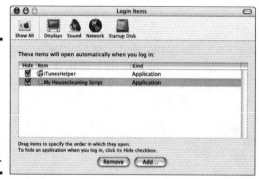

Figure 2-11: To launch scripts at login, add them to the Login Items in System Preferences.

Help is at your fingertips

If you would like to explore AppleScript further, you have many resources at your disposal. Sometimes the easiest way to use AppleScript is to copy what people before you have created. Other times, it's a good idea to read the documentation included in Apple's Help system. Whichever approach you use, with a little practice and guidance, you'll soon be doing stupendous tasks with your Mac.

Built-in AppleScript Help

The most readily available AppleScript reference is built into Mac OS X. Choose Help➪Mac Help to launch the Mac OS Help Guides from the Finder or choose Help➪Script Editor Help from the Script Editor. You'll find numerous Help topics, including help for AppleScript, by clicking the Help Center button as shown in Figure 2-12. This is a great place to begin your AppleScript exploration. It includes detailed documentation about the AppleScript language and loads of demonstration scripts for you to try (or alter) yourself.

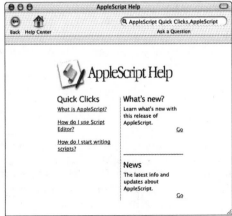

Figure 2-12: AppleScript Help is voluminous and easy to access: Look for it under the Help menu.

Book VII
Chapter 2

AppleScript Just Plain Rocks

AppleScript on the Web

In addition to the built-in AppleScript help in the Finder, the Internet has much to offer in the way of AppleScript training and examples. Like so many other excellent Web resources, AppleScripts are free!

Apple Computer

The first place on the Web that you should visit for AppleScript help is the mother ship: Apple Computer. Although the built-in OS X help offers a lot, Apple's Web site offers even more scripts, tutorials, and general AppleScript goodness. You can even find a list of all known scriptable applications, which can save you from searching for them with Script Editor. Furthermore, the site maintains an extensive list of links to other useful AppleScript sites.

`www.apple.com/applescript/`

AppleScript Central

AppleScript Central is no slouch when it comes to offering handy AppleScripts. Specializing in downloadable scripts, the site is organized according to application. Do you need a script to transfer your Eudora address book to Entourage; or maybe you need a script to display iTunes songs in your chat windows? AppleScript Central has it all. Whether you choose to use these scripts as-is or modify them for your particular needs, AppleScript Central is an AppleScript site you won't want to miss.

`www.applescriptcentral.com/`

ResExcellence

For the hacker in all of us, ResExcellence sports many unique system tweaks, modifications, and outright hacks. Among the ResExcellence bag of tricks is an extensive list of AppleScripts for you to download. Although not geared strictly towards AppleScript, ResExcellence offers many excellent scripts for customizing your desktop, doing things you didn't think possible, and generally making your Macintosh experience more fulfilling.

`www.resexcellence.com/applescripts/index.shtml`

MacScripter.net

MacScripter.net devotes its site to all Macintosh scripting. Because AppleScript is such a huge part of scripting the Mac OS, you can be certain that there's something here for you. Besides offering up-to-date news on scripting for the Mac OS, MacScripter.net also gives you access to many scripts, information about scripting books, as well as details on Apple's new AppleScript Studio software, which lets you create AppleScripts with interfaces. The sheer volume of information at this site makes it one you shouldn't skip.

`www.macscripter.net/`

Not all AppleScripts are created equal! When downloading scripts from the Internet, make sure that they are compatible with Mac OS X. While the majority of scripts made for Mac OS 9 will also work with Mac OS X, some simply won't. The converse is also true. Sometimes a script is meant solely for use with Mac OS X.

Chapter 3: Forget Hal! Talking and Writing to Your Macintosh

In This Chapter

✔ **Using handwriting recognition to control Mac OS X**

✔ **Speak to your Mac**

✔ **Your Mac speaks back**

*I*f typing on a keyboard makes you wince or leaves you thinking that there must be some better way to get information into your computer, you'll be happy to know that Apple has you in mind. Since the very first Mac rolled off the assembly line, Apple has had a keen interest in alternative modes of interaction with their computers. Mac OS X continues in this tradition of alternative computer controls, offering two options for controlling Mac OS X without the keyboard: handwriting and speech.

✦ **Handwriting:** By using a pen and computer tablet, you can enter text into your Mac by simply writing as you would on a sheet of paper.

✦ **Speech:** Talk to your Mac to make it listen and obey your commands. It even talks back!

This chapter guides you through the various options that you have for controlling your Macintosh without using the keyboard. First, I cover the new Inkwell features found in Mac OS X, which you use to write on a tablet to enter data into your computer. Think of it as digital paper. Whatever you write on the tablet appears on the screen as text. Then I look at the more space-age speech capabilities available to you in Mac OS X. By using your voice, you can command a Macintosh to perform all sorts of interesting feats. And just so you don't get lonely, the Mac will even talk back to you. Now you can control your computer the way the Star Trek crew does!

So, scoot away from your computer, lean that chair back, and let your Mac take care of the rest.

Using Ink with a Tablet

Typing on a keyboard can be a tedious and error-prone experience for even the best typists. To help out, Apple added some useful handwriting features to Mac OS X. Based in part on some of Apple's handheld software for the Newton (one of the first Personal Digital Assistants renowned for its recognition skills), the handwriting recognition in Mac OS X gives you the ability to write text on a compatible tablet for use in your favorite applications.

The basic process of working with handwriting on Mac OS X goes like this:

1. **Attach a tablet to your Mac.**

   Most tablets use a Universal Serial Bus (USB) connection, so connecting one to your computer is as simple as plugging in the cable from your tablet to the USB port on your Mac.

2. **Write on the tablet with the stylus that accompanies it.**

   A stylus is the name given the fake "pen" that accompanies most tablets. A stylus doesn't have any ink in it: It's simply a pen-shaped tool with a plastic tip meant for writing on a tablet.

3. **Your Mac interprets your handwriting.**

   After your Mac recognizes the handwriting, it sends that text to the foremost application at the cursor location where you would normally type with the keyboard. You're spared the whole training bit, too.

You aren't restricted to writing just text on the tablet, naturally. You can use it to control the interface of your Mac as you would a mouse. A tablet also works great for graphics applications like Procreate's Painter and Adobe's Photoshop. Many artists are frustrated when drawing with a mouse; when you use a tablet, you can feel right at home with the natural pen or brush movements that you've always used.

Although Inkwell pretty much takes care of preparing your Mac for handwriting recognition, it does offer you a few settings in the Inkwell pane of the System Preferences. To view the System Preferences, click the System Preferences icon in the Dock. From there, click the Inkwell icon to adjust settings for your tablet.

If you don't have a tablet connected to your Macintosh, you won't be able to view the System Preference pane for Inkwell. Mac OS X is smart enough to only show you the settings for your current hardware setup.

Computer, Can You Hear Me?

Remember that classic scene from the movie *Star Trek III: The Search for Spock* where Scotty picks up the mouse on a Macintosh and tries to talk directly to the computer? Since the very early days of the Mac OS, Apple has included some form of speech recognition in their computers. Mac OS X continues to improve on speech recognition by offering a host of tools that let you get more work done in a shorter amount of time. (We're not to that point yet, Scotty, but we're working on it.)

The Speech Recognition features of Mac OS X let you speak a word, phrase, or sentence. After you've spoken, your Mac goes to work translating what you said. If it understands the phrase, it then performs an action associated with that phrase. The great part about this system is that you can say any phrase in continuous speech and have your Mac perform any sort of action that you can imagine. In fact, you aren't limited to just one action. You could perform dozens of actions upon speaking a particular phrase, for example.

Before you get started using Speech Recognition, you need a microphone to get sound into your Mac. If you use one of the flat-screen iMacs, your microphone is built into the monitor. (Look for a little hole at the bottom-left corner of your monitor.) PowerBooks and iBooks have a similar microphone built into the screen. On the other hand, if you use a desktop machine, you'll need to purchase a microphone and connect it to the rear of your Macintosh by plugging it into the microphone jack.

The Speech Recognition tab

To get started with Speech Recognition in Mac OS X, open the System Preferences window by clicking its icon in the Dock. When it opens, click the Speech icon. This brings up the Speech Pane, as shown in Figure 3-1.

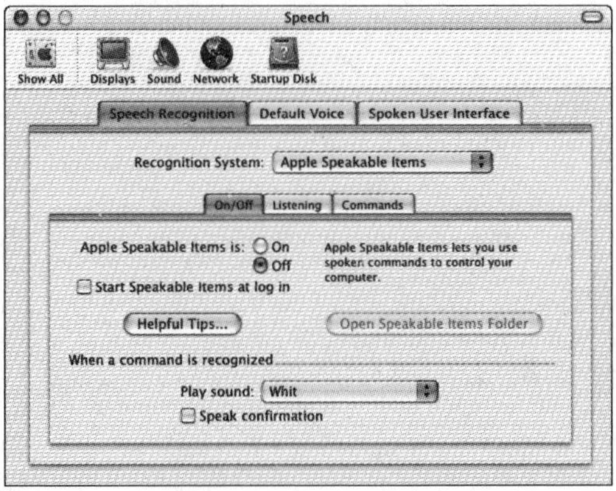

**Book VII
Chapter 3**

Forget Hal! Talking and Writing to Your Macintosh

Figure 3-1:
The Speech pane is the central location for adjusting Speech Recognition settings.

You'll find that three tabs comprise the speech settings of Mac OS X:

✦ Speech Recognition

✦ Default Voice

✦ Spoken User Interface

In this section, I'm only concerned with the Speech Recognition tab. Later, in the section "The Mac Talks Back!," I explore the other two tabs.

The Speech Recognition tab consists of three sub-tabs:

✦ **On/Off:** As you can probably guess, this tab lets you switch Speech Recognition features on and off. It lets you adjust some of the Speech Recognition settings as well.

✦ **Listening:** The Listening tab provides a number of settings that control how your Mac listens to Its Master's Voice. You can set the sound input, adjust the key on the keyboard that toggles speech recognition on and off, change microphone and volume settings, and name your computer. (You do want to call your computer by name like any techno-wizard, don't you?)

✦ **Commands:** When Speech Recognition is active, your Mac can understand any number of commands. In the Commands tab, you tell the Mac what type of command it should expect you to give. You can also specify whether you will be giving the commands word-for-word or whether your Mac should be prepared to interpret paraphrasing.

Besides the sub-tabs, note one other setting on the Speech Recognition tab: the Speech Recognition System drop-down list. At the time this book was published, the only available system was Apple Speakable Items.

The On/Off tab

The On/Off tab, shown in Figure 3-2, is your main control for starting and stopping Speech Recognition in Mac OS X.

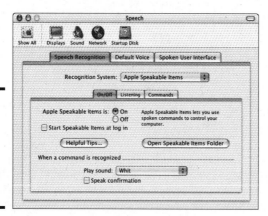

Figure 3-2:
Use the On/Off tab to toggle speech recognition on and off.

When you mark the On radio button, the Speech Recognition Feedback window appears on your screen, floating above all other windows. The Feedback window (as shown in Figure 3-3) is your friend and partner. If you use Speech Recognition often, it'll become a constant companion on your desktop. More on it in the next section.

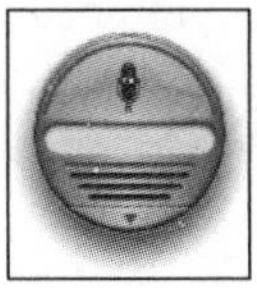

Figure 3-3:
The Feedback window appears automatically when you activate Speech Recognition.

When Speech Recognition is active, your Mac listens for whatever phrases appear in your Speakable Items Folder. The On/Off tab allows you to view the contents of the Speakable Items Folder, which is a directory on your hard drive that holds a number of scripts. When you speak a phrase that matches one of these file names, your Mac automatically executes that script. The script can perform any number of actions, which is what makes Speech Recognition so powerful. Apple includes a large number of scripts with Mac OS X, but you're free to create your own, too.

To view the contents of the Speakable Items Folder, click the Open Speakable Items Folder button. The Finder comes to the foreground and navigates to the folder that holds the scripts. This is handy because each item in the Speakable Items Folder is speakable.

To the left of the Open Speakable Items Folder button is another button: Helpful Tips. Click it to get some pointers on how to get the best performance from your microphone.

At the bottom of the On/Off tab is the When a Command is Recognized section. When your Mac comprehends one of your utterances, you can set it to respond by playing a sound, speaking a confirmation, or both. This is helpful when you're not sure whether your Mac understands you. One hundred percent recognition is not a reality on any computer at this point, so sometimes it helps to have any feedback that you can get. Otherwise, you might feel silly shouting at your machine while it sits there doing nothing.

The Listening tab

The second section of the Speech Recognition tab is the Listening tab, as shown in Figure 3-4. From this tab, you can control how you turn listening on and off. You can choose between two styles of listening with the Listening Method radio buttons:

✦ **Listen Only While Key Is Pressed:** Speech Recognition only works while the designated key is held down.

✦ **Key Toggles Listening On and Off:** Press a key to turn listening on. When you're finished speaking, press the key again to cease listening.

To change what key must be toggled or held down, click the Change Key button.

Figure 3-4: Use the Listening tab to determine when your Macintosh listens to your speech.

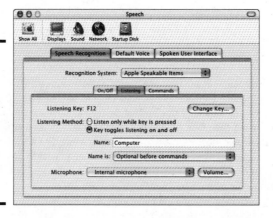

While your computer is listening for your spoken commands, you might want to preface each command with a word. For example, instead of saying, "Empty the Trash!," you might prefer, "Computer, empty the Trash!" This adds a little bit of personality to the interaction and also gives your computer a slightly longer time to react to your command. As a general rule, the longer the spoken phrase, the more likely your Mac will understand it. Below the Listening Method section of the Listening tab resides the name by which you'd like to address your computer. You can also choose to address by name all the time or only sometimes. These settings are located in the Name Is pop-up menu.

Finally, at the bottom of the Speech Recognition tab is where you set the microphone that you'd like to use for Speech Recognition. If you have more than one microphone connected to your machine, you can even select between the different ones.

The Commands tab

The Speech Recognition features of Mac OS X are not restricted to items in the Speakable Items Folder. Any application that supports Speech Recognition is also fair game for your verbal manipulation. To control commands within other applications, use the Commands tab, shown in Figure 3-5. Here you can enable the following check boxes:

✦ General Speakable Items Commands

✦ Specific Application Commands

✦ Application Switching Commands

✦ Front Window Commands

✦ Menu Bar Commands

Mark any one of these options to allow your Mac to listen to those kinds of commands.

At the bottom of the Commands tab, you can mark the Require Exact Wording of Speakable Item Command Names check box. If you enable this, you must speak the Speakable Items command exactly as it is named in the Finder. If you turn it off, you can speak some variation of the phrase, and Mac OS X will try to intelligently decide what you want to do.

Book VII Chapter 3

Forget Ha! Talking and Writing to Your Macintosh

Figure 3-5: The Commands tab lets you pick and choose which phrases you'd like your Mac to hear.

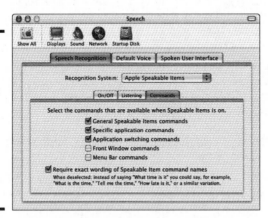

Feedback window

After you've activated Speech Recognition, you'll instantly see a Feedback window. The Feedback window, shown in Figure 3-6, is the small round window that floats above all applications.

Figure 3-6:
The Feedback window provides important visual information to assist your speech recognition activities.

 — Microphone Level Meter

The Feedback window includes controls and displays of its own:

✦ **Microphone Level Meter:** The Feedback window displays indicators to let you know how loud the input to your microphone is.

✦ **Visual Indicator:** The Feedback window displays visual feedback to let you know what mode it is in: idle, listening, or hearing a command. Refer to Figure 3-3 to see an example of a Feedback window in listening mode. (*Note:* When there are no arrows on either side of the microphone, this indicates listening mode.) Figure 3-6, with its microphone flanked by arrows, indicates that the computer is hearing a command spoken. When Speech Recognition is idle, no arrows are present, and the microphone is grayed out.

✦ **Quick-access Menu:** You can quickly access the Speech preferences for the System or view the Speech Commands window. Just click the downward-pointing arrow at the bottom of the Feedback window, and a menu appears giving you one-click access to both.

As soon as you disable speech recognition in the System Preferences, the Feedback window disappears.

Speech Command window

Because Speech Recognition might be listening for different sets of commands from the either Finder or many other applications, Mac OS X provides you with a single listing of all commands that you may speak at any given time: the Speech Commands window. To open the Speech Commands window, click the triangle at the bottom of the Feedback window. Choose Speech Commands window from the menu that appears, as shown in Figure 3-7.

Figure 3-7:
Open the
Speech
Commands
window
from the
Feedback
window.

The Speech Commands window is a simple one, but it serves an important purpose: to let you know what commands Mac OS X understands. The Speech Commands pane, shown in Figure 3-8, organizes commands into categories that match the settings in the Speech pane of the System Preferences.

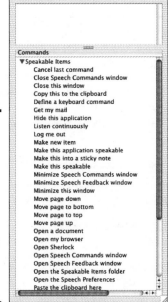

Figure 3-8:
The Speech
Commands
window
presents
you with
a list of
commands
that Speech
Recognition
under-
stands.

If you launch another application that supports Speech Recognition, Mac OS X adds that application's commands to the Speech Commands window. Speak any of these commands to make your Mac execute that function. Mac OS X ships with speech commands for Mail and Internet Explorer.

The Mac Talks Back!

Mac OS X is great at listening to your speech, but the fun doesn't stop there. Your Mac can talk to you, too! By using one of the many available voices, you can make your computer talk or even sing. And although Speech Recognition lets you speak to your Macintosh, *text-to-speech* (TTS, as the pros call it) gives your Mac the ability to speak text. This is an especially useful feature because it lets you listen to your e-mails, Web pages, or even your homework. Sometimes the eyes need a break. Text-to-speech gives you the opportunity to lean back in your chair or even get up and walk around while still using your Macintosh. There's no need to squint at the text on your computer screen.

Like Speech Recognition, you can adjust text-to-speech settings using the Speech pane of the System Preferences. The Speech pane has two tabs that pertain to text-to-speech.

✦ **Default Voice:** Lets you choose a voice for your Macintosh.

✦ **Spoken User Interface:** Permits you to automate some text-to-speech functions in Mac OS X.

The Default Voice tab

The text-to-speech engine that comes with Mac OS X has a collection of many different voices from which to choose. Some voices are male, some are female, and some aren't human at all. To begin working with the voices in Mac OS X:

1. **Open the System Preferences by clicking its icon in the Dock.**

2. **Click the Speech icon to display the Speech dialog, where you can change a number of Speech settings.**

3. **Click the Default Voice tab, shown in Figure 3-9, to reveal the voices available to you.**

On the left side of the Default Voice tab is the list of voices from which you can choose. When you select a voice, click the Play button to hear a demonstration of that voice. Above the Play button is a slider for adjusting the speed of the speech. Move the slider to the right to increase the speed at which your Mac speaks and to the left to slow it down.

Each voice has a set of characteristics associated with it. When you select voices, their properties appear in the top right of the Default Voice tab.

✦ **Language:** If you're reading this book, you'll probably see English here.

✦ **Gender:** Male, Female, or Other (which are robots or other nonliving entities).

✦ **Age:** How old is this voice, anyhow?

✦ **Description:** This is usually some cryptic title that is connected to the history of speech on the Macintosh. You can usually ignore this field.

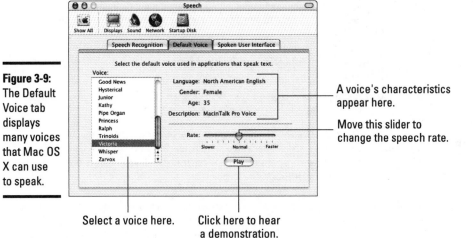

Figure 3-9:
The Default Voice tab displays many voices that Mac OS X can use to speak.

A voice's characteristics appear here.

Move this slider to change the speech rate.

Select a voice here.   Click here to hear a demonstration.

For what it's worth, Victoria, Kathy, and Ralph have some of the more intelligible (human-sounding) voices of the bunch.

The Spoken User Interface tab

After you select a voice, you have a variety of ways to make your Macintosh speak to you. The first one that you should check out is on the Spoken User Interface tab (see Figure 3-10). Here you can set your Mac to speak automatically to you based on some simple rules.

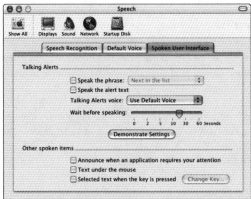

Figure 3-10:
Use the Spoken User Interface tab to automate some speech tasks.

The two sections on the Spoken User Interface tab are Talking Alerts and Other spoken Items.

Talking Alerts

If you use your Macintosh for any time at all, you will eventually run into an Alert dialog. An Alert dialog usually displays some kind of icon from the following list:

✦ **Stop sign:** Indicates that something particularly important requires your attention.

✦ **Yield sign:** Signals that you should cautiously proceed; not as severe as the Stop sign, but important nonetheless.

✦ **Notification:** Looks like the profile of a person speaking; displays an informative message, but not a warning. You could use this feature, for example, to have a calendar application alert you when you have a meeting or a deadline.

The Talking Alerts section of the Speech Pane in the System Preferences specifies what your Mac speaks whenever an Alert is showing. You can choose to have your Mac to speak a specific phrase or the contents of the Alert dialog by selecting one of the check boxes at the top of the tab. In the Talking Alerts voice drop-down list box, you can select a voice that is specific to the Talking Alerts: That is, it only applies to Talking Alerts. Use the Wait Before Speaking slider to control the increment of time that Mac allows to pass before it speaks. To hear what you're Talking Alert settings will sound like in use, click the Demonstrate Settings button.

If you click the Demonstrate Settings button and don't hear anything right away, remember that it won't begin speaking until the time has elapsed that you set with the Wait Before Speaking slider. To hear the Talking Alerts speak as soon as you click the Demonstrate Settings button, move the slider to 0 (zero).

Other Spoken Items

In addition to Talking Alerts, you can allow your Mac to speak when other actions occur. The Other Spoken Items section of the Spoken User Interface tab is where you make these settings. Your Mac can speak in the following circumstances:

✦ **Announce when an application requires your attention:** In case you have your Dock hidden from view, it's not always clear when an application needs your attention. In these instances, Mac OS X will grab your attention via speech.

✦ **Read the text that's directly under your mouse:** If you have trouble reading the text in word processing documents or Web pages, your Mac can read whatever text is below your mouse.

✦ **Read a selection of text when you press a particular key:** If you have a child who is learning to read, the Mac can help them by reading a selection of text. Kids can learn how to drag and select text often more quickly than they can read that text.

Apple might be a big, serious, computer company, but they aren't without a humorous side. With Speech Recognition enabled, say the phrase, "Tell me a joke." Your Mac will reply with a random joke. Say it again, and your Mac will tell you another joke.

Speaking Your Own Phrases

Because the speech engine is an integral part of Mac OS X, you can make your Mac speak whatever text you tell it to by using applications, services, and even AppleScript. This is useful for a variety of purposes: listening to your Address Book, hearing a Web page read to you, or even getting your Mac to call you by first name.

Speaking text through applications

One of the simplest ways to hear spoken text in Mac OS X is by using the TextEdit application. *TextEdit* is a simple text processor that accompanies every copy of Mac OS X. Besides its handy word processing features, TextEdit can also speak text. This is good for reviewing a document after you've written it by listening to it. To hear spoken text with TextEdit, follow these steps:

1. **Launch TextEdit from the Applications folder.**

To open the Applications folder, choose Go⇨Applications from the Finder. In the window that appears, double-click the TextEdit application.

This launches the TextEdit application and opens a new document.

2. **Enter some text.**

Either type some text on the keyboard or paste some into the document from the Clipboard.

3. **Choose Edit⇨Speech⇨Start Speaking.**

Your Mac will begin speaking the text from the document. The speech engine has some intelligence, so you can enter dollar amounts (such as $25,423.12) or Roman numerals (such as Chapter XIV), and these will read them back in plain English. The result of these two strings would be "Twenty-five thousand, four-hundred twenty-three dollars, and twelve cents" and "chapter fourteen."

4. **Choose Edit⇨Speech⇨Stop Speaking.**

   You Mac will stop speaking. It will also stop speaking when it reaches the end of the text.

Speaking text through services

Mac OS X introduced the new Services feature to Macintosh users, which are like miniature applications that are available to any application that supports Services. Located under the Apple Menu, the Services Menu lists all installed Services. To speak text from an application, first select that text. Then, choose Application⇨Services⇨Speech⇨Start Speaking to speak text from many applications (where *Application* is the name of the currently running application). This works great for doing things like

✦ Speaking a Web page aloud

✦ Reading your e-mail

✦ Listening to what your friends type on iChat

As you might expect, choosing Application⇨Services⇨Speech⇨Stop Speaking ceases the banter emanating from your Mac's speaker.

Alas, not all applications are created equal. Some applications cannot access the Services offered in the Services menu. This stems from the fact that Cocoa applications can and Carbon applications can't, although this might change in the future. In fact, this is one of the ways that you can guess whether an application is Cocoa or Carbon. If you don't understand (or care) about Cocoa versus Carbon applications, just keep in mind that Services are not always available, and that's why.

Speaking text through AppleScript

Besides the aforementioned methods for producing speech on the Mac, AppleScript offers other interesting possibilities. With AppleScript, you can command your Mac to say all sorts of things. How is this different than with an application or Services? AppleScript can speak text like most applications and so much more because it is *dynamic*. This means that it can speak text that it doesn't know about at the time that you create the script. For example, suppose you want your Mac to speak the day of the week. Each day that you run the script, your Mac will speak a different phrase: the name of that day of the week.

```
tell application "Finder"
  set today to weekday of the (current date)
  say (today as text)
end tell
```

This sort of task wouldn't be possible with TextEdit.

Of course, AppleScript isn't helpful only for speaking text. It works in conjunction with Speech Recognition, too. The Speakable Items folder holds various scripts that you can launch by using your own speech. (See the earlier section, "The On/Off Tab," to find out more about the Speakable Items folder.) Instead of simply double-clicking the previous script to hear the day of the week, you could save the script as an Application in the Speakable Items folder. Figure 3-11 shows the Save dialog with Application chosen from the Format menu.

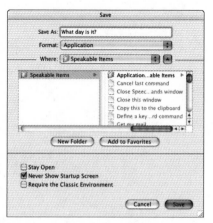

Figure 3-11: Save your scripts in the Application format if you want to use them in the Speakable Items folder.

Be sure to give the script a descriptive name because that name is what you will speak to execute the script later. For example, save the script with a name like this:

```
What day is it?
```

Then, when you want to know what day it is, simply ask your Mac! If all goes as planned, your Mac should speak the result. With a little imagination, it's not hard to dream up some fun or useful ideas for AppleScript.

Chapter 4: Hosting a Web Site à la OS X

In This Chapter

⤙ **Creating your own Web site**

⤙ **Using .Mac**

⤙ **Hosting your own Web server**

⤙ **Sharing files with FTP**

*I*n the last ten years, surfing the Internet has gone from a nerdy hobby to an activity enjoyed by the whole family. For children and grandparents alike, Web surfing has become one of the world's most popular spectator sports. At some point, you'll probably get the itch to become more involved. Everyone else has a Web site, so why not you?

Creating and hosting your own Web site can be a rewarding experience, and with some help from Apple and Mac OS X, it's a cinch to do. Whether you want to sell your favorite eggplant recipes, display pictures of your purple car, or just post a résumé (with a purple background), Mac OS X has you covered in more ways than one. So put on your seat belts because you are now entering a strange world of servers, mysterious codes, and things that go bump in the Net. Don't be scared, though. Apple has made the topic so simple that even a politician can do it.

Building a Site with .Mac

To get you up and running on the Web quickly, Apple offers a suite of online Web-publishing tools. The toolbox, collectively known as *.Mac,* gives you easy and fast access to a variety of Internet functions. A .Mac membership costs $99.95 per year and offers the following features:

✦ **iCards:** Send customized electronic postcards via the Internet.

✦ **HomePage:** Build and edit your own Web site.

✦ **iDisk:** Disk space on Apple's servers for you to post a Web site or files. This is where you'll be storing files for use in your own HomePage creations.

✦ **Email:** Web-based e-mail for your Mac.com e-mail account.

Registering as a .Mac user

You can visit Apple's home on the Internet to register as a .Mac user.

`http://www.mac.com/`

To register, you must create a username and password. The username that you select is an important part of the .Mac experience, so choose it carefully. Your username plays a part in your e-mail address, your Web address, your login name, and even the bar code on your forehead. (Maybe the bar code is a joke — for now, anyway — but the rest aren't.) Take a few minutes to carefully plan your .Mac user name. It will save you some typing, be easier for your friends to remember, and, like a customized license plate for your car, can convey a certain personality to others on the Web.

Setting up your site with HomePage

After you successfully register as a .Mac user, login to the .Mac section of the Apple Web site, as shown in Figure 4-1. You can find it in the toolbar at the top of the Web page.

Figure 4-1: Login from the .Mac tab of the Apple Web site.

Then click the <u>Account</u> link in the lower portion of the toolbar. This takes you to the login screen (see Figure 4-2). Enter your username and password that you entered upon registration and click the Enter button.

Figure 4-2: Log into .Mac here.

After you're logged in, click the HomePage icon that appears near the top of the page. HomePage is a complete publishing tool for building Web pages that's actually a Web site itself. HomePage lets you choose from a variety of styles which you can then apply to your Web site within a matter of seconds. HomePage is template driven, so even non-techies can produce impressive-looking Web sites. After you finished designing your Web pages by selecting one of the premade templates, HomePage automatically posts them to your .Mac Web site.

The HomePage interface includes two sections: the Pages section and the Create a Page section. The Pages section (see Figure 4-3) is where you manage the various pages of your site; here you can view a list of all pages on your site as well as password-protect any pages in your site. When you've completed your site, you can get spiffy and formal by sending an announcement to all of your friends from the Site section.

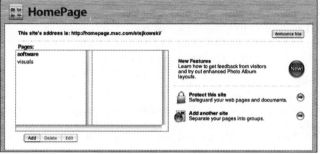

Figure 4-3: Manage the pages of your HomePage Web site.

Book VII
Chapter 4

Hosting a Web Site à la OS X

In the Create a Page section, shown in Figure 4-4, you can directly add a page to your site based on a variety of premade Web page templates. Apple offers a multitude of styles to suit your needs. Click any one of these styles to add it to your Web site. When you do, .Mac walks you through a series of questions that indicate what specific information, graphics, or movies you want on that Web page.

Figure 4-4: Add pages to your site.

✦ **Photo Album:** Display your favorite photos and images for your friends and family.

✦ **iMovies:** Post your home videos or iMovie creations on the Web. (To discover all about iMovies, read Chapter 4 of Book III.)

✦ **Resume:** Looking for a job? A Web-based résumé is a handy tool for impressing prospective employers.

✦ **Newsletter:** Want to update all those close and not-so-close relatives on your family's doings? Put out a newsletter.

✦ **Baby:** When your bundle of joy arrives, it's a cinch to post photos of the new baby to your HomePage site. This works great for long-distance relatives because they can cyber-visit the hospital without leaving home. It also works well for keeping those curious aunts and uncles out of the delivery room.

✦ **Education:** Schools are depending more and more on the Internet. To help the student and the teacher, Apple provides several useful education-related pages for you to use, including event calendars, homework pages, and an online school newspaper.

✦ **Invite:** The Web makes for a great tool when it comes to delivering invitations. Gone are the hassles of standing in line at the post office, licking 300 stamps (What? You don't have 300 friends?), and cards lost in the mail. Send your guests a Web-based invitation. Your guests will thank you. The trees that you save will thank you. Moreover, your tongue will thank you. The post office, however, might not thank you, but why should it start now?

✦ **File Sharing:** With HomePage, you can quickly post your favorite files for others to download.

Keep adding pages to your site as you see fit. Each type of page has a different layout. If a page requires media like images or movies, for example, HomePage will automatically list all media available on your iDisk. You simply select the desired media file, and HomePage adds them to the current page. The following section elaborates more on iDisk.

After you complete your Web site, you access it using a URL like this (with *your_username* replaced with your actual username):

```
http://homepage.mac.com/your_username/
```

Adding files with iDisk

If you create a Web page with HomePage that requires images or movies, you add them to your site by using iDisk. *iDisk* (see Figure 4-5) is a space on Apple's servers designated just for you. This is where HomePage stores the elements of your site when you add or change Web pages or any of the content within those pages.

Figure 4-5:
Add to your
Web page
with iDisk.

You aren't limited to iDisk access via HomePage: Simply choose the iDisk menu from the Finder's Go menu to mount your iDisk. (No need for a saddle — I explain more about mounting volumes in Book I.) When you mount an iDisk, it shows up as an icon on your Desktop, just like you might see when you insert a CD into your Mac. The icon for your iDisk, however, looks like a hard drive with a blue globe on top of it.

With your iDisk mounted, double-click its icon to view its contents. Apple organizes iDisk with a handful of folders that correspond to the page types in HomePage; you can't delete or rename these folders, however. If you need an image for your photo album page, stick it in the Pictures folder. If you need a movie for your Web page, copy it to the Movies folder. When you return to HomePage, your files will now appear in the list of items that you can use in a Web page.

Creating a Home Page with HTML and iDisk

For those folks who like driving automobiles while knowing nothing about what goes on under the hood, HomePage is perfect. Use it to create and post Web pages without knowing what makes it all work. On the other hand, some folks are grease monkeys and like to get under the hood. If you're one of those types, Apple gives you a chance to get your hands dirty. You don't *have* to use HomePage to work on your Web site. If you're well versed in HyperText Markup Language (HTML), you can edit your Web page files on your iDisk just like you would any file on your hard drive.

Open the Sites folder to see the various files that compose your Web page. If you're an old pro at HTML, you can even load the files on your iDisk with your favorite text editor, edit them, and resave to the iDisk. In other words, the iDisk acts much like any other disk that you're accustomed to using.

Logging into iDisk the Easy Way

You don't have to navigate to Apple's .Mac site and log in manually because .Mac is directly integrated into Mac OS X. However, your Mac first needs to know your .Mac username. Click System Preferences in the Dock and then click the Internet icon. The .Mac tab of the Internet pane appears on top by default (see Figure 4-6). Enter your .Mac username in the appropriate field and exit System Preferences to save your username and password.

Figure 4-6: Set up your .Mac login through System Preferences.

After Mac OS X has a handle on your .Mac username (horrible pun ignored), your iDisk is just one click away. Choose Go➪iDisk from the Finder (Figure 4-7), and your iDisk automatically mounts on your Desktop. Like other disks, you can unmount the iDisk by dragging it to the Trash.

Figure 4-7: Select Go➪iDisk to mount your iDisk instantly.

Using Mac OS X Web Sharing

With .Mac, Apple takes care of the Web server for you, but you aren't stuck with using .Mac: You have other options when it comes to posting Web pages. Mac OS X comes stocked with its own high-powered Web server, so you can run things without .Mac. Before you begin running your own Web server, consider why you might want to do so such a thing.

✦ **Privacy:** Everyone in the house wants access to the family phone book. You want all computers on your home network to see the telephone list but not the whole world. Posting it on the home network keeps it secure from prying eyes outside your home.

✦ **Speed:** Your friend needs a copy of your iMovies masterpiece for a class project. Rather than wait for you to post the file to your iDisk, he decides to download it directly from your computer.

✦ **Coolness factor:** It's fun, easy to do, and your mother will truly be proud. Seriously, it is fun and easy to run your own Web server. (And although your mother might not actually give a hoot, employers like employees who know useful skills; therefore, Web server stuff is good to know.)

I love Apache: Confessions of a UNIX Webmaster

Deep in the guts of Mac OS X lies one of the most popular Web servers around: Apache. *Apache* is the software that turns your Macintosh into a full-featured Web server. The Apache Web server is well respected around the world and comprises about half of all personal and commercial Web servers in use today. Yes, that's right! You have one of the world's most-used Web servers already installed on your Mac!

By now, you might be wondering what makes Apache so great that everyone uses it. Apache's first appealing feature is its price — absolutely free. Repeat after me: *Free is good!* Free isn't any good without quality, though. Fortunately, Apache delivers in this aspect as well. It's extremely reliable — and combined with the crash-proof Mac OS X, you can be almost certain that your Web server will always be available. Besides being rock-solid and free, Apache sports all the features you'd expect from a top-notch Web server, such as Server-Side Includes and integration with databases and scripting languages. It can serve anything you throw at it.

Configuring and running Apache

In addition to all its great qualities, Apache is dead simple to operate in Mac OS X. Open the System Preferences and click the Sharing icon; then mark the check box next to Personal Web Sharing to launch Apache. That's it! It doesn't get any easier than that. (See Figure 4-8.)

To begin using your Web server, it's time to visit the Finder. Open a Finder window and navigate to the Sites folder that resides in your Home folder; this is the root of your personal space on the Web server. Any files that you add to this folder will be accessible via your Web server.

Figure 4-8:
Start your
Web server
with only
one click in
the System
Preferences.

You might find a file named `index.html` already installed in the Sites folder.
This is the default file for your Web site. To view it, open your favorite Web
browser and load this URL, replacing *~username* with the username that
you're currently using:

`http://127.0.0.1/~username/`

The 127.0.0.1 address is a generic Internet Protocol (IP) address, which means
self. (In other words, your computer is connecting to your computer.) You can
also use your real IP address, which appears at the top of the Sharing panel
(next to the Network Address heading) in the System Preferences.

To see the Web page from another computer, you must use the real IP
address. The 127.0.0.1 address is merely a convenience for use when you're
using the actual machine that runs the Web server.

Because Mac OS X is a multi-user environment, each user can host a Web
site. Each Web site has a username found at the end of the URL. Replace it
with the appropriate username and you're ready to go. If everything goes
smoothly, you should be viewing the default Mac OS X Web page, as shown
in Figure 4-9. The default page displays a welcome message and some important information for Web-sharing beginners. Make sure you read the information carefully.

In addition to a main page for any individual that logs in, the Web server
also has a global default page. To find the global default page

1. **Open a new Finder window.**

2. **Click the Computer icon in the window's toolbar.**

3. **Double-click the drive that contains your Mac OS X installation.**

4. **Choose Library⇨WebServer⇨Documents.**

Figure 4-9:
The default
Apache
Web page
for your
username
greets you
upon your
first visit to
the site.

> **Your website here.**
>
> Now you can use Mac OS X Personal Web Sharing to publish
> web pages or share files on the Internet — or on your
> company's (or school's) local area network — from a folder
> on your hard disk.
>
> You can display your documents on the Internet — or
> restrict access to a chosen few within a local area network.
> Mac OS X Personal Web Sharing makes it a snap.
>
> Here's how it works: Once you're online, all you need to do
> is copy a file in HTML format to the Web Pages folder (in
> the Sites folder in your Home directory, on your computer's
> hard disk), and that's it. You're done — your page is ready
> for viewing. Make sure you have someone handy to
> exchange high fives with.

Here you'll find dozens of HTML files. These files are the default global home
pages for many different languages. For English versions of the Mac OS, this
means that the file named `index.html.en` serves as the default home page
for the server. To view this file in your browser, try this URL:

`http://127.0.0.1/`

This will display a Web page like the one shown in Figure 4-10.

Serving static information

To change the default Web page, simply open it in your favorite HTML editor
and start changing it. An *HTML editor* is an application that lets you lay out
your Web page with what-you-see-is-what-you-get (WYSIWYG) ease. If you're
familiar with a word processor, you're well on your way to using an HTML
editor. Of the many HTML editors available, VersionTracker (`www.`
`versiontracker.com`) will give you a good head start on finding some of
the most popular ones.

You aren't limited only to HTML editors, of course. Many word processors
support HTML export, so it's a cinch to create Web pages with them by
simply choosing File⇨Save As.

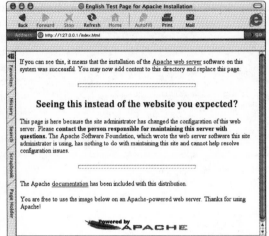

Figure 4-10:
Besides
the home
page for
each user,
Apache also
has a global
server page.

If you already know HTML (Webmasters might say, "If you can bang out raw HTML code"), you can edit your Web pages by hand. Simply open the existing `index.html` file with a text editor like TextEdit by choosing File⇨Open and change it to suit your needs. For example, a simple Web page might read like this:

```
<html>
<head><title>My First Web Page</title></head>
<body>

Welcome to my Web site!

</body>
</html>
```

If you're interested in improving your HTML skills, *HTML 4 For Dummies,* 4th Edition by Ed Tittle and Natanya Pitts (John Wiley & Sons, Inc.) makes a good starting point.

Serving information dynamically

It's cool to serve your own Web pages, but the fun doesn't stop there. Plain old HTML pages are handy for displaying the same information repeatedly. Computer Web-wizards call this type of information *static.* It doesn't change, so you can set it once and forget about it.

Although static displays are good for things like your copy of the Magna Carta or sports stats from the past 20 years, they're not so great for data that changes a lot *(dynamic).* Some good examples of dynamic information are the date, the time, your age, or the weather. If you were to display your age on a Web page using only HTML, you'd only have to change it once every year. This isn't so bad, but consider what happens if you want to post the date on a Web page: Now you have to update the Web page once per day. Add the time, and now you're down to HTML changes every hour, minute, or second, depending on how reliable you want to make the clock. Clearly, you need something besides static HTML for dynamic information.

The Apache Web server gives you the opportunity to use a variety of tools to produce dynamic Web pages. The most basic tool for serving dynamic data is called the *Serve Side Include.* The Web server executes a small piece of code in your HTML. Then the Web server replaces that code with some text and sends the page to whomever requested it. The result is dynamic text in your Web page.

Using Server Side Includes requires that you perform a few preparatory steps before you can take advantage of them. To alter Apache settings, you must change text in its settings file. The file is named `httpd.conf` and is located here:

```
/etc/httpd/httpd.conf
```

You probably won't be able to find this file if you go searching for it in the Finder because it's a hidden file. Some text editors like BBEdit can open hidden files, but you may not have that on hand. You do have the Terminal application, though. Launch the Terminal by double clicking its icon. (You can find it in the Utility folder that resides in your Applications folder.) Book VII, Chapter 1 has more information about the Terminal in case you need a refresher. At the prompt that appears, enter this command:

```
sudo pico /etc/httpd/httpd.conf
Password:
```

When prompted for a password, use a password of an administrator account on your machine. If you're the only user, this might be the password of the user that you're currently signed in as. Press Return and you will be looking at the innards of the Apache setup file. There's a lot of mumbo jumbo in this file, but don't be discouraged. Scroll down through the file and look for this chunk of text:

```
# Note that "MultiViews" must be named *explicitly* ---
    "Options All"
# doesn't give it to you.
#
    Options Indexes FollowSymLinks MultiViews
```

If you don't feel like scrolling through a bunch of text, you can jump to the text by pressing Control+W (shorthand for *where*), entering the text that you want to find (for example: *Options Indexes FollowSymLinksMultiViews*), and then pressing Return.

Whenever you find the desired text in the file, add the word **Includes** to the end of the last line of this text.

```
# Note that "MultiViews" must be named *explicitly* ---
    "Options All"
# doesn't give it to you.
#
    Options Indexes FollowSymLinks MultiViews Includes
```

One thing you might notice in this file is the many pound (#) characters. A pound character denotes a *comment*. If a comment character (#) precedes a line, that line of text performs no function. You can use this to your advantage to turn settings on and off for the server. Add a pound character to the beginning of a line, and that function stops working. Remove the character, and the function works again. Continue scrolling through the httpd.conf file by using the arrow keys or the Control+W search trick, looking for the following:

```
# To use server-parsed HTML files
#
AddType text/html .shtml
AddHandler server-parsed .shtml
```

Make sure that no # characters precede the AddType and AddHandler lines. After you finish, press Control+O to save the file. Then, press Control+X to exit the pico text editor. Now that you've edited Apache's settings, you have to restart it for the changes to take effect. Open the System Preferences and click the Internet tab. Deactivate Web Sharing and then reactivate it.

Next, open your favorite text editor and add some text to a new file:

```
<html>
<head><title>My First Web Page</title></head>
<body>

Welcome to my Web site!<br>
Today's date: <!--#echo var="DATE_LOCAL" -->

</body>
</html>
```

The `<!-#echo var="DATE_LOCAL" ->` part is a Server Side Include. The server understands the `"DATE_LOCAL"` message, and in its place, adds text that displays today's date. Save the text file and give it the name `index.shtml`.

Make sure that you include the `.shtml` extension. It's important for making the Server Side Includes work properly.

Save the file in your global Web folder, located here:

`/Library/WebServer/documents/index.shtml`

Finally, it's time to check out your handiwork. Open a Web browser and navigate to the URL of your global Web folder:

`http://127.0.0.1/index.shtml`

The result should be a Web page that displays today's date.

If you're not content with appending `.shtml` to your files to take advantage of Server Side Includes, you need to perform another step. When you view your Web site with a Web browser, it's customary to use default pages for a particular directory. For example, when loading the following URL:

`http://127.0.0.1/`

the server looks for a default page to load on the server because you didn't specify one. This is normally a file named `index.html`, which causes problems for Server Side Includes because they require a file name ending with `.shtml`. The easiest way to fix this is to tell the server that `index.shtml` can also be a default page. To fix this discrepancy, reload the Apache configuration file using this command line:

`sudo pico /etc/httpd/httpd.conf`

If you perform this step within 15 minutes of your last `sudo` command, you won't have to re-enter a password. If it's been longer, you might have to enter the password. Then scroll down through the `httpd.conf` file and find this bit of text:

```
# DirectoryIndex: Name of the file or files to use as a pre-
    written HTML
# directory index.   Separate multiple entries with spaces.
#
<IfModule mod_dir.c>
    DirectoryIndex index.html
</IfModule>
```

Change it by adding `index.shtml` to it:

```
# DirectoryIndex: Name of the file or files to use as a pre-
    written HTML
# directory index.  Separate multiple entries with spaces.
#
<IfModule mod_dir.c>
    DirectoryIndex index.shtml index.html
</IfModule>
```

Notice that `index.shtml` precedes `index.html`. This line indicates which file names you can use for the default file name of any folder on the Web server. In this case, I'm forcing `index.shtml` as the default file name before `index.html`. This means that when you load a Web page from your server without specifying a specific file, Apache is going to look for a file named `index.shtml` in that folder first. If it can't find one, it looks for a file named `index.html`. With that change in place, press Control+O to write the file to disk and then press Control+X to quit the pico text editor. To see your work in action, load this URL with your Web browser:

```
http://127.0.0.1/
```

The result should be that your `index.shtml` page loads with Server Side Includes intact.

Server Side Includes can perform a few other simple functions besides the date, including

✦ `DATE_GMT`: Today's date in Greenwich Mean Time.

✦ `DATE_LOCAL`: Today's date in your local time zone. (You're already an expert with this one.)

✦ `DOCUMENT_NAME`: The name of document.

✦ `LAST_MODIFIED`: The date that this document was last modified.

To see them all in action, alter your `index.shtml` file to read like this:

```
<html>
<head><title>My First Web Page</title></head>
<body>

Welcome to my Web site! <br><br>
GMT date: <!--#echo var="DATE_GMT" --> <br>
Today's date: <!--#echo var="DATE_LOCAL" --><br>
Name of this document: <!--#echo var="DOCUMENT_NAME" --><br>
Last Modified: <!--#echo var="LAST_MODIFIED" --><br>

</body>
</html>
```

Reload your Web server's main page to see the results.

Fancier dynamic stuff

Another common use of Server Side Includes gives you the chance to remove whole chunks of your HTML files and put them into another file. (Sounds messy, doesn't it?) You might want to do this for HTML that will appear on each page of your Web site: For example, you might like today's date and the page's last modified date to appear at the bottom of any page of your whole Web site. Webmasters, being the sedentary crowd that they can be, don't want to type this information repeatedly for each HTML page that they create. Furthermore, they don't want to have to retype all that information for every file if it should change. What's a lazy techno-wizard to do? Server Side Includes come to the rescue!

The first step is to modify your main page: in this case, index.shtml:

```
<html>
<head><title>My First Web Page</title></head>
<body>

Welcome to my Web site!<br>
<!--#include virtual="footer.shtml"-->

</body>
</html>
```

You might notice that I removed all the Server Side Includes from before and added a new one. The new line

```
<!--#include virtual="footer.shtml"-->
```

tells the Web server to load the file named footer.shtml and dump its contents into index.shtml in place of this Server Side Include. Save this file.

Next, create a new text file. To the new file, add this code:

```
<center>
<hr width="50%">

Today's date: <!--#echo var="DATE_LOCAL" --><br>
Last Modified: <!--#echo var="LAST_MODIFIED" --><br><br>

</center>
```

If you're familiar with HTML, the first thing that you might notice is that this file doesn't follow proper HTML formatting. Because this file is just a chunk of HTML that's going to be part of a fully formed HTML file, it doesn't need the full treatment. Otherwise, this code is standard HTML with a few Server

Side Includes tossed in for good measure. Just to spruce things up a bit, the text is centered with a small horizontal line above it. Save this file, giving it the name `footer.shtml`.

Now, whenever you want this footer to be at the bottom of any Web page on the server, add the `<!-#include virtual="footer.shtml"->` line from before. Besides saving you time from reconstructing the footer each time in a HTML file, you only have to add one line of code, and Server Side Includes take care of the rest. Even better, you can alter the footer file whenever you want, and the changes appear in the HTML of every page that contains the footer.

When bad things happen to good Webmasters

If you browsed the Web for any time at all, you've no doubt stumbled across a *dead link*. This phenomenon occurs when you attempt to load a Web page that no longer exists on a particular server. If you were lucky and the server still existed, you probably saw a boring error message telling you that the page no longer exists. Apache provides default error messages like this for you, but that doesn't mean you can't improve the messages that your visitors see.

Open your `httpd.conf` file for editing with pico like before.

```
sudo pico /etc/httpd/httpd.conf
```

Scroll through the file until you find the `ErrorDocument` directives.

```
#    2) local redirects
#ErrorDocument 404 /missing.html
#  to redirect to local URL /missing.html
```

Whenever a server can't find a page, it produces a 404 error. Normally, Apache directs itself to a default error message. By removing one comment (note the now-absent pound character at the beginning of the second line), you can dictate to Apache which file you would like to display (in the form of a page for the viewer) in the case of a 404 error.

```
#    2) local redirects
ErrorDocument 404 /missing.html
#  to redirect to local URL /missing.html
```

Press Control+O to save the `httpd.conf` file and then press Control+X to exit pico. Now whenever someone comes across a missing Web page on your site, your server will redirect him to a file named `missing.html`. Of course, you also need to create this `missing.html` file. Use your favorite text editor to create a new HTML file. To it, add this code:

```
<html>
<head><title>Uh-oh!</title></head>
<body>

Holy Toledo! <br><br>

We can't find the page you requested. <br>
Would you like to <a href="index.shtml">return to the main
    page</a>?


<!--#include virtual="footer.shtml"-->

</body>
</html>
```

Save this file, giving it the name `missing.html`. Save it in your Web server's root directory.

```
/Library/WebServer/Documents/missing.html
```

Return to the System Preferences Sharing panel, click the Internet tab, and toggle Web Sharing off and on again. This will force your Web server to read in the changes to the `httpd.conf` file.

**Book VII
Chapter 4**

To test it out, load a URL that you know doesn't exist. Anything will do.

```
http://1270.0.0.1/some_missing_page_I_forget_to_add.html
```

If you've configured things properly, you should see a Web page that looks like Figure 4-11.

**Hosting a Web Site
à la OS X**

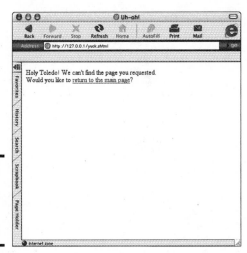

Figure 4-11:
Give your users a way out of dead links.

Sharing Files with FTP

Web sharing isn't the only way you can share files with Mac OS X, nor is it always the best way. You can also share files using FTP.

What does FTP mean and why should you care?

FTP is an acronym for *File Transfer Protocol*. It's simply an older term (dating back to the early days of the Internet) for a set of rules defining how to send files from one computer to another (hence the *protocol* designation). To use FTP, you need an *FTP server,* which is used to share files with anyone that you've allowed access. The person on the other end of the connection accesses your FTP server by using an *FTP client.*

One of the great things about using FTP is that any platform can access your files. This means that Windows, Linux, and, of course, Macintosh users can communicate and retrieve files from an FTP server. Of course, you can be selfish and decide not to share files with just anyone; you can restrict access to yourself or a select group of people. The choice is up to you.

Setting up and using FTP

Turning on the FTP server in Mac OS X is as simple as opening the Apache Web server. Click the System Preferences icon from the Dock and open the Sharing panel (see Figure 4-12). On the Service tab, select FTP Access from the list of options and then click the Start button to launch the FTP server. When you do, the Start button changes into a Stop button. Any easier, and the folks at Cupertino would be reading your mind.

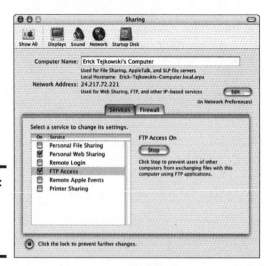

Figure 4-12:
Start the
FTP server
with one
click.

To see the files that are on your computer, you'll need an FTP client. There are many good ones, such as Anarchie and Fetch, but most of them cost money. If you aren't afraid of the command line, though, you already have access to an FTP client for free. Launch the Terminal application and enter this simple line of text:

```
ftp 127.0.0.1
```

When you do, the Terminal greets you with the following reply:

```
Connected to localhost.
220 localhost FTP server (lukemftpd 1.1) ready.
Name (127.0.0.1:erick):
```

Enter the appropriate user name and press Return. If it's a known user, the FTP session returns a message:

```
331 Password required for erick.
```

For this example, the username is `erick`. Enter the proper password for the current user. If it's valid, the server lets you in.

```
230-
   Welcome to Darwin!
230 User erick logged in.
Remote system type is UNIX.
Using binary mode to transfer files.
ftp>
```

Now you will see an alternate prompt: `ftp>`. This is where you issue commands to the FTP server. Many commands are available to you, some of which you may already know. If you check back to Chapter 1 of this minibook (about navigating the Mac OS X file system with UNIX commands), you'll be well on your way to navigating with FTP. All the usual commands are at hand, along with a few that are specific to FTP. Table 4-1 contains the basics.

Table 4-1	Basic FTP Commands
Command	*What It Does*
ls	Lists the contents of a directory
exit	Exits FTP and returns you to the command line
cd	Navigates to a different directory (change directory)
get	Downloads a file
put	Uploads a file

The first thing that you want to know is what files are available to you. Enter the following at the prompt:

```
ftp> ls
```

Because you're using FTP to navigate the files on your own hard drive, you probably won't be surprised at what's available. It's the contents of your Home folder!

```
-rw-r--r--    1 erick  staff        3 Nov 14  2000 .CFUserTextEncoding
-rwxr-xr-x    1 erick  staff    10244 Jul 11 17:55 .DS_Store
-rw-r--r--    1 erick  staff  1191936 Jun 11 05:10 .FBCIndex
drwxrwxrwx    3 erick  staff      102 Jun 11 05:10 .FBCLockFolder
drwx------   57 erick  staff     1938 Jul 11 20:26 .Trash
-rw-------    1 erick  staff     1273 Jun 23 17:18 .bash_history
drwx------    3 erick  staff      102 Jun 11 06:05 .ssh
-rw-------    1 erick  staff       62 Feb 16 02:16 .tcsh_history
-rw-rw-rw-    1 erick  staff       25 Jul  4 03:53 .tcshrc
-rw-r--r--    1 erick  staff        6 Feb  6 22:23 .xinitrc
drwxr-xr-x    7 erick  staff      238 Jun 11 07:26 Applications
drwx------   15 erick  staff      510 Jul 11 20:59 Desktop
drwx------   61 erick  staff     2074 Jul 10 07:16 Documents
drwx------   37 erick  staff     1258 Jul 10 22:10 Library
drwx------    2 erick  staff       68 May 12 20:50 Movies
drwx------    2 erick  staff       68 May 12 20:50 Music
-rw-rw-rw-    1 erick  staff       70 Jun 23 17:25 MyDocument
drwx------    9 erick  staff      306 May 12 20:50 Pictures
drwxr-xr-x    3 erick  staff      102 Nov 15  2000 Public
drwxr-xr-x    6 erick  staff      204 Jul 11 03:48 Sites
226 Transfer complete.
```

Normally, you'd probably be accessing this information from another computer, but for testing purposes, you can use FTP to access the same computer that you're currently using.

To download a file, use the `get` command. The `get` command can take either one or two parameters. For demonstration purposes, I'll stick with two. The first parameter is the file that you want to download, and the second parameter is the destination of the file that you're downloading. For example, if you want to download a file called `hello.txt` from the Desktop folder on the FTP server but you want it to have another name after it's saved on the root of your hard drive, do something like this:

```
ftp> get ~/desktop/hello.txt /goodbye.txt
```

The opposite of downloading, of course, is uploading. To upload a file with FTP, use the `put` command. It also requires one or two parameters. Again, I'll focus on two. The parameters work in the same manner as `get`, just in the reverse order.

```
ftp> put /goodbye.txt /users/erick/desktop/hello.text
150 Opening BINARY mode data connection for
  '/users/erick/desktop/ hello.text'.
100% |***************************| 58857        4.20 MB/s
226 Transfer complete.
58857 bytes sent in 00:00 (224.66 KB/s)
```

With only four commands, you can usually complete most FTP tasks. There are many more commands available to you. To read the manual for the command line FTP program, use the man command to display it:

man ftp

See the results in Figure 4-13.

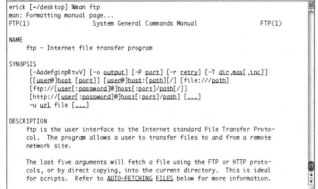

Figure 4-13:
The man page for FTP lists all available FTP commands.

```
erick [~/desktop] %man ftp
man: Formatting manual page...
FTP(1)                  System General Commands Manual                FTP(1)

NAME
     ftp - Internet file transfer program

SYNOPSIS
     [-AadefginpRtvV] [-o output] [-P port] [-r retry] [-T dir,max[,inc]]
     [[user@]host [port]] [user@]host:[path][/] [file:///path]
     [ftp://[user[:password]@]host[:port]/path[/]]
     [http://[user[:password]@]host[:port]/path] [...]
     -u url file [...]

DESCRIPTION
     ftp is the user interface to the Internet standard File Transfer Proto-
     col.  The program allows a user to transfer files to and from a remote
     network site.

     The last five arguments will fetch a file using the FTP or HTTP proto-
     cols, or by direct copying, into the current directory.  This is ideal
     for scripts.  Refer to AUTO-FETCHING FILES below for more information.
```

After you complete your FTP tasks, issue the exit command to log out of the FTP server. It's also a good idea to open the Sharing panel of the System Preferences to turn off the FTP when it's unnecessary. Although the security for your server is good, the best security is a server that's not operational. The same holds true for your Web server. If you don't need it on all the time, turn it off. Not only does it reduce your chances of security problems, but it also gives back some system performance.

Index

A

About This Mac dialog, 61
Abstract background options, 171
Accounts, 186, 210-217, 361–364,
    447–448
Accounts dialog, 362–363, 451
actions, undoing, 49
activate command, 604–605
Activision Web site, 563
Ad Hoc wireless networks, 474,
    479–481
Add Buddy (⌘+Shift+A) keyboard
    shortcut, 385
Add Movie as Favorite (⌘+D)
    keyboard shortcut, 334
Add Page to Favorites (⌘+D)
    keyboard shortcut, 407
Add Sender (⌘+Y) keyboard
    shortcut, 366
Add Sender to Address Book
    command, 92
Add to Favorites (⌘+T) keyboard
    shortcut, 155
Address Book, 91–94
  adding e-mail addresses, 366
  address card, 90
  addressing e-mail from, 370
  All group button, 95
  Buddies from, 386
  contact information, 90
  editing personal card, 186
  general information about, 89–90
  Group column, 95
  importing vCards, 99
  network directories, 96–97
  New Group icon, 95
  organizing contact cards, 95–96

personal card, 90
printing, 73, 97–98
resizing Group and Name
    columns, 90–91
US letter-size paper, 97
vCards, 98
Address Book command, 97
Adjust Colors effect, 300
Administrator accounts, 210
administrators, 110
Adobe Premiere, 502, 549
ADSL (Asynchronous Digital
    Subscriber Line) modems, 485
Advanced⇨Open Stream
    command, 261
AIFF files, 249, 291
AIM, 382, 387–388
airline schedules, 78
AirPort, 65, 480
AirPort Base Station, 488–489, 494–495
AirPort cards, 479, 483, 494
AirPort icon, 65
AirPort networks, 481–483
Aladdin Systems Web site,
    102, 519, 555
Album List, 270
Alert dialogs, 620
alerts and voices, 620
aliases, 37–39, 57, 125
American Heritage Dictionary, 78
animation and QuickTime, 324
antivirus software, 140–141, 423
AOL dial-up and Internet
    connections, 196
Apache Web server, 631–641
APIs (Application Program
    Interface), 122
Apple Background Images, 170
Apple dealer, 138, 146
Apple Knowledge Base, 78, 146
Apple logo, 123

Apple Mac OS X Support Web site, 146
Apple menu, 26, 60–61
  About This Macintosh command,
    103, 517
  Control Panels menu item, 128
  Dock command, 58
  Log Out command, 211, 212
  Magnification command, 59
  Recent Items menu, 57–58
  Startup Disk submenu item, 128
  System Preferences command, 179
Apple Speakable Items, 204
Apple System Profiler, 61
Apple User Group Support
    Web site, 135
Apple Web site, 78, 296, 325
  AirPort cards, 479
  controlling wireless networks, 483
  hardware installation
    instructions, 525
  help for AppleScript, 607–608
  Help topics, 130
  Hot News tab, 132
  Mac OS X tab, 132
  non-Apple 802.11 equipment and
    AirPort, 480
  registering as .Mac user, 626
AppleCare channel, 78
AppleMail, 18
AppleScript
  activate command, 604–605
  addressing application to
    automate, 604
  applications stop listening, 604
  automating
    application tasks, 596–597
    Finder tasks, 595–596
  built-in help, 607
  comments, 602
  end tell command, 604
  English-like commands, 605
  Internet help, 607–608

programming, 602–608
Script Editor, 598–599
scripts, 597–602
speaking text through, 622–623
tell command, 604
AppleScript Central Web site, 608
AppleScript dictionary, 603–604
AppleScript folder, 599
Apple⇨System Preferences⇨Network
    command, 446
AppleTalk, 449, 464–472
AppleTalk networks, 195
AppleTalk printers, 471–472, 536–538
AppleTalk servers, 467–470
AppleWorks, 45, 237–238
Application menu, 62
application windows, 46
applications. *See also* software and
    applications
  adding to Dock, 176
  addressing to automate, 604
  aliases, 57
  announcing attention needed, 620
  AppleScript dictionary, 603–604
  automatically launching, 185
  automating tasks, 596–597
  from CD-ROM or DVD-ROM, 42–43
  Close command, 28
  closing windows, 28
  copying, 38
  custom menus, 34
  deleting, 101–102
  documentation, 102
  drivers, 140
  exchanging contacts between, 98–99
  extensions, 105
  finding support files, 102
  force quitting, 60–61
  help, 132
  Help system, 134
  hidden or visible state, 186
  icons, 36

identifying which owns file, 36
limiting access, 219
linking to files, 55–56
listing, 64
merging information from, 62–63
minimum system requirements, 103
opening documents, 43–44
pico, 586–589
pop-up help for fields and
  controls, 133
printer drivers, 537
printing from, 73
quitting, 46
RAM (random access memory), 515
README file, 102
recently accessed, 57–58, 183
restricting access, 221–222
running, 30, 32, 42
saving documents, 45
speaking text through, 621–622
on start volume, 105
starting automatically after
  login, 214
stop listening, 604
swapping data between, 68
switching between, 43
upgrading Mac OS X and, 139
Applications folder, 153, 232, 400
Applications (Mac OS 9) folder, 125
Applications icon, 153
Applications window, 64
Applications⇨AppleScript⇨Script
  Editor command, 599
Application⇨Services⇨Speech⇨Start
  Speaking command, 622
Application⇨Services⇨Speech⇨Stop
  Speaking command, 622
Applications⇨Utilities command, 450
Applications⇨Utilities⇨Network
  Utility command, 422
Applications⇨Utilities⇨Terminal.app
  command, 570

Aqua, 12
ArKaos plug-in, 266
ArKaos Web site, 266
ascii command, 458
attachments, 368, 371, 373–374, 423
audio, 312–313, 324, 511–513
Audio box, 313
Audio CD volume icon, 69
audio CDs
  general information about,
    69, 188, 243
  importing sound from, 303–304
  iTunes, 263
  playing, 250–251
  recording, 550–551
audio controller, 193
audio files, 251–255, 257–258
Audio Palette, 289
audio player, 246
Audio shelf, 301–304
audio volume level, 65
Auto Login feature, disabling, 222
automated telephone operators, 243
automatic login, 201
automatically restarting after power
  failure, 191
automating tasks, 595–597

B

Back button, 153
backgrounds, 169–172, 181
backing up
  hard drives, 116–117
  troubleshooting, 138
Bare Bones Software Web site, 557
BBEdit, 556–558
BBS (Bulletin Board System), 418
bin command, 458
binary, 242

Birthday keyword, 275
Black and White effect, 300
Blizzard Web site, 560, 564
Book panel, 282–283
boot process, special keys for, 118
booting from CD or DVD disc, 118
BrickHouse, 422
BrickHouse Web site, 422
Brightness/Contrast effect, 300
broadband connections, 351
Buddies, 385–390
Buddies menu, 94
Buddies⇨Ignore *<username>*
    command, 391
Buddies⇨Send a File command, 390
Buddy List, 94, 385–390
Buddy List window, 381–382
burning
  CDs, 263–264
  DVDs, 308, 319–321
bus speed, 519
business address and telephone,
    78–80
buttons, colors of, 183

C

cable connections, 139
cable modems, 442, 485
cable/DSL modems, 490–491
cable/DSL routers, 488–489,
    491–492, 494–495
cables, 433–434, 531
cache folder, 415
cal command, 581–582
calendar in text form, 581–582
capabilities, 219–221
Carbon API, 125
Carbon application, 122
Casady & Greene Web site, 145

Cat5 (Category 5) cables, 433
Cat5E (Category 5 Enhanced) cables,
    433–434
CD and DVD Recording For Dummies,
    70, 320, 510, 550
cd command, 456, 572, 575, 578–579
CD devices, 104
CD recorders, 509–510
CD-R discs, 70–71, 188
CD-ROM, running applications
    from, 42–43
CD-RW discs, 70–71, 188
CDs
  booting from, 118
  burning, 263–264
  erasing, 111–112
  preferences, 188
CE Software Web site, 555
chapters, 341
Chat window, 388, 390
chatting
  AIM users, 388
  background display, 389
  Buddies, 385–386
  Buddy name and picture, 389
  closing, 390
  displaying text in balloons, 389
  first name, 381
  formatting text, 389
  ignoring someone, 391
  Instant Messages, 387
  invitations to, 387–390
  offline and online, 383
  Rendezvous messaging, 382
  saving discussion, 389
  surnames, 381
Checkmark keyword, 275
Choose Other Application dialog, 55
Chooser⇨AppleShare command, 398
Civilization III, 561–562
Classic Extensions Manager,
    125–126, 145

Classic mode
  Advanced tab, 125–126
  applications, 19
  automatically running, 123, 201–202
  background processes, 202
  checking what is running, 126–127
  Classic Extensions Manager, 125–126
  Classic Sleep option, 126
  configuring, 125–127
  debugging, 202
  default System Preferences
    settings, 125
  definition of, 121
  disabling extensions, 144–145
  extensions off, 125
  Mac OS version, 127
  memory and applications, 144
  moving start-up and shutdown
    files, 145
  older applications, 122–123
  preferences, 201–202
  Rebuild Desktop button, 126
  running, 122–123
  Show Background Processes check
    box, 127
  simulating Mac OS 9 startup
    keys, 126
  Sleep mode, 123, 126
  Startup Options area, 125–126
  stopping, 123
  troubleshooting, 144–145, 202
  Use Key Combination option, 126
  windows, 123
Classic System Preferences dialog,
    126–127
clicking, 28
clients, 454
client/server applications, 454
Clip Viewer, 289
Clips Palette, 289
Clips Shelf, 290–293
Clips Viewer, 287

clock, 66, 203
cloning items in folders, 50
Close AutoComplete (⌘+;) keyboard
    shortcut, 403
Close Finder Window (⌘+Option+W)
    keyboard shortcut, 41
closed networks, 482
coaxial cable, 433
Cocoa application, 122
Collapse/Expand Toolbars (⌘+B)
    keyboard shortcut, 401
collisions, 430–431
color matching technology, 189
Color menu, 175
color profiles, 189–190
colors, 183
  changing, 173–174
  number displayed, 189–190
  Stickies, 175
  title styles, 298
ColorSync preferences, 188–189
column view, 151, 164–165
Command key, 27
command line
  autocompletion, 576–577
  automation, 569–570
  calendar in text form, 581–582
  complex commands, 568–569
  copying files, 579–580
  deleting files or folders, 580–581
  downloadable tools, 591–594
  finding files, 584–585
  FTP (File Transfer Protocol) for
    transferring files, 456–459
  launching applications, 581
  moving files, 580
  opening documents, 581
  problems, 575–576
  remote control, 570
  renaming files, 580
  word count of files, 585

commands
  keyboard shortcuts, 34
  understood by Speech Recognition, 616–617
comments, 234, 602, 636
commercial software firewalls, 422–423
Compared Documents feature, 234
compiled scripts, 597–598
Compose window, 96
Computer icon, 153
computer operators, 66
Computer window, 63
computers
  controlling other types from Macintosh, 461–462
  determining exact model, 518–519
  listening for spoken commands, 614
  remotely controlling, 460–462
computer-to-computer networks, 474, 479–481
Conflict Catcher, 145
Connect to Server dialog, 397, 449–450, 452–453, 467–469
Connect to Server (Option+K) keyboard shortcut, 467
Connectix Web site, 552, 553
contact cards, 95–96
contacts
  entering Address Book information, 91–93
  exchanging between applications, 98–99
  exporting to iPod, 94
  information usage, 93–94
  Instant Messenger address, 94
  multiple items for same field, 92
  organizing cards, 95–96
  photographs, 92
  printing, 97–98
  searching through, 94

content searching, 158–159
Content window, 402
contextual menus, 34
Control Strip, 12
Controller, 340–342
controls, placement of, 12
Controls⇨Controller Type command, 341
cookies, 413–414
Copy (⌘+C) keyboard shortcut, 41, 293
copying
  applications, 38
  files and folders, 48–49
  files from command line, 579–580
  video clips, 293
copying and pasting information from Address Book, 93
cp command, 579–580
CPU, 105–107, 583
CPU Monitor, 106
CPU Monitor Preferences dialog, 106
credit card information, 418
cropping, 278–280, 293
Cross Dissolve transition, 295
crossover cables, 433
curl command, 590–591
Current Temperature by Zipcode script, 600
custom
  desktop background, 169–172
  keyboard shortcuts, 191
  menus, 34
Customize drawer, 315
Customize Toolbar dialog, 154–155
customizing
  Dock, 176–178
  DVD Menu titles, 318
  Favorites, 155
  Finder toolbar, 152–155
  Internet Explorer toolbar, 401
  keywords, 276–277

Movie Button, 315–316
prompt, 587–589
toolbar, 154–155
Cut (⌘+X) keyboard shortcut, 41
.cwk (AppleWorks) file extension, 54

D

daisy-chaining, 530
dangerous macros, 418
Dantz Development Corporation
    Web site, 21, 116
Darwin, 16, 571
DAT (Digital Audio Tape) drive, 510
data, backing up, 116–117
data CDs, 70–71, 550–551
data files, 37, 141
date and time preferences, 203–204
DATE_GMT message, 638
DATE_LOCAL message, 637, 638
dates, 184, 203
dead links, 640–641
debugging Classic mode, 202
defragmenting hard drives, 117, 547
Deimos Rising, 19
Delete key, 254, 274, 275, 295
Delete (⌘+Delete) keyboard
    shortcut, 51
Desktop
  arranging, 178
  automatically changing
      background, 181
  centering image, 171
  changing
    colors, 173–174
    screen saver, 172–173
  cleaning up, 160, 605
  current background, 181
  custom background, 169–172
  customizing Dock, 176–178

displaying icons, 166
Eject icon, 531
folders on, 48
iDisk icon, 396
Mac OS 9, 125
photos, 284
preferences, 181
resizing icons, 162
snapshot of, 172
Stickies, 174–176
stretching image to fit, 171
View Options, 178
Desktop Background command, 170
Desktop dialog, 170–171
destination drive, formatting, 23
Developer Tools, 593–594
DHCP (Dynamic Host Configuration
    Protocol), 24, 440–441, 493
dial-up connections, 351
dial-up modems, 490
Dictionary channel, 78
Dictionary protocol, 591
digital, 242–243
digital audio files, 246
digital cameras, 243, 245, 269, 500–501
digital extraction, 257
digital fingerprints, 243
digital hub, 241–242, 244–247
digital movies, 246
digital photo album, 245
Digital Photography Bible, 501
Digital Photography Handbook, 501
digital video, 243
digital video editing, 549–550
Digital Video For Dummies, 503
digitizing, 243–244
digits, 242
Dilbert Web site, 174
directional arrow keys, 39
directories, 572, 577. *See also* folders
Directory Services, 537–538
disabled users, 206–207

discs, 21, 118
Disk First Aid utility, 22
Disk Utility, 22, 108–115, 140, 144
display, 189–190. *See also* monitors
Display Favorites folder (⌘+Shift+F)
    keyboard shortcut, 155
Display Status window, 346
Displays icon, 64–65
DMZ (demilitarized zone), 454
DNS (Domain Name System)
    name, 538
.doc (Microsoft Word) file
    extension, 54
Dock, 176–178
  Address Book icon, 91
  application icon, 42, 43
  automatically hiding and displaying,
    60, 182
  Classic mode icon, 123
  configuring display, 106
  CPU Monitor window, 106
  Explorer page icon, 404
  Finder icon, 48
  iChat icon, 383
  icons, 59, 182
  Internet Explorer icon, 400
  minimizing, 29, 182
  preferences, 181–183
  Print Center, 471
  QuickTime Player icon, 325
  removing icon, 177
  repositioning on-screen, 182
  resizing, 182
  restoring, 182
  Script Editor icon, 601
  Sherlock icon, 76
  System Preferences icon,
    123, 127, 353
  Trash icon, 50, 51, 141
Document Properties dialog, 237
documentation, 102, 576
DOCUMENT_NAME message, 638

documents
  multiple versions, 236
  opening, 37, 43–44
  organizing, 151
  previewing, 72
  printing, 72–73
  recently accessed, 183
  saving, 45
  versions, 45
  write-protecting elements, 237
domain name service, 350
dotted notation, 435
Download Image to Disk
    command, 409
Download Manager window, 408–409
downloading files, 408–409,
    423, 454, 644
Drafts folder, 361, 371
Drawer, 360–361
drawing tablets, 508–509, 610
drilling, 44
Drive 10, 110, 546–547
drivers, 119, 139–140, 532, 537
drop-down list boxes, 183
DSL (Digital Subscriber Line),
    350, 442, 485
DSL (Digital Subscriber Line)
    providers, 65
dumb terminals, 219
Dummies Web site, 590
duplicating files, 50
DV (digital video) camcorders, 246,
    291–292, 305, 501–503
DV files, 291
DVD discs, booting from, 118
DVD Menus, 308, 312–318
DVD movie disc, 188
DVD movies, 247
DVD Player, 188, 320, 340–346
DVD Player⇨Preferences
    command, 343
DVD Preferences dialog, 343–346

DVD recorders, 509–510
DVD Studio Pro, 321, 549
DVD window, 312
DVD-compatible drive, 339
DVD-ROM, running applications
    from, 42–43
DVD-ROM drives, 339
DVDs
  accessing information on
    Internet, 344
  adding media, 308
  burning, 308, 319–321
  chapters, 341
  creation of, 307–308
  customizing menu, 308
  digitizing, 244
  DVD Menus, 308–314
  erasing, 111–112
  hardware for playing, 339
  image dimensions, 313
  mastering, 549–550
  multilanguage aware, 344
  navigating, 315
  preferences, 188
  previewing, 308, 319
  previewing movie, 315
  recordable, 188
  recording, 550–551
  saving, 319–321
dynamic Web pages, 634–640

E

EasyView plug-in, 266
eBay, 78, 83–84
eBay channel, 78
Edit Card (⌘+L) keyboard
    shortcut, 92
Edit panel, 278–280
Edit⇨Clear command, 293
Edit⇨Copy command, 293

Edit⇨Crop command, 293
Edit⇨Edit Keywords command, 277
Edit⇨Paste command, 293
Edit⇨Speech⇨Start Speaking
    command, 621
Edit⇨Speech⇨Stop Speaking
    command, 622
Edit⇨Split Video Clip at Playhead
    command, 293
Edit⇨Undo command, 295
Effects Palette, 289
Effects shelf, 299–300
EIDE (Enhanced Integrated Drive
    Electronics) hard drives, 523
Eject command, 67, 453, 470
Eject icon, 67, 453, 531
Eject key, 67
Eject (⌘+E) keyboard shortcut,
    67, 453, 531
Eject (Option+E) keyboard
    shortcut, 470
e-mail
  adding e-mail addresses to Address
    Book, 366
  addressing from Address Book, 370
  already sent or received, 361
  attachments, 368, 371, 373–374
  automatically checking for, 375
  automatically marking as
    junk mail, 372
  automating
    message deletion, 375
    with rules, 377–379
  carbon copies, 370
  checking for, 364–365
  composing and sending, 369–371
  default reader, 194
  deleted messages, 361
  deleting, 365–366
  disabling MIME, 368
  displaying

(continued)

e-mail *(continued)*
  all e-mail headers, 366
    contents, 360
  draft messages, 361
  filtered heading, 366
  formatting, 367–368, 370
  forwarding reply, 369
  grouped contact cards, 96
  information about current folder, 359
  junk mail, 361, 371–373
  listing folder contents, 359–360
  .Mac, 625
  manually
    checking for, 376
    marking as junk mail, 371
  MIME (Multipurpose Internet Mail
    Extensions), 368
  moving into Drawer folders, 361
  omitting text of original message, 369
  photos, 284
  reaching from Internet Explorer, 405
  reading, 365–366
  recipient's address, 370
  replying to, 366–369
  scanning, 365
  sending, 62
    from Address Book, 94
    from Drafts folder, 371
  settings, 24
  signatures, 376
  sound, 375
  subject, 370
  viruses and attachments, 423
  waiting to send, 361
e-mail accounts, 350, 361–365, 376
e-mail addresses, 363, 366
e-mail applications and
    attachments, 373
Empty Trash command, 51
Empty Trash (⌘+K) keyboard
    shortcut, 361

Empty Trash (⌘+Shift+Delete)
    keyboard shortcut, 51
emptying Trash can, 51, 605
end tell command, 604
Energy Saver, 187, 190–191
Entourage, 544
equalizer, 258–259
Equalizer (⌘+2) keyboard
    shortcut, 261
erasing, 111–112
escape characters (@%), 589
Ethernet, 430–432
Excel, 546
exit command, 645
Explorer bar, 403, 408, 411
Explorer Preferences dialog, 405, 409,
    411, 414–415
Explorer Preferences (⌘+;) keyboard
    shortcut, 406, 409
Explorer⇨Preferences command, 403,
    406, 409, 414, 415
Export dialog, 333
exporting
  files with QuickTime Player, 333
  movies for viewing, 305–306
  photos, 284
extensions, 54–55, 105, 144–145, 167
external
  devices, retracing installation
    steps, 139
  hard drives, 71, 520–521
  removable cartridge drives, 520

F

Fade In transition, 295
Fade Out transition, 295
Family keyword, 275
Family theme, 310

FAQs (Frequently Asked Question files), 68
Fast Forward playback control, 288
Favorite keyword, 275
Favorites
  creation of, 155
  customizing, 155
  deleting, 155, 408
  displaying, 153, 155
  Dock, 176
  general information about, 44, 63
  Internet Explorer, 403, 406–408, 407
  jumping to, 407–408
  Print Center, 471
  QuickTime movies, 334
  updating Web pages, 410–411
Favorites bar, 407–408
Favorites icon, 153
Favorites menu, 334
Favorites panel, 407–408
Favorites submenu, 63
Favorites window, 63
Favorites⇨Add Movie as Favorite command, 334
Favorites⇨Add Page to Favorites command, 407
Favorites⇨Favorites command, 407
Favorites⇨Organize Favorites command, 408
Favorites⇨Show Favorites command, 334
Favorites⇨Subscribe command, 407, 410
FaxSFT, 537
Feedback window, 612, 615–616
fiber-optic cable, 433
File menu
  Export vCards command, 98
  Print command, 72
  Save As menu option, 45
file selection controls, 12

file sharing
  accessing files on Windows computers, 452–453
  accounts, 447–448
  AppleTalk, 449
  connecting to shared resource, 449–450
  disconnecting Windows computers, 453
  enabling, 449
  firewalls, 459
  FTP (File Transfer Protocol), 642–645
  TCP/IP (Transmission Control Protocol/Internet Protocol), 449
  to Windows computers, 451–452
File⇨Add to Favorites command, 155
File⇨Eject command, 470
File⇨Export command, 333
File⇨Export Movie command, 305, 306
File⇨Get Info command, 257, 262
File⇨Go to Chat command, 387
File⇨Import command, 272, 291, 332
File⇨Import vCards command, 99
FileMaker Pro, 553–554
File⇨New command, 91, 483
File⇨New Finder Window command, 27
File⇨New Group command, 95
File⇨New Group From Selection command, 95
File⇨New Message command, 369
File⇨New Photo Album command, 273
File⇨New Playlist command, 255
File⇨New⇨New Keychain command, 225
File⇨Open command, 43, 332, 634
File⇨Open Dictionary command, 603
File⇨Page Setup command, 97

File⇨Quit command, 46
files
  access level for owner, 231
  accessing with FTP (File Transfer
    Protocol), 453–459
  adding to Dock, 176
  aliases, 57
  AppleTalk access, 466–472
  changing owner, 230–231
  checking for write-protection, 143
  command line, 579–581, 584–585
  comments, 53–54
  converting with QuickTime, 323–324
  copying, 48–49
  creation date, 53
  deleting, 50–51
  downloading, 454, 644
  duplicating, 50
  exporting with QuickTime Player, 333
  extensions, 54–55, 167
  formats, 45
  group permissions, 231
  icons, 36–37
  identifying application owning, 36
  importing with QuickTime Player,
    332–333
  indexing, 159–160
  information about, 52–56, 594
  Internet Explorer, 408–409
  languages for indexing, 167
  last-modified date, 53
  linking to applications, 55–56
  locking, 56
  moving, 49
  naming, 45
  paths, 44, 577–579
  permissions, 53, 229–233
  recently used, 57–58
  renaming, 52
  searching, 155–157, 157–160
  searching for, 153
  sending with iChat, 390–391
  size of, 53
  stationery, 54
  UNIX, 577–581
  uploading, 454
  word count, 585
File⇨Save a Copy As command, 389
File⇨Save As command, 69, 235, 412
File⇨Save command, 45, 69, 606
File⇨Versions command, 236
Final Cut Pro, 550
find command, 584–585
Find dialog, 157–160, 167
Find (⌘+F) keyboard shortcut, 157
Finder
  AppleScript dictionary, 603
  automating tasks, 595–596
  column view, 151, 164–165
  customizing toolbar, 154–155
  default toolbar icons, 153
  drag-and-drop files from, 273
  File menu, 53, 67
  Find dialog, 157–160
  general information about,
    27, 47–48, 71
  Get Info command, 53
  Go menu, 63–64
  hiding and showing, 152–155
  icon view, 149, 160–163
  list view, 150–151, 163–164
  locked items, 56
  preferences, 165–167
  Script Editor icon, 601
  scripts related to, 602
  search results, 158
  Search results list, 156
  services, 62
  toolbar customization, 152–155
  View menu, 178
  view option configuration, 160–165
Finder menu
  Burn CD command, 71
  Duplicate command, 50

Empty Trash command, 51
File command, 50, 51, 57, 71, 157
Finder command, 51
Help option, 129
Help Viewer option, 129
Hide (or Show) Toolbar
   command, 152
Mac Help option, 129
Make Alias command, 57
Move to Trash command, 51
Show/Hide Status Bar command, 153
View command, 152, 153
Finder Preferences dialog, 165–167
Finder toolbar, 50, 102
Finder window, 166
  Dock icon, 176
  Explorer page icon, 404
  icon view, 161
  images from, 172
  navigating to starting point for
    search, 156
  opening
    iDisk in, 396
    location, 176
  toolbar, 396
Finder⇨File⇨Get Info
   command, 229
Firaxis Web site, 560
Firewalk X 2, 422
firewalls, 200, 373, 419–423, 459–460
FireWire
  camcorder, 291–292
  CD-RW drives, 509
  common problems, 531–532
  connections advantages, 527–529
  control over connections, 528
  daisy-chaining, 530
  devices, 104, 528
  DVD-RW drives, 509
  hard drives, 521, 522–523
  hubs, 530
  large files and, 527–528

  powering devices through ports, 528
  speed, 527
FireWire 2, 529
First Aid, 109–110
First In, First Out technology, 58
First Use Wizard, 23–24
flags, 574–575, 590
Flash tracks, 330
flat-bed scanners, 503
Flights channel, 78
folders
  actual size, 164
  adding to Dock, 176
  changing, 572
  cloning items, 50
  copying, 48–49
  creation date, 53
  deleting from command line, 580–581
  on Desktop, 48
  within Home directory, 577
  icons, 37
  information about, 52–56, 359
  last-modified date, 53
  listing
    contents, 572
    e-mail in, 359–360
  moving, 49
  number of items in, 162
  opening, 37
  paths, 64
  permissions, 53, 231
  recently used, 64
  renaming, 52
  reviewing content before changing
    permissions, 232
  searching for, 153
  size of, 53
  spring-loaded, 166–167
  viewing thumbnails, 172
fonts, 184, 298
footer.shtml file, 639–640
force feedback joystick, 507

Force Quit Applications dialog, 60
Force Quit (⌘+Option+Escape)
    keyboard shortcut, 60
foreign languages, 86–87
Format⇨Make Plain Text
    command, 368
Format⇨Show Colors command, 389
Format⇨Show Fonts command, 389
formatting
  destination drive, 23
  e-mail, 367–368, 370
  text for chatting, 389
FQDN (Fully Qualified Domain
    Name), 453
frames, 432
frameworks, 104
free Acrobat, 14
FreeBSD kernel, 16
FreeBSD Web site, 16
FTP (File Transfer Protocol),
    436, 590–591
  accessing files, 453–459
  from CLI (command-line interface) to
    transfer files, 456–459
  connecting to another FTP
    server, 457
  downloading files, 644
  Internet, 453
  quitting sessions, 458
  setting up, 642
  sharing files, 642–645
  starting CLI (command line
    interface), 457
  uploading files, 644–645
  from Web browser to access files,
    454–456
FTP clients, 642, 643
ftp command, 456
FTP servers, 454–455, 457–458,
    642–643, 645
Full Screen Mode (⌘+O) keyboard
    shortcut, 342
full-duplex, 432

G

games, 559–564
gateways, 436
general preferences, 183–184
General Preferences dialog, 174, 336
generic file icons, 37
get command, 458, 644
Get Movie Properties (⌘+J) keyboard
    shortcut, 331, 332
GetFileInfo command, 594
Getty Images online image
    collection, 78
Gibson Research Corporation Web
    site, 423
GIF files, 291
Gigabit Ethernet, 431
global default page, 632–633
Global theme, 310
Go iDisk (⌘+Shift+I) keyboard
    shortcut, 396
Go menu, 63–64
Go to Chat (⌘+G) keyboard
    shortcut, 387
Go to Folder command, 64
Go⇨Applications command, 621
Go⇨Connect to Server command,
    397, 449, 452, 467
Go⇨iDisk command, 396, 630
Grab utility, 62, 172
graphics cards, 64–65
graphics engine, 13
Group Chat window, 387
group contact cards, 95–96
Group Contact Cards (⌘+Shift+N)
    keyboard shortcut, 95

H

hackers, 418–419
half-duplex, 432

handwriting, 609
handwriting recognition, 609–610
hard drives, 104
  backing up, 116–117
  cleaning off, 519
  cluttered, 151
  defragmenting, 117, 547
  determining needed capacity,
    522–523
  EIDE (Enhanced Integrated Drive
    Electronics), 523
  erasing, 111–112
  external, 520–521
  FireWire versus USB, 523
  free space on, 519
  importing photos from, 272–273
  installing yourself, 524–526
  internal, 521–522
  jumper settings, 525–526
  logical errors, 547
  Mac OS Extended (or HFS Plus)
    format, 23
  organizing documents, 151
  partitioning, 112–114
  physical, 107–108
  physical errors, 547
  physical size, 523
  repairing, 546–547
  requirements, 20–21
  running applications from, 42
  SCSI (Small Computer System
    Interface), 523
  shock-mounted, 521
  speed, 523
  thrashing, 516
  UFS (UNIX File System), 23
  used or refurbished, 523
  verifying and repairing errors,
    109–110
hardware, 499
  AirPort Base Station, 488–489
  audio, 511–513

cable/DSL routers, 488–489
  caring for old, 525
  CD recorders, 509–510
  dealer installation, 524
  digital cameras, 500–501
  drawing tablets, 508–509
  drivers, 119, 139, 532
  DV (digital video) camcorders,
    501–503
  DVD recorders, 509–510
  failure, 143
  firewalls, 421
  hard drives, 519–523
  icons, 35
  images and, 500–504
  information about, 103–105
  input, 504–509
  installing yourself, 524–526
  iPod, 512–513
  joysticks, 507
  keyboards, 504–505
  memory, 515–519
  microphones, 611
  MP3 players, 512–513
  networks, 430–434
  overview, 104
  playing DVDs, 339
  printers, 533–541
  retracing installation steps, 139
  scanners, 503–504
  sharing Internet connections,
    488–489, 491–494
  static electricity, 525
  subwoofer speaker systems, 511–512
  tape drives, 510–511
  testing, 526
  trackballs, 505–506
headers, 432
hearing problems, 207
help, 129–130, 132, 134–135, 607–608
Help (⌘+?) keyboard shortcut, 41
Help topics, 129–132

Help Viewer, 130–132, 146
Help Viewer (⌘+?) keyboard
    shortcut, 129
Help⇨Mac Help command, 607
Help⇨Script Editor Help
    command, 607
Hewlett-Packard PhotoSmart 912, 500
Hide Dock (⌘+Option+D) keyboard
    shortcut, 60
Hide Explorer Bar (⌘+T) keyboard
    shortcut, 402
Hide iMovie (⌘+H) keyboard
    shortcut, 285
Hide (⌘+H) keyboard shortcut, 41
Hide or Show Drawer (⌘+Shift+M)
    keyboard shortcut, 360
Hide or Show (⌘+B) keyboard
    shortcut, 152
Hide or Show Status Bar
    (⌘+Option+S) keyboard shortcut,
    359
highlighting, 39–40, 234
History (⌘+3) keyboard shortcut, 411
History list, 411
home directory (~), 63, 571, 577
Home folder, 153, 209, 229, 448, 572
Home icon, 153
home pages, 405–406, 629
Home playback control, 288
Home window, 63
HomePage, 395, 625, 627–629
Horizontal Controller (⌘+Shift+H)
    keyboard shortcut, 341
hosting Web site, 350
hot computers, 421
hot corners, 187
.htm and .html file extension, 55
HTML (HyperText Markup
    Language), 629
HTML 4 For Dummies, 634
HTML editors, 633

HTTP (HyperText Transfer
    Protocol), 437
httpd.conf file, 635–638
hubs, 430–432, 434, 530–531

1

IANA (Internet Assigned Numbers
    Authority), 435
iBooks, 22–23, 504, 524
iCal, 244
iCards, 625
iChat, 216, 382–387, 391
iChat icon, 383
iChat window, 385, 389–390
iChat⇨Buddies⇨Add a Buddy
    command, 385
icon labels, 162, 164
icon view, 149, 160–163
Icon View (⌘+1) keyboard
    shortcut, 161
icons
  aliases, 37–39
  aligning, 162
  applications, 36
  column view, 165
  displaying on Desktop, 166
  files and folders, 36–37
  hardware, 35
  highlighting, 39–40
  menu bar, 64–65
  selecting multiple, 39–40
  selecting single, 39
  size, 34
  sorting display, 162
  type of, 34
  typing first few letters, 39
id Software Web site, 560
identifying items, 53

iDisk, 18, 24, 63, 194, 393–398, 625, 628–630
iDisk file servers, 394
iDisk window, 63
iDVD, 18, 70, 244, 306–308, 549
  file formats, 313
  Movie Buttons, 314–315
  Preview mode, 319
  setting background, 311–314
  Show TV Safe Area option, 313
  Slideshow Button, 317–318
  themes, 309–311
  video clips, 321
iDVD window, 309, 311–313, 315, 318, 320
IEEE (Institute of Electrical and Electronics Engineers), 474
IEEE 802.11b standard, 474–475
iMac, 20
images
  adding to Web sites, 628–629
  dimensions, 313
  enhancing, 245
  from Finder window, 172
  hardware for, 500–504
  QuickTime, 324
  thumbnail icons, 162
iMovie, 19, 244, 246, 549
  adding video clips to movie, 294
  Audio button, 286
  Audio shelf, 290
  basic composition, 294–295
  camera capture mode, 291
  Camera/Edit Mode switch, 291
  Clip Viewer tab, 294
  Clips button, 286
  Clips shelf, 286, 290
  Clips Viewer, 287
  DV (digital video) camcorders, 502
  editing video clips, 293–294
  Effects button, 299

  exporting movies for viewing, 305–306
  file formats, 291
  hiding, 285
  importing
    different kinds of media files, 291
    movie clips, 290
  interface, 285–287
  launching, 285
  Monitor, 286–288
  playback controls, 288
  prerecorded sound effects, 302
  rearranging video clips in movies, 295
  recording voice-overs, 303
  removing video clips from movies, 295
  shelf, 286
  sound, 301–304
  special effects, 299–301
  stock effects, 299–300
  switching to other applications, 285
  Timeline Viewer tab, 287, 294, 301
  Title shelf, 297–299
  titles, 297–299
  Tool Palettes, 286, 288–289
  tracking progress of effect being built, 301
  transitions, 295–296
  Viewers, 287, 289
Import (⌘+I) keyboard shortcut, 93
Import text command, 175
Import vCards (⌘+I) keyboard shortcut, 99
importing
  files
    with QuickTime Player, 332–333
    into Stickies, 175
  media files, 291
  photos, 269, 271–273
  sound from audio CD, 303–304
  vCards, 93, 99

In folder, 361
inactive windows, 32
Incoming File Request pane, 391
index.html file, 632, 634
indexing files, 159–160, 167
index.shtml file, 637–639
Info dialog, 52–56, 144, 159–160,
    229–231, 594
Info (⌘+I) keyboard shortcut,
    52, 53, 519
Information dialog, 34
information files, 68
infrastructure mode, 474
Inkwell, 610
input hardware, 504–509
Instant Messages, 387
Intego Web site, 423
internal
  hard drives, 521–522
  modems, 353–354
Internal Modem dialog, 357
international options, 184–185
Internet, 349
  applications, 18
  FTP (File Transfer Protocol), 453
  help for AppleScript, 607–608
  instantaneous access to
    information, 75
  online storage, 393–398
  preferences, 193–194
  protocols, 18
  search engines, 84–85
  security, 417–426
  selecting ISPs (Internet Service
    Providers), 349–351
Internet channel, 78
Internet Connect, 65, 356–357,
    480, 482–483
Internet Connect window, 480, 482
Internet connections
  AOL dial-up, 196
  broadband connections, 351

cable modems, 442
DHCP (Dynamic Host Configuration
    Protocol), 355
dial-up connections, 351, 356–357
DSL, 442
easy configuration, 18
Ethernet hardware, 354–356
firewalls, 200
internal modem, 353–354
IP addresses, 486–487
ISDN (Integrated Services Digital
    Network), 351
manual connections, 357
modems, 65
NAT (Network Address Translation),
    486–487
network connections, 351
Point-to-Point connections, 196
PPP (Point-to-Point Protocol), 65, 196
PPPoE (Point-to-Point over
    Ethernet), 355
satellite connections, 351
searching control company
    directory, 97
setting up, 353
sharing, 200, 440–441, 485–495
speed, 337
verifying, 442–444
Internet Explorer
  adding Favorites, 407
  Address field, 455
  addresses for Web sites, 401
  AutoComplete feature, 402–403
  AutoFill button, 405
  Back button, 404
  changing cookie acceptance, 414
  cookies, 413–414
  customizing toolbar, 401
  deleting
    contents of cache folder, 415
    History list contents, 415

Download Manager window, 408–409
downloading files, 408–409
Explorer bar, 403
Explorer menu, 33
Favorites, 403, 406–408
Forward button, 404
FTP (File Transfer Protocol) to
    access files, 454–456
History list, 411
Home button, 403, 405
jumping
    directly to Web sites, 401
    to Favorites, 407–408
launching, 85, 400
location for downloaded files, 409
Mail button, 405
navigating World Wide Web, 404–405
Print button, 405
Refresh button, 404
saving Web pages, 411–413
security, 413–415
Services submenu, 33
setting up Home page, 405–406
Stop button, 404
subscriptions, 410–411
visiting Web sites, 402–404
Internet Explorer window, 400–403
Internet radio stations, 260–262
Internet server, checking
    availability, 62
Internet-based LDAP directories,
    96–97
Internet-savvy, 17–18
Internet-sharing devices, 486
invisible files, 588
Invite to Chat command, 387
Invite to Chat (⌘+Option+C)
    keyboard shortcut, 387
IP (Internet Protocol), 435
IP addresses
    automatic assignment, 440–441
    generic, 632

Internet connections, 486–487
ISPs (Internet Service
    Providers), 487
manually choosing range, 437–440
private, 436, 486
public, 436, 486
routers, 436
IP (Internet Protocol) printers,
    536–538
IPFW, 422
iPhoto, 18, 244–245
    Album List, 270
    Assign switch, 276
    black-and-white conversion, 280
    Book panel, 282–283
    changing image dimensions, 313
    Crop feature, 279–280
    editing photos, 270, 278–281
    graphics formats, 273
    Import mode, 272
    importing photos, 269, 271–273
    keywords, 275–278
    launching, 271–272
    Organize mode, 275–276
    organizing photos, 269–270
    Photo Album List, 281
    Photo Albums, 273–275
    Photo Library icon, 281
    printing photo albums, 281–283
    publishing photos, 270
    Red-Eye filter, 280
    Search switch, 277
    Share panel, 283
    sharing photos, 283–284
    Show Guides check box, 282
    tasks, 269–270
    toolbar, 270
    Viewer, 270, 276
iPhoto toolbar, 272, 276–278, 281–283
iPod, 246, 262–263, 512–513
ISDN (Integrated Services Digital
    Network), 351

ISPs (Internet Service Providers)
  AOL users, 354
  broadband service, 350
  dial-up connections, 356–357
  domain name service, 350
  DSL (Digital Subscriber Line), 350
  e-mail accounts, 350
  hosting Web site, 350
  IP addresses, 487
  local calling rates, 350
  manual connection, 354
  PPP (Point-to-Point protocol), 353
  public IP addresses, 436
  quality technical support, 350
  selecting, 349–351
  static IP addresses, 350
iSync, 245
iTunes, 18, 69, 244, 246
  AIFF files, 249
  audio CDs, 250, 263
  audio files, 249–250
  Browse button, 253
  burning CDs, 263–264
  converting file formats, 258
  default settings, 69
  equalizer, 258–259
  Equalizer button, 258
  Internet radio stations, 260–262
  iPods, 246, 262–263
  iTunes Radio, 252, 260–261
  keyboard shortcuts, 251
  manually setting or changing song
    information, 257
  MP3 CDs, 263
  MP3 files, 249
  New Playlist button, 255
  Next Song button, 251
  Play button, 250
  playing
    audio CD, 250–251
    audio files, 251–255
  Playlist feature, 255
  plug-ins, 266–267

  Previous Song button, 251
  Radio Station icon, 260
  radio stations, 262
  ripping audio files, 257–258
  Search function, 254
  Song Information dialog, 256
  Source list, 252, 255
  sources for music, 252
  Stop button, 250
  tracking songs, 256–257
  tuning in your own stations, 261
  Visualizer, 265–266
  visuals, 264–267
  Volume slider, 69
  WAV files, 250
iTunes Library, 251–256, 263
iTunes Preferences dialog, 264
iTunes Radio, 252, 260–261
iTunes window, 69
iTunes⇨Preferences command,
    258, 264

J

Jaguar, 1
Jobs dialog, 538–540
joysticks, 507
JPEG files, 291
.jpeg or .jpg file extension, 55
jumper settings, 525–526
jumping to location, 63–64
junk mail, 361, 371–373
Junk Mail filter, 372

K

kernel dump, 145
keyboard, 191, 504–505
  layouts, 185
  UNIX and, 567–570

keyboard shortcuts, 34, 40–41, 191, 207, 251

Keychain Access application, 223–224

Keychain dialog, 225

Keychain folder, 225

keychains, 223–225, 469

keywords, 275–278

Kids Blue theme, 310

Kids keyword, 275

Kids Pink theme, 310

`kill` command, 583

killing processes, 583

`locate` command, 584–585

locations, 61

Log Out (⌘+Shift+Q) keyboard shortcut, 212

logging out without shutdown, 212

login, 142, 185–186, 201

Login Items, 214, 606

Login items list, 42

login screen, 118, 186, 201, 211–213

Loop Movie (⌘+L) keyboard shortcut, 329

LPR (Line Printer Remote), 489

`ls` command, 456, 572, 578, 644

L

LAN connections, 24

LAN party, 433

languages, preferred, 184

LANs (local area networks), 486

`LAST_MODIFIED` message, 638

`lcd` command, 456

LDAP (Lightweight Directory Access Protocol), 96

LEAP (Lightweight Extensible Authentication Protocol), 478

libraries, 104

Library folder, 597, 599

Library⇨iMovie⇨Sound Effects command, 302

Library/Printer folder, 72, 73, 537

Library/Printer/PPD folder, 537

Library⇨Web Server⇨Documents command, 633

List view, 150–151, 163–164

List Web sites, The, 351

loading, 66

local networks, 437

LocalTalk, 463

M

.Mac, 116, 194, 394–395, 625–629

.Mac accounts, 24, 361, 382, 393–394

.Mac e-mail account, 194

Mac notebooks, 22–23

Mac OS, upgrading from earlier versions, 21–23

Mac OS 9

connecting to iDisk, 398

Control Strip, 12

crashes, 15

desktop, 125

Disk First Aid utility, 22

Info dialog, 144

problems running applications, 144–145

returning to, 127–128

returning to Mac OS X, 128

System Folder, 128

System folders, 205

virtual session, 19

Mac OS Help Guides, 607

Mac OS X, 1, 9–10
  accounts, 24
  Address Book, 89–90
  applications, 125
  Aqua, 12
  Aqua sheets, 12
  automatically restarting after power
    failure, 191
  built-in FTP server, 454
  Carbon application, 122
  changing colors, 173–174
  Cocoa application, 122
  country names and keyboard
    layouts, 23
  Darwin, 571
  Disk Utility, 22
  ease of use, 10
  First Use Wizard, 23–24
  forcing boot up in, 118
  free software, 18–19
  hardware requirements, 20–21
  help topics, 132
  Internet applications, 18
  Internet-savvy, 17–18
  IPFW, 422
  multitasking, 17
  multithreading, 17
  news, 130
  older programs, 19
  as Open Source project, 16
  PDF (Portable Document Format)
    files, 14
  personalizing, 23–24, 149
  placement of controls, 12
  Quartz Extreme, 13–14
  QuickTime, 15
  reasons for using, 10–19
  requirements, 2
  restarting, 26
  returning to Mac OS 9, 127–128
  services, 62–63
  shutting down, 26
  Sleep mode, 26
  solving problems by reinstalling, 145
  stability, 15–16
  standard user interface, 12
  streamlined appearance, 10
  System folders, 205
  uncovering UNIX core, 48
  UNIX applications, 16
  UNIX operating system, 15–16
  updating, 115–116
  upgrading and applications'
    behavior, 139
  upgrading to, 21–23
  version, 104
  Web sharing, 630–641
Mac OS X Chess, 560
Mac OS X System Folder, 128
MacAddict Web site, 135
@mac.com address, 24
MacConnection Web site, 519
MacFixIt Web site, 135
MacGamer Web site, 135
Macintosh
  checking current amount of memory,
    517–518
  controlling other computers from,
    461–462
  determining exact model, 518–519
  digital hub, 244
  Drive Open key, 27
  hardware upgrade, 103
  Power key, 27
  remote control of, 460–462
  restarting, 26
  shutting down, 26–27
  Sleep mode, 26
  time running since last reboot or
    login, 571
Macintosh Product Guide, 78
Macintosh publications, 135
Macintosh retailers, 135
Macintosh user groups, 135

MacMall Web site, 519
MacScripter.net Web site, 608
MacWarehouse Web site, 519
Macworld Web site, 135
Mail, 62, 96
  Accounts list, 361–362
  Add Account button, 362
  adding
    e-mail accounts, 362–364
    e-mail addresses to Address
      Book, 366
  automatically
    checking for e-mail, 375
    launching, 405
  automating
    message deletion, 375
    with rules, 377–379
  changing e-mail account status, 376
  checking for e-mail, 364–365
  composing and sending e-mail,
    369–371
  deleting
    e-mail, 365–366
    e-mail accounts, 364
  displaying all e-mail headers, 366
  Drafts folder, 361
  editing e-mail accounts, 364
  filtered heading, 366
  In folder, 361
  Junk folder, 361
  junk mail, 371–373
  Junk Mail filter, 372
  Message list, 365
  Message menu, 92
  MIME (Multipurpose Internet Mail
    Extensions), 368
  New Message window, 369–371
  omitting text of original
    message, 369
  Out folder, 361, 368
  page links, 403
  reading e-mail, 365–366

Reply window, 367–368
replying to e-mail, 366–369
scanning e-mail, 365
Sent folder, 361
setting up e-mail accounts, 361–364
signatures, 376
sound, 375
spell checking, 369
Trash folder, 361
Mail toolbar, 361, 369
Mail window, 359–360
Mail window toolbar, 360, 364, 366,
  368–369, 371
Mailbox⇔Erase Deleted Messages
  command, 361
Mailbox⇔Get New Mail command, 364
Mailbox⇔Get New Mail in Account
  command, 364, 376
Mailbox⇔New Mailbox command, 361
Mail⇔Preferences command,
  362, 364, 377
Mail⇔Preferences⇔Accounts
  command, 375
Mail⇔Preferences⇔Composing
  command, 369
Mail⇔Preferences⇔Signatures
  command, 376
mainframes, 66
Make Alias command, 57
Make Alias (⌘+L) keyboard
  shortcut, 57
Make Default (⌘+D) keyboard
  shortcut, 534
man command, 576
mappings, 537
Media Eject, 118
media files
  adding to DVD Menus, 314–318
  authentication, 337
  converting, 332–333
  importing, 291
  tracking, 334

megapixel, 500
Meier, Sid, 561
memory
  buying online, 519
  checking amount, 61
  checking current amount of, 517–518
  Classic applications, 144
  correct slot for, 525
  description of, 104
  installing yourself, 524–526
  processors, 518–519
  reasons for adding, 515–517
  Virtual PC, 553
memory cards, 501
memory module notches, 525
menu bar, 64–66, 192, 483
menus, 183
merging information from
    applications, 62–63
Message list, 365–366
Message⇨Add Sender command, 366
Message⇨Transfer command, 361
mget command, 458
Micromat, 546
Micromat Drive 10, 117
Micromat Web site, 110
microphones, 614, 616
MIME (Multipurpose Internet Mail
    Extensions), 368
MIME file types, 198
Minimize button, 29
Minimize Finder Window
    (⌘+Option+M) keyboard
    shortcut, 41
Minimize (⌘+M) keyboard
    shortcut, 41
minimizing windows, 29–30
Miramar Systems Web site, 468
missing.html file, 640–641
Modem status icon, 65
modems, 65, 196–197
modifier keys, 207

Monitor, 64–65, 286–288, 291, 300, 303
monitors, 189–190, 611
mounting, 66
mouse, 192
  buttons, 28
  numeric keypad to move mouse
      pointer, 207
  secondary button, 34
Mov files, 198
.mov format, 15
Move Properties window, 331–332
Move to Trash command, 51
Movie Buttons, 314–316
movie clips, adding special effects,
    300–301
Movie⇨Get Movie Properties
    command, 331
Movie⇨Hide Sound Controls
    command, 329
Movie⇨Loop Back and Forth
    command, 330
Movie⇨Loop command, 329
movies
  adding
    video clips, 290–292, 294
    to Web sites, 628–629
  editing video clips, 293–294
  exporting for viewing, 305–306
  importing or recording audio
      clips, 290
  information, 81–82
  listings and times, 78
  making, 289–290
  QuickTime, 324
  recording voice-overs, 303
  removing
    sound from, 304
    video clips, 295
  show times, 82
  sound, 301–304
  special effects, 299–301
  titles, 297–299

trailers, 78, 81–82
transitions, 290, 295–296
Movies channel, 78
Movie⇨Show Sound Controls
   command, 329
Movie⇨Show Video Controls
   command, 328
MP3 CDs, 263
MP3 files, 198, 249, 252, 291
MP3 players, 262–263, 512–513
mput command, 458
multiple users, 209–210, 213
multitasking, 17
multithreading, 17
multi-user accounts, 215
music
  altering volume of frequencies,
    258–259
  automatically setting song
    information, 256–257
  digitizing, 243
  QuickTime, 324, 337
  removing from iTunes Library,
    254–255
  tracking songs, 256–257
mv command, 580
My Housecleaning Script, 606

N

Name and Password sheet, 211
named menu, 62
NAT (Network Address Translation),
   486–487
NAT (Network Address Translation)
   devices, 421
NetBarrier X, 423
NetInfo Manager, 210
NetInfo Network, 96, 538

network connections, 104, 200, 351
Network dialog, 438–441, 446
network directories, 96–97
Network Preferences dialog, 464–465
Network Startup icon, 206
Network Utilities dialog, 422–423
Network Utility, 62, 442–444
networks
  AppleTalk, 195, 463–472
  best location for hub or switch, 434
  built-in firewall, 459–460
  cables, 433–434
  changing
    default names, 199
    folders on, 457
  closed, 482
  collisions, 430–431
  computer-to-computer, 474, 479–481
  configuration
    basics, 435–437
    problems, 446
  configuring system preferences,
    437–441
  default gateway, 436
  Dictionary protocol, 591
  document sharing, 227–229
  file sharing, 447–450
  FTP (File Transfer Protocol) to
    access files, 453–459
  gateways, 436
  hackers, 418
  hardware and software, 430–434
  hubs, 430–432
  IP addresses, 435
  local, 437
  locations, 61, 195
  manually choosing IP address range,
    437–440
  network ports, 197
  NIC (Network Interface Card), 430
  physical problems, 445

(continued)

networks *(continued)*
  Point-to-Point over Ethernet
    connections, 195
  preferences, 194–197
  private, 437
  protocols, 435, 436–437
  proxy servers, 195–196
  servers, 447
  setting up, 434
  sharing
    Internet connections, 485–495
    printers, 450–451, 540–541
  sniffing, 477
  software, 436–437
  subnet masks, 436
  switches, 432–433
  System folder, 206
  TCP/IP suite, 195, 435–436
  troubleshooting, 444–446
  UNIX, 590–591
  wireless, 473–483
New AppleScript Document (⌘+N)
    keyboard shortcut, 604
New Contact (⌘+N) keyboard
    shortcut, 91
New Finder Window (⌘+N) keyboard
    shortcut, 27
New Mail (⌘+Shift+N) keyboard
    shortcut, 364
New Message (⌘+N) keyboard
    shortcut, 369
New Message window, 369–371
New Playlist (⌘+N) keyboard
    shortcut, 255
New Script (⌘+N) keyboard
    shortcut, 601
New Window (⌘+N) keyboard
    shortcut, 63
New⇨Photo Album command, 281
newsgroups, 135
Next Web Page (⌘+]) keyboard
    shortcut, 404
NIC (Network Interface Card), 430

No access permission, 229
non-Apple 802.11 equipment and
    AirPort, 480
None keyword, 275
non-USB printers, 534, 536–538
Norton AntiVirus, 141, 423, 547
Norton Personal Firewall, 422
Norton Web site, 117, 547
NPR (National Public Radio) URL, 261
numbers, international, 185
numeric keypad moving mouse
    pointer, 207

O

octets, 435
Office v. X, 233–237, 544, 546
offline, 383
older applications, 19, 122–125
One Mouse, One Button, One King, 10
online, 141, 383, 393–398, 424–426
open command, 456, 581
Open dialog, 43–44, 68, 368
Open Dictionary dialog, 603
Open (⌘+O) keyboard shortcut,
    37, 41, 42, 43, 68
Open Stream dialog, 261
Open Stream (⌘+U) keyboard
    shortcut, 261
OpenGL graphics acceleration
    standard, 14
operands, 574–575
operating systems, 9, 12
Orange Micro Web site, 530
OrangeUSB 2.0 Hi-Speed PCI card, 530
Orb drives, 509, 520
OSXvnc, 461
Otto Matic, 19
Out folder, 361, 368, 371
Overlap transition, 295

p

Page Setup dialog, 97
Page Setup (⌘+Shift+P) keyboard shortcut, 97
Painter, 610
partitions, 107–108, 112–113
passthru port, 530
password verification sheet, 222
passwords
  accounts, 24
  adding to keychains, 469
  AppleWorks, 237–238
  changing, 186, 470
  composing, 213
  disabling hint, 213
  e-mail accounts, 363
  hints, 217
  keychains, 223
  login screen, 211
  .Mac, 194, 626
  Office v.X, 235–236
  screen savers, 187
  unencrypted, 469
  verifying, 217
  wireless networks, 480
Paste (⌘+V) keyboard shortcut, 41, 293
patch cables, 433
paths, 64, 577–579
pattern images, 171
PC MACLAN, 468
.pdf (Adobe Acrobat) extension, 54
PDF (Portable Document Format) files, 13–14, 37, 537
performance, tracking, 105–107
peripherals, ejecting, 531
permissions, 110, 229–233
personal information, 418
personalizing Mac OS X, 149–152
PGP Freeware, 425

PGP Web site, 425
Photo Album List, 273–274
Photo Albums
  adding photos, 273–274
  building with search tool, 278
  creation of, 273, 281
  deleting, 275
  naming, 273
  printing, 281–283
  removing photos from, 274
  as screen saver, 284
  text, 282–283
  viewing photos, 273–274
Photo Library, 273–274
photos
  adding to Photo Albums, 273–274
  assigning keywords, 277
  black-and-white conversion, 280
  brightness and contrast, 278, 280
  constraining, 279–280
  cropping, 278–280
  Desktop, 284
  digitizing, 243
  editing, 245, 270, 278–281
  e-mail, 284
  exporting, 284
  importing, 269
  iPhoto, 271–273
  keywords for organizing, 275–278
  ordering prints, 284
  organizing, 269–270, 273–278
  printing, 284
  publishing, 270, 284
  red-eye and black & white, 278
  removing
    from Photo Album, 274
    Red-Eye, 280
  rotating, 281
  sharing, 283–284
  slide show presentation, 284
Photoshop, 548–549, 610
Photoshop Elements 2.0, 549

physical disks, 107–108
pico, 586–589
picture CDs, 188
Pictures channel, 78
Pictures folder, 171–172
PID (Process ID), 583
ping utility, 442–444
pinging, 62
pipes (|), 585
Play Full Screen playback control, 288
Play playback control, 288
playback head, 288, 303
Playlists, 255, 262–264
Pliris-soft Web site, 422
plug-and-play, 528
plug-ins, 197–198, 266–267
Point-to-Point over Ethernet
    connections, 195
ports, 460
PostScript printers, 536
PostScript-compatible printers, 537
Power Mac G3, 20
Power Mac G4, 20
PowerBook, 22–23, 504
PowerPoint, 546
PPD (PostScript Printer Description)
    files, 536, 537
PPP (Point-to-Point Protocol),
    65, 196, 353
PPPoE (Point-to-Point over
    Ethernet), 355
PPPoE icon, 65
preemptive multitasking, 17
preferences
  accounts, 186, 200–201
  CD, 188
  Classic mode, 201–202
  ColorSync, 188–189
  CPU Monitor, 105–106
  date and time, 203–204
  Desktop, 181
  displays, 189–190

Dock, 181–183
DVD, 188
DVD Player, 343–346
Energy Saver, 190–191
Finder, 165–167
general, 183–184
hardware, 188–193
international, 184–185
Internet, 193–194
keyboard, 191
login, 185–186
mouse, 192
networks, 194–197
Print Center, 535
QuickTime, 197–199, 336
QuickTime Player, 336
saving, 180
sharing, 199–200
software update, 203–204
sound, 192–193
speech, 204–205
startup disk, 205–206
Universal Access, 206–207
Preferences command, 97
Preferences⇨Accounts command, 376
preset keywords, 275
Previous Web Page (⌘+[) keyboard
    shortcut, 404
Print Center, 450, 471–472,
    533–536, 538
Print Center Preferences dialog, 535
Print dialog, 72–74, 98, 537
print jobs, 538–540
Print (⌘+P) keyboard shortcut,
    41, 72, 98
printer drivers, 72, 537
Printer List dialog, 471–472
Printer List toolbar, 74
printers
  adding, 534
  AppleTalk, 466–472, 536–538
  compatible with TCP/IP printing, 489

configuring, 535
connecting with cable/DSL
  routers, 489
default, 72, 534
deleting, 534
Directory Services, 538
DNS (Domain Name System)
  name, 538
driver installation program, 73
drivers, 537
information about, 536
IP (Internet Protocol), 536–538
IP addresses, 538
job list for, 536
managing print jobs, 538–540
manually adding, 73–74
mappings, 537
name of application, 538
naming, 541
non-USB, 534, 536–538
PostScript, 536
PostScript-compatible, 537
PPD (PostScript Printer Description)
  files, 536–537
remote, 535
sharing on networks, 450–451,
  540–541
USB (Universal Serial Bus), 72, 534
printing, 72–73
  contacts, 97–98
  PDF files, 537
  photo albums, 281–283
  photos, 284
  search results, 80
  stopping, 540
  Web pages, 405
private
  IP addresses, 436, 486
  networks, 437
privileges, 110

processes, 583–584
processors, 61, 518–519
prompt, 571, 587–589
Properties pop-up menu, 331, 332
protocols, 18, 435, 436–437
proxy servers, 195–196
.psd extension, 55
PSD files, 291
Public folders, 394, 397
public IP addresses, 436, 486
publishing photos, 270
Push transition, 295
put command, 458, 644–645

Q

Quartz Extreme, 13–14
QuicKeys X, 555–556
QuickTime, 82, 198–199, 305–306,
  323–325
  media files, 332–333
  music, 337
  playback, 197, 324
  playing media, 324–332
  plug-in, 197–198, 324
  preferences, 197–199, 336
  Pro version, 325
  updating, 337
QuickTime 6 Player, 15
QuickTime movies, 15
  changing aspects, 332
  DVD Menus, 312, 314
  information about, 330–331
  opening, 325
  properties, 331–332
  resizing, 326
  tracks, 330
  Web pages, 335–336

QuickTime Player
  access to free multimedia content,
    334–335
  adjusting volume, 327
  advanced playback features, 328–330
  advancing through file, 327
  audio playback, 329
  changing image dimensions, 313
  Content Guide, 334–335
  exporting files, 333
  file types importable, 333
  importing files, 332–333
  information about movies, 330–331
  launching, 324–325
  location of controls, 327
  looping movies, 329–330
  movie properties, 331–332
  opening QuickTime movies, 325
  Play button, 327
  playback head, 327
  playback keyboard shortcuts, 328
  playing media, 327–328
  preferences, 336
  Stop button, 327
  tracking media files, 334
  video playback, 328
QuickTime Player window, 326
QuickTime Player⇨General
    Preferences command, 336
QuickTime Player⇨QuickTime
    Preferences command, 336
QuickTime Plug-In, 337
QuickTime Pro, 328–330
QuickTime Web plug-in, 335–336
quit command, 458
Quit (⌘+Q) keyboard shortcut,
    41, 46, 69
Quit System Preferences (⌘+Q)
    keyboard shortcut, 180
quitting applications, 46

R

RAID (Redundant Array of
    Independent/Inexpensive Disks),
    114–115
RAM (random access memory),
    20–21, 515–519
Read & Write permission, 229
Read only permission, 229
reading e-mail, 365–366
README file, 102
readme files, 68
README.curl file, 591
REAL Software Web site, 559
REALbasic, 558–559
REALbasic For Dummies, 559
real-time scanning, 423
rebooting, 138–139, 143–144
Recent Folders window, 64
Recent Items menu, 58
Recent Places, 44
recordable DVDs, 188
recording
  online radio stations, 592–593
  scripts, 600–602
  voice-overs, 303
Refresh Web Page (⌘+R) keyboard
    shortcut, 404
refreshing Web pages, 404
remote control of Macintosh, 460–462
remote printers, 535
removable cartridge drives, 520
removable media and viruses, 423
removable volumes, 66–67
renaming files from command line, 580
Rendezvous, 382, 387, 451, 537–538
Reply window, 367–368
replying to e-mail, 366–369
ResExcellence Web site, 608
Resize Stickie (⌘+M) keyboard
    shortcut, 175

resources, troubleshooting, 145–146
Restart command, 26
restoring windows, 29–30
retracing your steps, 139–140
Retrospect, 21, 116–117
Return to Castle Wolfenstein, 562–563
revision marks, 233
Rewind playback control, 288
ripping audio files, 257–258
rm command, 580–581
rmdir command, 580–581
Roget's II Thesaurus, 78
Root accounts, 210
root directory (/), 578
rotating photos, 281
routers and IP addresses, 436
Roxio Easy CD Creator, 70
Roxio Toast, 70–71, 550–551
Roxio Web site, 71, 551
RTF (Rich Text Format)
    documents, 37
Rules dialog, 377–379
rules for e-mail, 377–379
Run Script (⌘+R) keyboard
    shortcut, 600

S

Samba, 437
satellite connections, 351
Save As dialog, 235
Save Attachment command, 374
Save dialog, 45, 98, 412–413
Save (⌘+S) keyboard shortcut, 69
saving
  attachments, 373–374
  chat discussion, 389
  documents, 45
  DVDs, 319–321
  preferences, 180
  scripts, 606

text files, 68–69
Web pages in Internet Explorer,
    411–413
Scale Down transition, 295
scanners, 503–504
Scanners For Dummies, 84, 504
.scpt extension, 597
screen savers, 142, 172–173, 187, 284
Screen Savers folder, 172
screen snapshot, capturing, 62
script applications, 597
Script Editor, 598–603
scripts
  adding to Login items, 606
  compiled scripts, 597–598
  Current Temperature by Zipcode
    script, 600
  elements, 604–606
  executing, 599–600
  host applications, 598–599
  recording, 600–602
  related to Finder, 602
  saving, 606
  script applications, 597
  Speech Recognition, 612
  text files, 598
  types of, 597–598
  user-created, 600–602
scroll bar, 28–29, 183
scrolling windows, 28–29
scrubber bar, 288
SCSI (Small Computer System
    Interface) hard drives, 523
search engines, 76, 78, 84–85
searching
  Address Book contacts, 94
  business address and telephone,
    79–80
  content, 158, 159
  criteria, 158
  different types of, 76

(continued)

searching *(continued)*
  eBay, 83–84
  for files and folders, 153
  for files from toolbar, 155–157
  flight schedules, 87–88
  for keywords, 277–278
  movie information, 81–82
  movie trailers, 81–82
  network directories, 96–97
  printing results, 80
  results, 77
  search engines, 84–85
  stocks, 85
  summary of information, 77
  synonyms, 82
  topics, 76
  translations, 86–87
  Web sites, 76
  word definitions, 82
secure Web sites, 402
security
  802.11x standard, 478
  antivirus basics, 423
  credit card information, 418
  dangerous macros, 418
  firewall basics, 419–423
  hackers, 418
  Internet, 417–426
  Internet Explorer, 413–415
  keychains, 223
  LEAP (Lightweight Extensible
    Authentication Protocol), 478
  personal information, 418
  PGP Freeware, 425
  SSH, 469
  unsafe behavior online, 424–426
  unsavory individuals and, 418
  viruses, 418
  WEP (Wired Equivalency Protocol),
    477–478
  wireless networks, 476–478

Select All (⌘+A) keyboard
    shortcut, 41
selected text colors, 183
selection box, 39
Send a File (⌘+Option+F) keyboard
    shortcut, 390
sending e-mail, 62
Sent folder, 361
Sepia Tone effect, 300
Server Options dialog, 363
Server Side Includes, 635–640
servers, 447, 454
services, 62–63, 199, 622
Services menu, 62–63, 94
SetFile command, 594
Share panel, 283
share points, 467–470
shared files, 104
Shared folder, 232, 448, 468
sharing
  documents, 227–229, 233–234
  Internet connections, 200
  photos, 283–284
  preferences, 199–200
  printers, 537, 540–541
  services, 199
Sharing dialog, 449–450, 452, 459,
    489–490, 541, 631
sharing files. *See* file sharing
sharing Internet connections
  connecting elements up, 491–494
  DHCP (Dynamic Host Configuration
    Protocol), 493
  hardware, 488–489, 491–494
  Internet-sharing devices, 486
  LANs (local area networks), 486
  software, 489–494
  wireless support, 494–495
Sharing Preferences dialog, 454
Sharpen effect, 300
sheet-fed scanners, 503

Sherlock, 75
  All Airlines drop-down list, 87
  Arrival City or Airport Code
    drop-down list, 88
  business address and telephone,
    79–80
  Company Name or Ticker Symbol
    box, 85
  default channels, 78
  Departure City or Airport Code drop-
    down list, 87
  Dictionary channel button, 82
  displaying real-time information, 76
  Driving Directions From drop-down
    list box, 80
  eBay channel button, 83
  Flight Number box, 87
  flight schedules, 87–88
  Flights channel button, 87
  Internet channel button, 84
  language-to-language drop-down
    list box, 86
  Movies channel button, 81
  Original Text box, 86
  plug-ins, 76
  Print button, 80
  QuickTime movie trailer, 82
  running, 76
  Search button, 80, 88
  search engines, 84–85
  searching for word definitions, 82
  simplifying search engines, 76
  Stocks channel button, 85
  summary section, 85
  switching channels, 79
  text, graphics, and video, 76
  toolbar, 78
  Topic or Description box, 84
  Translation channel button, 86
  updating summary section, 84
  Yellow Pages channel button, 79
Sherlock window, 76–77, 84

ShieldsUp!, 423
Show All Headers (⌘+Shift+H)
  keyboard shortcut, 366
Show Colors (⌘+Shift+C) keyboard
  shortcut, 389
Show Fonts (⌘+T) keyboard
  shortcut, 389
Show Info dialog, 396, 541
Show Info (⌘+I) keyboard shortcut,
  535, 541
Show Jobs (⌘+O) keyboard
  shortcut, 538
Show Movie Info (⌘+I) keyboard
  shortcut, 330
Show Video Controls (⌘+K) keyboard
  shortcut, 328
Show View Options (⌘+J) keyboard
  shortcut, 161
Shut Down command, 26, 139
signature file, 141
signatures, 376
Simple Finder, 220
single Macintosh sharing documents,
  227–229
Sites folder, 629, 631
Size command, 332
Sky theme, 310
Sleep command, 26
Sleep mode, 26, 126, 187, 190–191
Slideshow Button, 317–318
Slideshow window, 317–318
sniffing, 477
Soft Focus effect, 300
software. *See also* applications
  digital hub, 244–247
  networks, 430–434
  retracing installation steps, 139–140
  sharing Internet connections,
    489–494
  update preferences, 203–204
  wireless support for sharing Internet
    connections, 494

software-based music synthesizer, 198
Song Information dialog,
 256, 257, 262, 593
Song Information (⌘+I) keyboard
 shortcut, 257, 262, 593
songs, tracking, 256–257
sorting
 Buddy List, 390
 help topics, 131
 icon display, 162
sound, 192–193, 301–304, 375
sound effects, 302–303
Sound Effects folder, 302
sound tracks, 330
Source List, 252, 255
spam. *See* junk mail
Speakable Items folder, 204, 612, 623
speaking text, 621–623
special effects, 299–301
speech, 62, 204–206, 609
Speech Commands window, 616–617
Speech dialog, 618–621
Speech Recognition, 610–617
Speed Disk, 117
spell checking e-mail, 369
Sports theme, 310
Spring Cleaning, 102, 519
SSH, 469
SSID (Service Set Identifier), 474
Standard accounts, 210
standard user interface, 12
standard-level accounts, 219
Standard-level users and capabilities,
 218–222
start-up applications, 118
start-up disk, 109, 113, 205–206
Startup Disk icon, 127
start-up keys, 118
start-up volume, verifying and
 repairing permissions, 110

static electricity, 525
static IP addresses, 350
static volumes, 66, 67
stationery file, 54
status bar, 152–153, 359
Stickie window, 175
Stickies, 174–176
stocks, 85
Stocks channel, 78
Stop Web Page Download (⌘+.)
 keyboard shortcut, 404
straight-through Cat5E cables, 433
Streamripper, 592–593
StuffIt, 554–555
stylus, 610
submenus, 33
subnet masks, 436
subscriptions, 410–411
subwoofer speaker systems, 511–512
sudo command, 579–580, 594
SuperDrive, 307, 339
swapping data between
 applications, 68
Switch Application (⌘+Tab) keyboard
 shortcut, 41, 43
switches, 432–434
switching between windows, 31–32
Symantec Web site, 141, 422
synonyms, 82
system, displaying top level, 153
System Administrator, 210
system alter sounds, 193
system boot menu, 118
system files, 145, 233
System Preferences
 changes and problems, 140
 Classic settings, 144
 Date & Time settings, 66
 Display settings, 65
 displaying panes, 179
 Dock settings, 59
 Login Items settings, 142

Network settings, 61
networks, 437–441
System Preferences Date & Time icon,
202–204
System Preferences dialog, 179
Accounts option, 211, 448
Accounts pane, 200–201, 213, 215,
216, 376
Activation tab, 142, 187
Advanced tab, 202
Allow User to Administer This
Computer check box, 217
Allow User to Log in from Windows
check box, 217
Animate Opening Applications check
box, 182
Appearance drop-down list, 183
Apple Speakable Items option, 612
AppleTalk tab, 195
Apply Now button, 180
Arrangement control, 181
Automatically Check for Updates
When You Have a Network
Connection check box, 115
Automatically Hide and Show the
Dock check box, 182
Built-in Ethernet option, 195, 355
Burn CDs or DVDs check box, 221
CDs & DVDs group, 188
Change Password check box, 221
Change Picture check box, 181
Classic mode group, 201–202
Click in the Scroll Bar To radio
buttons, 183
CMMs (Color Matching Methods)
tab, 189
Collection drop-down list, 181
Color tab, 190
ColorSync group, 188–189
Commands tab, 205, 612, 615
Configure drop-down list, 353–354

Connect Automatically When
Needed check box, 356
Connection tab, 198, 337
Current Desktop Picture well, 181
Date & Time tab, 203
Date tab, 184
Default Profiles tab, 189
Default Voice tab, 205, 611
Delete User button, 218
Desktop group, 181
DHCP (Dynamic Host Configuration
Protocol), 195, 355
Display tab, 189–190
Displays group, 189–190
Dock group, 181–183
Dock Size slider, 182
Double-Click Speed slider, 192
Duplicate button, 195
Edit Locations option, 195
Edit User button, 217
Email tab, 194
Energy Saver group, 190–191
Firewall tab, 200
Font Smoothing Style drop-down
list, 184
Full Keyboard Access tab, 191
General group, 183–184
General icon, 173
Hearing tab, 207
Helpful Tips button, 612
Hide the Restart and Shut Down
Buttons check box, 213
Highlight Color drop-down list, 183
Hot Corners tab, 187
iDisk tab, 194, 394
Import tab, 258
Inkwell pane, 610
Input Menu tab, 185
Input tab, 193
Installed Updates tab, 204
Internal Modem option, 196, 353, 356

(continued)

System Preferences dialog *(continued)*
International group, 184–185
Internet icon, 394, 630
Internet pane, 193–194, 630
Internet tab, 200
Key Toggles Listening On and Off
radio button, 614
Keyboard group, 191
Keyboard tab, 207
Language tab, 184
LDAP tab, 97
Listen Only While Key Is Pressed
radio button, 614
Listening tab, 204–205, 612, 614
Location drop-down list, 195
Login Automatically as username
check box, 213
Login Items icon, 214, 606
Login Items screen, 185–186
Login Options tab, 201, 212, 213
.Mac tab, 194, 630
Magnification slider, 182
Media Keys tab, 198, 337
Memory/Versions tab, 202
Menu Bar Clock tab, 203
Minimize button, 182
Minimize Using drop-down list, 182
Modem tab, 196
Mouse group, 192
Mouse tab, 207
MP3 Encoder option, 258
Music tab, 198, 337
Mute check box, 192
My Account icon, 217
My Account pane, 186, 212, 215
My Address Book Card option, 186
My Password area, 186
My Picture area, 186
Name text box, 216
Network group, 194–197
Network icons, 438, 464, 465
Network Port Configurations, 197
Network Time tab, 203

New Password text box, 217
New User button, 216, 448
Number of Recent Items drop-down
list boxes, 183
Numbers tab, 185
On/Off tab, 204, 612
Open All System Preferences
check box, 221
Open Speakable Items Folder
button, 612
Options tab, 191
Output tab, 193
Output Volume slider, 192
Passive FTP Mode check box, 196
Personal section, 180–188
Place Scroll Arrows radio
buttons, 183
Plug-In tab, 197–198, 337
Position on Screen options, 182
PPP tab, 196, 354, 356
PPPoE tab, 195, 355
Proxies tab, 195–196
QuickTime panel, 197–199, 325, 336
Random Order check box, 181
Remove Items from the Dock check
box, 221
Save Movies in Disk Cache check
box, 197
Screen Effects icon, 142, 172
Screen Effects tab, 187
Seeing tab, 207
Services tab, 199
Set Auto Login button, 211
Settings tab, 191
Sharing group, 199–200, 540
Sharing icon, 449, 489, 631
Sharing Preferences group, 449
Show drop-down list box, 195–197
Show PPPoE Status in Menu Bar
check box, 355
Show Volume in Menu Bar
check box, 192
Signatures pane, 376

Sleep tab, 190
Software Update group, 115, 203–204
Sound Effects tab, 193
Sound group, 192–193
Speech icon, 611
Speech pane, 204–205, 611, 618
Speech Recognition System
    drop-down list, 612
Speech Recognition tab, 204,
    611–612
Spoken User Interface tab, 205, 611
Start/Stop tab, 201–202
Startup Disk group, 205–206
System Preferences Date & Time
    icon, 202–204
TCP/IP tab, 195, 196
Time tab, 185
Time Zone tab, 203
toolbar, 179
Tracking Speed slider, 192
Turn off Text Smoothing for Font
    Sizes drop-down list, 184
Universal Access group, 206–207
Update Software tab, 203
Update tab, 199, 337
Use Only These Applications
    option, 221
Users list, 215
Users tab, 201, 213, 217, 218, 448
Verify text box, 217
Web tab, 194
When a Command Is Recognized
    section, 612–613
When You Insert a Blank CD
    drop-down list, 188
When You Insert a Blank DVD
    drop-down list, 188
When You Insert a Music CD
    drop-down list, 188
When You Insert a Picture CD
    drop-down list, 188

When You Insert a Video DVD
    drop-down list, 188
System Preferences icon, 179
System Preferences⇨Quit System
    Preferences command, 180
System Profiler, 103–105, 143, 517–519,
    523, 526
system time, 203
Systems folder, 232

T

Talking Alerts, 620
tape drives, 510–511
tasks, 68–71
TCP/IP (Transmission Control
    Protocol/Internet Protocol)
  networks, 24
TCP/IP (Transmission Control
    Protocol/Internet Protocol) suite,
    435–437, 449, 459–460
tcsh shell, 576–577
.tcshrc file, 588
technical support person, 103
tell command, 602, 604
Telnet, 436
Terminal, 48, 456–459, 568, 570–573,
    587–591, 643
text, 184, 282–283, 621–623
text editors, 586–589
text files, 37, 68–69, 598
TextEdit, 62, 68–69, 557, 621–622
themes, 309–311
Themes drawer, 309–310, 311–312, 315
third-party
  hard drives, 71
  media players, 198
  screen savers, 172
thrashing, 516

thumbnail icons, 162
.tiff or .tif extension, 55
tiling backgrounds, 171
time, international, 185
time zone, 203
Timeline, 298, 301
Timeline Viewer, 287, 289
Titanium PowerBook laptops, 524
title bar, 31
Title shelf, 297–299
title styles, 297–298
titles, 297–299, 318
Titles Palette, 289
Tool palette, 286, 288–289, 295, 300
toolbar, 31, 152–157, 179
top command, 583
Track pop-up menu, 331
trackballs, 505–506
tracking
  media files, 334
  performance, 105–107
  songs, 256–257
tracks, 330–331
Tracks pop-up menu, 332
transitions, 295–296
Transitions Palette, 289
Transitions shelf, 296
translations, 78, 86–87
Trash can, 50–52
  checking while troubleshooting, 141
  dragging Volume icon to, 67
  emptying, 605
  warning before emptying, 167
Trash folder, 361
Travan tape drive, 510
trimming video clips, 293
Trinfinity Software Web site, 266
troubleshooting
  antivirus software, 140–141
  Apple dealer, 146
  Apple Mac OS X Support
    Web site, 146

back-ups and, 138
cable connections, 139
checking
  online connections, 141
  Trash can, 141
  for write-protection, 143
Classic mode, 144–145, 202
disabling troublesome login
    items, 142
Disk Utility, 140
Help Viewer, 146
keywords, 78
networks, 444–446
panicking while, 137–138
physical network problems, 445
process, 138–144
rebooting
  curing problems, 138–144
  with Mac OS X Installation CD-ROM,
    143–144
reinstalling Mac OS X, 145
resources, 145–146
retracing your steps, 139–140
shutdown, 138–144
software, 139–140
System Profiler, 143
turning off screen saver, 142
TTS (text-to-speech), 618–619

U

UFS (UNIX File System), 23
Undo (⌘+Z) keyboard shortcut,
    41, 49, 295
undoing actions, 49
Universal Access preferences, 206–207
UNIX
  applications, 16, 586–594
  autocompletion on command line,
    576–577

cal command, 581–582
cd command, 572, 575, 578–579
command elements, 574–575
command line, 568–569
cp command, 579–580
documentation for commands, 576
downloadable command-line tools, 591–594
escape characters (%), 589
files, 577–581
find command, 584–585
flags, 574–575, 590
FTP (File Transfer Protocol), 590–591
general information about, 15–16
Home directory, 577
Home directory (~), 571
inequality of users, 580
invisible files, 588
keyboard and, 567–570
kill command, 583
locate command, 584–585
ls command, 572, 578
man command, 576
mv command, 580
networks, 590–591
open command, 581
operands, 574–575
paths, 577–579
performing functions as another user, 579
pico, 586–589
pipes (|), 585
piping commands, 585
problems with command line, 575–576
processes, 583–584
prompt, 571
ps command, 584
repeating commands, 573
retrieving Web pages, 590–591
returning to Home folder, 572
rm command, 580–581

rmdir command, 580–581
root directory (/), 578
space characters, 575–576
Streamripper, 592–593
sudo command, 579–580
tcsh shell, 576–577
.tcshrc file, 588
tell command, 602
text editors, 586–589
top command, 583
uploading and downloading files, 590–591
uptime command, 571
wc command, 585
unmounting, 66
unsafe behavior online, 424–426
Untitled CD volume icon, 71
Untitled Favorites (⌘+K) keyboard shortcut, 407
update files, 68
Update Subscribed Sites (⌘+U) keyboard shortcut, 410
uploading files, 454, 644–645
UPS (Uninterruptible Power Supply), 23
uptime command, 571
USB (Universal Serial Bus)
  CD-RW drives, 509
  common problems, 531–532
  connections, 501
  daisy-chaining, 530
  devices, 104
  hard drives, 521, 522–523
  hubs, 530
  network cards, 479
  port problems, 531
  printers, 72, 534
USB (Universal Serial Bus) 2.0, 529
user-created scripts, 600–602
username, 211
users, 201
  home directory (~), 63, 571
  Home folder, 209

/usr/bin directory, 581
utilities, 554–559
Utilities folder, 103, 105, 107, 232, 456

V

Vacation keyword, 275
vCards, 92-93, 98–99
.vcf extension, 92, 98
Version Tracker, 633
Version Tracker Web site, 633
Versions dialog, 236
Vertical Controller (⌘+Shift+V)
 keyboard shortcut, 341
video
 digitizing, 244
 editing, 246
 playback, 328
video clips, 290–295, 321
Video Track command, 332
video tracks, 330
View icon, 153
View menu, 129
view modes, 153
View Options dialog, 161–165, 178
View⇨As Icons command, 161
View⇨Clean Up command, 160
View⇨Collapse/Expand Toolbars
 command, 401
View⇨Columns⇨Attachments
 command, 373
View⇨Customize Toolbar command,
 154, 396, 401
Viewer, 270, 276, 282, 287, 289, 342, 346
View⇨Explorer Bar command, 402
View⇨Favorites bar command, 401
View⇨Show All Alphabetically
 command, 179
View⇨Show All Headers
 command, 366

View⇨Show View Options command,
 161, 163, 164
virtual memory, 516–517
Virtual PC, 552–553
viruses, 373, 418, 423, 547
Visualizer, 265–266
visuals, 264–267
Visuals⇨Full Screen command, 265
Visuals⇨Turn Visual Off
 command, 264
Visuals⇨Turn Visual On
 command, 264
VNC (Virtual Network Computer),
 461–462
VNC viewers, 461–462
voice-overs, 303
voices, 618–621
Volume icon, 64, 65
volumes, 107–108, 111–114, 152
Vortex plug-in, 266

W

WAP (Wireless Access Point),
 474, 488, 494
WarCraft III, 563–564
Water Ripple effect, 300
WAV files, 250
wc command, 585
Web browsers
 default, 194
 FTP (File Transfer Protocol) to
  access files, 454–456
 QuickTime Web plug-in, 335–336
Web pages, 628
 changing default, 633
 displaying, 402
 dynamic, 634–640
 editing, 634
 laying out, 633

next, 404
page links, 403
previous, 404
printing, 405
QuickTime Movies, 335–336
refreshing, 404
removing parts and putting in other
    pages, 639–640
retrieving, 590–591
saving in Internet Explorer, 411–413
static, 633–634
stopping download of, 404
templates, 627
updating, 410–411
using as Home page, 405–406
Web Archive format, 412–413
Web servers, 631–633
Web sharing, 630–641
Web sites
adding images and movies, 628–629
addresses for, 401
automatically completing forms, 405
building with .Mac, 625–629
cookies, 413–414
dead links, 640–641
default file for, 632
downloading files with Internet
    Explorer, 408–409
History list, 411
hosting, 350
index.html file, 632
jumping directly to, 401
publishing photos on, 284
searching, 76
secure, 402
visiting, 402–404
Web pages styles, 628
Wedding theme, 310
well, 171
WEP (Wired Equivalency Protocol),
    474, 477–478

Wi-Fi (Wireless Fidelity), 474–475
Window menu, 31
Window⇨Equalizer menu, 258
Window⇨History command, 411
windows, 28–32
aligning icons, 162
background, 163
colors, 183
column view, 151, 164–165
current, 153
default appearance, 149
hot corners, 187
icon view, 149, 152, 160–163
list view, 150–151, 163–164
previous, 153
sorting icon display, 162
spring-loaded, 166–167
toggling between view modes, 153
view modes, 149–152
write permissions, 152
Windows 98, 9
Windows accounts, 451
Windows computers, 451–453, 468
Windows Me, 9
Windows XP, 9, 552–553
Window⇨Show Movie Info
    command, 330
Window⇨Viewer command, 342
wireless networks
802.11 standard, 474
802.11a standard, 475–476
802.11g standard, 476
802.11x standard, 478
Ad Hoc mode, 474, 479–481
AirPort Base Station, 481–483
IEEE (Institute of Electrical and
    Electronics Engineers), 474
IEEE 802.11b standard, 474–475
infrastructure mode, 474
installing AirPort or 802.11b network
    card, 479

(continued)

wireless networks *(continued)*
  LEAP (Lightweight Extensible
    Authentication Protocol), 478
  passwords, 480
  security, 476–478
  setting up, 479–483
  SSID (Service Set Identifier), 474
  terminology, 473–474
  USB (Universal Serial Bus) network
    cards, 479
  WAP (Wireless Access Point), 474
  WEP (Wired Equivalency Protocol),
    474, 477–478
  WLAN (Wireless LAN), 474
wireless support for sharing Internet
    connections, 494–495
WLAN (Wireless LAN), 474
Word, 546
World Wide Web, navigating in
    Internet Explorer, 404–405
write-protect icon, 152
write-protected disks, 109

X-Y-Z

Yellow Pages channel, 78
Zip drives, 509, 520
zones, 466
Zoom button, 30
Zoomify plug-in, 267
Zoomify Web site, 267
zooming windows, 30–31

Notes

Notes

FOR DUMMIES®

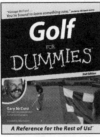

FOR DUMMIES®

A world of resources to help you grow

TRAVEL

0-7645-5453-0

0-7645-5438-7

0-7645-5444-1

Also available:

America's National Parks For Dummies
(0-7645-6204-5)

Caribbean For Dummies
(0-7645-5445-X)

Cruise Vacations For Dummies 2003
(0-7645-5459-X)

Europe For Dummies
(0-7645-5456-5)

Ireland For Dummies
(0-7645-6199-5)

France For Dummies
(0-7645-6292-4)

Las Vegas For Dummies
(0-7645-5448-4)

London For Dummies
(0-7645-5416-6)

Mexico's Beach Resorts For Dummies
(0-7645-6262-2)

Paris For Dummies
(0-7645-5494-8)

RV Vacations For Dummies
(0-7645-5443-3)

EDUCATION & TEST PREPARATION

0-7645-5194-9

0-7645-5325-9

0-7645-5249-X

Also available:

The ACT For Dummies
(0-7645-5210-4)

Chemistry For Dummies
(0-7645-5430-1)

English Grammar For Dummies
(0-7645-5322-4)

French For Dummies
(0-7645-5193-0)

GMAT For Dummies
(0-7645-5251-1)

Inglés Para Dummies
(0-7645-5427-1)

Italian For Dummies
(0-7645-5196-5)

Research Papers For Dummies
(0-7645-5426-3)

SAT I For Dummies
(0-7645-5472-7)

U.S. History For Dummies
(0-7645-5249-X)

World History For Dummies
(0-7645-5242-2)

HEALTH, SELF-HELP & SPIRITUALITY

0-7645-5154-X

0-7645-5302-X

0-7645-5418-2

Also available:

The Bible For Dummies
(0-7645-5296-1)

Controlling Cholesterol For Dummies
(0-7645-5440-9)

Dating For Dummies
(0-7645-5072-1)

Dieting For Dummies
(0-7645-5126-4)

High Blood Pressure For Dummies
(0-7645-5424-7)

Judaism For Dummies
(0-7645-5299-6)

Menopause For Dummies
(0-7645-5458-1)

Nutrition For Dummies
(0-7645-5180-9)

Potty Training For Dummies
(0-7645-5417-4)

Pregnancy For Dummies
(0-7645-5074-8)

Rekindling Romance For Dummies
(0-7645-5303-8)

Religion For Dummies
(0-7645-5264-3)

Available wherever books are sold. Go to www.dummies.com or call 1-877-762-2974 to order direct

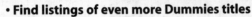

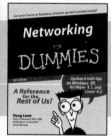